POWERSHIFT

ALVIN TOFFLER

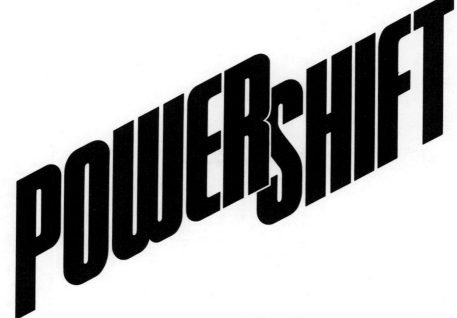

POWERSHIFT

KNOWLEDGE, WEALTH, AND VIOLENCE

AT THE EDGE OF THE 21st CENTURY

BANTAM BOOKS

NEW YORK • TORONTO • LONDON • SYDNEY • AUCKLAND

POWERSHIFT:
KNOWLEDGE, WEALTH, AND VIOLENCE AT THE EDGE OF THE 21ST CENTURY
A Bantam Book / November 1990

Library of Congress Cataloging-in-Publication Data

Toffler, Alvin.
 Powershift : knowledge, wealth, and violence at
the edge of the 21st century.

 Includes bibliographical references.
 1. Social history—1945–   . 2. Economic
history—1945–   . 3. Power (Social sciences)
4. Social change.   I. Title.
HN17.5.T6417 1990   303.4   90-1068
ISBN 0-553-05776-6

Published simultaneously in the United States and Canada

Foreign Editions of Powershift *(a partial list)*

Dutch	*Veen Publishers*
Finnish	*Otava Oy*
French	*Librairie Artheme Fayard*
German	*Econ Verlag*
Italian	*Sperling & Kupfer Editore*
Japanese	*Fuso Sha*
Korean	*Korea Economic Daily*
Portuguese	*Distribuidora Record (Brazil)*
Norwegian	*J. W. Cappelens Forlag*
Spanish	*Plaza y Janes*
Swedish	*Bokforlaget Bra Bocker*

PRINTED IN THE UNITED STATES OF AMERICA

BVG   0 9 8 7 6 5 4

For Karen
with love
from both of us

CONTENTS

A PERSONAL PREFACE

Powershift is the culmination of a twenty-five-year effort to make sense of the astonishing changes propelling us into the 21st century. It is the third and final volume of a trilogy that opened with *Future Shock,* continued with *The Third Wave,* and is now complete.

Each of these three books can be read by itself as an independent work. But together they form an intellectually consistent whole. Their central subject is change—what happens to people when their entire society abruptly transforms itself into something new and unexpected. *Powershift* carries forward the earlier analysis and focuses on the rise of a new power system replacing that of the industrial past.

In describing today's accelerating changes, the media fire blips of unrelated information at us. Experts bury us under mountains of narrowly specialized monographs. Popular forecasters present lists of unrelated trends, without any model to show us their interconnections or the forces likely to reverse them. As a result, change itself comes to be seen as anarchic, even lunatic.

By contrast, this trilogy starts from the premise that today's high-speed changes are not as chaotic or random as we are conditioned to believe. It contends that there are not only distinct patterns behind the headlines, but identifiable forces that shape them. Once we understand these patterns and forces, it becomes possible to cope with them strategically, rather than haphazardly on a one-by-one basis.

However, to make sense of today's great changes, to think strategically, we need more than bits, blips, and lists. We need to see how different changes relate to one another. Thus *Powershift,* like its two predecessors, sets out a clear and comprehensive

synthesis—an overarching image of the new civilization now spreading across the planet.

It then zeros in on tomorrow's flashpoints, the conflicts we face as the new civilization collides with the entrenched forces of the old. *Powershift* contends that the corporate takeovers and restructurings seen so far are only the first salvos in far larger, quite novel business battles to come. More important, it holds that the recent upheavals seen in Eastern Europe and the Soviet Union are mere skirmishes compared with the global power struggles that lie ahead. Nor has the rivalry among the United States, Europe, and Japan reached its full intensity.

In short, *Powershift* is about the crescendoing struggles for power that still face us as the industrial civilization loses world dominance and new forces arise to tower over the earth.

For me, *Powershift* is a high point reached after a fascinating journey. Before continuing, however, a personal note is required. For I did not make this journey alone. This entire trilogy, from inception to completion, has had an uncredited co-author. It is the combined work of two minds, not just one, although I have done the actual writing and have accepted the plaudits and criticisms for both of us.

My co-author, as many already know, is my best friend, spouse, and partner, my love for forty years: Heidi Toffler. Whatever the faults of this trilogy, they would have been far more serious without her skeptical intelligence, her intellectual insight, keen editorial sense, and general good judgment about ideas and people alike. She has contributed not merely to after-the-fact polishing but to the formulation of the underlying models on which the works are based.

While the intensity of her involvement varied from time to time, depending on her other commitments, these books required travel, research, interviews with hundreds of people around the world, careful organization, and drafting, followed by endless updating and revision, and Heidi took part at every stage.

Nevertheless, for reasons that were partly private, partly social, partly economic—and that varied at different times over the past two decades—the decision was made to credit only the actual writer.

Even now Heidi refuses to lend her name to a book jacket, out of integrity, modesty, and love—reasons that seem sufficient to

her, though not to me. I can only redress this shortcoming with these personal, prefatory words: I feel that the trilogy is as much hers as mine.

All three books probe a single lifetime—the period beginning, say, in the mid-1950s and ending approximately seventy-five years later, in 2025. This span can be called the hinge of history, the period in which smokestack civilization, having dominated the earth for centuries, is finally replaced by another, far different one following a period of world-shaking power struggles.

But, while focused on the same period, each of the three books uses a different lens with which to probe beneath the surface of reality, and it may be useful for readers to define the differences among them.

Thus *Future Shock* looks at the *process* of change—how change affects people and organizations. *The Third Wave* focuses on the *directions* of change—where today's changes are taking us. *Powershift* deals with the *control* of changes still to come—who will shape them and how.

Future Shock—which we defined as the disorientation and stress brought on by trying to cope with too many changes in too short a time—argued that the acceleration of history carries consequences of its own, independent of the actual directions of change. The simple speed-up of events and reaction times produces its own effects, whether the changes are perceived as good or bad.

It also held that individuals, organizations, and even nations can be overloaded with too much change too soon, leading to disorientation and a breakdown in their capacity to make intelligent adaptive decisions. They could, in short, suffer from future shock.

Against the then-current opinion, *Future Shock* declared that the nuclear family was soon to be "fractured." It also foreshadowed the genetic revolution, the rise of a throwaway society, and the revolution in education that may now, at long last, be beginning.

First published in the United States in 1970, and subsequently all over the world, the book touched an unsheathed nerve, became a surprise international best-seller, and generated avalanches of commentary. It became one of the most cited works in social science literature, according to the Institute for Scientific Information. The phrase *future shock* entered the daily language, turned up in many dictionaries, and today constantly appears in headlines.

The Third Wave, which followed in 1980, had a different focus. Describing the latest revolutionary changes in technology and society, it placed them in historical perspective and sketched the future they might bring.

Terming the agricultural revolution of 10,000 years ago the First Wave of transforming change in human history, and the industrial revolution the Second Wave, it described the major technological and social changes beginning in the mid-1950s as a great Third Wave of human change—the start of the new, post-smokestack civilization.

Among other things, it pointed at new industries to come—based on computers, electronics, information, biotechnology, and the like, terming these the "new commanding heights" of the economy. It foreshadowed such things as flexible manufacturing, niche markets, the spread of part-time work, and the de-massification of the media. It described the new fusion of producer and consumer and introduced the term *prosumer.* It discussed the coming shift of some work back into the home, and other changes in politics and the nation-state system.

Banned in some countries, *The Third Wave* became a best-seller in others, and for a time was the "bible" of the reform intellectuals in China. First accused of spreading Western "spiritual pollution," then released and published in vast quantities, it became the best-selling book in the world's most populous nation, second only to the speeches of Deng Xiaoping. The then–Prime Minister, Zhao Ziyang, convened conferences about it and urged policymakers to study it.

In Poland, after a legitimately abridged version was published, students and Solidarity supporters were so outraged at the cuts, they published an "underground" edition and also distributed pamphlets containing the missing chapters. Like *Future Shock, The Third Wave* inspired many responses among its readers, leading among other things to new products, companies, symphonies, and even sculptures.

Now, twenty years after *Future Shock* and ten years after *The Third Wave, Powershift* is at last ready. Picking up where its predecessors left off, it focuses on the crucially changed role of knowledge in relationship to power. It presents a new theory of social power, and explores the coming shifts in business, the economy, politics, and global affairs.

It seems hardly necessary to add that the future is not "knowable" in the sense of exact prediction. Life is filled with surrealistic surprise. Even the seemingly "hardest" models and data are frequently based on "soft" assumptions, especially where these concern human affairs. Moreover, the very subject of these books —accelerant change—makes the details in them subject to obsolescence. Statistics change. New technologies supplant older ones. Political leaders rise and fall. Nevertheless, as we advance into the terra incognita of tomorrow, it is better to have a general and incomplete map, subject to revision and correction, than to have no map at all.

While each of the works in the trilogy is built on a model different from, but compatible with, the others, all the books draw on documentation, research, and reportage from many disparate fields and many different countries. Thus, for example, in preparing this work, we attempted to study power at the pinnacle and in the depths of society.

We have had the opportunity to meet for hours with Mikhail Gorbachev, Ronald Reagan, George Bush, several Japanese Prime Ministers, and others whom most would count as among the most powerful men in the world.

At the opposite end of the spectrum, one or both of us also visited squatters in a South American "city of misery" and women prisoners under life sentence—both groups thought to be among the most powerless on earth.

In addition, we discussed power with bankers, labor unionists, business leaders, computer experts, generals, Nobel Prize–winning scientists, oil tycoons, journalists, and the top managers of many of the world's biggest companies.

We met with the staff people who shape decisions in the White House, in the Élysée Palace in Paris, in the Prime Minister's office in Tokyo, and even in the offices of the Central Committee of the Communist Party in Moscow. There a conversation with Anatoly Lukyanov (then on the staff of the Central Committee, later the second-highest official of the U.S.S.R. after Gorbachev) was interrupted by an unexpected call for a meeting of the Politburo.

Once, I found myself in a sunlit room surrounded by books in a small town in California. Had I been led into that room blindfolded, I might never have guessed that the intelligent young woman in T-shirt and jeans who faced me across an oak library table was a murderer. Or that she had been convicted of participation in a grisly sexual crime. Or that we were in a prison—a place where the realities of power are laid bare. From her I came to understand that even prisoners are by no means powerless. Some know how to use information for power purposes with all the manipulative finesse of Cardinal Richelieu in the court of Louis XIII, a point directly relevant to the theme of this book. (This experience led my wife and me, on two occasions, to teach a seminar for a class consisting mainly of murderers—from whom we learned much.)

Experiences like these, supplementing exhaustive reading and analysis of written source materials from around the world, made the preparation of *Powershift* an unforgettable time in our lives.

We hope that readers will find *Powershift* as useful, pleasurable, and enlightening as, we are told, they found *The Third Wave* and *Future Shock*. The sweeping synthesis started a quarter century ago is now complete.

—ALVIN TOFFLER

PART ONE

THE NEW MEANING OF POWER

Power grows out of
the barrel of a gun.
—MAO TSE-TUNG

Money talks.
—ANONYMOUS

Knowledge itself is power.
—FRANCIS BACON

1

THE POWERSHIFT ERA

This is a book about power at the edge of the 21st century. It deals with violence, wealth, and knowledge and the roles they play in our lives. It is about the new paths to power opened by a world in upheaval.

Despite the bad odor that clings to the very notion of power because of the misuses to which it has been put, power in itself is neither good nor bad. It is an inescapable aspect of every human relationship, and it influences everything from our sexual relations to the jobs we hold, the cars we drive, the television we watch, the hopes we pursue. To a greater degree than most imagine, we are the products of power.

Yet of all the aspects of our lives, power remains one of the least understood and most important—especially for our generation.

For this is the dawn of the Powershift Era. We live at a moment when the entire structure of power that held the world together is now disintegrating. A radically different structure of power is taking form. And this is happening at every level of human society.

In the office, in the supermarket, at the bank, in the executive suite, in our churches, hospitals, schools, and homes, old patterns of power are fracturing along strange new lines. Campuses are stirring from Berkeley to Rome and Taipei, preparing to explode. Ethnic and racial clashes are multiplying.

In the business world we see giant corporations taken apart and put back together, their CEOs often dumped, along with thousands of their employees. A "golden parachute" or goodbye package of money and benefits may soften the shock of landing for a top manager, but gone are the appurtenances of power: the corporate jet, the limousine, the conferences at glamorous golf resorts, and above all, the secret thrill that many feel in the sheer exercise of power.

Power isn't just shifting at the pinnacle of corporate life. The office manager and the supervisor on the plant floor are both discovering that workers no longer take orders blindly, as many once did. They ask questions and demand answers. Military officers are learning the same thing about their troops. Police chiefs about their cops. Teachers, increasingly, about their students.

This crackup of old-style authority and power in business and daily life is accelerating at the very moment when global power structures are disintegrating as well.

Ever since the end of World War II, two superpowers have straddled the earth like colossi. Each had its allies, satellites, and cheering section. Each balanced the other, missile for missile, tank for tank, spy for spy. Today, of course, that balancing act is over.

As a result, "black holes" are already opening up in the world system: great sucking power vacuums, in Eastern Europe for example, that could sweep nations and peoples into strange new—or, for that matter, ancient—alliances and collisions. Power is shifting at so astonishing a rate that world leaders are being swept along by events, rather than imposing order on them.

There is strong reason to believe that the forces now shaking power at every level of the human system will become more intense and pervasive in the years immediately ahead.

Out of this massive restructuring of power relationships, like the shifting and grinding of tectonic plates in advance of an earthquake, will come one of the rarest events in human history: a revolution in the very nature of power.

A "powershift" does not merely transfer power. It transforms it.

THE END OF EMPIRE

The entire world watched awestruck as a half-century-old empire based on Soviet power in Eastern Europe suddenly came unglued in 1989. Desperate for the Western technology needed to energize its rust-belt economy, the Soviet Union itself plunged into a period of near-chaotic change.

Slower and less dramatically, the world's other superpower also went into relative decline. So much has been written about America's loss of global power that it bears no repetition here. Even more striking, however, have been the many shifts of power away from its once-dominant domestic institutions.

Twenty years ago General Motors was regarded as the world's premier manufacturing company, a gleaming model for managers in countries around the world and a political powerhouse in Washington. Today, says a high GM official, "We are running for our lives." We may well see, in the years ahead, the actual breakup of GM.

Twenty years ago IBM had only the feeblest competition and the United States probably had more computers than the rest of the world combined. Today computer power has spread rapidly around the world, the U.S. share has sagged, and IBM faces stiff competition from companies like NEC, Hitachi, and Fujitsu in Japan; Groupe Bull in France; ICL in Britain, and many others. Industry analysts speculate about the post-IBM era.

Nor is all this a result of foreign competition. Twenty years ago three television networks, ABC, CBS, and NBC, dominated the American airwaves. They faced no foreign competition at all. Yet today they are shrinking so fast, their very survival is in doubt.

Twenty years ago, to choose a different kind of example, medical doctors in the United States were white-coated gods. Patients typically accepted their word as law. Physicians virtually controlled the entire American health system. Their political clout was enormous.

Today, by contrast, American doctors are under siege. Patients talk back. They sue for malpractice. Nurses demand responsibility and respect. Pharmaceutical companies are less deferential. And it is insurance companies, "managed care groups," and government, not doctors, who now control the American health system.

Across the board, then, some of the most powerful institutions and professions inside the most powerful of nations saw their dominance decline in the same twenty-year period that saw America's external power, relative to other nations, sink.

Lest these immense shake-ups in the distribution of power seem a disease of the aging superpowers, a look elsewhere proves otherwise.

While U.S. economic power faded, Japan's skyrocketed. But success, too, can trigger significant power shifts. Just as in the

United States, Japan's most powerful Second Wave or rust-belt industries declined in importance as new Third Wave industries rose. Even as Japan's economic heft increased, however, the three institutions perhaps most responsible for its growth saw their own power plummet. The first was the governing Liberal-Democratic Party. The second was the Ministry of International Trade and Industry (MITI), arguably the brain behind the Japanese economic miracle. The third was Keidanren, Japan's most politically potent business federation.

Today the LDP is in retreat, its elderly male leaders embarrassed by financial and sexual scandals. It is faced, for the first time, by outraged and increasingly active women voters, by consumers, taxpayers, and farmers who formerly supported it. To retain the power it has held since 1955, it will be compelled to shift its base from rural to urban voters, and deal with a far more heterogeneous population than ever before. For Japan, like all the high-tech nations, is becoming a de-massified society, with many more actors arriving on the political scene. Whether the LDP can make this long-term switch is at issue. What is not at issue is that significant power has shifted away from the LDP.

As for MITI, even now many American academics and politicians urge the United States to adopt MITI-style planning as a model. Yet today, MITI itself is in trouble. Japan's biggest corporations once danced attendance on its bureaucrats and, willingly or not, usually followed its "guidelines." Today MITI is a fast-fading power as the corporations themselves have grown strong enough to thumb their noses at it. Japan remains economically powerful in the outside world but politically weak at home. Immense economic weight pivots around a shaky political base.

Even more pronounced has been the decline in the strength of Keidanren, still dominated by the hierarchs of the fast-fading smokestack industries.

Even those dreadnoughts of Japanese fiscal power, the Bank of Japan and the Ministry of Finance, whose controls guided Japan through the high-growth period, the oil shock, the stock market crash, and the yen rise, now find themselves impotent against the turbulent market forces destabilizing the economy.

Still more striking shifts of power are changing the face of Western Europe. Thus power has shifted away from London, Paris, and Rome as the German economy has outstripped all the rest. Today, as East and West Germany progressively fuse their economies, all Europe once more fears German domination of the continent.

To protect themselves, France and other West European nations, with the exception of Britain, are hastily trying to integrate the European community politically as well as economically. But the more successful they become, the more of their national power is transfused into the veins of the Brussels-based European Community, which has progressively stripped away bigger and bigger chunks of their sovereignty.

The nations of Western Europe thus are caught between Bonn or Berlin on the one side and Brussels on the other. Here, too, power is shifting rapidly away from its established centers.

The list of such global and domestic power shifts could be extended indefinitely. They represent a remarkable series of changes for so brief a peacetime period. Of course, some power shifting is normal at any time.

Yet only rarely does an entire globe-girdling *system* of power fly apart in this fashion. It is an even rarer moment in history when all the rules of the power game change at once, and the very nature of power is revolutionized.

Yet that is exactly what is happening today. Power, which to a large extent defines us as individuals and as nations, is itself being redefined.

GOD-IN-A-WHITE-COAT

A clue to this redefinition emerges when we look more closely at the above list of apparently unrelated changes. For we discover that they are not as random as they seem. Whether it is Japan's meteoric rise, GM's embarrassing decline, or the American doctor's fall from grace, a single common thread unites them.

Take the punctured power of the god-in-a-white-coat.

Throughout the heyday of doctor-dominance in America, physicians kept a tight choke-hold on medical knowledge. Prescriptions were written in Latin, providing the profession with a semi-secret code, as it were, which kept most patients in ignorance. Medical journals and texts were restricted to professional readers. Medical conferences were closed to the laity. Doctors controlled medical-school curricula and enrollments.

Contrast this with the situation today, when patients have astonishing access to medical knowledge. With a personal computer and a modem, anyone from home can access data bases like Index Medicus, and obtain scientific papers on everything from Addison's disease to zygomycosis, and, in fact, collect more information about a specific ailment or treatment than the ordinary doctor has time to read.

Copies of the 2,354-page book known as the PDR or *Physicians' Desk Reference* are also readily available to anyone. Once a week on the Lifetime cable network, any televiewer can watch twelve uninterrupted hours of highly technical television programming designed specifically to educate doctors. Many of these programs carry a disclaimer to the effect that "some of this material may not be suited to a general audience." But that is for the viewer to decide.

The rest of the week, hardly a single newscast is aired in America without a medical story or segment. A video version of material from the *Journal of the American Medical Association* is now broadcast by three hundred stations on Thursday nights. The press reports on medical malpractice cases. Inexpensive paperbacks tell ordinary readers what drug side effects to watch for, what drugs not to mix, how to raise or lower cholesterol levels through diet. In addition, major medical breakthroughs, even if first published in medical journals, are reported on the evening television news almost before the M.D. has even taken his subscription copy of the journal out of the in-box.

In short, the knowledge monopoly of the medical profession has been thoroughly smashed. And the doctor is no longer a god.

This case of the dethroned doctor is, however, only one small example of a more general process changing the entire relationship of knowledge to power in the high-tech nations.

In many other fields, too, closely held specialists' knowledge is slipping out of control and reaching ordinary citizens. Similarly, inside major corporations, employees are winning access to knowledge once monopolized by management. And as knowledge is redistributed, so, too, is the power based on it.

BOMBARDED BY THE FUTURE

There is, however, a much larger sense in which changes in knowledge are causing or contributing to enormous power shifts. The most important economic development of our lifetime has been the rise of a new system for creating wealth, based no longer on muscle but on mind. Labor in the advanced economy no longer consists of working on "things," writes historian Mark Poster of the University of California (Irvine), but of "men and women acting on other men and women, or . . . people acting on information and information acting on people."

The substitution of information or knowledge for brute labor, in fact, lies behind the troubles of General Motors and the rise of Japan as well. For while GM still thought the earth was flat, Japan was exploring its edges and discovering otherwise.

As early as 1970, when American business leaders still thought their smokestack world secure, Japan's business leaders, and even the general public, were being bombarded by books, newspaper articles, and television programs heralding the arrival of the "information age" and focusing on the 21st century. While the end-of-industrialism concept was dismissed with a shrug in the United States, it was welcomed and embraced by Japanese decision-makers in business, politics, and the media. Knowledge, they concluded, was the key to economic growth in the 21st century.

It was hardly surprising, therefore, that even though the United States started computerizing earlier, Japan moved more quickly to substitute the knowledge-based technologies of the Third Wave for the brute muscle technologies of the Second Wave past.

Robots proliferated. Sophisticated manufacturing methods, heavily dependent on computers and information, began turning out products whose quality could not be easily matched in world markets. Moreover, recognizing that its old smokestack technologies were ultimately doomed, Japan took steps to facilitate the transition to the new and to buffer itself against the dislocations entailed in such a strategy. The contrast with General Motors—and American policy in general—could not have been sharper.

If we also look closely at many of the other power shifts cited above, it will become apparent that in these cases, too, the changed role of knowledge—the rise of the new wealth-creation system—either caused or contributed to major shifts of power.

The spread of this new knowledge economy is, in fact, the explosive new force that has hurled the advanced economies into bitter global competition, confronted the socialist nations with their hopeless obsolescence, forced many "developing nations" to scrap their traditional economic strategies, and is now profoundly dislocating power relationships in both personal and public spheres.

In a prescient remark, Winston Churchill once said that "empires of the future are empires of the mind." Today that observation has come true. What has not yet been appreciated is the degree to which raw, elemental power—at the level of private life as well as at the level of empire—will be transformed in the decades ahead as a result of the new role of "mind."

THE MAKING OF A SHABBY GENTILITY

A revolutionary new system for creating wealth cannot spread without triggering personal, political, and international conflict. Change the way wealth is made and you immediately collide with all the entrenched interests whose power arose from the prior wealth-system. Bitter conflicts erupt as each side fights for control of the future.

It is this conflict, spreading around the world today, that helps explain the present power shake-up. To anticipate what might lie ahead for us, therefore, it is helpful to glance briefly backward at the last such global conflict.

Three hundred years ago the industrial revolution also brought a new system of wealth creation into being. Smokestacks speared the skies where fields once were cultivated. Factories proliferated. These "dark Satanic mills" brought with them a totally new way of 'fe—and a new system of power.

Peasants freed from near-servitude on the land turned into n workers subordinated to private or public employers. With ange came changes in power relations in the home as well. n families, several generations under a single roof, all ruled rded patriarch, gave way to stripped-down nuclear families h the elderly were soon extruded or reduced in prestige nce. The family itself, as an institution, lost much of its social power as many of its functions were transferred to other institutions—education to the school, for example.

Sooner or later, too, wherever steam engines and smokestacks multiplied, vast political changes followed. Monarchies collapsed or shriveled into tourist attractions. New political forms were introduced.

If they were clever and farsighted enough, rural landowners, once dominant in their regions, moved into the cities to ride the wave of industrial expansion, their sons becoming stockbrokers or captains of industry. Most of the landed gentry who clung to their rural way of life wound up as shabby gentility, their mansions eventually turned into museums or into money-raising lion parks.

Against their fading power, however, new elites arose: corporate chieftains, bureaucrats, media moguls. Mass production, mass distribution, mass education, and mass communication were accompanied by mass democracy, or dictatorships claiming to be democratic.

These internal changes were matched by gigantic shifts in global power, too, as the industrialized nations colonized, conquered, or dominated much of the rest of the world, creating a hierarchy of world power that still exists in some regions.

In short, the appearance of a new system for creating wealth undermined every pillar of the old power system, ultimately transforming family life, business, politics, the nation-state, and the structure of the global power itself.

Those who fought for control of the future made use of violence, wealth, and knowledge. Today a similar, though far more accelerated, upheaval has started. The changes we have recently seen in business, the economy, politics, and at the global level are only the first skirmishes of far bigger power struggles to come. For we stand at the edge of the deepest powershift in human history.

2

MUSCLE, MONEY, AND MIND

An ultramarine sky. Mountains in the distance. The clatter of hoofbeats. A solitary rider draws closer, sun glinting from his spurs. . . .

Anyone who sat in a darkened theater enraptured by cowboy movies as a child knows that power springs from the barrel of a six-shooter. In film after Hollywood film, a lone cowboy rides in from nowhere, fights a duel with the villain, returns his revolver to its holster, and rides off once more into the hazy distance. Power, we children learned, came from violence.

A background figure in many of these movies, however, was a well-dressed, paunchy personage who sat behind a big wooden desk. Typically depicted as effete and greedy, this man also exerted power. It was he who financed the railroad, or the land-grabbing cattlemen, or other evil forces. And if the cowboy hero represented the power of violence, this figure—typically the banker—symbolized the power of money.

In many westerns there was also a third important character: a crusading newspaper editor, a teacher, a minister, or an educated woman from the "East." In a world of gruff men who shoot first and question later, this character represented not merely moral Good in combat with Evil, but also the power of culture and sophisticated knowledge about the outside world. While this person often won a victory in the end, it was usually because of an alliance with the gun-toting hero or because of a sudden lucky strike—finding gold in the river or inheriting an unexpected legacy.

Knowledge, as Francis Bacon advised us, is power—but for knowledge to win in a western, it usually had to ally itself with force or money.

Of course, cash, culture, and violence are not the only sources of power in everyday life, and power is neither good nor bad. It is a dimension of virtually all human relationships. It is, in fact, the reciprocal of desire, and, since human desires are infinitely varied, anything that can fulfill someone else's desire is a potential source of power. The drug dealer who can withhold a "fix" has power over the addict. If a politician desires votes, those who can deliver them have power.

Yet among the numberless possibilities, the three sources of power symbolized in the western movie—violence, wealth, and knowledge—turn out to be most important. Each takes many different forms in power play. Violence, for example, need not be actual; the threat of its use is often enough to bring compliance. The threat of violence can also lurk behind the law. (We use the term *violence* in these pages in a figurative, rather than literal, sense—to include force as well as physical coercion.)

Indeed, not only modern movies but also ancient myths support the view that violence, wealth, and knowledge are the ultimate sources of social power. Thus Japanese legend tells of *sanshu no jingi*—the three sacred objects given to the great sun goddess, Amaterasu-omi-kami—which to this day are still the symbols of imperial power. These are the sword, the jewel, and the mirror.

The power implications of sword and jewel are clear enough; the mirror's, a bit less so. But the mirror, in which Amaterasu-omi-kami's saw her own visage—or gained knowledge of herself—also reflects power. It came to symbolize her divinity, but it is not unreasonable to regard it as a symbol of imagination, consciousness, and knowledge as well.

Furthermore, the sword or muscle, the jewel or money, and the mirror or mind together form a single interactive system. Under certain conditions each can be converted into the other. A gun can get you money or can force secret information from the lips of a victim. Money can buy you information—or a gun. Information can be used to increase either the money available to you (as Ivan Boesky knew) or to multiply the force at your command (which is why Klaus Fuchs stole nuclear secrets).

What's more, all three can be used at almost every level of social life, from the intimacy of home to the political arena.

In the private sphere, a parent can slap a child (use force), cut an allowance or bribe with a dollar (use money or its equivalent), or—most effective of all—mold a child's values so the child *wishes* to obey. In politics, a government can imprison or torture a dissident, financially punish its critics and pay off its supporters, and it can manipulate truth to create consent.

Like machine tools (which can create more machines), force, wealth, or knowledge, properly used, can give one command over many additional, more varied sources of power. Thus, whatever other tools of power may be exploited by a ruling elite or by individuals in their private relationships, force, wealth, and knowledge are the ultimate levers. They form the power triad.

It is true that not all shifts or transfers of power are a result of the use of these tools. Power changes hands as a result of many natural events. The Black Death that swept Europe in the 14th century sent the powerful to the grave along with the powerless, creating many vacancies among the elite in the surviving communities.

Chance also affects the distribution of power in society. But as soon as we focus on purposeful human acts, and ask what makes people and whole societies acquiesce to the wishes of the "powerful," we find ourselves once more facing the trinity of muscle, money, and mind.

To stick as closely to plain-speak as possible, we will use the term *power* in these pages to mean purposeful power over people. This definition rules out power used against nature or things, but is broad enough to include the power exerted by a mother to prevent a baby from running in front of an onrushing car; or by IBM to increase its profits; or by a dictator like Marcos or Noriega to enrich his family and cronies; or by the Catholic Church to line up political opposition to contraception; or by the Chinese military to crush a student rebellion.

In its most naked form, power involves the use of violence, wealth, and knowledge (in the broadest sense) to make people perform in a given way.

Zeroing in on this trinity and defining power in this manner permit us to analyze power in a completely fresh way, revealing perhaps more clearly than before exactly how power is used to control our behavior from cradle to cremation. Only when this is understood can we identify and transform those obsolete power structures that threaten our future.

HIGH-QUALITY POWER

Most conventional assumptions about power, in Western culture at least, imply that power is a matter of quantity. But, while some of us clearly have less power than others, this approach ignores what may now be the most important factor of all: the *quality* of power.

Power comes in varying grades, and some power is decidedly low in octane. In the fierce struggles soon to sweep through our schools, hospitals, businesses, trade unions, and governments, those who understand "quality" will gain a strategic edge.

No one doubts that violence—embodied in a mugger's switchblade or a nuclear missile—can yield awesome results. The shadow of violence or force, embedded in the law, stands behind every act of government, and in the end every government relies on soldiers and police to en*force* its will. This ever-present and necessary threat of official violence in society helps keep the system operating, making ordinary business contracts enforceable, reducing crime, providing machinery for the peaceful settlement of disputes. In this paradoxical sense, it is the veiled threat of violence that helps make daily life nonviolent.

But violence in general suffers from important drawbacks. To begin with, it encourages us to carry a can of Mace, or to crank up an arms race that increases risks to everyone. Even when it "works," violence produces resistance. Its victims or their survivors look for the first chance to strike back.

The main weakness of brute force or violence, however, is its sheer inflexibility. It can only be used to punish. It is, in short, low-quality power.

Wealth, by contrast, is a far better tool of power. A fat wallet is much more versatile. Instead of just threatening or delivering punishment, it can also offer finely graded rewards—payments and payoffs, in cash or kind. Wealth can be used in either a positive or a negative way. It is, therefore, much more flexible than force. Wealth yields medium-quality power.

The highest-quality power, however, comes from the application of knowledge. Actor Sean Connery, in a movie set in Cuba during the reign of the dictator Batista, plays a British mercenary. In one memorable scene the tyrant's military chief says: "Major, tell what your favorite weapon is, and I'll get it for you." To which Connery replies: "Brains."

High-quality power is not simply clout. Not merely the ability to get one's way, to make others do what you want, though they might prefer otherwise. High quality implies much more. It implies efficiency—using up the fewest power resources to achieve a goal. Knowledge can often be used to make the other party *like* your agenda for action. It can even persuade the person that she or he originated it.

Of the three root sources of social control, therefore, it is knowledge, the most versatile, that produces what Pentagon brass like to call "the biggest bang for the buck." It can be used to punish, reward, persuade, and even transform. It can transform enemy into ally. Best of all, with the right knowledge one can circumvent nasty situations in the first place, so as to avoid wasting force or wealth altogether.

Knowledge also serves as a wealth and force multiplier. It can be used to augment the available force or wealth or, alternatively, to reduce the amount needed to achieve any given purpose. In either case, it increases efficiency, permitting one to spend fewer power "chips" in any showdown.

Of course, maximum power is available to those in a position to use all three of these tools in clever conjunction with one another, alternating the threat of punishment, the promise of reward, along with persuasion and intelligence. The truly skilled power players know intuitively—or through training—how to use and interrelate their power resources.

To assess the different contenders in a power conflict—whether a negotiation or a war—therefore, it helps to figure out who commands access to which of the basic tools of power.

Knowledge, violence, and wealth, and the relationships among them, define power in society. Francis Bacon equated knowledge with power, but he did not focus on its quality or on its crucial links to the other main sources of social power. Nor could anyone until now foresee today's revolutionary changes in the relationships among these three.

ONE MILLION INFERENCES

A revolution is sweeping today's post-Bacon world. No genius in the past—not Sun-Tzu, not Machiavelli, not Bacon himself—could have imagined today's deepest *powershift:* the astounding degree to which today both force and wealth themselves have come to depend on knowledge.*

Military might until not long ago was basically an extension of the mindless fist. Today it relies almost totally on "congealed mind"—knowledge embedded in weapons and surveillance technologies. From satellites to submarines, modern weapons are constructed of information-rich electronic components. Today's fighter plane is a flying computer. Even "dumb" weapons today are manufactured with the help of supersmart computers or electronic chips.

The military, to choose a single example, uses computerized knowledge—"expert systems"—in missile defense. Since subsonic missiles speed along at about 1,000 feet a second, effective defense systems need to react in, say, 10 milliseconds. But expert systems may embody as many as 10,000 to 100,000 rules elicited from human specialists. The computer must scan, weigh, and interrelate these rules before arriving at a decision as to how to respond to a threat. Thus the Pentagon's Defense Advanced Research Projects Agency (DARPA), according to *Defense Science* magazine, has set as a long-range goal the design of a system that can make "one million logical inferences per second." Logic, inference, epistemology—in short, brain work, human and machine—is today's precondition for military power.

Similarly, it has become a business cliché to say that wealth is increasingly dependent on brainpower. The advanced economy could not run for thirty seconds without computers, and the new complexities of production, the integration of many diverse (and constantly changing) technologies, the de-massification of markets, continue to increase, by vast leaps, the amount and quality of information needed to make the system produce wealth. Furthermore, we are barely at the beginning of this "informationalization" process. Our best computers and CAD-CAM systems are still stone-ax primitive.

*A power shift is a transfer of power. A "powershift" is a deep-level change in the very nature of power.

Knowledge itself, therefore, turns out to be not only the source of the highest-quality power, but also the most important ingredient of force and wealth. Put differently, knowledge has gone from being an adjunct of money power and muscle power, to being their very essence. It is, in fact, the ultimate amplifier. This is the key to the *powershift* that lies ahead, and it explains why the battle for control of knowledge and the means of communication is heating up all over the world.

FACTS, LIES, AND TRUTH

Knowledge and communication systems are not antiseptic or power-neutral. Virtually every "fact" used in business, political life, and everyday human relations is derived from other "facts" or assumptions that have been shaped, deliberately or not, by the preexisting power structure. Every "fact" thus has a power-history and what might be called a power-future—an impact, large or small, on the future distribution of power.

Nonfacts and disputed facts are equally products of, and weapons in, power conflict in society. False facts and lies, as well as "true" facts, scientific "laws," and accepted religious "truths" are all ammunition in ongoing power-play and are themselves a form of knowledge, as the term will be used here.

There are, of course, as many definitions of knowledge as there are people who regard themselves as knowledgeable. Matters grow worse when words like *signs, symbols,* or *imagery* are given highly technical meanings. And the confusion is heightened when we discover that the famous definition of *information* by Claude Shannon and Warren Weaver, who helped found information science, while useful for technological purposes, has no bearing on semantic meaning or the "content" of communication.

In general, in the pages ahead, *data* will mean more or less unconnected "facts"; *information* will refer to data that have been fitted into categories and classification schemes or other patterns; and *knowledge* will mean information that has been further refined into more general statements. But to avoid tedious repetition, all three terms may sometimes be used interchangeably.

To make things simple and escape from these definitional

quicksands, even at the expense of rigor, in the pages ahead the term *knowledge* will be given an expanded meaning. It will embrace or subsume information, data, images, and imagery, as well as attitudes, values, and other symbolic products of society, whether "true," "approximate," or even "false."

All of these are used or manipulated by power-seekers, and always have been. So, too, are the media for conveying knowledge: the means of communication, which, in turn, shape the messages that flow through them. The term *knowledge,* therefore, will be used to encompass all of these.

THE DEMOCRATIC DIFFERENCE

Besides its great flexibility, knowledge has other important characteristics that make it fundamentally different from lesser sources of power in tomorrow's world.

Thus force, for all practical concerns, is finite. There is a limit to how much force can be employed before we destroy what we wish to capture or defend. The same is true for wealth. Money cannot buy everything, and at some point even the fattest wallet empties out.

By contrast, knowledge does not. We can always generate more.

The Greek philosopher Zeno of Elea pointed out that if a traveler goes halfway to his destination each day, he can never reach his final destination, since there is always another halfway to go. In the same manner, we may never reach ultimate knowledge about anything, but we *can* always take one step closer to a rounded understanding of any phenomenon. Knowledge, in principle at least, is infinitely expandable.

Knowledge is also inherently different from both muscle and money, because, as a rule, if I use a gun, you cannot simultaneously use the same gun. If you use a dollar, I can't use the same dollar at the same time.

By contrast, both of us can use the same knowledge either for or against each other—and in that very process we may even produce still more knowledge. Unlike bullets or budgets, knowledge itself doesn't get used up. This alone tells us that the rules of the knowledge-power game are sharply different from the precepts relied on by those who use force or money to accomplish their will.

But a last, even more crucial difference sets violence and wealth apart from knowledge as we race into what has been called an information age: By definition, both force and wealth are the property of the strong and the rich. It is the truly revolutionary characteristic of knowledge that it can be grasped by the weak and the poor as well.

Knowledge is the most democratic source of power.

Which makes it a continuing threat to the powerful, even as they use it to enhance their own power. It also explains why every power-holder—from the patriarch of a family to the president of a company or the Prime Minister of a nation—wants to control the quantity, quality, and distribution of knowledge within his or her domain.

The concept of the power triad leads to a remarkable irony.

For at least the past three hundred years, the most basic political struggle within all the industrialized nations has been over the distribution of wealth: Who gets what? Terms like *left* and *right,* or *capitalist* and *socialist* have pivoted on this fundamental question.

Yet, despite the vast maldistribution of wealth in a world painfully divided between rich and poor, it turns out that, compared with the other two sources of worldly power, wealth has been, and is, the *least* maldistributed. Whatever gulf separates the rich from the poor, an even greater chasm separates the armed from the unarmed and the ignorant from the educated.

Today, in the fast-changing, affluent nations, despite all inequities of income and wealth, the coming struggle for power will increasingly turn into a struggle over the distribution of and access to knowledge.

This is why, unless we understand how and to whom knowledge flows, we can neither protect ourselves against the abuse of power nor create the better, more democratic society that tomorrow's technologies promise.

The control of knowledge is the crux of tomorrow's worldwide struggle for power in every human institution.

In the chapters immediately ahead we shall see how these changes in the nature of power itself are revolutionizing relationships in the world of business. From the transformation of capital to the growing conflict between "highbrow" and "lowbrow" businesses, from the electronic supermarket to the rise of family business and the emergence of startling new organizational forms, we will trace the new trajectory of power. These deep changes in business and the economy are paralleled by significant changes in politics, the media, and the global espionage industry. Finally, we will see how today's tremendous, wrenching powershift will impact on the impoverished nations, the remaining socialist nations, and the future of the United States, Europe, and Japan. For today's powershift will transform them all.

PART TWO

LIFE IN THE SUPER-SYMBOLIC ECONOMY

3

BEYOND THE AGE OF GLITZ

Business may be turning out products and profits. But it is hard to resist the suspicion that it is also becoming a popular form of theater. Like theater, it has heroes, villains, drama, and—increasingly—it has stars.

The names of business tycoons ricochet through the media like those of Hollywood celebrities. Surrounded by publicists, trained in all the arts of self-promotion, characters like Donald Trump or Lee Iacocca have become living symbols of corporate power. They are satirized in the comics. They (and their writers) crank out best sellers. Both men have even been mentioned—or perhaps arranged to have themselves mentioned—as potential candidates for the presidency of the United States. Business has arrived in the Age of Glitz.

Business had its stars in the past, too, but the very context of stardom is different today. The tinselly new glamour acquired by business is a superficial facet of the new economy, in which information (including everything from scientific research to advertising hype) plays a growing role. What is happening is the rise of an entirely new "system for wealth creation," which brings with it dramatic changes in the distribution of power.

This new system for making wealth is totally dependent on the instant communication and dissemination of data, ideas, symbols, and symbolism. It is, as we will discover, a super-symbolic economy in the exact sense of that term.

Its arrival is transformational. It is not, as some still belatedly insist, a sign of "de-industrialization," "hollowing out," or economic decay, but a leap toward a revolutionary new system of production. This new system takes us a giant step beyond mass production toward increasing customization, beyond mass marketing and distribution toward niches and micro-marketing, beyond the monolithic corporation to new forms of organization, beyond the nation-state to operations that are both local and global, and beyond the proletariat to a new "cognitariat."

The collision between forces favoring this new system of wealth creation and defenders of the old smokestack system is the dominant economic conflict of our time, exceeding in historical importance the conflict between capitalism and communism or among the United States, Europe, and Japan.

Moving from an economy based on smokestacks to one based on computers requires massive transfers of power, and it largely explains the wave of financial and industrial restructuring that has been ripping through the corporate world, throwing up new leaders, as companies desperately seek to adapt to fresh imperatives.

Takeovers, raids, acquisitions, leveraged buy-outs, corporate buy-backs, all made financial headlines throughout the 1980s, and involved not only U.S. firms but many foreign companies as well, despite legal and other restrictions that limit "unfriendly" takeovers in countries like West Germany, Italy, or Holland.

It would be an exaggeration to say that all these wild doings on Wall Street and the thrashing about in companies around the world are direct manifestations of the shift to a new kind of economy. Tax considerations, the integration of Europe, financial liberalization, old-fashioned greed, and other factors all play a role. Indeed, men like Trump and Iacocca represent, if anything, men of the past rather than heralds of the new. Successfully lobbying Washington to bail out a failing auto maker, Iacocca's chief claim to fame, or putting one's name on flashy skyscrapers and gambling casinos hardly make one a business revolutionary.

In a revolutionary period, however, all sorts of strange flora and fauna appear—atavists, eccentrics, publicity hounds, saints, and crooks, along with visionaries and genuine revolutionaries.

Beneath all the razzle-dazzle, the refinancings and reorganizations, there is an emerging pattern. For what we are seeing is a change in the structure of business and the beginnings of a shift of power from "smokestack money" to what might be called "super-symbolic money"—a process we will explore in more detail later.

This broad restructuring is necessary as the entire wealth-creation system, driven by competitive pressures, steps up to a more advanced level. Thus, to picture the takeover frenzy of the late eighties as nothing more than an expression of me-first greed is to miss its larger dimensions.

Nevertheless, the new economy has rewarded well those who first saw it coming. In the smokestack era any list of the richest people in the world would have been dominated by car makers, steel barons, rail magnates, oil moguls, and financiers, whose collective wealth ultimately came from the organization of cheap labor, raw materials, and the manufacture of hardware.

By contrast, *Forbes* magazine's latest list of the ten richest American billionaires includes fully seven whose fortunes were based on media, communications, or computers—software and services rather than hardware and manufacturing. They reflect what the Japanese call the new "softnomics."

The spasm of mergers, takeovers, divestitures, and financial reshufflings is, however, only one aspect of the transition to the new economy. At the same time that they are trying to fend off raiders or to make acquisitions, companies are also frantically striving to cope with an info-technological revolution, a restructuring of markets, and a host of other related changes. It adds up to the biggest shake-up the business world has known since the industrial revolution.

THE BUSINESS COMMANDOS

So deep a restructuring doesn't happen without anguish and confrontation. As happened at the start of the industrial revolution, millions find their incomes threatened, their ways of work made obsolete, their futures uncertain, their power slashed.

Investors, managers, and workers alike are thrown into conflict and confusion. Strange alliances spring up. New forms of judo are invented. In the past, labor unions exerted power by striking or threatening to do so. Today, in addition, they hire investment bankers, lawyers, and tax experts—purveyors of specialized knowledge—hoping to become part of a restructuring deal rather than its victim. Managers seeking to head off a takeover, or to buy out their own firm, along with investors seeking to profit from such upheavals, are increasingly dependent on timely, pinpointed information. Knowledge is a key weapon in the power struggles that accompany the emergence of the super-symbolic economy.

So is the ability to influence the media—thereby shaping what others know (or think they know). In this volatile environment, flashy personalities skilled at manipulating symbols have a distinct advantage. In France the epitome of the entrepreneur is Bernard Tapie, who claims to have built a privately held business with annual revenues of $1 billion. Tapie hosts his own TV show. In Britain, Richard Branson, who founded the Virgin Group, breaks speedboat records and, in the words of *Fortune,* enjoys "the sort of celebrity once reserved for rock stars or royalty."

As an old system cracks, the faceless bureaucrat-managers who run it are blown away by a guerrilla army of risk-taking investors, promoters, organizers, and managers, many of them antibureaucratic individualists, all of them skilled at either acquiring knowledge (sometimes illegally) or controlling its dissemination.

The arrival of the new super-symbolic system for creating wealth not only shifts power but changes its style as well. One need only compare the temperaments of, say, John DeButts, the slow, solemn man who ran the American Telephone and Telegraph Company in the 1970s before it was broken up, with that of William McGowan, who cracked AT&T's monopoly and created MCI Communications Corporation to compete with it. Impatient and irreverent, the son of a railroad unionist, McGowan began by peddling alligator purses, wound up raising funds for Hollywood producers Mike Todd and George Skouras when they made the wide-screen version of *Oklahoma,* and then founded a small defense contracting firm before zeroing in on AT&T.

Or compare the cautious "business statesmen" who ran General Electric for a decade or two, with Jack Welch, who gained the nickname "Neutron Jack" as he tore up the giant and reshaped it.

The stylistic shift reflects changed needs. For the task of restructuring companies and whole industries to survive in the super-symbolic economy is not a job for nit-picking, face-saving, bean-counting bureaucrats. It is, in fact, a job for individualists, radicals, gut-fighters, even eccentrics—business commandos, as it were, ready to storm any beach to seize power.

It has been said that today's risk-taking entrepreneurs and deal-makers resemble the "robber barons" who originally built the smokestack economy. Today's Age of Glitz, indeed, does bear a resemblance to the so-called Gilded Age, just after the American Civil War. That, too, was a time of fundamental economic restructure, following the defeat of agrarian slavery by the rising forces of the industrializing North. It was the era of conspicuous consumption, political corruption, wild spending, financial peculation and speculation, peopled by larger-than-life characters like "Commodore" Vanderbilt, "Diamond Jim" Brady, and "Bet a Million" Gates. Out of that era, marked by anti-unionism and contempt for the poor, came the decisive burst of economic development that thrust America into the modern industrial age.

But if today's new breed are more buccaneer than bureaucrat, they could be termed "electronic pirates." The power they seize is dependent on sophisticated data, information, and know-how, not just bags of capital.

Says California financier Robert I. Weingarten, describing the corporate takeover process, "The first thing you do is create a computer screen which lists your criteria. Then you search for a target company that meets them by running these criteria against various data bases until you identify the target. And the last thing you do? The last thing you do is call a press conference. You start with the computer and end with the media.

"In between," he adds, "you call in a host of highly specialized knowledge workers—tax lawyers, proxy war strategists, mathematical modelers, investment advisers, and PR experts—most of whom are also very dependent on computers, facsimile machines, telecommunications, and the media.

"Nowadays the ability to make a deal happen very often depends more on knowledge than on the dollars you bring to the table. At a certain level it's easier to obtain the money than the relevant know-how. Knowledge is the real power lever."

Because takeovers and restructure challenge power, they produce high drama, hence heroes and villains. Names like Carl Icahn and T. Boone Pickens become household words around the world. Feuds break out. Steve Jobs, co-founder of Apple Computer and once the boy wonder of American industry, resigns after a corporate *coup d'état* by John Sculley, despite Jobs's vast holdings in the company. Iacocca continues his interminable vendetta against Henry Ford II. Roger Smith of General Motors is satirized in a movie, *Roger & Me*, and savaged in public by Ross Perot, the computer millionaire whose company Smith acquired. The list lengthens each day.

To imagine that takeovers are peculiarly American, an artifact of inadequate regulation of Wall Street, is to miss their deeper significance. In Britain, Roland "Tiny" Rowland battles bitterly for control of Harrods department store and Sir James Goldsmith, the burly, brash financier launches a $21 billion raid on BAT Industries PLC. Carlo de Benedetti, head of Olivetti, battles with Gianni Agnelli of the Fiat empire and *il salòtto buono*—the inner circle of entrenched industrial power in Italy—and shocks all of Europe with a sudden bid for control of Société Générale de Belgique of Brussels, a group that controls a third of the entire Belgian economy.

Groupe Bull, the French computer firm, eyes the computer operation of Zenith in the United States. Groupe Victoire takes over Germany's second-largest insurer, Colonia Versicherung A.G., while the Dresdner Bank buys out the French Banque Internationale de Placement.

In Spain, where drama often turns into melodrama, the public has been treated to what the *Financial Times* has called "probably the most riveting and, ultimately, tasteless, display in decades," an explosive battle between "los beautiful people" and "los successful people"—old and new money.

Focused on control of the nation's three largest banks and their related industrial empires, the battle pitted Alberto Cortina and his cousin Alberto Alcocer against Mario Conde, a brilliant, Jesuit-trained lawyer who captured control of Banco Español de Crédito and tried to merge it with Banco Central, already the largest bank in the country. The battle hit the pages of the soft-porn press when one of "los Albertos" fell in love with a twenty-eight-year-old marquesa who was photographed in a nightclub wearing a miniskirt sans undies.

In the end the grand merger, touted by the Spanish Prime Minister as "possibly the economic event of the century," broke apart like shattered glass, leaving Conde fighting to survive in his own bank.

All this is exciting fodder for the media mills, but the international character of the phenomenon tells us that something more is involved than glitz, greed, and local regulatory failures. As we'll see, something more serious *is* happening. Power is shifting on a hundred fronts at once. The very nature of power—the mix of force, wealth, and knowledge—is changing as we make the transition to the super-symbolic economy.

DALE CARNEGIE AND ATTILA THE HUN

It is hardly surprising that even smart executives seem confused. Some rush out and read how-to books with silly titles like *Leadership Secrets of Attila the Hun*. Others peruse mystical tracts. Some take Dale Carnegie courses on how to influence people, while others attend seminars on the tactics of negotiation, as though power were purely a matter of psychology or tactical maneuver.

Still others privately bewail the presence of power in their firms, complaining that power-play is bad for the bottom line—a wasteful diversion from the push for profit. They point to energy dissipated in personal power squabbles and unnecessary people added to the payroll of power-hungry empire-builders. Confusion is redoubled when many of the most effective power wielders smoothly deny having any.

The bewilderment is understandable. Free-marketeer economists like Milton Friedman tend to picture the economy as an impersonal supply-and-demand machine and ignore the role of power in the creation of wealth and profit. Or they blandly assume that all the power struggles cancel one another out and thus leave the economy unaffected.

This tendency to overlook the profit-making importance of power is not limited to conservative ideologues. One of the most influential texts in U.S. universities is *Economics* by Paul A. Samuelson and William D. Nordhaus. Its latest edition carries an index that runs to twenty-eight pages of eye-straining fine print. Nowhere in that index is the word *power* listed.

(An important exception to this power-blindness or purblindness among celebrated American economists has been J. K. Galbraith, who, regardless of whether one agrees with his other views, has consistently tried to factor power into the economic equation.)

Radical economists do a lot of talking about such things as business's undue power to mold consumer wants, or about the power of monopolies and oligopolies to fix prices. They attack corporate lobbying, campaign contributions, and the less savory methods sometimes used by corporate interests to oppose regulation of worker health and safety, environment, progressive taxation, and the like.

But at a deeper level, even activists obsessed with limiting business power mistake (and underestimate) the role of power in the economy, including its positive and generative role, and seem unaware that power itself is going through a startling transformation.

Behind many of their criticisms lurks the unstated idea that power is somehow extrinsic to production and profits. Or that the abuse of power by economic enterprises is a capitalist phenomenon. A close look at today's powershift phenomenon will tell us, instead, that power is intrinsic to all economies.

Not only excessive or ill-gotten profits, but all profits are partly (sometimes largely) determined by power rather than by efficiency. (Even the most inefficient firm can make a profit if it has the power to impose its own terms on workers, suppliers, distributors, or customers.) At virtually every step, power is an inescapable part of the very process of production—and this is true for all economic systems, capitalist, socialist, or whatever.

Even in normal times, production requires the frequent making and breaking of power relationships, or their constant readjustment. But today's times are not "normal." Heightened competition and accelerated change require constant innovation. Each attempt to innovate sparks resistance and new power conflicts. But in today's revolutionary environment, when different systems of wealth creation collide, minor adjustments often no longer suffice. Power conflicts take on new intensity, and because companies are more and more interdependent, a power upheaval in one firm frequently produces reverberating shifts of power elsewhere.

As we push further into a competitive global economy heavily based on knowledge, these conflicts and confrontations escalate. The result is that the power factor in business is growing more and more important, not just for individuals but for each business as a whole, bringing power shifts that often have a greater impact on the level of profit than cheap labor, new technology, or rational economic calculation.

From budget-allocation battles to bureaucratic empire-building, business organizations are already increasingly driven by power imperatives. Fast-multiplying conflicts over promotions and hiring, the relocation of plants, the introduction of new machines or products, transfer pricing, reporting requirements, cost accounting, and the definition of accounting terms—all will trigger new power battles and shifts.

THE CONSULTANT'S HIDDEN MISSION

The Italian psychologist Mara Selvini Palazzoli, whose group studies large organizations, reports a case in which two men together owned a group of factories. The president hired a consulting psychologist, ostensibly to boost efficiency. Telling him that morale was low, he encouraged the consultant to interview widely to find out why the work force seemed riddled with ulcer-producing levels of anger and envy.

The vice-president and co-owner (30 percent, versus 70 percent owned by the president) expressed skepticism about the project. Hiring a consultant, the president shrugged, was merely "the thing to do" nowadays.

Analysis by Palazzoli's group revealed a snake pit of power relationships gone awry. The consultant's overt agenda was to increase efficiency. But his real task was different. In actuality, the president and vice-president were at dagger-points and the president wanted an ally.

Palazzoli and her group write: "The president's secret agenda was an attempt to gain control, through the psychologist, of the whole company, including manufacturing and sales [which were largely under the control of his vice-president and partner].... The vice-president's secret agenda was to prove himself superior to his partner and to show that his authority derived from his greater technical competence [i.e., better knowledge] and more commanding personality."

The case is typical of many. The fact is that all businesses, large and small, operate in a "power field" in which the three basic tools of power—force, wealth, and knowledge—are constantly used in conjunction with one another to adjust or revolutionize relationships.

But what the above case chronicles is merely "normal" power conflict. In the decades just ahead, as two great systems of wealth creation come into violent collision, as globalization spreads and the stakes rise, these normal contests will take place in the midst of far greater, more destabilizing power battles than any we have yet seen.

This doesn't mean that power is the only goal, or that power is a fixed pie that companies and individuals fight to divide, or that mutually fair relationships are impossible, or that so-called "win-

win" deals (in which both sides gain) are out of the question, or that all human relations are necessarily reduced to a "power nexus," rather than to Marx's famous "cash nexus."

But it strongly suggests that the immense shifts of power that face us will make today's takeovers and upheavals seem small by comparison, and will affect every aspect of business, from employee relations and the power of different functional units—such as marketing, engineering, and finance—to the web of power relations between manufacturers and retailers, investors and managers.

Men and women will make those changes. But the instruments of change will be force, wealth, and knowledge and the things they convert into. For inside the world of business, as in the larger world outside, force, wealth, and knowledge—like the ancient sword, jewel, and mirror of the sun goddess Amaterasu-omi-kami—remain the primary tools of power. Failure to understand how they are changing is a ticket to economic oblivion.

If that were all, business-men and -women would face a time of excruciating personal and organizational pressure. But it is not all. For a powershift, in the full sense, is more than a transfer of power. It is a sudden, sharp change in the nature of power—a change in the mix of knowledge, wealth, and force.

To anticipate the deep changes soon to strike, therefore, we must look at the role of all three. Thus, before we can appreciate what is happening to power based on wealth and knowledge, we must be prepared to take an unsettling look at the role of violence in the business world.

4

FORCE: THE YAKUZA COMPONENT

He is a celebrity. The business world's equivalent of a star. His marriages make the gossip pages. His name induces fear and fascination in the financial community. Still in his forties, he is a cocky man, by turns charming and choleric. He is a rabid reader whose Sunday afternoons may be spent wandering the Upper East Side of Manhattan, unrecognized in a turtleneck sweater, in search of a bookstore to browse in. He has butted heads with some of the mightiest corporate chieftains, made front-page business news, and built a personal fortune estimated at nearly half a billion dollars.

He is also a lawbreaker.

What's more, the law he has broken is not some wimpy law against stock market shenanigans or white-collar crime. It is the most macho of laws—that which prohibits violence.

Paraphrased for brevity's sake, here is his story.

After flames broke out in one of my company's computer centers in a nearby city, our investigators came to the conclusion the fire was set by a pissed-off employee. Trouble is, we didn't have evidence that would stand up in court, and we couldn't get the local cops interested. Even if we could, we knew it would take forever to get anything done about it.

So we wired up another employee with a hidden tape recorder and sent him to a bar, where he sidled up to the guy we suspected. He admitted it. Even bragged about it. When he did that, I wasn't going to take any chances. So our security men had a little talk with him and threatened to break his legs (or more) if he didn't quit his job in my company and get the hell out of town—fast!

Was that against the law? Sure. Would I do it again? You bet! The next fire he set could have killed some of my employees. Am I going to wait around for the cops and the courts to see what would happen?

This story reminds us that in every society there is what might be called a "secondary enforcement system," which operates around the edges of the formal, official law-enforcement system. But it also tells us that, under the smooth surface of business, things happen that few wish to speak about.

We seldom stop to think about force as a factor in business. Most of the trillions of business transactions carried out each day are so free of anything suggesting violence, so peaceful on the surface, that we seldom lift the lid to see what may be seething below.

Yet the same three sources of power we find in family life, government, or any other social institution operate in business as well, and much as we might prefer to think otherwise, violence has always been part of the economy.

BLOOD AND SNOW-MONEY

From the day the first paleolithic warrior smashed a rock into a small animal, violence has been used to produce wealth.

Taking preceded making.

It may be just a fluke, but *Roget's Thesaurus*, which devotes 26 lines to synonyms of the word *borrowing* and 29 lines to *lending*, devotes fully 157 lines to alternative descriptions of *taking*—including "capture," "colonize," "conquer," and "kidnap," not to mention "rape," "shanghai," and "abduct."

The agricultural revolution, starting some 10,000 years ago, represented a dramatic shift from taking—through fishing, foraging, or hunting—to making wealth. But even agriculture was steeped in violence.

Knout and knife, club and quirt were as much a part of the agricultural economy as the sickle, the scythe, or the spade.

Before the smokestack revolution, when our great-grandparents slaved away on the soil, the whole world was as economically underdeveloped as the poorest, most capital-starved countries today. There were no "developed" economies to turn to for billion-dollar loans or foreign aid. Where, then, did the first fortunes come from that financed the earliest smokestack industries?

Many of them flowed, directly or indirectly, from pillage, plunder, and piracy . . . from the slavemaster's whip . . . from the conquest of land . . . brigandage . . . extortion . . . terrorization of the peasant by the lord . . . forced Indian labor in gold and silver mines . . . from the vast tracts of land granted by grateful monarchs to their warriors and generals.

These pools of red-stained wealth turned pink and later snowflake-white as they passed from father to son and grandson, over the generations. Eventually they funded those first iron foundries, textile mills, shipping lines, and clock factories that came alive in the late 1600s and early 1700s.

Violence continued to play a role in the production of wealth in those early factories and mills, as children were shackled to machines and beaten, women miners brutalized or raped, men cudgeled into resignation.

ON ZEKS AND GOONS

The use of force to extract wealth did not end with the age of the steam engine. In the 20th century, violence was used on a truly grand scale.

In the Soviet Union's infamous camps, like Vorkuta, millions of "zeks" and other prisoners provided dirt-cheap labor for logging and mining. At first, writes the Soviet economist Vasily Selyunin, these were used to suppress political opposition to the 1917 revolution; later they "became a means of solving purely economic tasks." Hitler's factories during World War II, using slave labor from all over Europe, turned out munitions, chemicals—and corpses. And South Africa's brutal treatment of its black majority has been a form of labor control based on police dogs, truncheons, and tear gas.

The history of the labor movement in the United States, as in many other nations, is steeped in repressive violence and occasional terrorism. From the Molly Maguires, who tried to organize the Pennsylvania coal fields in the 1870s, to the Knights of Labor; from the Haymarket massacre in 1886 at the start of the campaign for an eight-hour workday, to the great textile strike in Gastonia, North Carolina, in 1929 and the Memorial Day massacre at Republic Steel in Chicago in 1937, employers and police attempted to prevent the organization of unions.

As recently as the late 1930s in the United States, companies hired strong-arm men to break strikes or to intimidate union organizers and their followers. Harry Bennett and his infamous "goon squads" were routinely called out to bust heads when Ford Motor Company employees asked for raises or threatened to organize. Not infrequently the Mafia helped employers "deal with" militant workers. In South Korea today many companies have set up "Save the Company" squads to break strikes and prevent unionization. At the Motorola plant in Seoul, violence reached the point at which two workers doused themselves with gasoline and set themselves on fire to protest the company's refusal to recognize a union.

Japanese employers in the early postwar period called on the Mafia-like Yakuza to intimidate union activists. And in Japan, even today, despite its advanced stage of economic development, the Yakuza factor has not completely vanished.

Yakuza-linked *sokaiya*—pointy-shoed hooligans and thugs—often turn up at stockholder meetings of Japanese corporations, either to embarrass or to protect the management. In 1987 the first meeting of shareholders following the privatization of the Nippon Telegraph and Telephone Company (NTT) was marked by disruption when a garishly dressed *sokaiya* accused a director of pinching his secretary. Dozens of others leaped to their feet to drag out the discussion. One demanded to know why he had to queue up for the toilets in the building. When an officer apologized, the man asked why an NTT employee had committed an indecent act. To groans from the audience, he hit his stride with questions about missing promissory notes worth a few thousand dollars and about telephone bugging.

The *sokaiya* did not stop this harassment, intended to embarrass rather than reform the company, until suddenly, as though from nowhere, a large number of husky young men surrounded the room—at which point the *sokaiya* quietly made their exit.

Not all business crime ends so peacefully, as Japan discovered when Kazuo Kengaku, a well-known investment fund manager with links to the Yakuza, was found encased in concrete in Osaka. The Yakuza are also involved deeply in real estate speculation and supply strong-arm men to frighten residents or small shop-owners reluctant to move out of the way of high-rise developments. So well known are these tactics that they provided the substance for Juzo Itami's 1989 movie, *A Taxing Woman's Return.*

Valuable real estate also lay behind a recent case in which the collapse of a financial deal led to fraud litigation. An American lawyer in Tokyo, Charles Stevens of Coudert Brothers, representing a U.S. firm, received threatening calls and wound up keeping a baseball bat at his desk.

Violence in the business demimonde takes on bizarre forms on occasion—especially on the fringes of the entertainment business. In South Korea local film distributors have tried to frighten customers away from theaters showing U.S. films by releasing snakes in the theaters. In France, when Saudi Arabian investors, together with the French government, built Mirapolis, a $100 million amusement park, carnival workers, fearing competition, poured sand in the gears of thrill rides. (The park turned out to be a disaster for other reasons.)

Similarly, Japanese *sarakin,* like loan sharks the world over, sometimes rely on physical "persuasion" to coerce borrowers into repaying usurious debts—the money from these activities flowing smoothly into major banks and other financial institutions.

In the United States, as in many other countries, force is sometimes used to shut the mouths of corporate "whistle blowers" —employees who call attention to the questionable practices of their bosses.

This was the role Karen Silkwood chose for herself. Silkwood was killed in a car crash after protesting her employer's handling of nuclear materials, and there are those who still, years after the event, question whether the crash was accidental. They will never stop believing that her company had her killed.

Of course, all these cases are dramatic precisely because they are exceptions in the advanced economies. The daily experience of an American executive with a sheaf of printout in hand, the Japanese salaryman on his telephone, or the salesperson spreading a sample on a counter is so remote from any hint of violence that even to mention it is to draw skeptical looks.

Yet just because most transactions in business involve no direct violence does not mean that violence has vanished.

The reality is that violence has been contained, transmuted into another form—and hidden.

A MONOPOLY OF FORCE

One reason that overt corporate or business violence is now so rare is that over the years it has been increasingly "contracted out." Instead of businesses producing their own violence, they have, in effect, bought the services of government. In all industrial nations, state violence replaces private violence.

The first thing any government tries to do, from the moment it is formed, is to monopolize violence. Its soldiers and police are the only ones legally permitted to exert violence.

In some cases the state is politically controlled by the corporations, so that the line between the exercise of private and public power is hair-thin. But the old Marxist idea—that the state is nothing more than the "executive committee" of the ruling corporate power—ignores what we all know: that politicians more often act on their own behalf than on the behalf of others.

Moreover, the Marxist assumed that only capitalist corporations or governments would ever use force against unarmed workers. That was before communist police, armed with tear gas, fire hoses, and more ominous equipment, tried to stamp out Poland's Solidarity union movement in the early 1980s, and China massacred its students and workers near Tiananmen Square, behaving exactly like the soldiers and police of Pinochet's Chile or any number of other vehemently anticommunist countries.

By seizing into its own mailed fist the technologies of violence, and attempting to eliminate or control all violence, the state reduces the independent manufacture of violence by the corporation and other institutions.

THE HIDDEN GUN

A second reason why direct physical aggression seems to have almost vanished from ordinary business life is that violence has been sublimated into law.

All business, capitalist and socialist alike, depends upon law. Every contract, every promissory note, every stock and bond, every mortgage, every collective bargaining contract, every insurance policy, every debit and credit is ultimately backed by the law.

And behind every law, good or evil, we find the barrel of a gun. As tersely put by former French President Charles de Gaulle, "The law must have force on its side." Law *is* sublimated violence.

Thus when one company sues another, it asks the government to bring the *force* of law to bear. It wants the government's guns (concealed behind obscuring layers of bureaucratic and judicial rigmarole) stuck into the ribs of its adversary to compel certain actions.

It is not entirely accidental that corporate lawyers in the United States are often called "hired guns."

The very frequency of recourse to law (as distinct from other ways of resolving business disputes) is a fair measure of force in the economy. By this criterion, the United States has a "force-full" economy. Today there are 5.7 million business establishments in the United States and 655,000 lawyers—i.e., approximately one for every nine businesses. More than a thousand civil lawsuits are painfully processed by the clogged district court systems every business day of the year.

U.S. businessmen complain loudly about the allegedly unfair intimacy between Japanese business and government. Yet ironically, when it comes to settling disputes, it is the Americans, not the Japanese, who rush to litigate, thereupon calling upon the power of the state to intervene on their behalf.

From the smallest commercial litigation to the multibillion-dollar lawsuit involving a dispute between Pennzoil and Texaco over a takeover bid, law masks force—which, in the end, implies the potential application of violence.

Corporate campaign contributions can be seen as another camouflaged way of getting a government to pull a gun out of its holster in the interest of a company or industry.

In Japan, when Hiromasa Ezoe, chairman of the Recruit company, passed out huge amounts of stock at below-market price to top politicians in the ruling Liberal Democratic Party, his attempt to curry favor was so blatant it outraged the press and public and led to the resignation of Prime Minister Noboru Takeshita. The scandal bore some resemblance to the earlier case of the Flick empire in West Germany, whose executives channeled illegal funds to various political parties.

The Japanese also spend over $60 billion a year—more than they spend for their automobiles—in 14,500 garishly lit "pachinko parlors," where they play a game that involves guiding a stainless-steel ball downward past obstacles into an appropriate slot. Winners receive prizes, some of which they can exchange for money. Like game arcades in the United States, pachinko is a cash business, made to order for tax evasion and money laundering. Criminal gangs siphon off protection money from the parlors and sometimes war with one another for control of the most lucrative one. To ward off legislation aimed at opening their books to the police, parlor operators have made large contributions to both leading parties.

Whenever business funds are passed to candidates or political parties, the presumption is that a quid pro quo is expected. In the United States, despite repeated reforms and changes in the laws governing campaign contributions, every important industry pipes funds to one or both of the parties to buy, at a minimum, a hearing for its special point of view; and ingenious methods—inflated speaking fees, the purchase of otherwise unsalable books, the "loan" of real estate, the granting of low-interest loans—are constantly invented to avoid or evade the legal restrictions.

The mere existence of government creates a set of indirect, often hidden, and unintentional cross-subsidies and cross-penalties in the economy. To the extent that government actions are ultimately backed by force—by guns and soldiers and police—the notion of power-free or violence-free economics is puerile.

But the last, and most important, reason why corporations—and even governments—resort to open violence less often than in the preindustrial past is that they have found a better instrument with which to control people.

That instrument is money.

THE TRAJECTORY OF POWER

That power, and even violence, remain part of the world of business should not surprise us. What should raise our eyebrows is the remarkable change in the *way* force is applied.

A slavemaster or feudal lord transplanted from antiquity into today's world would find it hard to believe, even astonishing, that we beat workers less—and they produce more.

A ship's captain would be amazed that sailors are not physically abused and shanghaied into service.

Even a journeyman carpenter or tanner from the 18th century would be nonplussed at the idea that he could not legally bash his fist into a sassy apprentice's mouth. See, for example, William Hogarth's color engraving entitled "Industry and Idleness," printed in England in 1796. In it we see two " 'prentices"—one working happily at his loom, the other dozing. At the right, the boss approaches angrily brandishing a stick with which to beat the idler.

Both custom and law now restrain this open use of force in the modern world. This vestigialization of violence in the economy, however, did not spring from Christian charity or gentle altruism.

What happened is that, during the industrial revolution, the elites in society shifted from a primary reliance on the low-quality power produced by violence, to the mid-quality power produced by money.

Money may not produce the immediate results of a fist in the face or a gun in the ribs. But, because it can be used both to reward *and* punish, it is a far more versatile, flexible tool of power—especially when the ultimate threat of violence remains in place.

Money could not become the main tool of social control earlier, because the vast majority of humans were not part of the money system. Peasants in the preindustrial ages basically grew their own food, made their own shelter and clothing. But as soon as factories replaced farms, people no longer grew their own food and they became desperately dependent on money for survival. This total dependence on the money system, as distinct from self-production, transformed all power relationships.

Violence, as we've just seen, did not disappear. But its form and function changed as money became the prime motivator of the work force and the main tool of social control during the three industrial centuries.

It is this which explains why smokestack societies, capitalist and socialist alike, have proved more grasping and acquisitive, more money-obsessed than far poorer, preindustrial cultures. Greed no doubt goes back to Paleozoic times. But it was industrialism that made money into the prime tool of power.

In sum, the rise of the industrial nation-state brought the systematic monopolization of violence, the sublimation of violence into law, and the growing dependence of the population on money. These three changes made it possible for the elites of industrial societies increasingly to make use of wealth rather than overt force to impose their will on history.

This is the true meaning of powershift. Not simply a transfer of power from one person or group to another, but a fundamental change in the mix of violence, wealth, and knowledge employed by elites to maintain control.

Today, just as the industrial revolution transmuted violence into law, so we are transmuting money—indeed, wealth in general— into something new. And just as the smokestack age saw money assume a primary role in gaining or maintaining power, so today, at the edge of the 21st century, we face another twist in the history of power. We are on the brink of a new powershift.

5

WEALTH: MORGAN, MILKEN . . . AND AFTER

When a man has got vast power, such as you have—you admit you have, do you not?"

"I do not know it, sir."

The man in the witness chair, who "did not know" he held power, was a bull-necked, bristle-browed banker with a fierce mustache and an outsized nose. The congressional committee investigator pressed him: "You do not feel [powerful] at all?"

"No," he replied smoothly, "I do not feel it at all."

The time was 1912. The witness, in a dark suit and wing collar, with a gold watch chain draped across his generous paunch, dominated three or four giant banks, three trust companies, an equal number of life insurance companies, ten railroad systems, plus, among a few other odds and ends, United States Steel, General Electric, AT&T, Western Union, and International Harvester.

John Pierpont Morgan was the quintessential financial capitalist of the industrial era, the very symbol of turn-of-the-century money power.

A womanizing churchgoer and moralizer, he lived in conspicuous opulence and gluttony, holding business meetings amid damask and tapestries from the palaces of Europe, next to vaults containing Leonardo da Vinci notebooks and Shakespeare folios. Morgan looked down his monumental nose at Jews and other minorities, hated trade unions, sneered at new money, and fought ceaselessly with the other "robber barons" of his era.

Born enormously rich in an era of capital scarcity, he was imperious and driven, savagely repressing competition, sometimes relying on methods that would probably now have landed him in jail.

Morgan assembled huge sums and poured them into the great smokestack industries of his time—into Bessemer furnaces and Pullman cars and Edison generators and into tangible resources like oil, nitrates, copper, and coal.

But he did more than simply seize targets of opportunity. He planned strategically and helped shape the smokestack age in the United States, accelerating the shift of political and economic power from agricultural to industrial interests, and from manufacturing to finance.

Furthermore, he was said to have "Morganized" industry in the United States, creating a hierarchically ordered, finance-driven system and, according to his critics, a "money trust," which essentially controlled the main flows of capital in the country.

When Morgan blandly denied having any power, the cartoonists had a field day, one picturing him sitting astride a mountain of coins marked "Control over $25,000,000,000"; another as a dour emperor in crown and robes, with a mace in one hand and a purse in the other.

While to Pope Pius X he was a "great and good man," to the *Boston Commercial Bulletin* he was a "financial bully, drunk with wealth and power, who bawls his orders to stock markets, directors, courts, governments and nations."

Morgan concentrated capital. He consolidated small companies into ever larger and more monopolistic corporations. He centralized. He regarded top-down command as sacred and vertical integration as efficient. He understood that mass production was the coming thing. He wanted his investments to be protected by "hard" assets—plants, equipment, raw materials.

In all this he was a near-perfect reflection of the early smokestack age he helped to create. And whether Morgan "felt powerful" or not, his control of vast sums in a period of capital scarcity gave him immense opportunities to reward and punish others and to make change on a grand scale.

THE X-SHAPED DESK

When his name first exploded into the headlines, Michael Milken was an intensely private, work-obsessed man in his early forties, nominally a senior vice-president of Drexel Burnham Lambert, an investment banking firm actually co-founded by Morgan in 1871. Despite this deceptive title, Milken was more than just another senior vice-president. He was the architect of a whole new order in American finance. He was, as many soon recognized, the J. P. Morgan of our time.

In the 1980s, Drexel became one of Wall Street's hottest investment banking firms. And because Milken's hard-driving efforts were mainly responsible for its spectacular growth, he was allowed to run his own largely independent shop, three thousand miles from the firm's headquarters in the East. His office was just across from the Beverly Wilshire Hotel in Beverly Hills, California.

Milken would arrive at his office as early as 4:30 or 5:00 A.M., in time to squeeze in a few meetings before the opening of the New York Stock Exchange, three time zones away. CEOs of major corporations, trekking in from New York or Chicago, would drag themselves red-eyed to these conferences, hat in hand, seeking financing for their companies. One might want to build a new plant; another might wish to expand into new markets; a third might wish to make an acquisition. They were there because they knew Milken could find the capital for them.

Throughout the day Milken would sit at the center of a huge X-shaped trading desk, whispering, wheeling, dealing, shouting, surrounded by a frenzy of employees working the telephones and computer screens. It was from this desk that he and his team reshaped modern American industry, as Morgan had done in an earlier day.

A comparison of how each did it tells a lot about how the control of capital—and hence the power of money in society—is changing today. And it begins with the personal.

MILKEN VERSUS MORGAN

While J. P. Morgan was paunchy, fierce-looking, and imposing, Milken is tall, slender, clean-shaven, with curly black hair and the look of a startled doe. While Morgan was born with the proverbial silver spoon in his baby mouth, Milken, son of a CPA, collected soiled spoons off tables at the coffee shop where he worked for a time as a busboy.

Morgan commuted between Wall Street, mid-Manhattan, an estate on the Hudson, and palatial residences in Europe. Milken still lives in a far-from-palatial wood and brick home in Encino, in the not-quite-fashionable San Fernando Valley of Los Angeles. Seldom far from the Pacific Ocean, he keeps his eyes focused on Japan, Mexico, and the developing economies to the south.

Morgan surrounded himself with compliant young ladies and left his wife and family to languish in his absence; Milken is, by all accounts, a family man. Morgan disliked Jews. Milken is Jewish.

Morgan despised trade unions; Milken has served as a financial consultant for rail, airline, and maritime unions. The idea that employees might own their own firms would have struck Morgan as arrant communism. Milken favors worker-ownership and believes it is going to play a major role in American industry in the years to come.

Both men accumulated vast power for themselves, became notorious in the press, came under government investigation for real and/or alleged wrongdoing. But, far more important, they shifted the *structure* of power in America in remarkably different ways.

OPENING THE GATES

When Milken was born on July 4, 1946, the American economy was still dominated by huge companies formed, for the most part, in the Morgan era. These were the General Motors and Goodyear Tires, the Burlington Mills and Bethlehem Steels of the world. These smokestack firms, the so-called Blue Chips, along with their lobbyists, political fund-raisers, and trade associations, plus organizations like the National Association of Manufacturers, had enormous political, as well as economic, clout. Collectively, they sometimes acted as though the country belonged to them.

This corporate power was magnified by their influence on the media through the control of immense advertising budgets, and their ability, at least in theory, to shut down a plant in a recalcitrant congressman's district, and shift the investments and jobs to another where the political climate was more favorable. Often they were able to induce the labor unions representing their blue-collar workers to join them in a lobbying effort.

This "smokestack power," moreover, was further protected by a financial industry that made it difficult for competitors to challenge Blue Chip dominance. As a result, the basic structure of industrial power remained largely unchanged through mid-century in the United States.

Then something happened.

Milken was still in elementary school in 1956, when, for the first time, service and white-collar workers came to outnumber blue-collar workers in the United States. And by the time he began his career as a young investment banker the economy had already begun its rapid transition to a new system of wealth creation.

Computers, satellites, vastly varied services, globalization, were creating a totally new, change-filled business environment. But the financial industry, hidebound and protected by legislation, formed a major barrier to change.

Until the 1970s, long-term capital was readily available for Blue Chip dinosaurs, but much more difficult for smaller, innovative and entrepreneurial firms to obtain.

Wall Street was the financial Vatican of the world, and in the United States two "rating services"—Moody's and Standard & Poor's—guarded the gates of capital. These two private firms assigned risk ratings to bonds, and only some 5 percent of American companies were considered by them to be of "investment grade." This locked thousands of companies out of the long-term debt market or sent them to banks and insurance companies for loans rather than to investors in the bond market.

A student, first at the University of California in Berkeley and later at the Wharton School of the University of Pennsylvania, Milken studied investor risk. He discovered that many of the smaller firms frozen out of Wall Street had good records for paying their debts. They seldom defaulted and were prepared to pay higher than usual interest if anyone would buy bonds from them.

From this counterintuitive insight came the so-called high-yield or "junk" bond, and Milken, now a young underling at Drexel, proceeded to sell them to investors with missionary zeal.

The details of the story are not important for our purposes. What matters is that Milken succeeded beyond anyone's wildest expectations. The result was that he almost single-handedly broke the financial isolation that had hitherto been imposed on this secondary tier of companies. It was like a dam bursting. Capital poured into these companies, passing through Drexel on its way. By 1989 the junk-bond market reached an astronomical $180 billion.

Rather than creating a "money trust," therefore, as Morgan had done, Milken made finance more competitive and less monopolistic, opening the gates, as it were, and freeing thousands of companies from dependence on banks and insurance companies. They also bypassed the snooty Wall Street firms that existed to serve the Blue Chips. Milken's bonds permitted managers to go directly to the public and to institutional lenders like pension funds for the capital with which to build new plants, to expand markets, to do research and development—or to take over other firms.

Roughly 75 percent of junk bonds were quietly used for investment in new technology, or to open new markets, and for other noncontroversial purposes. Drexel's advertising made much of the fact that while employment in the Blue Chips, the old giants, was not keeping pace with the economy's expansion, jobs in the smaller firms they financed multiplied more rapidly than in the economy at large. But some of the capital Milken supplied was used in pitched takeover battles.

These dramatic financial showdowns filled the headlines and kept the stock market and the nation itself spellbound. Stock prices soared and plunged on rumors of more, and still more, takeovers and raids affecting some of the nation's best-known companies. Deals were made that no longer provided a reasonable balance of risk and reward for the investor. Debt was pyramided on top of unrealistic debt in an orgy of speculation. Taxi drivers and waitresses knowingly discussed the latest news and called their stockbrokers, hoping to cash in on the killings to be made as competing raiders bid up the stock of corporations marked for takeover. As other Wall Street firms entered the junk-bond market, the money machine created by Milken and Drexel, no longer in their hands alone, became a runaway juggernaut.

Such violent upheavals, often involving highly personal power struggles, led to a slaughter of the innocents. Companies were "downsized," workers ruthlessly laid off, executive ranks decimated. Not surprisingly, a massive counterattack was launched with Milken as the principal target.

THE COUNTERATTACK

By forcing open the sluice gates of capital, Milken had rattled the entire structure of smokestack power in America. While enriching Drexel Burnham (and feathering his own nest to the amazing tune of $550 million in 1987 alone), he also made bitter enemies of two extremely powerful groups. One consisted of the old-line Wall Street firms who previously had had a stranglehold on the flow of capital to American corporations; the other consisted of the top managers of many of the largest firms. Both had every reason to destroy him if they could. Both also had powerful allies in government and the media.

First savaged in the press, which pictured him as the very embodiment of capitalist excess, Milken was then hit with a ninety-eight-count federal indictment charging him with securities fraud, market manipulation, and "parking" (illegally holding stock that belonged to Ivan Boesky, the arbitrageur who was jailed for insider trading). Threatening to use sweeping legal powers designed to deal with the Mafia, rather than with stock market wrongdoing, the federal government forced Drexel to sever its relationship with Milken and pay a crushing $650 million fine to Uncle Sam.

At the same time, some of the worst-case buy-outs began to come apart, panicking investors and pushing down the value of most junk bonds, safe and unsafe alike. Soon Drexel, struggling to stabilize itself after the $650 million fine, and itself holding $1 billion in junk bonds, found itself driven to the wall. Drexel collapsed with a thunderous crash. Milken, already tried and convicted in the press, ultimately pled guilty to six violations in a complex deal that erased all other criminal charges.

However, as in the case of Morgan, the question of whether or not he broke the law is far less important for the country than his net impact on American business. For while finance was restructuring other industries, Milken was restructuring finance.

The conflict between those, like Morgan, who wanted to restrict access to capital so that they could themselves control it, and those like Milken, who fought to widen access, has a long history in every country.

"There has been a long struggle," writes Professor Glenn Yago of the State University of New York (Stony Brook), "to innovate U.S. capital markets to make them more accessible. Farmers fought for credit in the 19th century, and agricultural productivity increases . . . were the outcome. In the '30s, small businessmen got relief from being squeezed out from bank credit windows. After World War II, workers and consumers sought credit for home ownership and college education. In spite of resistance by those who would restrict popular access to credit, financial markets responded to demand and the country flourished."

While an excess of credit can unleash inflation, there is a difference between excess and access. By broadening access, Milken's firm could, as Connie Bruck, one of his most savage critics, admits, "reasonably sustain the claim . . . that it had furthered the 'democratization of capital,' " which is why some trade unionists and African-Americans rallied to his defense in his time of trouble.

Morgan and Milken, in short, changed American finance in contrary ways.

TAMPONS AND CAR RENTALS

Furthermore, while Morgan was the ultimate centralizer and concentrator, operating on the assumption that the whole was worth more than its parts, Milken and the people he financed often started from the opposite assumption. Thus the 1960s and 1970s had seen the formation of gigantic, unwieldy, unfocused "conglomerates"—huge companies built on bureaucratic management and a blind belief in "economies of scale" and "synergy." The bonds Milken sold financed takeovers designed to bust up these behemoths and create slimmer, more maneuverable and more strategically focused firms.

Virtually every Milken-funded takeover resulted in the sell-off of divisions or units, because, in fact, the parts *were* worth more than the whole; the synergy, less than imagined.

A striking case in point was the breakup of the Beatrice Companies, an ungainly agglomeration that combined, with little logic, Avis car rentals, Coca-Cola bottling, Playtex brassieres, the manufacture of tampons, along with the food processing that had once formed its core business. After its parts were sold to other companies, Beatrice was a much smaller firm operating more sensibly in the food, cheese, and meat business. Borg-Warner, an industrial firm, sold off its financial operations. Revlon, after takeover, sold off its medical business and other units unrelated to its central skills—the cosmetic industry.

Milken's easing of access to capital also helped nourish upstart firms in the new service and information sectors that are key to the advanced economy.

Surely this was not Milken's primary purpose. He was more than willing to fund rust-belt industries as well. But, operating at a moment when the entire economy was in transit out of the smokestack era, he was certainly aware of this fundamental change and, in some ways, helped spur it on. Thus at one point he told *Forbes* magazine that much of the restructuring going on had to do with the country's transition out of the industrial age, adding that "in an industrial society, capital is a scarce resource, but in today's information society, there's plenty of capital."

Since Milken's high-yield or junk bonds worked to the advantage of newer, less established companies rather than the Blue Chips, all of whom had easy access to conventional financing, it is not surprising that many of his beneficiaries were in the fast-expanding service and information sectors where newer companies were likely to be found.

Thus Milken helped reorganize or channeled capital into cellular telephones, cable television, computers, health services, day care, and other advanced business sectors—whose growing power challenged the dominance of the old smokestack barons.

In short, Morgan and Milken alike, but in almost diametrically different ways, shook the established power structure in their time and for this reason, quite apart from legal issues, called down upon themselves hailstorms of controversy and calumniation. For good or ill, legally or not, each changed finance in ways that corresponded to the emerging needs of the economy in their time.

THE POST–WALL STREET ERA

Dramatic as they seemed at the time, the upheavals wrought by Milken were only part of a much larger revolution. For today's changes in the control and channeling of capital—still one of the primary sources of power in society—parallel even deeper changes in the entire economy.

In Morgan's time, and throughout the heyday of Wall Street power, the mass production of millions of identical products was symbolic of "modern times." Today, exactly as first suggested in *Future Shock* in 1970 and elaborated in *The Third Wave* in 1980, we are standing the principle of mass production on its head.

Computer-driven technologies are making it possible to turn out small runs of increasingly customized goods aimed at niche markets. Smart companies are moving from the production of long runs of commodity products to short runs of "higher value added products" like specialty steels and chemicals. Meanwhile, constant innovation shortens product life cycles.

We find precisely parallel changes in the financial service industry, which is also diversifying product lines and shortening product life cycles. It, too, is spewing out a stream of niche products—new types of securities, mortgages, insurance policies, credit instruments, mutual funds, and endless permutations and combinations of these. Power over capital flows toward firms capable of customization and constant innovation.

In the new Third Wave economy, a car or a computer may be built in four countries and assembled in a fifth. Markets, too, expand beyond national boundaries. In the current jargon, business is becoming global. Once more, in direct parallel, we find the financial services—banking, insurance, securities—all racing to "globalize" in order to serve their corporate clients.

The Third Wave economy operates at super-high speeds. To keep pace, financial firms are pouring billions into new technologies. New computers and communications networks not only make possible the variation and customization of existing products, and the invention of new ones, but also drive transaction speeds toward instantaneity.

As new-style factories shift from "batch processing" to round-the-clock or "continuous flow" operations, finance follows suit, and shifts from "banker's hours" to twenty-four-hour services. Financial centers crop up in multiple time zones. Stocks, bonds, commodities, and currencies trade nonstop. Electronic networks make it possible to assemble and disassemble billions in what seems like nanoseconds.

Speed itself—the ability to keep pace or stay ahead—affects

the distribution of profit and power. A good example is the shrink-age of the "float" once enjoyed by banks. "Float" is the money in customers' accounts on which a bank can earn interest while cus-tomer checks are waiting to clear. As computers accelerate the clearing process, banks gain less advantage from these funds and are forced to find alternative sources of revenue—which leads them into frontal competition with other sectors of the financial industry.

As capital markets expand and interlink, from Hong Kong and Tokyo to Toronto and Paris, crossing time zones, money runs faster. Velocity and volatility both rise, and financial power in society shifts from hand to hand at faster and faster speeds.

Taken together, all these changes add up to the deepest re-structure of world finance since the early days of the industrial era. They reflect the rise of a new system of wealth creation, and even the most powerful firms, once controlling vast flows of capital, are tossed about like matchsticks in a gale.

In 1985, America's largest investment banker, Salomon Broth-ers, committed itself to build an impressive $455 million headquar-ters on Manhattan's Columbus Circle. By spring of 1987 Salomon became the target of a possible takeover; in October it had to shut down the municipal bond business it had dominated for twenty years; its commercial paper department went, too; 800 of its 6,500 employees were laid off; the October 1987 stock market crash slammed into the firm, and by December it was ignomini-ously forced to back out of the big headquarters deal at a cost of $51 million.

As profits plummeted and its own stock price fell, internal schisms rent the firm apart. One faction favored sticking to its traditional role as a capital supplier to the Blue Chips. Another sought to enter the high-yield or junk bond business that Milken had pioneered and reach out to second-tier firms. Defections and chaos followed. "The world changed in some fundamental ways," rued its chairman, John Gutfreund, "and most of us were not on top of it. We were dragged into the modern world."

The "modern world," however, is a volatile, hostile place for the old dragons. Not only individuals and companies, but whole sectors of the financial industry totter. The collapse of more than five hundred savings-and-loans banks in the United States, requiring the government to pump hundreds of billions into an emergency rescue plan, reflects the rising instability. Government regulatory agencies designed for a simpler, slower smokestack world proved unable to anticipate and avert the looming disaster, as hundreds of these "thrift institutions," caught off guard and crushed by rapidly shifting interest rates, went down in a welter of corruption and stupidity.

THE ZIGZAG OF POWER

As the global economy grows, the financial marketplace itself becomes so vast that it dwarfs any single institution, company, or individual—even a Milken. Tremendous currents rip through the system causing eruptions and perturbations on a global scale.

From the dawn of the industrial era, money power was centered in Europe. By the end of World War II it had shifted decisively to North America, and more specifically to the southern tip of Manhattan island. U.S. economic dominance went unchallenged for nearly three decades. From then on, money—and the power that flows from it—has been zigzagging unsteadily across the planet like a pachinko ball gone mad.

In the mid-seventies, seemingly overnight, the OPEC cartel sucked billions out of Europe, North America (and the rest of the world), and sent them zigging into the Middle East. Immediately, these petrodollars were zagged into bank accounts in New York or Zurich, zigged out once more in the form of gigantic loans to Argentina, Mexico, or Brazil, shot right back to U.S. and Swiss banks. As the value of the dollar fell and trade patterns shifted, capital zagged again to Tokyo, and zigged back into real estate, government bonds, and other holdings in the United States—all at speeds that stagger the experts struggling to understand what is happening.

With each such lurch of capital comes a corresponding redistribution of power at the global and local levels. As oil money fire-hosed into the Middle East, Arab nations began to wield a huge cudgel in international politics. Israel found herself increasingly isolated in the U.N. African countries, needing oil and eager for foreign aid from the Arabs, broke off diplomatic relations with Jerusalem. Petrodollars began to influence the media in various parts of the world. And the lobbies of hotels in Riyadh, Abu Dhabi, and Kuwait were jammed with attaché-case-carrying supplicants—salesmen, bankers, executives, and wheeler-dealers from around the world, pleading ignominiously with this or that spurious relative of a royal family for contacts and contracts.

However, by the early 1980s, as OPEC unity fell apart and oil prices collapsed, the frenzy waned, and so did Arab political power. Today the horde of supplicants, often representing the largest banks and corporations in the world, mill about the lobbies of hotels like the Okura or the Imperial in Tokyo.

The growing volatility of the world capital market, dramatized by such huge swings and punctuated by stock market crashes and recoveries, as in the "Two Octobers"—October 1987 and October 1989—are a sign that the old system is increasingly going out of control. Old safety mechanisms, designed to maintain financial stability in a world of relatively closed national economies, are as obsolete as the rust-belt world they were designed to protect.

Globalized production and marketing require capital to flow easily across national boundaries. This, in turn, demands the dismantling of old financial regulations and barriers erected by nations to protect their economies. But the step-by-step relaxation or removal of these barriers in Japan and in Europe has negative consequences as well.

The result is a larger and larger pool of capital instantly available anywhere. But if this makes the financial system more flexible and helps it overcome localized crises, it also raises the ante, escalating the risk of massive collapse.

Modern ships are built with watertight compartments so that a leak in one part of the hull can't flood and sink the entire vessel. Liberalization of capital so that it can flow freely is the equivalent of eliminating these fail-safe compartments. Essential for the advance of the economy, it increases the danger that a serious collapse in one country will spread to others. It also threatens the power of one of the most important economic institutions of the industrial age: the central bank.

THE LOOMING FIGHT FOR GLOBAL CONTROL

Until a decade or so ago, a relative handful of central bankers and government officials could decisively affect the price of everything from Danish hams to Datsun cars by manipulating interest rates and intervening in foreign currency markets.

Today this is becoming harder for them to do. Witness the explosive growth of the "forex," or foreign exchange, markets and the electronic networks that facilitate them.

Only a few years ago the Bank of Japan could influence the yen–dollar ratio by buying or selling 16 billions' worth of dollars. Today such sums are laughable. An estimated 200 billion dollars' worth of currencies are traded every day in London, New York, and Tokyo alone—more than a trillion a week. (Of this, no more than 10 percent is associated with world trade; the remaining 90 percent is speculation.)

Against this background the role of individual central banks, and even of the major ones acting in concert, is limited at best.

Because power is rapidly shifting out of the hands of central bankers and the governments they nominally represent, we hear urgent calls for new, more centralized regulation at a supra-national level. These are attempts to control a post-smokestack financial system by using essentially the same tools used during the smokestack age—merely raised to a higher power.

In Europe some political leaders call for the elimination of national currencies and the creation of a single all-European central bank. France's former finance minister Édouard Balladour and West Germany's foreign minister Hans Dietrich Genscher are joined by many French, Belgian, and Italian officials in pushing for this higher level of centralization. Though still some time off in the future, says economist Liane Launhardt of Commerzbank A.G. in Frankfurt: "We will eventually have to have a European central bank."

Against this supra-nationalism, Prime Minister Margaret Thatcher of Britain has waged a rear-guard action in defense of national sovereignty. But even at the world level we begin to see increasing attempts by the G-7, the group of seven largest industrial economies, to synchronize and coordinate their policies with respect to currencies, interest rates, and other variables. And academics and some financial experts argue for a "world central bank."

If the globalizers win, it will mean further weakening of the power of existing central banks—the key regulators of capital in the noncommunist world since the dawn of the smokestack age.

The decades to come will therefore see a titanic power struggle between the globalizers and the nationalists over the nature of new regulatory institutions in the world capital markets. This struggle reflects the collision between a moribund industrial order and the new global system of wealth creation that is replacing it.

Ironically, however, these proposals to centralize control of global finance at a higher level run counter to developments at the actual level of economic production and distribution, both of which are becoming more dispersed, diverse, and decentralized. This suggests that the outcome of this historic power struggle may satisfy neither nationalists nor globalists. History, full of surprises, could force us to reframe the issues in novel ways and to invent wholly new institutions.

One thing seems clear. When the battle to reshape global finance reaches its climax in the decades ahead, many of the greatest "powers that be" will be overthrown.

Yet even these upheavals in the distribution of world money-power reveal less than the whole story. They will be dwarfed in history by a revolution in the nature of wealth itself. For something odd, almost eerie, is happening to money itself—and all the power that flows from it.

6

KNOWLEDGE: A WEALTH OF SYMBOLS

Once upon a time, wealth was elemental. You had it or you didn't have it. It was solid. It was material. And it was easy to understand that wealth gave power, and power wealth.

It was simple because both were based on the land.

Land was the most important capital of all. Land was finite—meaning that if you used it, no one else could use it at the same time. Better yet, it was eminently touchable. You could measure it, dig it, turn it, plant your feet on it, feel it between your toes, and run it through your fingers. Generations of our ancestors either had it or (literally) hungered for it.

Wealth was transformed when smokestacks began to stab the skies. Machines and materials for industrial production, rather than land, now became the most critically needed form of capital: steel furnaces, textile looms and assembly lines, spot welders and sewing machines, bauxite, copper, and nickel.

This industrial capital was still finite. If you used a furnace in a steel foundry making cast-iron engine blocks, no one else could use that furnace at the same time.

Capital was still material as well. When J. P. Morgan or other bankers invested in a company, they looked for "hard assets" on its balance sheet. When bankers considered a loan, they wanted "underlying" physical, tangible collateral. Hardware.

However, unlike most landowners who knew their wealth intimately, who knew each hill, each field, each spring and orchard, few industrial-age investors ever saw, let alone touched, the machines and minerals on which their wealth was based. An investor received paper instead, a mere symbol, a bond or stock certificate representing some fraction of the value of the corporation using the capital.

Marx spoke of the alienation of the worker from his or her product. But one might also have spoken of the alienation of the investor from the source of his or her wealth.

Today, at a pace that would have blinded Marx and/or Morgan, capital is being transformed again.

INSIDE THE SKULL

As service and information sectors grow in the advanced economies, as manufacturing itself is computerized, the nature of wealth necessarily changes. While investors in backward sectors of industry still regard the traditional "hard assets"—plant, equipment, and inventories—as critical, investors in the fastest growing, most advanced sectors rely on radically different factors to back their investments.

No one buys a share of Apple Computer or IBM stock because of the firm's material assets. What counts are not the company's buildings or machines, but the contacts and power of its marketing and sales force, the organizational capacity of its management, and the ideas crackling inside the heads of its employees. The same is of course true throughout the Third Wave sectors of the economy—in companies like Fujitsu or NEC in Japan, Siemens of West Germany, France's Groupe Bull, in firms like Digital Equipment, Genentech, or Federal Express. The symbolic share of stock represents, to a startling degree, nothing more than other symbols.

The shift to this new form of capital explodes the assumptions that underpin both Marxist ideology and classical economics, premised alike on the finite character of traditional capital. For unlike land or machines, which can be used by only one person or firm at a time, the same knowledge can be applied by many different users at the same time—and if used cleverly by them, it can generate even more knowledge. It is inherently inexhaustible and nonexclusive.

Even this, however, only hints at the full scope of the revolution in capital. For if the shift toward knowledge-capital is real, then capital itself is increasingly "unreal"—it consists largely of symbols that represent nothing more than other symbols inside the memories and thoughtware of people and computers.

Capital has therefore gone from its tangible form, to a paper form that symbolized tangible assets, to paper symbolizing symbols in the skulls of a continually changing work force. And, finally, to electronic blips symbolizing the paper.

At the very same time that capital increasingly comes to rest on intangibles (a relentless process temporarily disguised by obsolete accounting rules and tax regulations), the instruments traded in the financial markets are similarly growing ever more remote from tangibility.

In Chicago, London, Sydney, Singapore, and Osaka, billions are traded in the form of so-called "derivative" instruments—such as securities based not on the stock of individual companies but on various indices of the market. A step even further removed from "fundamentals" are options based on these indices. And beyond that, in a kind of shadow world, are so-called "synthetics," which, through a series of complex transactions, offer an investor results that simulate or mirror those of an existing bond, stock, index, or option.

We are speeding toward even more rarified investments based on indices of indices of indices, derivatives of derivatives, synthetics mirroring synthetics.

Capital is fast becoming "super-symbolic."

Just as much of the power of modern science lies in longer and longer chains of reasoning, just as mathematicians build more and more extended structures, piling theorem upon theorem to yield a body of knowledge that yields still more abstract theorems, precisely as artificial intelligencers and "knowledge engineers" construct dizzying architectures of inference, so, too, we are creating a capital of progressive derivation, or—some might say—of infinitely receding mirrors.

AN EPITAPH FOR PAPER

If this were all, it would be revolutionary. But the process is pushed even further by parallel changes in the nature of money.

Most of us hear the rustle of paper when we think of dollars, francs, yen, rubles, or deutsche marks. Yet nothing would have seemed odder to one of our great-great-grandparents who miraculously time-traveled into the present. He or she would never have accepted "useless" paper for a bolt of wearable calico or a bushel of edible corn.

Throughout the agricultural age or First Wave civilization, money consisted of some material substance that had a built-in value. Gold and silver, of course. But also salt, tobacco, coral, cotton cloth, copper, and cowrie shells. An endless list of other useful things also served, at one time or another, as money. (Paper, ironically, had only limited use in daily life prior to the spread of mass literacy, and was therefore seldom—if ever—used as money.)

At the dawn of the industrial era, however, strange new ideas began to circulate about money. In 1650, for example, a man named William Potter published a prescient tract in England suggesting something previously unthinkable—that "symbolic wealth was to take the place of real wealth."

Forty years later, when people like Thomas Savery were tinkering with early steam engines, the idea was actually tried out.

It was the American colonists, forbidden by the British to mint gold or silver coins, who for the first time—in the Western world at least—began printing money.

This switch, from an inherently valuable commodity like gold or tobacco or furs to virtually worthless paper, required a tremendous leap of faith on the part of users. For unless a person believed that others would accept paper, and deliver goods for it, it had no value at all. Paper money was based almost entirely on trust. And paper money dominated the industrial society—the civilization of the Second Wave.

Today, as a more advanced Third Wave economy emerges, paper money faces near-total obsolescence. It is now clear that paper money, like assembly lines and smokestacks, is an artifact of the dying industrial era. Except for economically backward countries and quite secondary uses, paper money will go the way of the coral shell and copper bracelet currency.

DESIGNER CURRENCIES AND PARA-MONEY

There are today some 187 million Visa credit card holders in the world, using their cards at some 6.5 million retail stores, gas stations, restaurants, hotels, and other businesses, and running up bills at the rate of $570 million per day, 365 days a year. Visa is only one credit card firm.

When a restaurant owner transmits your card number to Visa or American Express, the credit card company's computers credit the restaurant account with the appropriate amount, deduct an amount from its own books, and increase the amount you owe to it. This, however, is still primitive card play.

With what is called a "smart card," the very act of handing it to a cashier who runs it through an electronic device would result in the price of the dinner being instantly debited from your bank account. You don't pay at the end of the month. Your bank account pays right away. It is like a check that clears instantaneously. Patented by Roland Moreno, a French inventor, the smart card has been pushed by French banks, along with the French postal and telecommunications services. The card, made by the Bull group, has a microchip embedded in it, and is claimed to be virtually fraud-proof. Some 61 million are already in use in Europe and Japan.

Eventually, as electronic record keeping and banking become more integrated, the store's cashless cash register will link directly to the store's bank. As charges are deducted from the customer they will instantly be credited to the retailer's account and start earning interest immediately—reducing the bank's "float" to zero.

Simultaneously, instead of customers paying bills at fixed intervals—say once a month—rents, charge accounts, and similar regular expenses may be paid, bit by bit, bleeding electronically from one's bank account in tiny droplets, as it were, on a minute-by-minute basis. Paralleling developments in the manufacturing sector, such changes promise to move the financial system further from batch processing to continuous-flow operation and toward the ultimate goal of real-time or instantaneity.

Someday, with the even smarter cards to come, you may, if you so wish, deduct the price of a meal or a new car not from your bank account but from the equity in your home—or even, in theory, from the value of jewelry or Japanese prints you may own.

Coming down the pike is the "super-smart card," otherwise called the "electronic bank-in-your-wallet." Made experimentally by Toshiba for Visa International, the plastic card contains a microchip that allows the user to check his or her bank balances, buy and sell shares, make airline reservations, and perform a variety of other tasks.

The new technologies also make possible a dialectical return to a condition that existed before the industrial revolution—the coexistence of multiple currencies in a single economy. Money, like breakfast foods and a thousand other artifacts of daily life, is becoming more diversified. We may be approaching the age of "designer currencies."

"Suppose," writes *The Economist,* "a country had privately issued money alongside the official stuff. . . . Consumers in some countries already have this parallel money—otherwise known as the pre-paid magnetic card, whose store of value runs down as it is used."

Japan is awash in this para-money. Customers buy 10 million cards a month from NTT, the phone company. They pay a sum in advance, then use the cards for making telephone calls. NTT loves it because it gets money in advance—and thus enjoys a "float" of the kind that banks used to enjoy before the speedup of check clearing began shrinking it. As of 1988, NTT had sold 330 million cards for some 214 billion yen. Consumers can also get cards for all sorts of other things, such as rail tickets and video games.

One can imagine many highly specialized types of para-money. The U.S. Department of Agriculture is piloting a program that would ultimately replace food stamps issued to the poor with a smart card programmed with one month's worth of benefits and a personal identification number. The user would run it through the supermarket checkout terminal, which would verify identification before deducting the purchase from the user's remaining balance. The system is aimed at providing better accounting while reducing fraudulent use, black marketing, and counterfeiting. This is only a step away from what might be called a "Basics Card" for all welfare recipients, which would be usable only for food, rent, and public transit.

Another example of para-money is as close as the nearest school cafeteria. Thirty-five U.S. school districts are already preparing to launch a school lunch card system designed by Prepaid Card Services, Inc., of Pearl River, New York. Paid for weekly or monthly in advance by the parent, the kiddie-card is linked to a school computer, which keeps a running account of purchases at the lunch counter.

(By stretching the imagination only a little, one can also picture a programmable card, for example, that would permit parents to customize diet. One child's card might be invalid, say, for soft drinks. If a child had a milk allergy, the card would be invalid for foods containing dairy products, and so forth.)

One can also picture special cards issued to children that could be used in movie theaters or video stores but would be electronically unacceptable for X-rated films. All kinds of custom currencies are possible, including what might be called "programmable money."

In short, once a symbol of middle-class arrival, cards are becoming ubiquitous. Millions of elderly Americans who for years received a monthly Social Security check (a piece of paper worth a certain number of paper dollars) have stopped getting it. Instead, the government sends an electronic blip to each recipient's bank, which then credits his or her account with the amount of the Social Security payment.

U.S. federal agencies also use credit cards for both buying and collecting funds. In fact, according to Joseph Wright, deputy director of the White House Office of Management and Budget, Uncle Sam is "the largest credit card user in the world."

Nowhere in any of these transactions does anything remotely like "money" in the traditional sense change hands. Not a single coin or piece of paper money is exchanged. The "money" here consists of nothing more than a string of zeros and ones transmitted by wire, microwave, or satellite.

All this is now so routine, and accepted with such confidence, that we hardly stop to doubt it. On the contrary, it is when we see large sums of paper money change hands that we suspect something is fishy. We assume that cash payment is intended to cheat the tax collector or that someone is in the drug racket.

POWER FAILURES

Such deep changes in the money system cannot occur without threatening entrenched institutions that have, until now, enjoyed positions of extraordinary power.

At one level the substitution of electronic money for paper money is a direct threat, for example, to the very existence of banks as we know them. "Banking," according to Dee Hock, former chairman of Visa International, "will not retain its position as the primary operator of payment systems." Banks have had a government-protected monopoly in check-clearing services. Electronic money threatens to supplant this system.

In self-defense, some banks have entered into the credit card business themselves. More important, they have extended their reach with automatic teller machines. If banks issue debit cards and put ATMs at millions of retail locations, they may repel the attack of the credit card companies. Since debit cards make it possible for the shopkeeper to receive payment instantly, instead of waiting for Diner's Club or American Express or Visa to remit payment, store owners may not wish to continue paying them a percentage of each sale.

On another front, banks face attack from a wide variety of nonbanks. In Japan, for example, the Ministry of Finance has qualms about the idea that private companies like NTT can issue value-bearing plastic "notes"—a kind of currency—and operate outside the banking system and its rules. If a company can take in money for a prepaid card, it is accepting a "deposit," exactly like a bank. When the user spends, he or she is making the equivalent of a "withdrawal." And when the card company pays the vendor, it is operating a "payment system." These are functions that once only banks could perform.

Moreover, if card companies can issue credit to users, as they and the cardholders see fit, unconstrained by the kind of limits and reserves that govern banks, central banks risk losing their grip on monetary policy. In South Korea, plastic money has expanded so rapidly that the government fears it is feeding inflation.

In brief, the rise of electronic money in the world economy threatens to shake up many long-entrenched power relationships. At the vortex of this power struggle is knowledge embedded in technology. It is a battle that will redefine money itself.

21ST-CENTURY MONEY

Of course, money, whether in the form of metal or paper (or paper backed by metal), is unlikely to vanish completely. But barring nuclear holocaust or technological cataclysm, electronic money will proliferate and drive out most alternatives, precisely because it combines exchange with real-time record-keeping, thus eliminating many of the costly inefficiencies that came with the traditional money system.

If we put this all together now, a rather striking pattern becomes plain. Capital—by which we mean wealth put to work to increase production—changes in parallel with money, and both take on new forms each time society undergoes a major transformation.

As they do so, their knowledge content changes. Thus agricultural-era money, consisting of metal (or some other commodity), had a knowledge content close to zero. Indeed, this First Wave money was not only tangible and durable, it was also *pre-literate*—in the sense that its value depended on its weight, not on the words imprinted on it.

Today's Second Wave money consists of printed paper with or without commodity backing. What's printed on the paper matters. The money is symbolic but still tangible. This form of money comes along with mass literacy.

Third Wave money increasingly consists of electronic pulses. It is evanescent . . . instantaneously transferred . . . monitored on the video screen. It is, in fact, virtually a video phenomenon itself. Blinking, flashing, whizzing across the planet, Third Wave money *is* information—the basis of knowledge.

Increasingly detached from material embodiments, capital and money alike change through history, moving by stages from totally tangible to symbolic and ultimately today to its "super-symbolic" form.

This vast sequence of transformations is accompanied by a deep shift of belief, almost a religious conversion—from a trust in permanent, tangible things like gold or paper to a belief that even the most intangible, ephemeral electronic blips can be swapped for goods or services.

Our wealth is a wealth of symbols. And so also, to a startling degree, is the power based on it.

7

MATERIAL-ISMO!

One day while Ronald Reagan was still in the White House a small group assembled around the table in the Family Dining Room to discuss the long-range future of America. The group consisted of eight well-known futurists and was joined by the Vice President and three of Reagan's top advisers, among them Donald Regan, the President's newly appointed chief of staff.

The meeting had been convened by the author at the request of the White House, and opened with the statement that while futurists differed on many technological, social, and political issues, there was common agreement that the economy was going through a deep transformation.

The words were hardly voiced when Donald Regan snapped, "So you all think we're going to go around cutting each other's hair and flipping hamburgers! Aren't we going to be a great manufacturing power anymore?"

Remembered more for his "kiss and tell" memoirs than his performance in office, Regan subsequently was sacked after a nasty fight with Nancy Reagan, the First Lady. But this was his very first day on the job, and he hurled the gauntlet onto the highly polished table amid the dishes.

The President and Vice President looked around expectantly for a reply. Most of the males at the table seemed taken aback by the brusqueness and immediacy of his attack. It was Heidi Toffler, co-author of *Future Shock, The Third Wave,* and this book as well, who took Regan on. "No, Mr. Regan," she replied patiently. "The United States will continue to be a great manufacturing power. There just won't be as high a percentage of people working in factories."

Explaining the difference between traditional manufacturing

methods and the way Macintosh computers are produced, she pointed out that the United States was surely one of the great food producers in the world—with fewer than 2 percent of the work force engaged in agriculture. In fact, throughout the past century, the more its farm labor force shrank relative to other sectors, the stronger, not weaker, the United States became as an agricultural power. Why couldn't the same be true of manufacture?

The startling fact remains that after many ups and downs, manufacturing employment in the United States in 1988 was almost exactly the same as it was in 1968: slightly over 19 million. Manufacturing contributed the same percentage of national output as it did thirty years earlier. But it was doing all this with a smaller fraction of the total work force.

Moreover, the handwriting is clear: Because American population and the labor force are both likely to expand, and because many American manufacturers automated and reorganized in the 1980s, the shrinkage of factory employment relative to the total must continue. While the United States, according to some estimates, is likely to generate 10,000 new jobs a day for the next decade, few if any will be in the manufacturing sector. A similar process has been transforming the European and Japanese economies as well.

Nevertheless, even now Donald Regan's words are still occasionally echoed by captains of badly run American industries, union leaders with dwindling membership rolls, and economists or historians who beat the drum for the importance of manufacture—as though anyone had suggested the reverse.

The self-perpetuated myth that America is going to lose its manufacturing base has led to loony proposals like those in a recent business magazine which called for the United States to impose a 20 percent tariff on "all imports" and to prohibit the foreign purchase of any American company.

Behind much of this hysteria is the notion that the shift of employment from manual work to service and mental-sector jobs is somehow bad for the economy and that a small manufacturing sector (in terms of jobs) leaves the economy "hollowed out." Such arguments recall the views of the French physiocrats of the 18th century who, unable to imagine an industrial economy, regarded agriculture as the only "productive" activity.

THE NEW MEANING OF JOBLESSNESS

Much of the lamentation over the "decline" of manufacture is fed by self-interest and based on obsolete concepts of wealth, production, and unemployment.

As early as 1962, a seminal work called *The Production and Distribution of Knowledge in the United States* by the Princeton economist Fritz Machlup laid the foundation for an avalanche of statistics documenting the fact that more workers now handle symbols than handle things. Throughout the late fifties and early sixties, in books, articles, reviews, monographs, and in at least one internal white paper prepared for IBM, a small band of futurists in the United States and Europe forecast the transition from muscle work to mental work or work requiring psychological and human skills. At the time, these early warnings were largely written off as too "visionary."

Since then, the shift away from manual labor toward service work and super-symbolic activity has become widespread, dramatic, and irreversible. In the United States today these activities account for fully three quarters of the work force. The great transition is reflected globally in the surprising fact that world exports of services and "intellectual property" are now equal to that of electronics and autos combined, or of the combined exports in food and fuels.

Because the early signals were ignored, the transition has been unnecessarily rocky. Mass layoffs, bankruptcies, and other upheavals swept through the economy as old rust-belt industries, late to install computers, robots, electronic information systems, and slow to restructure, found themselves gutted by more fleet-footed competition. Many blamed their troubles on foreign competition, high or low interest rates, overregulation, and a thousand other factors.

Some of these, no doubt, played a role. But equally to blame was the arrogance of the most powerful smokestack companies—auto makers, steel mills, shipyards, textile firms—who had for so long dominated the economy. Their managerial myopia punished those in the society least responsible for industrial backwardness and least able to protect themselves—their workers. Even middle managers felt the hot scorch of joblessness and saw their bank accounts, egos, and sometimes their marriages collapse as a result. Washington did little to cushion the shocks.

The fact that aggregate manufacturing employment in 1988 was at the same level as 1968 doesn't mean that the workers laid off in between simply returned to their old jobs. On the contrary, with more advanced technologies in place, companies needed a radically different kind of work force as well.

The old Second Wave factories needed essentially interchangeable workers. By contrast, Third Wave operations require diverse and continually evolving skills—which means that workers become less and less interchangeable. And this turns the entire problem of unemployment upside down.

In Second Wave or smokestack societies, an injection of capital spending or consumer purchasing power could stimulate the economy and generate jobs. Given one million jobless, one could, in principle, prime the economy and create one million jobs. Since the jobs were either interchangeable or required so little skill that they could be learned in less than an hour, virtually any unemployed worker could fill almost any job. Presto! The problem evaporates.

In today's super-symbolic economy this is less true—which is why a lot of unemployment seems intractable, and neither the traditional Keynesian or monetarist remedies work well. To cope with the Great Depression, John Maynard Keynes, we recall, urged deficit spending by government to put money into consumer pockets. Once consumers had the money, they would rush out and buy things. This, in turn, would lead manufacturers to expand their plants and hire more workers. Goodbye, unemployment. Monetarists urged manipulation of interest rates or money supply instead, to increase or decrease purchasing power as needed.

In today's global economy, pumping money into the consumer's pocket may simply send it flowing overseas, without doing anything to help the domestic economy. An American buying a new TV set or compact-disc player merely sends dollars to Japan, Korea, Malaysia, or elsewhere. The purchase doesn't necessarily add jobs at home.

But there is a far more basic flaw in the old strategies: They still focus on the circulation of money rather than knowledge. Yet it is no longer possible to reduce joblessness simply by increasing the number of jobs, because the problem is no longer merely numbers. Unemployment has gone from quantitative to qualitative.

Thus, even if there were ten new want ads for every jobless worker, if there are 10 million vacancies and only one million unemployed, the one million will not be able to perform the available jobs unless they have skills—knowledge—matched to the skill requirements of those new jobs. These skills are now so varied and fast-changing that workers can't be interchanged as easily or cheaply as in the past. Money and numbers no longer solve the problem.

The jobless desperately need money if they and their families are to survive, and it is both necessary and morally right to provide them with decent levels of public assistance. But any effective strategy for reducing joblessness in a super-symbolic economy must depend less on the allocation of wealth and more on the allocation of knowledge.

Furthermore, as these new jobs are not likely to be found in what we still think of as manufacture, what will be needed is not just a question of mechanical skills—or, for that matter, algebra, as some manufacturers contend—but a vast array of cultural and interpersonal skills as well. We will need to prepare people, through schooling, apprenticeships, and on-the-job learning, for work in such fields as the human services—helping to care, for example, for our fast-growing population of the elderly, providing child care, health services, personal security, training services, leisure and recreation services, tourism, and the like.

We will also have to begin according human-service jobs the same respect previously reserved for manufacture, rather than snidely denigrating the entire service sector as "hamburger flipping." McDonald's cannot stand as the symbol for a range of activities that includes everything from teaching to working at a dating service or in a hospital radiology center.

What's more, if, as often charged, wages are low in the service sector, then the solution is not to bewail the relative decline of manufacturing jobs, but to increase service productivity and to invent new forms of work-force organization and collective bargaining. Unions—primarily designed for the crafts or for mass manufacturing—need to be totally transformed or else replaced by new-style organizations more appropriate to the super-symbolic economy. To survive they will have to stop treating employees en masse and start thinking of them as individuals, supporting, rather than resisting, such things as work-at-home programs, flextime, and job-sharing.

In brief, the rise of the super-symbolic economy compels us to reconceptualize the entire problem of unemployment from the ground up. To challenge outworn assumptions, however, is also to challenge those who benefit from them. The Third Wave system of wealth creation thus threatens long-entrenched power relationships in corporations, unions, and governments.

THE SPECTRUM OF MIND-WORK

The super-symbolic economy makes obsolete not only our concepts of unemployment, but our concepts of work as well. To understand it, and the power struggles that it triggers, we will even need a fresh vocabulary.

Thus, the division of the economy into such sectors as "agriculture," "manufacturing," and "services" today obscures, rather than clarifies. Today's high-speed changes blur the once-neat distinctions. It might surprise Mr. Regan, who is concerned about too many Americans cutting each other's hair, that the founder of one of Europe's largest computer manufacturers has repeatedly said, "We are a service company—just like a barbershop!"

Instead of clinging to the old classifications, we need to look behind the labels and ask what people in these companies actually have to do to create added value. Once we pose this question, we find that more and more of the work in all three sectors consists of symbolic processing, or "mind-work."

Farmers now use computers to calculate grain feeds; steelworkers monitor consoles and video screens; investment bankers switch on their laptops as they model financial markets. It matters little whether economists choose to label these as "agricultural," "manufacturing," or "service" activities.

Even occupational categories are breaking down. To label someone a stockroom attendant, a machine operator, or a sales representative conceals rather than reveals. The labels may stay the same, but the actual jobs don't.

It is a lot more useful today to group workers by the amount of symbolic processing or mind-work they do as part of their jobs, regardless of the label they wear or whether they happen to work in a store, a truck, a factory, a hospital, or an office.

At the top end of what might be called the "mind-work spectrum" we have the research scientist, the financial analyst, the computer programmer, or for that matter, the ordinary file clerk. Why, one might ask, include file clerks and scientists in the same group? The answer is that, while their functions obviously differ and they work at vastly different levels of abstraction, both—and millions like them—do nothing but move information around or generate more information. Their work is totally symbolic.

In the middle of the mind-work spectrum we find a broad range of "mixed" jobs—tasks requiring the worker to perform physical labor, but also to handle information. The Federal Express or United Parcel Service driver handles boxes and packages, drives a van, but now also operates a computer at his or her side. In advanced factories the machine operator is a highly trained information worker. The hotel clerk, the nurse, and many others have to deal with people—but spend a considerable fraction of their time generating, getting, or giving out information.

Auto mechanics at Ford dealers, for example, may still have greasy hands, but they will soon be using a computer system designed by Hewlett-Packard that provides them with an "expert system" to help them in trouble-shooting, along with instant access to one hundred megabytes of technical drawings and data stored on CD-ROM. The system asks them for more data about the car they are fixing; it permits them to search through the masses of technical material intuitively; it makes inferences and then guides them through the repair steps.

When they are interacting with this system are they "mechanics" or "mind-workers"?

It is the purely manual jobs at the bottom end of the spectrum that are disappearing. With fewer manual jobs in the economy, the "proletariat" is now a minority, replaced increasingly by a "cognitariat." More accurately, as the super-symbolic economy unfolds, the proletariat *becomes* a cognitariat.

The key questions about a person's work today have to do with how much of the job entails information processing, how routine or programmable it is, what level of abstractions is involved, what access the person has to the central data bank and management information system, and how much autonomy and responsibility the individual enjoys.

To describe all this as "hollowing out" or to write it off as "hamburger slinging" is ridiculous. Such catch phrases devalue exactly that part of the economy that is growing fastest and generating the most new jobs. They ignore the crucial new role of knowledge in the production of wealth. And they fail to notice that the transformation of human labor corresponds precisely to the rise of super-symbolic capital and money, sketched in the previous chapter. It is part of the total restructure of society as we race into the 21st century.

LOWBROWS VERSUS HIGHBROWS

Such immense changes cannot come without power conflict, and to anticipate who will gain and who will lose, it may help to think of companies on a similar mind-work spectrum.

We need to classify companies not by whether they are nominally in manufacturing or services—who really cares?—but by what their people actually do. CSX, for example, is a firm that operates railroads throughout the eastern half of the United States, along with one of the world's biggest oceangoing containerization businesses (CSX brings Honda auto parts to the United States). But CSX increasingly sees itself as in the information business.

Says Alex Mandl of CSX: "The information component of our service package is growing bigger and bigger. It's not just enough to deliver products. Customers want information. Where their products will be consolidated and de-consolidated, what time each item will be where, prices, customs information, and much more. We are an information-driven business." Which means that the proportion of CSX employees in the middle and higher ranges of the mind-work spectrum is increasing.

What this suggests is that companies can be roughly classified as "highbrow," "midbrow," or "lowbrow," depending on how knowledge-intensive they are. Some firms and industries need to process more information than others, in order to produce wealth. Like individual jobs, they can be positioned on the mind-work spectrum according to the amount and complexity of the mind-work they do.

Psychiatrist Donald F. Klein, director of research of the New York State Psychiatric Institute, carries this idea one step further and insists that these differences, in turn, are reflected in the general levels of intelligence required of workers. "Do you really think that the average worker at Apple is not smarter than the average worker at McDonald's?" he asks. "The top management at McDonald's may be just as smart as the top management at Apple (although I doubt it), but the proportion of the staff of these corporations who require high IQ and symbolic skills surely differs considerably."

According to this reasoning, one should be able to arrive at a collective IQ score for each company. Are Chrysler workers inherently smarter than those at Ford or Toyota? (Not are they better educated, but are they natively more intelligent?) What about IQ rankings, say, for Apple versus Compaq, or General Foods versus Pillsbury? Carried to absurdity, one might imagine a new ranking for the Fortune 500—according to collective IQ.

But do high-IQ firms necessarily produce more wealth than low-IQ firms? Are they more profitable? Surely, other qualities, like motivation and drive or, for that matter, the intensity of competition, may have more to do with corporate success. And how should one measure intelligence in any case? There are strong reasons to believe that conventional IQ tests are culturally biased and take too few aspects of intelligence into account.

We don't need to entertain fanciful scenarios, however, to notice that, quite apart from the intelligence level of individual employees, highbrow firms behave differently from firms that are less knowledge-dependent.

Lowbrow firms typically concentrate mind-work in a few people at the top, leaving muscle work or mindless work to everyone else. Their operating assumption is that workers are ignorant or that, in any case, their knowledge is irrelevant to production.

Even in the highbrow sector today one may find examples of "de-skilling"—simplifying jobs, reducing them to their smallest components, monitoring output stroke by stroke. These attempts to apply methods designed by Frederick Taylor for use in factories at the beginning of the 20th century are, however, the wave of the lowbrow past, not the highbrow future. For any task that is so repetitive and simple that it can be done without thought is, eventually, a candidate for robotization.

In contrast, as the economy moves more toward super-symbolic production all firms are being compelled to rethink the role of knowledge. The smartest firms in the highbrow sector are the first to rethink the role of knowledge and to redesign work itself. They operate on the assumption that productivity and profits will both skyrocket if mindless work is reduced to a minimum or transferred to advanced technology, and the full potential of the worker is tapped. The goal is a better-paid but smaller, smarter work force.

Even midbrow operations that still require physical manipulation of things are becoming more knowledge-intensive, moving up the mind-work spectrum.

At GenCorp Automotive in Shelbyville, Indiana, a spanking-new $65 million plant soon to employ five hundred workers making plastic body panels for Chevrolets, Pontiacs, and Oldsmobiles is being completed. Each worker, not just supervisors and managers, will receive $8,000–$10,000 worth of training. In addition to learning the physical tasks required, they will be trained in problem solving, leadership skills, role playing, and organization processes. Workers are to be divided into teams. Supported by computer, they will learn statistical process control methods. Each team will learn many different tasks, so that they can switch jobs and minimize boredom. Team leaders receive a full year's training, including visits abroad.

GenCorp is not investing so heavily for altruistic reasons. It expects payback in the form of quick start-up at the plant, as well as better quality, less waste, and more output per worker.

Highbrow firms, in general, are not charitable institutions. Although the work in them tends to be less physically onerous than in lowbrow operations, and the surroundings more agreeable, these firms typically demand *more* of their employees than lowbrow firms do. Employees are encouraged to use not only their rational minds, but to pour their emotions, intuitions, and imagination into the job. This is why Marcusian critics see in this an even more sinister "exploitation" of the employee.

LOWBROW IDEOLOGY

In lowbrow industrial economies, wealth was typically measured by the possession of goods. The production of goods was regarded as central to the economy. Conversely, symbolic and service activities, while unavoidable, were stigmatized as nonproductive. (They sometimes still are by economists applying routine measures of productivity designed for the manufacturing sector and inapplicable to the services, which are, by their very nature, harder to measure.)

The manufacture of goods—autos, radios, tractors, TV sets— was seen as "male" or macho, and words like *practical, realistic,* or *hardheaded* were associated with it. By contrast, the production of knowledge or the exchange of information was typically disparaged as mere "paper pushing" and seen as wimpy or—worse yet—effeminate.

A flood of corollaries flowed from these attitudes. For example, that "production" is the combination of material resources, machines, and muscle . . . that the most important assets of a firm are tangibles . . . that national wealth flows from a surplus of the trade in goods . . . that trade in services is significant only because it facilitates trade in goods . . . that most education is a waste unless it is narrowly vocational . . . that research is airy-fairy . . . and that the liberal arts are irrelevant or, worse yet, inimical to business success.

What mattered, in short, was matter.

Incidentally, ideas like these were by no means limited to the Babbitts of capitalism. They had their analogs in the communist world as well. Marxist economists, if anything, have had a harder time trying to integrate highbrow work into their schema, and "socialist realism" in the arts produced thousands of portrayals of happy workers, their Schwarzenegger-like muscles straining against a background of cogwheels, smokestacks, steam locomotives. The glorification of the proletariat, and the theory that it was the vanguard of change, reflected the principles of a lowbrow economy.

What all this added up to was more than a welter of isolated opinions, assumptions, and attitudes. Rather it formed a self-reinforcing, self-justifying ideology based on a kind of macho materialism—a brash, triumphant "material-ismo!"

Material-ismo, in fact, was the ideology of mass manufacture.

Whether voiced by captains of capitalism or by conventional economists, it reflects, as the *Financial Times* wryly commented, "a view of the primacy of material product that would be appreciated by Soviet planners." It is a cudgel used in the power struggle between the vested interests of the smokestack economy and those of the fast-emerging super-symbolic economy.

There was a time when material-ismo may have made sense. Today, when the real value of most products lies in the knowledge embedded in them, it is both reactionary and imbecile. Any country that, out of choice, pursues policies based on material-ismo condemns itself to becoming the Bangladesh of the 21st century.

HIGHBROW IDEOLOGY

The companies, institutions, and people with a strong stake in the super-symbolic economy haven't yet fashioned a coherent counter-rationale. But some of the underlying ideas are falling into place.

The first fragmentary foundations of this new economics can be glimpsed in the still-unrecognized writings of people like the late Eugen Loebl, who during eleven years in a communist prison in Czechoslovakia, deeply rethought the assumptions of both Marxist and Western economics; Henry K. H. Woo of Hong Kong, who has analyzed "the unseen dimensions of wealth"; Orio Giarini in Geneva, who applies the concepts of risk and indeterminacy in his analysis of services of the future; and the American Walter Weisskopf, who writes on the role of non-equilibrium conditions in economic development.

Scientists today are asking how systems behave in turbulence, how order evolves out of chaotic conditions, and how developing systems leap to higher levels of diversity. Such questions are extremely pertinent to business and the economy. Management books speak of "thriving on chaos." Economists rediscover the work of Joseph Schumpeter, who spoke of "creative destruction" as necessary to advance. In a storm of takeovers, divestitures, reorganizations, bankruptcies, start-ups, joint ventures, and internal reorganizations, the entire economy is taking on a new structure that is light-years more diverse, fast-changing, and complex than the old smokestack economy.

This "leap" to a higher level of diversity, speed, and complexity requires a corresponding leap to higher, more sophisticated forms of integration. In turn, this demands radically higher levels of knowledge processing.

Without this higher coordination, and the mind-work it requires, no value can be added, no wealth created by the economy. Value, therefore, is dependent on more than the mixture of land, labor, and capital. All the land, labor, and capital in the world won't meet consumer needs if they cannot be integrated at a far higher level than ever before. And this changes the entire notion of value.

A recent report by Prométhée, an independent think tank in Paris, put it this way: "Value is in fact 'extracted' throughout the production/provision of a product/service. So-called service economies . . . are not characterized by the fact that people have suddenly begun to fulfill their lives through non-tangible consumption but rather by the fact that activities pertaining to the economic realm are increasingly integrated."

Drawing heavily on the 17th-century writings of René Descartes, the culture of industrialism rewarded people who could break problems and processes down into smaller and smaller constituent parts. This disintegrative or analytic approach, when transferred to economics, led us to think of production as a series of disconnected steps.

Raising capital, acquiring raw materials, recruiting workers, deploying technology, advertising, selling, and distributing the product were all seen as either sequential or as isolated from one another.

The new model of production that springs from the supersymbolic economy is dramatically different. Based on a systemic or integrative view, it sees production as increasingly simultaneous and synthesized. The parts of the process are not the whole, and they cannot be isolated from one another.

Information gained by the sales and marketing people feeds the engineers, whose innovations need to be understood by the financial people, whose ability to raise capital depends on how well satisfied the customers are, which depends on how well scheduled the company's trucks are, which depends in part on employee motivation, which depends on a paycheck plus a sense of achievement, which depends . . . et cetera, et cetera.

Connectivity rather than disconnectedness, integration rather than disintegration, real-time simultaneity rather than sequential stages—these are the assumptions that underlie the new production paradigm.

We are, in fact, discovering that "production" neither begins nor ends in the factory. Thus, the latest models of economic production extend the process both upstream and downstream—forward into aftercare or "support" for the product even after it is sold, as in auto-repair warrantees or the support expected from the retailer when a person buys a computer. Before long, the conception of production will reach even beyond that to ecologically safe disposal of the product after use. Companies will have to provide for post-use cleanup, forcing them to alter design specs, cost calculations, production methods, and much else besides. In so doing they will be performing more service, relative to manufacture, and they will be adding value. "Production" will be seen to include all these functions.

Similarly, they may extend the definition backward to include such functions as training of the employee, provision of day care, and other services. An unhappy muscle-worker could be compelled to be "productive." In high-symbolic activities, happy workers produce more. Hence, productivity begins even before the worker arrives at the office. To old-timers, such an expanded definition of production may seem fuzzy or nonsensical. To the new generation of super-symbolic leaders, conditioned to think systemically rather than in terms of isolated steps, it will seem natural.

In brief, production is reconceptualized as a far more encompassing process than the economists and ideologists of lowbrow economics imagined. And at every step from today on, it is knowledge, not cheap labor; symbols, not raw materials, that embody and add value.

This deep reconceptualization of the sources of added value is fraught with consequence. It smashes the assumptions of both free-marketism and Marxism alike, and of the material-ismo that gave rise to both. Thus, the ideas that value is sweated from the back of the worker alone, and that value is produced by the glorious capitalist entrepreneur, both implied in material-ismo, are revealed to be false and misleading politically as well as economically.

In the new economy the receptionist and the investment banker who assembles the capital, the keypunch operator and the salesperson, as well as the systems designer and telecommunications specialist, all add value. Even more significantly, so does the customer. Value results from a total effort, rather than from one isolated step in the process.

The rising importance of mind-work will not go away, no matter how many scare stories are published warning about the dire consequences of a "vanishing" manufacturing base or deriding the concept of the "information economy." Neither will the new conception of how wealth is created.

For what we are watching is a mighty convergence of change— the transformation of production coming together with the transformation of capital and money itself. Together they form a revolutionary new system for wealth creation on the planet.

8

THE ULTIMATE SUBSTITUTE

Anyone reading this page has an amazing skill called literacy. It comes as a shock sometimes to remember that all of us had ancestors who were illiterate. Not stupid or ignorant, but invincibly illiterate.

Simply to read was a fantastic achievement in the ancient world. Saint Augustine, writing in the 5th century, refers to his mentor, Saint Ambrose, the Bishop of Milan, who was so learned that he could actually read without moving his lips. For this astonishing feat he was regarded as the brainiest person in the world.

Not only were most of our ancestors illiterate, they were also "innumerate," meaning they couldn't do the simplest arithmetic. Those few who could were deemed downright dangerous. A marvelous warning attributed to Augustine holds that Christians should stay away from people who could add or subtract. It was obvious they had "made a covenant with the Devil to darken the spirit and to confine man in the bonds of Hell"—a sentiment with which many a fourth-grade math student today might agree.

It wasn't until a thousand years later that we find "reckoning masters" teaching pupils bound for commercial careers.

What this underscores is that many of the simplest skills taken for granted in business today are the product of centuries and millennia of cumulative cultural development. Knowledge from China, from India, from the Arabs, from Phoenician traders, as well as from the West, is an unrecognized part of the heritage relied on today by business executives all over the world. Successive generations have learned these skills, adapted them, transmitted them, and then slowly built on the result.

All economic systems sit upon a "knowledge base." All business enterprises depend on the preexistence of this socially constructed resource. Unlike capital, labor, and land, it is usually neglected by economists and business executives when calculating the "inputs" needed for production. Yet this resource—partly paid for, partly exploited free of charge—is now the most important of all.

At rare moments in history the advance of knowledge has smashed through old barriers. The most important of these break-throughs has been the invention of new tools for thinking and communication, like the ideogram ... the alphabet ... the zero ... and in our century, the computer.

Thirty years ago anyone with the slenderest ability to use a computer was described in the popular press as a "mathematical wizard" or a "giant brain," exactly as Saint Ambrose was in the age of moving lips.

Today we are living through one of those exclamation points in history when the entire structure of human knowledge is once again trembling with change as old barriers fall. We are not just accumulating more "facts"—whatever *they* may be. Just as we are now restructuring companies and whole economies, we are totally reorganizing the production and distribution of knowledge and the symbols used to communicate it.

What does this mean?

It means that we are creating new networks of knowledge ... linking concepts to one another in startling ways ... building up amazing hierarchies of inference ... spawning new theories, hypoth-eses, and images, based on novel assumptions, new languages, codes, and logics. Businesses, governments, and individuals are collecting and storing more sheer data than any previous genera-tion in history (creating a massive, confusing gold mine for tomor-row's historians).

But more important, we are interrelating data in more ways, giving them context, and thus forming them into information; and we are assembling chunks of information into larger and larger models and architectures of knowledge.

None of this implies that the data are correct; information, true; and knowledge, wise. But it does imply vast changes in the way we see the world, create wealth, and exercise power.

Not all this new knowledge is factual or even explicit. Much knowledge, as the term is used here, is unspoken, consisting of assumptions piled atop assumptions, of fragmentary models, of unnoticed analogies, and it includes not simply logical and seemingly unemotional information data, but values, the products of passion and emotion, not to mention imagination and intuition.

It is today's gigantic upheaval in the knowledge base of society— not computer hype or mere financial manipulation—that explains the rise of a super-symbolic economy.

THE ALCHEMY OF INFORMATION

Many changes in the society's knowledge system translate directly into business operations. This knowledge system is an even more pervasive part of every firm's environment than the banking system, the political system, or the energy system.

Apart from the fact that no business could open its doors if there were no language, culture, data, information, and know-how, there is the deeper fact that of all the resources needed to create wealth, none is more versatile than these. In fact, knowledge (sometimes just information and data) can be used as a replacement for other resources.

Knowledge—in principle inexhaustible—is the ultimate substitute.

Take technology.

In most smokestack factories it was inordinately expensive to change any product. It required highly paid tool-and-die makers, jig-setters, and other specialists, and resulted in extended "downtime" during which the machines were idle and ate up capital, interest, and overhead. That's why cost per unit went down if you could make longer and longer runs of identical products.

Instead of these long runs, the latest computer-driven manufacturing technologies make endless variety possible. Philips, the giant Dutch-based electronics firm, manufactured one hundred different models of color TV in 1972. Today the variety has grown to five hundred different models. Bridgestone Cycle Company in Japan is promoting the "Radac Tailor-Made" bike, Matsushita offers a semicustomized line of heated carpets, and the Washington Shoe Company offers semicustomized women's shoes—thirty-two designs for each size—depending on the individual customer's feet as measured by computer in the shoe store.

Standing the economics of mass production on their head, the new information technologies push the cost of diversity toward zero. Knowledge thus substitutes for the once-high cost of *change* in the production process.

Or take materials.

A smart computer program hitched to a lathe can cut more pieces out of the same amount of steel than most human operators. Making miniaturization possible, new knowledge leads to smaller, lighter products, which, in turn, cuts down on ware-housing and transportation. And as we saw in the case of CSX, the rail and shipping firm, up-to-the-minute tracking of ship-ments—i.e., better information—means further transportation savings.

New knowledge also leads to the creation of totally new mate-rials, ranging from aircraft composites to biologicals, and increases our ability to substitute one material for another. Everything, from tennis rackets to jet engines, is incorporating new plastics, alloys, and complex composites. Allied-Signal, Inc., of Morristown, New Jersey, makes something called Metglas, which combines features of both metal and glass and is used to make transformers far more energy-efficient. New optical materials point to much faster com-puters. New forms of tank armor are made of a combination of steel, ceramics, and uranium. Deeper knowledge permits us to cus-tomize materials at the molecular level to produce desired thermal, electrical, or mechanical characteristics.

The only reason we now ship huge amounts of raw materials like bauxite or nickel or copper across the planet is that we lack the knowledge to convert local materials into usable substitutes. Once we acquire that know-how, further drastic savings in transporta-tion will result. In short, knowledge is a substitute for both re-sources and shipping.

The same goes for energy. Nothing illustrates the substitut-ability of knowledge for other resources than the recent break-throughs in superconductivity, which at a minimum will drive down the amount of energy that now must be transmitted for each unit of output. At present, according to the American Public Power Association, up to 15 percent of electricity generated in the United States is lost in the process of moving it to where it is needed, because copper wires are inefficient carriers. This trans-mission loss is the equivalent of the output of fifty generating plants. Superconductivity can slash that loss.

Similarly, Bechtel National, Inc., in San Francisco, along with Ebasco Services, Inc., of New York, is working on what amounts to a giant, football-field-sized "battery" for storing energy. Down the road such storage systems can help eliminate the power plants that are there to provide extra electricity in peak periods.

In addition to substituting for materials, transportation, and energy, knowledge also saves time. Time itself is one of the most important of economic resources, even though it shows up nowhere on a company's balance sheet. Time remains, in effect, a hidden input. Especially when change accelerates, the ability to shorten time—for instance, by communicating swiftly or by bringing new products to market fast—can be the difference between profit and loss.

New knowledge speeds things up, drives us toward a real-time, instantaneous economy, and substitutes for time expenditure.

Space, too, is conserved and conquered by knowledge. GE's Transportation Systems division builds locomotives. When it began using advanced information-processing and communications to link up with its suppliers, it was able to turn over its inventory twelve times faster than before, and to save a full acre of warehouse space.

Not only miniaturized products and reduced warehousing, but other savings are possible. In one year the United States turns out 1.3 trillion documents—sufficient, according to some calculations, to "wallpaper" the Grand Canyon 107 times. All but 5 percent of this is still stored on paper. Advanced information technologies, including document scanning, promise to compress at least some of this. More important, the new telecommunications capacity, based on computers and advanced knowledge, makes it possible to disperse production out of high-cost urban centers, and to reduce energy and transport costs even further.

KNOWLEDGE VERSUS CAPITAL

So much is written about the substitution of computerized equipment for human labor that we often ignore the ways in which it also substitutes for capital. Yet all the above also translate into financial savings.

Indeed, in a sense, knowledge is a far greater long-term threat to the power of finance than are organized labor or anticapitalist political parties. For, relatively speaking, the information revolution is reducing the need for capital per unit of output. In a "capital-ist" economy, nothing could be more significant.

Vittorio Merloni is a fifty-seven-year-old Italian businessman whose family owns 75 percent of a company called Merloni Elettrodomestici. In a small side room at the education center of the Banca Nazionale del Lavoro in Rome, he converses candidly about his firm. Ten percent of all the washing machines, refrigerators, and other major household appliances sold in Europe are made by Merloni's company. His main competitors are Electrolux of Sweden and Philips of Holland. For four turbulent years Merloni served as head of Confindustria, the Italian confederation of employers.

According to Merloni, Italy's recent economic advances are a result of the fact that "we need less capital now to do the same thing" that required more capital in the past. "This means that a poor country can be much better off today with the same amount of capital than five or ten years ago."

The reason, he says, is that knowledge-based technologies are reducing the capital needed to produce, say, dishwashers, stoves, or vacuum cleaners.

To begin with, information substitutes for high-cost inventory, according to Merloni, who uses computer-aided design and shoots data back and forth via satellite between his plants in Italy and Portugal.

By speeding the responsiveness of the factory to the market and making short runs economical, better and more instantaneous information makes it possible to reduce the amount of components and finished goods sitting in warehouses or railroad sidings.

Merloni has cut a startling 60 percent from his inventory costs. Until recently, his plants needed an inventory of 200,000 pieces for 800,000 units of output. Today they turn out 3 million units a year with only 300,000 in the pipeline. He attributes this massive saving to better information.

Merloni's case is not unique. In the United States, textile

manufacturers, apparel makers and retailers—organized into a Voluntary Inter-Industry Communications Standards (VICS) committee—are looking forward to squeezing $12 billion worth of excess inventory out of their system by using a shared industry-wide electronic data network. In Japan, NHK Spring Company, which sells seats and springs to most of the Japanese carmakers, is aiming to synchronize its production lines to those of its customers so perfectly as to virtually eliminate buffer stocks.

Says one NHK official: "If this system can be implemented, we can theoretically reduce our inventories to nil."

Cuts in inventory, of course, not only translate back into the smaller space and real estate costs mentioned earlier, but also into reduced taxes, insurance, and overhead. Similarly, Merloni points out, he is able to transfer funds from London or Paris to Milan or Madrid in minutes, saving significant interest charges.

Even though the initial cost of computers, software, information, and telecommunications may itself be high, he says, the overall savings mean that his company needs less capital to do the same job it did in the past.

These ideas about capital are spreading around the globe. In the words of Dr. Haruo Shimada of Keio University in Tokyo, we are seeing a shift from corporations that "require vast capital assets and a large accumulation of human capital to carry out production" to what he calls "flow-type" corporations that use "much less extensive capital assets."

As though to underscore this shift and the importance of knowledge in the economy of tomorrow, the major Japanese corporations are now, for the first time, pouring more funds into research and development than into capital investment.

Michael Milken, who, for better or worse, knows a thing or two about investment, has summed it up in six words: "Human capital has replaced dollar capital."

Knowledge has become the ultimate resource of business because it is the ultimate substitute.

What we've seen so far, therefore, is that in any economy, production and profits depend inescapably on the three main sources of power—violence, wealth, and knowledge. Violence is progressively converted into law. In turn, capital and money alike are now being transmuted into knowledge. Work changes in parallel, becoming more and more dependent on the manipulation of symbols. With capital, money, and work all moving in the same direction, the entire basis of the economy is revolutionized. It becomes a super-symbolic economy, which operates according to rules radically different from those that prevailed during the smoke-stack era.

Because it reduces the need for raw materials, labor, time, space, and capital, knowledge becomes the central resource of the advanced economy. And as this happens, its value soars. For this reason, as we'll see next, "info-wars"—struggles for the control of knowledge—are breaking out everywhere.

PART THREE

THE INFORMATION WARS

9

THE CHECKOUT BATTLE

Not long ago it was announced that the Smithsonian Institution of Washington, D.C., one of the most prestigious museums in the world, was considering the purchase of a small diner in New Jersey. It was the plan of the Smithsonian to move this little restaurant to Washington, make it part of the museum, perhaps even operate it, to illustrate the synthetic materials used during a certain period in American life. The plan was never carried out.

For many Americans the roadside diner exercises a nostalgic fascination. Many a 1930s Hollywood scene took place in a diner. Hemingway's famous story "The Killers" is set in a diner. So, quite beyond illustrating the uses of vinyl and Formica, there was a certain logic to the Smithsonian's surprising idea.

But if the Smithsonian ever wishes to show what America meant to the outside world in the 1950s, the dead center of the 20th century, it should buy and relocate not a diner but a supermarket.

Pushing a cart down a brightly lit supermarket aisle was a weekly ritual for a majority of American families. The supermarket with its glistening, packed shelves became a symbol of plenty in a hungry world. It was a marvel of American business and was soon emulated the world over.

Today the supermarket is still there, but, largely unnoticed by the public, it has become a battlefield in the information wars—one of many raging throughout the business world today.

BEHIND THE SHOOT-OUTS

From one end of the United States to the other, a multibillion-dollar tug-of-war today pits giant manufacturers like Nabisco, Revlon, Procter & Gamble, General Foods, and Gillette, once at the top of the industrial heap, against the lowly retail stores that put their products into the customer's shopping bag. Fought at the checkout counter, this battle gives a glimpse of things to come in the super-symbolic economy.

In the early days of the supermarket the big food processors and manufacturers would send their thousands of salespeople across the country to call on these stores and push their various lines of food, cosmetics, soft drinks, cleaning supplies, and the like. Every day, thousands of negotiations occurred.

In this day-to-day dickering, sellers had the edge. They carried with them the clout of their giant firms, which even the largest supermarket chains could not match. Each of these mega-firms was a commanding presence in its chosen markets.

The Gillette Company, for instance, until the late 1970s sold six out of every ten razor blades used in the United States. When the French firm Bic, the world's largest maker of ballpoint pens and disposable cigarette lighters, challenged Gillette on its home turf with a line of disposable razor blades, Gillette fought back and wound up with 40 to 50 percent of the U.S. disposable market. Bic was left with under 10 percent. Gillette operated outside its own country too. Today, Gillette has company locations in forty-six countries and manufacturing plants in twenty-seven, spread across the globe from Germany and France to the Philippines.

When a Gillette salesperson came to call, the supermarket listened hard—or else.

From the 1950s into the 1980s, the balance of power, with the giant manufacturers at the top and the wholesalers and retailers at the bottom, remained essentially unchanged. One of the reasons for manufacturer-power was control of information.

THE SCENT OF MISS AMERICA

At the peak of this dominance, these manufacturers were among the heaviest mass advertisers in America. This gave them effective command of the information reaching the consumer.

Gillette was particularly astute. It spent heavily to advertise razor blades or shaving cream on TV broadcasts of baseball's World Series. It plugged its perfumes on the televised Miss America Pageant.

Gillette typically ran six "marketing cycles" in the course of a year, each with a big backup ad campaign. This was called "pull-through" marketing—designed to "pull" customers into the store aisles and wipe the shelves clean in no time. These campaigns were so effective, supermarkets could hardly afford *not* to carry the Gillette products.

In turn, success at the cash register meant that Gillette, like the other big firms, could order its own supplies in bulk, at reduced prices. In this way, by coordinating production and distribution with the mass media, manufacturers by and large came to dominate all the other players in the production cycle—farmers and raw material suppliers as well as retailers.

In fact, the Gillette man (rarely a woman) could often dictate to the store how many blades it would buy, what types, how they would be displayed, when they would be delivered, and, not infrequently, what the price would be.

This was economic power in action, and it could not have existed without the pivotal control of information. It was Gillette, after all, not the retailer, who touted the advantages of Foamy shaving cream on television, or showed stubble-faced athletes using Gillette blades to get a clean shave. What the world knew about these products it learned from Gillette.

Moreover, if Gillette controlled the information going *to* the consumer, it also collected information *from* the consumer. At every stage, Gillette simply knew more than any of its retailers about how, when, and to whom its products would sell.

Gillette knew when its advertising would appear on television, when new products were to be launched, what price promotions it would offer, and it was able to control the release of all this information. In short, Gillette and the other mass manufacturers stood *between* the retailer and the customer, feeding information under their exclusive control, to both.

This control played a critical, though largely overlooked, role in maintaining the traditional dominance of the manufacturer vis-à-vis the store. And it paid off.

There was a time when Campbell Soup didn't even take the trouble to list a phone number on its salespeople's calling cards. "No use calling them," a vice-president of the Grand Union supermarket chain points out. "They never made deals."

Similarly, when Gillette's salesman came to the store to sell, he knew what he was talking about. The buyer did the listening.

THE "PUSH-MONEY" PLOY

The weapon used by retailers to hurl the big manufacturers back on their heels is a small black-and-white symbol.

Ever since the mid-sixties a little noticed committee of retailers, wholesalers, and grocery manufacturers had been meeting with companies like IBM, National Cash Register, and Sweda to discuss two common supermarket problems: long checkout lines and errors in accounting.

Couldn't technology be used to overcome these difficulties?

It could—if products could somehow be coded, and if computers could automatically "read" the codes. Optical scanning technology was still in its infancy, but the computer companies, sensing a major new market, gladly worked with the retailers.

On April 3, 1973, the "symbol selection committee" agreed on a single standard code for their industry. The result was the now familiar "Universal Product Code" or "bar code"—the shimmery black lines and numbers that appear on everything from detergent to cake mix—and the swift spread of optical scanning equipment to read them.

Today, bar coding is becoming near universal in the United States, with fully 95 percent of all food items marked with the UPC. And the system is fast spreading abroad. By 1988 there were 3,470 supermarkets and specialty and department stores in France using it. In West Germany, at least 1,500 food stores and nearly 200 department stores employed scanners. All told, not counting the United States, there were 78,000 scanners at work from Brazil to Czechoslovakia and Papua New Guinea.

In Japan, where the new retail technologies spread like fire in a high wind, 47 percent of all supermarkets and 72 percent of all convenience stores were already equipped by 1987.

The bar code did more, however, than speed the checkout line for millions of customers or reduce errors in accounting. It transferred power.

The average U.S. supermarket now stocks 22,000 different items, and with thousands of new products continually replacing old ones, power has shifted to the retailer who can keep track of all these items—along with their sales, their profitability, the timing of advertising, costs, prices, discounts, location, special promotions, traffic flow, and so on.

"Now," says Pat Collins, president of the 127 Ralph's stores in southern California, "we know as much, if not more than, the manufacturer about his product." Ralph's scanners scoop up vast volumes of data, which then helps its managers decide how much shelf space to devote to what products, when.

This is a crucial decision for competing manufacturers who are hammering at the doors, pleading for every available inch of shelf on which to display their products. Instead of the manufacturer telling the store how much to take, the store now compels manufacturers to pay what is known as "push money" for space, and staggering sums for particularly desirable locations.

Says *USA Today:* "The result [of such changes] is a war over turf: product makers battling grocers—and fighting each other—to win and keep their spots in supermarkets."

And it is clear who is winning—at the moment.

Says Kavin Moody, formerly corporate director of Management Information Systems at Gillette: "We want to control our own destiny . . . but the trade is getting more powerful. . . . They're looking for smarter deals and cooperative relationships. They're looking for better prices, which squeezes our margins. . . . The buyer used to be the flunky. Now he's backed up by all kinds of sophisticated tools."

Retail data become a more potent weapon when computer-analyzed and run through models that permit one to manipulate different variables. Thus, buyers use "direct product profitability" models to determine just how much they actually make on each product. These models examine such factors as how much shelf space is occupied by a square package as against a round one, what colors in the packaging work best for which products.

A version of this software is provided to retailers, in fact, by Procter & Gamble, one of the biggest manufacturers, in the hope of ingratiating itself with them. Armed with this software, P&G's sales force offers to help the store analyze its profitability if it, in turn, will share consumer information with P&G.

Retailers also use "shelf management" software and "space models" to help them decide which manufacturer's lines or goods to carry and which to reject, which to display in prime eye-catching space and which to put elsewhere. "Plan-a-Grams" printed out by computer give shelf-by-shelf guidance.

Having seized control of the main flow of data coming *from* the customer, retailers are also beginning to influence, if not control, the information going *to* the customer.

According to Moody, "The buyer can control the fate of a promotion. . . . To a large extent, they dictate what the consumer is going to see."

At both ends, therefore, the big food and package-goods companies have lost control of the information that once gave them power.

BEYOND THE SUPERMARKET

Beginning in the supermarket, the high-tech battle for control of information has caught fire elsewhere too. Scanners, lasers, hand-held computers, and other new technologies are pouring into drugstores, department stores, discount stores, bookstores, electrical appliance stores, hardware stores, clothing stores, specialty shops, and boutiques of all kinds. In these markets, too, manufacturers suddenly face antagonists who are keener, more confident, sometimes just short of arrogant.

"If you don't have Universal Product Codes on your goods, don't sit down, because we're not going to write the order," declares a peremptory sign in the buying office of Toys-R-Us, the 313-store chain.

As power shifts, retailer demands grow more aggressive. Bypassing the country's 100,000 independent manufacturers' representatives, dealing direct with its suppliers, Wal-Mart, the United States' fourth-biggest chain, insists that companies like Gillette change how they ship. Once more accommodating, Wal-Mart now demands that all its orders be filled 100 percent accurately—down to the numbers, sizes, and models of the products—and that deliveries be made to *its* schedule, not the supplier's. Failure to fill the order or deliver precisely on time could result in a supplier's payments being held ransom or a "handling cost" being deducted.

This puts manufacturers up against the wall: Either they increase inventories or they install new, more advanced technologies for de-massifying their factory output, moving to shorter rather than longer factory runs and faster turnaround times. Both are costly options. At the same time, retailers are imposing tighter quality standards—right down to the quality of the print on the packaging.

This seemingly trivial matter is in fact critical, since much of the information on which retail power now increasingly depends is found in the bar code, and bad printing means that the scanners may not be able to read the code accurately. Some retailers are threatening to hold the supplier responsible if the bar code on the package cannot be read properly by their scanning equipment.

Millions of customers have waited at checkout lines while clerks have passed the same package over the electronic scanner again and again before the scanner picked up the print message properly. All too often the clerk is forced to ring the product price up manually on the cash register.

Some storekeepers, in effect, are now threatening, "If my scanner can't read your code, it's your problem. I'm not telling my clerk to try again and again, and keep the customer waiting. If it doesn't scan, and we have to enter it manually, we're going to toss the product into the customer's bag and not charge for it. We'll give the product away and stop payment to you!"

Nobody ever talked back to the big companies that way. But then, nobody had the information that retailers now have.

So vital is this information that some manufacturers are now paying the retailers for it—either directly, or in exchange for services, or through intermediary firms who buy the data from retailers and sell them to manufacturers.

THE DOUBLE PAYMENT

This contest at the checkout counter has important implications for the consumer as well—and for the economy generally. Among other things it should help us rethink our obsolete assumptions about the respective roles of producers and consumers.

For example, in a world in which money is "informationalized" and information "monetized," the consumer pays for every purchase twice over: first with money and a second time by providing information that is worth money.

The customer typically gives this away for nothing. It is this valuable information that the retailers, manufacturers, banks, credit card issuers (and a lot of other people) are now fighting to control. In Florida and California, retail chains have fought blistering legal battles with banks over this issue. The central question their lawyers are asking one another is: "Who owns the customer data?"

The legal answers are not yet in. But one thing is certain: No one is asking the customer.

In theory, the customers' reward for providing data will be lower prices deriving from greater efficiency in the system. But it is by no means guaranteed that any part of this saving will be passed on, and, to the degree that the customer is the source of this crucial information, it is like giving the retailer an interest-free "information loan" in the hopes of future payback.

Since data originating with the customer are increasingly needed for the design and production (as well as distribution) of goods and services, the customer is in fact becoming a contributor to, if not an actual part of, the production process. The consumer, in a sense, is a co-producer of his or her own purchases.

But does the customer in fact "own" this information? Or does it acquire value only after it is collected and processed?

We lack the vocabulary, let alone laws and economic concepts, with which to deal with these unfamiliar questions arising from the information wars. But the issues involve the transfer of billions of dollars—and a subtle shift of economic and social bargaining power.

What does a customer give away free to the store, the manufacturer, or his or her credit card company?

Take the simplest of cases: A mother, home from work, in haste to make dinner, discovers she is out of margarine.

Dashing into the nearest store, she snatches a pound of

Fleischmann's sweet unsalted margarine made by Nabisco off the shelf. Hurrying to the checkout counter, she waits her turn, grabbing a copy of *TV Guide* from the rack near the register, and hands her purchases to the clerk, who passes them over the scanner.

In principle, she has communicated the following to the store computer: (1) a type of product she uses; (2) its brand; (3) its size or amount; (4) the fact that she preferred unsalted margarine to the regular; (5) the time of the purchase; (6) what other items, brands, sizes, etc., she bought at the same time; (7) the size of her total bill; (8) the kind of magazine in which an advertiser might reach her; (9) information about where additional shelf space is now available; and much more besides.

If a customer buys several bagfuls of different products, the same data become available for each item, and it becomes theoretically possible to *interrelate* these items to one another, in order to infer a *pattern* of purchasing—a consumption "signature" of each individual or group of customers.

If the shopper pays with a credit card, of course, much more is revealed.

Now the customer is also providing: (1) name; (2) address and postal code (important for segmenting markets); (3) credit information; (4) a basis for inferring the family income; and, potentially, much more besides.

By combining all this, it will soon become possible to construct a surprisingly detailed picture of the individual's life style, including driving habits, travel, entertainment and reading preferences, the frequency of meals outside the home, purchases of alcohol, condoms or other contraceptives, and a list of favored charities.

Marui, a leading Japanese general-goods retailer which issues its own credit card, uses a system called M-TOPS. This permits Marui to zero in on families who have just changed residence. It does this by identifying purchases that usually go with furnishing a new home. On the assumption that a family buying air conditioners or kitchen cabinetry might be in the market for new beds as well, Marui has been able to achieve astonishingly high direct-mail responses.

Leaving aside for a time the unsettling issues this raises about privacy in a super-symbolic economy, much of this information, once in the hands of any commercial enterprise—supermarket chain, bank, manufacturer—can also be sold for a price or bartered for a discount on services. The market for such information is huge.

"Data protection" laws in many countries now seek to regulate the uses of computerized information, but the data banks are filling up, the possibilities of integration are increasing, and the economic value of the information is soaring.

All this, however, is only a primitive first approximation of the future.

THE INTELLIGENT SUPERMARKET

Consumers may soon find themselves in supermarkets lined with so-called "electronic shelves." Instead of paper tags indicating the prices of canned goods or paper towels, the edge of the shelf itself will be a blinking liquid crystal display with digital readouts of the prices. The magic of this new technology is that it permits the store to change the price of thousands of products automatically and instantaneously as data streak in from the scanners at the front of the store.

Prices might plummet for slow-selling goods, climb for the hot items, rising and falling continuously in real-time response to supply and demand. Telepanel, Inc., a Toronto firm, estimates that such a system, capable of pricing 8,000 to 12,000 items, would cost the store in the range of $150,000 to $200,000 and pay for itself within two years.

Carried only a short step further, the electronic shelf might also provide shoppers with nutritional and price information at the touch of a button. Nor are such systems contemplated only for supermarkets. Says *Business Week:* "Drug chains, convenience stores, and even department stores already are planning their own versions of the system."

Down the line are even "smarter" shelves that would not merely send information to the customer, but elicit information from him or her. Hidden sensors, for example, make it possible to know when a customer passes a hand over a particular shelf or item, or when traffic exceeds or falls below expectation at a particular display.

Soon the customer will hardly be able to blink in the store, or move his or her arms, without providing the storekeeper with more and yet more usable or salable data.

The moral and economic implications of all this have hardly been explored by business or by consumer advocates. (Those interested in organizing consumer power had better start thinking about all this quickly, before the systems have been laid in place.) For now, it is only necessary to understand that profit margins today increasingly depend on information judo.

A THREAT TO THE "SHOGUNS"

Many of these same forces are changing power relationships in Japan as well. According to Alex Stewart, author of a definitive report on the Japanese distribution system, "retailers are now the dominant force within the distribution industry," while "manufacturers have to rely increasingly on retailers to interpret the needs of the marketplace."

George Fields is chairman and CEO of ASI Market Research (Japan). According to Fields, in Japan "distribution no longer means putting something on the shelf. It is now essentially an information system." Distribution anywhere, he notes, "will no longer be a chain of inventory points, passing goods along the line, but an information link between the manufacturer and the consumer."

What Fields is perhaps too polite to say, and what the Japanese in particular feel uncomfortable in making explicit, is that this transformation will dethrone many of the "shoguns" of industry in Japan. In Japan, too, power will shift toward those firms or industrial sectors that know best how to win the info-wars.

But the battle between manufacturers and retailers is only beginning, and it is not a two-sided struggle. The real-life tug-of-war has drawn many others into the battle zone—everyone from banks and computer manufacturers to truckers and telephone companies.

Squeezed between manufacturers and retailers are wholesalers, warehousers, transport firms, and others, each engaging in a fiercely competitive war-against-all, wielding advanced information and communications technologies as the main weapons.

Moreover, what we've seen so far is only the opening skirmish, and manufacturers themselves are mounting important counter-offensives—selling through alternative channels outside the store (direct mail, for example), using computers and telecommunications to set up their own vertically integrated distribution systems, buying up retail stores, and attempting to leapfrog technologically, to get ahead of the retailers.

Information flowing from these technologies will transform all our production and distribution systems, creating vast power vacuums that completely new groups and institutions are already racing to fill.

10

EXTRA-INTELLIGENCE

In 1839 a down-at-heels artist who gave lessons in drawing was asked by a pupil whether payment of a ten-dollar fee would be helpful. The art teacher—a sometime dabbler in the mysteries of electromagnetism—replied, "It would save my life, that's all."

Samuel F. B. Morse had already proved that he could send coded messages along an electric wire. But it wasn't until four years later, by dint of strenuous lobbying, that Morse managed to persuade the U.S. Congress to appropriate $30,000 to build a telegraph line between Washington and Baltimore. It was on the opening of that earliest line that Morse sent his historic telegram—"What hath God wrought!" With that Morse opened the age of telecommunications and triggered one of the most dramatic commercial confrontations of the 19th century. He started a powerful process that is still unfolding in our time.

Today, even as the battle of the supermarket checkout counters intensifies, a larger conflict is shaping up, centered on control of what might be called the electronic highways of tomorrow.

BACH, BEETHOVEN, AND WANG

Because so much of business now depends on getting and sending information, companies around the world have been rushing to link their employees through electronic networks. These networks form the key infrastructure of the 21st century, as critical to business success and national economic development as the railroads were in Morse's era.

Some of these are "local area networks," or LANs, which merely hook up computers in a single building or complex. Others are globe-girdling nets that connect Citibank people the world over, or help Hilton reserve its hotel rooms and Hertz its cars.

Every time McDonald's sells a Big Mac or a McMuffin, electronic data are generated. With 9,400 restaurants in 46 countries, McDonald's operates no fewer than 20 different networks to collect, assemble, and distribute this information. Du Pont's medical sales force plugs laptops into its electronic mail network, and Sara Lee depends on its nets to put L'eggs hosiery onto the shelves. Volvo links 20,000 terminals around the world to swap market data. DEC's engineers exchange design information electronically worldwide.

IBM alone connects 355,000 terminals around the world through a system called VNET, which in 1987 handled an estimated 5 trillion characters of data. By itself, a single part of that system—called PROFS—saved IBM the purchase of 7.5 million envelopes, and IBM estimates that without PROFS it would need nearly 40,000 additional employees to perform the same work.

Networking has spread down to the smallest businesses. With some 50 million PCs in use in the United States, Wang now advertises its networking equipment over the radio, sandwiching its commercials about "connectability" between Bach suites and Beethoven symphonies.

Companies daily grow more dependent on their electronic nets for billing, ordering, tracking, and trading; for the exchange of design specifications, engineering drawings, and schedules; and for actually controlling production lines remotely. Once regarded as purely administrative tools, networked information systems are increasingly seen as strategic weapons, helping companies protect established markets and attack new ones.

The race to build these networks has taken on some of the urgency that accompanied the great age of railroad construction in the 19th century, when nations became aware that their fate might be tied to the extensiveness of their rail systems.

Yet the power-shifting implications of this phenomenon are only dimly perceived by the public. To appreciate their significance, it helps to glance back to what happened after Samuel Morse strung the first telegraph network.

THE TELEPHONE FAD

By the mid-19th century Morse franchises had built thousands of miles of telegraph lines. Competing companies sprang up, networks grew, and an intense race began to connect major cities to one another across the continent. Stringing its wires along railroad rights of way, a company called Western Union began gobbling up smaller companies. Within eleven years its lines reached from one end of America to the other, and its capital had shot up from $500,000 to $41 million—a bank-boggling amount in those days.

Soon its subsidiary, the Gold & Stock Telegraph Company, was providing high-speed information for investors and gold speculators—paving the way for today's Dow Jones or Nikkei.

At a time when most messages were still carried across the continent in saddlebags or railway cars, Western Union had a stranglehold on the means of advanced communication.

Success, as usual, bred corporate arrogance. Thus, in 1876, when a voice teacher named Alexander Graham Bell patented the first telephone, Western Union tried to laugh it off as a joke and a fad. But as public demand for telephone service soared, Western Union made it clear it was not about to surrender its monopoly. A knockdown conflict ensued, and Western Union did everything possible to kill or capture the newer technology.

It hired Thomas Edison to invent alternatives to the Bell technology. Its lawyers fought Bell in court.

"At another level," writes Joseph C. Goulden, author of *Monopoly*, "Western Union barred Bell from the right-of-way monopolies it owned for its wires along highways and railroads. Western Union had its instruments in every major hotel, railway station, and newspaper office in the nation, under terms which forbade installations of telephones. A Bell manager in Philadelphia was forbidden to erect lines anywhere in the city; his workers frequently were jailed on complaints sworn by Western Union. The telegraph company's political influence in Washington kept Bell phones from federal offices."

Despite all this, Western Union failed, swept aside not so much by its smaller antagonist as by the business world's desperate hunger for better communications. In turn, the winner of that corporate power struggle grew into the biggest privately owned business the world had ever seen—the American Telephone & Telegraph Company (AT&T).

SECRETS AND SECRET-ARIES

The benefits of communication—whether Morse's telegraph, Bell's telephone, or today's high-speed data networks—are relative. If no one has them, all competing firms operate, as it were, at the same neural transmission rate. But when some do and others don't, the competitive arena is sharply tilted. So companies rushed to adopt Bell's new invention.

Telephones changed almost everything about business. They permitted operations over a greater geographical area. Top executives could now speak directly with branch managers or salesmen in distant regional offices to find out, in detail, what was going on. Voice communication conveyed far more information, through intonation, inflection, and accent, than the emotionless dah-dits of Morse code ever could.

The phones made big companies bigger. They made centralized bureaucracies more efficient. Switchboards and operators proliferated. Secretaries overheard calls and learned when to keep mum. They learned to screen calls, thereby partially controlling access to power.

At first the phone also abetted secrecy. A lot of business could now be transacted without the incriminating evidence of a piece of paper. (Later came technologies for wiretapping and bugging, tipping the scales in the never-ending battle between those who have business secrets and those who want to penetrate them.)

The indirect benefits of this advanced communications system were even greater. Phones helped integrate the industrializing economy. Capital markets became more fluid; commerce, easier. Deals could be made swiftly, with a confirming letter as follow-up.

Phones accelerated the pace of business activity—which, in turn, stepped up the rate of economic development in the more technically advanced nations. In this way, one might argue that telephones, over the long term, even affected the international balance of power. (This claim is less outrageous than it might seem at first glance. National power flows from multiple sources, but one can crudely track the rise of America to a position of global dominance by looking at its communications system relative to other nations. As late as 1956, half of all the telephones in the world were in the United States. Today, as America's relative dominance declines, that percentage has slipped to about one-third.)

ELECTRONIC HIGHWAYS

As more and more of the economy came to depend on phones, the companies or government agencies that provided or regulated them became enormously powerful too. In the United States, AT&T, otherwise known as the Bell System or Ma Bell, became the dominant supplier of telecommunications services.

It is hard for those accustomed to decent telephone service to imagine operating an economy or a business without it, or to function in a country where the telephone company (usually the government) can deny even basic phone service or delay its installation for years. This bureaucratic power gives rise to political favoritism, payoffs, and corruption, slows down national economic development, and frequently determines which enterprises have a chance to grow and which must fail. Yet such is the situation still prevailing in many of the formerly socialist and nonindustrial nations.

Even in the technologically advanced nations, phone service suppliers and regulators can control the fate of entire industrial sectors, by providing or refusing specialized services, setting differential prices, and through other means.

Sometimes angry or frustrated users strike back. In fact, the biggest corporate restructuring in history, the court-ordered breakup of AT&T in 1984, can illustrate the point.

The U.S. government had been trying without success to dismantle AT&T since the 1940s on grounds that it was charging customers too much. Government attorneys hauled the company into court, cases dragged on interminably, but nothing fundamental changed. Warning shots were fired across the corporation's bow, but even during Democratic administrations pledged to strong antitrust action, nothing cracked the AT&T grip on the U.S. communications system.

What ultimately shifted the power balance was a combination of new technology and the irrepressible demand of business phone users for more and better service.

Starting in the 1960s, a large number of American businesses had begun installing computers. Simultaneously, satellites and many other new technologies erupted from the laboratories—some of them out of AT&T's own Bell Labs. Soon corporate computer users began demanding a great variety of new data network services. They wanted computers to be able to talk to one another. They knew the necessary technology was feasible. But the diverse data services they desperately needed represented, at the time, too small a market to whet Ma Bell's appetite.

As a protected monopoly the phone company had no competition, and was therefore slow to respond to these new needs. As computers and satellites spread, however, and more companies needed to link them up, business disgruntlement with AT&T intensified. IBM, the prime supplier of mainframes, presumably lost business because AT&T was dragging its feet, and had other reasons for wishing to see AT&T's monopoly cracked. All these unhappy corporations were politically savvy.

Gradually anti-AT&T sentiment in Washington mounted. Ultimately, it was the combination of new technologies and rising hostility to Ma Bell that provided the political climate for the climactic bust-up that occurred. Breaking AT&T into pieces, the court, for the first time since the early decades of the century, opened telecommunications in the United States to competition. There were, in other words, structural forces, not merely legal reasons, behind the massive breakup.

Just as an overwhelming business demand for better communications had defeated Western Union a century earlier, so again, new technologies and an overwhelming unmet demand for new services ultimately defeated AT&T. By now the rate of technological change has become white-hot and companies are far more dependent on telecommunications than ever in history.

The result is that airlines, car makers, and oil companies are all engaged in a many-sided war for control of the emerging communications systems. Indeed, as we'll shortly see, truckers, warehousers, stores, factories—the entire chain of production and distribution—are being shaken.

Moreover, as money becomes more like information, and information more like money, both are increasingly reduced to (and moved around by) electronic impulses. As this historic fusion of telecommunications and finance deepens, the power inherent in the control of networks increases exponentially.

All this explains the fierce urgency with which companies and governments alike are hurling themselves into the war to control the electronic highways of tomorrow. Amazingly, however, few top business leaders actually understand the stakes, let alone the fantastic changes restructuring the very nature of communications in our time.

THE SELF-AWARE NETWORK

Anyone can see and touch the telephone or computer on the nearest desk. This is not true of the networks that connect them to the world. Thus we remain, for the most part, ignorant about the high-speed advances that are fashioning them into something resembling the nervous system of our society.

The networks that Morse, Western Union, Bell, and others set up when they first began stringing wires were unintelligent, if not downright stupid. Common sense taught that a straight line is the shortest distance between two points. So engineers sought this straight line, and messages sent from one city to another were always sent over this pathway.

As these first-stage networks expanded, however, it was discovered that in the world of the network, a straight line is not necessarily the best way to get a message from one place to another. In fact, more messages could flow faster if, instead of always sending a call, say, from Tallahassee to Atlanta via the same route, the network could count the calls in each leg of the system and then shunt the Atlanta-bound call onto available lines, sending it as far away as New Orleans or even St. Louis, rather than delaying it because the shortest straight-line route happened to be busy.

Primitive though it was, this was an early injection of "intelligence" or "smarts" into the system, and it meant, in effect, that the network was beginning to monitor its own performance. With this the entire system leaped to a second stage of development. This breakthrough led to many additional innovations, often of marvelous ingenuity, that eventually allowed the telephone network to monitor many more things about itself, to check its components and anticipate and even diagnose breakdowns.

It was as though a once-dead or inert organism suddenly began checking its own blood pressure, pulse, and breathing rate. The network was becoming self-aware.

Crisscrossing the entire planet, with wires running into hundreds of millions of homes, with whole copper mines of cable snaking under the streets of cities, with complex switching systems and transmission technologies in them, these second-stage networks, constantly refined, improved, extended, and given more and more intelligence, were among the true marvels of the industrial age.

Because they are largely invisible to the ordinary user, our civilization has radically underestimated the congealed brilliance and conceptual beauty of these hidden networks as well as their evolutionary significance.

For while some human populations still lack even the most rudimentary telephone service, researchers are already hard at work on another revolutionary leap in telecommunications—the creation of even more sophisticated third-stage networks.

Nowadays, as millions of computers are plugged into them, from giant Crays to tiny laptops, as new networks continually spring up, as they are linked to form a denser and denser interconnected mesh, a still higher level of intelligence or "self-awareness" is needed to handle the incredibly vast volumes of information pulsing through them.

As a result, researchers are racing to make networks even more self-aware. Their goal is so-called neural networks. These will not only route and reroute messages, but actually learn from their own past experience, forecast where and when heavy loads will be, and then automatically expand or contract sections of the network to match the requirements. This is as though the San Diego Freeway or a German *Autobahn* were clever enough to widen and narrow itself according to how many cars it expected at any moment.

Yet even before this major effort is complete, another even more gigantic leap is being taken. We are moving not into a fourth-stage system, but to another kind of intelligence altogether.

MESSING WITH THE MESSAGE

Until now, even the smartest networks, including the new neural networks, had only what might be called "intra-intelligence." All their "smarts" were aimed inward.

Intra-intelligence is like the intelligence embedded in our own autonomic nervous system, which regulates the involuntary operations of the body, such as heartbeat and hormonal secretions—the functions we seldom think about, but which are necessary to sustain life.

Intra-intelligent networks deliver the message precisely as sent. Scientists and engineers struggle to maintain the purity of the message, fighting to eliminate any "noise" that might garble or alter the message. They may scramble it or digitize it or packetize it (i.e., break it into short spurts) to get it from here to there. But they reconstitute it again at the receiving end. And the message content remains the same.

Today we are reaching beyond intra-intelligence toward networks that might be called "extra-intelligent." They do not just transfer data. They analyze, combine, repackage, or otherwise alter messages, sometimes creating new information along the way. Thus massaged or enhanced, what comes out the other end is different from what is fed in—changed by software embedded in the networks. These are the so-called "Value Added Networks," or VANs. They are extra-intelligent.

At present most VANs merely scramble and rescramble messages to adapt them to different media. For example, in France the Atlas 400 service of France Telecom accepts data from a mainframe computer, say, then repackages it in a form that can be received by a PC, a fax machine, or a videotex terminal.

Not very exciting, it would appear. But the concept of adding value to a message doesn't stop with altering its technical characteristics. The French Minitel network, which links 5 million homes and businesses, offers Gatrad, Mitrad, Dilo, and other services that can accept a message in French and automatically deliver it in English, Arabic, Spanish, German, Italian, or Dutch—and vice versa. While the translations are still rough, they are workable, and some services also have the specialized vocabularies needed for subjects involving, say, aerospace, nuclear, or political topics.

Other networks receive data from a sender, run them through a computerized model, and deliver an "enhanced" message to the end-user.

A simple hypothetical example illustrates the point.

Imagine that a trucking firm based in the outskirts of Paris must regularly dispatch its trucks to forty different European distributors, restocking their shelves with a product. Road conditions and weather differ in various parts of Europe, as do currency exchange rates, gasoline prices, and other factors. In the past each driver calculated the best route, or else phoned the transport company each day for instructions.

But imagine instead that an independent VAN operator—a common carrier—not only can send signals to truck drivers all over Europe, but also collects current information on road conditions, traffic, weather, currencies, and gas prices. The Paris trucker can now load its daily messages and routing instructions onto the VAN for distribution to its drivers. But the messages, before reaching the drivers, are run through the network's software program, which automatically adjusts routes to minimize driving time, mileage, gas costs, and currency expenses in light of the latest data.

In this case, the instructions sent by the transport firm to its drivers are altered en route and "enhanced" before reaching them. The telecommunications carrier firm—the operator of the Value Added Network—has added value by integrating the customer's message with fresh information, transforming it, and then distributing it.

This, however, suggests only the simplest use of an extra-intelligent net. As the networks come to offer more complex services—collecting, integrating, and evaluating data, drawing automatic inferences, and running input through sophisticated models—their potential value soars.

In short, we are now looking toward networks whose "smarts" are no longer aimed at changing or improving the network itself but which, in effect, act on the outside world, adding "extra-intelligence" to the messages flowing through them.

Still largely a gleam in their architects' eyes, extra-intelligent nets represent an evolutionary leap to a new level of communication. They also raise to a higher level the sophistication required of their users. For a company to load its messages on a VAN and permit them to be altered without a deep understanding of the assumptions buried in the VAN's software is to operate on blind faith, rather than rational decision. For hidden biases built into the software can cost a user dearly.

Foreign airlines, for example, have complained to the U.S. Department of Transportation that they are discriminated against in the electronic network that thousands of U.S. travel agents use in choosing flights for their clients. Called Sabre, the computerized reservation system is run by AMR Corp., which also owns American Airlines. The system, which monitors reservations on many airlines, has extra-intelligence embedded in it in the form of a software model that tells the travel agent the best available flights. At issue in the complaint were the assumptions built right into this software.

Thus, when a travel agent searches, say, for a flight from Frankfurt to St. Louis, Missouri, her computer screen displays the flights in order depending upon the length of time they take. The shorter the flight the better. But the Sabre software automatically assumed that changing planes and transferring from one airline to another takes ninety minutes, irrespective of the actual time required. Since many of their flights to the United States required a change of plane and transfer to a domestic American airline, the foreign carriers charged that the hidden premises of the software unfairly penalized those whose interline transfers require less than ninety minutes. For this reason, they argued, their flights were less likely to be chosen by travel agents. In short, the extra-intelligence was biased.

Imagine, soon, not a handful of such disputes and networks, but thousands of VANs with tens of thousands of built-in programs and models, continually altering and manipulating millions of messages as they whiz through the economy along these self-aware electronic highways. Britain alone already boasts eight hundred VANs, West Germany seven hundred, and more than five hundred companies in Japan have registered with the Ministry of Posts and Telecommunications to operate VANs.

The existence of VANs promises to squeeze untold billions of dollars out of today's costs of production and distribution by slashing red tape, cutting inventory, speeding up response time. But the injection of extra-intelligence into these fast-proliferating and interlinked nets has a larger significance. It is like the sudden, blinding addition of a cerebral cortex to an organism that never had one. Combined with the autonomic nervous system, it begins to give the organism not merely self-awareness and the ability to change itself, but the ability to intervene directly in our lives, beginning first with our businesses.

Because of this, networks will take on revolutionary new roles in business and society. And even though, so far as we know, no one has yet used extra-intelligence for pernicious or even criminal purposes, the spread of extra-intelligent networks is still in its infancy, with rules and safeguards yet to be defined.

Who knows what will follow? By creating a self-aware electronic neural system that is extra-intelligent, we change the rules of culture as well as business.

E-I, as we may call it, will raise perplexing questions about the relationships of data to information and knowledge, about language, about ethics and the abstruse models concealed in software. Rights of redress, responsibility for error or bias, issues of privacy and fairness will all cascade into executive suites and the courts in the years to come as society tries to adapt to the existence of extra-intelligence.

As the implications of E-I will someday reach far beyond mere business matters, they should cause deep social, political, and even philosophical reflection. For prodigies of labor, intellect, and scientific imagination that dwarf anything involved in constructing Egyptian pyramids, medieval cathedrals, or Stonehenge are now being poured into the construction of the electronic infrastructure of tomorrow's super-symbolic society.

E-I, as we shall see next, is already upsetting power relationships in whole sectors of the emerging economy.

11

NET POWER

Japan worries. To the outside world it often seems economically invincible. But things look different from inside. It has no energy supplies of its own, grows little food, and is highly sensitive to trade restrictions. If the yen goes down, it worries. If the yen goes up, it worries. But individual Japanese do not just worry about the economy in general. They also worry about their own future. So they are among the world's biggest savers. And they buy massive amounts of insurance.

For a long time the chief beneficiaries of all this anxiety were the giant insurance companies. Today, however, it is the insurers who are doing the worrying.

The government is opening the door that once kept out competition from Japan's aggressive securities brokers. Tough, world-class companies like Nomura and Daiwa, the Merrill Lynches or Shearsons of Japan, are preparing to move in on the insurance industry's turf.

Topping that off, the entire insurance field is in an uproar of change. Customers are demanding all sorts of newfangled policies and financial services which these venerable giants—Nippon Life is over one hundred years old—find hard to create and manage.

To deal with threats like these, the big insurance firms have begun laying down an electronic line of defense. Nippon Life is betting nearly half a billion dollars on a new information system that adds 5,000 PCs, 1,500 larger computers for its satellite offices, mega-machines for branches and headquarters, plus optical scanners and other equipment, all plugged together in a single network.

Rival Dai-Ichi Mutual is also running hard, building a network that will allow agents in the field to dial up central data banks, respond to synthesized voice commands on the phone, and get facsimile printouts of the data they need about customers or policies. Meanwhile, Meiji Mutual, with its 38,000 field agents, mainly women, is also racing to arm itself with the weaponry of communications.

Nor are the insurance companies alone. All of Japan, it would seem, is going electronic. Writes *Datamation:* "Major service companies are installing networks with 5,000 or more PCs and workstations in every corner of Japan." Says Meiji's Toshiyuki Nakamura: "If we don't . . . we might lose everything."

Nakamura is right. For as electronic networks spread, power is beginning to shift. And not just in Japan. The United States and Europe, too, are wiring up as never before. It is the electronic race of the century.

THE SEARCH FOR DENIM

Consider a pair of jeans. The denim in them may well have come from Burlington Industries. This giant American textile firm sends its customers free software that allows them to communicate directly with Burlington's mainframe, to paw through its stock of denims electronically, to find the particular batch of fabric they want, and to order it—all at instantaneous speeds.

Manufacturers like Burlington hope such services will distinguish them from their competitors, make life easier for customers— and simultaneously lock those customers into the new "electronic data interchange" (EDI) systems so tightly that it will become hard for them to escape.

At their simplest, EDI systems simply permit the electronic exchange of documents between companies or business units— invoices, specifications, inventory data, and the like. But leaving it at that is rather like calling Mozart a tunesmith. For by wedding one another's data bases and electronic systems, companies are able to form highly intimate partnerships.

For example, while Burlington opens its inventory files to its customers, Digital Equipment, the computer maker, opens its design secrets to its suppliers. When DEC places an order for components, it may electronically transfer its entire Computer-Aided-Design file to the supplier firm, so that both buyer and seller can work more closely together, step by step. The object is intimacy.

The big auto companies now virtually refuse to do business with suppliers who are not equipped for electronic interaction. At Ford, fifty-seven parts plants have been told they must electronically exchange shipping schedules, material requisitions, releases, and receipts with both customers and suppliers.

The benefits of EDI are not only a reduction in paperwork and inventory, but quicker, more flexible response to customer needs. Together these can amount to massive savings.

But the worldwide shift to electronic interchange also implies radical changes in the business system. Companies are forming into what might be called "information-sharing groups." More communication is crossing—and sometimes blurring—organizational boundaries.

Whether in a Japanese insurance company or an American automaker, EDI forces major changes in accounting and other control systems. When a company goes electronic, jobs change; people move around; some departments gain clout, others lose. The entire relationship of the firm to its suppliers and customers is shaken up.

Such power shifts, however, are not merely limited to individual firms. Whole sectors of the economy are already feeling the impact of EDI. For EDI can be used as a weapon to wipe out go-betweens and intermediaries.

THE BINGO-ED WHOLESALER

Shiseido, Japan's top cosmetics firm, for example, uses its networks to sidestep the traditional distribution chain. Shiseido's powders, creams, eye shadows, lotions, and what-have-you are everywhere in Japan and are beginning to make a splash in U.S. and European markets as well.

By connecting its computers directly to those of its customers, Shiseido end-runs wholesalers and warehousers, delivering from its own distribution centers directly to the stores. If Shiseido and other manufacturers can "talk" directly with their retailers, and retailers can electronically access information in the manufacturer's own computers, who needs an intermediary?

"The wholesaler? Bingo! Bypassed," says Monroe Greenstein,

a retail industry analyst at the Bear, Stearns securities firm in New York. To avoid that fate, wholesalers, too, are turning to electronic weaponry.

The most publicized, by now classic case of a wholesaler taking the offensive—and capturing new power in the marketplace—involves American Hospital Supply, now a part of Baxter Health Care Corporation. Starting as early as 1978, AHS began placing terminals inside hospitals and allowing them to dial directly, through a network, to its computers. It was much simpler for hospitals to order supplies from AHS by pushing a button than to deal with other, less sophisticated suppliers.

In turn, AHS used the network to zap all sorts of useful information about products, usage, costs, inventory control, etc., to its customers. Because AHS's system was so responsive and reliable, hospitals were able to cut back on their own inventories, saving them substantial money. And if a hospital placed all its business with AHS, the company provided an entire management information system for the hospital. AHS's business skyrocketed.

Consultant Peter Keen, from whose study, *Competing in Time*, some of these data are drawn, describes how Foremost McKesson, a pharmaceutical wholesaler, applied the AHS strategy to its own field.

As customer orders flow into Foremost McKesson's computers electronically from hand-held terminals placed in 15,000 stores, they are instantly sorted and consolidated. This generates Foremost McKesson's own orders, fully half of which are then, in turn, instantly and automatically transmitted to *its* supplier firms.

Such high-speed systems allow AHS, Foremost, and many other firms to wire themselves so snugly into their customers' daily operations that it becomes costly and complex for them to shift their business elsewhere. In return, the systems save their customers significant sums and help them manage more smartly all around. All this pays off in negotiating power.

But AHS and McKesson are still exceptions. Most wholesalers could face an electronic squeeze play, caught between manufacturers and increasingly sophisticated retailers.

REAL ESTATE AND RAILS

Warehouse companies are next in line for trouble as extra-intelligence spreads through the economy.

The increasing customization and flexible manufacture made possible by computers, means, among other things, a shift from a few big orders for uniform products to many smaller orders for diversified products. Simultaneously, the speedup of business encouraged by electronic networking increases pressures for just-in-time delivery to factories and stores.

All this implies fewer bulk shipments, shorter storage times, faster turnaround, and more insistence on precise information about the whereabouts of every stored item—less space, more information.

This substitution reduces the clout of the space merchant and pushes smart warehousers into a search for alternative functions. Some are using networks and computers to sell customers data software services, transportation management, packing, sorting, inspecting, knockdown and assembly services, and the like. Still others—Sumitomo Warehouse in Japan, for instance—are moving into real estate development as the traditional functions of the warehouser dry up.

The super-symbolic economy and the spread of extra-intelligence also shake up the transportation sector—railroads, shippers, and truckers. Like warehousers, many truckers are also turning to electronic networks to save themselves.

In Japan the move toward short-run factory production and the push for just-in-time delivery means a big surge in short-haul work. And instead of delivering big loads on a once-a-week schedule, the pressure is toward smaller but far more frequent dropoffs. The most rapid growth is seen in door-to-door delivery.

What we see, therefore, are all the traditional sectors of the production and distribution system wielding extra-intelligence to stay alive, or as an offensive weapon to extend their power.

MOBILIZING FOR ELECTRONIC WAR

The scale of the electronic war rises when whole industries mobilize to do battle.

Rather than individual firms, industry-wide groups are taking collective action. Such industry-wide networks are especially notable in Japan, where their formation is strongly encouraged by the ubiquitous Ministry of International Trade and Industry. Thus MITI is prodding the petroleum industry to complete a net that will link refiners, oil tank facilities, and retailers. Industry-wide Value Added Networks have already appeared in fields as disparate as frozen foods, eyeglasses, and sporting goods.

Similar industry-wide nets are springing up elsewhere. In Australia two competing Value Added Networks, Woolcom and a service offered by Talman Pty., Ltd., for wool brokers and exporters, are vying for business and looking ahead to link-ups with Tradegate, an international trade net, and EXIT, an export clearance system.

In the United States a major drive is under way to complete a network that will tie together not only textile manufacturers like Burlington, but apparel makers and the giant retailers like Wal-Mart and K Mart. To stoke up support for this effort, business leaders like Roger Millikin, chairman of Millikin & Company, make speeches, hold seminars, fund studies, and preach the network gospel.

A key problem in the industry has been slow response time. Clothing fashions change swiftly, so the industry wants to compress the time between order and delivery from weeks to days by installing an electronic network that runs from the textile mill to the retail checkout counter. By speeding response, huge cuts in inventory become possible.

The electronic system allows retailers to order smaller batches and replace the fast-sellers more frequently as styles and consumer tastes change, instead of sitting on slow-moving merchandise. Milliken cites the experience of one department store chain that was able to sell 25 percent more slacks while, at the same time, carrying 25 percent fewer slacks in its inventory. Indeed, with the system only partly in place, results have been dramatic. The campaign began in 1986. By 1989, according to Arthur Andersen & Company, more than seventy-five retailers had invested an estimated $3.6 billion in the system, called Quick Response, and had already benefited to the tune of $9.6 billion.

In fact, Millikin and many others believe so many more billions can be saved that electronic intelligence can serve as a weapon in international trade wars. If efficiency can be raised enough, and rapidly enough, the reasoning goes, the American textile and apparel industries would be able to compete more effectively against cheap labor imports.

As individual companies and entire industries race to position themselves for the future by building their own special-purpose networks, other giants are racing to lay in place global multipurpose networks that will carry messages for anyone.

What we are seeing, therefore, is the emergence of several types or layers of electronic networks: private nets primarily designed for the employees of a single firm; EDI hookups between individual companies and their customers and/or vendors; and industry-wide networks. To these, however, must now be added generic networks—so-called common carriers—which are needed to connect these lower-level networks to one another and to transport messages for everyone else.

The volume of messages and data now surging through this neural system is so huge that an even larger-scale battle has erupted among big companies who wish to dominate this common carrier service. Giants like British Telecom, AT&T, and Japan's KDD are racing to expand their capacity and speed up data flows. To complicate matters, large companies that have their own global nets sell services to outsiders and compete with the common carriers. Thus Toyota, for example, and IBM fight for business that might otherwise go to one of the old telephone companies. General Electric operates a network in seventy countries, and Benetton, based in Italy, relies on GE to connect 90 percent of its employees.

What is forming under our eyes, therefore, is an entirely new, multilayered system, the economy's infrastructure for the 21st century.

THE CUSTOMER LOOP

Its growth is causing new struggles for the control of knowledge and communication, struggles that are shifting power among people, companies, industries, sectors, and countries. Yet the "neuralization" of the economy has scarcely begun and new players enter the power game every day. They include credit card companies, the great Japanese trading houses, equipment manufacturers, and many others.

Crucial to this emerging system is the plastic card in the consumer's wallet. Whether it is an automatic teller machine card, a conventional credit card, or a "smart" debit card, the card is a network's link to the individual. That link can, in principle, be expanded vastly.

As everyone from banks and oil companies to local merchants moves more deeply into the electronic age . . . as the cards themselves become smarter, carrying and conveying vast amounts of information . . . and as money itself becomes "super-symbolic," no longer pegged to either metal or paper . . . the card provides the missing link in the emerging neural system.

Whoever controls the card—bankers or their rivals—has a priceless channel into the home and daily life. Thus we see a push to link individual customers to the specialized networks. In Japan, JCB Co., a credit card firm, together with NTT Data Communications, is launching a card women can use at their hairdressers'. It hopes to connect 35,000 hairdressers with 10 million card-carrying customers in a two-year period.

The long-range dream of the world's network builders is a single integrated loop, running from the customer (who will electronically tell business what goods or services to make) . . . to the producer . . . through what remains of distribution intermediary firms . . . to the retailer or the electronic home shopping service . . . to the ATM or the credit card payment system . . . and ultimately back into the home of the consumer.

Any company or industrial group that can seize control of the main steps in this cycle will wield decisive economic power—and hence considerable political power as well. But seizing it will depend less on capital than on brains—intelligence embedded in computers, software, and electronic networks.

BUSINESS BLITZKRIEG

Economies of the past, whether agricultural or industrial, were built around long-lasting structures.

In place of these, we are laying the electronic basis for an accelerative kaleidoscopic economy capable of instantly reshuffling itself into new patterns without blowing itself apart. The new extra-intelligence is part of the necessary adaptive equipment.

In the confusing new flux, businesses can use extra-intelligence to launch surprise attacks on entirely fresh territory, which means that companies can no longer be sure where the next competitive push will come from.

The classic blitzkrieg—much analyzed in the network literature— was Merrill Lynch's launch of its Cash Management Account in 1977, an early use of information technology for a strategic, as distinct from merely administrative, purpose.

The Cash Management Account, or CMA, was a new financial product that combined four previously separate services for the customer: a checking account, a deposit account, a credit card, and a securities account. The customer could move money back and forth among these at will. There was no float and the checking account paid interest.

The integration of these previously disparate products into a single offering was made possible only by Merrill Lynch's sophisticated computer technology and electronic networks. In twelve months, Merrill sucked in $5 billion of customer funds and by 1984, according to consultant Peter Keen, $70 billion had flooded into Merrill Lynch's hands. Keen calls it a "preemptive strike" against the banks, which saw vast sums withdrawn by customers who preferred the CMA to an ordinary bank checking account. A securities house, not subject to bank regulation and not regarded as a bank, devastated the banks.

Since then, many banks and other financial institutions have offered similar packages, but Merrill had a several-year head start on them.

The strange new hybrid patterns of competition—which reflect a restructuring of markets as a result of extra-intelligence— are seen in the move of retailers like Japan's Seibu Saison group into the financial services business. A Seibu subsidiary is planning to install electronic cash dispensers in railroad stations. British

Petroleum, having set up its own internal bank, sells banking services to outsiders.

Extra-intelligent networks help explain the widespread push for deregulation of industry, and they suggest that existing government regulations will prove less and less effective. For existing regulations are based on categories and divisions among industries that no longer exist in the age of extra-intelligence. Should banking regulations apply to nonbanks? What, after all, is a bank these days?

By linking actual operations across company lines, by making it possible for companies to compete in fields once regarded as alien, extra-intelligent networks break up the old specializations, the old institutional division of labor.

In their place come new constellations and clusters of companies, densely interrelated not merely by money but by shared information.

Ironically, it is the disruption caused by this drastic restructuring of the economy around knowledge that explains many of today's breakdowns and inefficiencies—the misplaced bills, the computer errors, the inadequate service, the sense that nothing works properly. The old smokestack economy is disintegrating; the new super-symbolic economy is still being built, and the electronic infrastructure on which it depends is still in a primitive stage of development.

Information is the most fluid of resources, and fluidity is the hallmark of an economy in which the production and distribution of food, energy, goods, and services increasingly depend on symbolic exchange.

What emerges is an economy that itself looks more like a nervous system than anything else, and which runs according to rules no one has as yet formulated coherently.

Indeed, the unprecedented rise of extra-intelligence raises profound, sometimes chilling questions for society as a whole, quite different from those raised by earlier communications revolutions.

THE RISE OF INFO-MONOPOLIES?

Extra-intelligence can squeeze untold billions of fat and waste out of the economy. It potentially represents an enormous leap forward—the substitution of brainpower and imagination not merely for capital, energy, and resources, but for brutalizing labor as well.

But whether extra-intelligence produces a "better" way of life will depend partly on the social and political intelligence that guides its overall development.

The more automated and extra-intelligent our networks become, the more human decision-making is hidden from view, and the more dependent we all become on preprogrammed events based on concepts and assumptions that few understand and that are sometimes not even willingly disclosed.

Before long the power of computers will leap forward because of parallel processing, artificial intelligence, and other stunning innovations. Speech recognition and automatic translation will, no doubt, come into wide use, along with high-definition visual displays and concert-class sound. The same networks will routinely carry voice, data, images, and information in other forms. All this raises profound philosophical questions.

Some see in all this the coming monopolization of knowledge. "The moment of truth," wrote Professor Frederic Jameson of Duke University at an earlier stage in the rise of the symbolic economy, ". . . comes when the matter of the ownership and control of the new information banks . . . [strikes] with a vengeance." Jameson raises the specter of a "global private monopoly of information."

That fear is now far too simple. The issue is not whether one giant global private monopoly will control all information—which seems highly unlikely—but who will control the endless *conversions and reconversions* of it made possible by extra-intelligence, as data, information, and knowledge flow through the nervous system of the super-symbolic economy.

Baffling new issues about the uses and misuses of knowledge will arise to confront business and society as a whole. They will no longer simply reflect Bacon's truth that knowledge is power, but the higher level truth that, in the super-symbolic economy, it is knowledge *about* knowledge that counts most.

12

THE WIDENING WAR

Umbrellas and automobiles are different. Not just because of size, function, and cost. But for a reason we seldom stop to consider. A person can use an umbrella without buying another product. An automobile, by contrast, is useless without fuel, oil, repair services, spare parts, not to mention streets and roads. The humble umbrella, therefore, is a rugged individual, so to speak, delivering value to its user irrespective of any other product.

The mighty auto, by contrast, is a team player completely dependent on other products. So is a razor blade, a tape recorder, a refrigerator, and thousands of other products that work only when combined with others. The television set would stare blankly into the living room if someone somewhere were not transmitting images to it. Even the lowly closet hanger presupposes a rack or bar to hang it on.

Each of these is part of a product *system*. It is precisely their systemic nature that is their main source of economic value. And just as "team players" must play by certain agreed-on rules, systemic products need standards to work. A three-pronged electrical plug doesn't help much if all the wall sockets have only two slots.

This distinction between stand-alone and systemic products throws revealing light on an issue that is widening today's information wars all around the world. The French call it *la guerre des normes*—"the war over standards." Battles over standards are raging in industries as diverse as medical technology, industrial pressure vessels, and cameras.

Some of the most explosive—and public—disputes are directly related to the ways in which data, information, knowledge, images, and entertainment are created and distributed.

In essence a global battle over dollars and political power, its outcome will reach into millions of homes. It will radically shift power among the industrial giants of the world: companies like IBM, AT&T, Sony, and Siemens. And it will affect national economies.

Nowhere is this battle more public than in the three-way fight to determine what kind of television the world will watch in the decades to come.

THE HALF-TRILLION-DOLLAR STAKE

Three basic television standards are in use in different parts of the world at present: NTSC, PAL, and SECAM, each slightly different but incompatible. Because of this, an American program like *The Cosby Show* usually has to be converted from one system to another before it can be telecast abroad. But the images produced by all three systems are fuzzy by contrast with what is known as HDTV—the television of tomorrow.

"High-definition TV" is to today's home video screens what the compact disc is to the scratchy platter played on great-grandma's gramophone. High definition can put pictures on the TV screen that match the quality of the best big-screen movies. It can make an image blast off the computer monitor looking as bright and sharp as the finest printed page.

Congressman Mel Levine has pointed out in testimony before the telecommunications subcommittee of the U.S. House of Representatives that, despite its name, more is involved than just TV. HDTV, he said, "represents a new generation of consumer electronics, one that will drive technological developments in dozens of areas, from chip to fiber-optic to battery to camera technology."

Because HD image quality is so good, it could even make it possible for cinemas all over the world to receive their movies via satellite, rather than on film as at present, which would open an additional immense market for satellite receivers and other equipment.

In total, therefore, the decision as to which HDTV standard(s) to use will shape a world market estimated to be worth half a trillion dollars.

Japanese engineers have worked on HDTV for nearly twenty years. Now high definition is about to burst on the world economic scene. And when it does, writes Bernard Cassen in *Le Monde Diplomatique*, "the Japanese and the Americans threaten to render all European television sets obsolete—and to be the only ones with the power to replace them."

The Japanese hoped the world would adopt a single standard for HDTV. This would have simplified matters and saved them a lot of money. With their head start, had they been able to sell this basic international standard, the way would have been open for a massive expansion of the Japanese consumer electronics industry.

To head off this onslaught, however, European governments and TV networks (in many cases one and the same) have agreed to stick with broadcast standards that are incompatible with the Japanese system. This, they hope, will give European manufacturers a chance to play technological catch-up. High definition could then be introduced in stages by the Europeans themselves.

Thirty-two European broadcasters, universities, and manufacturers hastily formed themselves into the Eureka 95 project and began developing a complete set of high-definition technologies, covering everything from studio and transmission equipment to television sets. Thomson, S.A., of France coordinated the team working on technical standards for TV production; Robert Bosch GmbH of West Germany focused on studio equipment; Thorn/EMI of Britain, on TV receivers.

The Europeans, meanwhile, also began courting the United States. West Germany's minister of posts and telecommunications, Christian Schwarz-Schilling, flew to Washington and proposed a formal alliance, arguing that "we should not permit Japan to get supremacy in the next generation of standards."

By now the Japanese began to worry that the Europeans might steal a march on them, actually launching a counterattack on both the U.S. and Japanese domestic markets with their Euro-version of HDTV. To block this, Japanese manufacturers have lobbied strongly in the United States against the European system.

Given all this uncertainty, the Japanese are also quietly preparing to market different sets for different parts of the world, as a fallback in the event they cannot impose a single standard.

Economic paranoia is rampant in the United States as well, where the entire HDTV issue is bogged down in hairsplitting technical debate, political controversy, and commercial rivalry.

The three big U.S. broadcast networks want to slow down HDTV. They argue for a single U.S. standard that could carry current signals as well as the new HDTV pictures. By contrast, the U.S. cable industry and direct satellite broadcasters argue that this single standard would paralyze research into better cable and satellite transmission.

Congress, in the meantime, wants to make sure that when new sets start pouring into American homes, they will come from American plants. "Right now," says Congressman Edward J. Markey, "Japanese and European companies are far out in front . . . while our domestic consumer electronics industry is moribund."

Amid charges of "techno-nationalism," the TV tug-of-war will wax hotter for years to come. But even as the battle for the future of television heats up, a parallel struggle is under way to shape the future of the computer.

STRATEGIC STANDARDS

Today's blistering pace of innovation forces manufacturers to choose a strategy: either invent and impose a standard on your industry, or piggyback on someone else's standard—or be driven into a commercial Siberia in which your products have limited uses and markets.

IBM has been the dominant force in the computer industry since its inception. It was IBM's blue-suited and buttoned-down salespeople who first put mainframes into government offices and corporations. And for nearly two decades IBM faced only weak and disorganized competition.

Much of IBM's monumental success could be traced to its early ability to set—and enforce—a standard for what goes on inside computers.

At first it was the hardware that counted most. But gradually it became clear that software is the most important element in any computer system. So-called "applications programs" were sets of instructions to the machine to perform tasks like accounting or word-processing, printing, displaying graphics, and communicating. But every computer has built into it a kind of meta-program called an "operating system," which determines what other kinds of programs it can or cannot run.

The key to dominating the computer industry lies in software—

without which the machines are inert and useless. But the key to dominating software is the operating system. And the ultimate lever of control—the key to dominating operating systems—lies in the standards to which they, in turn, are held. It was IBM's control of these that made it the superpower of the computing world.

Despite IBM's efforts, however, other operating systems have sprung up over the years, from Ada, which is promoted by the U.S. Department of Defense, to Unix, originally offered by AT&T, plus many variations of these. When Apple Computer started the microcomputer revolution in the mid-seventies, it specifically opted to create non-IBM-compatible machines, choosing a different operating system.

Today an all-out battle is being fought internationally between IBM and its chief competitors to set the operating systems standard for the future. The struggle is highly technical, with experts arguing with other experts. But the implications reach far beyond the computer industry itself, and governments see it as directly related to their economic development plans for tomorrow.

Because IBM still dominates the field, and because its operating systems constrain users and competitors alike, a London-based organization called X/Open has been set up to create a standard for the operating systems of mini-computers, workstations, and PCs—the newer fields in which IBM is most vulnerable. Originally set up by AT&T, Digital Equipment, and the German Siemens, it now includes Fujitsu as well, all demanding a new standard that is "open," rather than a barrier to non-IBM equipment.

Since then the pressure on IBM has become so strong, it has been compelled to join the group and to pledge, cross its heart, that it will in the future commit itself to "open" policies.

Even before this setback had fully sunk in, IBM faced another challenge, this time pitting it directly against Ma Bell, the American Telephone & Telegraph Company. As long ago as the 1960s, AT&T software engineers had developed an operating system called Unix for their own use. It had certain characteristics that made it attractive to universities and to some of the smaller computer makers. Not yet in the computer business itself, AT&T let them use Unix for pennies. They, in turn, produced their own customized variations of Unix. Since then Unix has become increasingly popular, with Sun Microsystems selling Unix-based machines to the fast-growing workstation market.

In a shrewd strategic stroke, AT&T promptly bought into Sun

and formed an alliance with Xerox, Unisys, Motorola, and other companies to create a single Unix standard under AT&T's leadership.

Backed by AT&T and these allies, Unix's growing popularity presented a direct threat to the dominance of IBM and other computer manufacturers with proprietary operating systems. Thus IBM, the new convert to operating-system glasnost, or openness, counterattacked.

Faced with the danger that a unified version of Unix would be available on AT&T machines before anyone else's, IBM now formed its own alliance to fight back. Called the Open Software Foundation, this group now includes DEC, Groupe Bull from France, Siemens and Nixdorf from West Germany, and many others. It is working to formulate its own alternate standard for Unix.

Charges and countercharges blare from full-page ads in *The Wall Street Journal* or the *Financial Times* as the battle over computer operating-system standards heats up. Once more the fate of giant corporations and whole industries hinges on a war over standards.

THE MAIN BOUT

One of the most important things computers do today is talk to one another. In fact, computers and communication are so closely fused today as to be inseparable.

This means that computer companies must defend not only their operating systems, but also their access to, or control of, telecommunications networks. If operating systems control what goes on *inside* computers, telecommunications standards control what goes on *between* computers. (The distinction, in reality, is not so neat, but good enough for our purposes here.) And here again we find companies and countries locked in a bitter struggle over the main systems that process our information.

Because more data, information, and knowledge now flow across national boundaries, the info-war over telecommunications is, if anything, even more politically fraught than the war over operating systems.

General Motors, for example, in trying to tie together its

global production, has devised its own standard to allow its machines to communicate with one another even though they come from different makers. It calls this standard MAP (for Manufacturing Automation Protocol) and has tried to promote its worldwide adoption by other manufacturers and its own suppliers.

To block GM, the European Community has talked thirteen giant manufacturing companies, including BMW, Olivetti, British Aerospace, and Nixdorf, into supporting a counter-standard called CNMA. If European machines are going to talk to one another, the EC seems to be saying, it will not be on terms defined by General Motors—or the United States.

This toe-to-toe over electronic communication in the factories of the planet, however, is only part of the even larger battle for control of the world's extra-intelligent networks.

As Japanese firms began to connect up electronically with plants and offices around the world a host of companies rushed to sell them the necessary computers and telecommunications links. This is a field in which U.S. technology still outstrips that of Japan; and IBM, once again, was a major player. But the Japanese Ministry of Posts and Telecommunications announced that any networks linking Japan with the outside world would have to conform to a technical standard set by an obscure United Nations consultative committee on telecom policy. This ruling would have kept IBM in Japan from using equipment and systems designed to its own proprietary standard. The result was a massive lobbying effort in Washington and Tokyo, negotiations between the two governments, and ultimately, a back-off by Japan.

When each country's telephone system was controlled by a single company or ministry, national standards were set and international standards were then decided by the International Telecommunications Union.

Life was simple—until computers wanted to talk to one another.

By the 1980s, as new technologies avalanched into the market, businesses and individuals alike were using machines built by different manufacturers, using different operating systems, running programs written by different software houses, and trying to send messages around the world through a patchwork of cables, microwaves, and satellites belonging to different countries.

The result today is the much-bewailed electronic Tower of Babel, and it explains why desperate cries for "connectivity" and "interoperability" echo around the business world. And here yet again the main struggle has shaped up as IBM versus The World.

IBM has long promoted a standard called System Network Architecture. The problem with SNA is that while it allows (some, not all) IBM machines to talk to other IBM machines, it is decidedly deaf to a great many non-IBM computers.

As *The Wall Street Journal* once put it: "Hooking any non-SNA computers into those networks is a programmer's nightmare. Rivals wanting to sell their computers to IBM's legion of customers must mimic SNA in their own machines." This indirect control of access to information may have been tolerable when most computers *were* IBMs, but not today. Hence the cry has gone up for computer democracy.

COMPUTER DEMOCRACY

No longer ready to accept IBM's dominance, competitors have searched for a weapon with which to strike down Goliath. And they found one.

That mighty slingshot is a counter-standard called OSI (Open System Interconnection), which is intended to permit all kinds of computers to talk freely to one another. Heavily promoted by the European computer makers, OSI has forced IBM to retreat from its restrictive policies.

The conflict heated up when a dozen European computer manufacturers, appalled by IBM domination, reached agreement in 1983 that they would jointly undertake the incredibly complex work needed to design the specifications for an open system. Sensing the implications, European governments leaped to support them.

On the other side, Uncle Sam, watching this gang-up of forces against IBM, cried foul. Charging the Europeans with discrimination in their decisions, Donald Abelson of the Office of U.S. Trade Representative, stated that "Americans suspect . . . that we are the subject of a conspiracy."

Since then the anti-IBM campaign has expanded. Support for it has come from Esprit, the Common Market's program for the support of science and technology. At the end of 1986 the Council of Ministers of the European Community ruled that a subset of OSI options would be the standard for computer sales to governments in the community.

IBM responded to this attack with an offering confusingly called System Applications Architecture, or SAA, which included a version of SNA, and by offering customers a choice of either SNA or OSI products.

Then faced with this formidable opposition, IBM once more followed the principle "If you can't lick 'em, join 'em." Joining these various groupings, IBM pledged on scout's honor that it will henceforth support the open standard. It was, as in the case of operating systems, a last-minute religious conversion called into question by IBM's critics and competitors.

Like General Motors and many other giants of the industrial age, IBM expanded to fill every available inch of its ecological niche, adapted itself all too comfortably to it, and now finds itself in an increasingly hostile, fast-changing environment in which sheer size, once an advantage, is now often a handicap. To some it appears that the battle over telecommunications standards is the beginning of the post-IBM era.

On the surface, IBM's main rivals, American and foreign, have won. It might also appear that Europe has won. The war, however, is not yet over. The battle over standards is never won.

THE PARADOX OF NORMS

There is a hidden paradox in these power struggles. As business produces more diversified products, there is, in addition to a mounting pressure for more standards,. a countereffort to make products more and more versatile by accommodating multiple standards. (This is why some portable TV sets provide a button that allows the user to switch back and forth among the European PAL and SECAM standards and the American NTSC standard.)

Another technique used to make products more versatile is to break them down into smaller and more numerous modular components. This reduces the importance of the external standard. But at the same time, it increases the number of "micro-standards" embedded *inside* the product and needed to make the components work together.

However, no sooner is one standard established—OSI, for example—than new technologies drive it into obsolescence or irrelevancy. And as soon as we have arrived at standards for networks, or for software, the battleground shifts to a still higher and more complex plane. Thus, where two or more standards compete, new equipment appears that permits a user to convert from one system to another. But the appearance of adaptors gives rise to a need for standards for adaptors. Today, therefore, we are even seeing attempts to create what might be termed "standards for standards"—a group called the Information Technology Requirements Council was established not long ago for precisely this purpose in the field of communications.

The fight to control standards, in other words, shifts from higher to lower levels and back up again. But it does not go away. For the battle is part of the larger, continuing war for the control, routing, and regulation of information. It is a key front in the struggle for power based on knowledge, and it is raging not just in the technical thickets of television, computers, and communication, but in the nearest *bierstube* and, indeed, in the kitchen itself.

THE BEER AND SAUSAGE MINUET

Standards have long been set by industries or governments to assure the safety or quality of products and, more recently, to safeguard the environment. But they are also designed by protectionist governments to keep competitive foreign products out or to advance an industrial policy. West Germany, for instance, conveniently enough for local industry, effectively barred foreign beer on grounds that it was "impure."

And what good is beer without sausage? So Italian canned luncheon meats were also excluded, as were many other imported foods that happened to contain an additive widely used to improve the consistency of the jelly in canned ham and beef.

It took a minuet of negotiations and ultimately the threat of legal action by the European Community to make the Germans back down. By now it should come as no surprise that GATT, the General Agreement on Tariffs and Trade, has devised yet another standard—this one intended to reduce the use of standards for unfair trade purposes.

But even beyond their competitive purpose and their use as

weapons in today's blistering trade wars, there is another, deeper reason why *la guerre de normes* is heating up.

A provocative article by the French writer Philippe Messine has suggested that fights over standards must multiply, because in advanced economies the ratio of systemic products to stand-alone products rises, putting standards "at the center of great industrial battles."

This important insight is underlined by the fact that computer-based manufacture leads to a tremendous increase in the variety of products, which means that systems must link more products into wholes or gestalts, and that, in turn, explains why demands for standards *must* skyrocket.

It also helps us understand Messine's remark that the new systemic products increasingly include "an important non-material component, gray matter." For the manufacture of many goods in small runs aimed at segments or niches of the market increases the amount of information needed to coordinate the economy, making the entire cycle of production and distribution more knowledge-dependent.

Then, too, as science and technology advance, technical standards themselves reflect our deeper knowledge. The tests and technologies employed to measure standards become more precise; tolerances, narrower. More information and ever-deeper knowledge are embedded in the standards.

Finally, as competitive innovations drive more new products into the marketplace, filling (and simultaneously creating) new consumer needs, the push for the definition of standards itself propels research forward.

Thus, on every front—scientific, political, economic, and technological—the battle over standards can be expected to intensify as the new system for wealth creation replaces the fast-fading smokestack world of the past.

Victors in the widening wars over standards will wield immense, high-quality power in the fast-arriving world of tomorrow.

13

THE EXECUTIVE THOUGHT
POLICE

Tom Varnum is forty-eight years old and still married to his first wife. He works nearly sixty hours a week, in return for which he receives $162,000 a year. He also has some stock options and extra life insurance, but travels tourist or business class when he flies. He's been with his company for more than ten years and in his present job for nearly five. Just below the top rank in his firm, he dreams of someday becoming a Chief Executive Officer, but knows his chances are remote. In the meantime, he wants parity with his company's Chief Financial Officer.

The problem is that Tom is a specialist and his superiors think he doesn't know enough about general management. So he feels trapped in his specialty, and he reads enviously about colleagues who have left the profession behind and broken into the mainstream of corporate management at the highest levels—people like Art Ryan, who is now vice-chairman of Chase Manhattan Bank, or Ed Schefer, a vice-president and group manager at General Foods USA, or Josephine Johnson, executive vice-president at Equicor, a joint venture of Equitable Life and Hospital Corporation of America.

Tom is sharp, bright, clean-cut, and articulate, but he tends to lapse into a jaw-breaking jargon that leaves co-workers and superiors suitably puzzled and instantly brands him a "techie."

While Ryan, Schefer, and Johnson are real people who began as computer specialists and "migrated" outward from Information Systems, or "IS," and upward into senior management, Tom is a fictional composite whose traits, according to a recent survey, match those of an increasingly restive and assertive group of executives known as "chief information officers." In the United States today more than two hundred big corporations use the title "Chief Information Officer" or some close approximation of it. Not many years ago there was no such thing. Nomenclature varies, but in many firms the CIO title is a notch or two up from such related designations as "Manager of Data Processing," "Vice-President of Information Systems," or "Director, Management Information Systems."

CIOs are the men—only a few, so far, are women—who are responsible for spending the huge budgets corporations now allocate for computers, data processing, and information services. Because of this they find themselves at the hot center of the info-wars.

LEVELS OF COMBAT

Eavesdrop on a group of CIOs at a conference, and chances are that before long you will hear their standard complaints: That they are misunderstood by top management. Bosses view them as budget-busting cost centers, whereas they believe that effective high-tech Information Systems can actually cut costs and bring in a profit. Bosses are too uninformed—*ignorant* is the *mot juste*—about computers and communications to make intelligent judgments. And they aren't patient enough to learn. In fact, only one CIO in thirteen actually gets to report directly to his president or chief executive officer.

But while CIOs may grumble, they are far from powerless. As the super-symbolic economy expands, business expenditures for knowledge-processing soar. Only a fraction of these are for computers and related information systems. But that fraction represents enormous amounts of money.

By 1988 sales of the world's top one hundred information technology firms, according to *Datamation* magazine, topped the $243 billion mark. A conservative projection shows this rising to $500 billion within a decade. Anyone who helps direct these purchases and allocate these funds is hardly bereft of clout. What CIOs scarcely mention, however, is that they also allocate information—the source of power for others and, not incidentally, for themselves.

As soon as a company budgets mega-dollars for information technology, struggles break out as different factions try to bite a chunk off the budget. But in addition to traditional turf and money conflicts, CIOs also find themselves smack in the middle of fights over information itself. Who gets what kinds of information? Who has access to the main data bases? Who can *add* to that data base? What assumptions are built into the accounting? Which department or division "owns" what data? And even more important, who dictates the assumptions or models built into the software? The conflicts over such questions, while seemingly technical, clearly affect the money, status, and power of individuals and businesses.

Moreover, these conflicts escalate. As the CIO and his staff redirect flows of information, they shake existing power relations. To use the expensive new computers and networks effectively, most companies are compelled to reorganize. Major restructurings are thus set in motion—and these trigger repercussive power struggles throughout the firm.

Before long, smart management, prodded by the CIO, discovers that new information technology isn't just a way to cut paperwork or speed service. It can sometimes be used strategically to capture new markets, create new products, and enter entirely new fields. We've already seen Citibank selling software to travel agents in the United States, or Seino Transport in Japan peddling software to truckers. Such forays into new businesses begin to change the shape and mission of the organization. This, however, triggers even more dangerous power struggles in the executive suite.

To complicate matters, as computers and communications fuse and networks proliferate, a new power group begins to poke its head under the managerial tent: the telecommunications managers and their staff, who often jockey with the IS people for resources and control. Should communications be subordinate to Information Systems or independent?

Chief information officers thus find themselves at the vortex of many disputes, some of which lead to, or become part of, revolutions at the highest level.

THE TWO-PARTY CAMPAIGN

This is what happened several years ago inside Merrill Lynch, the best known American securities firm and one with a staggering budget for information services.

In 1976, Merrill Lynch's total revenues, after ninety-one years of doing business, reached the magic billion-dollar mark. Ten years later, information and information technology had become so important that DuWayne Peterson, Merrill's head of Systems Operations and Telecommunications, by himself presided over an annual budget of $800 million—and that was only part of the total spent on information services and systems.

Merrill Lynch was basically divided into two parts. Its Capital Markets people created "products"—specialized funds, underwritings, stock and bond offerings—a dizzying profusion of investment vehicles. They also disbursed the capital raised by the firm. Its Retail people, by contrast—some 11,000 securities brokers in 500 branches—sold the products to investors.

These two sides of the house were almost like two different political parties or tribes. Each had its own culture, leaders, and specialized needs. Each placed different demands on Merrill's information systems.

In the words of Gerald Ely, a Merrill vice-president: "On the Capital Markets side, it's all real-time. . . . It all happens now, the profit and loss, the inventories, the prices . . . everything has to be there, real time. . . . I thought it was bad on the Retail side. When I got to the Capital Markets side I walked into a whole different world . . . different people . . . with different attitudes. The data center runs differently, obviously. The programmers and the people who manage them are different. The talents they need, the knowledge of the business, the understanding of the products, the integration of product and technology—I've never seen it quite as intense."

Not surprisingly, there was a fundamental tension between the two sides of the house, and they wanted quite different things from the huge budget for information services and technology. Capital Markets was constantly demanding instantaneous, highly analyzed and sophisticated data, while Retail needed more transactional data, but less refined and complex information.

A similar tension is found in many of the other big financial firms. Thus, those mostly concerned with assembling and providing capital—the Salomon Brothers, First Bostons, Morgan Stanleys, and Goldman, Sachses—invest more heavily in information and communications systems, as a rule, than those firms, like Merrill, Shearson, or Hutton, that are still primarily oriented toward retail securities.

At Merrill the collision between the two sides of the house ended with a political battle royal and the departure of the CEO, a man regarded as sympathetic to the Capital Markets people and their informational needs.

While the budget for information systems was not the critical factor in the Merrill case, it is likely to become more and more central to corporate politics as computers and communication begin to change strategies and missions at the very highest levels.

STRATEGIC RETREAT

An exact illustration of this was provided by Bank of America when it decided on a strategic expansion of its trust business.

In 1982, BofA had assets of $122 billion, employed 82,000 people in more than 1,200 branches and offices from Sacramento to Singapore. Its trust department alone managed $38 billion in funds for some 800 large institutional investors and pension funds. Among its trust customers were the Walt Disney Company, AT&T, Kaiser Aluminum, and other industrial heavyweights. But the bank had fallen behind technologically. At that point it decided to expand its beachhead in the trust business, in competition with Bankers Trust, State Street of Boston, and the other East Coast financial giants.

BofA's head of trust operations, Clyde R. Claus, realized he would need a state-of-the-art computer system. The old system, though recently given a botched $6 million face-lift, would be hopelessly inadequate.

The day of the proverbial "widows and orphans," who went to the bank's trust department, timidly asked the bank to invest their funds, and were satisfied with terse semiannual or annual reports— that day was long past. Trust customers now were far more sophisticated. Some had huge accounts. They wanted detailed information broken down every which way. The big ones had their own powerful computers, telecommunications nets, and sophisticated financial analysis software, and they demanded complex up-to-the-instant data.

So Claus and BofA's information systems group hired consultants and contractors to build the most advanced information system in the trust field. Some 3.5 million lines of programming code were written; and 13,000 hours of training were devoted to preparing employees to use the new information system.

Despite this crash effort, the new system lagged behind its deadlines. Endless bugs plagued the project. Worse yet, the existing system was falling further and further behind, too. Customers were muttering. The pressures rose.

In 1986 the trust department's in-house newsletter, *Turtle Talk*, received an anonymous letter warning Claus not to implement the new system. It was, the letter writer claimed, not ready. If Claus thought so, it was because someone had "pulled the wool" over his eyes.

But Claus couldn't wait. Customers were already three months behind on their statements. Things had got so bad that BofA officials were paying out huge sums to customers on the "honor" system, because they couldn't locate the records needed to verify the amounts. Crisis followed crisis. Battle followed battle. Upheavals in the bank's top management, sudden changes in policy, layoffs, staff relocations, all took a disastrous toll on the trust division. By 1988, having poured an estimated $80 million down the sump, the entire project collapsed. Bank of America backed ignominiously out of the trust business.

The rout was complete.

Heads rolled down the carpeted corridors in the months that followed. Out went Claus. Out went several senior VPs. (Out, too, went 320 of the 400 employees of the main software and system design contractor.)

Out went customers—taking with them about $4 billion worth of assets. Out went parts of the trust operation, one piece having previously been sold off to Wells Fargo, another turned over to State Street of Boston, one of the industry leaders that BofA had intended to challenge.

It was Napoleon's retreat from Moscow all over again.

Systems experts, whether called CIOs or directors of systems engineering or managers of management information systems, are point men in the info-wars, vulnerable to bullets from any direction. A brief look at their rise, fall, and resurrection provides a keen insight into how power shifts as the control of information changes hands.

THE GIANT BRAIN ERA

When computers first arrived in corporate offices about three decades ago, the press was filled with speculation about the coming of the "giant brain." This electronic mega-brain would contain all the information needed to manage a firm.

(This first-phase fantasy of a total, all-inclusive data bank and decision system led, in the Soviet Union, to an even more extended version. There, it was thought, a few giant electronic brains controlled by Gosplan, the state planning agency, would direct not a single enterprise but the entire national economy.)

Order would once and for all replace informational disorder or chaos. No more sloppiness. No more bursting file cases. No more lost memos. No more uncertainty.

Such megalomaniac fantasies vastly underestimated the increased diversity and complexity in a super-symbolic economy. They arrogantly underrated the role of chance, intuition, and creativity in business. Most important, they also assumed that the people on top of a business knew enough to specify what information was, or was not, needed by the people working below them in the hierarchy.

The title of Chief Information Officer did not yet exist in American firms, but there was a small "Data Priesthood"—the data-processing professionals. Because no one else could make the "giant brain" do anything, these few professionals essentially "owned" the firm's mainframes, and anyone who wanted information processed had to come to them. The priests enjoyed the blessings of an info-monopoly.

Then came the micros.

Desktop computers arrived with the force of a whirlwind in the late 1970s. Immediately sensing that these cheap new machines would erode their power, many data professionals threw everything they had into a campaign to keep them out of their companies. The DP priests sneered at the microcomputers' limited capacity and small size. They fought against budgeting funds for them.

But just as an entrenched monopoly, Western Union, could not keep telephones out of the hands of Americans in the 19th century, the business community's voracious hunger for information swept aside all opposition from the data professionals. Soon thousands of executives were end-running the data priests, buying their own machines and programs, beginning to network with one another.

It became clear that companies would need dispersed computer power, not just a few centrally controlled mainframes. The "giant brain" fantasy was dead, and with it the concentrated power of the DP staff. Today, in many big firms more than half of all computer processing power is outside the Information Systems department, and, as a senior manager of Deloitte & Touche puts it, the computer professionals still have "worlds more to lose."

Executives no longer came, tugging their forelocks and shuffling their feet, to beg for a few minutes of computer time. Many, no longer under the control of the DP priesthood, had their own sizable departmental budgets for computers.

The priests now faced a situation not unlike that of the medical doctors, who lost their godlike status as more and more medical knowledge seeped into the lay press and the media. Instead of dealing with computer illiterates, the DP professionals now confronted a large number of "end-users" who knew some of the basics of simple computing, read computer magazines, bought machines for their kids at home, and were no longer awestruck by anyone who rattled on about RAM and ROM.

The "micro revolution" demonopolized computer information and shifted power out of the hands of the priesthood.

The micro revolution, however, was soon followed by the connectivity revolution—and power shifted once again.

Like most revolutions, the micro revolution was a messy affair. With individuals and their departments rushing out to buy whatever kind of machines, software, and services they wanted, the result was an electronic Tower of Babel. So long as these were mainly stand-alone systems, it didn't matter much. But once it became necessary for these machines to talk to the mainframes or to one another and the outside world, the drawbacks of unrestrained liberty became starkly apparent.

Computer professionals carried a grave warning to their bosses. Computer democracy could end by shrinking the power of top management itself. How could anyone responsibly run a company when its entire computerized information system was out of control? Different machines, different programs, different data bases, everyone "doing his own thing" raised the specter of anarchy in the office. It was time to clamp down.

In every revolution there is a period of upheaval and extremism, followed by a period of consolidation. Thus the DP staff, backed by senior management, now set about institutionalizing the revolution and, in the process, recouping some of the priesthood's erstwhile influence.

To impose order on computers and communications, the new CIOs were handed far greater resources and responsibilities than ever before. They were told to integrate systems, connect them up, and formulate what might be called "rules of the electronic road." Having originally been hoarders of centralized information, and later having lost control of the system for a time, the new information systems people and the CIOs who lead them have now re-emerged as data police, enforcing new rules that, together, define the firm's information system.

These rules, which cover technical standards and types of equipment, also usually govern access to central data banks, priorities, and many other matters. Ironically, the latest surprising twist of the screw finds many CIOs singing the virtues of the very microcomputers they once despised.

The reasons are clear. Micros are no longer the 98-pound weaklings they once were. Together with minis and workstations, they are now so powerful they can actually take over many of the old functions of the mainframe. Hence, many CIOs are calling for "downsizing" and further decentralization.

"Downsizing is a phenomenal trend," reports Theodore Klein of the Boston Systems Group, Inc. "I was recently at a conference of sixty MIS directors and just about every one was doing this in some form." In the words of *CIO* magazine, the journal of the CIOs, "Downsizing puts control in the hands of business-unit managers." But that control is now firmly governed by rules set by computer professionals. Many CIOs, in fact, with support from above, are attempting to recentralize control under the flag of "network management."

Says Bill Gassman, a marketing specialist for DEC: "Network management is more than a technical issue; it's political." His view is shared by others who believe, in the words of *Datamation* magazine, that "the argument for centralized network management . . . frequently masks a desire by some within MIS organizations to regain personal operational control lost during the past few years."

In short, while info-wars rage in the corporation's external environment—pitting, as we saw, retailers versus manufacturers, or industries and even nations against one another—info-wars on a smaller scale are raging internally as well.

CIOs and their staffs become, whether they mean to or not, info-warriors. For though they may not conceive of their function in these terms, their largely unrecognized task is to redistribute power (while trying, not surprisingly, to expand their own).

Functioning as both highway engineers and state troopers on our fast-growing electronic highways—they build as well as attempt to manage the systems—they are put in the distasteful position of being, in a sense, the corporation's "executive thought police."

THE ETHICS OF INFORMATION

As such, they earn their paychecks. Their jobs are filled with stress and difficulty. Indeed, it is hard to exaggerate the staggering complexity of the rules needed in engineering and integrating a large-scale corporate information system that delivers information to those who need it . . . that prevents fraud, sabotage, or invasion of personal privacy . . . that regulates access to various networks and data banks by employees, customers, and suppliers . . . that sets priorities among them . . . that produces numberless specialized reports . . . that allows users to customize their software . . . that meets dozens of other requirements, does it all within budgetary constraints—and then does it over and again as new technologies, competitors, and products appear.

Devising rules to guide such a system requires such high-level technical expertise that CIOs and their staffs often lose sight of the human implications of their decisions. Who gets access is, in fact, a political issue. Privacy is a political issue. Designing a system so that it serves one department better than another is a political act. Even timing is political, if one unit gets a lower communications priority than another, so that it must wait for service. The allocation of cost is always a power issue.

Thus, as soon as we begin to speak of policing information, all sorts of disquieting "para-political" questions pop up.

Two employees are caught up in a bitter personal feud. One of them learns the appropriate computer passwords, enters the personnel files, and puts damaging material into an adversary's records. None of this comes to light until the victim has already left and gone to work for another firm, where discovery of the damaging information leads to dismissal. What happens? Who is responsible? The first company?

Are a worker's chances for promotion unfairly reduced if he or she lacks or loses access to an important data base?

With only a trace of imagination, it is possible to multiply scores of such questions. In the absence of comprehensive public policies, it is left to private firms to think through the personal and political implications of all the rules governing their information systems. But should such questions, with their human rights implications, be left entirely to private companies? And if so, who in any particular firm should write the rules? The chief information officer?

We are, here, on thin and alien ice. Few have much experience with the ethical, legal, and ultimately political questions arising from the need to impose constraints on the flow of business information. Top management, as a rule, delegates the task. But to whom?

Should the rule-writing power be shared? And with whom? Should companies establish internal "information councils" or even "legislatures," to write the laws governing information rights, responsibilities, and access? Should unions share in this decision-making? Do we need "corporate courts" to settle disputes over security and access? Do we need "information ethicists" to define a new informational morality?

Will the rules regulating information in industry condition public attitudes toward freedom of information in the larger society? Might they accustom us to censorship and secrecy? Will we eventually need an explicit Bill of Electronic Information Rights?

Every one of these is a power issue, and the decisions about them will shift power within the firm and, ultimately, in society at large.

THE PARADOX BOMB

The more turbulent, unstable, and non-equilibrial tomorrow's business environment becomes, the more unpredictable the needs of users.

Rapid change means chance. It means uncertainty. It means competition from the least-expected quarter. It means big projects that collapse and small ones that stun one with their success. It means new technologies, new kinds of skills and workers, and wholly unprecedented economic conditions.

All this is amplified when the competition is blistering hot and comes, very often, from countries or cultures that are drastically different from the one the business was designed to serve.

How, in this kind of world, can even the cleverest CIO accurately pre-specify what information will be needed by whom? Or for how long?

In today's high-turbulence environment, business survival requires a stream of innovative products or services. Creativity requires a kind of corporate glasnost—an openness to imagination, a tolerance for deviance, for individuality, and the serendipity that has historically accounted for many creative discoveries, from nylon and latex paint to products like the NutraSweet fat substitute.

There is, therefore, a profound contradiction between the need for careful channeling and close control of information, on the one hand, and the need for innovation on the other.

The safer and surer a business information system, and the better it is protected, pre-defined, pre-structured, and policed, the more it will constrain creativity and constipate the organization.

What we learn, therefore, is that the information wars now raging in the outside world—over everything from supermarket scanners and standards to television sets and technonationalism—are mirrored inside the corporation as well.

Power, in the business of tomorrow, will flow to those who have the best information about the limits of information. But before it does, the info-wars now intensifying will alter the very shape of business. To know how, we need to take a closer look at this crucial resource—knowledge—whose pursuit will shake the powers-that-be from New York to Tokyo, from Moscow to Montevideo.

14

TOTAL INFORMATION WAR

Anew concept of business is taking shape in response to the info-wars now raging across the world economy. As knowledge becomes more central to the creation of wealth, we begin to think of the corporation as an enhancer of knowledge.

We speak of adding value by upgrading information. We talk about improving the firm's human resources. And we begin poking our noses into information that doesn't belong to us. All, it would seem, is fair in love and info-war.

On April 25, 1985, the telephone rang at the offices of Texas Instruments in Dallas, Texas. A voice with a foreign accent asked for a meeting with a company security executive. A Syrian electrical engineer who sought political asylum in the United States, Sam Kuzbary had once worked at TI before being fired as a security risk. Rumor had it that the CIA had helped him get out of Syria, where he had once worked for the Syrian military. Kuzbary carried a gun in his car. Now, he said, he wanted to ingratiate himself with TI and get his job back. He had information, he said, about important secrets that had been stolen from TI.

That call led to an early morning raid by Dallas police on the offices of a small high-tech firm called Voice Control Systems, Inc., founded originally by a real estate developer who wound up in jail for drug smuggling. Now owned by a different investment group and headed by a former president of U.S. Telephone, VCS, it turned out, employed numerous former TI researchers, including Kuzbary.

What the police found were 7,985 files copied from the computers at TI's advanced research project on speech recognition. A scorching race was (and still is) under way among major computer firms, including IBM and Texas Instruments, to find a way for computers to understand human speech. (They can already, but only in limited and costly ways.) Everyone knows that whoever wins this race will have the potential for fabulous profits. In fact, at the time, Michael Dertouzos, head of computer science at the Massachussetts Institute of Technology, considered that "whoever breaks the logjam to make machines understand spoken words will gain control over the information revolution."

Were the engineers who jumped ship at TI and joined VCS really guilty of stealing research worth $20 million, as TI charged?

In the trial that followed, Dallas prosecutors Ted Steinke and Jane Jackson insisted a crime had been committed. Lawyers for defendants Tom Schalk and Gary Leonard, however, pointed out that none of the material taken was marked with the words TI— STRICTLY PRIVATE which were supposed to be on all secret material. What's more, the lab in which the work was done was headed by Dr. George Doddington, a brilliant maverick who often described his lab as "free and open" and argued that major breakthroughs would come only if researchers from different companies and universities shared their knowledge. Even more to the point, VCS didn't seem to be using any of the TI material.

Schalk insisted to the jury that at no time during his work at TI had he regarded any of this material as secret. Leonard said he merely wanted to keep a historical record of research he had done, and that he had copied a TI computer directory because it contained a list of the people in his Sunday-school class.

To all of which Steinke, the prosecutor, replied: "One thing they can't change. They snuck these programs out without telling anyone."

The Dallas jury, some of its members crying as the verdict was read, found the men guilty. They were sentenced and fined, then placed on probation. Both appealed the ruling and immediately went back to work, trying to make computers understand speech.

RUSTY TRACKS AND HOTEL LOVE-SOUNDS

It is hard to know if industrial espionage is actually on the rise, because, in the words of Brian Hollstein of the American Society for Industrial Security's committee on the protection of information, "Being a victim of industrial espionage is a lot like getting venereal disease. Many may have it, but nobody wants to talk about it." On the other hand, more lawsuits are being filed against information thieves and pirates.

Hollstein has thought about the value of information more than most. "Many corporations," he said a few years ago, "really don't understand. . . . They still think in terms mainly of moving around men and materials," as though still locked into the smoke-stack economy. "What it amounts to," he has said, "is a failure to recognize that information has value."

That attitude is changing swiftly. As wars for the control of information heat up, many companies have decided they need more information about the plans, products, and profits of their adversaries. Thus the dramatic rise of what is known as "competitive intelligence."

Smart companies, of course, have always kept an eye cocked at their competitors, but today adversarial knowledge is prime ammunition in the info-wars.

Several factors account for the changed attitude. The speed with which any market can now be invaded from outside, the long lead times needed for research (in contrast with shorter product life-cycles), and stiffer competition all have contributed to the much-publicized systematization and professionalization of business spying.

The pressure for continual innovation means more resources are flowing into new products, some requiring extremely heavy research expense. "Designing a chip can take hundreds of labor-years and millions of dollars. Simply copying the competition is both faster and cheaper," writes John D. Halamka in *Espionage in Silicon Valley*, explaining why companies now engage in reverse engineering—taking apart a rival product to learn its secrets. Xerox reverse-engineers competitive copiers. Companies reverse-engineer services to find out what makes them profitable.

Yet another factor promoting the rise of competitive intelligence has been the widespread reorganization of strategic planning. Once a highly centralized activity carried out by staff personnel reporting to top management, planning has been pushed down into the operating units, where it is often carried out by practical line managers geared to rough-and-tumble competition. Knowing what competitors are up to has immediate tactical advantage as well as possible strategic use.

All this helps explain why 80 percent of the thousand largest

U.S. firms now have their own full-time sleuths and why the Society of Competitor Intelligence Professionals alone claims members from at least three hundred companies in six nations. Their companies keep them busy.

Before the Marriott Corporation committed itself to launching the Fairfield Inn chain of low-cost hotels, reports *Fortune*, it sent a team of snoops into nearly four hundred rival hotels to check on what soaps and towels they supplied, how good the front desk was in dealing with special problems, and whether the sounds of love-making could be heard in adjoining rooms. (The sounds were simulated by one of Marriott's CI agents while another in the next room listened for them.)

Marriott also hired executive headhunters to interview (and pump) the regional managers of rival chains, to find out how much its competitors were paying, what training they offered, and whether their managers were happy.

When the Sheller-Globe Corporation, maker of heavy truck cabs, wanted to design a new cab, it systematically called on potential customers, asking them to rank the opposition on seven scales covering gasoline mileage, comfort, windshield visibility, ease of steering, seating, accessibility of controls, and durability. The information set targets for the Sheller-Globe design team to beat.

Like real spies, business intelligence agents begin their hunt with a careful scan of "open" sources. They pore over trade journals, newsletters, and the general press for clues to a competing firm's plans. They read speeches, study recruiting ads, attend meetings and seminars. They interview former employees, many of whom are eager to talk about their old companies.

But CI snoops—among them, paid outside consultants—have also been known to fly a helicopter over a plant for clues to a competitor's capacity, to scour trash baskets for discarded memos, and to employ more aggressive measures as well. A look at a rival's internal phone directory can help one construct a detailed map of its organization, from which it is possible to estimate its budget. One Japanese company sent experts to look at the rail tracks leaving the plant of an American competitor. The thickness of the rust layer—presumably indicating how often or how recently the tracks were used—was a clue to the factory's production.

On occasion, zealous practitioners bug hotel rooms or offices where rivals are negotiating a deal. Even less savory are the U.S. defense contractors who paid "consultants" to learn in advance how much their competitors were bidding on a Pentagon project, thus permitting them to underbid. In turn, some of the consultants reportedly bribed military personnel to get the facts.

Of course, competitive intelligence professionals define CI as the *legal* pursuit of information. But a recent Conference Board survey of senior managers suggests that 60 percent of them think anything goes when it comes to corporate spying.

The hotting-up of today's info-wars is part of a growing recognition that knowledge, while central to the new economy, violates all the rules that apply to other resources. It is, for example, inexhaustible. We know how to add value to ingots of steel or bolts of cloth. But how to add value to a good idea is much more problematic. We lack the new accounting and management theories needed to grapple with super-symbolic realities.

We do not yet know how to manage a resource that is salable, but much of which is supplied (often at no charge) by customers themselves. Or, for that matter, either willingly or unwittingly, by competitors. Nor have we yet come to understand how the corporation as a whole engages in knowledge enhancement.

INS AND OUTS

The info-wars cast the corporation—and the work that goes on in it—into a new light.

Forget, for a moment, all conventional job descriptions; forget ranks; forget departmental functions. Think of the firm, instead, as a beehive of knowledge processing.

In the day of the smokestack it was assumed that workers knew little of importance and that relevant information or intelligence could be gathered by top management or a tiny staff. The proportion of the work force engaged in knowledge processing was tiny.

Today, by contrast, we are finding that much of what happens inside a firm is aimed at replenishing its continually decaying knowledge inventory, generating new knowledge to add to it, and upgrading simple data into information and knowledge. To accomplish this, employees constantly "import," "export," and "transfer" data and information.

Some employees are essentially importers. These "OUT-IN" people gather information from outside the company and deliver it to their co-workers inside. Market researchers, for example, are OUT-INers. Studying consumer preferences in the external world, they add value by interpreting what they learn, and then deliver new, higher-order information to the firm.

Public relations people do the reverse. They market the firm to the world by collecting information internally and disseminating or exporting it to the outside world. They are IN-OUTers.

House accountants are basically IN-IN people, gathering most of their information from inside the firm and transferring it internally as well.

Good salespeople are two-way RELAYS. They disseminate information, but also collect it from outside and then report it back to the firm.

These functions relate to *flows* of data, information, or knowledge. Cutting across them is a set of functions that have to do with upgrading the *stock* of data, information, and knowledge that the firm and its people already possess.

Some mind-workers are creators, capable of finding new, surprising juxtapositions of ideas, or putting a fresh spin on an old idea; others "edit" new ideas by matching them against strategic requirements and practical considerations, then deleting those that are irrelevant.

In reality, we all do all these things at various times. But while different functions emphasize one or another, no conventional job descriptions or management texts deal with such distinctions—or their implications for power.

At almost every step in this knowledge processing, some people or organizations gain, and others lose, an edge. Thus, conflicts—tiny, sometimes highly personal info-wars—are fought over things like who will or will not be invited to a meeting, whose names appear on the routing slip, who reports information to a superior directly and who, by contrast, is asked to leave it with a secretary, and so forth. These organizational battles—"micro info-wars," so to speak—are hardly novel. They are a feature of all organizational life. They take on new significance, however, as the super-symbolic economy spreads.

Since the value added through smart knowledge-processing is critical in the new system of wealth creation, 21st-century accountants will find ways to assess the net economic value added by various informational activities. The performance ratings of individuals and units may well take into account their contribution to knowledge enhancement.

Today, a geologist who finds a huge oil strike is likely to be well rewarded by the company for adding to its reserves. Tomorrow, when knowledge resources are recognized as the most important of all, employee remuneration may well come to hinge, at least in part, on the success of each individual in adding value to the corporate knowledge reserve. In turn, we can expect even more sophisticated power struggles for the control of knowledge assets and the processes that generate them.

WHOLISTIC ESPIONAGE

We are already witnessing the beginnings of a change in management assumptions about the functions of the work force. Thus, all employees are increasingly expected to add not merely to the firm's knowledge assets in general, but to its competitive intelligence arsenal as well.

According to Mindy Kotler, president of Search Associates, a company that does CI work for both U.S. and Japanese firms, the Japanese take a far more wholistic view of intelligence than do the Americans. While Japanese executives regard information collection as a routine part of their job, she says, "If you ask a typical Harvard M.B.A., he says it's the company librarian's job."

That narrow assumption, however, is fading. At General Mills every employee is expected to engage in competitive intelligence gathering. Even janitors when buying supplies are supposed to ask vendors what competing firms are buying and what they are doing.

Telephone companies in the United States run seminars and distribute literature explaining the methods and benefits of CI to their executives. Bayer even rotates executives through its CI staff to teach them the importance of this kind of information collection. GE links CI directly into its strategic planning.

Pushed to extremes, such measures inch us toward the notion of the corporation as a total info-war fighting machine.

A 75-CENT ERROR

While the business press has paid superficial attention to the rise of business spying, little has been said about the relationship of CI to the spread of information systems and the rise of the chief information officer.

Yet the connection is not hard to find.

It is easy enough to picture the espionage branch of a business requesting cooperation from the chief information officer in gathering information about a competitor. The CIO is increasingly responsible not merely for information systems inside the firm, but for electronic links into the data bases of other companies. This means he controls systems that penetrate, at least to some limited degree, the electronic perimeter of suppliers, customers, or others, and information from or about a competitor may be no more than one electronic synapse away.

For more than a year three West German computer spies were able to access data relating to nuclear weapons and the strategic defense initiative (SDI) by breaking into 430 computers. They rifled at will through more than 30 of them linked in a network set up by the Pentagon's Defense Advanced Research Projects Agency. They were spotted only after Clifford Stoll, an ex-hippie computer system manager at the Lawrence Berkeley Laboratory, noticed a 75-cent discrepancy between two files.

Many business networks are still highly vulnerable to penetration by determined thieves or spies, including disgruntled current or former employees suborned by a competing firm. According to *Spectrum,* the journal of the Institute of Electrical and Electronics Engineers, "Members of most [local area networks] can add modems to their personal computers, creating new passageways in the system unbeknownst to system administrators."

With customers able to access a manufacturer's inventory records electronically, with suppliers made privy to their customers' design secrets, the possibilities for the diversion of information to a competitor are real, despite access limits and passwords.

This access, moreover, can be direct or through intermediaries—including intermediaries who are unaware of what they are doing. In CIA jargon, some informants are "witting" and others not. Business spies, too, can make use of third parties to gain access to information useful as ammunition in the info-wars.

If, say, two retailers like Wal-Mart and K Mart are both electronically plugged into the computers of the same supplier, how long will it be before an overzealous CI unit, or one of a growing horde of CI consultants, proposes breaking through the ID numbers and passwords on the manufacturer's mainframe, or tapping into the telecommunications lines and foraging through its data banks? If a U.S. government's defense research network could be compromised by Soviet intelligence, relying on a few spies armed with personal computers and working from their homes in West Germany, how secure are the commercial networks and corporate data bases on which our economy now depends?

The example is purely hypothetical, with no implication that either Wal-Mart or K Mart has actually done this or would even consider it. But there are now thousands of electronic data interchange systems, and new technologies open stunning opportunities for both licit and illicit data collection.

With only a little imagination, one can picture a competitive intelligence firm planting equipment across the street from a major store and tapping into the signals sent by optical scanners to its cash registers, thus supplying rich, real-time data to a competitor or manufacturer. As discoveries in the U.S. Embassy in Moscow have shown, it is already technologically possible for one firm to rig devices that will literally print out a duplicate of every letter typed by the CEO's secretary in a rival firm.

But total information war might not end with passive information collection. The temptation to engage in "commercial covert action" is growing. Consultant Joseph Coates of J. F. Coates, Inc., has suggested the day may come when a hard-pressed competitor feeds false orders into a rival firm's computers, causing it to overproduce the wrong models and undersupply those that are directly competitive.

Revolutions in video, optics, and acoustics open the way to spy on or interfere with human-to-human communication as well. Speech synthesis may make it possible to fake the voice of a manager and use it to give misleading telephone instructions to a subordinate. The imaginative possibilities are endless.

All this, of course, has led to a race to develop counterintelligence technologies. Some networks now require users to have a card that generates passwords in synchronization with those demanded by a host computer. Other systems rely on fingerprints or other physical and behavioral traits to confirm the identity of a user before allowing access. One system shoots a beam of low-intensity infrared light into a person's eye and scans the unique blood vessel patterns in the back of the retina to confirm identity. Another identifies a user by the rhythm of his or her key-strokes.

Because of its cost, sophisticated encryption or coding is largely limited today to the defense industries and financial institutions—banks, for example, making electronic funds–transfers. But GM already codes information moving on its electronic interchange links, and the toy-maker Mattel encodes certain data when they are down-loaded to a customer's computers or when they are physically transported from place to place.

Seesaw battles between offense and defense are a reflection of the info-war.

At every level of business, therefore—at the level of global standards for television and telecommunications . . . at the level of the retailer's checkout counter . . . at the level of the automatic teller machine and the credit card . . . at the level of extra-intelligent electronic networks . . . at the level of competitive intelligence and counterintelligence—we are surrounded by info-war and info-warriors fighting to control the most crucial resource of the Powershift Era.

PART FOUR

POWER IN THE FLEX-FIRM

15

THE CUBBYHOLE CRASH

The war for economic supremacy in the 21st century has already begun. The main tactical weapons in this global power struggle are traditional. We read about them in the daily headlines—currency manipulation, protectionist trade policies, financial regulations, and the like. But, as in the case of military competition, the truly strategic weapons today are knowledge-based.

What counts for each nation in the long run are products of mind-work: scientific and technological research . . . the education of the work force . . . sophisticated software . . . smarter management . . . advanced communications . . . electronic finance. These are key sources of tomorrow's power, and among these strategic weapons none is more important than superior organization—especially the organization of knowledge itself.

This, as we shall see next, is what today's attack on bureaucracy is mainly about.

THE BUREAUCRACY-BUSTERS

Everyone hates a bureaucrat.

For a long time businessmen maintained the myth that bureaucracy was a disease of government. Civil servants were called lazy, parasitic, and surly, while business executives were pictured as dynamic, productive, and eager to please the customer. Yet bureaucracy is just as rampant in business as in the public sector. Indeed, many of the world's largest corporations are as arthritic and arrogant as any Soviet ministry.

Today a search is on for new ways to organize. In the Soviet

Union and Eastern Europe the political leadership is at war with elements of its own bureaucracy. Other governments are selling off public enterprises, experimenting with things like merit pay and other innovations in the civil service.

But it is in business that the drive for new organizational formats is most advanced. Hardly a day passes without some new article, book, or speech decrying the old top-down forms of pyramidal power.

Management gurus publish case histories of companies experimenting with new organizational approaches, from "underground research" at Toshiba to the antihierarchical structure of Tandem Computers. Managers are advised to take advantage of "chaos," and a thousand formulas and fads are tried and discarded as fast as new buzz-phrases can be coined.

Of course, no one expects bureaucratic organization to disappear. It remains appropriate for some purposes. But it is now accepted that companies will wither under competitive fire if they cling to the old centralized bureaucratic structures that flourished during the smokestack age.

In smokestack societies, even when ultimate power is in the hands of charismatic and even antibureaucratic leaders, it is typically exercised on their behalf by bureaucrats. The police, the army, the corporation, the hospital, the schools, all are organized into bureaucracies, irrespective of the personality or style of their top officers.

The revolt against bureaucracy is, in fact, an attack on the dominant form of smokestack power. It coincides with the transition to the super-symbolic economy of the 21st century, and it explains why those who create "post-bureaucratic" organizations are truly revolutionary, whether they are in business, government, or the civil society.

AN INFINITY OF CUBBYHOLES

Any bureaucracy has two key features, which can be called "cubbyholes" and "channels." Because of this, everyday power—routine control—is in the hands of two types of executive: specialists and managers.

Specialized executives gain their power from control of information in the cubbyholes. Managers gain theirs through their control of information flowing through the channels. It is this power system, the backbone of bureaucracy, which is now coming under fire in large companies everywhere.

We think of bureaucracy as a way of grouping people. But it is also a way of grouping "facts." A firm neatly cut into departments according to function, market, region, or product is after all a collection of cubbyholes in which specialized information and personal experience are stored. Engineering data go to the engineers; sales data to the sales department.

Until the arrival of computers, this "cubbyholism" was the main way in which knowledge was organized for wealth production. And the wondrous beauty of the system was that, at first, it appeared to be endlessly expandable. In theory, one could have an infinity of cubbyholes.

In practice, however, companies and governments are now discovering that there are strict limits to this kind of specialization. The limits first became apparent in the public sector as government agencies grew to monstrous proportions, reaching a point of no return. Listen, for example, to the lament of John F. Lehman, Jr., a recent U.S. Navy Secretary.

In the Pentagon, Lehman confessed to his colleagues, so many specialized cubbyhole-units had sprung up that it is "impossible for me or anyone at this table to accurately describe . . . the system with which, and within which, we must operate."

As private companies grew to gargantuan size they, too, began to smack up against the limits of organizational specialization. Today, in company after company, the cubbyhole system is crashing under its own weight. Nor is it just bigness that makes it unworkable.

POWER VERSUS REASON

As we leave the industrial era behind, we are becoming a more diverse society. The old smokestack economy serviced a mass society. The super-symbolic economy services a de-massified society. Everything from life styles and products to technologies and the media is growing more heterogeneous.

This new diversity brings with it more complexity, which, in turn, means that businesses need more and more data, information, and know-how to function. Thus, huge volumes of the stuff are being crammed into more and more cubbyholes—multiplying them beyond comprehension and stretching them to the bursting point.

Today's changes also come at a faster pace than bureaucracies can handle. An uptick of the yen in Tokyo causes instantaneous purchases and sales in Zurich or London. A televised press conference in Tehran triggers an immediate reply in Washington. A politician's off-the-cuff remark about taxes sends investors and accountants instantly scurrying to reevaluate a takeover deal.

This speedup of change makes our knowledge—about technology, markets, suppliers, distributors, currencies, interest rates, consumer preferences, and all the other business variables—perishable.

A firm's entire inventory of data, skills, and knowledge is thus in a constant state of decay and regeneration, turning over faster and faster. In turn, this means that some of the old bins or cubbyholes into which knowledge has been stuffed begin to break into parts. Others are crammed to overload. Still others become useless as the information in them becomes obsolete or irrelevant. The relationships of all these departments, branches, or units to one another constantly change too.

In short, the cubbyhole scheme designed for Year One becomes inappropriate for Year Two. It is easy to reclassify or sort information stored in a computer. Just copy a file into a new directory. But try to change organizational cubbyholes! Since people and budgets reflect the scheme, any attempt to redesign the structure triggers explosive power struggles. The faster things change in the outside world, therefore, the greater the stress placed on bureaucracy's underlying framework and the more friction and infighting.

The real trouble starts, however, when turbulence in the marketplace, the economy, or society stirs up completely new kinds of problems or opportunities for the firm. Suddenly decision-makers confront situations for which no cubbyholed information exists. The more accelerated the rate of change in business—and it is speeding up daily—the more such one-of-a-kind situations crop up.

On December 3, 1984, the executives of Union Carbide awoke

to discover that their pesticide plant in Bhopal, India, had released a toxic cloud and caused the single worst accident in industrial history. The disaster killed more than 3,000 and injured another 200,000. Decisions had to be made instantly, rather than through the usual tortuous processes.

Equally unique, though far less disastrous, events are hitting business executives like hailstones. In Japan, the managers at Morinaga Chocolate learn that a mysterious killer is poisoning their product . . . Guinness in Britain is struck by a stock manipulation scandal . . . Pennzoil and Texaco are flung into a titanic legal struggle . . . the Manville Corporation is forced to bankrupt itself in dealing with lawsuits arising from having exposed its workers to asbestos . . . CBS has to fend off a blitzkrieg raid by Ted Turner . . . United Airlines faces an unprecedented buy-out bid from its own pilots, which then falls apart and triggers a crash on Wall Street. Such events—and many that are smaller and less publicized—hurl managers into situations for which nothing has adequately prepared them, or their bureaucracies.

When situations arise that can't easily be assigned to pre-designated informational cubbyholes, bureaucrats get nasty. They begin to fight over turf, money, people—and the control of information. This unleashes tremendous amounts of energy and raw emotion. Instead of solving problems, however, all this human output is burned up in the *Sturm und Drang*. What's still worse, these fratricidal battles make the firm behave irrationally. The vaunted "rationality" of bureaucracy goes out the window. Power, always a factor, now replaces reason as the basis for decision.

"CAMELEPHANTS" AND HOT POTATOES

When a real fluke arises—something that doesn't fit naturally into anyone's informational bailiwick—the company's first instinct is to ignore it. This ostrich response is what happened the first time foreign cars began appearing in the United States. The earliest little Opels and Citroën Deux Chevaux that turned up on American streets in the late 1950s drew a shrug from Detroit's bureaucrats. Even when floods of Volkswagens began to arrive, the giant bureaucratic auto makers preferred not to think about the unthinkable. There were no units inside their companies whose task was to fight foreign competition, no cubbyholes loaded with the necessary information.

When bureaucracies are forced to deal with a problem that fits into no one's existing cubbyhole, they behave in certain stereo-typed ways. After some initial fencing, someone inevitably suggests setting up a new unit (with himself or herself at its head). This is instantly recognized for what it could easily become: a budget-eating rival of the older units. Nobody wants that, so a compromise is arrived at. This compromise is that familiar bureaucratic "camelephant," the interdepartmental committee or task force. Washington is filled with them. So are big companies.

Combining the slow, lumbering gait of the elephant with the IQ of the camel, this new unit is, in effect, yet another cubbyhole, only this one is typically staffed by junior people, sent by their permanent departments not so much to solve the problem as to make sure that the new unit doesn't chip away at existing jurisdic-tions or budget allocations.

Sometimes the new problem is such a hot potato that nobody wants to deal with it. It is either dumped on someone young, inexperienced, and luckless, or it becomes an orphan: another problem on its way to becoming a crisis.

Faced by all this infighting, an exasperated CEO decides to "cut through the red tape." He does this by appointing a "czar," who theoretically will get the cooperation of all the relevant agen-cies, branches, and departments. But, lacking the information needed to cope with the problem, the czar, too, winds up depending on the pre-existing cubbyhole system.

Next the CEO decides frontal assault on the bureaucrats be-low will do no good. So he or she tries another standard ploy, quietly assigning the problem to a "troubleshooter" on his or her personal staff, rather than waiting for the slow, resistant bureau-cratic machine to act. This attempt to end-run the existing depart-ments only further outrages them, at which point the offended units begin working diligently to assure staff failure.

Something like this happened when Ronald Reagan assigned staff from his National Security Council, not traditionally an oper-ational unit, to take on functions more normally carried out by the Defense, State, or CIA bureaucracies. The resulting attempt to deal with "moderates" in Iran, in the hope that they would help release American hostages, blew up in the President's face. (Afterward, the Tower Commission, investigating the Irangate fiasco, solemnly concluded that the scandal could have been avoided if the White House had "used the system"—meaning relied on the line bureaucracies rather than the White House staff. It left unsaid whether the bureaucracies, which had previously failed either to negotiate the hostage release or to rescue them with military force, would have succeeded where the staff failed.)

Similar power games are played *within* each department, as its subunits also jockey for control of money, people, and knowledge. One might think that infighting stops at moments of dire crisis. Instead, the reverse happens when executive heads are on the block. In politics and even the military, crisis frequently brings out the worst, rather than the best, in organizations.

One has only to read the history of military interservice rivalry in the heat of battle, or the life-and-death struggles between rival British intelligence and covert action agencies during World War II, to glimpse the fanaticism that purely bureaucratic struggles can generate—especially during crisis. Businesses are not exempt from this destructive game-playing and fanaticism. For the image of the "rational" bureaucracy is false. It is power, not reason, that drives the classical pyramids that still litter the business landscape.

Any hope of replacing bureaucracy, therefore, involves more than shifting people around, laying off "fat," clustering units under "group vice-presidents," or even breaking the firm into multiple "profit centers." Any serious restructure of business or government must directly attack the organization of knowledge—and the entire system of power based on it. For the cubbyhole system is in crisis.

CHOKED CHANNELS

As change speeds up, this "cubbyhole crisis" is deepened by a parallel breakdown in the "channels" of communication.

Smart business people have always known that a company succeeds only when its parts work together. If the sales force is terrific but manufacturing can't deliver on time . . . or if the ads are wonderful but not tied to the right price policy . . . if engineers have no sense of what the marketers can sell . . . if all the accountants do is count beans and the lawyers just look at the law, without asking business questions . . . the firm cannot succeed.

But smart managers also know that people in one department or unit seldom speak to their counterparts in another. In fact, this lack of cross-communication is precisely what gives mid-rank managers their power. Once more it is the control of information that counts.

Middle managers coordinate the work of several subordinate units, collecting reports from the executive-specialists who run them. Sometimes the manager receives information from one subordinate and passes it back down to another, thus serving as a formal link between cubbyholes. At other times he or she may pass information laterally to the manager heading another group of units. But a middle manager's main task is to collect the disparate information that the specialists have cut into fragments and synthesize it before passing it through channels to the next higher level in the power pyramid.

Put differently, in every bureaucracy, knowledge is broken apart horizontally and put back together vertically.

The power structure based on control of information was clear, therefore: While specialists controlled the cubbyholes, managers controlled the channels.

This system worked marvelously when business moved slowly. Today, change is so accelerated and the information needed is so complex that the channels, too, exactly like the cubbyholes, are overwhelmed, clogged with messages (many of them misrouted).

Because of this, more executives than ever are stepping outside channels to circumvent the system, withholding information from their bosses and peers, passing it sideways unofficially, communicating through "back channels," operating on "dual tracks" (one formal, the other not), adding fire and confusion to the internecine wars now tearing up even the best-managed bureaucracies.

One overlooked reason why Japanese corporations have been better so far in managing the breakdown of bureaucracy is the existence in them of a backup system lacking in American and European firms.

While Western firms are dependent on cubbyholes and channels, Japanese firms also have, overlaid on these, what is known as the *dokikai* system. The *dokikai* system is a deviation from formal bureaucracy—but one which makes it far more effective.

In a large Japanese firm all recruits hired at the same time—what might be called an "entering class" or a "cohort"—maintain contact with one another throughout their employment by the firm, rising up the ranks as they grow more senior. After a time the members of the *dokikai* are scattered through the various functions, regions, and sections of the firm. Some have risen up the grades faster than others.

But this fraternity, as it has been called, hangs out together, socializing in the evenings, swilling much beer and sake, and—most important—exchanging information from many different cubbyholes outside the formal hierarchical channels.

It is through the *dokikai* that the "real" facts or "true" facts of a situation are communicated, as distinct from the official party line. It is in the *dokikai* that men, lubricated with alcohol, speak to one another with *honto*—expressing their true feelings—rather than with *tatemae*—saying what is expected.

It is a mistake to take at face value the picture of the Japanese corporation as smoothly run, efficient, consensual, and conflict-free. Nothing is further from the truth. But the information matrix—the *dokikai* laid on top of the bureaucracy—allows know-how and know-who to flow through the company even when the formal channels and cubbyholes are overloaded. It gives the Japanese corporation an information edge.

Yet this is no longer sufficient for organizational survival, and even this system is breaking down. Thus, companies race to build electronic alternatives to the old bureaucratic communication systems, and with these come fundamental reorganization as well, not only in Japan, but in the United States, Europe, and all the advanced economies.

What we see, then, is a burgeoning crisis at the very heart of bureaucracy. High-speed change not only overwhelms its cubbyhole-and-channel structure, it attacks the very deepest assumption on which the system was based. This is the notion that it is possible to pre-specify who in the company needs to know what. It is an assumption based on the idea that organizations are essentially machines and that they operate in an orderly environment.

Today we are learning that organizations are not machinelike but human, and that in a turbulent environment filled with revolutionary reversals, surprises, and competitive upsets, it is no longer possible to specify in advance what everyone needs to know.

FREE-FLOW KNOWLEDGE

We saw in Chapter 13 how companies attempt to impose order on information by designing computerized management information systems (MIS). Some of these, it turns out, are intended to buttress the old system by employing computer and communication links merely to expand the cubbyholes and the capacity of the communication channels. Others are truly revolutionary in intent. They seek to crush the cubbyhole-and-channels system and replace it with free-flow information.

To appreciate the full significance of this development, and the power shift it implies, it helps to note the quite remarkable (though largely unremarked) parallels between bureaucracies and our early computers.

The first big mainframes ministered to by the data priests supported the existing bureaucracies in business and government. This accounts for the initial fear and loathing they aroused in the public. Ordinary people sensed that these monster machines were yet another tool of power that might be used against them. The very data bases they held resembled the bureaucracies they served.

Early business computers were used chiefly for routine purposes like keeping thousands of payroll records. John Doe's record was made up of what the computer experts called "fields." Thus his name might be the first field, his address the second, his job title the third, his base salary the fourth, and so on.

Everyone's address went into his or her second "field." Everyone's base salary figure went into his or her fourth field.

In this way, all information entered into the payroll files went to pre-specified locations in the data base—just as information in a bureaucracy was addressed to pre-specified departments or cubbyholes.

Moreover, the first computerized data systems were largely hierarchical, again like the bureaucracies they were designed for. Information was stored hierarchically in memory, and the actual hardware itself concentrated computer power at the top of the company pyramid. Brains resided in the mainframe, while at the bottom the machines were unintelligent. The jargon referred to them appropriately as "dumb terminals."

The microcomputer revolutionized all this. For the first time, it placed intelligence on thousands of desk tops, distributing data bases and processing power. But while it shook things up, it did not seriously threaten bureaucratic organization.

The reason for this was that even though there were now many computerized data banks instead of one giant central bank, the knowledge stored in them was still crammed into rigid pre-designated cubbyholes.

Today, however, we are at the edge of a further revolution in how information is organized in computerized data bases.

So-called "relational" data bases now permit users to add and subtract fields and to interrelate them in new ways. Says Martin Templeman, senior vice-president of SPC Software Services, whose products are designed for financial firms: "Taking all . . . dimensions of change into account, we realized upfront that . . . hierarchical . . . relationships between the data would be a disaster." The new data bases "had to allow new relationships to emerge."

But such systems today are still so cumbersome they cannot be easily run on microcomputers.

The next step has come with the introduction recently of "hyper-media" data bases capable of storing not merely text but also graphics, music, speech, and other sounds. More important, hyper-media combine data bases and programs to give the user far greater flexibility than earlier data base systems.

Even in the relational systems, data could be combined in only a few pre-specified ways. Hyper-media vastly multiplies the ways in which information from different fields and records can be combined, recombined, and manipulated. Information in the original data bases was structured like a tree, meaning that to go from a leaf on one branch to a leaf on another, you had to go back to the trunk. "Hyper" systems are like a web, making it possible to move easily from one piece of information to another contextually.

The ultimate goal of the hyper-media pioneers—admittedly still a distant grail—is systems in which information can be assembled, configured, and presented in an almost infinite number of ways. The goal is "free-form" and "free-flow" information.

A striking example of the genre (called "HyperCard" and popularized by Apple) was first demonstrated at a Boston computer show by its author, Bill Atkinson. What he showed stunned the audience at the time.

First to appear on his screen was a picture of a cowboy. When Atkinson indicated the cowboy's hat, other hats began to appear on the screen, one of which was the hat on a baseball player. When

Atkinson indicated the player's hat, other images associated with baseball began to appear, one after another, on the screen. He was able to extract information from the data base and detect patterns in it, in highly varied ways.

This was so different from earlier data base systems that it gave the illusion that the computer was free-associating—much like a person.

By crossing conventional categories, reaching across different collections of data, hyper-media makes it possible for, say, a designer creating a new product to let her mind weave through the stored knowledge naturally and imaginatively.

She might instantly shift, for instance, from technical data to pictures of earlier products that preceded it in the market . . . to chemical abstracts . . . to biographies of famous scientists . . . to video clips of the marketing team discussing the product . . . to transportation tariff tables . . . to clips of relevant focus groups . . . to spot prices for oil . . . or lists of the components or ingredients the new product will need . . . plus the latest study of political risk in countries from which its raw materials will have to come.

In addition to vastly increasing the sheer quantity of accessible knowledge, hyper-media also permits a "layering" of information, so that a user can first access the most or least abstract form of it, and move by stages up or down the abstraction ladder. Or, alternatively, generate innovative ideas by creating novel juxtapositions of data.

Conventional data bases are good for getting information when you know exactly what you want. Hyper systems are good for searching when you are not certain. Ford Motor Company is developing a "Service Bay Diagnostic System" for mechanics, so that they can search and browse for answers when they are not sure what's wrong with your car.

The U.S. Environmental Protection Agency makes available a "hyper-text" data base to help companies sort through and interrelate complex regulations governing 2 million underground storage tanks. Cornell University uses a hyper system for its second-year medical curriculum, permitting students to browse and search for patterns interactively. The University of Toledo is developing a hyper-text-based course in Spanish literature.

We are still far from being able to throw different kinds of data or information into a single pot and then search it entirely free of a programmer's preconceptions about what pieces are or are not related. Even in hyper systems the cross-connections a user can make are still dependent on previous programming. But the direction of research is clear. We are inching toward free (or at least freer) forms of information storage and manipulation.

Bureaucracies, with all their cubbyholes and channels pre-specified, suppress spontaneous discovery and innovation. In contrast, the new systems, by permitting intuitive as well as systematic searching, open the door to precisely the serendipity needed for innovation.

The effect is a dazzling new freedom.

The significant fact is that we are now moving toward powerful forms of knowledge processing that are profoundly antibureaucratic.

Instead of a little bureaucracy inside a machine, as it were, where everything is sequential, hierarchical, and pre-designated, we move toward free-style, open information. And instead of a single mainframe or a few giant processors having this enormous capacity, companies now have thousands of PCs, which before long will all have this capacity.

This form of information storage and processing points toward a deep revolution in the way we think, analyze, synthesize, and express information, and a forward leap in organizational creativity. But it also eventually means the breakup of the rigid little information monopolies that overspecialization created in the bureaucratic firm. And that means a painful shift of power away from the guardians of those specialized monopolies.

Even this tells only a fraction of the tale. For to these truly revolutionary ways of storing and using knowledge, we must now add the nonhierarchical communication networks that crisscross companies, crash through departmental perimeters, and link users, not merely between the specialized departments but also up and down the hierarchy.

A young employee at the very bottom of the ladder can now communicate directly with top-level executives working on the same problem; and, significantly, the CEO at the touch of a button can access any employee down below and jointly call up images, edit a proposal together, study a blueprint, or analyze a spreadsheet—all without going through the middle managers.

Is it surprising therefore that recent years have seen such savage reductions in the number of middle managers in industry?

Just as the new forms of information storage strike a blow

against specialization, the new forms of communication end-run the hierarchy. The two key sources of bureaucratic power—cubbyholes and channels—are both under attack.

KNOWLEDGE IS POWER IS KNOWLEDGE

Here then we glimpse one of the most fundamental yet neglected relationships between knowledge and power in society: the link between how a people organize their concepts and how they organize their institutions.

Put most briefly, the way we organize knowledge frequently determines the way we organize people—and vice versa.

When knowledge was conceived of as specialized and hierarchical, businesses were designed to be specialized and hierarchical.

Once a bureaucratic organization of knowledge finds concrete expression in real-life institutions—corporations, schools, or governments—political pressures, budgets, and other forces freeze the cubbyholes and channels into place. Which then tend to freeze the organization of knowledge into place, obstructing the reconceptualizations that lead to radical discovery.

Today, high-speed change requires equally high-speed decisions—but power struggles make bureaucracies notoriously slow. Competition requires continual innovation—but bureaucratic power crushes creativity. The new business environment requires intuition as well as careful analysis—but bureaucracies try to eliminate intuition and replace it with mechanical, idiot-proof rules.

Bureaucracy will not vanish, any more than the state will wither away. But the environmental conditions that permitted bureaucracies to flourish—and even made them highly efficient engines—are changing so rapidly and radically, they can no longer perform the functions for which they were designed.

Because today's business environment is convulsing with surprise, upsets, reversals, and generalized turbulence, it is impossible to know precisely and in advance who in an organization will need what information. In consequence, the information needed by both executives and workers to do their jobs well, let alone to innovate and improve the work, cannot reach the front-line managers and employees through the old official channels.

This explains why millions of intelligent, hardworking employees find they cannot carry out their tasks—they cannot open new markets, create new products, design better technology, treat customers better, or increase profits—except by going around the rules, breaking with formal procedures. How many employees today need to close their eyes to violations of formal procedure to get things done? To be a doer, a fixer, a red-tape cutter, a go-getter, they must trash the bureaucracy.

Thus, information begins to spill out of the formal channels into all those informal networks, gossip systems, and grapevines that bureaucracies seek to suppress. Simultaneously, corporations spend billions to construct electronic alternatives to the old communication structures. But all these require enormous changes in the actual organization, the way people are ranked and grouped.

For all these reasons the years ahead will see a tsunami of business restructuring that will make the recent wave of corporate shake-ups look like a placid ripple. Specialists and managers alike will see their entrenched power threatened as they lose control of their cubbyholes and channels. Power shifts will reverberate throughout companies and whole industries.

For when we change the relations between knowledge and production we shake the very foundations of economic and political life.

That is why we are on the edge of the greatest shift of power in business history. And the first signs of it are already evident in the new-style organizations fast springing up around us. We can call them the "flex-firms" of the future.

16

THE FLEX-FIRM

Meet some of today's business heroes—people like Sergio Rossi. Rossi is not some strutting bureaucrat or tycoon ensconced in a glass-sheathed skyscraper. He works instead from his home in the Val Vibrata, in eastern Italy, with three employees who use high-tech machines to turn out fine-quality purses and pocketbooks for sale in New York City department stores.

Not so far away one finds Mario D'Eustachio, who heads up Euroflex, a 200-employee firm that makes luggage for Macy's. Euroflex is a collaborative effort. Pia D'Eustachio, Mr. E.'s wife, is in charge of sales; Tito, a son, guards the finances; Tiziana, a daughter, designs the luggage; and a nephew, Paolo, runs the production side of things.

These, according to *The Christian Science Monitor*, are only 2 of the 1,650 small firms in the valley, each averaging only 15 workers, but collectively turning out over $1 billion a year in clothing, leatherware, and furniture. And Val Vibrata is only one small region—part of what is now known as the Third Italy.

Italy Numero Uno was the agricultural South. Italy Numero Due was the industrial North. Italy Numero Tre is composed of rural and semirural regions, like Val Vibrata, using high-tech and small, usually family-based enterprise to contribute to what has been called the "Italian miracle."

A similar pattern is seen in smaller cities. Modena, for example, boasts 16,000 jobs in the knitwear industry. Whereas the number of workers in firms employing more than 50 has plummeted since 1971, employment in firms with 5 or fewer workers rose. Most of these are family-run.

The virtues of family business are being discovered elsewhere too. In the United States, writes *Nation's Business*, "after years of being considered small-time, family businesses are hot." François

M. de Visscher, of the financial firm Smith Barney, says he wants his company to become "the premier investment banker to family businesses," and everyone from management consultants to marriage counselors are gearing up to sell services to what might be called "the fam-firm sector."

The smallest of these family firms are short on titles and formality; larger ones combine informality among family members at the top with formality and bureaucratic organization below.

It is glib to suggest that small is always beautiful or that an advanced economy can function without very large enterprises, especially as the global economy grows more integrated. Italian economists, for example, worry that Italy's dynamic small firms may not cut the mustard in an integrated European market, and the European Community, long an advocate of bigness, favors large-scale mergers and urges small firms to form alliances and consortia. But while consortia may make sense, the EC's infatuation with superscale may prove shortsighted—a failure to recognize the imperatives of the super-symbolic economy.

Thus, there is mounting evidence that giant firms, backbone of the smokestack economy, are too slow and maladaptive for today's high-speed business world. Not only has small business provided most of the 20 million jobs added in the U.S. economy since 1977, it has provided most of the innovation. Worse yet, the giants are increasingly lackluster as far as profits go, according to a *Business Week* study of the thousand largest firms. "The biggest companies," it reports, "are the most profitable—on the basis of return on equity—in only four out of 67 industries. . . . Well over half the time the biggest corporate player fails to attain even the industry average return on invested capital."

In many fields the savings that sheer size once made possible are fading as new technologies make customization cheap, inventories small, and capital requirements low. According to Donald Povejsil, former vice-president of corporate planning at Westinghouse, "Most of the classical justifications of large size have proved to be of minimal value, or counterproductive, or fallacious."

Small firms now can gain access to huge amounts of capital from Wall Street. They have ready access to information. And it is easier for them to use it, since they tend to be less bureaucratic.

Conversely, the "diseconomies of scale" are catching up with many of the bloated giants. It is clear, moreover, that in the economy of tomorrow huge firms will become more dependent than in the past on a vast substructure of tiny but high-powered and flexible suppliers. And many of these will be family-run.

Today's resurrection of small business and the family firm brings with it an ideology, an ethic, and an information system that is profoundly antibureaucratic.

In a family, everything is understood. By contrast, bureaucracy is based on the premise that nothing is understood. (Hence the need for everything to be spelled out in an operational manual and for employees to work "by the book.") The more things are understood, the less has to be verbalized or communicated by memo. The more shared knowledge or information, the fewer the cubbyholes and channels needed in an organization.

In a bureaucratic company, position and pay are ostensibly determined by "what you know," as though "who you know" didn't matter. Yet the reality is that "who you know" *is* important, and grows in importance as one moves up in the world. Who you know determines access to crucial knowledge—namely, information about who owes whom a favor, and who is to be trusted (which, in turn, means whose information is reliable).

In a family firm nobody kids anyone. Too much is known by all about all, and helping a son or daughter succeed by using "pull" is natural. In the bureaucratic firm, pull is called nepotism and is seen as violation of the merit system that purportedly prevails.

In a family, subjectivity, intuition, and passion govern both love and conflict. In a bureaucracy, decisions are supposed to be impersonal and objective, although, as we've seen, it is internecine power struggles that determine important decisions, rather than the cool clear rationality described in textbooks.

Finally, in a bureaucracy it is often difficult to know who has power, despite the formal hierarchy and titles. In the family enterprise, everyone knows that titles and formality don't count. Power is held by the patriarch or, occasionally, the matriarch. And when he or she passes from the scene, it is usually conferred on a hand-picked relative.

In short, wherever family relationships play a part in business, bureaucratic values and rules are subverted, and with them the power structure of the bureaucracy as well.

This is important, because today's resurgence of family business is not just a passing phenomenon. We are entering a "post-bureaucratic" era, in which the family firm is only one of many alternatives to bureaucracy and the power it embodies.

THE END OF THE COOKIE-CUT COMPANY

Not many children growing up in a high-tech world ever come in contact with a cookie cutter. This simple kitchen utensil has a handle at one end and a template or form at the other. When pressed into rolled dough, it cuts out the shape of the cookie-to-be. Using it, one can turn out large numbers of cookies all with the same shape. For an older generation, the cookie cutter was a symbol of uniformity.

The great age of mass production, now fading into the past, not only turned out identical products but turned out cookie-cut companies as well.

Glance at any Table of Organization. Chances are it consists of straight lines connecting neat little boxes, each exactly like the other. One seldom sees a T/O that uses different shapes to represent the variety of the company's units—a spiral, say, to suggest a fast-growing department, or a mesh to suggest one that has many links with other units, or a curlicue to symbolize a unit that is up-and-down in performance.

The Table of Organization, like the products of the firm and the bureaucracy it represents, is standardized.

Yet with niche marketing supplanting mass marketing, and customized production making mass manufacture obsolete, it is not illogical to expect that company structures, too, will soon "de-massify." Put differently, the day of the cookie-cut company is over. And so are the cookie-cut power structures that ran large corporations.

In *The Third Wave* we wrote about such innovations as flexible hours, flexible fringe benefits, and other "flex" arrangements that begin to treat workers as individuals and, at the same time, give the firm far greater flexibility too. Today such ideas are so commonplace that *Newsweek* headlines a story "A Glimpse of the 'Flex' Future."

What companies have not yet grasped, however, is that flexibility must cut far deeper—right to the very structure of the organization. The rigid, uniform structure of the firm must be replaced by a diversity of organizational arrangements. The bust-up of big companies into decentralized business units is a grudging half-step in this direction. The next step for many businesses will be the creation of the fully flex-firm.

THE DE-COLONIZATION OF BUSINESS

Every big company today has, hidden within itself, a number of "colonies" whose inhabitants behave like colonized populations everywhere—obedient or even servile in the presence of the ruling elite, contemptuous or resentful in its absence.

Many of us, at one time or another, have seen supposedly "big shot" managers choke back their own thoughts in the presence of their bosses, nod approval of imbecilic ideas, laugh at bad jokes, and even assume the dress, manner, and athletic interests of their superiors. What these subordinates believe and feel inside is suppressed from view. Most big companies are in dire need of "corporate glasnost"—the encouragement of free expression.

Under the smooth surface of male camaraderie and (at least in the United States) a show of equality, the "bwana" or "sahib" mentality still thrives. But the taint of colonialism in business runs even deeper.

Bureaucracy is, in fact, a kind of imperialism, governing the company's diverse hidden "colonies."

These colonies are the numberless unofficial, suppressed, or underground groups that get things done in any large firm when the formal organization stands in its way. Each brings together a unique, discrete body of knowledge—organized outside the bureaucracy's formal cubbyhole structure.

Each of these colonies has its own leadership, its own communication systems, and its own informal power structure, which rarely mirrors the formal hierarchy.

The struggle to rebuild business on post-bureaucratic lines is partly a struggle to de-colonize the organization—to liberate these suppressed groupings. In fact, one might say that the key problem facing all big companies today is how to unleash the explosive, innovative energies of these hidden colonies.

DANCING ON TABLES

When Sears, Roebuck & Company, the largest U.S. retailer, announced a major reorganization of its merchandise group not long ago, the group chairman and CEO, Michael Bozic, said it was needed because "We are competing in many diverse businesses . . . and have essentially been using one organizational format to compete in all of these businesses." This, critics implied, had made the firm sluggish and noncompetitive.

But even top managers who sense they need to "let go" or loosen the reins, in order to free up the energies of their people, drastically underestimate how far they will need to go to break the grip of bureaucracy.

Scores, if not hundreds of companies have broken themselves into numerous "profit centers," each of which, it is hoped, will act like a small, market-driven enterprise. Even some staff operations have now been designated as profit centers and must finance themselves (and thus justify their existence) by selling their in-house services. But what good is it to break a firm into profit centers if each of these is merely a cookie-cut miniature of the parent firm—a mini-bureaucracy nestling inside the mega-bureaucracy?

What is beginning now is a much more profound and revolutionary shift, which will alter the entire nature of power in business.

Most American managers still think of the organization as a "machine" whose parts can be tightened or loosened, "tuned up," or lubricated. This is the bureaucratic metaphor. By contrast, many Japanese are already using a post-bureaucratic metaphor—the corporation, they say, "is a living creature."

This implies, among other things, that it undergoes birth, maturation, aging, and death or rebirth in a new form. The Japanese term for company birth is *sogyo* and many companies today speak of experiencing a second or third or "new" *sogyo*.

It is precisely at this moment of rebirth that long-term success or failure is determined. For if the new reborn firm is still organized along bureaucratic lines, like the old one it replaces, it may have a short and unhappy second life. By contrast, if at this moment firms are permitted to reach out in new directions and to assume whatever organizational forms are most appropriate, chances for adaptation to the new, innovation-rich environment are much better.

The flex-firm concept does not imply structurelessness; it does suggest that a company, in being reborn, may cease being a mule and turn into a team consisting of a tiger, a school of piranhas, a mini-mule or two, and who knows, maybe even a swarm of information-sucking bees. The image underlines the point. The business of tomorrow may embody many different formats within a single frame. It may function as a kind of Noah's Ark.

To grasp the "flex-firm" concept, it helps to remind ourselves that bureaucracy is only one of an almost infinite variety of ways of organizing human beings and information. We actually have an immense repertoire of organizational forms to draw on—from jazz combos to espionage networks, from tribes and clans and councils of elders to monasteries and soccer teams. Each is good at some things and bad at others. Each has its own unique ways of collecting and distributing information, and ways of allocating power.

A company could conceivably have within it a monastery-style unit that writes software . . . a research team organized like an improvisational jazz combo . . . a compartmentalized spy network, with need-to-know rules, operating within the law, to scout for merger or acquisition possibilities . . . and a sales force organized as a highly motivated "tribe" complete with its own war songs and emotional membership rituals. (The author has attended the sales meeting of a major corporation where the tribal form was incipient and the members so psyched up about their jobs they quite literally danced on tabletops.)

This new way of conceiving of a company as a collection of very different organizations, many of them counterbureaucratic, reflects what already exists in some firms in a semi-smothered or embryonic form. Many businesses will find themselves moving toward this free-form model simply to stay alive in the de-massified economy of tomorrow.

The term *flex-firm* is needed because there is no handy word in the English language to describe such an entity. The French economist Hubert Landier uses the mouth-cracking term *polycellular* to describe the business of the future. Others describe it as "neural" or nervous-system-like rather than machinelike. Still others refer to the emerging business organization as a "network."

Though all these words capture some facet of the new reality, none are adequate, because the dawning business form of the future embraces them all, and more. They may *include* elements that are polycellular or neural. They may (or may not) be networked. But the organization may also include within it units that remain thoroughly bureaucratic because, for some functions, bureaucracy remains essential.

A key feature of post-bureaucratic firms is that the relationships of their parts are not closely pre-specified, like information force-fitted into an old-fashioned data base.

Instead, the units of a flex-firm may draw information, people, and money from one another and from outside organizations as needed. They may be next door to one another or continents apart. Their functions may partly overlap, like information in a hyper-media data base; for other purposes, the functions may be logically, geographically, or financially divided. Some may use many central services provided by headquarters; others may choose to use only a few.

In turn this requires freer, faster flows of information. This will mean crisscrossing, up, down, and sideways conduits—neural pathways that bust through the boxes in the table of organization so that people can trade the ideas, data, formulae, hints, insights, facts, strategies, whispers, gestures, and smiles that turn out to be essential to efficiency.

"Once you connect the right people with the right information you get the extra value added," says Charles Jepson, director of office marketing, Hewlett-Packard Company, adding that "information is the catalyst for effecting change at every level. That's what makes its power so awesome."

FAM-FIRMS OF THE FUTURE

One of the suppressed business forms struggling hardest to break free from old-style managerial bureaucracy is the mom-and-pop enterprise symbolized by people like the Rossis and D'Eustachios in Italy.

There was a time when virtually all businesses were, in fact, small family-owned firms. Beginning mainly in the 19th century, as companies grew larger, they transformed themselves into professionally managed bureaucracies.

Today, as we've seen, independent family-run units are once more multiplying. But in addition, we have witnessed the spread of franchising, which links mom-and-pop operators to the financial and promotional clout of large firms. The next logical step will come when family enterprises crop up as respected, powerful units *within* large corporations as well.

Most large firms engage in a cynical rhetoric about "family." A well-tailored chairman smiles at us from the pages of the annual report as his ghostwritten text assures us that everyone in the firm, from the chairman to the janitor, is a member of "one big family."

Yet nothing is more inimical to family forms of organization and, indeed, hostile to family life itself than the typical business bureaucracy. This accounts for the widespread corporate ban against hiring both husbands and wives.

Such rules, intended to guard against favoritism and exploitation, are now beginning to crack in the United States, as the number of highly qualified women in the work force increases and companies face difficulty in relocating one spouse when the other has a good job locally.

We can expect to see couples hired by companies—as couples. Before long we will no doubt see a wife-husband team placed in charge of a profit center and permitted—in fact, encouraged—to run it like a family business.

The same result is likely to come from the acquisition of companies like the D'Eustachios' Euroflex. If that firm were to be acquired, would it make sense to break up the family team that built it into a success in the first place? Smart acquirers would lean over backward to leave the family form intact.

Familialism, sometimes overglamorized, presents many challenges for top management.

A high-powered husband-wife team can be a formidable political force in the firm. The sublimation of expressed emotion—a corporate norm—may well give way to the shouts, tears, and seeming irrationality that often go with family life. Male-dominated companies may have to make room for women managers backed by husbands or other relatives. How in this system does one make sure important jobs are not handed off to the idiot son? How should succession be handled? None of these problems is easily solved.

On the other hand, fam-firms have great advantages. In contrast to large bureaucratic firms, they can make quick decisions. They often are willing to take daring entrepreneurial risks. Family firms can change faster, and adapt better to new market needs. Communication through constant face-to-face interaction and even pillow talk is swift and rich, conveying much with only a grunt or a grimace. Family members typically enjoy a deep sense of "ownership" in the firm, evince high motivation, are strongly loyal, and often work superhuman hours.

For all these reasons, we can expect family firms to proliferate inside as well as outside the smarter giant firms.

The Pakistani management expert Syed Mumtaz Saeed has acutely observed, "The dehumanization of the industrial era in the West has been a consequence of the relegation of the family to a purely social and non-economic role. Thus, the manager and the worker of the modern age are torn between the work-place and the home in a physical sense, and between the family and the organization in an emotional sense. . . . This conflict is central to the problems of motivation, morale and productivity in modern Western societies."

Saeed argues that Third World countries should reject bureaucratic impersonality and Western antifamilialism and build economies that are, in fact, based on family.

What he is arguing for is the retention of a classic paternalism that not only was wiped out in most big companies in the West, but is diminishing even in Japan. But this is quite different from the flex-firm, in which it is theoretically possible to have one profit center that is thoroughly paternalistic and others that are decidedly not, one unit that is run like a Marine boot camp, another like a commune. In the coming shift toward diverse organizational forms, corporate anti-colonialism, as it were, will lead to the liberation of the family business within the frame of the flex-firm.

Yet, as we see next, the family firm is only one of a host of colorful business formats that will shift power away from manager-bureaucrats in the years ahead.

17

TRIBAL CHIEFS
AND CORPORATE COMMISSARS

Every ten years the United States is invaded.
Recently an army of 400,000 fanned out from twelve beachheads and moved across the nation in a six-week campaign. At the end of that period the army withdrew, vanishing into the surrounding society along with all the logistics, telecommunications, and computers that linked its units together during its field operations.

Though seldom studied, the plans for this massive campaign hold lessons for many American businesses. For the goal of this "army" is to collect the detailed intelligence on which millions of business decisions will be based. Moreover, the very way in which the campaign is organized will provide insight to many an executive.

The organization involved is, of course, the U.S. Bureau of the Census, and its decennial operations cast revealing light on that future form of enterprise, the flex-firm. As the post-smokestack economy grows increasingly diverse, companies will be compelled to invent new, more varied business formats.

This is not just an academic theory. It has to do with survivability. Cybernetician W. Ross Ashby coined the phrase "requisite variety" many years ago to describe one of the preconditions for the survival of any system. Today's businesses simply lack the requisite variety to make it in the 21st century.

As they cast about for more adaptive ways of doing business, they will uncover—or rediscover—many arrangements now overlooked, suppressed, misunderstood, or misused by bureaucratic management. They will look for ideas everywhere: in other businesses, as well as in nonbusiness institutions like governments, political parties, universities, the military—and census bureaus.

Here is a sampling of what they will find.

The Pulsating Organization

This is an organization that expands and contracts in a regular rhythm. A good example is the U.S. Census Bureau, which swells to enormous size every ten years, then shrinks, starts planning for the next decennial count, and swells again.

Ordinarily staffed by about 7,000 regular employees, the Bureau maintains twelve regional centers around the United States. But to conduct a complete census, it sets up a parallel or "shadow" center for each of the twelve. Through them, more than 1.2 million applicants are interviewed to find the 400,000 "troops" who actually fan out and knock on every American door. These shadow centers are designed to last one year or a year and a half, and then to be dismantled. The staff then shrivels back to around 7,000. At which point planning begins for the next count ten years in the future.

Carrying this operation through successfully ought to earn the managerial equivalent of an Olympic gold medal. The 1990 census was fraught with bugs and bloopers. But the task would clearly daunt many a senior business executive. Indeed, many firms will notice that their own problems, though smaller in scale, are not entirely dissimilar. For "pulsating organizations" are present in many industries as well.

We see them in companies that gear up for annual model changes, then gear down again; in retail firms that staff up for Christmas and lay off in January; and in pickup crews used for film and television production.

In fact, one of the most rapidly proliferating formats in business today is the task force or project team, examples of what, in *Future Shock,* we termed "ad-hocracy." These, however, are only variants of the pulsating organization. While true "pulsers" grow and shrink repetitively, a project team normally carries out a single task. It therefore grows and declines once and then is dismantled. It is, in effect, a "single-pulse" organization.

Pulsing organizations have unique information and communication requirements. For its 1990 census, the Census Bureau's shadow centers, for example, were linked by some $80 million worth of computers and telecommunications equipment in a temporary network designed to be disposed of, or folded back into the permanent organization.

Executives in charge of pulsing companies or units often find their power pulsing too. Funds dry up as the unit shrinks. People disappear. The available pool of knowledge or talent diminishes. The power of rival units in the company expands relatively as the unit continues to shrink. In a pulsating power structure, the executive who commands a large project may be a "700-pound gorilla" one day—and a monkey the next. As many pulsating organizations interact, they lend a kind of rhythm to the economy.

Pulsing, however, isn't only a matter of size. Some companies pulse back and forth between centralization and decentralization. With each swing or pulse, information structures are changed—and power therefore shifts. The speedup and growing unpredictability of change point toward faster pulsing in the years ahead.

The Two-faced Organization

Another format likely to find a place in many flex-firms is a completely two-faced unit capable of operating in two modes, depending upon circumstance. The pulsating unit differs in size and organization from time to time. The Janus-like organization may remain the same in size, but shift from hierarchical to nonhierarchical command as needs demand.

A prime example is the famed British military unit, the Special Air Service, or SAS. Used for surgical antiterrorist strikes, hostage rescue, and other missions demanding surprise and deception, the SAS operates in two diametrically opposed modes. On the parade ground it is all spit, polish, and blind obedience. Regimental protocol is enforced by screaming sergeants. The privileges of rank and hierarchy are brutally upheld.

In action, however, a totally different kind of behavior is expected from the same people. SAS troops fight in tiny units, often cut off from their base, and without any officer present. There is a unit commander, but he may not hold a formal rank and is likely to be referred to simply as the "boss." The men, derisively called "sir" on the parade ground, now become "mister" or are addressed simply by first name. The same sergeant who cursed a trooper for some trivial infraction of the dress code may now tolerate jokes about those "parade ground idiots." Rank, hierarchy, and privilege are replaced under fire by a different set of ground rules.

In fact, Colonel David Stirling, who initially proposed formation of the SAS, pointed out that the smallest unit in paratroop or commando organizations consisted of eight or ten men led by a noncommissioned officer who did the thinking for the unit. Stirling insisted on something unique in military history—a four-man fighting module.

In the SAS, Stirling has written, "Each of the four men was trained to a high general level of proficiency in the whole range of the SAS capability and, additionally, each man was trained to have at least one special expertise according to his aptitude. In carrying out an operation—often in pitch-dark—each SAS man in each module was exercising his own individual perception and judgment at full stretch."

In fact, Stirling insisted on the number four to prevent orthodox leadership from arising. The danger of each person acting as a loose cannon is minimized through the selection of extremely motivated team players. The result is an organization that has been described as "a unique military democracy . . . in which, if he succeeds, a man exchanges his former class and even identity for membership [in] a caste as binding as any family." It is this intense training and commitment that make it possible for the same unit to operate in both an authoritarian and a democratic mode, as the occasion demands.

Business, too, needs different behavior during normal operations and in the midst of crisis. In fact, many firms today are creating crisis centers, contingency plans, and fallback arrangements. But few actually train all their employees to operate in two contrasting modes.

The present conception of crisis management is to create a "shadow management," which waits in reserve, prepared to assume power during the emergency. Its ability to do so depends heavily on access to information and control of communications. Southern California Edison, for example, which operates the San Onofre Nuclear Generating Station, has set up a complex emergency information system that uses remote sensing, voice and video links, to tie its crisis command center to field units.

As we move further into a period of economic and political turbulence, punctuated erratically by technological breakthroughs and disasters, we can expect crises to crowd in on one another—

everything from terrorist attacks and product failures to sudden international crises. The Exxon oil spill, the collapse of the Continental Illinois bank, the wave of savings-and-loan failures, the bankruptcy of the A. H. Robins Company after the discovery of health problems related to its Dalkon Shield intrauterine contraceptive device only begin to suggest the diversity of crises that can face businesses.

Each one brings enormous power shifts with it as scapegoats are blamed, new leaders arise, and others are discredited and replaced. But the increased likelihood of crisis in a period of revolutionary change suggests we will see crisis teams and two-faced organizations spread through the business world and become a regular part of the flex-firm of tomorrow.

The Checkerboard Organization

In Austria after World War II a deal was struck between the two main political parties assuring that whichever party won the top spot would install a member of the opposition party in the second spot, and so on all the way down to the shop floor. This *proparz* system has meant that throughout the key posts in state-owned companies, banks, insurance companies, and even in schools and universities, Socialist "reds" alternated with Conservative "blacks."

Today we find an adaptation of this in, say, the Japanese bank in California that alternates Japanese and Americans at each level of the hierarchy, thus guaranteeing that Tokyo receives a flow of information seen through Japanese eyes, not simply from the top, but from many levels of the organization. Power at the pinnacle is reinforced by a constant stream of insight originating at many layers at once. As firms go global, many will no doubt try the Austrian and Japanese approach.

The Commissar Organization

Soviet Army units have traditionally had not only military commanders but political officers attached to them. While the military officer reported up the military line of command, the political officers also report to the Communist Party. The object was to keep the army subject to the party. In business, too, we often see "commissars" chosen from above and planted in subordinate units to keep an eye on things and report to the top through separate channels rather than through the normal hierarchy.

Here there are two main information channels, instead of one, violating the strict single-channel character of bureaucracy. It also reflects the deep distrust with which top management regards information flowing up through normal channels.

As change speeds up and predictability declines, CEOs will use "commissars" to end-run the bureaucracy in a desperate attempt to maintain control.

The Buro-baronial Organization

The best surviving example of feudal organization today is found in the university, where each department is a barony, professors are ranked and rule over graduate assistants, who make up the body of serfs. This feudal holdover is embedded within (and often at war with) the bureaucratic administrative structure of the university. Another example is the Congress of the United States, where 535 elected "barons" rule over a huge bureaucratic staff.

A similar combination of industrial bureaucracy and feudal barony is found in the Big Eight accounting firms, in large law offices, in brokerage houses, and in the military, where each service—army, navy, or air force—is a fiercely independent fiefdom. Generals and admirals in charge of these fiefdoms may have more real power than higher-ranked officers in staff positions who command no troops.

In "buro-baronies" the barons war with one another, often forming alliances to weaken central control. Such feudal elements are still found in business as well, along with what we might call "vestigial vassalage."

George Masters is a veteran engineer who has worked for several U.S. electronics manufacturers and now serves as the administrative aide to Philip Ames, a corporate VP in one of the world's largest computer firms. If anyone in personnel took the trouble to check, they would discover that Masters came into the company shortly after Ames arrived. And if they were to check further, they would discover the same thing happened in the company that employed both of them before they took their present jobs. And the one before that.

Hard-drinking buddies as well as workmates, Masters and Ames socialize together. They and their wives take vacations together. In fact, Masters and Ames (the people are real, the names are not) have worked together for more than fifteen years, Masters always following Ames as Ames hopped to successively higher positions.

This pattern, whether called "hitching your wagon to a star" or "riding on someone's coattails," is found in almost every large firm. Because it sharply reduces the need for communication—the two men know each other so well they can anticipate each other's reactions—it is highly efficient for some purposes, even though it violates formal personnel rules that call for "objective" selection.

The psychology of "vassalage" is extremely complex, involving everything from mentorships to the exchange of financial, sexual, or other favors. At its heart, however, the system is feudal and subjective, rather than bureaucratic and impersonal.

The power relationships are similarly complicated. At one level the "vassal," or junior, is dependent upon the "lord," or senior, who is higher up in the table of organization. Yet the top dog can be totally dependent upon his or her underling, whose chief unofficial function may be to conceal from others the weaknesses of the boss. This may be as common as fronting for the boss when he is too drunk to do his job. It may be as unusual as reading to him and making presentations for him because, unbeknownst to the company, the boss is dyslexic.

As bureaucracy weakens and its channels and cubbyholes become clogged, other neo-feudal forms and practices are likely to proliferate also, and find a place in the flex-firm.

The Skunkworks Organization

Here a team is handed a loosely specified problem or goal, given resources, and allowed to operate outside the normal company rules. The skunkworks group thus ignores both the cubbyholes and the official channels—i.e., the specialization and hierarchy of the existing corporate bureaucracy.

Tremendous energies are released; information is exchanged at high speed outside normal channels. Members develop strong emotions toward their work and one another, and very often, enormously complex projects are completed in record time.

According to Hirotaka Takeuchi and Ikujiro Nonaka of Hitotsubashi University in Japan, writing about "The New New Product Development Game," when Honda wanted to design a car that would appeal to young people, it put together a team—average age twenty-seven—and turned it loose. In the words of one young engineer: "It's incredible how the company . . . gave us the freedom to do it our way."

When Nippon Electric Company (NEC) developed its PC8000, it turned the project over to a group of former microprocessor sales engineers who had no previous experience with PCs. Says the project head: "We were given the go-ahead from top management to proceed with the project, provided we would develop the product by ourselves and also be responsible for manufacturing, selling, and servicing it on our own."

IBM's PC, which became the industry standard, was developed by a nearly autonomous group working in Boca Raton, Florida. Apart from quarterly reviews by corporate headquarters in Armonk, New York, the team was free to operate as it wished. It was also permitted to break normal corporate policy about buying from outside suppliers. Similar examples can be found at Apple, Hewlett-Packard, Xerox, and other high-tech firms.

The skunkwork format is inherently and militantly antibureaucratic.

As described by Takeuchi and Nonaka, "A project team takes on a self-organizing character as it is driven to a state of 'zero information'—where prior knowledge does not apply. . . . Left to stew, the process begins to create its own dynamic order. The project team begins to operate like a start-up company—it takes initiatives and risks, and develops an independent agenda."

Successful skunkworks develop their own leadership, based on skill and competence rather than formal rank. These newly empowered leaders often come into direct frontal conflict with the formal leader appointed by the bureaucracy to initiate and oversee the skunkwork unit.

The Self-start Team

We are also beginning to see the rise of "self-starting" teams or groups. Rather than being handed an assignment from above, they are typically drawn together by the electronic network. These "information clusters" go beyond even the skunkwork in their antihierarchical nature.

They spring up when people intensely interested in a common problem find one another electronically and begin to exchange information across departmental lines, irrespective of either geography or rank.

So long as it is compatible with a very general statement of the corporation's goals, the team sets its own objectives, often through democratic exchange.

For example, in David Stone's engineering management group at Digital Equipment Corporation, members dispersed around the world hold an electronic "conference" in which each team member puts forward her or his draft objectives.

"Each person," says Stone, "is then required by me to comment on each other's objectives with respect to whether they believe them or not, whether they are appropriate, and what support might be needed from that person that should be incorporated in their objectives. After a month and a half of this dialogue . . . we each rewrite them, based on the input, and we now have created a shared set, a team set, of objectives."

The process, antibureaucratic to its roots, can function only in an atmosphere that gives individuals considerable autonomy. The result can be a chain reaction of creativity. Because of this, such units are most common where competitive innovation is highest. As electronic nets spread and link flex-firms together, such self-start units will spring up, even across company lines.

A DIVERSITY OF POWERS

To manage the high diversity of the flex-firm will require new styles of leadership wholly alien to the bureaucrat-manager.

Senior officials will be far less homogeneous. Instead of look-alike (and think-alike) executives from central casting, the power group in the flex-firm will be heterogeneous, individualist, antibureaucratic, impatient, opinionated, and as a group, probably far more creative than today's bureaucratic committees.

Instead of neat lines of authority, the flex-firm presents a far more complex, transient, and fuzzy picture. A CEO may have to deal with what, from today's bureaucratic perspective, may appear to be a motley mixture of tribal chieftains, commissars, egotistical divas, smart and self-important barons, cheerleaders, silent technocrats, Holy Roller–style preachers, and fam-firm patriarchs or matriarchs.

Pulsing organizations, for example, need executives who can lead small organizations as well as large—or else they need an orderly system of succession that permits control to be handed off to leaders with different skills, depending upon the phase in which the organization finds itself.

In firms where the checkerboard and commissar principles are used, dual lines of communication compete. In the checkerboard, both lines terminate in the CEO's office. In the commissar arrangement, the two lines terminate in different places—one carrying reports to the CEO; the other, say, directly to the board.

All arrangements that affect the flow of information allocate or reallocate power. In baronial organizations the CEO must continually negotiate with his or her executive barons, playing them off against one another to avoid being neutered or ousted by a coalition of them.

Leadership under such conditions is less likely to be impersonal and spuriously "scientific," and more dependent, instead, on intuitive sensitivity, empathy, along with guile, guts, and plenty of old-fashioned emotion.

The flex-firm becomes increasingly political, in the sense that managing multiple constituencies is political. It is political in the sense that conscious application of power is political.

Power—the control of company money and information backed by the force of law—is shifting out from under those with legal or formal position and toward those with natural authority based on knowledge and certain psychological and political skills.

THE MISSING PANACEA

Finally, a word on networks. This form of organization has received so much attention in recent years, has been so heavily hyped, and has been defined so broadly that a touch of caution is warranted. For many, the network is a panacea.

Societies and business are riddled with networks of many kinds. We normally think of them as the informal pathways along which information and influence flow. Feminists complain that an "old boys' network" frequently operates to deprive women managers of promotion. Ex-military men often have their own network of contacts, as do former police and members of the Federal Bureau of Investigation, many of whom take jobs as corporate security officers after their retirement from government service.

Homosexuals have networks that are particularly strong in certain industries like fashion and interior design. Ethnic minorities have strong networks—the overseas Chinese throughout Southeast Asia, Jews in Europe and America, West Indians in Britain. Transplanted people in general—New Yorkers in Texas, the so-called Georgia Mafia that came to Washington when Jimmy Carter was President, the Ukrainians who came to Moscow with Leonid Brezhnev—also form their own communication networks.

In short, informal networks of many kinds crop up in virtually all complex societies. To these one must add formal networks—Masons, for example, Mormons, or members of the Catholic order Opus Dei.

For a long time the role and structure of such networks were ignored by economists and business theorists. Today they are much studied as potential models for corporate structure.

This recent interest can be traced to deep social changes. One is the previously noted breakdown of formal communication in companies. When the firm's bureaucratic channels and cubbyholes get clogged, unable to carry the heavy volumes of communication and information needed nowadays to produce wealth, the "right information" doesn't get to the "right person" as it once did, and employees fall back on the informal networks to help carry the information load.

Similarly, the de-massification of the economy compels companies and work units to interact with more numerous and varied partners than before. This means more personal and electronic

contact with strangers. But when a stranger tells us something, how do we know if it is accurate? When possible, skeptical managers check in with their personal networks—people they have known or worked with for years—to supplement and verify what they learn through formal channels.

Finally, since an increasing number of business problems today require cross-discipline information, and the broken-down cubbyhole-and-channel system stands in the way, employees rely on friends and contacts in the network whose membership may be scattered across many departments and units.

These networks, formal or not, share common characteristics. They tend to be horizontal rather than vertical—meaning they have either a flat hierarchy or none at all. They are adaptive—able to reconfigure themselves quickly to meet changed conditions. Leadership in them tends to be based on competence and personality rather than on social or organizational rank. And power turns over frequently and more easily than in a bureaucracy, changing hands as new situations arise that demand new skills.

All this has popularized the notion of the corporate network among both academics and managers. Corning, Inc., which operates in four sectors—telecommunications, housewares, materials, and laboratory sciences—describes itself as a "global network." Says Chairman James R. Houghton:

"A network is an interrelated group of businesses with a wide range of ownership structures. . . . Within each sector there are a variety of business structures that range from traditional line divisions to wholly owned subsidiaries and alliances with other companies. . . .

"A network is egalitarian. There is no parent company. A corporate staff is no more, or less, important than a line organization group. And being part of a joint venture is just as important as working at the hub of the network."

Networks can be enormously useful, flexible, and antibureaucratic. But in the recent enthusiasm, elementary distinctions are often ignored.

In the 1970s one of the earliest and deepest analysts of network organization, Anthony Judge, then based in Brussels at the Union of International Associations, examined the density and response times of people networks, the structure of nets and their social functions, and the degree of connectedness they exhibit. He also compared human networks with such inanimate networks as

pipelines, electric grids, railways, and transaction networks handling foreign exchange, commodity trading, and so on. Judge developed a whole little-known but useful vocabulary for the network concept.

He also brilliantly matrixed global networks against global problems, showing in a vast volume how networks of ideas or problems were linked, how networks of organizations overlapped, and how ideas and organizations were related.

More recently Netmap International, an affiliate of KPMG Peat Marwick, has developed a methodology for identifying the hidden communication networks in organizations as varied as the Republican Party and a giant accounting firm, in the course of its work for businesses and governments from Malaysia to Sweden. Says Netmap vice-president Leslie J. Berkes: "Organizations are redesigned daily by their members to get the job done. That's the real structure. It's the informal organization—the anti-organization. . . . It is the primary organization." If you cannot identify it, and track its changes, Berkes asks, "how are you going to manage it? You'll be satisfied with manipulating the formal organization with titles, hierarchies and tables of organization."

Such tracking can provide deep insight into existing organizations, but to enthuse blindly today over networks and assume that networks are "the" basic form of the future is to imply much the same uniformity that bureaucracy imposed, albeit at a higher, looser level.

Like any other type of human organization, the network has its limitations along with its virtues. Network organization is superb for fighting terrorism or a decentralized guerrilla war, not marvelous at all for the control of strategic nuclear weapons where the last thing we want is for local commanders to be free and unrestrained. The flex-firm is a broader concept, which implies an organization capable of encompassing both the formal and informal, the bureaucratic and the networked suborganizations. It implies even greater diversity.

THE LIMITS OF CONTROL

There are, however, limits to how far even a flex-firm can go toward diversity.

The spread of the "profit center"—which has seen many once-monolithic companies broken into semiautonomous, independently accounted units, each responsible for its own operations and its own profit and loss—can be seen as only a first step toward the eventual dissolution of the company altogether, atomized into a network or consortium of completely independent contractors or free entrepreneurs. In this model, every worker is a free lance, freely contracting with other free lances, to get specific jobs done.

But no social process continues forever, and the day of the total individualization of work, the ultimate dream of the theologically committed free-marketeer, is far distant. Instead, we can expect profit centers to become smaller—and more diverse—without disappearing into millions of one-person firms.

There is, after all, only so much diversity that any organization can tolerate and any managerial team manage. The argument here, therefore, is not that companies should maximize the variety of their organizational formats, but that today's companies, in their flight from the rigor mortis of bureaucracy, need to explore far more diverse options than ever before. They need, in short, to liberate their "colonies" and even to invent new formats.

In doing so, they—and we—move away from the idea that an organization is like a machine, each of its actions predictable and determinist, toward a conception of organization that is closer to the biological. Living systems are only partly deterministic, only sometimes predictable.

This is why the new electronic networks are increasingly tending toward neural rather than preplanned architectures. It is why David Stone, vice-president of international engineering at Digital Equipment, says, "You cannot tell in advance how the traffic will operate. . . . If you break a link between two places, provided that the network is still connected to those two points, it will find its own way. . . . We believe," he adds, "in the value of communication between any two individuals based on what they know rather than what their place is in the hierarchy."

Just as hyper-media, the new form of data base, permits knowledge to be arranged in extremely varied ways, the concept of the flex-firm points toward companies that can adapt in myriad ways to the twisty, quirky high-change competition that lies ahead.

The emerging flex-firm of the future, however, cannot function without basic changes in the power relationships of employees and their bosses. As we shall see next, these changes are well on their way. For power is shifting on the shop floor as well as in the executive suite.

18

THE AUTONOMOUS EMPLOYEE

During years spent working as a factory and foundry worker, we put in time on an auto assembly line. Even now, more than a third of a century later, it is impossible to forget what it felt like—especially the harrowing impact of the speedup. Every day, from the moment the bell started our shift, we workers raced to do our repetitive jobs while desperately trying to keep pace with the car bodies moving past us on the clanking, fast-jerking conveyor. The company was forever trying to accelerate the line.

Suppressed rage so filled the plant that every once in a while, for no apparent reason, an eerie wordless wail would issue from the throats of hundreds of workers, swell into a keening, ear-knifing sound as it was picked up and passed from department to department, then fade away into the clatter and roar of the machines.

As the cars sped past we were supposed to prepare them for the paint shop, hammering out dents and dings, and grinding them smooth. But the bodies flew by before we could do a good job. After they left us, they passed in front of inspectors who chalk-circled the remaining problems to be cleaned up afterward. Eight or ten hours a day of this was enough to numb us to any calls for "quality."

Somewhere there were "managers"—men in white shirts and ties. But we had almost no contact with them.

The power of these men in white shirts came not merely from our need for a paycheck, but from their superior knowledge about the factory, its goals, procedures, or plans. By contrast, we knew almost nothing about our job, except the few preprogrammed steps necessary to do it. Apart from exhortations to work harder, we received almost no information from the company. We were the last to find out if a shop or plant was to be closed down. We were given no information about the market or the competition.

We were told nothing about new products soon to be introduced, or new machines.

We were supposed to take on faith that our superiors knew what they were doing. (As the decline of the U.S. auto industry suggests, they didn't.) We were expected to show up on time, work, keep our muscles moving and our mouths shut. Even with a strong union in place, we felt powerless. A faceless "they" had us in their power. *They* were the men in white shirts. Managers. We were, during our work shift, citizens of a totalitarian state.

We are reminded of these experiences as reports arrive almost daily describing the newest plants now going up. For power is shifting in the workplace, and things will never be the same.

UNBLOCKING MINDS

General Electric makes electricity-distribution equipment in Salisbury, North Carolina. The plant is a model that GE wants to replicate at three hundred other factory locations.

In the past, if a piece of equipment broke down, a machine operator like Bob Hedenskog would have had to report it to his foreman and wait for help. Today Hedenskog makes the necessary decisions himself. He telephones a GE engineer in Plainville, Connecticut, for advice and takes responsibility for repair. On his own initiative he has ordered $40,000 worth of replacement parts, which he anticipated his machinery would need. He is part of a group of about seventy-five employees who, through committees of their own, make production, scheduling, and even some hiring decisions. Together they have cut worker-hours per unit of production by two thirds, and have slashed the time to customer delivery by 90 percent.

Some workers quit when this system was introduced, explaining that they didn't want to carry the additional responsibility it entailed. But employee turnover has fallen from 15 percent in the first year of the new system's operation to 6 percent four years later.

Similar stories are flowing in from all parts of the high-tech world. Ford Australia recently built its EA Falcon with an innovative work system that, according to the *Financial Times,* "contradicts the traditional Western way of assuring quality—namely, that management checks the output of workers who are following engineers' minutely detailed instructions."

Ford concluded that detecting defects first and correcting them later was not working. Only by allowing workers more discretion—no longer preprogramming their every move—could the goal of zero defects be approached. And this, according to the article, meant "recognizing the power of the operators right down to shop floor level."

Instead of one repetitive task, workers at the Chrysler-Mitsubishi Diamond-Star plant in Normal, Illinois, are told before being hired that they will need to handle several different jobs. They will be expected to come up with fresh ideas for improving production, and in that connection, they must be prepared to give, as well as take, constructive criticism.

At the Mazda Motor Manufacturing factory in Flat Rock, Michigan, ordinary plant workers get three weeks of training, including sessions on psychology. A small group of new hires are given six minutes to dream up twenty-five ideas on how to improve the common garden-variety bathtub, and then get only two minutes to come up with thirty more suggestions. Says Mazda's head of training, "We're trying to loosen people up and unblock them." After the initial three weeks, workers spend additional weeks on more job-specific training. Mazda estimates it spends $13,000 to hire and train the average employee.

These increasingly commonplace accounts underscore the historic shift currently taking place from "manufacture" to "mentifacture"—the progressive replacement of muscle by mind in the wealth creation process. But giving employees more say-so over the details of their work is only the tip of a more significant iceberg.

THE FECKLESS FARMER

To put this power shift into perspective, it is helpful to read the early history of the industrial revolution in England and Western Europe, and the complaints made by the earliest employers about the fecklessness, unreliability, drunkenness, and ignorance of the agrarian people from whom the early factory work force was drawn.

Every society imposes its own distinct work discipline or "regimen." Workers are supposed to obey certain rules, often unspoken. Their performance on the job is monitored, policed, and a structure of power is in place to enforce the rules.

In First Wave or agricultural societies, most peasants toiled endlessly, yet barely survived. This agrarian work force, organized into family production teams, followed a regimen set by the rhythms of season, sunrise, and sunset.

If a peasant was absent or lazy, his own relatives disciplined him. They might ostracize him, beat him, or cut his food rations. The family itself was the dominant institution in society, and, exceptions aside, it imposed the work regimen. Its dominance over the individual family member was reinforced by social pressures from the villagers.

Local elites might hold the power of life and death over the peasantry. Tradition might restrict social, sexual, and religious behavior. Peasants often suffered the cruelest hunger and poverty. And yet in their daily work lives they seemed less minutely restricted than those in the small but growing industrial labor force.

The agrarian work regimen had lasted for millennia, and until only a century or two ago, the vast majority of human beings knew no other and assumed it to be the *only* logical and eternal way of organizing work.

THE NEW CHAINS

As the first factories began to appear, a totally different work regimen came into being, at first affecting a tiny fraction of the population, then spreading as agricultural labor declined and industrial work expanded.

The urban industrial worker in a Second Wave society might be freer socially in the great, teeming anonymity of the urban slum. But in the factory itself, life was more tightly regimented.

Brute technology was designed for illiterates—which most of our ancestors were. Intended to amplify human muscle power, it was heavy, rigid, and capital-intensive. Before the invention of small electric motors, the machines were typically positioned all in a row and driven by overhead belts that set the pace for the whole factory. Later came the mechanical conveyor line that compelled armies of workers to perform motions in sync, chaining them to the production system.

It is no accident that the French term for "assembly line" is *chaine* or that everyone, from the manual laborer to the topmost managers, operated in a "chain of command."

Work was "de-skilled" or dumbed-down, standardized, broken into the simplest operations. And as white-collar work spread, offices were organized along parallel lines. Because they were not harnessed to an assembly line, clerical employees had a bit more physical freedom of movement. But the goal of management was to increase efficiency in the office by making it resemble the factory as much as humanly—or inhumanly—possible.

The smokestack factories and mills were severely criticized for their dehumanization of the worker. But even the most radical thinkers of the time regarded them as "advanced" and "scientific."

Less commented on was a change in the police function. Instead of the family policing work and pressuring its members to perform, a new power structure—hierarchical management—came into being to enforce the new rules.

This new Second Wave work regimen was at first bitterly resisted even by employers, who tried to keep the old agrarian system and to transplant it into the factory. Because families had long sweated together in the fields, early manufacturers hired whole families at once. But this system, efficient in agriculture for 10,000 years, proved totally inefficient in the factory.

Old people could not keep up with the machines. Children had to be beaten and often manacled to prevent them from running off to play. Families arrived at different times, straggling in as they had in the fields. Inevitably, the attempt to maintain a family production team in the new technological environment collapsed, and the smokestack regimen was imposed.

The lesson became clear: You couldn't organize work around a steam engine or textile loom the way you did around a hoe or a team of oxen. A new technical environment required a different discipline—and a different structure of power to police and enforce it.

THE ELECTRONIC PROLETARIAT

Today, as the super-symbolic economy develops, a new work regimen is once more supplanting an old one.

In our remaining smokestack factories and offices, conditions today are still largely the same as they were decades ago. Around the world, and especially in the newly industrializing nations, hundreds of millions of workers are still chained to a Second Wave industrial discipline.

And today, too, exactly as in the past, we still see employers underestimating the revolution taking place around them. They introduce computers and other advanced, Third Wave technologies—but attempt to retain yesterday's Second Wave work rules and power relationships.

Trying to turn their employees into "electronic proles," as George Orwell might have put it, they count keystrokes, monitor breaks, and listen in on employee phone calls. They attempt to control the most minute details of the work process. These methods, characteristic of industrial work, are especially prevalent in the processing of insurance claim forms and routine data entry in other businesses. But they can also be applied to higher-level work.

According to a report by the U.S. Congressional Office of Technology Assessment, they are "increasingly being directed to . . . more skilled technical, professional and managerial positions. The jobs of commodities broker, computer programmer and bank loan officer . . . could lend themselves to monitoring."

How long such methods will pay off, however, remains doubtful, for the work rules of the past contradict the new possibilities brought by advanced technology. Wherever we see radical new technology and an old work system, it is likely that the technology is misapplied and its real advantages wasted. History has shown repeatedly that truly advanced technologies require truly advanced work methods and organization.

Employers today who still think they need electronic proles resemble those reactionary ironmasters and textile-mill owners who thought they could run the new steam-driven factories with methods designed for ox power. They either quickly corrected their mistake or were driven out of business by smarter competitors who learned how to reorganize the work process itself, matching the work regimen to the most advanced technologies of the time.

Today in thousands of workplaces, from auto plants to offices, smart companies are experimenting with, or actually exploiting, the new regimen. Its key characteristic is a changed attitude toward both knowledge and power.

TOMORROW'S WORK REGIMEN

The changes now transforming work are not a result of woolly-headed altruism. They are a consequence of much heavier loads of information and communication needed for wealth production.

In the past, when most businesses were still tiny, an entrepreneur was able to know virtually all that needed to be known. But as firms grew and technology became more complicated, it was impossible for any one person to carry the entire knowledge load. Soon specialists and managers were hired and formed into the characteristic compartments and echelons of the bureaucracy. The knowledge load had to be diffused throughout the managerial ranks.

Today a parallel process is at work. Just as owners became dependent on managers for knowledge, managers are becoming dependent on their employees for knowledge.

The old smokestack division of the firm into "heads" and "hands" no longer works. In the words of Teruya Nagao, professor of information and decision sciences at the University of Tsukuba, "The separation of thinking and doing in the traditional model . . . may well be appropriate for constant technology but is hardly in keeping with rapid technological progress."

Because technologies are more complicated and turn over more frequently than in the past, workers are expected to learn more about adjacent and successive jobs. Thus, a General Motors ad proudly speaks of workers' helping to choose the lighting in their plants, selecting the sandpaper, the tools, and even "learning how the plant runs, what things cost, how customers respond to their work." In computer-integrated manufacture, says consultant David Hewitt of United Research Company, workers "need not only to know how the specific machines work, but . . . how the factory works."

What is happening is that the knowledge load and, more important, the decision load are being redistributed. In a continual cycle of learning, unlearning, and relearning, workers need to master new techniques, adapt to new organizational forms, and come up with new ideas.

As a result, "submissive rule-observers, who merely follow instructions to the letter, are not good workers," says Nagao, quoting an earlier study of Sony. In fact, in today's fast-change environment, he points out, rules, too, need to be changed more frequently than in the past, and workers need to be encouraged to propose such changes.

This is so because the worker who helps frame new rules will also understand why they are necessary and how they fit into the larger picture—which means the worker can apply them more intelligently. In fact, says Reinhard Mohn, chairman of Bertelsmann A.G., one of the world's largest media conglomerates, "only regulations which are endorsed by the majority of the work force have a chance of being abided by."

But to invite workers into the rule-making process is to share power once held exclusively by their bosses. It is a power shift not all managers find easy to accept.

Workplace democracy, like political democracy, does not thrive when the population is ignorant. By contrast, the more educated a population, the more democracy it seems to demand. With advanced technology spreading, unskilled and poorly educated workers are being squeezed out of their jobs in cutting-edge companies. This leaves behind a more educated group, which cannot be managed in the traditional authoritarian, don't-ask-me-any-questions fashion. In fact, asking questions, challenging assumptions are becoming part of everyone's job.

Lowell S. Bain is the plant manager of GenCorp Automotive's new plant in Shelbyville, Indiana. Describing the role of the manager, he says, "Here the pressure comes from inside the work force—a work force that challenges management and doesn't accept its dictates or authority. Here people question objectives. . . . Just because you're a member of management doesn't make your ideas holy."

What we see, therefore, is a clear pattern. Workplace power is shifting, not because of fuzzy-minded do-goodism, but because the new system of wealth creation demands it.

THE NON-INTERCHANGEABLE PERSON

Another key factor shifting power on the job has to do with the concept of interchangeability. One of the most important innovations of the industrial revolution was based on the idea of interchangeable parts. But workers, too, came to be regarded as interchangeable.

Much of the relative powerlessness of the industrial working class derived precisely from this fact. So long as jobs required little skill, and workers could be trained in a few minutes to do some rote task, one worker was as good as another. Especially in periods of labor surplus, wages would drop and workers, even when unionized, had little bargaining power.

A "reserve army of the unemployed" usually was standing by to step into any available jobs. By contrast, as pointed out in Chapter 7, the jobless today cannot step into available jobs unless they happen to have the right mixture of skills at the right moment.

Moreover, as the knowledge content of work rises, jobs grow more individualized—i.e., less interchangeable. According to consultant James P. Ware, vice-president of Index Group, Inc., "Knowledge workers are less and less replaceable. The tools are used differently by each knowledge worker. One engineer uses the computer differently from the next. One market analyst analyzes things one way; the next is different."

When a worker leaves, either the company must find another with matching skills, which becomes mathematically harder (and more costly) as the variety of skills increases, or else it must train a new person, which is also expensive. Hence, the costs of replacing any one individual grow, and his or her bargaining power rises correspondingly.

The boss of a giant project team in the defense industry puts it this way: "Years ago you might have everybody doing the same thing. . . . Today it's different. Now if we lose somebody, it takes six months to train an individual to understand our system." Furthermore, because work is team-based, "When we pluck an individual out, the whole team becomes dysfunctional."

The net result of such changes is that companies tend to use fewer but better-paid workers than in the past, and in the fast-growing, leading-edge industries, the old authoritarian command structure is phasing out, replaced by a new, more egalitarian or collegial style of work.

Seen in its historical context, this represents a significant shift of power in the workplace.

TWO IMPERATIVES

The new work regimen will not wipe out all trace of the older ones. It will be a long time before the last sweatshop disappears. But two imperatives make its spread largely unstoppable.

The first is the "innovation imperative." No existing market share is safe today, no product life indefinite. Not only in computers and clothing, but in everything from insurance policies to medical care to travel packages, competition tears away niches and whole chunks of established business with the weapon of innovation. Companies shrivel and die unless they can create an endless stream of new products.

But free workers tend to be more creative than those who work under tightly supervised, totalitarian conditions. As David Stone, vice-president of international engineering at DEC, puts it, "When you're watching someone else watching your performance, you don't create much." Thus the need for innovation encourages worker autonomy.

It also implies a totally different power relationship between employer and employee. It means, for one, that intelligent error needs to be tolerated. Multitudes of bad ideas need to be floated and freely discussed, in order to harvest a single good one. And this implies a new, liberating freedom from fear.

Fear is the primary idea-assassin. Fear of ridicule, punishment, or loss of job destroys innovation. Smokestack management saw as its main task the ruthless elimination of error. Innovation, in contrast, requires experimental failure to achieve success.

A possibly apochryphal story about Tom Watson of IBM has an executive asking him if he is going to fire another executive whose $5 million project failed. "Fire him," Watson is supposed to have said. "I've just paid his tuition!" Whether true or not, it represents an attitude toward work diametrically opposed to the industrial system, and it underscores, yet again, the importance of learning.

The push toward a new work regimen is also furthered by a second imperative: speed. Advanced economies are accelerative. In the new environment, therefore, innovation is not enough. The business has to get its new products to market fast—before a competitor beats it to the punch or copies the products.

This accelerative pressure also shifts power by undermining the fixed, bureaucratic chain of command.

Not only do the new electronic networks frequently make it possible to communicate up, down, and sideways in the organization, so that an employee can skip across hierarchical levels, a similar effect is seen in personal or face-to-face communication.

In the past, a worker with a problem or a new idea got into trouble by going over the head of a superior. But acceleration forces employees to end-run the hierarchy. So employees are actually encouraged to ignore rank when necessary. At the Brother Industries headquarters in Nagoya this is routine. Says one BI personnel manager: "If a middle manager felt insulted in seeing any of his subordinates go over his head without permission, that man would immediately lose respect from both downstairs and upstairs."

Acceleration and innovation both play havoc with the power hierarchies of the smokestack past and promote the spread of the advanced, Third Wave work regimen.

THE DEMAND FOR ACCESS

For all these reasons, the new work regimen will, in time, sweep across the main sectors of the economy. And as the work force is continually ceded more autonomy, it will demand increased access to information.

During the smokestack era, arguments for the humane treatment of employees were crushed by the realities of brute technology that paid off even when workers were kept ignorant (and powerless).

Today, workers are demanding more and more access to information because they can't do their jobs effectively without it. We are thus seeing a redistribution of knowledge (and power) made necessary by new market conditions and by the new technologies themselves.

"As computer programs mimic the skills that have long set managers apart, workers in lower-level jobs can do tasks once reserved for executives," reports *The New York Times*. It quotes Charles Eberle, a former vice-president of Procter & Gamble, saying: "You suddenly have information in the hands of the people who run the machines; it's no longer reserved for people two or three rungs up the hierarchy.

"The first-level supervisors don't appreciate the power of this information until it gets into workers' hands. Then their resistance is enormous."

Clearly not all workers fit well in jobs that demand initiative, full participation, and a sharing of responsibility. Nor can all managers cope with the new-style work. But, as work units grow smaller and educational levels higher, the pressure from below mounts. The result is a fundamental shift in power relationships.

This is not the first time since the dawn of the industrial age that managers have been confronted with changing models of human relationships in the workplace. For many years the old Taylorite notions that turned the worker into an appendage of the machine were challenged by a school of "good-guy" theorists who argued that more humane treatment of employees would prove more efficient in the end.

The new regimen, increasingly espoused by management itself, is, however, more radical. In the words of Teruya Nagao: "This idea goes far beyond the assumptions of the human-relations model, where employees were made to feel important. Now they are acknowledged truly *to be* important."

It is true that the overriding power—greater than that of any individual—is that of the labor market. A shortage or surplus of some skills determines the outer parameters of the new autonomy. Many programmers or space engineers have learned that they, exactly like punch-press operators and assembly-line hands, can be pink-slipped without ceremony, while their bosses vote themselves "golden parachutes." Those cast out of work suffer a devastating decline in personal and collective power—which is a subject for a totally different book.

What is relevant here, however, is how things are changing for those *inside* the work force. And within that framework, a change of historical proportion is taking place.

In the smokestack era no individual employee had significant power in any contest with the firm. Only a collectivity of workers, massed and threatening to withhold their muscles, could force a recalcitrant management to improve the pay or status of the employee. Only group action could slow or stop production, for any individual was easily interchangeable and, hence, replaceable. This was the basis for the formation of labor unions.

If unions, with their traditional emphasis on "solidarity" and "unity," are losing membership and power in virtually all the advanced technological nations, it is precisely because workers are no longer as interchangeable as they once were.

In the world of tomorrow it will not take masses of workers to bring a company's production to a standstill, or to damage it in other ways. A "computer virus" slipped into a program, a subtle distortion of the information in a data base, the leakage of information to a competitor—these are only the most obvious of a whole range of new methods of sabotage available to the angry, the irresponsible, or the justifiably outraged individual.

The "information strike" of the future could turn out to be a one-person protest. And no laws, clever programs, and security arrangements can totally protect against this. The best defense is likely to be social pressure from one's peers. Or the simple feeling that one is treated with dignity and justice.

But far more important is the shift toward non-interchangeability. As work grows more differentiated, the bargaining position of individuals with crucial skills is enhanced. Individuals, not only organized groups, can exert clout.

Marxist revolutionists argued that power flows to those who own the "means of production." Contrasting the factory worker with the preindustrial craftsman who owned his own tools, Marx contended that workers would be powerless until they seized the "means of production" from the capitalist class that owned them.

Today we are living through the next power shift in the workplace. It is one of the grand ironies of history that a new kind of autonomous employee is emerging who, in fact, does own the means of production. The new means of production, however, are not to be found in the artisan's toolbox, or in the massive machinery of the smokestack age. They are, instead, crackling inside the employee's cranium—where society will find the single most important source of future wealth and power.

19

THE POWER-MOSAIC

In 1985, General Motors, America's largest car maker, bought control of Hughes Aircraft, the company founded by that reclusive, eccentric billionaire Howard Hughes. GM paid $4.7 billion dollars—the single largest amount ever paid for a corporate acquisition until then.

A merger mania had begun in the early 1980s, the fourth since 1900, and each year saw more corporate marriages in America, until by 1988 there were 3,487 acquisitions or mergers involving an astronomical $227 billion. Then in 1989, all the old records were smashed again when RJR-Nabisco was taken over for $25 billion.

In short, in a single four-year period the maximum size of these mergers increased more than five times. Even allowing for inflation, the growth in scale was colossal.

Of the twenty largest deals in U.S. history, all consummated between 1985 and 1989, most involved a wedding of American firms. By contrast, hardly a day now goes by without new headlines proclaiming "mixed marriages"—mergers that cross national frontiers. Thus Japan's Bridgestone acquires Firestone Tire & Rubber. Sara Lee gulps the Dutch company Akzo. England's Cadbury Schweppes swallows up France's Chocolat Poulain. France's Hachette buys up America's Grolier. Sony buys Columbia Pictures.

"The extraordinary increase in world takeover activity . . . is showing no signs of abatement," writes the *Financial Times*. "Indeed, the scramble to reorganize several key industries is likely to accelerate . . . driven by factors that go way beyond the asset-stripping moves that first sparked the U.S. merger boom."

As this suggests, while many mergers were originally based on get-rich-quick exploitation of financial or tax quirks, others were strategic. Thus, as Europe raced toward total economic integration, many of its biggest companies merged, hoping to take advantage of the pan-European market and to stave off the advances of Japanese and American giants. American and Japanese grooms looked for European brides.

Some companies were thinking on an even bigger scale, preparing themselves to operate all across the so-called "triad market" —Europe, the United States, and Japan. And beyond that, a few firms dreamed of truly conquering the "global market."

All this frenetic activity led to deep concern over the concentration of economic power in a few hands. Politicians and labor unions attacked the so-called "deal mania." Financial writers compared it to the feeding frenzy of sharks.

Looking only at the question of financial size, one might be led to believe that power in the economy of the future will eventually be controlled by a tiny handful of enormous, hierarchical monoliths, not unlike those depicted in the movies.

Yet that scenario is far too simple.

First, it is a mistake to assume all these mega-firms will stay pasted together. Previous merger manias have been followed, a few years later, by waves of divestiture. A new round of divorces looms ahead. Sometimes the anticipated market evaporates. Sometimes the cultures of the merged firms clash. Sometimes the basic strategy was wrong in the first place. Indeed, as we saw earlier, many recent buy-outs have actually been designed with divestiture in mind, so that after a gigantic merger various units are spun off from a central core, shrinking, rather than enlarging, the scale of the resultant firm.

Second, we are witnessing a growing disjuncture between the world of finance and the "real" economy in which things and services are produced and distributed. As two heart-stopping stock market crashes in the late 1980s proved, it is sometimes possible for the financial markets to collapse, at least temporarily, without significantly disrupting the actual operations of the larger economy. For capital itself is growing less, not more, important in economic wealth production.

Third, bulk doesn't necessarily add up to power. Many giant firms possess enormous power resources but cannot deploy them effectively. As the United States learned in Vietnam, and the Soviets in Afghanistan, sheer size is no guarantee of victory.

More important, however, to know how power in any industry or economy is going to be distributed, we need to look at *relation-*

ships, not just structures. And when we do, we discover a surprising paradox.

At the same time that some firms are swelling (or bloating) in size, we also see a powerful countermovement that is breaking big businesses into smaller and smaller units and simultaneously encouraging the spread of small business. Concentration of power is thus only half the story. Instead of a single pattern, we are witnessing two diametrically opposed tendencies coming together in a new synthesis.

Rising out of the explosive new role of knowledge in the economy, a novel structure of power is emerging: the power-mosaic.

FROM MONOLITHS TO MOSAICS

In the 1980s, at the very height of the merger mania, business "discovered" the profit center.

With an enthusiastic rush, companies began to break themselves into a large number of units, each of which was told to operate as though it were an independent small business. By doing so, the largest corporations began shifting from monolithic internal structures to mosaics made of scores, often hundreds of independently accounted units.

While few managers realized it, this restructure was propelled by changes in the knowledge system.

The idea of setting up separate profit centers inside the same firm was hardly new. But it was resisted in the pre-computer age because it implied a significant loss of control by top management.

Even after the mainframe computer arrived on the scene, it was difficult for companies to monitor the operations of large numbers of separately accounted "centers." It wasn't until personal computers began showing up in businesses en masse that the profit-center idea began to win serious attention in executive boardrooms. But one more precondition was needed. The micros had to be networked to mainframes. Once this began to happen in the 1980s, the profit-center concept caught fire.

At first, stand-alone microcomputers shifted power downward.

Armed with these new tools, junior executives and even rank-and-file employees tasted an unaccustomed degree of power and autonomy. But once the micros were connected to central mainframes, they also allowed top management to keep tabs on key parameters in a multiplicity of small units. It became practical to grant these units considerable freedom while still holding them financially accountable.

The information revolution thus began to widen the gulf between finance and operations, making it possible for financial concentration to go hand in hand with a considerable de-concentration of operational power.

At present, most profit centers are still only mirror images of the parent firm, baby bureaucracies hived off from the mother bureaucracy. As we advance toward the flex-firm, however, these will begin to diversify organizationally, and form themselves into mosaics of a new kind.

At S. Appolinare Nuovo in Ravenna a procession of saints is pictured on a mosaic wall. Imagine, however, a kind of kinetic mosaic, a moving mosaic composed not on a flat solid wall, but on many shifting see-through panels, one behind the other, overlapping, interconnected, the colors and shapes continually blending, contrasting, and changing.

Paralleling the new ways that knowledge is organized in data bases, this begins to suggest the future form of the enterprise and of the economy itself. Instead of a power-concentrating hierarchy, dominated by a few central organizations, we move toward a multidimensional mosaic form of power.

MEAT-CLEAVER MANAGEMENT

Indeed, inside the firm the nature of hierarchy itself is changing. For along with the creation of profit centers, the 1980s witnessed a so-called "flattening of the hierarchy," otherwise known as the massacre of the mid-ranks. Like the shift to profit centers, this change, too, was driven by the need to regain control of the knowledge system in business.

As large companies slashed their middle ranks, managers, academics, and economists who once had chorused that "bigger is better" began to sing a different tune. They suddenly discovered the "diseconomies" of scale.

These diseconomies are chiefly a result of the collapse of the old knowledge system—the bureaucratic allocation of information to departmental cubbyholes and to formal channels of communication.

As suggested earlier, much of the work of middle managers in industry consisted of collecting information from their subordinates, synthesizing it, and passing it up the line to their own superiors. As operations accelerated and became more complex, however, overloading the cubbyholes and channels, the entire reporting system began to break down.

Screw-ups and misunderstandings proliferated. Catch-22's multiplied, driving customers crazy. More people end-ran the Kafkaesque system. Transaction costs skyrocketed. Employees ran harder to accomplish less. Motivation plummeted.

Few managers understood what was happening. Show most chief executives a defective part or a broken machine on the factory floor, and they know what to do about it. Show them an obsolete, broken-down knowledge system, and they don't know what you are talking about.

What was clear was that top management couldn't wait for the step-by-step synthesis of knowledge down below, with messages slowly making their way up the chain of command. Moreover, so much knowledge fell outside the formal cubbyholes and moved outside the formal channels, and so much began moving instantaneously from computer to computer, that the masses of middle managers increasingly came to be seen as a bottleneck, rather than as a necessary aid to swift decision.

Facing competitive pressures and takeover threats, the same managers who allowed the knowledge infrastructure to become antiquated in the first place now searched desperately for ways to cut costs.

A frequent first reaction was to cut costs by padlocking plants and throwing rank-and-file workers out on the street, seldom considering that, by doing so, they were tampering with the firm's knowledge system.

Professor Harold Oaklander of Pace University, an expert on work-force reductions, points out that many "cost-cutting" layoffs are actually counterproductive for this reason.

Where union contracts call for senior workers to "bump" junior workers at layoff time, he notes, the result is a cascade of job changes. For every worker actually laid off, three or four others are transferred downward into jobs for which they lack the necessary knowledge. Long-established communication links are ruptured. The result is a fall-off, rather than the expected increase, in post-layoff productivity.

Undaunted, the top officials next zero in on the armies of middle managers they added over the years to handle the information avalanche.

American bosses who chop the payroll without regard for social consequence, or understanding of what that does to the firm's knowledge structure, are commended for "getting rid of fat." (The same is not true for managers in Japan who consider it a failure to lay people off. It is also different in many parts of Europe, where unions are represented on the board and must be persuaded that all other options have been exhausted.)

These meat-cleaver layoffs of middle managers are a belated, mostly unconscious attempt to redesign the firm's information infrastructure and speed up communication.

It turns out that many of mid-management's uncreative tasks can now be done better and faster by computers and telecommunications networks. (IBM, as we saw, estimates that just one part of its internal electronic network—the PROFS sub-net—replaces work that would otherwise have required 40,000 additional middle managers and white-collar workers.)

With new networks being laid in place daily, communications are flowing sideways, diagonally, skipping up and down the levels, ignoring rank. Thus, whatever top management may have *thought* it was doing, one result of the retrenchments has been to change the information infrastructure in the firm—and with it the structure of power.

When we create profit centers, flatten the hierarchy, and shift from mainframes to networked desktop computers, linked both to mainframes and to one another, we make power in the company less monolithic and more "mosaic."

THE MONOPOLISTS INSIDE

The information revolution pushes us still further in the direction of mosaic power by encouraging businesses, as it were, to go out shopping.

Instead of trying to do more work in-house, and thus "vertically integrating" themselves, many large firms are shifting work to outside suppliers, making it possible to scale their size down even further.

The traditional way to coordinate production was the way John D. Rockefeller did it with Standard Oil at the turn of the century—by trying to control and perform every step in the production-distribution cycle. Thus Standard, before it was broken up by the U.S. government in 1911, pumped its own oil, transported it in its own pipelines and tankers, cracked it in its own refineries, and sold it through its own distribution network.

When, to choose another example at random, Ernest T. Weir built National Steel into the most profitable U.S. steel producer in the 1930s, he started with a single ramshackle tin mill. From the start, he knew he wanted a "completely integrated" operation. Eventually, National controlled its own iron ore sources, dug its own coal, and operated its own transportation system. Weir was regarded as one of the "great organizers" of American industry.

In these companies, at each stage, a monolithic hierarchy of executives determined schedules, fixed inventories, fought over internal transfer prices, and made decisions centrally. This was command management—a style perfectly familiar to Soviet planning bureaucrats.

By contrast, today Pan American World Airways contracts out to others all "belly freight" space on its transcontinental flights. GM and Ford announce they will increase their "outsourcing" to 55 percent. An article in the American Management Association's journal, *Management Today,* is headlined "Vertical Integration of Multinationals Becomes Obsolete." Even large government agencies are increasingly farming out operations to private contractors.

The alternative to vertical integration allows competition to coordinate production. In this system, firms must negotiate with one another to win the right to carry out each successive stage of production and distribution. Decisions are decentralized. But a lot of time, energy, and money is spent on setting and monitoring specifications and in gathering and communicating the information needed in negotiation.

Each method had its pros and cons. A benefit of doing things in-house is control over supply. Thus, during a recent worldwide shortage of D-RAM semiconductor chips, IBM emerged unscathed because it made its own.

Today, however, the costs of vertical integration, in terms of money and additional bureaucracy, are both soaring, while the costs of gathering market information and negotiating are plummeting—largely because of electronic networking and the information revolution.

Better yet, the company that buys from many outside suppliers can take advantage of a breakthrough in technology without having to buy the new technology itself, retrain its workers, and make thousands of small changes in procedure, administration, and organization. In effect, it pushes much of the cost of adaptation out the front door. By contrast, doing things in-house produces dangerous rigidity.

Often, doing it inside is also more expensive. Unless forced to compete against outside suppliers, the in-house provider of components or services becomes, in effect, an "internal monopoly" able to foist higher prices on its own in-house customers.

To keep this monopoly going, inside suppliers typically hoard the knowledge they control, making it difficult to compare their performance objectively against outside competitors. This control of technical and accounting information makes it politically difficult to break the internal monopoly.

But here again we find information technology driving change by undermining these knowledge-monopolies.

A recent M.I.T. study in companies like Xerox and General Electric points out that "computerized inventory control systems and other forms of electronic integration allow some of the advantages" of vertical integration to be retained when work is shifted outside.

The plummeting cost per unit of computerized information also improves the position of small outside suppliers, which means that, increasingly, goods or services become the product not of a single monolithic firm but of a mosaic of firms. The mosaic created by profit centers inside the firm is paralleled by the creation of a larger mosaic without.

IN THE BELLY OF THE BEHEMOTH

The same forces help account for today's surprising population explosion of small business in general, which moves us still further from an economy of monoliths.

Small and medium-sized firms have won recognition as the new centers of employment, innovation, and economic dynamism. The small business entrepreneur is the new hero (and often heroine) of the economy.

In France, reports the *Financial Times,* "big business support schemes have been jettisoned for programmes more likely to help the small business." The United Kingdom provides subsidized management consulting services to increase small business organizational efficiency. In the United States, *Inc.* magazine, which measures the activity of the one hundred top small businesses, reports an average five-year growth rate that "approaches the incomprehensible—high enough to astonish (us) and to stagger (the companies that experience it)."

In place of an economy dominated by a handful of giant monoliths, therefore, we are creating a super-symbolic economy made up of small operating units, some of which may, for accounting and financial reasons, be encapsuled inside large businesses. An economy built of boutiques, rather than behemoths (though some of the boutiques remain inside the belly of a behemoth).

This many-shaped, multi-mosaic economy requires entirely new forms of coordination, which explains the ceaseless split-up and formation of so-called strategic alliances and other new arrangements.

Kenichi Ohmae, brilliant head of the McKinsey office in Tokyo, has called attention to the growth of triangular joint ventures involving companies or parts of companies in all three—Japan, the United States, and Europe. Such "trilateral consortia," he writes, "are being formed in nearly every area of leading edge industry including biotechnology, computers, robots, semiconductors, jet engines, nuclear power, carbon fibers, and other new materials." These are manufacturing mosaics, and they are redrawing business boundaries in ways that will redefine national boundaries as well.

In Italy, Bruno Lamborghini, vice-president for corporate economic research, Olivetti, speaks of the "networking of companies" based on "alliances, partnerships, agreements, research and technical cooperation." Olivetti alone has entered into fifty such arrangements.

Competitive position, says Lamborghini, "will no longer depend solely on . . . internal resources," but on the pattern of relationships with outside units. Like data bases, success is increasingly "relational."

And, significantly, the new relations of production are not fixed, rigid, and prespecified—like the position of names and addresses in an old-fashioned data base. They are fluid and free-form as in hyper-media. The new mosaic organization of companies and the economy thus begins to reflect (and promote) changes in the organization of knowledge itself.

To understand power in the business world of tomorrow, therefore, forget fantasies of near-total concentration, a world dominated by a few mega-firms. Think, instead, about power-mosaics.

RELATIONAL WEALTH

In the bustling city of Atlanta, Georgia, the single largest enterprise employs some 37,000 workers. This mainstay of the economy has a payroll of over $1.5 billion a year. Its key facilities occupy 2.2 million square feet of space.

This massive service enterprise is not, however, a company or corporation. It is the Atlanta airport.

It is a giant mosaic consisting of scores of separate organizations —everything from airlines, caterers, cargo handlers, and car rental firms to government agencies like the Federal Aviation Administration, the Post Office, and the Customs Service. Employees belong to many different unions, from the Air Line Pilots Association to the Machinists and Teamsters.

That the Atlanta airport creates wealth is not doubted by hotelkeepers, restaurants, real estate interests, auto dealers, and others in the city, not to mention the 56,000 other employees in Atlanta whose jobs are indirectly generated by the airport operations.

Little of this wealth results from the effort of any individual firm or agency. The wealth flowing from this meta-mosaic is precisely a function of *relationships*—the interdependence and coordination of all of them. Like advanced computerized data bases, the Atlanta airport is "relational."

Though relationships have always been important in the creation of wealth—being implied in the very concept of the division of labor—they become far more important as the number and diversity of "players" in the mosaic system increase.

As this number rises arithmetically, relationships increase combinatorially. Moreover, these relationships can no longer be based on simple command, in which one participant imposes behavior on the others. Because of interdependence, the players increasingly rely on consensus, explicit or otherwise, which takes account of the interests of many.

As knowledge itself is organized relationally or in hyper-media form—meaning that it can be constantly reconfigured—organization, too, must become hyper-flexible. This is why an economy of small, interacting firms forming themselves into temporary mosaics is more adaptive and ultimately more productive than one built around a few rigid monoliths.

POWER IN MOSAICS

A generation ago, mosaics had a different structure. Typically, they looked like pyramids or wheel-and-spoke arrangements. A big company was surrounded by a ring of suppliers and distributors. The giant dominated the other firms in its grouping, dealers and suppliers alike serving essentially as its satellites. Customers and labor unions were also weak in comparison with the jumbo company.

It goes without saying that large firms today still carry tremendous clout. But things are rapidly changing.

First, suppliers today are no longer just selling goods or services. They are also supplying critical information and, conversely, sucking information out of the buyer's data bases. They are, as the buzzword has it, "partnering" with their clients.

At Apple Computer, says CEO John Sculley, "We're able to . . . rely on an independent network of third-party business partners—independent software developers, makers of peripheral equipment, dealers and retailers. . . . Some critics wrongly assert that such arrangements have led to the emergence of the 'hollow corporation,' a vulnerable shell whose survival is dependent on outside companies."

Sculley challenges this view, pointing out that this mosaic arrangement permits Apple itself to be lean, fleet, and adaptive, and that especially in times of crisis it was the "partners" who helped Apple pull through. In fact, he contends, "for every dollar of revenue in the catalyst company, the external infrastructure may generate three to four additional dollars of sales. . . . Of far greater import is the enhanced flexibility to turn change and chaos into opportunity."

In the past, companies often mouthed the rhetoric of partnership. Today they are finding themselves thrust into it.

By tracing information patterns in a power-mosaic, we gain a clue to where real power and productivity lie. For example, communication flows might be densest between a parts supplier and a manufacturer (or more accurately between a specific unit of each). The shipping operation of one and the stock-intake operation of the other form, in effect, a single organic unit—a key relationship. The fact that for accounting purposes, or for financial reasons, one is part of Company A and the other a part of Company B is increasingly divorced from the productive reality. In fact, the people in each of these departments may have more common interest in and loyalty to this relationship than to their own companies.

At Matsushita in Japan the partnering process has been formalized into something called "high productivity through investment of total wisdom."

Matsushita meets with its subcontractors at an early stage of a product's design and asks them to help improve it, in order to shorten time lags and get the product to market faster.

Kozaburo Sikata, chairman of Kyoei-kai, the association of Matsushita subcontractors, expects this system to become standard practice. Sharing previously unshared information at the start is not something Matsushita does out of the goodness of its heart, but because competition demands it. And one can be sure that, as big as Matsushita is, its executives listen carefully when its 324 organized suppliers speak.

Beyond this, suppliers these days aren't just linked electronically to the big company, like spokes to a wheel-hub; they are, and increasingly will be, linked to one another as well, which means they are in a far stronger position to form coalitions when necessary to apply pressure on the big firm.

There is still another reason why the emerging mosaics no longer necessarily consist of dominators and dominated. With the breakup of the monolithic corporation into profit centers, many supplier or customer firms find themselves dealing not with the full force and power of a giant, but with a profit center smaller and often weaker than themselves. The size of the parent firm, once a major factor, is increasingly irrelevant.

It is, therefore, no longer sensible, as power shifts from monoliths to mosaics, to take for granted that giant firms dominate the mosaics of which they are a part.

Indeed, the large firm is also pressured from the other side, by customers who are increasingly organized into "users councils." Ostensibly these groups are in business to exchange technical data. In reality, they are a new form of consumer lobby.

Proliferating rapidly and arming themselves with high-powered legal, technical, and other expertise, users' organizations represent countervailing power, and can often compel their supplier firms, regardless of size, to meet their demands.

Such groups are especially active in the computer field, where, for example, users of VAX and Lotus software are organized. IBM customers are organized into many groups, joined in a single international council that represents some 10,000 companies, including some of the biggest in the world. IBM now boasts that it listens to its users. It better.

Members of these groups may at one and the same time be customers, competitors, and joint venturers. Business life is becoming confusingly poly-relational.

The idea, therefore, that a few monolithic giants will command the economy of the future is simple-minded.

BEYOND THE CORPORATION

Such largely unnoticed changes will also force us to rethink the very functions of the firm. If much of the value added derives from *relationships* in the mosaic system, then the value a firm produces and its own value comes, in part, from its continually changing *position* in the super-symbolic economy.

Accountants and managers who attempt to quantify added value and assign it to specific subsidiaries or profit centers are compelled to make arbitrary, often quite subjective judgments, since conventional accounting typically ignores the value-generating importance of "organizational capital" and all these complex, ever-changing relationships. Accounting categories like "good will" only crudely and inadequately reflect the mounting importance of such assets.

Management theorists are belatedly beginning to speak of "organizational capital." But there is also what might be called "positional capital"—the strategic location of the firm in the overall web-work of mosaics and meta-mosaics.

In any given industry, a crucial position in one of these wealth-producing systems is money in the bank—and power in the pocket. To be frozen out or forced to the periphery can be disastrous.

All this suggests that the big corporation or company is no longer necessarily the central institution for the production of material wealth in the capitalist world and the advanced economies generally.

What we are seeing is the divorce of the big corporation from the key material processes of wealth creation. These are performed by small and medium-sized business or by the subcorporations called profit centers. With so much of the hands-on work done in these units, the functions of top management in the large corporation have less and less to do with ensuring production and more to do with setting very general strategic guidelines; organizing and accounting for capital; litigating and lobbying; and substituting information for all the other factors of production.

This delegation or contracting-out of many of the functions of the large corporation—once the central production institution in the economy—has a historical precedent.

The industrial revolution stripped away many of the functions from the traditional family—that other key institution of society. Education went to the schools, care of the elderly went to the state, work was transferred to the factory, and so forth. Today, since many of its former functions can be carried out by small units armed with high-powered information technology, the large business firm is being similarly stripped of some of its traditional reasons for being.

The family did not disappear after the industrial revolution. But it became smaller, took on more limited responsibility, and lost much of its power vis-à-vis other institutions in the society.

The same is happening to the large corporation as we transit out of the smokestack era dominated by Brobdingnagian business.

In short, even as big corporations expand, the significance of the corporation, as an institution, contracts.

It is still too early for any of us fully to understand the power-mosaics that are now rapidly taking form and the long-term destiny of the corporation. But one thing is certain: The notion that a tiny handful of giant companies will dominate tomorrow's economy is a comic-book caricature of reality.

CODA:

THE NEW SYSTEM
FOR WEALTH CREATION

Not long ago Wendy's International, whose 3,700 fast-food restaurants stretch from the United States and Japan to Greece and Guam, introduced an "Express Pak" order for drive-in customers. It consists of a hamburger, French fries, and a Coke. But the customer has to utter only the words *Express Pak* instead of specifying each item separately. The idea was to accelerate service. In the words of one Wendy's spokesperson, "We may be talking three seconds. But the cumulative effect can be significant."

This seemingly trivial business innovation tells us a lot about the future of power. For the speed with which we exchange information—even seemingly insignificant information—is related to the rise of a completely new system for wealth creation. And that lies behind the most important power shifts in our time.

THE NEW ECONOMIC METABOLISM

In itself, of course, how quickly Wendy's sells hamburgers is not exactly a matter of earth-shaking significance. But one of the most important things to know about any system, and particularly any economic system, is its "clock-time," the speed with which it operates.

Every system—from the human body's circulatory system to the society's wealth creation system—can operate only at certain speeds. Too slow and it breaks down; too fast and it flies apart. All

233

systems consist of subsystems, which likewise function only within a certain speed range. The "pace" of the whole system can be thought of as the average of the rates of change in its various parts.

Each national economy and each system of wealth creation operates at its own characteristic pace. Each has, as it were, a unique metabolic rate.

We can measure the speed of a wealth-making system in many ways: in terms of machine processes, business transactions, communication flows, the speed with which laboratory knowledge is translated into commercial products, or the length of time needed to make certain decisions, lead times for delivery, and so on.

When we compare the overall pace of First Wave or agrarian systems of wealth creation with that of Second Wave or industrial systems, it becomes clear that smokestack economies run faster than traditional agricultural economies. Wherever the industrial revolution passed, it shifted economic processes into a higher gear.

By the same token, the new system of wealth creation described in these pages operates at speeds unimaginable even a generation or two ago. Today's economic metabolism would have broken the system in an earlier day. A new "heterojunction" microchip that switches on and off in two trillionths of a second symbolizes the new pace.

In *Future Shock*, first published in 1970, we argued that the acceleration of change would transform society, and showed what happens to systems when speeds exceed their adaptive capabilities. We demonstrated that acceleration itself has effects independent of the nature of the change involved. Hidden within this finding is an economic insight that goes beyond the old "time is money" cliché. The acceleration effect, indeed, implies a powerful new law of economics.

This law can be stated simply: When the pace of economic activity speeds up, each unit of time comes to be worth *more* money.

This powerful law, as we shall see, holds profound implications not just for individual businesses, but for whole economies and for global relations *among* economies. It has special meaning for the relations between the world's rich and poor.

A HAILSTORM OF PLEAS

Returning from broad economic theory to the practicalities of everyday life makes it clear that Wendy's managers, in speeding up their business, are reacting to customers who demand instant responses. They want fast service, and they want products that save time in their lives. For in the emerging culture, time itself becomes a valuable product.

Beyond this, in today's increasingly competitive world economy, the ability to bring products to market fast is essential. The blistering speed with which fax machines or VCRs or other consumer electronic items sweep the market astonishes makers and customers alike.

In small numbers, facsimile machines existed for decades. As long ago as 1961, Xerox research laboratories demonstrated what was called an LDX machine—for long-distance xerography—which did much of what today's faxes do.

Several things blocked its commercialization. Thus, postal systems still functioned with reasonable efficiency, while telephone systems were still comparatively backward and long-distance services expensive.

Suddenly, in the late 1980s, several things came together. Fax machines could be produced at low cost. Telecommunications technologies vastly improved. AT&T was broken up, helping to cut the relative cost of long-distance services in the United States. Meanwhile, postal services decayed (slowing transaction times at a moment when the economy was accelerating). In addition, the acceleration effect raised the economic value of each second potentially saved by a fax machine. Together these converging factors opened a market that then expanded with explosive speed.

In the spring of 1988, as though overnight, Americans received a hailstorm of phone calls from friends and business associates pleading with them to install a fax. Within a few months, millions of fax machines were buzzing and bleeping all over America.

Under today's competitive conditions, the rate of product innovation is so swift that almost before one product is launched the next generation of better ones appears. Having recently bought twenty megabytes of hard disc storage for a personal computer, should one now buy forty, seventy—or just twenty more, in anticipation of the fact that CD-ROM storage will soon be available? (By the time these figures reach print, they may look primitive.)

In terminology reminiscent of space flight or nuclear war, marketers now speak of the "launch window"—the all-too-brief interval after which a new product is likely to fail because of competition from more advanced models.

These accelerative pressures lead to new production methods. Thus one way to move faster is to do simultaneously what you used to do sequentially. Hence the recent appearance of the term *simultaneous engineering*.

In the past a new product was designed first, manufacturing methods worked out later. Today, says David W. Clark, vice-president of engineering for the Jervis B. Webb Company, a maker of materials-handling equipment, "You're defining and designing the manufacturing process concurrently with designing the end product."

"S.E.," as it is known, requires unprecedented precision and coordination. Says Jerry Robertson of Automation Technology Products: "The concept of simultaneous engineering . . . has been around for over fifteen years." Only recently, however, has "progress in computing power and data base capability" begun to make it feasible.

Another accelerative step is to eliminate or redesign parts—to make products with fewer components and to modularize them. This requires more exquisite tolerances and higher levels of information and knowledge. IBM redesigned one component of its 4720 printer and not only cut its cost from $5.95 per unit to $1.81 but also reduced manufacture time from three minutes to seconds. As at Wendy's, seconds count.

Still another accelerative step is the introduction of "just-in-time" delivery of components, pioneered by the Japanese. Instead of suppliers' making long runs of a part and delivering them in big batches at infrequent intervals, the system requires the frequent delivery of small numbers of each part, precisely when they are required for assembly. The effect of this innovation is to speed production and slash the capital tied up in inventory. Britain's Rolls-Royce, for example, reports that its just-in-time system has cut lead times and inventory by 75 percent.

Speed of response to customer demand has become a critical

factor differentiating one company's product or service from that of another. Travel agents, banks, financial services, fast-food franchisees, all vie with one another to provide instant information and gratification.

In the past, employers sought to accelerate production through the speedup of the workers. One of the great humanizing contributions of the old trade union movement was its battle to limit the speedup. In thousands of backward factories and offices, this battle has not yet been won.

Under the new system of wealth creation, however, hands-on labor costs plummet as a percentage of overall cost, and speed is gained not by sweating the work force but through intelligent reorganization and sophisticated electronic information exchange. Knowledge substitutes for sweat as the entire system picks up speed.

In June 1986, Motorola, Inc., formed a twenty-four-member team—code-named Team Bandit—and gave it a seemingly impossible assignment. Its goal was to design a new radio-pager and a world-class computer-integrated manufacturing facility for producing it. The new plant would have to meet super-high quality requirements, defined as a 99.9997 percent probability that each unit of output would be perfect.

The time limit: eighteen months.

Today at Boynton Beach, Florida, the plant turns out customized radio pagers in production runs as small as one of a kind. Twenty-seven robots do the physical work. Of forty employees, only one actually touches the product. The Team Bandit operation succeeded—with seventeen days to spare.

Even the automotive industry, a slow-paced dinosaur by comparison with the camera industry or electronics, is struggling to shorten time frames.

The success of Japan's car industry is partly a reflection of the fact that Japanese manufacturers can design and introduce an entirely new model in half the time it takes European and American car makers.

At Toyota, which Joseph L. Bower and Thomas M. Hout in the *Harvard Business Review* characterize as a "fast-cycle company," simultaneous engineering, advanced information systems, self-organizing teams, and the sharing of information with suppliers at an early stage, result, according to Hout and Bower, in "an ever-faster development cycle . . . frequent new product introductions, and a constant flow of major and minor innovations on existing models."

Similarly, they cite the case of a bank that cut the time needed to make a decision on a loan from several days to thirty minutes, by presenting the necessary information to a group of loan specialists simultaneously, rather than routing it in sequence from one specialist to the next.

So powerful is the "accelerative effect," according to consultant Howard M. Anderson, founder of the Yankee Group, that companies must now have "one overriding goal: speed. Speed at all costs . . . hyper-speed."

What is emerging is a radical new economic system running at far faster speeds than any in history.

TOMORROW'S WEALTH

In earlier pages we sketched elements of this new wealth-creation system. It is now possible to put all the pieces together into a single coherent frame. Doing so makes clear how revolutionary this new way of making wealth really is—and how starkly different it is from the ways wealth was produced in the past.

1. The new accelerated system for wealth creation is increasingly dependent on the exchange of data, information, and knowledge. It is "super-symbolic." No knowledge exchanged, no new wealth created.

2. The new system goes beyond mass production to flexible, customized, or "de-massified" production. Because of the new information technologies, it is able to turn out short runs of highly varied, even customized products at costs approaching those of mass production.

3. Conventional factors of production—land, labor, raw materials, and capital—become less important as symbolic knowledge is substituted for them.

4. Instead of metal or paper money, electronic information becomes the true medium of exchange. Capital becomes extremely

fluid, so that huge pools of it can be assembled and dispersed overnight. Despite today's huge concentrations, the number of sources of capital multiply.

5. Goods and services are modularized and configured into systems, which require a multiplication and constant revision of standards. This leads to wars for control of the information on which standards are based.

6. Slow-moving bureaucracies are replaced by small (de-massified) work units, temporary or "ad-hocratic" teams, increasingly complex business alliances and consortia. Hierarchy is flattened or eliminated to speed decision-making. The bureaucratic organization of knowledge is replaced by free-flow information systems.

7. The number and variety of organizational units multiply. The more such units, the more transactions among them, and the more information must be generated and communicated.

8. Workers become less and less interchangeable. Industrial workers owned few of the tools of production. Today the most powerful wealth-amplifying tools are the symbols inside workers' heads. Workers, therefore, own a critical, often irreplaceable, share of the "means of production."

9. The new hero is no longer a blue-collar worker, a financier, or a manager, but the innovator (whether inside or outside a large organization) who combines imaginative knowledge with action.

10. Wealth creation is increasingly recognized to be a circular process, with wastes recycled into inputs for the next cycle of production. This method presupposes computerized monitoring and ever-deeper levels of scientific and environmental knowledge.

11. Producer and consumer, divorced by the industrial revolution, are reunited in the cycle of wealth creation, with the customer contributing not just money but market and design information vital for the production process. Buyer and supplier share data, information, and knowledge. Someday, customers may also push buttons that activate remote production processes. Consumer and producer fuse into a "prosumer."

12. The new wealth creation system is both local and global. Powerful microtechnologies make it possible to do locally what previously could be done economically only on a national scale.

Simultaneously, many functions spill over national boundaries, integrating activities in many nations into a single productive effort.

These twelve elements of the accelerative economy are inter-related, and mutually reinforce the role of data, information, and knowledge throughout the economy. They define the revolution-ary new system of high-tech wealth creation. As pieces of this system come together, they undermine power structures designed to support the wealth-making system of the industrial age.

The new system of wealth creation as summarized here helps explain the tremendous upheavals now spreading across the planet—premonitory shudders that herald a collision of wealth creation systems on a scale never before seen.

PART FIVE

POWERSHIFT POLITICS

20

THE DECISIVE DECADES

In Bluefield, West Virginia, on November 9, 1989, a schoolteacher wept. All across the world, millions shared her moment of joy. Glued to their television screens, they saw the Berlin Wall brought down. For an entire generation, East Germans had been imprisoned, maimed, or shot for trying to get past that twenty-eight-mile wall. Now they were pouring through it into West Germany, eyes gleaming, faces registering everything from exhilaration to culture shock. Soon the hammers went to work. And today remnants of the wall that once bisected Berlin, and indeed all of Germany, are souvenirs of stone and cement gathering dust on countless mantelpieces.

Because it concretized, one might say, the end of Soviet-imposed totalitarianism throughout Central and Eastern Europe, the downfall of the wall drew an elated response in the West. Shortsighted intellectuals and politicians joined in an ode to joy that would have done Beethoven proud. With Marxism on the ropes, they chorused, the future of democracy was now assured. We had reached the very end of ideology itself.

Today Eastern Europe seethes with instability. Poland faces total economic breakdown. Romanian crowds clash in the streets. And Yugoslavia's president warns that "extremist right parties" and "revanchist forces" could ignite "civil war and the possibility of foreign armed intevention." Anti-Semitism and ancient ethnic hatreds run rampant. Post-war borders are called into question. The collapse of Soviet power over Eastern Europe, far from assuring democracy, has opened a combustive vacuum into which fools and firebrands seem ready to rush. Western Europe's drive toward integration has been thrown into confusion.

Looming over this vast continental spectacle are threats of

a Soviet split-up that could easily trigger a generation of wars, raising anew nuclear dangers that were supposed to have been relaxed.

Ironically, even as millions who have never had it grope for freedom, the established democracies in North America, Western Europe, and Japan themselves face an expected internal crisis. Democracy is entering its decisive decades. For we are at the end of the age of mass democracy—and that is the only kind the industrial world has ever known.

DYNASTIES AND DEMOCRACIES

In any system, democratic or not, there needs to be some congruence between the way a people make wealth and the way they govern themselves. If the political and economic systems are wildly dissimilar, one will eventually destroy the other.

Only twice before in history have we humans invented a wholly novel way of creating wealth. Each time we invented new forms of government to go with it.

The spread of agriculture wiped out tribal groupings, hunting bands, and other social and political arrangements, replacing them with city-states, dynastic kingdoms, and feudal empires. The industrial revolution, in turn, wiped out many of these. With mass production, mass consumption, and mass media there arose in many countries a counterpart system: "mass democracy."

Mass democracy, however, met bitter resistance. The old forces of feudal agrarianism—the landed gentry, the hierarchical church, and their intellectual and cultural apologists—resisted, co-opted, and battled the rising industrialism and the mass democracy it often brought with it.

Indeed, in all smokestack societies the central political struggle has not been, as many imagine, between left and right. It has been between admirers of First Wave agrarianism and "traditionalism" on the one side and the forces of Second Wave industrialism or "modernism" on the other.

Such power struggles are frequently fought under other banners—nationalism, for example, or religion, or civil rights. They run through family life, gender relations, schools, the professions, the arts, as well as politics. Today that historic conflict, still raging, is being overshadowed by a new one—the struggle of a Third Wave, postmodern civilization against both modernism and traditionalism.

And if it is true that a new knowledge-based economy is superseding smokestack production, then we should expect a historic struggle to remake our political institutions, bringing them into congruence with the revolutionary post-mass-production economy.

All the industrial societies already face convergent crises—crises in all their most basic systems: urban systems, health systems, welfare systems, transport systems, ecological systems. Smokestack politicians continue to respond to these crises one at a time, with variations of the old approaches. But they may be insoluble given existing institutions, designed for the mass society.

In addition, the rising economy hurls totally new problems and crises at us that shatter the conventional assumptions and alliances of the mass democratic era.

SHIFTING LEVELS

The age of mass democracy was also the age of immense concentrations of power at the level of the nation. This concentration reflected the rise of mass-production technology and national markets. Today's short-run technologies change things.

Take a loaf of bread.

Baked goods originally came from local bakeries. But with industrialization, mom-and-pop bakeries were overwhelmed by supermarkets that bought baked goods from giant national companies like Nabisco in the United States. Today, surprisingly, many U.S. supermarkets, in addition to selling the national brands, have begun to bake on their own premises. We are coming full circle—but on the basis of more sophisticated technology.

Photos, once sent to Rochester, New York, to be centrally processed by Kodak, can now be developed and printed on every street corner. Commercial printing, which once required heavy investment and complex machinery, can now be done using small, advanced copying equipment in shops in every neighborhood. New technologies are thus making local production competitive again.

Simultaneously, however, the advanced economy transfers other forms of production to the global level. Cars, computers, and many other products are now no longer made in a single country, but require components and assembly in many nations. These twin changes, one driving production down and the other up, have direct political parallels.

Together they explain why we see pressures for political decentralization in all the high-tech nations, from Japan and the United States, across Europe—along with simultaneous attempts to shift power upward to supra-national agencies.

The most significant of the latter is the European Community's drive to re-centralize power at a higher level by creating a single integrated market, along with a single currency and a single central bank.

But even as the EC steamroller attempts to flatten differences and concentrate political and economic decision-making, various regions are taking advantage of its attack on national power from above to launch a parallel attack from below. "The single European market," says Jean Chemain, head of the economic development agency for the area around Lyon in France, "offers us a great opportunity to break the centralization of Paris." In fact, the entire Rhône-Alpes region, of which Lyon is a part, is hooking up with regions outside France—Catalonia, Lombardy, and Baden-Württemberg—in pursuit of mutual interests.

As the super-symbolic economy spreads, it will create constituencies for radical shifts of power among local, regional, national, and global levels. The "politics of levels" can be expected to split voters into four distinct groupings: "globalists," "nationalists," "regionalists," and "localists." Each will defend its perceived identity (and its economic interests) with ferocity. Each will seek allies.

Each group will attract different financial and industrial supporters, depending on self-interest, but each will also attract talented artists, writers, and intellectuals who will manufacture appropriate ideological rationales for them.

What's more—contrary to conventional opinion—regions and localities, instead of becoming more uniform, are destined to grow more diverse. "You make a serious error if you look at the U.S. as an entity. Different parts of the United States are as different as night and day," says James Crupi, president of the Dallas-based International Leadership Center.

One might not go as far as Crupi, who suggests "The U.S. is

on its way to becoming a nation of city-states." But a close look at statistics for the 1980s already shows widening differences between the two coasts, the Midwest, and the oil patch, and between the big urban centers and the suburbs. Whether measured in housing starts, rates of growth, employment levels, investment, or social conditions, these differences are likely to widen further, rather than narrow, under the impact of a new economy that runs counter to the homogenization of the smokestack era.

As regions and localities take on their own cultural, technological, and political character, it will be harder for governments to manage economies with the traditional tools of central bank regulation, taxation, and financial controls. Raising or lowering interest rates or setting a new tax rate will produce radically different consequences in different parts of the same country.

And as these disparities widen, they may well trigger an explosion of extremist movements demanding regional or local autonomy or actual secession. The bombs are present, waiting to be detonated in all the advanced economies.

In every nation some regions already regard themselves as economically cheated by the central authorities. Promises to reduce regional differences have delivered little, as any resident of Glasgow will tell you. (The renewal of secessionist sentiment in Scotland, according to press reports, has worried the Queen enough for her to express private fears about the breakup of the United Kingdom.) Canada hangs together by a thread.

Apart from economic inequalities, moreover, there are also long-festering linguistic and ethnic cells of secession in places like South Tyrol, Brittany, Alsace, Flanders, Catalonia. A united Western Europe will have to grant increasing regional and local autonomy—or smash all these movements with a steel fist.

In Central Europe, so long as the Hapsburgs ruled, in the 19th and early 20th centuries, hostilities among their German, Italian, Polish, Magyar, Slovak, and Austrian subjects were suppressed (barely) by the central power. Once Hapsburg power disintegrated after World War I, these groups hurled themselves at one another's throats with a vengeance. The collapse of Soviet power in Central Europe has raised age-old ghosts. Already we see a sharp intensification of the conflict over the Hungarian minority in Romania and the Turks in Bulgaria.

Farther south, Yugoslavia could break apart as its Serbs, Albanians, Croats, and other nationalities war with one another.

And all this ignores the gigantic centrifugal forces that threaten to splinter the Soviet Union itself.

The smokestack era was the great age of nation-building, which led to central control over small communities, city-states, regions, and provinces. It was this consolidation that made national capitals the centers of enormous state power. The decline of the smokestack era will set loose bone-deep resentments, vast and violent emotional tides, as the locus of power is transferred. In many parts of the world it will multiply extremist groups for whom democracy is a bothersome obstacle, to be destroyed if it stands in the way of their fanatic passions.

EARTH POLITICS

During the period of mass democracy, people, parties, and policies were typically categorized as either left-wing or right-wing. Issues were usually "domestic" or "foreign." They fit into a neat framework.

The new system of wealth creation makes these political tags, and the coalitions that went with them, obsolete. Ecological catastrophes are neither right-wing nor left-wing, and some are both domestic *and* international.

Many of our most serious environmental problems—from air pollution to toxic waste—are by-products of the old, industrial methods of creating wealth. By contrast, the new system, with its substitution of knowledge for material resources, its dispersal, rather than concentration, of production, its increasing energy efficiency, and its potential for dramatic advances in recycling technologies, holds out the hope of combining ecological sanity with economic advance.

It is unlikely, however, that the next decade or two will pass without new Chernobyls, Bhopals, and Alaska oil spills, legacies of the smokestack era. These, in turn, will lead to bitter conflicts over new technologies and their possible consequences. Social groups inside each country (and, indeed, whole countries) will demand "ecological indemnification" from one another and fight over the allocation of clean-up costs. Others will demand "ecological blackmail" or "ransom" to abstain from actions that could send fallout, acid rain, weather changes, toxic wastes, or other dangerous products across their neighbors' borders.

Will the advanced economies wind up making "ecological welfare payments" to the Brazils and Indias of the world to deter them from destroying rain forests, jungles, or other environmental resources? What about natural disasters in a newly networked world economy? An earthquake in Tokyo can now send Wall Street reeling into chaos. Should Wall Street contribute to Tokyo's earthquake-preparedness programs? Are such issues left-wing or right-wing? Domestic or foreign?

The attempt to deal politically with such problems will not only fragment old alliances, but breed more zealots—world savers for whom environmental requirements (as they define them) supersede the niceties of democracy.

AN EXPLOSION OF ETHNICS

As the super-symbolic economy develops, it is accompanied by population shifts and migrations. Immigration politics—fiercely controversial at any time—will be fought against a background marked by atavistic nationalism and ethnicism, not merely in remote places like Armenia and Azerbaijan, or in Albania and Serbia, but in New York and Nagoya, Liverpool and Lyon.

In industrial mass societies, racism typically took the form of a majority persecuting a minority. This form of social pathology is still a threat to democracy. White street toughs, skinheads, admirers of the Nazis, says Morris Dees of the Southern Poverty Law Center, "are on their way to becoming . . . domestic terrorists."

But the new system for creating wealth brings with it economic de-massification and much higher levels of social diversity. Thus, in addition to traditional conflict between majority and minorities, democratic governments must now cope with open warfare *between* rival minority groups, as happened in Miami, for example, between Cuban and Haitian immigrants, and elsewhere in the United States between African-Americans and Hispanics. In Los Angeles, Mexican-Americans fight for jobs held by Cuban-Americans. In affluent Great Neck, on Long Island, near New York City, tensions rise between American-born Jews and Iranian

Jewish immigrants who refuse to surrender their old life-ways. African-American rap groups sell anti-Semitic records. Korean shopkeepers and African-Americans collide in the inner cities.

Under the impact of the new production system, resistance to the "melting pot" is rising everywhere. Instead, racial, ethnic, and religious groups demand the right to be—and to remain—proudly different. Assimilation was the ideal of industrial society, corresponding to its need for a homogeneous work force. Diversity is the new ideal, corresponding to the heterogeneity of the new system of wealth creation.

Governments may, in an atmosphere of hostility, have to accommodate certain groups who insist on preserving their cultural identity—everyone from Turks in Germany, or Koreans, Filipinos, and South Sea Islanders in Japan, to North Africans in France. At the same time, governments will also have to mediate among them.

This will become progressively harder to do, because the ideal of homogeneity (in Japan, for example) or of the "melting pot" (in the United States) is being replaced by that of the "salad bowl"—a dish in which diverse ingredients keep their identity.

Los Angeles with its Koreatown, its Vietnamese suburbs, its heavy Chicano population, its roughly seventy-five ethnically oriented publications, not to mention its Jews, African-Americans, Japanese, Chinese, and its large Iranian population, provides an example of the new diversity. But the salad-bowl ideal means that governments will need new legal and social tools they now lack, if they are to referee increasingly complex, potentially violent disputes. The potential for antidemocratic extremism and violence rises even as regions, nations, and supra-national forces battle for power.

MOSAIC DEMOCRACY

Mass democracy implies the existence of "masses." It is based on mass movements, mass political parties, and mass media. But what happens when the mass society begins to de-massify—when movements, parties, and media all splinter? As we move to an economy based on noninterchangeable labor, in what sense can we continue to speak of the "masses"?

If technology permits the customization of products, if markets are being broken into niches, if the media multiply and serve continually narrowing audiences, if even family structure and culture are becoming increasingly heterogeneous, why should politics still presume the existence of homogeneous masses?

All these changes—whether rising localism, resistance to globalization, ecological activism, or heightened ethnic and racial consciousness—reflect the increased social diversity of advanced economies. They point to the end of the mass society.

But with de-massification, people's needs, and therefore their political demands, diversify. Just as market researchers in business are finding more and more differentiated segments and "micromarkets" for products, reflecting the rising variety of life styles, so politicians are bombarded by more and more diverse demands from their constituencies.

While mass movements may fill Tiananmen Square in Beijing or Wenceslas Square in Prague, in the high-technology nations mass movements, while still a factor, increasingly tend to fragment. Mass consensus (on all but a handful of high-priority issues) becomes harder to find.

The initial result, therefore, of the breakup of the mass society is a tremendous jump in the sheer complexity of politics. In terms of winning elections, the great leaders of the industrial era faced a comparatively simple task. In 1932, Franklin D. Roosevelt could assemble a coalition of half a dozen groups—urban workers, poor farmers, the foreign-born, the intellectuals. With it, his Democratic Party was able to command power in Washington for a third of a century.

Today an American presidential candidate must piece together a coalition composed not of four or six major blocs, but of hundreds of groupings, each with its own agenda, each changing constantly, many surviving only a matter of months or weeks. (This, not just the cost of television advertising, helps explain the rising cost of American elections.)

What is emerging, as we'll see, is no longer a mass democracy but a highly charged, fast-moving "mosaic democracy" that corresponds to the rise of mosaics in the economy, and operates according to its own rules. These will force us to redefine even the most fundamental of democratic assumptions.

Mass democracies are designed to respond mainly to mass input—mass movements, mass political parties, mass media. They do not yet know how to cope with mosaics. This leaves them doubly vulnerable to attack by what we might call "pivotal minorities."

PIVOTAL MINORITIES

Scientists exploring turbulence, instability, and chaos in nature and society know that the same system—whether it is a chemical system or a country—behaves differently depending on whether it is in an equilibrial or a non-equilibrial condition. Push any system—a digestive system, a computer system, an urban traffic system, or a political system—too far, and it violates its traditional rules and acts bizarrely.

When the environment becomes too turbulent, systems become non-linear, and this creates vast opportunities for tiny groups. We are, in fact, rapidly moving into a new stage of politics that might be called "opportunity time" for the pivotal minorities.

As politics becomes increasingly de-massified, leaders who once dealt with a few big, more or less predictable political constituencies are seeing these splinter into countless small, temporary, single-issue grouplets, continually forming, breaking, and re-forming alliances—all at high speeds.

Any one of these, finding itself at a strategic political intersection at just the right moment, can leverage its clout. In 1919 a railroad machinist named Anton Drexler headed a tiny political group in Munich—a group so small it was no more than a fringe of the fringe. At its first public meeting it managed to attract only 111 listeners. The speaker at that meeting held the floor for thirty minutes. His name was Adolf Hitler.

There are many explanations for Hitler's rise, but one can be found in the new science of non-equilibrial systems. This new science teaches us that in moments of extreme instability of the kind found in Germany at the time, three things happen. Sheer chance plays an enlarged role. Pressures from the outside world carry more weight. And positive feedback creates gigantic snowball effects.

An example of the snowball effect as it operates in today's world is provided by the media. By focusing a hand-held camera, a reporter can instantly project even the tiniest group of political cranks or terrorists onto the world's consciousness, and give it far more importance than it could garner on its own. Once this happens, the group becomes "news," and other media cover its activities, which, in turn, makes it still bigger news. A "positive feedback loop" is set up.

Snowballing can also come about in other ways. In a globally linked economy, a foreign political or commercial interest can pump money and resources into a tiny group, which suddenly explodes in size and, in turn, attracts more resources.

Chance, outside help, and the snowballing process help explain why—throughout the history of mass democracy—extremist cults, revolutionary cabals, juntas, and conspiracies have flourished in times of seething turmoil, and why a once-insignificant group can suddenly become "pivotal." The difference for mosaic democracies is that, in the past, a majority could sometimes restrain or overwhelm dangerous extremists. But what if there is no coherent majority?

Some pivotal minorities may, of course, be good. But many are toxic to democracy. They vary. The P-2 Masonic lodge in Italy sought to take power in the country. The Jewish Defense League, with support from U.S. citizens, seeks power in Israel. Nazi-esque groups, some of them heavily armed, spew anti-Semitic and racist hate, and dream of taking over Washington. Some of their members have engaged in gun battles with the Federal Bureau of Investigation. An African-American organization in the United States, headed by an admirer of Hitler, saw its ranks swell with the aid of a $5 million interest-free loan from Libya's Qaddafi. Add to this witch's brew the megalomaniac LaRouchite movement with its "intelligence operations," its branches and front groups reaching from the United States to West Germany and Mexico.

In the United States, hate groups will proliferate as social unrest grows in the decade ahead, according to Dr. William Tafoya, the FBI's outstanding expert on the future. These groups will attempt to infiltrate U.S. police agencies to facilitate acts of domestic terrorism. "If I were a racist, what better place to initiate my hidden agenda than behind the shield of a badge?" Tafoya asks.

Citing unemployment, poverty, homelessness, and illiteracy as breeding grounds of social unrest, Tafoya has catalogued the rising frequency of race-related crimes, riots, and beatings and warns that the framework for social justice has become "loose dry straw" waiting for a spark to ignite it.

Nor are domestic social conditions the only ones that matter. Emigré groups, like the Kurds in Sweden or the Sikhs in Canada, carry their political passions and sense of injustice from the "old country" into the new. In the past, emigrants were largely cut off from their original homelands. Today, with instant communication and jet travel, the old culture retains its grip and its political movements live on abroad. Such groups want to seize power, too, not in the host country but in the homeland, creating complex, strained international relations.

Insignificant in normal times, such groups reach a "takeoff" stage when the cultural and social soil is right and when the mainstream political parties are paralyzed or so evenly matched that a tiny coalition partner can tip the power balance.

Healthy democracies should tolerate the widest possible diversity, and there is nothing unusual or particularly frightening about the existence of such grouplets—so long as the political system remains equilibrial. But will it?

We already live in a world of barely contained fanaticisms. Groups seek to impose totalitarian dogma not merely on one nation, but on the entire world. Ayatollahs incite murder, calling for the assassination of Salman Rushdie, a writer whose words offend them. Anti-abortion protesters bomb clinics. Separatist movements leave a trail of car bombs and blood in defense of their national identity. And religio-political terrorists think nothing of hurling a grenade into a café or downing a 747, as if the death of a vacationing secretary or a salesman with his case full of catalogues would somehow win points from God.

Because of an out-of-date conception of progress, many in the West assume that fanatic, irrational, hate-mongering ideologies will vanish from the earth as societies become more "civilized." Nothing, says Professor Yehezkel Dror of Hebrew University in Jerusalem, is more misleadingly smug. An internationally respected policy analyst and futurist, Dror contends that "confessional conflicts, 'holy wars,' committed crusaders and martyrdom-seeking warriors" are not merely relics of the past. They are portents of the future.

His study of "high-intensity aggressive ideologies" analyzes the international threat posed by them. But for the democracies, the threat is domestic as well, for as culture and economics are fused in the new economy, and new emotionally charged issues arise, the dangers of pivotal minorities and global fanaticism escalate in tandem.

The rise of a new kind of economy, never before known, threatening to many, demanding rapid changes in work, life style, and habits, hurls large populations—terrified of the future—into spasms of diehard reaction. It opens cleavages that fanatics rush to fill. It arms all those dangerous minorities who live for crisis in the hopes of catapulting themselves onto the national or global stage and transporting us all into a new Dark Age.

Instead of the much-touted "end of ideology," we may, in both global and domestic affairs, see a multiplicity of new ideologies spring up, each inflaming adherents with its single vision of reality. Instead of President Bush's famous "thousand points of light," we may well face a "thousand fires of fury."

While we are busy celebrating the supposed end of ideology, history, and the Cold War, we may find ourselves facing the end of democracy as we have known it—mass democracy. The advanced economy, based on computers, information, knowledge, and deep communication, calls into question all the traditional defenses of democracy, challenging us to redefine them in 21st-century terms.

To do that, we need a clearer picture of how the system works and how it is already changing.

21

THE INVISIBLE PARTY

Shortly after Ronald Reagan was elected to the American presidency, Lee Atwater, one of his chief aides (later successively George Bush's campaign manager and chairman of the Republican National Committee), met with friends for lunch at the White House. His candor at that table was remarkable.

"You will hear a lot in the coming months about the Reagan Revolution," he said. "The headlines will be full of the tremendous changes Reagan plans to introduce. Don't believe them.

"Reagan does want to make a lot of changes. But the reality is, he won't be able to. Jimmy Carter pushed the 'system' five degrees in one direction. If we here work very hard and are extremely lucky, Reagan may be able to push it five degrees in the opposite direction. That's what the Reagan Revolution is really about."

Despite a media focus on individual politicians, Atwater's remark underlines the degree to which even the most popular and highly placed leader is a captive of the "system." This system, of course, is not capitalism or socialism, but bureaucratism. For bureaucracy is the most prevalent form of power in all smokestack states.

Bureaucrats, not democratically elected officials, essentially run all governments on an everyday basis, and make the overwhelming majority of decisions publicly credited to Presidents and Prime Ministers.

"All Japanese politicians . . ." writes Yoshi Tsurumi, head of the Pacific Basin Center Foundation, "have become totally dependent on the central bureaucrats for drafting and passing bills. They stage Kabuki plays of 'debates' on bills according to scenarios created by the elite bureaucrats of each ministry."

Similar descriptions apply with varying degrees of force to the civil services of France, Britain, West Germany, and the other countries routinely described as democratic. Political leaders regularly bemoan the difficulty they face in getting their bureaucracies to carry out their wishes. The fact is that, no matter how many parties run against one another in elections, and no matter who gets the most votes, a single party always wins. It is the Invisible Party of bureaucracy.

THE MINISTRY OF THE 21ST CENTURY

The revolutionary new economy will transform not only business but government. It will do this by altering the basic relationship between politicians and bureaucrats, and by dramatically restructuring the bureaucracy itself.

It is already causing power to shift *among* the various bureaucracies.

A prime example is the rise of the Japanese Ministry of Posts and Telecommunications (MPT). From 1949 on this ministry had three basic functions. It handled the mail and, like many European postal services, offered customers insurance and savings accounts. (These were originally set up to serve people living in remote rural regions largely ignored by the banks and insurance companies.) In power-conscious Tokyo, the Teishin-sho, as it was called, was regarded as a minor ministry.

Today the renamed MPT is one of the giants, often hailed as the "Ministry of the 21st Century." It achieved this new status after 1985, when—in what must have been a knockdown *nawabari-arasoi,* or turf battle—it won responsibility for the development of the entire Japanese telecommunications industry, from radio and television broadcasting to data communication.

It thus combines in a single agency financial functions (which are increasingly dependent on advanced telecommunications) and the telecommunications functions themselves. No organizational intersection is likely to be more strategic.

Explaining MPT's rise to power, the *Journal of Japanese Trade and Industry* writes:

"A sophisticated information-oriented society in which information circulates smoothly thanks to telecommunications is not complete in itself. When information flows, people, goods and money also flow. When information about a product is disseminated, as in advertising, people go and buy it. The flow of information is accompanied by 'physical flow' and 'cash flow.' The MPT alone among the ministries has a direct interest in all three of these phenomena."

Other governments, of course, divide the functions of their ministries and departments differently, but it hardly needs a wizard to anticipate that power will flow toward those agencies that regulate information in the super-symbolic economy and win jurisdiction over expanding functions.

As education and training become central to economic effectiveness, as scientific research and development become more significant, as environmental issues gain importance, agencies with jurisdiction in those fields will gain clout relative to those that deal with declining functions.

But these inter-bureaucratic power shifts are only a minor part of the unfolding story.

THE GLOBAL BUZZWORD

After half a century in which governments continually took on more tasks, the decades since the start of the super-symbolic economy have seen a truly remarkable development.

In the advanced economies, leaders as different as Republican Ronald Reagan and Socialist François Mitterand began to systematically strip away governmental operations or functions. They have been emulated by Carlos Salinas de Gortari in Mexico, Saddam Hussein in Iraq, by dozens of other leaders around the world, and most important by reformers throughout Eastern Europe, all of whom suddenly began calling for key government enterprises to be denationalized or their tasks contracted out to be performed by others. *Privatization* became a global buzzword.

This is widely taken to be a sign of the triumph of capitalism over socialism. But the push toward privatization cannot be simply written off as a "capitalist" or "reactionary" policy, as it so often is. Opposition to privatization and similar measures is not "progressive." Whether recognized or not, it is a defense of the unelected Invisible Party, which holds massive power over people's lives, irrespective of whether their governments are "liberal" or "conservative," "right-wing" or "left-wing," "communist" or "capitalist."

Moreover, few observers have noticed the hidden parallels between the privatization push in the public sector and today's restructuring of business in the private sector.

We've already seen big firms splitting themselves into small profit centers, flattening their pyramids, and installing free-form information systems that break up bureaucratic cubbyholes and channels.

Few seem to have considered that if we change the structure of business and leave government unchanged, we create a gaping organizational mismatch that could damage both. An advanced economy requires constant interaction between the two. Thus, like a long-married couple, government and business eventually must take on some of each other's characteristics. If one is restructured, we should expect corresponding changes in the other.

STRIPPING FOR ACTION

In 1986, when Allen Murray took over as chairman, the Mobil Corporation was America's third-largest company. Like other oil companies, Mobil had, during the early eighties, launched a major drive to diversify. It bought Montgomery Ward, the giant retail firm, and Container Corporation, the packager.

No sooner did Murray take charge than the axe began to chop. In less than two years he had sold off $4.6 billion in assets, including both Montgomery Ward and Container Corp. "We have gotten back to basics at Mobil," declared Murray. "We're in the businesses we know how to run." Petroleum engineers, it turned out, were not terrific marketers of women's clothing or paperboard boxes.

The same questioning of functions has now begun in government as well. What business calls "divestiture," politicians the world over now call "privatization."

Thus, Japan's government decided it didn't need to be in the railroad business. When it announced plans to sell off the Japan National Railways, the employees struck. In a coordinated campaign of sabotage widely attributed to the Chukaku-ha, or "Middle

Core," radical group, signaling equipment was damaged in twenty-four places in seven regions, and travel in the Tokyo area was paralyzed. Fire broke out in a station. The railway union denounced the sabotage. Some 10 million commuters were inconvenienced. But the plan went through, and the rail lines are now privately owned.

The Japanese government also decided it didn't need to be in the telephone business. This led to the sell-off of Nippon Telephone and Telegraph, Japan's biggest single employer (with some 290,000 jobs). When ownership of NTT was shifted from the public to the private sector, it swiftly became, for a time, one of the world's most highly valued corporations.

Headlines outside Japan tell a similar story: Argentina privatizes thirty companies . . . West Germany sells off Volkswagen . . . France divests itself of Matra, a defense manufacturer, along with such giant state enterprises as St.-Gobain, Paribas, Compagnie Générale d'Électricité, and even Havas, an advertising agency.

Britain sells shares in British Aerospace and British Telecom. . . . Heathrow, Gatwick, and other airports are now run by a privatized BAA (once the government-owned airport authority), and the government-operated bus services are now private. Canada sells stock in Air Canada to the public.

Seen in perspective, the privatizations to date amount to no more than a fleabite on a dinosaur's hide, and even recently privatized firms could be renationalized in the event of a sudden change in political fortunes or a world-scale economic collapse.

Nevertheless, a deep reconceptualization is under way—a first nervous step toward slimming down and restructuring governments in ways that roughly parallel organizational changes in the private economy.

None of this is to say that privatization is the panacea claimed by Margaret Thatcher and free-market purists. It often carries its own long list of shortcomings. Yet, at a time when all governments face a kaleidoscopic, bewildering world environment, privatization helps leaders focus on strategic priorities rather than dissipating the taxpayers' resources on a hodgepodge of distracting sidelines.

Still more significant, it speeds up response times in both the divested and the retained operations. It helps bring government back into sync with the rising pace of life and of business in the symbolic economy.

Privatization, however, is not the only way in which governments are, consciously or not, trying to cope with the new realities.

DISAPPEARANCE OF THE HIERARCHS

We saw earlier that many corporations, from auto makers to airlines, are struggling to cut down on the degree of "vertical integration"—the reliance on their own people, keeping everything in-house, rather than contracting tasks to outside supplier firms.

Many governments, too, are clearly reexamining their "make or buy" decisions and questioning whether they should actually be running laboratories and laundries and performing thousands of other tasks that could be shifted to outside contractors. Governments are moving toward the principle that their task is to assure the delivery of services, not to perform them.

Whether the specific function is, or is not, appropriate for private-sector contractors to perform, the drive toward contracting out is the mirror image of industry's reappraisal of vertical integration.

Again, exactly like businesses, governments are also beginning to bypass their hierarchies—further subverting bureaucratic power. "There are fewer hierarchies in Washington today than in Roosevelt's time," says political scientist Samuel Popkin of the University of California at San Diego. There are "fewer leaders with whom a President can cut a deal and reasonably expect them to be able to enforce it in their agency or committee."

Power has shifted away from the old hierarchs, creating a far more fluid, confusing system, with continually shifting centers of power.

New communications technologies also undermine hierarchies in government by making it possible to bypass them entirely. "When a crisis occurs anywhere in the world," states Samuel Kernell, a colleague of Popkin's at UCSD, "the White House can instantaneously communicate with persons who are on the spot. . . . These instantaneous relays to the President from on-the-spot observers and commanders disrupt the traditional channels of information and the chain of command."

Kernell adds: "Specialists who do not yet have access to the last-minute information cannot address the President's concerns."

However, despite such changes, as complexity grows, change accelerates, and bureaucratic responses lag as more and more problems pile up that bureaucracies cannot handle.

SECRET TEAMS AND PLUMBERS

Under normal circumstances, much of the work of, let us say, Presidents of the United States or Prime Ministers of Japan has been

• to make choices among options (prepared in advance for them by their respective bureaucracies),
• about issues they understand only superficially,
• and then only when the different parts of their bureaucracy are unable to reach agreement.

There are, of course, decisions that only top leaders can take—crash decisions that cannot wait for the bureaucratic mills to grind, turning-point decisions, war and peace decisions, or decisions that require extraordinary secrecy. These are non-programmable, as it were, decisions that come directly from the leader's viscera. But these are comparatively rare when things are running "normally."

When, however, we enter a revolutionary period, and a new wealth system clashes with the power structures built around an old one, "normalcy" is shattered. Each day's headlines report some new unpredicted crisis or breakthrough. Global and domestic affairs alike are destabilized. Events accelerate beyond any reasonable capacity to stay on top of them.

In conditions like these, even the best bureaucracies break down, and serious problems are allowed to fester into crises. The "homeless problem," in the United States, for example, is not a problem of inadequate housing alone, but of several interlinked problems—alcoholism, drug abuse, unemployment, mental illness, high land prices. Each is the concern of a different bureaucracy, none of which can deal effectively with the problem on its own, and none of which wants to cede its budget, authority, or jurisdiction to another. It is not merely the people who are homeless, but the problem.

Drug abuse, too, requires integrated action by many bureaucracies simultaneously: police, health authorities, the schools, the foreign ministry, banking, transportation, and more. But getting all these to act effectively in concert is almost impossible.

Today's high-speed technological and social changes generate precisely this kind of "cross-cutting" problem. More and more of them wind up in limbo, and more turf wars break out to consume government resources and delay action.

In this environment, political leaders have the opportunity to seize power from their own bureaucrats. Conversely, as they see problems escalating into crises, political leaders are often tempted to take extreme measures, setting up all kinds of task forces, "czars," "plumber's groups," and "secret teams" to get things done.

Driven by frustration, some political leaders come to despise their bickering civil servants, and rely ever more heavily on intimates, on secrecy, informal orders, and arrangements that end-run and actually subvert the bureaucracy.

This is, of course, exactly what the Reagan White House did so disastrously in the Irangate case, when it set up its own secret "enterprise" to sell arms to Iran and pipe the profits to the contra forces in Nicaragua, even at the risk of violating the law.

Less dramatically, when George Bush asked the State Department and the Pentagon to prepare proposals for him to present to NATO, in mid-1989, the usual hordes of mid- and senior-level bureaucrats put on their green eyeshades and masticated the ends of their pencils. But what ultimately came up the line from them were a series of warmed-over, trivial proposals.

Bush was under political pressure, at home and abroad, to come up with something more dramatic—something that would steal the thunder from the latest proposals made by Soviet leader Gorbachev. To get it, he threw away the bureaucratic script, called in Cabinet members and a handful of senior aides, and drew up a plan to withdraw some U.S. troops from Europe. It won instant approval from the allies and the American public.

Similarly, West German Chancellor Helmut Kohl simply ignored his foreign ministry when he first outlined his list of ten conditions for uniting the two Germanys.

Whenever a leader end-runs the bureaucracy in this way, dire warnings that disaster looms rise from its ranks. This is often followed by leaks to the press designed to undermine the new policy.

Nevertheless, in times of rapid change, requiring instant or imaginative responses, cutting ministries or departments out of the loop comes to be seen as the only way to get anything done, which accounts for the proliferation of *ad hoc* and informal units that increasingly honeycomb governments, competing with and sapping the formal bureaucracy.

All this, when combined with privatization and the looming redistribution of power to local, regional, and supra-national levels, points to basic changes in the size and shape of government tomorrow. It suggests that, as we move deeper into the super-symbolic economy, mounting pressures will force governments, like corporations before them, into a process of painful restructure.

This organizational agony will come even as politicians attempt to cope with a wildly unstable world system, plus all the dangers outlined in the previous chapter, from unprecedented environmental crises to explosive ethnic hatreds and multiplying fanaticisms.

What we can expect to see, therefore, is sharpened struggle between politicians and bureaucrats for control of the system as we make the perilous passage from a mass to a mosaic democracy.

22

INFO-TACTICS

Today we live in the age of instant media, a bombardment of contending images, symbols, and "facts." Yet the more data, information, and knowledge are used in governing as we penetrate deeper into the "information society," the more difficult it may become for anyone—political leaders included—to know what is really going on.

Much has been written about how TV and the press distort our image of reality through conscious bias, censorship, and even in inadvertent ways. Intelligent citizens question the political objectivity of both print and electronic media. Yet there is a deeper level of distortion that has been little studied, analyzed, or understood.

In the coming political crises that face the high-tech democracies, all sides—politicians and bureaucrats, as well as the military, the corporate lobbies, and the swelling tide of citizens groups—will use "info-tactics." These are power plays and ploys based on the manipulation of information—for the most part before it ever gets to the media.

With knowledge in all its forms becoming more central to power, with data, information, and knowledge piling up and pouring out of our computers, info-tactics will become ever more significant in political life.

Before we can understand the sophisticated techniques that will shape political power in the future, we need to look at the methods used by today's most successful power players. These "classic" techniques are not taught in any school. Shrewd players of the political power game know them intuitively. The rules have not been formalized or set down systematically.

Until this is done, talk about "open government," an "informed citizenry," or "the public's right to know" remains rhetorical. For these info-tactics call into question some of our most basic democratic assumptions.

ALFALFA SECRETS AND GUIDED LEAKS

On July 4, 1967, in the White House, President Lyndon Johnson signed a measure called the Freedom of Information Act. At the signing ceremony he declared, "Freedom of information is so vital that only the national security, not the desire of public officials or private citizens, should determine when it must be restricted."

No sooner had Johnson spoken than a reporter asked if he could obtain a copy of the original draft of these remarks. It was the first request made in the full radiant flush of the new freedoms guaranteed by the act.

Johnson turned him down cold.

The "Secrecy Tactic" is the first, probably oldest, and most pervasive info-tactic. Today the U.S. government classifies as secret some 20 million documents a year. Most of these pertain either to military and diplomatic affairs—or to matters that might embarrass officialdom. But if that seems undemocratic and even hypocritical, most other countries are far more secretive, defining everything from alfalfa yields to population statistics as state secrets. Some governments are positively paranoid. Virtually everything they do is secret unless specifically declared otherwise.

Secrecy is one of the familiar tools of repressive power and corruption. But it also has its virtues. In a world filled with bizarre generalissimos, narco-politicians, and killer-theologians, secrets are necessary to protect military security. Moreover, secrecy makes it possible for officials to say things they would not dare utter in front of a TV camera—including things that need saying. They can criticize their bosses' policies without embarrassing them publicly. They can compromise with adversaries. Knowing how and when to use a secret is a cardinal skill of the politician and bureaucrat.

Secrets give rise to the second most common info-tactic, another classic tool of power: the "Guided Leak Tactic."

Some secrets are kept; others leak. When the leak is inadvertent it is merely an ineffectually kept secret. Such leaks drive officials into deep dementia. "Why," one CIA official is supposed to have asked, "do we have to send the China estimate to U.S. military commands overseas just because that's where the action is? That's where the leaking is, too." In short, better to keep information secret than to send it to those who need it.

By contrast, "guided leaks" are informational missiles, consciously launched and precision-targeted.

In Japan targeted leaks have produced spectacular effects. The Recruit-Cosmos financial scandal, which led to the ouster of Prime Minister Noboru Takeshita in 1989, offered a field day for leakers mainlining inside information from the office of the chief prosecutor, Yusuke Yoshinaga, to the daily press. "Without these press leaks," says Takashi Kakuma, author of books on corruption in Japan, "I'm sure their investigation would have been stopped. . . ."

Reporters received carefully timed spurts of information, which were moves in an exquisite power ballet. By releasing details to the press, the prosecutors prevented higher-ups in the Ministry of Justice from emasculating the investigation and protecting the upper reaches of the Takeshita government and the Liberal Democratic Party. Without these guided leaks, the government might have survived.

In France, too, leaks have historically played a major political role. Recounting France's difficulties in disentangling from the Indochina War, a White House document states: "Leak and counter leak was [sic] an accepted domestic political tactic. . . . Even highly classified reports or orders pertaining to the war were often published verbatim in the pages of political journals."

So prevalent are leaks in London that, according to Geoffrey Pattie, a minister of state for trade and industry, they have created a pall of suspicion inimical to innovation. Officials hesitate to voice a new idea, he charges, for fear it will be leaked instantly and its author made to look ridiculous before the idea has had a chance to be considered.

"But unless someone thinks," said Pattie, "which sooner rather than later entails thinking aloud, no new thinking will be done and no old thinking will be brought up to date."

In Washington, where guided leaks from a still unidentified source called Deep Throat forced Richard Nixon to resign the presidency, and where guided leaks are still a daily phenomenon, leak-phobia is rampant. Says Dave Gergen, a former director of communications in the White House:

"Fifteen years ago presidential aides felt free to write candid memos and have serious, far-reaching disagreements with each other—and the President. Watergate put a stop to that. One quickly learned never to write anything on paper that you would be unhappy to see on page one of *The Washington Post.* . . . Never say anything controversial in a conversation where more than one other person was present."

The ironic consequence, he pointed out, is that "when the really inconsequential issues come along, an army of bureaucrats moves in to consider it [*sic*]. But the more important the issue, the fewer the numbers involved—almost solely because of the fear of leaks."

Of course, the same officials who excoriate leakers are themselves very often the best source of guided leaks. While serving in the White House as national security adviser, Henry Kissinger once wanted the telephones of his staffers wiretapped to find out whether they were leaking embarrassing information to the press and Congress. But Kissinger himself was—and remains—a "leakmaster."

Secrets and guided leaks, however, are only the two most familiar info-tactics used in political and bureaucratic war. They may not be the most important.

THE MASKED SOURCE

Any data, information, or knowledge that is communicated requires (1) a source or sender; (2) a set of channels or media through which the message flows; (3) a receiver; and of course (4) a message. Power players intervene at each of these points.

Take the Sender.

When a letter arrives in the mail, the first thing we usually want to know is who sent it. The identity of the Sender is, in fact, a crucial part of any message. Among other things, it helps us decide how much credence to give the message.

This is why the "Masked Source Tactic" is so frequently used. An ostensibly nonpartisan citizens group that sends out millions of fund-raising letters may actually be financed and controlled covertly by a political party. A political action committee with a fine-sounding name may be run by the lobbyist for a rapacious industry. A patriotic-sounding organization may be controlled by a foreign country. Both the KGB and the CIA covertly channel funds into publications, labor unions, and other institutions in targeted countries and help set up friendly organizations. The "Masked Source Tactic" is the basis for front groups of all political stripes.

But masking the message-sender can take many forms, in many different settings, from business boardrooms to prison cells.

An imprisoned murderer once described how she could bring power to bear on a jail guard who was harassing her. She could, she said, write a letter of complaint to the prison warden. However, if the guard found out, life would be made even more miserable for her. She could also, she said, go over the warden's head and write to a politician complaining of brutal treatment, and pleading with him to put pressure on the warden to call off his guard. But this was even more risky.

"Fortunately," she observed in a memorable phrase, "prisons are filled with idealists. And so," she said, "I could get another inmate to write to the politician for me," thus concealing the real source of the message.

Officials throughout business and government play variations of this game. When an underling "pulls rank," using a superior's name (often without authorization) to gain an advantage, he or she is using the Masked Source Tactic.

A classic twist on the Masked Source Tactic influenced U.S. policy during the Vietnam War. It was used in 1963, when a report prepared by Robert McNamara and General Maxwell Taylor advised the President and the nation that "it should be possible to withdraw the bulk of U.S. personnel" by the end of 1965.

This forecast was bolstered by data supposedly originating in Saigon. What readers of the report were not told is that much of what was datelined Saigon had been prepared in Washington, then transmitted to Saigon so it could be sent back to Washington looking as though the data actually came from the field. The source was disguised to lend the data greater authenticity.

A special class of Masked Source messages are outright forgeries.

Seldom used in everyday bureaucratic warfare, it is well known in international affairs where strange forgeries have on occasion changed history—like the Zimmermann Telegram that helped propel the United States into World War I.

In 1986 the U.S. State Department publicly exposed as forged a document that described a "confidential" meeting at the Pentagon. It quoted then Secretary of Defense Caspar Weinberger as saying that SDI, the Strategic Defense Initiative, would "give the United States . . . the ability to threaten the Soviet Union with a knockout blow." If true, the quotation would have bolstered Soviet arguments against the SDI program.

But the document was a fake circulated in West Germany (presumably by the Soviets) as part of the public campaign drumming up sentiment against SDI. Another forged document about SDI turned up in the Nigerian press.

More recently an anti-Japanese forgery turned up in Washington when Congressman Tom McMillen rose in the House of Representatives to read what he called an "internal, high-level Japanese government memo."

Ostensibly addressed to the Prime Minister from his "Special Assistant for Policy Coordination," the memo called for Japanese investments in the United States to be planted in congressional districts where they could be used to influence U.S. politics.

Nothing could have been better calculated to intensify Japan-bashing in the United States. But rather than a Japanese government document, it turned out to be an embarrassing fiction traced to Ronald A. Morse, an official of the Asian program of the Woodrow Wilson Center for Scholars. Morse said he had written it merely to illustrate, in a dramatic way, what he believed to be current Japanese attitudes. He claimed he had told its recipients the document was bogus.

BACK-STABBERS AND BACK-CHANNELS

All messages move through channels. But some channels are more equal than others.

All executives know that the "routing slip" which determines who gets to see a memo is a tool of power. Keeping someone "out of the loop" is a way of clipping his or her wings. Sometimes the person kept out of the loop is the person on top.

When John H. Kelly was the U.S. ambassador in Beirut, he sent messages direct to the White House National Security Council, using the facilities of the CIA, rather than through the normal

State Department chain of command. This meant he was end-running his own boss, Secretary of State George P. Shultz.

Kelly, while in Washington, also met numerous times with Oliver North and other NSC officials in connection with their plan to trade arms to Iran in return for hostages—a plan Shultz had advised against.

Shultz was so furious when he learned about the Beirut incident that he blasted Kelly publicly, and formally prohibited State Department personnel from communicating outside departmental channels without express instructions from either himself or from the President. It is unlikely, however, that any such order will ever wipe out the practice. Back-channels are too useful to power-shifters.

On hearing of this case, Congressman Lee Hamilton, chairman of the House Intelligence Committee, blurted, "I don't think I have ever heard of that happening before—totally bypassing an American Secretary of State."

Irritation may have fogged his memory. A precisely parallel case of back-channeling took place when the American ambassador to Pakistan communicated secretly with the White House National Security Council, again bypassing a Secretary of State. In this earlier case, the back channel was set up by Henry Kissinger, then serving as head of the NSC. Kissinger used it in arranging President Nixon's secret mission to China, which resulted in restoring relations between the two countries.

Kissinger was an enthusiastic back-channeler, eager to keep information out of the official bureaucratic system and in his own hands. Claiming he had the President's approval, he once invited William J. Porter, the U.S. ambassador to South Korea, to communicate directly with him without going through Porter's boss, William Rogers, then Secretary of State.

Porter's diary notes his reaction: "Here's the Nixon-Kissinger secret diplomatic service shaping up, secret codes and all. . . . If the President agreed to create a super-net of ambassadors under his security adviser without the knowledge of the Secretary of State something new was happening in American history. . . . I concluded that I was just a country boy and I'd keep my head down."

When the SALT treaty was being negotiated with the Soviets, the American team in Geneva was headed by Gerard C. Smith. But Kissinger and the Pentagon's Joint Chiefs of Staff set up a private channel so that certain staff people could communicate with them directly without Smith's knowledge.

Kissinger also maintained a back-channel to Moscow, again bypassing the State Department, sending messages to the Politburo through Anatoli Dobrynin, rather than through the appropriate State Department specialists or their counterparts in the Soviet Foreign Ministry. Only a few people in Moscow—in the Politburo, the secretariat, and the Soviet diplomatic corps—were ever aware that messages were being passed back and forth this way.

The most celebrated—and perhaps most fateful—use of the Back-Channel Tactic helped prevent World War III.

This occurred during the Cuban missile standoff. Formal messages ricocheted back and forth between President Kennedy and Soviet leader Khrushchev while the world held its breath. Russian missiles in Cuba were pointed at American soil. Kennedy ordered a naval blockade. It was at that moment of high tension that Khrushchev sent Aleksandr Fomin, his KGB chief in Washington, to call on an American newsman, John Scali, whom Fomin had earlier met.

On the fourth day of the crisis, with danger escalating by the moment, Fomin asked Scali whether he thought the United States would agree not to invade Cuba if the Soviets pulled out their missiles and bombers. That message, relayed by the journalist to the White House, proved to be a key turning point in the crisis.

THE DOUBLE-CHANNEL PLOY

But even such uses of the Back-Channel Tactic are simple by comparison with the more sophisticated method that might be called the Double-Channel Tactic—the sending of alternative or contradictory messages through two different channels to test reactions or to sow confusion and conflict among the recipients.

Twice during negotiations over the antiballistic missile system, Kissinger and Soviet Foreign Minister Alexei Gromyko each relied on a back-channel to bypass their own normal chain of command. During these talks, in May 1971 and April 1972, Kissinger had reason to suspect that the Russians were using the Double-Channel Tactic against him.

Years later Arkady Shevchenko, a former Gromyko assistant, defected to the United States and wrote in his autobiography that

Kissinger's suspicion had been unwarranted. It was not a deliberate ploy but confusion, arising because one of the Soviets had been "operating on outdated instructions from Moscow, knowing no better." Whether or not this is correct is irrelevant here. What is clear is that Back- and Double-Channeling are much-used techniques to shift power.

ON THE RECEIVING END

There is also a dazzling variety of games played at the receiving end of the communication process.

The most familiar of these is the Access Tactic—meaning the attempt to control access to one's superior, and thereby to control the information he or she receives. Top executives and lowly secretaries alike know this game well. Access conflicts are so common they hardly merit further comment.

Then there is the Need-to-Know Tactic, much favored by intelligence agencies, terrorists, and underground political movements, by means of which data, information, and knowledge are compartmentalized and carefully kept away from all but specified receivers with a validated "need to know."

The exact converse of this is the Need-Not-to-Know Tactic. A former Cabinet Secretary in the White House explains it this way:

"Should I, as a White House official, know something? Does knowing it mean I have to take action? Can the person telling me then go to someone else and say, 'I've already discussed this with the White House'? That could put me in a pissing contest between two other players I don't know anything about and have nothing to do with. . . . There was a lot I didn't *want* to know about."

The Need-Not-to-Know Tactic is also used by subordinates to protect a superior, leaving the leader in a position to claim ignorance if things go sour. During the Irangate investigation a joke that went the rounds in Washington made the point.

QUESTION: How many White House aides does it take to screw in a light bulb?
ANSWER: None. They like to keep Reagan in the dark.

By the same token, there is also a Forced-to-Know Tactic,

more popularly known as the CYA, or "cover your ass," memo. Here the power player makes sure that another player has been notified of something, so that if things fall apart, the recipient can share the blame.

Variations are numerous, but for every game played with sources, channels, and receivers, there is a multitude of ploys and stratagems directed at the message itself.

MASSAGING THE MESSAGE

Infinite varieties of deception (and self-deception) are found in the masses of data, information, and knowledge that flow through the government's mind-work mill every day. Space constraints make it impossible to continue illustrating and classifying them here. Instead, we will list just a few more in abbreviated form.

• THE OMISSION TACTIC. Because politics is so intensely adversarial, political messages are even more consciously selective than most. Typically, they have gaping holes where someone applied the Omission Tactic and ripped relevant or balancing facts out of them.
• THE GENERALITY TACTIC. Here details that might lead to bureaucratic or political opposition are glossed over with airy abstraction. Diplomatic communiqués are rife with examples—which accounts for their frequently brain-numbing style.
• TIMING TACTICS. Here the most common approach is to delay sending a message until it is too late for the receiver to do anything about it. Thick budget documents are dumped in the laps of legislators who are supposed to respond to them in a few days—well before they can intelligently digest and analyze them. White House speechwriters are known to deliver their drafts of a presidential speech at the latest possible moment, allowing other staffers minimum time to monkey with the text.
• THE DRIBBLE TACTIC. Here, data, information, and knowledge are doled out in tiny takes at different times, rather than compiled into a single document. In this way the pattern of events is broken up and made less visible to the receiver.

• THE TIDAL WAVE TACTIC. When someone complains about being kept uninformed, the shrewd player ships him or her so much paper that the recipient is drowned and cannot find the essential facts in all the froth.

• THE VAPOR TACTIC. Here a host of vaporous rumors are released, along with some true facts, so that receivers cannot distinguish the latter from the former.

• THE BLOW-BACK TACTIC. Here a false story is planted overseas so that it will be picked up and reprinted by the domestic press. This tactic is employed by intelligence and propaganda agencies. But sometimes the blow-back is inadvertent—or seems to be.

The CIA once planted a story in the Italian press about the terrorist Red Brigade. This account was picked up and incorporated in a book published in the United States, the galley proofs of which were read by then-Secretary of State Al Haig. When Haig commented on the story in a press conference, his remarks were then, in turn, incorporated in the finished version of the book. This self-referential process is more common than imagined.

• THE BIG LIE TACTIC. Made famous by Hitler's propaganda minister, Josef Goebbels, it is based on the idea that if a lie is macro enough it will be believed more readily than any number of mere micro-lies. In this category was the 1987 report spread by Moscow claiming that the world AIDS epidemic was launched by the CIA in the course of experiments with biological warfare agents in Maryland. Widely disseminated around the world, the story is utterly repudiated by Soviet scientists.

• THE REVERSAL TACTIC. Few examples of tampering with, or massaging, the facts require as much chutzpah as the Reversal Tactic. This simply turns a given message inside out. An example occurred not long ago in Israel, where no love was lost between Prime Minister Yitzhak Shamir and Foreign Minister Shimon Peres. At one point Shamir instructed the Foreign Ministry to notify its embassies around the world that Peres had no authority to promote an international conference aimed at resolving the Arab-Israeli problem.

Peres's staff at the Foreign Ministry received the Prime Minister's message, but simply scrapped it and sent out cables saying the exact opposite. When a senior official was later asked how that could happen, he replied: "How can you ask me such a question? This is a war."

IN-FIGHTERS AND SAVVY STAFFERS

Given this lengthy list of techniques widely used for doctoring the messages that flow through government offices, it becomes apparent that few statements, messages, or "facts" in political or governmental life can be taken at face value. Almost nothing is power-neutral. Most data, information, and knowledge circulating in government are so politically processed that even if we ask, *Cui bono?*—whose interest is served?—and even if we think we've got the answer, we may still not be able to cut through the "spin" to the reality beneath it.

And all this occurs before the media further reprocesses reality to fit its own requirements. Media massage merely further denatures the "facts."

The implications of what we have just seen go to the crux of the relationship between democracy and knowledge. An informed public is held to be a precondition for democracy. But what do we mean by "informed"?

Restricting government secrecy and gaining public access to documents are necessary in any democracy. But these are only feeble first steps. For to understand those documents we need to know how they have been doctored along the way as they passed from hand to hand, level to level, and agency to agency in the bureaucratic bowels of government.

The full "content" of any message does not appear on the page or the computer screen. In fact, the most important political content of the document may be the history of its processing.

At a still deeper level, the ubiquity of these most commonly exploited info-tactics casts doubt on any lingering notion that governing is a "rational" activity or that leaders are capable of "objectively based" decision.

Winston Churchill was right when he refused to read "sifted and digested" intelligence analyses, insisting instead on seeing the "authentic documents . . . in their original form," so he could draw his own conclusions. But it is obviously impossible for any decision-maker to read all the raw data, all the information, and grapple with all the knowledge needed for decision.

What we have seen here are just a few of the tricks of the trade exploited by streetwise political in-fighters and savvy staffers in world capitals from Seoul to Stockholm or Bonn to Beijing.

Smart politicians and bureaucrats know in their bellies that data, information, and knowledge are adversarial weapons—loaded and ready to be fired—in the power struggles that constitute political life.

What most of them do *not* yet know, however, is that all these Machiavellian ploys and devices must now be regarded as kindergarten stuff. For the struggle for power changes when knowledge *about* knowledge becomes the prime source of power.

As we see next, we are about to enter the era of "meta-tactics" in the mind-work mills we call government, moving the entire power game to an even higher level.

23

META-TACTICS

An unnoticed "first" in politics was marked in 1989. That was the year John Sununu moved into the White House as its chief of staff, making him in all likelihood the world's most highly placed "computernik." In a world bristling with microchips, he was the first computer-literate person ever to occupy one of the pinnacles of political power.

A mechanical engineer by training, Sununu had done doctoral work at the Massachusetts Institute of Technology and was known as a whiz who could spot and correct programming errors and question the mathematical model underlying an environmental impact statement. Whatever one may think of his political views, Sununu undeniably understood the power-potential of computerized information.

Before arriving in Washington, Sununu had served as governor of New Hampshire. When Sununu installed an electronic fiscal and financial control system for the state, members of the legislature demanded access to the data stored in the IBM mainframe. Sununu sidetracked their proposals, declaring, "They'll get what we think they need."

According to *Time* magazine, Sununu "seemed to be trying to shift the balance of political power" by "holding the state's computerized financial data close to his chest."

In the end, the governor was forced to give one legislative official a password providing access to some (but not all) of the disputed data. Similarly, though a state court had held that citizens had a right to see and copy public documents, Sununu insisted that this did not apply to computerized data. Sununu, as governor, fully understood the power of knowledge about knowledge.

ESKIMOS AND MIND-WORKERS

Sununu's action in New Hampshire was hardly subtle. Stamping something *confidential* or withholding access is an age-old tactic. New, more potent tools—many of them computer-based—are now available to those who wish to control data, information, and knowledge.

In fact, we are witnessing a shift to a higher—and less visible—level of power struggle that reflects the rising level of abstraction and complexity in society generally as the super-symbolic economy spreads.

Take, for example, computers. We now use computers to build computers. We are also developing CASE—computer-assisted software engineering. This is based on what might be termed "meta-software"—software designed to produce software. One can imagine a future in which CASE is used to produce the meta-software, itself, in a kind of infinite regress, as the process moves to higher and higher levels of abstraction.

Similarly, in the early 1980s, "spreadsheet software" spread rapidly through the business world. These computer programs permitted hundreds of thousands of users to put numbers into columns and rows, as in a ledger book, and to manipulate them easily. Because they could automatically show how a change in one number or variable would affect all the others, they accustomed a whole generation of users to think in terms of "what if" scenarios. What would happen if we raised the price of a product by 2 percent? What if interest rates fell by half a point? What if we could get the new product to market a month sooner? But spreadsheets, like traditional ledgers, were two-dimensional, flat as a chessboard.

In 1989, Lotus Development Corporation, the main spreadsheet supplier, introduced its 1-2-3 Release 3.0. This program can be used to create three-dimensional spreadsheets—the accounting equivalent of moving chess pieces up and down as well as backward and forward on the conventional board. It permits users to simulate change in a business or a process in far more complex and revealing ways. It leads users to ask much smarter what-if questions at a much higher level.

The new system of wealth creation requires a symbol-drenched work force. Constant exposure to the data deluge—to media, computers, paperwork, fax machines, telephones, movies, posters, advertisements, memos, bills, invoices, and a thousand other symbolic stimuli, with millions spending their time attending meetings, presenting ideas, persuading, negotiating, and otherwise exchanging images—makes for an increasingly "info-savvy" population.

Just as Eskimos develop high sensitivity to differences in the properties of snow, and farmers can almost intuitively sense weather and soil changes, mind-workers become attuned to this informational environment.

This rising sophistication compels those in power to seek new, higher-level instruments of persuasion and/or social control.

Satellites, videocassettes, narrow-casting, niche-identification, cluster-targeting, extra-intelligent networks, instant polling, simulation, mathematical modeling, and other such technologies are becoming a taken-for-granted part of the political environment in the affluent nations. And along with these come new ways of manipulating computerized information that make all the conventional info-tactics of the politician or bureaucrat look crude and klutzy by comparison.

Along with changes in the general population, therefore, fed by the shift to the new wealth-creation system, comes a parallel upgrading of the tools of manipulation used by politicians and government officialdom to hold on to their power. That is what meta-tactics are all about.

TRUTH VERSUS POWER

To grasp what is meant here by "meta-tactics," think for a moment about business. Naïve investors look at a company's "bottom line" to assess its soundness and profitability. But, as *Fortune* magazine put it, "profits, like sausages . . . are esteemed most by those who know least about what goes into them." Sophisticated investors, therefore, study not merely the bottom line but what lies behind it—the so-called "quality of earnings."

They look at the numbers that make up the numbers; at the assumptions that underlie them; and even at the accounting and computer models that manipulate them. This is analysis at a higher level. It is, we might say, an example of simple meta-analysis.

When GM can legally add nearly $2 billion to its (ostensible) profits in one year by changing the length of time over which it depreciates its plants, altering the way it reports on its pension plan, monkeying with the value assigned to its inventories, and changing the supposed worth of the cars it leases, think of what governments or their agencies can do with their accounting.

Governments, of course, have been "cooking their books" at least since the invention of double-entry ledgers by the Venetians in the 14th century. They have been "cooking" all sorts of data, information, and knowledge, not just budgetary or financial, since Day One. What's new is the ability to fry, broil, or microwave the stuff with the help of computers.

Computers do good things. They vastly increase the know-how potentially available to decision-makers. They improve the efficiency of many services. They help integrate complex processes.

The computer revolution makes it possible to model—and therefore better understand—various social problems, from unemployment to rising health costs and environmental threats, in ways never before possible. We can apply multiple models to the same phenomenon. We can examine the interplay of many more factors. We can create data bases on an unprecedented scale, and analyze the data in extremely sophisticated ways.

Wherever the new system of wealth creation takes root, governments cannot run without computers any more than businesses can. Nor should we want them to. Governments were less, not more, democratic before the arrival of computers and other advanced information technologies.

But politics is about power, not truth. Decisions are not based on "objective" findings or profound understanding, but on the conflict of forces, each pursuing its perceived self-interest. Computers cannot eliminate this necessary (and useful) parry, thrust, and cut of power struggle. They raise it, instead, to a higher level.

Political leaders and senior bureaucrats themselves underestimate how dependent they have become on computers—and how vulnerable, therefore, to those who know how to manipulate them for power purposes. The reason for this is that most governmental computer processing typically occurs at the lowest rather than highest levels of the mind-work hierarchy. We don't see Presidents or party chiefs punching keyboards or gazing at screens. Yet the people on top make scarcely a decision, from the choice of a warplane to the determination of tax policy, that does not rest on "facts" that have at some point been manipulated by specialists using computers.

Whether it has to do with hospital beds, import controls, or meat inspection, by the time any problem or policy comes up for a vote or a decision, it has been described (and counter-described) in terms that are quantified, aggregated, abstracted, and pre-formatted for the computer.

And at every point in this process, from the creation of a data base to the way information in it is classified, to the software used to analyze it, the information is open to manipulation so subtle and frequently invisible it makes such standard political info-tactics as secrecy or leaks look crude by comparison.

When we add the distortions produced by meta-tactics to all those deliberately introduced by officials and politicians who play the conventional "info-games" described in the last chapter, we can reach only one conclusion:

Political knowledge reaches the decision-maker only after passing through a maze of distorting mirrors. Tomorrow the mirrors themselves will reflect still other mirrors.

THE KIDNAPPED FINGER

A rapidly accumulating international literature tells lurid stories about computer crime—about bank swindles, espionage, viruses sent from one computer to destroy the contents of others. Movies like *WarGames* have dramatized the dangers from unauthorized entry to the computer and communication systems that control nuclear weapons. According to a published report in France, the Mafia has kidnapped an IBM executive and cut off his finger because it needed his fingerprint to breach a computer security system.

The U.S. Department of Justice has defined a dozen different methods used in computer-based criminal activity. They range from switching or altering data as they enter the computer, to putting self-concealing instructions into the software, to tapping the computers. Widely publicized cases of "computer viruses" have illustrated the potential for sabotage of military and political communications and computation.

But relatively little thought has been given so far to the ways in which similar techniques might alter political life.

One day in 1986, Jennifer Kuiper, a staff aide of Congressman Ed Zschau, saw her computer screen go blank. When she got her machine up and running again, two hundred letters had disappeared. Four days later hundreds of letters and addresses disappeared from the computer of Congressman John McCain. Capitol Hill police, claiming to have eliminated the likelihood of staff error, launched a criminal investigation.

According to Zschau, himself the founder of a computer software firm before entering politics, "Every office on Capitol Hill can be broken into in this way. . . . It can bring the work that a member of Congress does to a complete halt."

Writing in the *Information Executive,* specialist J. A. Tujo pointed out that, with 250,000 word processors used in the offices of American lawyers, it "becomes feasible for a lawyer's unscrupulous opposing counsel to glean compromising information by illegal access" to his or her computer—and that this can be accomplished with cheap electronic equipment purchasable in the corner Radio Shack.

Politicians and officials, however, may be even more vulnerable. Thousands of computers, many of them linked in networks, are now found in congressional offices, the homes of elected officials and lobbyists, as well as on the desk tops of hundreds of thousands of civil servants who regulate everything from soybean quotas to air travel safety standards. Unauthorized and secret entry could cause endless troubles and shift power in unexpected ways.

Computers also increasingly populate election campaign headquarters. Thus new, virtually undetectable games can be played in the ballot box itself.

CHERNOBYL IN THE BALLOT BOX

In Seoul, South Korea, in December 1987, after sixteen years of military rule, a general election took place. The results of this bitterly fought three-way contest were ultimately accepted and the country got on with its business. But in the immediate aftermath, political observers noted certain peculiarities in the balloting.

The winner's percentage of margin, established in the earliest returns, remained strangely unchanged throughout the night and across regions. A highly popular opposition candidate cast doubt on the size of his own victory in Kwangju Province, saying he couldn't believe that he had actually garnered 94 percent of the votes. At best, he claimed, he should have won a maximum of 80 percent. The suspicion grew that someone was tampering not with the ballot boxes, but with the computers that compiled the results.

This suspicion was never confirmed, so far as we know, but Maggie Ford, the *Financial Times* correspondent in Seoul, citing a Washington political analyst, pointed out that "it would be extremely easy to draw up a computer model of an acceptable decision result. This could be adjusted for people's perceptions of voter choice, regional, class, and age background, and events during the campaign. Such a model could design the size of a majority."

Such a model could also, presumably, be used to tailor the results so subtly in key districts as to provide a victory without leaving an overt trail. This is possible if a sophisticated programmer, gaining access to the right password, instructs the computer to credit some percentage of the votes of one candidate to another and then to spring a "trapdoor"—which, in effect, erases any record of what has been done.

The Election Watch project of the Urban Policy Research Institute, basing itself in part on work done by two Princeton University computer scientists, Jon R. Edwards and Howard Jay Strauss, concludes that "the advent of computerized vote counting over the past two decades has created the potential for election fraud and error on a scale previously unimagined."

Many current election officials disagree, but Election Watch gains support from Willis H. Ware, a senior researcher at the Rand Corporation. Ware puts it even more dramatically: The vulnerability of electronic voting systems is such that "there is probably a Chernobyl or a TMI [Three Mile Island] waiting to happen in some election, just as a Richter-8 earthquake is waiting to happen in California."

Give these admittedly speculative scenarios a further twist. Imagine what might be done if the computer were "fixed" by technicians, programmers, or systems integrators working for a multinational corporation that wants a particular senator, say, driven from office. Or imagine that the electronic ballot box is under the indirect, secret control not of a party or corporation but of a foreign power. An election could be swung by adding or subtracting a tiny—unnoticed—number of votes from each precinct. No one might ever know.

Caveat candidate!

GIMME A NUMBER!

The vulnerability isn't just inside the computers, or at election times, but in the way computer-generated data, information, and knowledge are used and misused.

Smart politicians and officials, of course, do what smart people in general have always done when presented with new information. They demand to know more about its sources and the reliability of the data behind it; they ask how samples were drawn in polls and what the response rates were; they note whether there are inconsistencies or gaps; they question statistics that are too "pat"; they evaluate the logic, and so forth.

Smarter power players also take into account the channels through which the information arrived and intuitively review in their minds the various interests who might have "massaged" the information in transit.

The smartest people—a minority of a tiny minority—do all the above, but also question assumptions and even the deeper assumptions on which the more superficial assumptions are based.

Finally, imaginative people—perhaps the fewest of all—question the entire frame of reference.

Government officials are found in all four categories. However, in all the high-tech countries they are so harried, so pressured, that they typically lack the time and attention span, if not the brains, to think past the surface "facts" on which they are pressed to make decisions. Worse yet, all bureaucracies discourage out-of-frame thinking and the examination of root premises. Power-players take advantage of this fact.

When David Stockman, who headed the U.S. Office of Management and Budget, proposed budget cuts to the President and White House staff, he carefully chose the reductions from programs accounting for only 12 percent of the total budget. In discussing these cuts with his higher-ups, he never provided context.

Telling tales out of school, he later wrote:

"What they didn't realize—because I never made it clear—was that we were working in only a small corner of the total budget. ... We hadn't even looked at three giant programs that accounted for over *half* of the domestic budget: Social Security, veterans' benefits, and Medicare. Those three alone cost $250 billion per year. The programs we had cut saved $25 billion. The President and White House staff were seeing the tip of the budget iceberg; they weren't finding out about the huge mass which lurked below the waterline. . . .

"No one raised any questions about what *wasn't* being reviewed."

Were they willfully ignorant, too much in a hurry to ask, or blinded by Stockman, a master of statistical legerdemain? Or were they just "snowed" by all the computer-generated numbers?

A political speech is barely worth making these days unless it is stuffed with computer-derived statistics. Yet most decision-makers seldom question the numbers that have been crunched for them.

Thus Sidney Jones, a former Under Secretary of Commerce, once proposed setting up a Council of Statistical Advisers to serve the President. Presumably they would have been able to tell the President how the notorious "body count" statistics during the Vietnam War were being massaged. Or why the CIA and the Pentagon couldn't agree on how powerful Soviet nuclear tests were, and therefore on whether or not the U.S.S.R. was violating the Threshold Test Ban Treaty of 1975. Or why the Commerce Department figures on gross national output were wildly exaggerated at one time, then corrected down to show the economy in a near-recession.

The reasons in every case were highly technical—but they were also, inevitably, political. Even the most objective-seeming numbers have been hammered into shape by the push and pull of political power struggle.

The U.S. Census Bureau takes more pains than most agencies

to make public its definitions and statistical procedures so that users can form their own judgments about the validity of its figures. Its top experts readily admit, however, that such reservations and footnotes are routinely ignored in Washington.

According to one Census staffer: "The politicians and the press don't care. All they say is 'Gimme a number!' "

There are two reasons for this. One is mere naïveté. Despite all we have learned in the past generation about the spurious quality of much seemingly hard computer data, according to the Census official responsible for automatic data processing and planning, "Computer output is still regarded as Gospel."

But there is a deeper reason. For political tacticians are not in search of scholarly "truth" or even simple accuracy. They are looking for ammunition to use in the info-wars. Data, information, and knowledge do not have to be "accurate" or "true" to blast an opponent out of the water.

DATA BASE DECEPTION

Governments rely increasingly on computer-stored data bases. While Sununu's withholding of access to data is an example of ordinary info-tactics at work, subtle tampering with the data base is an example of meta-tactics.

Meta-tacticians attack the data base not by controlling access to it, but by determining what may or may not be included in it in the first place.

The ten-year census questionnaire used in the United States must be approved by Congress. Says a senior Census official: "Congress puts various pressures on us. We do a sample survey on farm finance. We've been directed by Congress *not* to collect that data because it might have been used to cut federal support for farmers." Companies in every industry also pressure the Census Bureau to ask, or to avoid asking, certain questions. For example, it has been asked to include a question about mobile homes in its housing survey to supply data needed by a company in that business. Since the number of questions that can be included in the questionnaire is always limited, lobbyists fight one another and apply fierce pressure on the Bureau.

No matter how computerized and seemingly "objective," data bases thus reflect the values and power relationships of society.

Controlling what goes into today's endlessly multiplying data bases is, however, only the simplest of meta-tactics. Far more subtle are attempts to control the way data are broken into categories or classes.

Well before the computer era, at a time when the U.S. government was concerned about overconcentration in the auto industry, General Motors employed a lobbyist who sat in a little-known body, the Federal Statistics Users Council. His job was to assure that figures for the industry were lumped together so they could never be publicly disaggregated—thus, the degree of economic concentration might be given in terms of how large a share of the industry was controlled by the "top three" companies, but never by the top company alone—General Motors.

Today, advanced systems are used to index, classify, and categorize the data flowing into computer data bases. With the help of computers the same data can be "cut" or recategorized many different ways. Thus, intense political battles are waged over more and more obscure, abstract, seemingly technical questions.

Many power struggles take place over the indicators used in data bases and the relative importance assigned to them. If you want to know how many angels can dance on the tip of a warhead, do you count their haloes or their harps? Hospital beds, which are easily counted, are sometimes presumed to be an indicator of the level of health services in a community. But would the number of doctors per thousand residents be a better measure? And what do either of these reveal about the actual health of local residents? The number of beds may reflect government subsidy programs that reward or penalize hospitals based on bed-count, rather than on the provision of real services to the community.

To get a true picture of the population's health needs, should one count patients? Cures? Life expectancy? Infant mortality? The choice of an indicator or group of indicators will heavily affect the output.

Meta-tacticians know the WYMIWYG Principle—What You Measure Is What You Get.

Panels of experts, teams of government specialists, lobbyists, and others wrestle frequently with such questions. While some participants are not clever enough to ask deep-probing questions or to understand the hidden significance, others can and do. In so doing, they typically fight for their own commercial or departmental interests. While couched in highly technical jargon, the conflicts are often, in fact, strongly political.

Most of this skirmishing takes place out of sight of the public, and well below the level of senior officials and Cabinet members, who rarely have the time or inclination to understand the hidden issues in any case. Lacking these and the training needed to cut through the barrage of facts and pseudo-facts themselves, decision-makers are forced to rely more on technical specialists.

The monitoring of more variables, plus the enormous jump in data processing capacity made possible by computers, changes the problem facing political decision-makers from information underload to information overload.

This overload also means that interpretation becomes more important than simple collection. Data (of varying quality) are plentiful. Understanding is rare. But shifting the emphasis to interpretation means more processing at higher levels in the mindwork hierarchy. This alters power relationships among the experts themselves. It also shifts the info-tacticians' playing field to a much higher, meta-level.

A perfect example has to do with the latest satellite observation systems used to monitor U.S.-Soviet arms control agreements. Recently launched satellites deliver such a deluge of data—from their locations in space they can detect objects as small as a few inches—that interpreters drown in the flood. Says Thomas Rona, deputy director of the White House Science Office, "In the past the problems have been mostly connected with sensing the data. Now, they are more in filtering and interpreting it."

The sheer volume, reports *Science* magazine, threatens "to overwhelm even armies of analysts," leading to pressures to automate the interpretation function.

This, in turn, encourages a reliance on artificial intelligence and other "knowledge engineering" tools. But their use raises the level of abstraction still further, and buries the critical assumptions of the system under still heavier layers of inference.

In business, according to *Datamation* magazine, "corporations are looking to embed the inferencing capabilities" of expert systems into their existing computer systems. Some 2,200 such expert systems are already operating in North America, doing everything from diagnosing factory tools that malfunction to analyzing chemical spills and evaluating applications for life insurance. Expert systems are spreading in government, too, where they have even been used by the FBI to help investigate serial murders.

What this implies is a dependence on complex rules elicited from experts of various kinds, weighted, systematized, and installed in computers to support the making of decisions. We can expect the spread of similar technologies throughout government—including in political life itself, where decisions often have to be taken on the basis of a mass of complex, imprecise, cross-related, ambiguous facts, ideas, images, and proposals, and just plain deceits intended to produce power shifts.

What these tools mean, however, is that the logic driving decisions is further "embedded" and, so to speak, invisibilized. Paradoxically, the very system that delivers clarifying information itself becomes more opaque to most of its end-users.

This is no reason to avoid artificial intelligence and expert systems. But it points to a deep process with important ramifications for democracy.

Politics were no purer in some earlier Golden Age. From China's Lord Shang to the Borgias of Italy, those in power have always manipulated the truth to serve their needs. What is changing dramatically today is the level at which these mind-games are played.

The world will face staggering new problems in the decades ahead—dangers of global ecological catastrophe, the breakup of longstanding military balances, economic upheavals, technological revolutions. Every one of these requires intelligent political action based on a clear apprehension of the threats and potentials.

But how accurate are the images of reality on which governments base their survival decisions? How accurate can they be when all the data and information on which they are based are vulnerable to repeated and invisible "meta-massage"?

PHANTOM PEOPLE

In the spring of 1989, when Dr. James T. Hansen, chief of NASA's Goddard Institute for Space Studies, prepared to testify before the U.S. Congress on the "greenhouse effect"—the overheating of the global climate—he submitted his text for clearance to the White House Office of Management and Budget. Hansen firmly believed that the time had come for the U.S. government to take significant action to prevent drought and other severe effects of climatic warming.

When he got his text back, however, he discovered that the OMB had added a paragraph throwing doubt on the scientific evidence about planetary warming, and considerably softening his position. He protested, lost the internal battle, and then made his personal views public through the press.

Behind this collision between the administration and one of the government's top scientists lay a little-noticed bureaucratic battle. The U.S. State Department and the Environmental Protection Agency both wanted the United States to take the international lead in combating the greenhouse problem. By contrast, the OMB and the Department of Energy backed a go-slow approach.

When Hansen took his protest to the media, Senator Al Gore, one of the few technologically sophisticated members of the U.S. Congress, demanded that the OMB "testify about the basis for their conclusions. I want to determine . . . the climatic models they have used."

This reference to "models" is a sure tip-off that the struggle would be waged at the meta-tactical level. For more and more government programs and policies are shaped by the assumptions and sub-assumptions buried inside complex computer models.

Thus while Gore in the Senate was questioning the models relied on by the go-slow camp, Sununu in the White House was challenging the reliability of the models that provided ammunition for the other side. Wrote *Insight* magazine: "He is on top of the scientific literature and thinks the computer models predicting significant warming are too primitive to form a reliable basis for action."

Today, whether dealing with the economy, health costs, strategic arms, budget deficits, toxic waste, or tax policy, behind almost every major political issue we find teams of modelers and countermodelers supplying the raw materials for this kind of political controversy.

A systematic model can help us visualize complex phenomena. It consists of a list of variables, each of which is assigned a weight based on its presumed significance. Computers make it possible to build models with much larger numbers of variables than the unaided intellect alone. They also help us to study what happens when the variables are given different weights or are interrelated in alternative ways.

But no matter how "hard" the final output may appear, all models are ultimately, and inescapably, based on "soft" assumptions. Moreover, decisions about how much importance to assign to any given variable, or its weighting, are frequently "soft," intuitive or arbitrary.

As a result, political in-fighters, skilled at meta-tactics, battle fiercely over weights, variables, and the way they are linked. Despite the political pressures that tilt and bias the outcome, the results of such conflicts normally come packaged in impressive, seemingly neutral and value-free computer printout.

Models are used in developing and choosing policies, in evaluating program effectiveness, and in asking "what if . . ." questions. However, as we learn from *Data Wars,* a recent study of government modeling, they can also be used to "obscure an issue or to lend credence to a previously made policy position . . . to delay decision-making; to give symbolic rather than real attention to a decision; to confuse or obfuscate decision-making," and so on.

The authors conclude: "Model use occurs as much for political and ideological need as for technical [substantive decision] need." This, they note, is necessarily so because "computer models influence 'who gets what.' "

A study by the U.S. Congressional Research Service, for example, pointed out that government cuts in social programs during the 1980s threw at least 557,000 Americans into poverty. The number provided ammunition to politicians who opposed such cuts. But this figure was not based on counting the poor. Instead, like an increasing number of other statistics, it was a result of politically contentious premises built into a model that attempted to show what might have happened had the budget cuts not taken place.

Just how rarefied meta-tactics become as computer data spreads in government is illustrated by the controversy that broke out over missing people and what the Census Bureau technicians call "hot deck imputation."

In November 1988 the cities of New York, Houston, Chicago, and Los Angeles filed a lawsuit against the U.S. Bureau of the Census to force a change in the way it counts. They were joined by civil rights groups, the Conference of Mayors, and other organizations.

In any census, some groups are undercounted. Poor, transient, and homeless groups are harder to count. Undocumented aliens may not wish to be counted. Others escape the information net for other reasons. Whatever its reason, undercounting can have potent political consequences.

Because Washington sends billions of tax dollars back to the cities and states, cities can be deprived of federal funds to which they might otherwise be entitled. Since seats in the House of Representatives are apportioned on the basis of population, states with large uncounted populations may be cheated of full representation. This, in turn, can cost them many other benefits. Inadequate information can thus shift power.

To compensate for undercounting, the Census Bureau's computers, on finding a house for which information is lacking, are now programmed to assume that the unaccounted-for people have characteristics similar to people who live nearby. The computers then fill in the missing data, as though it had been provided by the missing people.

The result is that millions of persons, presumed to exist, are really a phantom population whose characteristics we are guessing at. Hot deck imputing may be a better way of compensating for the unknown than previously used statistical methods, but, as with all such techniques, its assumptions are open to challenge. On the strength of these assumptions—informed as they might be—voters in Indiana lost one member in Congress whose seat was reassigned to Florida instead. "Hot deck imputation" shifted political power.

In sum, therefore, a new stage of political conflict is developing—a battle over the assumptions that lie behind assumptions that lie behind still other assumptions, often embedded in complex computer software. It is a conflict over meta-questions. It reflects the rise of the super-symbolic economy. This new economy could not run for a second without human contact, imagination, intuition, care, compassion, psychological sensitivity, and other qualities we still identify with people rather than machines. But it also requires ever more complex and abstract knowledge, based on vast avalanches of data and information—all of which is subject to increasingly refined political manipulation.

What this look at info-tactics, and especially the new meta-tactics, teaches us is that laws that set limits on governmental secrecy only touch the outermost skin of democracy's knowledge problem. The new economy, by its very nature, requires a free exchange of ideas, innovative theories, and a questioning of authority. And yet . . .

Despite glasnost, despite "freedom of information" legislation, despite leaks and the difficulty today's governments face in keeping things secret—despite all these and more—the actual operations of those who hold power may well be growing more, not less, opaque.

That is the "meta-secret" of power.

24

A MARKET FOR SPIES

One of America's funniest humorists, Art Buchwald, once imagined a meeting of spies in the Café Mozart in East Berlin, including George Smiley, John le Carré's famous fictional character. "Does anyone know who'd like to buy the plans for the Warsaw Pact defense of the northern corridor?" Buchwald has Smiley ask.

"Forget it, Smiley," comes the reply. "There's no market for defense secrets anymore. The Cold War is over and Moscow is giving away Warsaw Pact plans, not buying them."

The Buchwald column was amusing, as usual. But the loudest laugh must have come from the world's real, as distinct from fictional, spies. For among the boom businesses of the decades ahead, espionage will be one of the biggest. Spies are not only here to stay, we are about to see their entire industry revolutionized.

As the entire society shifts toward a new system of wealth creation based on knowledge, informational functions of governments mushroom, and certain types of stolen knowledge, secret knowledge, are worth more, not less, to those who need them.

In turn, this will challenge all conventional ideas about democracy and information. For even if we leave aside covert action and domestic surveillance, and focus instead on the "pure" work of the spy—the collection and interpretation of foreign intelligence—we find a system emerging that goes beyond anything we have previously known as espionage.

Just how far beyond becomes clear when we glance briefly backward.

BUTTERFLIES AND BOMBS

Spies have been busily at work at least since the Egyptian *Book of the Dead* termed espionage a soul-endangering sin. But from the Pharaohs to the end of World War II the technologies available for espionage remained primitive, and early spies, like early scientists, were largely untrained amateurs.

In the first years of the 20th century, Robert Baden-Powell, later the founder of the Boy Scout movement, masqueraded as a dotty butterfly collector when he hiked through the Balkans, sketching fortifications and hiding their outlines in drawings of complicated butterfly wings. (Baden-Powell insisted that enthusiastic amateurs, who regarded spying as sport, would do the best work.)

Another self-taught spy was the Japanese Captain Giichi Tanaka. After serving on the staff of the Japanese military attaché in Moscow, learning to speak Russian and claiming adherence to the Russian Orthodox church, Tanaka took a leisurely two-month trip back to Tokyo so he could reconnoiter the Trans-Siberian and Chinese Eastern railroads, bringing back with him intelligence used by Tokyo in planning for the Russo-Japanese war of 1905. Much spy literature today still focuses on the derring-do of intrepid individuals pursuing military secrets.

The industrial revolution, however, transformed war. The conscripted mass army, the mechanization of transport, the machine gun, mass-produced tanks and airplanes, and the concept of total war were all products of the Second Wave or smokestack era. The potential for mass destruction grew, right along with the rise of mass production, reaching its final point of no return in the U.S.-Soviet nuclear stalemate.

The industrialization of intelligence followed that of war. In the early 20th century, spying became more systematic and bureaucratic, with the Tsar's fearsome Okhrana, forerunner of the KGB, leading the way. Espionage schools were set up. Spies began to be trained as professionals.

But a handful of even well-trained spies could no longer satisfy the growing market for intelligence. Thus, just as individual craft took a back seat to assembly-line production in the factory, attempts were made to mass-manufacture intelligence.

By early in the 20th century, the Japanese were no longer relying exclusively on a handful of full-timers like Tanaka but on thousands of foot-soldier spies, as it were—emigrants settled in China or Siberia, cooks, servants, and factory workers who reported on their host countries. Japanese intelligence, following the factory production model, used unskilled "espionage workers" to mass-produce information, then built a growing bureaucracy to process the "take."

After the 1917 revolution in Russia, Lenin promoted the idea of "rabcors" or "people's journalists"—thousands of ordinary workers were encouraged to write to the newspapers denouncing supposedly antirevolutionary saboteurs and traitors. The idea of masses of amateur correspondents was applied to foreign intelligence, too, and by 1929 there were three thousand so-called "rabcors" in France, including workers in state arsenals and the defense industries who were told to write to the Communist press to expose their poor working conditions. These contributions, however, provided useful insights into war production, and the most revealing letters were not published, but sent on to Moscow. It was another attempt at mass collection of low-level intelligence by amateurs.

High-level espionage, however, was entrusted to carefully trained professionals. Richard Sorge, born in Baku and raised in Berlin, became one of the most brilliant Soviet agents in history. Because of his German boyhood, Sorge was able to penetrate the Nazi Party and get himself sent to Japan posing as the enthusiastically pro-Hitler correspondent for the *Frankfurter Zeitung*—a cover that won him access to top German and Japanese officials and diplomats in Tokyo.

The Soviets were terrified of a Japanese surprise attack on Siberia. Sorge correctly told them it would never happen, but that the Soviet Union would be attacked by Germany instead. In 1941, Sorge actually sent Moscow advance news of the coming Nazi invasion of the U.S.S.R., warning that 150 German divisions were concentrating in preparation. He even pinpointed the date—22 June 1941. But his information was ignored by Stalin.

Sorge was about to tip off Moscow about the coming Japanese attack on Pearl Harbor—once again naming the exact date—when he was captured and later executed by the Japanese. Sorge was subsequently described by General Douglas MacArthur as "a devastating example of a brilliant success of espionage." Sorge's career surely underscored the continuing value of the courageous and resourceful individual spy and spymaster.

But World War II also saw remarkable breakthroughs in everything from coding and deciphering equipment to reconnaissance aircraft, radio, and radar—technologies that laid the basis for true mass production of intelligence, some of it high-level stuff indeed.

THE KREMLIN'S LIMOUSINES

Since then, fantastic technical advances have filled the sky with eyes and ears automating the collection of mass data. Satellites, advanced optics, and other imaging equipment constantly monitor the earth. Acoustical sensors blanket strategic sea lanes. Listening stations, giant radars, and other electronic devices dot the planet from Australia to Norway.

Technological intelligence, or "Techint," now includes: Signals Intelligence, or "Sigint" (which, in turn, embraces communications, electronics, and telemetry); "Radint" (which sweeps up signals sent by or to radars); and "Imaging intelligence" (which includes photography, infrared, and other detection tools). All use the biggest and most advanced computers on earth. So vast, costly, and powerful are these systems that they have shoved intelligence gathered by humans, or "Humint," into a second-class position.

William E. Burrows, author of a study of space espionage, has summed up these high-tech systems in the following terms:

"The remote sensing systems with which each side monitors the other and most of the rest of the world are so many, so redundant, and so diffuse that no preparation for an all-out attack could take place without triggering multiple alarms. . . . Orders for armies to march, planes to fly, and civilians to hide must be communicated relatively quickly over vast areas, and what is communicated can be intercepted; everything necessary to wage the war must be moved, and what is moved can be photographed."

The big eavesdroppers in the sky can monitor all military, diplomatic, and commercial messages sent by phone, telex, radio, teletype, or other means via satellites or microwave systems. They have even been able to listen in on Kremlin bigwigs in their limousines and Chinese scientists at the Lop Nor nuclear weapons site. (The Chinese subsequently quit using over-the-air communications and installed secure below-ground lines.)

There are serious limits on all this. Despite its vaunted "spy-in-the-sky" capabilities, the United States was red-faced to discover that the Soviets, who were supposed to have destroyed 239 SS-23 missiles, had secretly transferred 24 of them to East Germany. There are other failings too. An increasing number of codes can no longer be cracked because of computer advances in coding. Weather still interferes with some photoreconnaissance. Adversaries can use their own electronic countermeasures to blind or deceive the collection systems. Nevertheless, factory-style mass collection of data has been spectacularly achieved.

Naturally, not all intelligence involves either high technology or trench-coated snoops. A vast amount is derived from "open sources"—careful reading of the press, monitoring of foreign broadcasts, study of officially released statistics, attendance at scientific and commercial conferences—all of which, when added to the secret materials, becomes raw material for the intelligence mill.

To handle all these data, from both human and technical sources, a dizzying bureaucracy has grown up which applies the factory principle of the division of labor, breaking production into a sequence of steps. The process begins with the identification of client needs, the collection of raw material from both open and secret sources, translation, decoding, and other preparation, followed by analysis and its packaging into reports which are then disseminated to clients.

Many corporations today are learning that this form of sequential production is inadequate. As we saw, in the new economy steps are eliminated or made simultaneous. Bureaucratic organization is too slow and cumbersome. Markets change rapidly. Mass production itself is giving way to "flexible production" of more and more customized products. The result for many industries has been a profound crisis.

Not surprisingly, intelligence, too, finds itself at a crisis point. The new collection technologies have been so effective, they now vacuum up so much computerized imagery and listen in on so many phone calls, they deluge intelligence agencies with so much information it can no longer be processed adequately. They now increasingly cause "analysis paralysis."

Finding the right piece of information, analyzing it correctly, and getting it to the right customer in time are turning out to be bigger problems than collecting it in the first place.

Today, therefore, as the world moves toward a new system of

producing wealth, superseding the smokestack system, intelligence operations face a crisis of restructure paralleling that which has overtaken the economy itself.

THE MAIN COMPETITORS

It helps to think of spying as a gigantic business. In fact, it is not inappropriate that the U.S. Central Intelligence Agency is nicknamed The Company.

As in any industry, there are a few giant firms and many smaller ones. In the global espionage industry, U.S. producers are dominant. These include, apart from the CIA, the Pentagon's Defense Intelligence Agency and, above all, the National Security Agency and the National Reconnaissance Office, which together are responsible for most of the "techint" data collection. In addition there are specialized military intelligence units attached to various military commands. Less known are the small intelligence units, frequently staffed by CIA people on loan, in the State Department, the Energy Department, the Treasury, the Commerce Department, and sprinkled throughout the government. Together they form the U.S. "intelligence community."

The Soviets, on their side, rely on part of the KGB (the other part has domestic security functions) to collect foreign intelligence, and on the GRU, which specializes in military and technological espionage. The Soviets, too, possess a vast system of satellites, ground stations, giant radar, reconnaissance aircraft, and other means to monitor international communications and nuclear activities around the world.

The British—famed for excellent analytic skills and for the number of Soviet moles who succeeded in worming their way into their intelligence agencies—depend on their Secret Intelligence Service, known as MI6, and their own NSA counterpart, called Government Communications Headquarters, or GCHQ.

The French CIA is the DGSE, also known as La Piscine or "the swimming pool," and is supplemented by the GCR, or Groupement de Contrôles Radioélectrique. Frequently on the outs with other Western services, it is rising in prestige, despite its Keystone Kops performance in the so-called Greenpeace incident, which led to the sinking of the *Rainbow Warrior,* a ship belonging to anti-nuke protesters.

The highly rated Israeli Mossad, often called "The Institute," and the West German Bundesnachrichtendienst are also important producers, as are the three main Japanese services. The first of these is the Naicho, or Cabinet Research Office, a small organization that reports directly to the Japanese Prime Minister. The Naicho pulls together information from military intelligence; from private organizations and news media like Kyodo News Service and Jiji Press; and from the Chosa Besshitsu, or "Chobetsu," which handles electronic and aerial reconnaissance, focusing mainly on North Korea, China, and the U.S.S.R. (In 1986, eighty-four years after Giichi Tanaka's firsthand look-see at the Trans-Siberian Railroad, the Soviets discovered an odd Japanese container on the railroad. Techint had supplanted Humint.)

In short, virtually every nation has some semblance of an agency for the collection of foreign intelligence. Additionally, certain nongovernmental institutions, from giant oil companies to the Vatican, conduct extensive intelligence operations. In aggregate, these organizations form one of the world's greatest "service" industries.

SWAPPING SECRETS

All these "companies" are part of a massive information marketplace. Part of any industrial economy consists of sales of goods or services, not to "end consumers" but from one business to another. In the same way, spies have long traded with one another.

Edward Gleichen, a British spy at the turn of the 20th century, surveyed Moroccan fortifications, sometimes with the good-natured help of local populations who, he reported, "assisted me in 'shooting' angles and slopes." This intelligence was later handed over to the French, who were busy "pacifying the natives." What the British received in exchange is not recorded, but this kind of truck and barter, as Adam Smith might have termed it, is not only rampant behind the scenes, but growing.

Much like today's global corporations, spy agencies are linked in consortia and alliances. Ever since 1947, a secret pact known as the UKUSA Security Agreement has linked the NSA, the British GCHQ, and their Canadian, Australian, and New Zealand counterparts. Later, the NATO organization joined the pact. (Since 1986, however, New Zealand has been excluded from the intelligence-sharing arrangement because it prohibited nuclear-armed American vessels from entering its ports.) Members of such consortia maintain uneasy links, sharing information and misinformation, accusing one another of leaking secrets or having been penetrated by an adversary, or of holding out some secrets.

The modern world's second great intelligence consortium, from the end of World War II until the 1990s, was, of course, controlled from Moscow and included most of the East European nations plus Cuba and North Vietnam.

One case that illustrates their relationships involved James D. Harper, a retired electrical engineer in California whose wife worked for Systems Control, a U.S. defense contractor. For $250,000, Harper sold a large number of Systems Control documents to Zdzislaw Przychodzien, supposedly an employee of the Polish Ministry of Machine Industry, but actually an agent of the Polish SB, the Sluzba Bezpieczenstwa.

The papers, dealing with U.S. ballistic missile defenses, were quickly shipped to Warsaw, sorted, copied, and then picked up by case officers of the Soviet KGB. The KGB is said to have routinely "tasked" the satellite services with specific assignments.

The Harper story was repeated many times with the agencies of East Germany, Bulgaria, Hungary, and Romania when Eastern Europe was under Soviet domination. While all these countries also pursued their own perceived self-interests, they were so organically linked to the Soviets, they even continued collaborating with the Soviets for a time after the overthrow of their communist governments.

But not everyone was a member of the two big intelligence camps. Nor did members trade only with one another. Many other buyer-seller relationships exist. In many nations when a new regime or different party takes over the government, one of its most important decisions (never discussed publicly) is the choice of an "intelligence vendor" or "wholesaler."

A good example was the case of President Raul Alfonsin, who headed the first democratic government of Argentina after the military junta fell. In 1985 insiders in his civilian government were debating the problem. The main suppliers that Argentina could hook up with were the CIA, the French, the British, or the Israeli Mossad. Under the deal, Argentina's spies would feed its supplier with information about certain countries, in return for a stream of information about countries that Argentinian intelligence could not afford to cover or couldn't penetrate.

The British were out, because of the then still-fresh Falklands/ Malvinas war, which pitted them against the Argentinians. The CIA? It had had relations with the previous regime in Buenos Aires, and anyway it might be best to avoid both the superpowers. The French were a possibility, but while strong in Africa, they were weak on the ground in South America, where, after all, Argentina's main interests lie. "Alas," said one Argentine official, "the problem is that in intelligence matters, one never knows with whom one is dealing."

Similar questions are, no doubt, being debated in all the Eastern European nations that have loosened their ties with Moscow and are even now searching for new spy-partnerships in Western Europe and elsewhere.

Even in the United States, intelligence-sharing practices change with the arrival of a new administration. South Africa, lacking satellites of its own, has received intelligence about neighboring black nations from both the United States and the British. This included information about the African National Congress, the main black opposition movement in South Africa. President Jimmy Carter banned any exchange of U.S. intelligence data with South Africa. The Reagan administration opened the pipeline again.

If the secret history of world intelligence were ever opened, all sorts of odd cross-linkages would turn up. The Australians working in Chile under CIA direction to overthrow the Allende government. The French working with the Portuguese and the Moroccans, for example, or the Romanians with the PLO. The Soviets have collected information about Israeli air and sea operations and have passed it on to Libya. The Israelis supply information to the United States.

Perhaps the most astonishing cross-linkage of all is implied in the 1989 visit of two former top KGB officials—Deputy Director Fiodor Sherbak and Valentin Zvezdenkov, chief of KGB antiterrorist operations—to the United States, where they met with former CIA Director William Colby and current officials to work out an information-sharing agreement with respect to narcotics and terrorism.

Such secret criss-cross arrangements make it possible for one nation to hide behind another and to do things that its own laws might declare illegal or questionable. The GCHQ, for example, maintains a list of Americans whose phone calls interest the NSA. The international swapping of secrets subverts all domestic restrictions on intelligence gathering.

THE LOOMING GIANTS

As the world of intelligence adapts to the emerging super-symbolic economy, this ravenous information market will demand new products, and new giants will arise to dominate it.

Looming in the not-too-distant future is the breakup or terminal enfeeblement of the UKUSA-NATO espionage alliance. As the Soviet Union's former satellites in Eastern Europe rush off, each to make its own separate deal with Western spy agencies, the world "intelligence balance" is further tilted.

In addition, as Japan and Germany take on much larger diplomatic and political (and perhaps military) roles, consonant with their enormous economic strength, they can be expected to beef up their intelligence activities, which in turn will stimulate intelligence and counter-intelligence among their neighbors, trading partners, allies, and adversaries. (We must assume, for example, that German reunification has delivered to Bonn at least some spy networks and "assets" previously run by the East Germans in the United States, France, Britain, or other nations.)

The Japanese and the Germans may themselves form the nuclei of new consortia, to which lesser powers will attach themselves. In any event, it would be surprising if both the Bundesnachrichtendienst and the Chobetsu were not enjoying substantial budget increases (no doubt disguised or hidden in the budgets of other agencies).

These power-shifting changes in the hidden world of intelligence reflect the new "correlation of forces" (to use a favorite Soviet phrase). As the new system of wealth creation intensifies competition among the high-tech nations, it will also shift the priorities of the main spy services. Three specific topics will command top-level attention from spies in the future: economics, technology, and ecology.

WARPLANES AND "WATCH LISTS"

In 1975 a Palestinian consultant to the Iraqi government was given a blunt message. Iraq, in the process of switching its political orientation from the Soviet Union to the West, was in the market for sixty military aircraft, then worth about $300 million. The consultant, Said K. Aburish, tried to negotiate the purchase with a British firm, but the government wouldn't guarantee that spare parts would be available. The Iraqis thus turned to the French, who agreed to sell them F-1 Mirages and to guarantee spare parts. But the Iraqis sensed the French were overcharging them. According to Aburish, he was then called in by the Iraqis and told: "Drop whatever you are doing, and find out what the bastards charged other countries. You have unlimited expenses—use them to bribe, buy or bully anyone."

Ironically, as he tells the story, he ultimately found the information he needed in the files of the Peace Institute in Stockholm, not exactly a friend of warplane merchants. When France's then-Prime Minister Jacques Chirac visited Baghdad shortly thereafter, Saddam Hussein, the Iraqi strongman, shoved a paper in front of him with the prices charged other countries. According to Aburish, Chirac "volunteered, on the spot, a reduction of $1,750,000 in the price of each plane." The planes went on to fly during the Iran-Iraq war that ended in 1988.

This was traditional commercial intelligence activity carried out on behalf of a government. The size of the return—i.e., $1.75 million times 60 planes, or a bit over $100 million—against the modest bribe Aburish claims he paid indicates the immense profit possibilities inherent in economic intelligence gathering. It is frequently a low-risk, high-return operation. But the Aburish case is small potatoes. It is an example of what might be termed "micro-intelligence."

Compare the potential rewards of "macro-intelligence."

When Britain negotiated its entry into the Common Market in 1973, its negotiators were armed with information from the intercepted messages of the other European countries. It is impossible to measure the bargaining edge thus gained, but it would make Iraq's $100 million look like petty cash. That was macro-intelligence.

Today the National Security Agency and the British GCHQ both maintain so-called "watch lists" of companies or organizations they monitor with more than routine interest. These include banks, petroleum companies, and commodity traders whose activities might swing the world price of, say, oil or grain.

The Soviets, too, pay a lot of attention to economic data. Says Raymond Tate, a former official of the National Security Agency, "The Soviet Union has for many years manipulated a lot of commercial markets in the world" by using its intelligence capabilities.

But it is the Japanese, according to Lionel Olmer, a former Under Secretary of Commerce in the United States, who "have the most refined and organized system of economic intelligence in the world through a network of 'operatives'—a word I do not use disparagingly—in their export trade offices. JETRO [the Japanese External Trade Organization] is the main collector. But Japanese trading companies live and die on information, and they are active everywhere, from Africa to Eastern Europe. We do not know how much of the information they collect is shared with government, but we assume almost all of it is."

When Olmer was at Commerce, he says, "We spent a year once trying to prove that the Japanese were secretly manipulating the value of the yen—in the period around 1983. We could find no hard evidence to demonstrate that the government was orchestrating up and down moves in the value of the currency. But we certainly would have liked to know." That is macro-intelligence.

In 1988–89 a major commercial tug-of-war broke out between Japan and the United States over terms for the joint production of the FSX fighter plane. In those negotiations, says Olmer, "It would have been very helpful if our government were better informed as to the Japanese government's true intentions. . . . Was it looking to the FSX project as a springboard to help Japan develop a commercial passenger jet business in competition with our own? All we got were a lot of inconsistencies." Here, too, what was at stake was not the sale of a few planes, but the fate of whole industries.

These are only the opening skirmishes, however, of an economic intelligence war that will grow more systematic, more central to government policy and corporate strategies alike in the decisive decades ahead.

The world's leading intelligence producers are being driven deeper into economic espionage by several converging factors. First, with the breakup of the Cold War, all the major agencies are searching for new missions to justify their budgets. Second, as the new wealth-creation system forces more industries to globalize, more and more companies have overseas interests to nurture or protect. These firms step up the pressure on governments for political backup and economic intelligence that may be beyond the reach of an individual firm. Whether or not public intelligence should be used for private gain, these pressures can only mount as globalization proceeds.

Beyond this, however, is a startling, largely overlooked fact. As companies, in order to operate in the new super-symbolic economy, become ever more dependent on electronics, building extensive, earth-spanning networks, transmitting data across borders, exchanging data directly between their computers and those of other companies, the entire business system becomes more vulnerable to electronic penetration by outfits like the NSA or GCHQ, Chobetsu, and their Soviet counterparts. Immense flows of fine-grained business data, once less accessible, will present a vast, irresistible target for intelligence agencies.

Finally, as the stakes rise in global trade rivalries, intelligence rivalries will heat up in parallel, leading to the intelligence equivalent of the arms race. A breakthrough by one country's spy service will immediately set all the others racing to outdo it, raising the stakes at each move.

Spying, to a greater extent than at any time in the past century, will be pressed into service in support not only of government objectives but of corporate strategy as well, on the assumption that corporate power will necessarily contribute to national power. That's why we must expect more refined monitoring of crops and mining activities in target nations, more eavesdropping on crucial trade negotiations, more stealing of engineering software, more purloined bidding data, and so on. The entire armamentarium of electronic surveillance may be pressed into commercial service, along with armies of trained human operatives determined to answer precisely the kind of questions Olmer found unanswerable during his years in the U.S. Commerce Department.

All this will lead to a boom in cryptography or coding and code-breaking, as companies and individuals seek to protect their secrets from prying eyes and ears. It will also open the door to corruption—the back-door sale of government-acquired data to private parties by agents or former agents. In the absence of enforceable international law, it will also spark bitter international conflicts.

LINE X VERSUS JAMES BOND

Like military force, economic clout is increasingly based on knowledge. High technology is congealed knowledge. As the super-symbolic economy spreads, the value of leading-edge technology soars.

In January 1985 nearly 200,000 tons of Romanian 96-inch carbon steel arrived in North America and went on sale for 40 percent less than comparable Canadian steel. The story of that shipment began thirteen years earlier, when the Romanian dictator Nicolae Ceausescu placed his country's nuclear development program under the aegis of the DIE, his foreign intelligence organization.

According to Ion Pacepa, the former head of the DIE, who later defected to the West, teams of intelligence-trained engineers were provided with false papers and sent abroad to find jobs in the nuclear industry. According to Pacepa, these techno-spies actually landed positions in General Electric, Combustion Engineering, their Canadian counterparts or affiliates, as well as in Siemens, Kraftwerke Union, and AEG in West Germany and Ansaldo Nucleari Impiante in Italy. Soon technical intelligence began barreling into Bucharest.

Knowing that the Canadians were having difficulty selling their CANDU reactor, Ceausescu, through the DIE, hinted that he might buy as many as twenty CANDUs. In fact, on October 27, 1977, the Romanians signed an agreement with the Canadians under which four reactors would be entirely built by Canadians, the remainder with Romanian help. Canada thereupon laid down the welcome mat for Romanian nuclear engineers, many of them DIE agents.

The result, according to Pacepa, was that "the DIE soon obtained intelligence covering approximately 75 percent of CANDU-600 technology, a modern security system for nuclear plants, technology and equipment for producing heavy water, and architectural and construction plans for nuclear plants built in Canada, West Germany, and France."

Better yet, Romania was able to sweet-talk Canada into putting up a $1 billion loan, supposedly to be partly used as payments to Canadian firms involved in the project, the remaining Romanian costs to be paid to Canada in the form of countertrade or barter.

By March 1982, the entire commercial deal melted down, as it were. But Romania had already pocketed an advance tranche amounting to $320 million. Moreover, Romania also already had most of the technology it needed. All it needed to do now was send Canada goods under terms of the barter deal. Which is why Romanian steel entered Canada and began to undersell the domestic product.

The Romanian scam, combining technological espionage with an economic rip-off, is less unusual than it might appear in a world in which research costs are skyrocketing and the cost of stolen technology is dirt-cheap by comparison.

In fact, according to Count de Marenches, former chief of French intelligence: "In any intelligence service worthy of the name you would easily come across cases where the whole year's budget has been paid for in full by a single operation. Naturally, intelligence does not receive actual payment, but the country's industry profits."

This—not just military considerations—explains why spies swarm around any center of new technology, why the Soviets and others have focused on Silicon Valley, why the Russians even tried to buy three California banks, one of which made loans to many Silicon Valley companies. It is why Japan, too, is a major target today. (According to a former KGB officer stationed there, "Even the special audio equipment used by the KGB residency to monitor radio communications between Japanese National Police surveillance teams was stolen from Japan.")

The entire Romanian system was modeled after the much bigger technology espionage apparatus constructed by the Soviet Union and centered in the so-called Line X of the KGB, its Directorate T, the scientific and technological section.

A 1987 U.S. State Department report based on CIA data charged that one third of all the officials of the Soviet Chamber of Commerce and Industry are, in fact, known or suspected KGB or GRU officers. "Hosting over 200 trade exhibitions and about 100 Western business delegations annually, and inspecting thousands of goods each year give its employees extraordinary access to imported equipment. . . ." The Soviets pay special attention to robots, deep-sea marine technology, and industrial chemicals.

As the lack of hard currency makes it difficult for many nations to afford legal purchases of technology and the know-how in it, they are irresistibly drawn to illegal acquisition. This suggests a coming step-up in technological espionage by the poor countries of Africa, Asia, and South America. If they themselves cannot use the knowledge their engineers or students steal, they can at least sell it. Indeed, one of the frequently ignored aspects of technological espionage is what might be termed the "resale" market.

Furthermore, as knowledge becomes ever more central to economic, military, and political power, techno-espionage causes increasing friction among former allies.

Note the recent charges that French intelligence has intercepted IBM transatlantic communications, passed them to Groupe Bull, and also planted agents in American computer firms.

Witness, too, CoCom.

CoCom is the Paris-based Coordinating Committee on Multilateral Export Controls set up by sixteen nations to prevent the seepage of Western high technology to what was then the Soviet bloc. CoCom, the scene of escalating dissension among its members, now faces possible disintegration. Members increasingly resent its restrictions on trade, and accuse one another of using it to gain commercial advantage.

At the initiative of the Europeans and Japanese, moves are under way to shorten the list of restricted technologies and embargoed countries. But in 1983, when the United States, the main force behind CoCom, proposed that China be struck from the list, a howl arose. According to Professor Takehiko Yamamoto of Shizuoka University, Western European nations, "fearing . . . that the U.S. would take over the Chinese market . . . vehemently opposed this proposal and kept it from ever seeing the light of day."

Japan had recently been embarrassed by the Toshiba affair. This centered on a Toshiba subsidiary's illegal sale to the Soviets of highly sophisticated equipment for grinding submarine propeller blades. Under heavy U.S. pressure, Japan tightened its own domestic export controls to prevent a recurrence. One result, however, was to cut itself off from part of its Chinese market. Thus, Japanese machine tool exports to China plummeted by 65.9 percent in the single year 1987. Japan was furious, therefore, when a Cincinnati Milacron machining center turned up in Shanghai.

This kind of commercial war now threatens to explode CoCom altogether. Moreover, European economic integration means that the export controls of individual European nations are weakened, since goods can flow freely among the twelve EC nations.

The rise of the super-symbolic global economy also brings

with it, as we saw, the creation of transnational or multinational business groups, along with multiple, boundary-crossing commercial alliances and joint ventures. These increase the cross-flows of knowledge, and make it far harder to police.

For all these reasons, technology will join economics as a top-priority target for the world's spies. The spy of the future is less likely to resemble James Bond, whose chief assets were his fists, than the Line X engineer who lives quietly down the block and never does anything more violent than turn a page of a manual or flick on his microcomputer.

THE COMING ECO-WARS

A third growth business for tomorrow's spies is the environment. Environmental problems increasingly cross national boundaries, so that pollution from the Rhine affects Holland as well as Germany, acid rain ignores frontiers, and the deforestation of the Amazon has become a global concern.

Increasing environmental knowledge can help reduce such problems, but it also opens the way to sophisticated manipulation of one country's environment by another's political policy-makers. A crude example was the 1989 announcement by Turkey that it would shut off the flow of Euphrates River water to Iraq and Syria for a month. The shutdown threatened Iraqi agriculture and Syrian electrical supplies. Its purpose, according to the Turks, was to do repair work on the Ataturk Dam. But skeptics insisted there was more to the story.

Across Turkey's southern border in Iraq and Syria are the remote bases of Kurdish separatists belonging to the Marxist Kurdish Workers Party. KPW guerrillas have been slipping across into Turkey. In turn, Turkey has been demanding that Iraq and Syria guard the border and prevent such penetrations. The incursions did not stop, and were followed by the Turkish announcement of a dam shutdown. This, in turn, was followed four days later by a guerrilla raid that left twenty-eight dead in a Turkish village on the Iraqi line. The Turkish press clamored for a reprisal against the guerrilla bases in Syrian-controlled territory.

Whether the water cutoff was or was not intended to prod the

Iraqi and Syrian governments into military action against the guerrillas, it was an event with significant ecological implications, an
opening shot, one might say, in the eco-warfare that will become
more common and far more sophisticated in the decades ahead.
Someday nations may unleash genetically altered insects against
an adversary, or attempt to modify weather.

When that day comes, intelligence will provide ammunition
for the eco-wars.

On a more positive note, however, because of their satellite
remote sensing systems, intelligence agencies may be well placed to
take on the task of verifying compliance with environmental treaties, as they now verify arms control agreements.

Eco-intelligence will be integrated more closely with political
and military planning as both eco-war and eco-treaties become
part of the new global system.

The spread of the new system of wealth creation thus begins
to transform one of the universal functions of the nation-state—
the collection of foreign intelligence. What we have glimpsed so
far, however, are only the most superficial changes. Far deeper
ones lie in store.

THE PRIVATIZATION OF SPYING

We are about to see a fusion of government and private
business intelligence on a scale never before known in the capitalist
economies.

Governments and companies have long had truck with one
another. Some giant firms have long provided "cover" for government agents. For example, the Bechtel Corporation, the San
Francisco–based construction firm that had hundreds of millions of
dollars' worth of contracts in the Middle East, gave nominal jobs to
CIA operatives. In return, Bechtel received commercially valuable
intelligence from the CIA.

At one time U.S. businesses provided cover for some two
hundred intelligence agents posted abroad who pretended to be
executives. The companies were reimbursed for their costs. On the
other hand, while many countries simply "expect" their business
people to cooperate with intelligence and may apply pressure if

they refuse, the United States does not. American business executives, including those who have had contacts with high-level foreign politicians, are seldom debriefed.

The line between public and private espionage will continue to blur. As multinational corporations proliferate, many grow their own private intelligence networks—"para-CIAs," as it were. This is as true for European oil companies or banks and for Japanese trading houses as it is for American construction firms. Contact between some of these para-CIAs and the intelligence units of their own or their host countries must be assumed.

Paralleling "para-intelligence" operations abroad is the recent spread of so-called "competitive intelligence" units in domestic industry, described in Chapter 14. While designed to operate within the law, these apply, at least on a rudimentary level, many of the same methods and skills used by government intelligence operations. The possibilities for informal links with government increase as these business firms hire former spies and analysts from the ranks of government.

Such incestuous relationships will multiply as a consequence of the restructuring of world business now taking place, which is leading to complex cross-national business alliances. The company entering into a "strategic alliance" with another firm may never know that some of its partner's operations are actually espionage activities run for the benefit of some government. Or it may want to know—and demand that its own government's spies find out.

Inevitably, such changes will drag many formerly "private" business activities into the public purview, politicizing them, and firing off a succession of charges, countercharges, upheavals, and explosive scandals.

Another change that parallels recent developments in business will be a shift of emphasis from mass production to customization of intelligence. Government policy-makers are demanding more and more targeted, particularized, and precise information. This requires either customized collection of information or, at a minimum, customized analysis.

To meet this demand—especially in the fields of economics, technology, and environment—requires pinpointed tactical information about so vast a variety of matters that not even the largest intelligence producers, like the CIA, will be able to recruit, maintain, and pay for all the necessary specialists. Intelligence agencies will therefore do what companies are doing: They will contract more work out, breaking up the vertical integration characteristic of mass-production operations.

Espionage agencies have always done some contracting out. The CIA and French intelligence have both hired gangsters and Mafiosi to carry out unpleasant tasks for them. Intelligence agencies have often set up pseudo-businesses—like the famous "Foreign Excellent Trench Coat Company," used as a cover by the Red Orchestra spy network during its work against the Nazis in World War II, or the CIA's "proprietary" airlines used during the Vietnam War. But spies will soon be forced to rely on independent outside suppliers and consultants to a greater extent than ever.

The basis for this "out-sourcing" is already being laid by the proliferation of private research boutiques specializing in everything from political risk analysis to technical information searches. Business Environment Risk Information, a Long Beach, California, firm, has made whopping mistakes on occasion, but it is also credited with having told its business subscribers in December 1980 that Egyptian president Anwar Sadat would be assassinated. He was, ten months later. It also correctly forecast Iraq's invasion of Iran nine months ahead of time. As long ago as 1985, even before the boom in such shops, there were scores of these info-boutiques.

Many employ former senior officials or intelligence agents. The most prominent is Kissinger Associates, which at one time or another has employed Brent Scowcroft, national security adviser to President Bush; Lawrence Eagleburger, the number two man in the State Department; William Simon, a former Secretary of the Treasury; and, of course, Henry Kissinger himself, a former national security adviser and once Secretary of State. Officials with intelligence connections move in and out of such firms—among them William F. Colby, former director of the CIA, who set up his own shop in Washington after leaving the agency. Said Colby: "The assessment business is a lot like the intelligence business."

Private intelligence enterprises can provide "deniability" to the governments that hire them; they can attract the best professionals at free-market, rather than civil service, wages; they can also perform the niche tasks for which large, bureaucratic spy shops are inherently ill-fitted.

What we may well see, therefore, is a far closer fusion or interpenetration of business and government intelligence-seeking.

THE NEW MEANING OF "PRIVATE EYE"

However, by far the most dramatic evidence of what might be called the growing "privatization" of intelligence is occurring not on earth but in space. Five nations—the United States, France, Japan, India, and even the Soviet Union—now peddle data collected by their space satellites.

The process began in 1972, when NASA launched the first Landsat for civilian use. There are now two—Landsats 4 and 5—with a third scheduled to be launched soon. Orbiting at 438 miles above the earth's surface, the Landsats send down data that are routinely used in mineral exploration, crop forecasting, forestry operations, and similar tasks.

Landsat images are also automatically down-linked to some fifteen countries, each of which, for a fee of $600,000 per year, gets a steady stream of digitized images. Some of these have military significance. Thus, the U.S. Department of Defense is itself a purchaser of Landsat data. Landsat is also used by the Japanese military to keep an eye on Eastern Siberia. In 1984 an American scientist, Dr. John Miller at the University of Alaska, using Landsat photos, was able to detect what appeared to be Soviet tests designed to show if nuclear missiles could be launched by submarines operating under the Arctic ice.

On February 21, 1986, the French launched the SPOT satellite and went into competition with Landsat. Since then scholars, scientists, and the public have been able to study military and industrial operations anywhere on earth. The American and Soviet monopoly of space-based intelligence was cracked wide open.

While SPOT and Landsat imaging is not as good as that available to the military, it is plenty good enough. Thus, governments lacking satellites of their own are a market for SPOT's commercially available military intelligence.

More to the point, customers can now buy images and data tapes from several suppliers, then merge and manipulate the data on computers, and come up with inferential information that goes far beyond that which might be available from a single source.

Indeed, there is a thriving industry that does little but process data from one or more of these satellites. These range from the Environmental Research Institute of Michigan, to the Saudi Center for Remote Sensing in Riyadh, and the Instituto de Pesquisas

Espaçiais in São Paulo. A company in Atlanta named ERDAS, Inc., in turn, writes software for these "value added" image enhancers—two hundred of them in the world.

Perhaps the best example of the de-monopolization of intelligence data is the work of the Stockholm-based Space Media Network, which buys data from both SPOT and Landsat, crunches it through computers, and comes up with images it provides to the world press. Just so the intelligence aspect of its work is not overlooked, an SMN handout describes its work as reporting on "every part of the world where normal media access is limited or out of bounds, i.e., closed borders, critical war zones, current crises or catastrophes."

SMN has made public images showing secret Soviet preparations for a shuttle program in Tyuratam, data about a giant Soviet laser that could form part of an antimissile system, a site for Chinese missiles in Saudi Arabia, Pakistan's nuclear weapons project in Kahuta, and continuous monitoring of the Persian Gulf during the military confrontation there.

The handwriting is not on the wall, but in the sky. Space-based intelligence will continue to be de-monopolized as additional satellites and additional computer technology become available. Countries like Iraq and Brazil are deep in satellite development. Others, including Egypt and Argentina, are developing missile launch capability, and Inscom, a Brazil-China joint venture, aims to combine Brazilian satellite know-how with Chinese rocket-launch capabilities.

What was once available only to superpowers and their spies is increasingly available to lesser powers and, at some level at least, to private users and to the world media.

Indeed, with this, the media itself becomes a prime competitor to the manufacturers of intelligence. Says a former senior White House official: "When I first arrived I was a victim of the 'secrecy mystique'—if it was stamped 'secret' it was going to be really valuable. I soon found that I was often reading something I had previously read in the *Financial Times*. Even faster, instant television coverage normally beats the spies to the punch."

The continuing privatization and "media-ization" of intelligence or "para-intelligence" will force the spymasters to restructure their operations, just as many corporate CEOs have had to do. Espionage, too, will have to adapt to the new system of wealth creation on the planet. But espionage faces problems that other industries do not.

CONTRADICTIONS AT THE CORE

The clients who use intelligence—government officials and policy-makers—no longer suffer from any shortage of information. They are glutted with it.

The deluge of mass-produced data now available and the overload it causes means that, for many purposes, collection is no longer the spies' main problem. The problem is to make sense of what is collected and to get the results to the decision-makers who need it.

This is driving the spy business to rely more heavily on expert systems and artificial intelligence as computerized aids to analysis. But technology alone can't solve analysis paralysis. That requires a completely new approach to knowledge.

Since leaks of secret information can have dire consequences, including the death of informants, the CIAs and mini-CIAs of the world apply the principle of "compartmentation." Analysts working on a problem seldom get to see the whole picture, but are fed limited bits of information on a strict need-to-know basis, often with no way of evaluating the credibility of the fragments they get. In theory, the information is pieced back together and raised to a higher level as it moves up the hierarchy.

But we have seen this theory before—in bureaucratic corporations. And we have also seen that as change accelerates and the environment becomes more stormy, this system is too slow and ignores too many factors.

This is not an idle issue. Senator Sam Nunn, the leading expert on the military in the U.S. Senate, has publicly blasted the intelligence agencies for falling behind fast-moving events in Europe, making it impossible for Congress to make rational decisions about the U.S. military budget. The costs of falling behind could be calamitous.

It is precisely to overcome such problems that the smartest corporations now give employees access to more information, let them communicate freely outside channels and skip around the hierarchy at will. Such innovations, however, clash directly with the need for extreme secrecy in the espionage industry. The spies are in a double bind.

This "bind" is knotted to another. For much intelligence is not merely late, but irrelevant to the needs of the decision-makers who are the "customers."

Says Lionel Olmer, the former Under Secretary of Commerce: "We need sounder supervision by policy-level officials, so that they are not just consumers, but shapers of the process." Throughout industry, as we have seen, customers are being drawn into the design process, and users' groups are organized into networks of support for the producers. The line between production and consumption is blurring.

Olmer's suggestion that senior policy-makers help "shape" the intelligence process is logical. But the more politicians and officials help "reshape the process," the greater the danger that the estimates handed to Presidents and Prime Ministers will tell them only what they want to hear—or else reflect the narrow views of one faction or party. This would still further distort information that has already been pretzel-bent by the info-tacticians and meta-tacticians who work it over in the beginning.

If intelligence is twisted by a nation's adversary, as sometimes happens when spies are "doubled," the results can be disastrous. But the same is potentially true when it is twisted for political convenience by someone on one's own side.

The historic revolution now facing the intelligence industry, carrying it beyond mass production, places it squarely in the path of the advancing new wealth-creation system. Like other industries, the intelligence industry faces competition from unlikely quarters. Like other industries, it must form new, continually changing alliances. Like other industries, it must recast its organization. Like other industries, it must customize its products. Like other industries, it must question its deepest missions.

"A man's most open actions," wrote Joseph Conrad, "have a secret side to them." Democracies, too, no matter how open, have a secret side.

If intelligence operations, already difficult for parliaments and even Presidents to control, become so intertwined with the everyday activities of the society, so decentralized, so fused with business and other private interests as to make effective control impossible, democracy will be in mortal peril.

Conversely, so long as some nations are led by aggressive terrorists, torturers, and totalitarians, or by fanatics armed with ever more lethal weaponry, democracies cannot survive without secrets—and secret services.

How we manage those secrets—and, indeed, knowledge in general—becomes the central political issue in the Powershift Era.

25

THE INFO-AGENDA

The man with the Irish passport waited endlessly in his Tehran hotel room for the signal that never came.

Improbably armed with a chocolate cake shaped like a key, the man, as the world soon learned, was actually Robert McFarlane, former national security adviser to Ronald Reagan. Intended as a gift, the cake remained undelivered. For, as we recall, McFarlane's ill-fated attempt to free American hostages and open a back door to Iranian "moderates" exploded into the Irangate scandal, the most damaging event in the entire eight years of the Ronald Reagan presidency.

With a colorful cast of Middle Eastern arms merchants, CIA operatives, mysterious ex-generals, a handsome Marine officer and his gorgeous secretary, the congressional hearings that followed kept world television audiences spellbound.

Yet what many viewers, especially those outside the United States, missed was the crux of the case.

For the political struggle in Washington actually had little to do with terrorism, secret bank accounts, Iranian moderates, or Nicaraguan rebels. It was, rather, a showdown between the White House and an outraged U.S. Congress for control of American foreign policy. This battle for power pivoted on the refusal of the White House to inform Congress of its covert activities.

Democrats wanted to prove that the plan had been ordered by the President. The Republican White House insisted the fiasco was the work of an overzealous staff operating without presidential approval. Thus the investigations and massive media coverage focused less on foreign policy issues themselves, and more on the question of "who knew what when." Irangate became an info-war.

The lapsed memories, shredded documents, secrets, leaks, and lies still provide a rich lode of insight into the traditional tactical uses and abuses of information. But more important, the scandal offers a foretaste of the politics of the future—one in which data, information, and knowledge will become more highly politicized than ever in history. For quite apart from spies and spying, the new system of wealth creation is propelling us headlong into the era of info-politics.

A HUNGER FOR KNOWING

The power of the state has always rested on its control of force, wealth, and knowledge. What is profoundly different today is the changed relationship among these three. The new super-symbolic system of wealth creation thrusts a wide range of information-related issues onto the political agenda.

These range from privacy to product piracy, from telecommunications policy to computer security, from education and insider trading to the new role of the media. Even these touch only the tip of an emerging iceberg.

Although not yet widely noticed, this emerging info-agenda is expanding so rapidly that, in the United States, the 101st Congress saw the introduction of more than a hundred proposed laws dealing with info-issues. Twenty-six dealt with how the federal government should disseminate data and information collected at taxpayer expense. Today anyone with a personal computer and a modem can dial into a number of government data bases for information on a dizzying number of topics. But how should this dissemination work? Should the government contract with outside private firms to do the electronic distribution and sell access for a fee? Many librarians, university researchers, and civil liberties advocates argue that government information should not be sold but made available freely to the public. On the other hand, the private companies serving as intermediaries claim they provide additional services that justify charging a fee.

The info-agenda extends far beyond such concerns, however.

As we drive deeper into the new super-symbolic economy, info-issues no longer remain remote or obscure. A public whose livelihood increasingly derives from the manipulation of symbols is also increasingly sensitive to their power significance. One of the things it is already doing is asserting a wider and wider "right to know"—especially about circumstances directly related to its welfare.

In 1985 a survey by the U.S. Bureau of Labor Statistics found that more than half of 2.2 million workers involved in large-scale layoffs got less than twenty-four hours notice before being heaved out on the street. By 1987 organized labor was pushing for a law that would require large firms planning substantial layoffs to give their workers sixty days' notice, and to inform state and city authorities as well.

Employers strongly fought the proposed law, arguing that going public with this information would undermine a firm's efforts to save the plant. Who would want to invest in it, or merge with it, or contract work to it, or refinance it once the word was out that mass layoffs were about to occur?

Popular support for the measure grew, however. In the words of the Democratic Party leader in the Senate: "It's not a labor issue. It's a fairness issue."

By 1988 the battle was raging all across Washington, with the Congress lined up in favor and the White House against. Ultimately the law passed, despite the threat of presidential veto. American employees now do have a right to know in advance when they are about to lose their jobs because of a plant close-down.

Americans want more information about conditions off the job as well. Across the United States environmental groups and whole communities are clamoring for detailed data from companies and government agencies about toxic waste and other pollutants.

They were outraged not long ago to learn that at least thirty times between 1957 and 1985—more than once a year—the Savannah River nuclear weapons plant near Aiken, South Carolina, experienced what a scientist subsequently termed "reactor incidents of greatest significance." These included widespread leakage of radioactivity and a meltdown of nuclear fuel. But not one of these was reported to local residents or to the public generally. Nor was action taken when the scientist submitted an internal memorandum about these "incidents." The story did not come to light until exposed in a Congressional hearing in 1988.

The plant was operated by E. I. du Pont de Nemours & Company for the U.S. government, and Du Pont was accused of covering up the facts. The company immediately issued a denial, pointing out that it had routinely reported the accidents to the Department of Energy.

At this point, the DoE, as it is known, accepted the blame for keeping the news secret. The agency was steeped in military secrecy and the traditions of the Manhattan Project, which led to the invention of the atomic bomb in World War II. Public pressures for disclosure, however, touched off an internal struggle between Secretary of Energy John S. Herrington, fighting for higher safety standards and greater openness, and his own field managers who resisted.

But even as that conflict raged within the agency, a revolutionary new law went into effect, requiring for the first time that communities all over the United States be given explicit, detailed information about toxic wastes and other hazardous materials to which they are exposed. "For the first time," said Richard Siegel, a consultant whose firm has helped three hundred factories gear up for compliance, "the public is going to know what the plant down the street is releasing." It was another clear victory for public access.

The rising pressure for openness is not just an American phenomenon, nor is it limited to national issues.

In Osaka, Japan, citizens have formed a "Right to Know Network Kansai," which has since organized what they call "tours" of municipal and prefectural governments, for the purpose of demanding access to hitherto restricted information. Of twelve requests made at the prefectural offices, six were granted, the others quickly denied. Among these was a request for information about the governor's expense account.

The response of the Osaka city government was, so to speak, more artful. When the group demanded files relating to the city's purchase of a painting by Modigliani, now proudly hanging in the Osaka City Museum of Modern Art, officials did not say no. They just never replied. But pressures for access to public documents, local as well as national, won't go away.

The growth of what might be called info-awareness, paralleling the rise of an economy based on computers, information, and communication, has forced governments to pay more and more attention to knowledge-related issues like secrecy, public access, and privacy.

From the time the United States passed its Freedom of Information Act in 1966, broadening the right of citizens to access government documents, the concept has spread steadily through the advanced economies. Denmark and Norway followed suit in

1970; France and the Netherlands, in 1978; Canada and Australia, in 1982. This list, however, hardly tells the full story. For an even larger number of states, provinces, and cities have also passed legislation—sometimes even before the nation itself acted. This is the case in Japan, where five prefectures, five cities, two special districts, and eight towns had done so as early as 1985.

The same period has also seen the rapid diffusion of laws defining the right to privacy. Privacy laws were passed in Sweden in 1973, in the United States in 1974. In 1978, Canada, Denmark, France, and West Germany all followed suit, with Britain joining the parade in 1984. Numerous nations set up "data protection" agencies specifically designed to prevent computer abuses of privacy. The terms and methods naturally vary from nation to nation, as does their effectiveness. But the overall pattern is plain: Everywhere, as the super-symbolic economy develops, information issues became more significant politically.

TERRORIST BOMBS AND AIDS VICTIMS

Everywhere, too, there is a continuing info-war between the cult of secrecy and citizens groups fighting for even wider access. These battles cross party lines and are often so complex that they confuse the participants themselves.

For example, demands for openness get tangled when they conflict with publicly acknowledged needs for safety or security. After a terrorist bomb exploded on Pan Am Flight 103 over Lockerbie, Scotland, killing 259 passengers and crew on December 21, 1988, the press revealed that authorities had been forewarned. An outraged world demanded to know why the public at large had not been warned at the same time. Much of the anger toward the terrorists was siphoned off and directed at the authorities instead.

This anger soon led to an investigation by a subcommittee of the U.S. House of Representatives. The subcommittee made public a long list of security bulletins previously issued to airlines by the Federal Aviation Administration. In turn, this breach of secrecy angered the Secretary of Transportation, who charged that the subcommittee's action "could jeopardize lives by disclosing security methods."

Congresswoman Cardiss Collins, the subcommittee chairperson, stood by her guns, however, and labeled the Secretary's blast "misleading." In fact, she said, publicly disclosing the FAA's bulletins showed up dangerous flaws in the entire warning system and thereby served the public. But it was also clear that, with U.S. airlines alone receiving some three hundred bomb threats a year, publicizing every terrorist threat could paralyze air travel—and give the terrorists the power to upset the system at any moment for the price of a phone call.

Soon the executive branch, the legislature, the airlines, the regulatory agencies, the police, and others were all joined in a still-continuing free-for-all over control of this information.

In December 1989, just a year after the Lockerbie tragedy, Northwest Airlines received a bomb threat against its Paris-to-Detroit Flight 51. Aware of the outrage the year before, Northwest decided it would have to inform passengers ticketed on the flight. It intended to tell them at the gate before boarding. But after a Swedish newspaper broke the story, Northwest began systematically notifying passengers by telephone in advance and agreed to help them make alternate arrangements if they wished. (Not all did, and the flight was made safely.)

Demands for more open information also clash with the above-mentioned demands for privacy. Among the most emotional of all info-issues are those raised by the AIDS epidemic. As AIDS spread swiftly through many countries, carrying hysteria with it, some extremists urged that victims of the disease literally be tattooed and sequestered. Fearful parents tried to bar AIDS-infected children from the schoolroom. William Bennett, then the tough-talking U.S. Secretary of Education, called for compulsory AIDS-testing of several specified groups, including all hospital patients, couples seeking a marriage license, immigrants, and prisoners. Bennett urged further that whenever an individual's test showed positive, all spouses and past sex partners should automatically be notified.

His position provoked a storm of opposition from public health authorities, lawyers, and civil libertarians who favored voluntary testing instead. Ironically, many of those who fought for privacy in this case were among those most committed to open information in other matters.

The tests, some claimed, were indecisive. If results were made public, victims would be discriminated against on the job, in school, and mistreated in other ways. Moreover, if the tests were compulsory, many potential victims might hide or refuse to seek medical care. Bennett's position was publicly attacked by Surgeon General C. Everett Koop, the nation's top medical official.

Controversy still rages over the AIDS-testing issue, not just in Washington but in many state capitals as well. The relative rights of the individual versus those of the community, and the contradiction between privacy and openness, both remain fuzzily unresolved.

Still more cross-interests arise from the existing morass of laws governing such things as copyright, patents, trade secrets, commercial secrecy, insider trading, and the like—all part of the fast-emerging info-agenda of politics. As the super-symbolic economy continues to expand, an information ethic may emerge appropriate to the advanced economies. Today that coherent ethic is missing and political decisions are made in a bewildering moral vacuum. There are few rules that do not contradict other rules.

Many parts of the world still lack the most elementary freedom of information, and face cultural repression, brutal press censorship, and governments paranoid about secrecy. In the high-tech democracies, by contrast, where freedom of expression is moderately protected, info-politics has begun to move to a higher, more subtle level.

We are, however, only at the beginning of info-politics in the technologically advanced societies. So far we have been struggling with the easy questions.

THE NEW GLOBAL FEEDBACK

Because of the growing global character of technology, environmental problems, finance, telecommunications, and the media, new cultural feedback systems have begun to operate that make one country's information policies a matter of concern for others. The info-agenda is going global.

When Chernobyl sent radioactive clouds over parts of Europe, a great wave of anti-Soviet anger was aroused, because Soviet officials delayed notifying countries in the path of the fallout. These nations insisted that they had a *right* to know the facts, and to know them immediately.

The implication was that no nation, by itself, had the right to withhold the facts, and that an unspoken information ethic transcends national interests. By the time another disaster struck—an earthquake in Armenia—chastened Soviet authorities instantly reported it to the entire world press.

But by the terms of that implicit principle the Soviet Union was not the only transgressor. Shortly after Chernobyl, Admiral Stansfield Turner, former director of the CIA, publicly criticized the United States for failing to divulge sufficient information about the disaster gathered by its "eye-in-the-sky" satellites. Without giving away secrets, Turner declared, "Our intelligence collection capabilities . . . give us the opportunity to keep people well-informed worldwide."

In fact, as new media for dissemination of information encircle the earth, facilitating the globalization required by the new wealth-creation system, it becomes harder to contain specific information within national borders, or even to keep it out.

This is what the British government forgot during the so-called *Spycatcher* controversy in Britain. When Peter Wright wrote a book with that title, in which he made serious accusations against former officials of British counterintelligence, the Thatcher government moved to bar its publication. Wright thereupon published the book in the United States and elsewhere. The British attempt to suppress the book turned it into an international best-seller. Television and newspapers everywhere carried stories about it— thus guaranteeing that information the British government wanted to conceal would find its way back into Britain. Because of this feedback process, the British government was compelled to back down, and Wright's book went on to become a best-seller in Britain too.

The use of the media outside a country to influence political decisions inside it is also becoming more common. When the Kohl government in Bonn denied that German firms were helping Libya's strongman, Muammar el-Qaddafi, to build a chemical weapons plant fifty miles outside Tripoli, U.S. intelligence leaked its satellite and aerial reconnaissance evidence to American and European media. This led the German magazine *Stern* to undertake its own in-depth investigative report, which in turn forced a red-faced government to admit that it had known all along what it claimed not to know.

In case after case, then, we find information—who has it, how it was obtained, how it was arrived at—at the heart of both national and international political conflict. The underlying reason for the new importance of info-politics is the growing reliance of power, in all its forms, on knowledge. As this historic powershift is more widely understood, info-politics will take on added intensity.

Yet all these are mere skirmishes alongside what could turn out to be the most important info-war of the decades to come.

THE INDIANA JONES CODE

Among the most common sights in Thailand, especially in the tourist quarters, are street stalls. From these one may buy video-tapes, musical tapes, and other products at knockdown prices. One reason is that these, like all sorts of other products circulating in the world today, are pirated—meaning that the original artists, publishers, and record companies are cheated of the payments due them.

In Egypt, so-called underground publishers churn out West-ern books in Arabic illegally and without payment to the authors or publishers. "Book piracy in the Middle East has reached pro-portions second only to that in the Far East and Pakistan," accord-ing to the *Middle East* monthly published in London. In Hong Kong, police arrested 61 people after raiding 27 bookstores where they found 647 books ready to be reproduced illegally. But in many countries piracy is not merely legal but encouraged for its export potentials. New technologies make piracy cheaper and easier.

Driven by piracy that cost the American movie industry an estimated $750 million annually in the mid-1980s, Hollywood coun-terattacked. When *Indiana Jones and the Temple of Doom* first hit the theaters, every print of the film had subliminal coding in it that gave it a unique identifier so that, if illegal copies were made, investigators would be able to trace their origin. From then on, similar coding began to be used by many of the major studios.

Nonetheless, as late as 1989, Taiwan, for example, was home to 1,200 so-called "Movie-TV" lounges—small private rooms in which groups of teenagers could gather to watch pirated video-tapes of the latest American movies, a kind of micro-version of the drive-in movie. Teenagers formed block-long lines to patronize them. The illegal showings were so popular, they cut into ticket sales at conventional theaters. Ultimately, Hollywood pressures led to a government crackdown.

In parallel with actual piracy came the patent-wars—the refusal of various countries to pay fees or royalties, say, on a new pharmaceutical developed and tested by research scientists at enormous cost.

In addition to outright piracy, counterfeiting has become a major global industry, with cheap fakes of designer fashions and other products pouring into world markets. Ultimately even more important is the theft or illegal copying of computer software, not by individuals for their own use, but on a large scale by pirate distributors throughout the world. All these problems are heightened by the latest technologies that make copying and theft easier.

By 1989, the question of how to protect "intellectual property" —the basis of much of the new system of wealth creation—was causing political friction among nations. Intellectual property—the term itself is fraught with controversy—implies ownership of intangibles resulting from creative efforts in science, technology, the arts, literature, design, and the manipulation of knowledge in general. With the spread of the super-symbolic economy, these become more economically valuable and, hence, more political.

In Washington, political battles broke out between various trade lobbies, backed by the U.S. Trade Representative, who demanded firm U.S. action against Thailand for failing to suppress piracy and counterfeiting of U.S. creative products. They demanded that, if Thailand refused to crack down, the United States should retaliate. Specifically, this meant lifting import duty exemptions on such Thai exports as artificial flowers, tiles, dried mung beans, and telecommunications equipment.

Opposing this demand were other agencies of the U.S. government—the State Department and the National Security Council—both of which argued for leniency, placing the interests of diplomacy and military security over those of the copyright and patent owners.

On his last day as President of the United States, Ronald Reagan rejected even more stringent proposals for a crackdown, and removed the Thai exemption from import duties on the listed products.

But Thailand is hardly the worst offender against copyright and patent laws as they are understood in the advanced economies, and the minor struggle in Washington only illustrates what is happening on a hundred fronts as products of creative activity become more and more central to all the high-tech economies.

In 1989, American copyright holders, including the music industry, the computer industry, and book publishers, demanded that the U.S. government take action against twelve nations that, they claimed, were costing the American economy $1.3 billion a year in sales. The twelve included China, Saudia Arabia, India, Malaysia, Taiwan, and the Philippines.

The protection of intellectual property, though most aggressively pushed by the Americans, is also of strong concern to the European Community and Japan. The EC has called for customs authorities around the world to seize counterfeit goods and to impose criminal penalties on pirates who operate on a commercial scale.

The political battle over intellectual property is waged, among other places, in the council of the General Agreement on Tariffs and Trade, where the advanced economies face determined opposition from the nations with less developed economies, whose negotiators sometimes reflect the attitude voiced by Arab students who buy pirated books and insist that "the West's idea of copyright is elitist and designed to line the pockets of publishers."

But it is not this attitude that is most threatening to the high-tech nations. It is the gnawing philosophical question of whether intellectual property can be owned in the same sense that tangible assets are—or whether the entire concept of property needs to be reconceptualized.

Futurist and former diplomat Harlan Cleveland has written of the "folly of refusing to share something that can't be owned." Cleveland points out: "What builds a great company or a great nation is not the protection of what it already knows, but the acquisition and adaptation of new knowledge from other companies or nations. How can 'intellectual property' be 'protected'? The question contains the seeds of its own confusion: it's the wrong verb about the wrong noun."

This line of argument is often used to support the vision of a world in which all information is free and unfettered. It is a dream that dovetails neatly with the plea of the earth's poorer nations for the science and technology needed to break free of economic underdevelopment. What is not yet answered, however, is the counterquestion raised by the high-tech nations: What happens to either the poor *or* the rich if the world's stream of technological innovation runs dry? If, because of piracy, a pharmaceutical firm cannot recoup the vast sums spent in developing new drugs, it is hardly likely to invest further funds in the search. Cleveland is right that all nations will need knowledge, culture, art, and science from abroad. But if so, there must be some civilized ground rules for the exchange, and these must promote, rather than restrict, further innovation.

Arriving at these new rules, and an underlying informational ethic, in a world trisected into agrarian, smokestack, and post-smokestack economies, is already proving extremely difficult. What is obvious is that these issues can do nothing but grow in importance. The control of intangibles—ideas, culture, images, theories, scientific formulae, computer software—will consume greater and greater political attention in all countries as piracy, counterfeiting, theft, and technological espionage threaten increasingly vital private and national interests.

In the words of Abdul A. Said and Luiz R. Simmons, in *The New Sovereigns,* a study of multinational corporations: "The nature of power is undergoing a truly radical transformation. It is increasingly defined in terms of the maldistribution of information. Inequality, long associated primarily with income, is coming to be associated with technological factors and the political and economic control over knowledge."

In the 19th and early 20th centuries, nations went to war to seize control of the raw materials they needed to feed their smokestack economies. In the 21st century, the most basic of all the raw materials will be knowledge. Is that what the wars and social revolutions of the future might be about? If so, what role will the media of the future play?

26

THE IMAGE MAKERS

Benjamin Day was a twenty-three-year-old printer with wild ideas when he changed the history of what we now call the media. The year was 1833 and New York had grown to a population of 218,000. But the largest daily newspaper in the city claimed only 4,500 subscribers. At a time when the average urban worker in America earned 75 cents a day, a New York newspaper cost 6 cents, and not many people could afford them. The papers were printed on handpresses capable of turning out no more than a few hundred copies an hour.

Day took a crazy chance.

On September 3, 1833, he launched the New York *Sun* and sold it for only one penny a copy. Day unleashed a horde of newsboys into the streets to sell his paper—an innovation at the time. For $4 a week he hired another printer to go to the courthouse and cover police cases. It was one of the earliest uses of a "reporter." Within four months the *Sun* had the biggest readership in the city. In 1835 he bought the latest technology—a steam-driven press—and the *Sun* reached the unheard-of circulation of 20,000 daily. Day had invented the popular press, crime stories and all.

His innovations were paralleled at about the same time by other "wild men"—Henry Hetherington with his *Twopenny Dispatch* in England and Émile de Girardin with *La Presse* in France. The down-scale "penny paper"—called the "pauper press" in England—was more than just a commercial affair. It had lasting political effects. Along with the early trade unions and the beginnings of mass education, it helped bring the poorer classes into the political life of nations.

By the 1870s something called "opinion" had to be taken into account by politicians of every stripe. "There is, now," wrote one

French thinker, "no European government which does not reckon with opinion, which does not feel obliged to give account of its acts and to show how closely they conform to the national interest, or to put forward the interest of the people as the justification for any increase in its prerogatives."

A century and a half after Benjamin Day, another wild man came up with an idea sure to bankrupt him. Tall, gutsy, impatient, and brilliant, Ted Turner had inherited a billboard company when his father committed suicide. Turner built it, acquired radio and television stations, and was wondering what to do next when he noticed something odd. Cable television stations were springing up around the United States, but they were starving for programs and advertising. Meanwhile, up in the heavens were things called "satellites."

Turner put two and two together and turned it into five. He beamed the programming from his Atlanta station up to a satellite and down to the program-hungry cable stations. At the same time, he offered a "one-buy" national market for advertisers who wouldn't trouble to purchase time on scores of small individual cable systems. His Atlanta "superstation" became the cornerstone of a growing empire.

On June 1, 1980, Turner took the next, even loonier step. He formed what critics labeled the "Chicken Noodle Network"—for CNN, or Cable News Network. CNN became the laughingstock of every media pundit from the canyons of Manhattan to the studios in Los Angeles. Wall Street was sure it would collapse, probably taking his other businesses down with it. No one had ever even tried to create a twenty-four-hour news network.

CNN today is perhaps the most influential broadcast news source in the United States. TV monitors are constantly tuned to CNN in the White House, in the Pentagon, in foreign embassies, as well as in millions of homes all over America.

But Turner's wild dreams went far beyond the United States, and today CNN operates in eighty-six countries, making it the most global of all television networks, mesmerizing Middle East sheiks, European journalists, and Latin American politicians with its extended firsthand coverage of such events as the assassination of Egyptian President Anwar Sadat, the Chinese repression of the 1989 Tiananmen Square protests, or the American invasion of Panama. CNN is carried over the air, or over cable, into hotel rooms, offices, homes, even staterooms on the *Queen Elizabeth II*.

One of Turner's little-known prize possessions is a videotape of his private meeting with Cuba's Fidel Castro. In the course of the visit, Castro mentions that he, too, routinely watches CNN. Turner, never shy about promoting his companies, asks Castro if he would be willing to say as much on camera for a commercial. Castro puffs on his cigar and says, in effect, why not? The commercial has never run on the air, but Turner hauls it out to show to visiting friends now and then.

Turner is one of a kind. Handsome, raucous, funny, erratic, he owns a buffalo ranch, the Atlanta Braves baseball team, MGM's library of old movies, and, according to critics, the biggest mouth in the South.

A fierce exemplar of free enterprise, he was also a peace activist long before he and actress Jane Fonda began a highly-publicized romance. He launched the "Goodwill Games" in Moscow at a time when it took political, as well as financial, courage to do so. His networks also run a heavy schedule of pro-ecology programming.

Today Turner is by far the most visionary of a dozen or so hard-driving media barons who are revolutionizing the media even more deeply than Benjamin Day—and whose collective efforts will, over the long term, shift power in many countries.

THE MULTI-CHANNEL SOCIETY

The basic direction of change in the media since at least 1970, when *Future Shock* foreshadowed the coming de-massification of the airwaves, has been toward the breakup of mass audiences into segments and subgroups, each receiving a different configuration of programs and messages. Along with this has come a vast expansion of the sheer amount of imagery transmitted by television in the form of both news and entertainment.

There is a reason for this image-explosion.

Humans, of course, have always exchanged symbolic images of reality. That is what language is all about. It is what knowledge is based on. However, different societies require either more or less symbolic exchange. The transition to a knowledge-based economy sharply increases the demand for communication and swamps the old image-delivery systems.

Advanced economies require a labor force with high levels of symbolic sophistication. This work force needs instant and largely free access to all sorts of information hitherto considered irrelevant to its productivity. It needs workers who can quickly adapt to, and even anticipate, repeated changes in work methods, organization, and daily life.

The very best workers are worldly, alert to new ideas and fashions, customer preferences, economic and political changes, aware of competitive pressures, cultural shifts, and many other things previously regarded as pertinent only to managerial elites.

This wide-scan knowledge does not come out of classrooms or from technical manuals alone, but from exposure to a constant barrage of news delivered by TV, newspapers, magazines, and radio. It also comes indirectly from "entertainment"—much of which unintentionally delivers information about new life styles, interpersonal relationships, social problems, and even foreign customs and markets.

Some shows, like *Murphy Brown*, which stars the actress Candice Bergen, deliberately build drama or comedy around current news. But even when this is not the case, television shows, sometimes despite themselves, convey images of reality.

It is true that the intentional content of a television show—the plot and the behavior of the principal characters—often paints a false picture of social reality. However, there is in all television programs and commercials, as well as in movies, an additional layer of what we might call "inadvertent content."

This consists of background detail—landscape, cars, street scenes, architecture, telephones, answering machines, as well as barely noticed behavior, like the banter between a waitress and a customer as the hero seats himself at a lunch counter. In contrast with the intended content, the inadvertent detail frequently provides a quite accurate picture of quotidian reality. Moreover, even the tritest "cop shows" picture current fads and fashions, and express popular attitudes toward sex, religion, money, and politics.

None of this is ignored or forgotten by the viewer. It is filed away in the mind, forming part of a person's general bank of knowledge about the world. Thus, good and bad alike, it influences the bag of assumptions brought to the workplace. (Ironically, much of the worker's image of the world, which increasingly affects economic productivity, is thus absorbed during "leisure" hours.) For this reason, "mere entertainment" is no longer "mere."

In short, the new economy is tightly tied not only to formal knowledge and technical skills but even to popular culture and the expanding market for imagery. This seething market is not only growing, but is simultaneously being restructured. Its very categories are re-forming. For better or worse, the old lines between show business and politics, leisure and work, news and entertainment, are all crashing, and we are exposed to a hurricane of often fragmented, kaleidoscopic images.

THE ARRIVAL OF CHOICE

The main producers of this imagery until recently were the major broadcast networks. Today, in the United States, where de-massification is most advanced, their power is plummeting. Where ABC, NBC, and CBS once stood virtually alone, there are now seventy-two national services of various kinds, with more coming on line. "A new crop of networks serving 'niche' markets is the big news in cable," according to *The Hollywood Reporter*. Soon to be added are a comedy network, a consumer-business news network, and a science-fiction network. In addition, Channel One pipes programs into school classrooms, and National College Television uses satellite to target special programs to university students.

In 1970, *Future Shock* declared that "the invention of electronic video recording, the spread of cable television, the possibility of broadcasting direct from satellite . . . all point to vast increases in program variety."

Today, cable TV is available in 57 percent of American homes and is conservatively projected to reach 67 percent within the decade. The average cable user has more than twenty-seven channels to choose from, and that will soon top fifty. In a small town like Rochester, Minnesota, viewers can choose from more than forty different channels offering a wide range of material, from the Black Entertainment Network and programs in Spanish, to specialized medical training programs aimed at the larger medical community around the famed Mayo Clinic.

Cable was the first to begin fractionalizing the mass audience. Videocassette and direct broadcast satellite (delivering signals not only to cable stations but into the home itself) fractionalize the fractions. Thus videocassette offers viewers a choice of thousands of movies and programs. And recently four major companies banded together to deliver 108 channels of standard and high-definition TV to American viewers by shooting signals from the world's most powerful commercial satellite to "napkin-size" receiver dishes in the home.

Furthermore, the number of stations operating independently of the three big networks has quadrupled since the late 1970s. Many have formed themselves into syndicates or temporary groupings that compete with the majors for top-rated programming. The impact of all these de-massifying forces on the once-mighty networks has been, as *Newsweek* put it, little short of "catastrophic."

Says Robert Iger, head of ABC's entertainment division, "The key words in all of this are choice and alternatives. It's what people didn't have back in 1980. It's what they do have today." But these are precisely what the main networks were designed to prevent. For CBS, ABC, and NBC were Second Wave smokestack companies, accustomed to dealing with masses, not heterogeneous micromarkets, and are having as much difficulty adapting to the post-smokestack Third Wave economy as are General Motors and Exxon. A measure of the networks' concern was the decision of NBC to join in the direct broadcast satellite venture.

Asked what will happen to the Big Three, Al Burton, a top independent TV producer, says: "Once upon a time there were three big radio networks too. Today hardly anyone even remembers they existed."

THE COMING EUROVISION

While the de-massification of the media began earliest in the United States, Europe is now catching up.

In the United States broadcasting has been a private industry, while in most European countries radio and, especially, television were for many years either government-run or financed by special taxes paid by listeners and viewers. As a result, Europeans had even less choice of programming than Americans had when the big networks dominated.

Today's changes are remarkable. There are now more than fifty satellite TV services in Europe. British Satellite Broadcasting (BSB) plans five direct broadcast satellite services, while Sky Television, another contender, plans six distinct services.

Sky and BSB are fiercely battling, each threatening to pull the other down, each spending pots of money without any likelihood of immediate return. Both have their eye fixed on the bonanza that awaits if an estimate by Saatchi & Saatchi, Britain's biggest ad agency, proves even partly correct. According to Saatchi, within a decade more than half of Britain's homes will be equipped to receive satellite-to-home transmissions, and satellite TV will be supported by about $1.3 billion in advertising revenues. At first slow to catch on, home dishes are now selling rapidly, and number over 700,000.

British viewers, who at one time were limited to two BBC channels and who got their fourth network only in 1982, are likely to have some fifteen satellite channels available to them before long.

France, in a politically explosive move, ended its monopoly control of television in 1986, when La Cinq (Channel 5) went into service with a glitzy grand opening that featured singer-actor Charles Aznavour cutting the ribbon. In a short time France went from a country with three government-run networks to one with six networks, of which four are private. Pay-TV channels like Canal Plus in France are growing in Switzerland and the Low Countries as well.

In Italy, RAI, the state radio and television corporation, now faces competition from at least four networks. Rome boasts perhaps twenty-five channels of television.

West Germany has added two new commercial channels and has been busy cabling up since 1985, when its first private cable channel went on the air to the strains of Dvorak's *New World Symphony*. Today 6 million West German homes are already cabled. And Spain, not to be outraced, is opening three new private networks to compete with its state networks.

The situation is changing so swiftly that these estimates may be out of date by the time they see print. And no one knows for sure how many more new channels Europe will add in the years to come, doubling or perhaps tripling its total. And this is without the explosion of television and radio likely to occur in the Eastern

European countries freed of their communist governments. There, multiple networks will spring up like dandelions.

Japan, meanwhile, which has pioneered high-definition television, has been much slower, so far, to spread cable or to multiply channels. If, however, it remains true to historical precedent, when it finally makes the decision to do so, it will move with blinding speed.

Two seemingly contradictory things are happening, therefore. At the financial level: consolidation. At the actual level of what audiences get to see: increasing diversity fed by a dizzying variety of new channels and media.

THE GLOBAL SELL

The existence of a global image market has led some companies, including media companies, to a simple, linear conclusion. The time had come to "globalize," meaning they would now try doing on a global scale what they had successfully done before on a national scale.

This straight-line strategy has turned out to be a loser.

Advanced wealth creation presupposes the globalization of a good bit of manufacturing and the parallel development of global means of distribution. Thus, as manufacturing and distribution corporations began forming cross-border alliances, or merging across national frontiers, ad agencies followed suit. Taking advantage of the low dollar, Britain's WPP, for example, swallowed up both J. Walter Thompson and Ogilvy & Mather, each an American giant in its own right. In its drive to become the world's biggest agency, Saatchi & Saatchi gulped down Compton Advertising and Dancer Fitzgerald Sample, among other firms.

In theory, transnational ad agencies would be in a position to channel standardized advertising from transnational corporations into transnational media with minimum effort. The same commercials would be translated into many languages. Presto! Bigger commissions for the agency.

The rationale for the "global sell" strategy was supplied in part by marketing guru Theodore Levitt of Harvard, who preached that "the world's needs and desires have been irrevocably homogenized," and who celebrated the coming of "global" products and brands—implying that the same product, backed by the same advertising, which once sold nationally could now be sold to the whole world. The same industrial-style standardization that earlier took place on the national level would now take place on a global level.

What's wrong with the global sell theory is that it makes little distinction among the world's regions and markets. Some are still in a pre-mass-market condition; others are still at the mass-market stage; and some are already experiencing the de-massification characteristic of an advanced economy. In these last, consumers demand greater individualization and customization of products and positively shun certain homogeneous goods or services. The same marketing or advertising can hardly be expected to work in all of them.

The Levitt theory also drastically underestimates the economic impact of cultural preferences and assumptions at a time when culture is growing more, not less, important. A 1988 study by the Hill Samuel merchant bank for the Confederation of British Industry suggests that even a unified Europe cannot be regarded as uniform. According to its report, French housewives prefer washing machines that load from the top, while the British like front-loaders better. Germans regard low blood pressure as a problem needing heavy medication, while British doctors don't. The French, the Hill Samuel study notes, worry about a "heart/digestive condition known as 'spasmophilia,' the existence of which U.K. doctors don't even recognise." Are attitudes toward food, beauty, work, play, love—or, for that matter, politics—any less diverse?

In practice, the simplistic "global sell" theory proved disastrous for firms that applied it. *The Wall Street Journal,* in a front-page lead article, described the theory as a costly fiasco. The paper detailed the agonies of Parker Pen when it tried to follow the formula. (It went into the red, sacked the responsible executives, and eventually had to sell off its pen division.) When an attempt was made to peddle an Erno Laszlo skin-care brand to fair-skinned Australians and dark-skinned Italians alike, the pitch, not surprisingly, flopped. Even McDonald's, it turns out, accommodates national differences, selling beer in Germany, wine in France, and even, at one time, mutton pot pie in Australia. In the Philippines it offers McSpaghetti. If diversity is necessary in consumer products, is it likely to be less necessary in culture or political ideology? Will global media really homogenize away the differences among peoples?

The fact is that with some exceptions, cultures, too—like products—are de-massifying. And the very multiplicity of media accelerates the process. Thus it is high diversity, not uniformity, that the marketers of political candidates or ideas will be forced to confront. If products, with only rare exceptions, fail when they try to sweep the world market, why should politicians or policies succeed?

Rather than homogenizing the planet, as the old Second Wave media did, the new global media system could deepen diversity instead. Globalization, therefore, is not the same as homogeneity. Instead of a single global village, as forecast by Marshall McLuhan, the late Canadian media theorist, we are likely to see a multiplicity of quite different global villages—all wired into the new media system, but all straining to retain or enhance their cultural, ethnic, national, or political individuality.

THE NEW BARONS

The globalization of the media, necessary for the new economy, is in fact moving rapidly.

When Japan's Sony bought up Columbia Pictures Entertainment for $5 billion, acquiring Hollywood's largest library of films, including such quality products as *On the Waterfront, Lawrence of Arabia,* and *Kramer vs. Kramer,* along with 220 movie houses and 23,000 TV episodes, it shook the entertainment industry. Sony is preparing a big push to sell its 8mm video players and recorders and wanted the "software" to go with its "hardware." But the deal is only one of many that are changing the structure of the image industry.

Thus Fujisankei Communications Group has bought into Virgin Music. Britain's TV South has bought MTM Enterprises, the TV firm founded by Mary Tyler Moore. Germany's Bertelsmann Group, one of the biggest media companies of them all, owns properties in more than twenty countries. Rupert Murdoch's span reaches across three continents, and encompasses newspapers and magazines, book publishing, movies, and a TV network in the United States.

One side effect of all this activity is the rise of a colorful group of global media barons, among whom the Australian-American Murdoch was a pioneer.

Charged (sometimes unfairly) with debasing the newspapers he owns, riding roughshod over trade unions, and being a ruthless competitor, he is also a long-range thinker who systematically studies the latest technologies. Apart from the newspapers he owns or controls in Australia, the United States, and Britain, Murdoch has been carefully piecing together a vertically integrated global media empire.

He owns a significant chunk of 20th Century-Fox Broadcasting, which owns the rights to thousands of hours of films and TV programs. He owns the Fox TV network and *TV Guide* magazine in the United States. In Europe he has pioneered satellite broadcasting, and owns 90 percent of Sky Channel, a new sports network, and a twenty-four-hour news channel which draws some of its material from his London newspapers, *The Times* and *The Sunday Times*. Beyond this, he has formed a fifty-fifty joint venture with Amstrad, a British firm, to manufacture cheap satellite dishes designed to pick up broadcasts beamed into the home.

Whether this vertical integration will ultimately produce the desired "synergy" remains to be seen. Other industries, as we've seen, are moving away from vertical integration. But win or lose, Murdoch has already pumped new energy into the entire publishing and broadcast industries.

In Britain, Robert Maxwell, a swaggering bulldozer of a man—sometimes called, behind his back, the "Bouncing Czech," the "Black Hurricane," or "Captain Bob"—started out by publishing a tiny chain of obscure academic journals. Born in Czechoslovakia, Maxwell served as an officer in the British Army in World War II and later was elected to Parliament.

From his tiny scholarly publishing base, he has, in fact, built an empire made up of pieces of many existing television properties, including TF1 in France, Canal 10 in Spain, Central Television in Britain, a movie channel, and an MTV channel. His extensive operations include magazines, newspapers, and the Macmillan book publishing firm in the United States.

In sharp contrast to Maxwell and Turner, Reinhard Mohn is a modest man with a philosophical turn of mind and carefully thought-out ideas about management, employee participation, and the social responsibilities of ownership.

A German prisoner of war in Concordia, Kansas, during World War II, Mohn was impressed by American democracy and, among other things, the Book-of-the-Month Club. He returned to the small town of Guetersloh, took over the family's Bible publishing house, and proceeded to build the Bertelsmann Group into a media powerhouse. In addition to book and record clubs in Germany, Spain, Brazil, the United States, and eighteen other countries, Bertelsmann owns the Bantam Doubleday Dell Publishing Group in the United States, Plaza y Janes book publishers in Spain, as well as thirty-seven magazines in five countries, plus record labels like RCA/Ariola, and more than a few radio and television properties.

Italy's Silvio Berlusconi, meanwhile, whose TV stations account for 60 percent of all Italian ad revenues, has reached across into France, where he is part-owner of La Cinq; Germany, where he owns a major chunk of Tele-5; and into Moscow, which has named him the exclusive purveyor of advertising for the Soviet Union in Europe. Berlusconi is making eyes at Yugoslavia, Spain, and Tunisia as well.

THE FORGING OF GLOBAL OPINION

Shifts of financial power over the media always spark hot controversy. Today the sheer size of the media empires provokes anxiety. Established networks and other media are threatened. Moreover, the concentration of financial control in the hands of the Murdochs and Berlusconis conjures up memories of the great press lords of the past, such as William Randolph Hearst in the United States or Lord Northcliffe in Britain, men whose political influence was enormous and by no means universally admired.

The first and most common criticism heard today is that the new global media will homogenize the world. The failure of the "global marketing" theory, however, suggests this fear is overdrawn.

The mass media had their strongest homogenizing effects when there were only a few channels, few different media, and hence little audience choice. In the future, the reverse situation will prevail. While the content of each individual program may be good or bad, the most important new "content" of all is the existence of diversity itself. The shift from a low-choice to a high-choice media environment holds not only cultural but political implications.

High-tech governments face a future in which multiple, conflicting, custom-tailored commercial, cultural, and political messages will bombard their people, rather than a single message repeated in unison by a few giant media outlets. The old "politics of mass mobilization" and the "engineering of consent" both become far more difficult in the new media environment.

Expanded media choice is itself inherently democratic. It makes life difficult for politicians who offer their followers a choiceless environment.

A second set of complaints about the new media barons relates to their personal political views. Murdoch is charged with being too conservative. Maxwell is too close to the British Labour Party. Turner is an unpredictable maverick. This one has sold his soul to French President Mitterand, while that one is in bed with someone else. If all these charges were true, they would soon cancel one another out.

Far more important than their personal political views and alliances are the interests they hold in common. Of course, all are capitalists operating in a capitalist framework. As such, we can assume that, in general, the bottom line interests them more than any political line.

What matters most about these media lords is not whether they favor left-wing or right-wing policies and politicians. Far more significant is their support, through their actions more than their words, of the ideology of globalism. Globalism, or at least supranationalism, is a natural expression of the new economy, which must operate across national boundaries, and it is in the self-interest of the new media moguls to spread this ideology.

This self-interest, however, collides with another. For if their television and radio stations, their newspapers and magazines are to succeed financially, they will have to de-massify—which means they will have to search for niches, carry specialized material, and appeal to very local audience interests. The familiar slogan "Think global, act local" perfectly describes the new media imperatives.

The very existence, however, of powerful media of communication capable of spanning continents will shift power as between national political leaders and the global community. Thus, without necessarily intending it, the new media barons are drastically changing the role of "global opinion" in the world.

Just as in the past century national leaders were compelled to justify their actions before the court of national "public opinion," tomorrow's national leaders will confront a much-enhanced "global opinion." And just as the work of Benjamin Day or Henry Hetherington or Émile de Girardin brought the poorer classes into the political life of nations, the activities of today's media lords will bring new millions into the global decision-making process.

Today, nations flout global opinion without worrying overmuch about the consequences. World opinion did not save the victims of Auschwitz, the people of Cambodia, or, more recently, the boat people fleeing hunger and oppression in Asia. Nor did it prevent the Chinese from murdering their protesting students in Beijing.

Nevertheless, global opinion has sometimes stayed the hand of killer regimes. The history of human rights is filled with cases in which global protests have prevented the torture or murder of a domestic political prisoner. It is unlikely that Anatoly Shcharansky would have survived his encounter with Soviet prison camps had the outside world not put pressure on Moscow to release him. Andrei Sakharov's chances for survival were improved when he won the Nobel Prize and became a household word because of constant media attention around the world.

The global media system will not make nations behave like Boy Scouts. But it raises the costs of defying world opinion. In the world being constructed by the media barons, what outsiders say about a nation will carry more weight inside than it ever did before.

Governments will no doubt invent more sophisticated lies with which to rationalize their self-serving actions and manipulate the increasingly systemic media. They will also step up propaganda efforts to improve their global image. But if such efforts fail, they could suffer significant economic penalties for behavior frowned on by the rest of the world.

South Africa may deny that sanctions hurt its economy or that its pariah image also damaged the country economically. But its senior officials know better. Global opinion sets the stage for global action.

Even if an outraged world does not impose formal trade sanctions on a rogue regime, international agencies like the World

Bank may reject their pleas for multibillion loans. Private banks may shy away, foreign investors and tourists go elsewhere. Worse yet, companies and countries still willing to do business with a pariah nation are in a position to drive a harder bargain than might have been the case otherwise. Power in the negotiations shifts as a result of global imagery.

What's more, as the importance of global opinion grows in parallel with the spread of the systemic media, shrewd power-players will wield it as an unconventional weapon. It will be used not only to save some political prisoners, or to direct instant relief to disaster zones, but to spare us from some, at least, of the ecological ravages that might otherwise be inflicted on a bleeding planet.

When Armenians are attacked by Azeris in Baku, Armenians in Los Angeles know it instantly and begin mobilizing political action. When Jesuits are murdered by a death squad in El Salvador, the entire world knows it. When a trade unionist is jailed in South Africa, the word gets out. The new global media are basically in business to make a profit. But they are inadvertently raising the level of cross-national political action by a dazzling diversity of activist groups.

Without even intending it, Murdoch and Maxwell, Turner and Mohn, Berlusconi and other new media magnates are creating a powerful new tool and placing it in the hands of the global community.

But that hardly scratches the surface of what is happening. As we'll see next, the new global media system has, in fact, become the prime tool of revolution in today's fast-changing world.

27

SUBVERSIVE MEDIA

On June 30, 1988, in Victorville, California, near Los Angeles, the Sheriff's Department received a complaint. Five Mexican men were blasting loud music, drinking beer, and urinating on the lawn in a party that lasted over twelve hours. When six sheriff's deputies came to investigate and tried to quiet the men down, fists and night sticks began to fly. For the sheriff's men, it was hardly a unique event. Except for one thing.

Unknown to them, as they struggled to subdue the five, using night sticks and choke holds, a next-door neighbor pointed a videocamera out the window.

Public outrage against alleged police brutality erupted instantly after the four-minute tape was shown to the town's Latino community. Civil rights protests followed, then a lawsuit against the deputies, charging them with the use of excessive force. Said Armando Navarro, executive director of the Institute for Social Justice, a local civil rights organization, "I've dealt for twenty-one years in community activism, but I've never had something so classic, showing the violence in living color."

Lawyers for the deputies, on the other hand, contended that the tape did not tell the truth because it didn't show what happened before the camera was turned on—when, the deputies say, violence was used against *them*.

The case took on larger dimensions when the person who shot the tape disappeared and when a representative of Mexico's consulate in Los Angeles began showing up in the courtroom to monitor the trial, evidencing concern about anti-Mexican discrimination in the United States. In the end, a federal court ruled against the sheriff's men and awarded the Mexicans $1 million.

It is unlikely that the revolutionaries who overthrew the communist government in Czechoslovakia in 1989 ever heard of the case of the "Victorville Five." But in the streets of Prague, students set up TV monitors on street corners and played videotapes showing the brutality of Czech authorities trying to suppress antigovernment street rallies. The students also played tapes of speeches by dramatist Vaclav Havel, who went from being a political prisoner to the presidency. Elsewhere, in Taiwan, too, the political opposition has used videocameras and monitors to expose what they called government violence.

All across the world, new communication media, or new ways of using old ones, are being exploited to challenge—and sometimes overthrow—the power of the state. In the words of Solidarity founder Lech Walesa, describing the political upheavals in Eastern Europe, "These reforms are a result of civilization—of computers, satellite TV [and other innovations] that present alternative solutions."

THE NASTY LITTLE MAN ON TV

It is clear that the domino-wave of revolutions that swept Eastern Europe in 1989 was a consequence of three convergent forces: the long-term failure of socialism to deliver the economic wealth it promised; the announcement by the Soviet Union that it would no longer prop up communist governments with the threat of military intervention; and the avalanche of information that poured into communist countries despite all the efforts of their censors—information carried by the new means of communication.

During the quarter-century dictatorship of Nicolae Ceausescu, Romania imposed the harshest censorship of any communist regime in Eastern Europe, controlling everything that appeared in the press and especially on television. Ceausescu himself was a television fan, and especially liked episodes of *Kojak*, the American cop-show starring Telly Savalas. But for all his viewing, Ceausescu failed to understand the world media revolution and paid with his life on Christmas Day, 1989.

Had Ceausescu studied the role of the new global media system, for example, in the overthrow of Ferdinand Marcos in the Philippines, he would have known that control of the domestic media is no longer enough to keep a people in ignorance, and that domestic political events are increasingly played out on a global stage.

"What happened in the Philippines," said Professor William Adams, a media expert at George Washington University, "was an epic step toward a new kind of revolution—a revolution via the media and via symbols."

Because of historically close connections between the Philippines and the United States and the continuing presence of U.S. military bases there, Marcos and his main political opposition courted U.S. support. Both sought out foreign journalists to tell their story.

As opposition mounted, Marcos reluctantly agreed to hold an election in 1986. The ensuing campaign was given saturation coverage by the American TV cameras, drawn by the drama of Cory Aquino, widow of an assassinated hero, confronting the corrupt old dictator.

At first President Reagan supported Marcos. But as the U.S. TV coverage continued, Americans saw nice middle-class peaceful demonstrators opposed by Marcos goons, and Reagan's position began to shift. Wrote the television critic of *The Washington Post:* "It didn't look good to be allied with this nasty little man on TV."

Reagan sent an official team to Manila to monitor the elections for corruption and fraud. Led by Senator Richard Lugar, the team found ample evidence of both and disclosed its conclusions to television audiences even before reporting back officially to the President. Its reports further hurt the Marcos campaign, and what Americans saw on their TV screens instantly seeped back into the Philippines.

The TV coverage also influenced the White House, which ultimately backed an anti-Marcos military faction, and with that, the combination of force and information squeezed Marcos out of office. In the end, faced with the inevitable, Marcos fled the country and was permitted to settle in Hawaii.

Said one political analyst afterward: "If he had been one of the twentieth century's great tyrants, he would have kicked out the media and opened up with the machine guns."

Yet the reverse might well have been true for Ceausescu. Had he allowed the media in and not opened up with machine guns, he might conceivably have survived. The initial overthrow of communist regimes in other Eastern European countries in the dramatic winter of 1989 was peaceful. Only in Romania did the machine guns stutter.

One of the dictator's last acts was to order the massacre of protestors in the city of Timisoara. As Romanians swarmed into the streets of Bucharest after that, fighting broke out between the military and Ceausescu's feared security forces, the Securitate. The strife continued for days, the Securitate battling on even after Ceausescu and his wife were given a drumhead trial and shot by a firing squad.

By now the revolution was centered in Studio 4 of "Free Romanian Television." Even as snipers and commandos tried to retake the studio from them, leaders of the revolution, in control of the airwaves, played and replayed pictures of the corpses of the dictator and his wife. Only after that did the bloodshed cease.

Shortly afterward, *The New York Times* declared that his dictatorship had been replaced by a "videocracy."

Following the overthrow of communist regimes all across Eastern Europe, the *Financial Times* exulted: "The medium which George Orwell saw as the tool of enslavement has proved the liberator; not even a Ceausescu could blindfold his people."

Yet by overfocusing on television, many observers miss the larger story. For it isn't just television that is revolutionary, but the combined *interplay* of many different technologies.

Millions of computers, fax machines, printers and copying machines, VCRs, videocassettes, advanced telephones, along with cable and satellite technologies, now interact with one another and cannot be understood in isolation. Television is only a part of this much larger system, which links up at points with the intelligent electronic networks that business and finance use to exchange computerized data.

This new overarching media system is a cause of (and a reaction to) the rise of the new, knowledge-based economy, and it represents a quantum jump in the way the human race uses symbols and images. No part of this vast web is entirely cut off from the rest. And that, in turn, is what makes it potentially subversive—not just for the remaining Ceausecus of the world but for all power-holders. The new media system is a powershift accelerator.

THREE MEDIA MODES

The best way to understand its power is to place today's media revolution in historical perspective, and to distinguish clearly among three different modes of communication.

In highly oversimplified terms, we can say that in First Wave or agrarian societies, most communications passed mouth-to-ear and face-to-face within very small groups. In a world without newspapers, radio, or television, the only way for a message to reach a mass audience was by assembling a crowd. The crowd was, in fact, the first mass medium.

A crowd may "send a message" upward to its ruler. In fact, the very size of the crowd is itself a message. But whatever else the crowd may communicate, it also sends an identical message to all its participants. This message—which can be profoundly subversive—is simple: "You are not alone." The crowd, therefore, has played a crucial role in history. The problem with the crowd or mob as a communications medium, however, is that it is usually ephemeral.

The crowd was not the only pretechnological mass medium. In the West during the medieval era, the Catholic Church, because of its extensive organization, was the closest thing to a durable mass medium—and the only one able to transmit the same message to large populations *across political boundaries*. This unique capacity gave the Vatican immense power vis-à-vis Europe's feuding kings and princelings. It accounts in part for the seesaw power struggles between church and state that bloodied Europe for centuries.

The Second Wave system of wealth creation, based on factory mass production, needed more communication at a distance and gave rise to the post office, telegraph, and telephone. But the new factories also needed a homogeneous work force, and technologically based mass media were invented. Newspapers, magazines, movies, radio, and television, each capable of carrying the same message to millions simultaneously, became the prime instruments of massification in the industrial societies.

The new Third Wave system, by contrast, reflects the needs of the emerging post-mass-production economy. Like the latest "flexible manufacturing" plants, it customizes its image products and sends different images, ideas, and symbols to closely targeted population segments, markets, age categories, professions, ethnic or life-style groupings.

This new high diversity of messages and media is necessary because the new system of wealth creation requires a far more heterogeneous work force and population. The de-massification foreshadowed in *Future Shock* and elaborated in *The Third Wave* thus has become a key characteristic of the new media system. But this is only one of its aspects.

MEDIA-FUSION

Unlike the Second Wave media, each of which operated more or less independently of the other, the new media are closely interlinked and fused together, feeding data, images, and symbols back and forth to one another. Examples of this fusion abound.

A radio call-in show, which links listeners and broadcasters via the telephone lines, becomes the subject of a 1988 movie, *Talk Radio,* which in turn is shown on cable television and reviewed in the print media and then—who knows?—discussed on radio call-in shows.

Or take *Broadcast News,* a movie about television newscasters, which after being shown in many cinemas is itself shown on television and advertised in the newspapers.

Newsweek describes "the now almost commonplace spectacle of an Iowa farmer being interviewed by a print reporter who is being shot by a still photographer who is being taped by a TV crew, all of which is the subject of a magazine's media story." A still photograph of precisely that scene illustrates the *Newsweek* account.

At a deeper level, newspaper newsrooms watch TV monitors to keep abreast of the latest events. Many European correspondents in Washington watch CNN's live coverage and write their newspaper stories based on what television shows them. From serving as the medium, TV becomes the source.

TV talk-show producers get ideas for subjects and guests from the newspapers. All of them depend on fax, computers, word processors, electronic typesetters, digitized imagery, electronic networks, satellites, or other interlinked technologies.

It is this dense interpenetration that transforms the individual media into a *system*. Combined with globalization, it reduces the clout of any single medium, channel, publication, or technology relative to all the others. But it endows the media system-as-a-whole with an enormously enhanced power that permeates the planet. What is at work, therefore, is not "videocracy" but "media-fusion."

VALLEYS OF IGNORANCE

To "fusion" must be added "diffusion," for no part of the world is now completely cut off from the rest. Messages get through the most tightly guarded borders.

Despite Ceausecu's cruel censorship, many Romanians were able to pick up Bulgarian television from across the border. (Many Bulgarians, in turn, preferred Soviet television to their own.) Even before the revolution, Romanians knew the names of the anti-Ceausescu dissidents who risked imprisonment by calling for human rights. Their names were familiar from foreign broadcasts beamed into Romania.

Most East Germans were able to watch West German television stations, which told them things their Communist government would have preferred to suppress. Thus in 1989, when big anti-government demonstrations occurred in Leipzig, East Germans learned about it from West German transmissions. In the same way, they found out when Hungary opened its borders to East German refugees and where cracks were opening in the Berlin Wall. Those out of reach of these West German TV transmissions lived mainly in the Dresden region, which was spoken of as the "Valley of Ignorance." These "valleys" are getting smaller.

Cross-border television "leakage" is hardly new, nor is the fact that Voice of America and Radio Free Europe, the British Broadcasting Corporation (BBC), and others beamed shortwave programming into the communist countries. During the China democracy protests preceding the massacre near Tiananmen Square, the Voice of America broadcast eleven and a half hours a day, reaching an estimated 100 million Chinese listeners. It even broadcast simple instructions on how to avoid government attempts to "jam" the transmissions.

What is different now, however, is the subversive media strategy employed by today's revolutionaries.

THE REVOLUTIONISTS' MEDIA STRATEGY

What Ceausescu was not alone in missing were the strategic ways in which First Wave, Second Wave, and Third Wave communications can sometimes be combined or opposed to one another.

A good example is provided by religion.

One of the biggest gainers from the 1989 revolutions in Eastern Europe has been the Catholic Church, long suppressed but never destroyed by the communist regimes. The church, as suggested above, was itself a mass medium, long before today's Jim Bakkers and Jimmy Swaggerts hit the Protestant televangelical circuit, and long before Pat Robertson built so large a TV following that he was able to mount a campaign for the presidency of the United States.

The church wields power in the world today partly because of its moral influence and economic resources, but also because it continues to serve as a mass medium. Able to reach numberless millions every Sunday morning, it makes the audience for some of the world's top-rated television shows seem small indeed. Of course, it communicates with its members the other six days of the week as well, and in today's world the church makes use of newspapers, magazines, and other media in support of its face-to-face communications.

So long as the Catholic Church—or any other organized religion—can gather enormous flocks, and thus reach a mass audience, no government can ignore it. Some governments, as we know, have tried to extirpate the church (which is almost impossible). Others have tried peddling a substitute religion based on nationalism, Marxism, or some other doctrine. Still others compromise and try to co-opt the church.

In totalitarian states the existence of an unco-opted or unsuppressed mass medium in the hands of the church is a constant threat, for there is always the danger that this channel will be made available to the political opposition. This accounts for the ferocity with which communist states tried to kill off the church or to buy it off when that proved impossible.

The recognition that organized religion, whatever else it might be, is also a mass medium helps explain many recent shifts of power.

It helps explain why, so often in history, in countries as different as Iran under the Shah or South Korea under Chun Doo Hwan, economic and other popular discontents are channeled into religious movements. In Iran, of course, this canalization of protest into a religious form led to the overthrow of the Shah's secular regime. In South Korea it led to a spectacular growth of Christianity, both Catholic and Protestant. In both countries organized religion took the place of, or merged with, a political opposition.

Ironically, the more successfully a totalitarian government censors and controls all the other media of expression, the more important the church medium becomes as a potential vehicle for dissidence. It may be the only way to express opposition to a regime.

But when the church opens its "channel" and expresses popular resentment from the pulpit, the medium alters the message, and the protest, which may originate in hunger or other material grievances, is recast in religious terms. This explains why movements that start out fighting for goals having little to do with religion, per se, become transmuted into religious crusades.

In Iran, the Ayatollah Khomeini fused class resentment and nationalist rage with religious fervor. Love of Allah + hatred of imperialism + anticapitalism = a triple-charged brand of fanaticism that turned the Middle East into a tinderbox.

But Khomeini did more than combine these three elements into a single passion. He also combined First Wave media—face-to-face exhortation by his mullahs to the faithful—with Third Wave technology—audio tapes with political messages, smuggled into the mosques, where they were played and duplicated on cheap tape recorders.

To counter Khomeini, the Shah used the Second Wave media—press, radio, and television. Once Khomeini managed to overthrow the Shah and take control of the state, he also took command of these centralized Second Wave media as well.

This strategy of using First and Third Wave media to combat those who control Second Wave media is common among revolutionary movements, and was even more conspicuous in China during the pro-democracy protests of 1989. The old men in Beijing who trembled when Ceausescu fell in Bucharest, six months after they massacred students near Tiananmen Square, underestimated the power of this strategy.

THE CHINA SYNDROME

In China, too, three modes of communication clashed in the battle for control of the mind.

Wall posters were a traditional First Wave tool of protest in China. Early in 1989 posters began showing up on the walls near Beijing University, lashing out at corruption, making fun of the privileged children of the party's top leaders, urging broadened democracy, calling for the ouster of Premier Li Peng and others.

By late spring, that other First Wave communications weapon, the crowd, came into play. Using the memorial service for the late Hu Yaobang, a reformist Communist Party leader, students from Beijing universities gathered in Tiananmen Square on April 22. The protesters' initial demands were moderate, focusing mainly on freedom of expression and an end to corruption. But as the government rebuffed the student demands, the demonstrators stayed on in the square and began a hunger strike. The peaceful crowds grew.

Soon they were joined by industrial workers bearing banners that proclaimed "Here come your elder brothers." And as the government stonewalled, the momentum grew until, at its peak on May 18 and 19, more than a million still-peaceful marchers from every walk of life took to the streets. The massive size of this crowd was itself a clear message.

During this same period, a fierce struggle broke out among the Chinese authorities over how to respond. The government, headed by Li Peng, tried to turn the Second Wave media— newspapers, radio, and television—against the protesters. But the party, headed by its reformist chairman, Zhao Ziyang, controlled much of the media, including the party organ, *People's Daily*.

As this power struggle tilted back and forth, the news coverage in the Second Wave media seesawed. When Zhao's supporters gained, *People's Daily* and Chinese television showed sympathy for the strikers' demands. By contrast, when the hard-liners gained, newscasters, editors, and journalists were forced to slant news against the protesters, thus using the Second Wave media to blunt the message carried by First Wave media.

Simultaneously, however, a battle began for control of the more advanced Third Wave media: satellites, fax machines, hand-held TV cameras, computers, copiers, and global communication networks.

The hard-liners now faced a double problem. They had to win decisive control not only over the domestic media, but over foreign press coverage as well. A wild card in the situation was the presence of a vast corps of foreign journalists and broadcasters who had come to China to cover the Gorbachev-Deng summit meeting. These journalists, many relying on satellites, computers, and other advanced Third Wave tools, stayed to cover events in the streets.

Particularly important was the Cable News Network, whose round-the-clock coverage went not merely into the White House and to millions of viewers around the world but, equally important, into hotels in Beijing itself. As the political battle raged, Chinese officials cut off its satellite links to the outside world, then restored them, then told foreign broadcasters to use China TV's own up-links. Confusion reigned.

Aware that global opinion is growing more important, the hard-liners tried desperately to cut all connections between the protesters and their supporters outside China. But because China in recent years had opened extensive economic relations with the outside world, and had permitted students to study abroad, this proved very difficult.

The protesters aimed many messages directly at foreign audiences. They patiently repeated their demands for the reporters and TV crews from abroad. They translated. They painted slogans in foreign languages so television viewers outside China could instantly understand them. "Le 1789 de Chine" compared their uprising to the French Revolution. For American consumption, they sang "We Shall Overcome" and adapted the words of Patrick Henry—"Give me democracy or give me death." These efforts to reach out were rewarded by sympathy marches in Hong Kong, Taiwan, Australia, and all across the United States.

Meanwhile, at Harvard University, a Chinese student set up a Beijing-to-Boston "hot line"—an open telephone link that brought round-the-clock news from Tiananmen Square to his small apartment near Harvard. From there it went by phone, fax, and computer to Chinese students all over the United States.

In turn, students at Stanford and Berkeley created what they termed a "news-lift"—using fax machines to send back to the strikers the latest news stories appearing in the U.S. press. These were addressed to the offices of companies in Beijing and other cities, in the hope that friendly hands would deliver them to the striking students. There were an estimated 30,000 fax machines in China and 3 million phone lines into Beijing.

The Chinese students in the United States, many of them the sons and daughters of high government and party officials, also tape-recorded telephone interviews with strikers and immediately delivered these to the Voice of America, which broadcast them back into China. When the government began jamming, the VOA switched to new frequencies.

This global battle for control of knowledge and the means of communication continued even after the hard-liners, having called out troops, killed many demonstrators and smashed the strike. Again relying on the Second Wave mass media, the government now broadcast pictures of student and worker "ringleaders" and displayed telephone numbers for informers to use if they spotted the fugitives.

But the same video was broadcast outside China, and from Canada to Italy, televiewers using international direct-dial phones tried to jam the lines so Chinese informers could not reach the government. It was the first known attempt at citizen-jamming across national borders.

In China, power once more blasted out of the barrel of a gun, as Mao Tse-tung said it would. But it was clear, as the events in Eastern Europe and elsewhere underscored, that the hard-liners who seized control could not rest easy in victory. China's move into the 21st century had only just begun.

What the China story also revealed, however, with startling clarity, were the media strategies of revolution and counterrevolution. Today, the Second Wave mass media still exert enormous influence. As the world speeds deeper into the Powershift Era, however, the Second Wave tools of mind control, once so overwhelming, will themselves be overwhelmed by the subversive media of tomorrow.

28

THE "SCREENIE" GENERATION

At almost the precise midpoint of the 20th century, George Orwell published *1984*, his scorching indictment of totalitarianism. The book pictured a government in total control of the mass media. Orwell's brilliant neologisms, like *newspeak* and *doublethink,* entered the language. The book became a powerful assault weapon in the fight against censorship and mind-manipulation, which is why it was banned for decades in the Soviet Union.

While it helped rally forces opposed to dictatorship of the mind, however, the book's projection of the future turned out to be highly questionable.

Orwell correctly envisioned such technologies as two-way television screens that could be used to deliver the state's propaganda to viewers while simultaneously spying on them, and his warnings about potential invasions of privacy are, if anything, understated. But he did not foresee—nor did anyone else at the time—the most important revolution of our era: the shift from an economy based on muscle to one dependent on mind.

He did not, therefore, anticipate today's astonishing proliferation of new communication tools. The number and variety of these technologies is now so great, and changing so swiftly, that even experts are bewildered. To confront the army of technical abbreviations, from HDTV and ISDN to VAN, ESS, PABX, CPE, OCC, and CD-I, is to sink into alphabetical asphalt. Even to scan the advertisements for consumer electronics is to come away dazed.

Rise above this clutter, however, and the basic outlines of tomorrow's Third Wave media become strikingly clear.

The electronic infrastructure of the advanced economies will have six distinct features, some of which have already been foreshadowed. These half-dozen keys to the future are: interactivity, mobility, convertibility, connectivity, ubiquity, and globalization.

When combined, these six principles point to a total transformation, not merely in the way we send messages to one another, but in the way we think, how we see ourselves in the world, and, therefore, where we stand in relationship to our various governments. Put together, they will make it impossible for governments —or their revolutionary opponents—to manage ideas, imagery, data, information, or knowledge as they once did.

THE SLAVE GOLFER

In a long low building on Los Angeles's Santa Monica Boulevard, a former president of the 20th Century-Fox movie studios, Gordon Stulberg, banters with Bernard Luskin, a psychotherapist. Luskin is a former community college president and a past head of the California Educational Computing Consortium. Together they run American Interactive Media's team of educators, artists, and computer programmers who plan to launch upon the world the next advance in compact-disc technology—CD-I, as in "Interactive."

AIM plans to release discs that play on the home television screen and make it possible for the viewer to interact with the visuals. Holding a remote in the palm of the hand and using one's thumb on a tiny "joystick," the owner of a disc called "Interactive Golf" can tee off against another player, manipulating a slave golfer on the screen as he lines up his shot. You can choose his clubs and determine the power and the arc of the drive. You can make him turn to the right or left and alter his swing. You control what happens on the screen.

The "Grolier Encyclopedia" disc makes it possible to call up audiovisual information about any of its listings. The text, animation, and visuals explain, say, a car engine or a DNA molecule, and can be moved and manipulated by the user.

Other interactive AIM discs include games, Bible stories, a new kind of atlas, a course in photography developed with Time-Life, and a disk that takes you on a tour of the Smithsonian and lets you manipulate the exhibits as you stroll through.

Owned by Polygram Records, a subsidiary of N.V. Philips, the

Dutch electronics giant, AIM is just one of several firms working with interactive video technology. Their goal is to make the TV experience active, rather than passive—to put the couch potato out of business.

Meanwhile, Interactive Game Network, a Northern California firm partly funded by United Artists, Le Groupe Videotron, Ltd., and General Electronics, Ltd., is taking a different path toward the same goal. It is building a device that will allow the home viewer to participate in popular TV game shows like *Jeopardy* or *Wheel of Fortune*. Players will communicate their answers to a central computer which will check all the home scores and choose a prizewinner.

But the most radical leap toward interactivity—still a gleam in the eye—consists of a vast network of what author George Gilder has called "telecomputers": interactive TV sets that are, in effect, personal computers too.

In addition to discs or cassettes, the TV set itself will come alive in the hands of its user, according to Gilder, who has looked closely at the technological frontiers in video and computing. "The line between 'television'—a business where Japan now reigns supreme—and 'computers'—where American industry holds the best cards—is blurring every day," he reports. The coming merger of these two technologies will shift power from the old television networks to the users, allowing them "to reshape the images as they wish." This new hybrid could also shift power from Japan to the United States, Gilder claims.

Whether that is true or not, two powerful streams of technical development are both pushing toward a vast extension of video interactivity.

A DECADENT LUXURY

A second principle of the new system is mobility. The phone in the airplane cabin and, even more, the cordless phone and the mobile car phone have begun to accustom users to the idea of communication from anywhere to anywhere while in motion.

At first regarded as a decadent luxury (the earliest telephones themselves were similarly regarded in the 19th century), car phones based on cellular radio have come into widespread use in the United States.

A consortium called Phonepoint, representing the German Bundespost, France Telecom, and Nynex, the New York telephone company, as well as British Telecom, is speeding the introduction of sophisticated "pocket phones" in England as well. Nor are mobile units purely decorative status symbols. For salespeople, plumbers, physicians, and others they have become a productivity-enhancing work tool.

As people work and play on the move, the demand for even cheaper, simpler, always-there communications is soaring, which provides the basis for the coming leap to that comic-strip invention, the Dick Tracy wristwatch phone.

But the phone is only one of a host of new devices that are becoming unplugged from the wall. Sony offers a 4.6-ounce pocket-size copier. The fax machine in the car, the vest-pocket video, the laptop computer, the portable printer are all spreading fast. Mobility is a second fundamental trait of the new system.

Convertibility is next—the ability to transfer information from one medium to another. For example, we are moving toward speech-based technologies that can convert an oral message into printed form and vice versa. Machines that can take dictation from several executives at the same time and spew out typed letters are well on the way toward practicality.

Such tools may shake up everything from employment and the organization of the office, to the role of literacy in daily life. But they are trivial compared with another form of conversion: automatic translation. Automatic conversion of commercial documents from one language to another, at least in a rough-and-ready form, is already available on France's Minitel system, as we saw in Chapter 10. More sophisticated translation is the object of intense research in Japan (which regards its language as an economic barrier). Similarly, the EC, which faces the need to translate into the languages of its twelve member nations, is eager for breakthroughs.

The fourth principle of the new infrastructure, connectivity, is a buzzword among computer and telecommunications users the world over, who are demanding the ability to connect their devices to a dazzling diversity of other devices, regardless of which manufacturer made them in what country.

Despite the heated political battles over standards, immense efforts are now driving toward connectibility, so that the same mobile, interactive, video-voice telecomputer of tomorrow can tie into an IBM mainframe in Chicago, a Toshiba laptop being used in Frankfurt, a Cray supercomputer in Silicon Valley, or a housewife's Dick Tracy phone in Seoul.

MORE THAN COMPASSION

Ubiquitization, the fifth key, is something else. By this we mean the systematic spread of the new media system around the world and down through every economic layer of society.

A potential nightmare facing high-tech governments derives from the split-up of populations into the info-rich and the info-poor. Any government that fails to take concrete action to avoid this division courts political upheaval in the future. Yet this dangerous polarization is hardly inevitable.

In fact, one can imagine considerable equality of access in the emerging society, not because of compassion or political good sense on the part of the affluent elites, but because of the workings of what might be called the Law of Ubiquity.

This law holds that strong commercial, as well as political, incentives will arise for making the new electronic infrastructure inclusive, rather than exclusive.

In its infancy the telephone was regarded as a luxury. The idea that everyone would someday have a phone was simply mystifying. Why on earth would everybody want one?

The fact that almost everyone in the high-tech nations now has a phone, rich and poor alike, did not stem from altruism but from the fact that the more people plugged into a system, the more valuable it became for all users and especially for commercial purposes.

The same proved true, as we've seen, in the early development of postal services. The industrial economy needed a way to send bills to, or advertise to, or sell newspapers and magazines to everyone, not just the rich. And today, once more, as fax machines begin to replace the industrial-era post office, similar pressures are accelerating the spread of the new technology.

There were 2.5 million fax machines in the United States in 1989, churning out billions of pages of faxed documents per year.

The fax population was doubling yearly, partly because early users were importuning friends, customers, clients, and family to buy a fax quickly, so that the early users could speed messages to them. The more faxes out there, the greater the value of the system to all concerned.

It is, therefore, in the distinct self-interest of the affluent to find ways of extending the new systems to include, rather than exclude, the less affluent.

Like phones and VCRs, faxes will begin to appear in even the humblest homes, driven by the Law of Ubiquity. And so will fiber optic cables and other advanced technologies, whether paid for by the individual, the public, or by other users whose fees will subsidize service to those who can't afford it.

The widest diffusion of communication capabilities is an inseparable part of the new system of wealth creation. The direction is almost inevitably toward what the old Bell phone company called "universal service"—i.e., ubiquity—combined with interactivity, mobility, convertibility, and connectibility.

Finally, the new infrastructure is global in scope. As capital flows electronically across national borders, zipping back and forth from Zurich to Hong Kong, Hong Kong to Norway, Norway to Tokyo, Tokyo to Wall Street in milliseconds, information traces equally complex pathways. A change in U.S. T-bill rates or the yen–deutsche mark ratio is instantly known around the world, and the morning after the big event in Los Angeles, youngsters in Ho Chi Minh City discuss the latest Grammy winners. The mental borders of the state become as permeable as its financial frontiers.

The combination of these six principles produces a revolutionary nervous system for the planet, capable of handling vastly enlarged quantities of data, information, and knowledge at much faster transmission and processing rates. It is a far more adaptable, intelligent, and complex nervous system for the human race than ever before imagined.

ELECTRONIC ACTIVISM

The rise of a new media system, corresponding in form with the requirements of a wholly new way of creating wealth, challenges those in power, giving rise to new political methods, constituencies, and alliances.

Just as people at, say, the beginning of the 18th century could not imagine the political changes that flowed from the spread of a smokestack economy, so today it is almost impossible, short of science-fiction-style speculation, to foresee the political uses to which the still emerging media system will be put.

Take, for example, interactivity.

By allowing TV viewers to use, rather than merely view, the screen, interactivity could someday change political campaigning and candidates. Interactive media make possible far more sophisticated opinion polling than ever before, not simply asking yes-no questions, but allowing respondents to make trade-offs among many options.

But the possibilities go beyond polling. Would a candidate, once elected, trade off jobs for environmental improvement—and if so, how many? How would the candidate respond to a hostage crisis, a race riot, or a nuclear disaster under differing sets of circumstances? Instead of trying to test the values and judgment of a potential President by listening to thirty-second commercials, the interactive video users of tomorrow could tune into a program, or insert a diskette, that would visually show the candidate discussing and making decisions under a variety of conditions programmed in by the voter. Political platforms could be issued in a spreadsheet format, so that the voters could manipulate their underlying budgetary assumptions and ask "what if" questions.

If large numbers can participate in a mass-appeal game show like *Jeopardy* with a computer tallying their responses, it doesn't take too much imagination to see how similar technology could be adapted to political polling or collective decision-taking—and political organizing of a new kind.

Futurists, simulation experts, and others have long speculated about the possibility of organizing very large numbers of citizens in political "games." Professor José Villegas at Cornell University developed models for such activity as far back as the late 1960s, including games that ghetto residents and squatters could engage in as a form of political education—and protest.

What was missing was the technology. The spread of networked interactivity will place the tools for political "games" in millions of living rooms. With them, citizens could, in principle at least, conduct their own polls, and form their own "electronic parties" or "electronic lobbies" and pressure groups around various issues.

One can also easily imagine electronic sabotage, not as the act of individual hackers or criminals, but for the purposes of political protest or blackmail. At 2:25 P.M. on the afternoon of January 15, 1990, engineers in Bedminster, New Jersey, noticed red lights flashing on the seventy-five screens that display the status of AT&T's long-distance telephone network in the United States. Each light indicated trouble.

"It just seemed to happen. Poof, there it was," said William Leach, manager of AT&T's network operations center. That "poof" added up to a massive breakdown in the U.S. long-distance phone system lasting for nine hours, during which an estimated 65 million calls were blocked.

AT&T investigators concluded that the breakdown resulted from a faulty computer program. But they could not "categorically rule . . . out" the possibility that it resulted from sabotage. It so happened that January 15 was the national holiday celebrating the birth of Dr. Martin Luther King, Jr. It also happened to be true that some racist Americans bitterly hated King and were outraged that a national holiday should commemorate him. The AT&T "blackout" may simply have been a random occurrence. But it doesn't stretch credulity too far to imagine electronic political protests and sabotage in the future.

One needn't engage in sci-fi speculation, however, to recognize some of the profound social tensions already arising from the introduction of a new form of economy—problems related to the way knowledge is disseminated in society.

THE INFORMATION DIVIDE

Today, because the Law of Ubiquity has not yet completed its action, high-tech societies, and especially the United States, suffer from a maldistribution of information—an "information divide" as deep as the Grand Canyon.

A seemingly intractable problem in many of the high-tech nations is the existence of what has come to be called an "underclass." The presence of this underclass is not only a moral affront to affluent societies but a menace to social peace, and ultimately a threat to democracy. It is simple-minded to assume that all those in the underclass are "victims" of society or unemployment. Many, perhaps most, are there for other reasons.

What is increasingly clear, however, is that work requires higher and higher informational skills, so that even if jobs are available, most of the members of this group cannot match the knowledge requirements.

Moreover, the knowledge needed goes beyond task-specific job skills. To be truly employable a worker must share certain implicit cultural understandings about things like time, dress, courtesy, money, causality, and language. Above all, the worker must be able to get and exchange information.

These generalized cultural skills cannot come out of textbooks or training sessions alone. They presuppose a familiarity with how the world-beyond-one's-own-street functions. That kind of knowledge comes increasingly from the media environment. It is from the media that people infer both social norms and "facts" about how things work.

The nature of the media, the pictures they deliver, the groups they target, and the feedback they permit are directly related, therefore, both to employment and to the problems of the underclass. Furthermore, the cultural divide between the underclass and the mainstream society actually widens as the new media system spreads.

Jeffrey Moritz is president of National College Television, which uses satellites to distribute specialized programming to college students for forty-two hours a week. NCT claims a student audience of 700,000. Ranging in age from eighteen to thirty-four, these are citizens today and potential leaders tomorrow. They represent, if anything, the polar opposite of the young people in the underclass. (As Moritz points out, the U.S. college population of today probably includes within it two future Presidents, a hundred senators, and thousands of corporate CEOs.)

Here is how Moritz describes them:

"Today's college student of age 20 is the most 'video-sophisticated audience' in history. . . . Twenty years ago *Sesame Street* went on the air, specifically designed to educate infants and pre-school children with sophisticated television techniques including short (90-second) segments, dazzling video effects, interactive involvement, new heroes, easy daily access, etc. This audience migrated [as it grew older, to other programs like] *Electric Company, Zoom,* to *Nickelodeon,* MTV—each a move representing an inexorable progression. . . .The audience created by *Sesame Street* now reshaped all of television!"

The TV programs he cites are all either shown on the public—i.e., educational—network or on cable channels, rather than on the major Second Wave networks.

Moritz uses the term *screenie* to describe this video-drenched generation, which has digested thousands of hours of television, imbibing its "video-logic." To that must be added, for many of them, more hours of interactive video games and, even more important, of work on their own personal computers. They not only follow a different logic, but are accustomed to make the screen do things, thus making them good prospects for the interactive services and products soon to hit the market. Above all, they are accustomed to choice.

The vast divide between the youth of the underclass and the screenie, which now characterizes the United States, will widen in Europe, Japan, and other high-tech nations, too, unless steps are taken to bridge the informational Grand Canyon.

THE NEW ALLIANCE

In a knowledge-based economy the most important domestic political issue is no longer the distribution (or redistribution) of wealth, but of the information and media that produce wealth.

This is a change so revolutionary it cannot be mapped by conventional political cartography. The new wealth-creation system will compel politicians, activists, and political theorists—whether they still regard themselves as left-wing or right-wing, radical or conservative, feminist or traditionalist—to rethink all political ideas developed during the smokestack era. The very categories are now obsolete.

Social justice and freedom both now increasingly depend on how each society deals with three issues: education; information technology (including the media); and freedom of expression.

In the case of education, the reconceptualization now required is so profound, reaching so far beyond questions of budgets, class size, teacher pay, and the traditional conflicts over curriculum, that it cannot be dealt with here. Like the Second Wave TV networks (or for that matter all the smokestack industries), our mass education systems are largely obsolete. Exactly as in the case of the media, education will require a proliferation of new channels and a vast expansion of program diversity. A high-choice system will have to replace a low-choice system if schools are to prepare people for a decent life in the new Third Wave society, let alone for economically productive roles.

The links between education and the six principles of the new media system—interactivity, mobility, convertibility, connectivity, ubiquity, and globalization—have scarcely been explored. Yet to ignore the relationships between the educational system of the future and the media system of the future is to cheat the learners who will be formed by both.

Significantly, education is no longer merely a priority for parents, teachers, and a handful of education reformers, but for the advanced sectors of business as well, since its leaders increasingly recognize the connection between education and global competitiveness.

The second priority involves the speedy universalization of access to computers, information technology, and the advanced media. No nation can operate a 21st-century economy without a 21st-century electronic infrastructure, embracing computers, data communications, and the other new media. This requires a population as familiar with this informational infrastructure as it is with cars, roads, highways, trains, and the transportation infrastructure of the smokestack period.

Not everyone, of course, needs to be a telecom engineer or a computer expert, just as not everyone needs to be a car mechanic. But access to the media system, including computers, faxes, and advanced telecommunications, must be as free and easy as access is today to the transportation system. A key objective of those who want an advanced economy, therefore, should be to accelerate the workings of the Law of Ubiquity—that is, to make sure that all citizens, poor and rich alike, are guaranteed access to the widest possible range of media.

Finally, if the essence of the new economy is knowledge, the democratic ideal of freedom of expression becomes a top political priority, rather than a peripheral matter.

The state—any state—is in business to stay in power. Whatever the economic costs to the rest of us, it will seek ways to harness the latest communications revolution to its purposes, and it will set limits on the free flow of information.

Just as the state invented new forms of mind control when the industrial revolution brought mass media into being, it will search for new tools and techniques to retain at least some control over the images, ideas, symbols, and ideologies reaching its people through the new electronic infrastructure.

Enthusiasm over the way the media were used to overthrow totalitarian regimes in Eastern Europe should not blind citizens to the more sophisticated mind manipulations that governments and politicians will attempt in the future.

No society can tolerate total freedom of information. Some secrecy is necessary to all social life. Total freedom of information would mean total lack of individual privacy. There are moments of extreme crisis, moments of "clear and present danger," when absolute freedom invites arsonists to spread gasoline on a raging fire. Absolute freedom of expression is, therefore, no more possible than absolute anything else.

But the more the society advances toward a super-symbolic economy, the more important it becomes to permit an extremely wide range of dissent and free expression. The more any government chokes off or chills this rich, free flow of data, information, and knowledge—including wild ideas, innovation, and even political dissent—the more it slows down the advance of the new economy.

For the vast extension of the global neural system coincides with the most important change in the function of free expression since at least the French and American revolutions.

In the agrarian past, new ideas were often a threat to survival. In communities living on the thin edge of subsistence, using methods honed over the centuries, any deviation was dangerous to an economy that left little margin for risk. The very notion of freedom of thought was alien.

With the rise of science and the industrial revolution, a radical new notion came into being: that minds free of state or religious shackles were necessary for "progress." But the population to whom this applied was a fraction of the total.

With the revolutionary rise of the new wealth-creation system, it is not a fraction of the working population but a substantial and ever-expanding number whose productivity depends precisely on the freedom to create everything from new product designs to new computer logics, metaphors, scientific insights, and epistemologies.

Super-symbolic economies grow from cultures constantly provoked by new, often dissenting ideas, including political ideas.

The fight for free expression, once the province of intellectuals, thus becomes a matter of concern to all who favor economic advance. Like adequate education and access to the new media, freedom of expression is no longer a political nicety, but a precondition for economic competitiveness.

This discovery lays the basis for an unusual political coalition of the future—one that brings together two groups who have, since the early days of the industrial revolution, been frequent adversaries: intellectuals, scientists, artists, and civil libertarians, on the one side, and advanced managers and even shareholders and capitalists on the other, all of whom will now find that their interests depend on revolutionizing the education system, widening the access of the entire population to computers and the other new media, and protecting—even extending—freedom of expression.

Such a coalition is the best guarantee of both intellectual and economic advance in the economies of the 21st century.

For Marx, freedom was the recognition of necessity. Those who wish to build 21st-century economies could find that necessity is the mother of freedom.

CODA:

YEARNINGS FOR A NEW DARK AGE

We now face the ultimate political power shift. We can redesign democracy for the 21st century—or descend into a new Dark Age.

One path moves power from the state toward the individual. The other threatens to shrink the individual to zero.

Nothing in the foreseeable future is about to take the gun out of the hands of the state. Nothing will prevent the state from siphoning wealth into its hands and disposing of it for its own power-enhancing purposes. What *is* likely to change, as we've already begun to see, is the state's ability to control knowledge.

The new economy thrives on freer expression, better feedback between rulers and ruled, more popular participation in decision-making. It can produce a less bureaucratic, more decentralized and responsive government. It can create a greater independence for the individual, a power shift away from the state—not its "withering away" but its humanization.

Yet any new alliance of democratic groups will face three giant forces now racing toward convergence in a worldwide crusade that could, if we are not careful, sweep us into a new Dark Age.

HOLY FRENZY

Organized religion, in one form or another, had a virtual monopoly on the production and distribution of abstract knowl-

372

edge in the pre-smokestack era, the time before the Enlightenment, before the birth of democracy in the West. Today, forces are at work seeking to restore that monopoly control of the mind.

The resurgence of religio-politics around the world may seem to have little to do with the rise of the computer and the new economy. But it does.

The knowledge-based wealth-creation system, of which the computer is the symbol, rings down the curtain on three centuries during which the industrial nations dominated the earth. Within the smokestack nations, this period was marked by a war for the mind between the forces of religion, aligned with the power elites of the agrarian age, and secular forces that fought for industrial "modernism" and mass democracy.

By the middle of the industrial era, these secular forces had managed to subdue organized religion, weakening its hold on the schools, on morality, and on the state itself.

By the 1960s a *Time* magazine cover was asking "Is God dead?" and a tormented Catholic Church convened the Second Vatican Council, one of its most important events in centuries. The three great religions of the West, where industrialism had triumphed, had all seen their social, moral, and political power diminish.

It was, however, precisely at this moment that the computer actually began to change the way wealth was produced. The technology that would most radically undermine the blue-collar, factory-based economy began to move more rapidly out of the laboratories and a few corporate and government installations, and into general use.

Coinciding with this revolutionary development, most advanced in the United States, there arose the hippie movement, which launched a savage attack on the cultural premises of the industrial age, including its secularism.

With the long hair came a bitter technophobia and a widespread interest in mysticism, drugs, Eastern cults, astrology, and off-brand religion. The movement looked at industrial society, hated what it saw, and urged a return to some haloed, mythical past. Its back-to-the-earthism, granny glasses, Indian beads, and headbands symbolized the hippies' rejection of the entire smokestack era and their yearning for a return to preindustrial culture. This was the seed from which sprang today's sprawling, burgeoning New Age movement, with its myriad mysticisms and its search for the sacral.

By the 1970s and 1980s, signs of crisis in the old industrial society were everywhere. Its ecological by-products threatened life itself. Its basic industries began to shrink in the face of new, high-tech goods and service production. Its urban systems, health systems, education systems, all plunged into crisis. Its greatest corporations were forced to restructure. Its labor unions declined. Its communities were torn by moral conflict, devastated by drugs, crime, family breakup, and other agonies.

Outraged by the hippies' pagan rejection of traditional Christianity, upset by the breakup of the familiar world, Christian fundamentalists also began a powerful counterattack on secularism that soon took the form of highly effective political action. Here, again, was a violent rejection of the messy, painful present and a search for the absolutist certainties of the past. Hippie and counterhippie, pagan and Christian, whatever their differences, joined in the assault on secular society.

Those launching this assault did not see themselves as enemies of democracy. Most would no doubt be offended at the very idea. Some among the hippies were, if anything, libertarians. Yet the secularism they attacked was one of the pillars of democracy in the modern era.

Meanwhile, there were signs of religious revival, followed by fundamentalist extremism, in many other parts of the world.

In the Middle East, starting at the end of World War I, leaders like Ataturk in Turkey, Reza Shah and the Shah in Iran, had come to power. These were men committed to "modernizing" their societies. They began building secular societies in which the mullahs and religious firebrands were forced to take a back seat.

These secular regimes, however, were identified with continued Western colonialism. Exploitation and corruption flourished, producing moral outrage. Ruling elites spent more time skiing in Gstaad and conferring with their private bankers in Zurich than in distributing income widely. During the Cold War, the intelligence agencies of various industrial powers, capitalist and communist alike, sometimes found it in their interest to subsidize Middle Eastern religious extremists.

All these factors kept relighting the fires of religious fundamentalism, ultimately symbolized by the holy frenzy of Khomeiniism, with its all-out attack on the modern world and the secularism it flaunted.

This fanatic attack might have carried less punch if industrial civilization, the home of secularism, were not itself in moral and social crisis, no longer offering a very attractive model for emulation by the rest of the world. Indeed, the industrial states, now torn apart internally, no longer seemed as invincible as they once had. Now hostage-takers, terrorists, and petroleum sheiks were able to jerk them around, seemingly at will.

As the smokestack era ended, therefore, its reigning secular philosophy was attacked from within and without, from many sides at once, and fundamentalism and religion in general took wing.

In the U.S.S.R., where Mikhail Gorbachev attempted to transform the economy and political system, the fires of Islamic fundamentalism began licking around the entire southern edge of the Soviet state. Soon Muslim Azeris and Christian Armenians were killing each other throughout the Caucasus, and when Soviet troops and militia were sent to restore order, the Iranian government warned Moscow not to use force against Muslims. The flames grew stronger. With Gorbachev's reforms allowing greater freedom of expression, there came signs of a revival of Christian fundamentalism as well.

Elsewhere, there were similar phenomena. In Israel, meanwhile, secular Jews were beaten and their cars stoned by Jewish fundamentalists whose ideas and social models were shaped by centuries of life in the tiny preindustrial *shtetls* of Eastern Europe and in Middle Eastern communities. In India, Muslim fundamentalism ripped across Kashmir, and Hindu fundamentalism across the rest of the subcontinent.

In Japan, where Buddhism and Shinto coexist, it is not possible to describe religion in Western terms, so the very concept of fundamentalism may be inapplicable. Nevertheless, there are evidences of a new interest in ancient forms of Shinto that the pre–World War II militarist regime exploited for its own political purposes. In 1989 the Ministry of Education issued a controversial order that pupils be taught respect for the Emperor, who is the high priest of Shinto.

What is happening is a sky-darkening attack on the ideas of the Enlightenment which helped usher in the industrial age.

While all these religious movements are, of course, different, and frequently clash with one another, and while some are extremist and others not, all of them—Christian or New Age, Judaic or Islamic—are united in one thing—their hostility to secularism, the philosophical base of mass democracy.

Today, therefore, in country after country, secularism is in retreat. What do advocates of democracy have to put in its place? So far. the new, high-tech democracies have renovated neither their outdated mass democratic political structures nor the philosophical assumptions that underlie them.

Religion is not the enemy of democracy. In a secular multireligious society, with a clear separation of state and church, the very variety of beliefs and nonbeliefs adds to the vibrance and dynamism of democracy. In many countries religious movements provide the only countervailing force against state oppression. Nor is fundamentalism, as such, a threat. Yet within the giant religious revival, in every country, not just Iran, fanatics are breeding who are committed to theocratic control of the mind and behavior of the individual, and others lend them unwitting support.

Tolerance of diversity is the first commandment of the demassified society, including tolerance of the intolerant—up to a point.

Religions that are universalistic, that wish to spread all over the world and embrace every human being, may be compatible with democracy. Even religions that insist on totalitarian control over every aspect of their own members' lives, but do not try to impose their control on nonmembers, may be compatible with democracy.

What is *not* compatible are those religions (and political ideologies as well) that combine totalitarianism with universalism. Such movements are at war with any possible definition of democracy.

Yet some of the fastest-growing and most powerful religious movements in the world today exhibit precisely this lethal combination.

They are determined to seize power over the lives and minds of whole nations, continents, the planet itself. Determined to impose their own rule over every aspect of human life. Determined to seize state power wherever they can, and to roll back the freedoms that democracy makes possible.

They are the agents of a new Dark Age.

ECO-THEOCRACY

Across the world, meanwhile, a green tide is gathering momentum too. This movement for ecological sanity is essential—a positive example of ordinary people around the world leading their leaders. Propelling ecology to the top of the world agenda have been a succession of sensational catastrophes, from Three Mile Island and Chernobyl to Bhopal and the Alaska oil spill. Clearly, more lie ahead.

Industrial society has reached its outer limits, making it impossible to continue putting toxic wastes in our backyards, stripping the land of forests, dumping Styrofoam debris in our oceans, and punching holes in the ozone. The worldwide environmental movement is therefore a survival response to planetary crisis.

But this movement, too, has an antidemocratic fringe. It has its own advocates of a return to darkness. Some of them are ready to hijack the environmental movement in pursuit of their private political or religious agendas.

The issues are so complex and recalcitrant that the Green movement is likely to split into at least four parts. One part will continue to be the very model of legal, nonviolent democratic action. But, given a succession of ecological crises and tragedies, a second wing, which already exists in embryonic form, might well step up from eco-vandalism to full-scale eco-terrorism to enforce its demands.

A further split will intensify the key ideological war already dividing the environmental movement. On one side: those who favor technological and economic advance within stringent environmental constraints. Unwilling to give up on imagination and intelligence, they believe in the power of the human mind—and therefore in our ability to design technologies that will use smaller amounts of resources, emit less pollution, and recycle all wastes into reusable resources. They argue that today's crisis calls for revolutionary changes in the way the economy and technology are organized. Oriented toward tomorrow, these are the mainstream environmentalists.

Battling them for ideological control of the movement, however, are self-described "fundamentalists," who wish to plunge society into pre-technological medievalism and asceticism. They are "eco-theologues," and some of their views dovetail with the thinking of religious extremists.

The eco-theologues insist that there can be no technological relief, and that we are therefore destined to slide back into pre-industrial poverty, a prospect they regard as a blessing rather than a curse.

In a seminal series of articles in *New Perspectives Quarterly*, the main lines of debate are clearly laid out. For these reversionist thinkers, the issues are not primarily ecological but religious. They wish to restore a religion-drenched world that has not existed in the West since the Middle Ages. The environmental movement provides a convenient vehicle.

This group reduces the history of our relations with nature to biblical allegory. First there was an ecological "Golden Age," when humans lived in harmony with nature and worshipped it. The species fell from this "Eden" with the arrival of the industrial age, in which the "Devil"—technology—ruled human affairs. Now we must transit to a new "Paradise" of perfect sustainability and harmony. If not, we face "Armageddon."

This imposition of a Western, indeed Christian, parable on the far more complex history of our relations with nature is common to the "eco-theologues" who glamorize life in the medieval village.

Rudolf Bahro, an influential Green theorist now living in West Germany, explicitly holds that what is needed is "theology, not ecology—the birth of a new Golden Age which cultivates . . . the nobility in man."

He reaches back into the 13th century to quote Meister Eckhart, the founder of German mysticism, "who lived in the now despoiled Rhine River valley" and who told us that all creatures have God within them. Bahro finds the same idea in the poetic words of Mechtild of Magdeburg, another 13th-century Christian thinker, quoting her beautiful line to the effect that all creatures are "a flash of grace."

Ecological salvation thus, for him, is a matter of religion, something the secular world will never be able to offer. Bahro even approves of the Ayatollah Khomeini's remark to Gorbachev that the Soviet leader should look to Allah rather than economic reforms to solve Soviet problems.

Another theorist, Wolfgang Sachs of the University of Pennsylvania, attacks the Worldwatch Institute, a leading environmentalist research center, for its "specifically modern outlook" and dismisses Amory Lovins, the conservationist, for urging greater energy efficiency, whereas what is wanted by Sachs is "good house-keeping" in the tradition of "subsistence-oriented households."

Ivan Illich, one of our most imaginative social critics and author of several brilliant works bearing on ecological theory, is opposed to "managerial fascism" and simple-minded Ludditism. What he proposes, however, is "sustainability without development" —in short, stasis.

For Illich, poverty *is* the human condition and should be accepted as such; hence, who needs development? The new system of wealth creation, he says, has "injected new life into what would otherwise have been the exhausted logic of industrialism." He fails to see that the new knowledge-based technological system actually contradicts the old logic of industrialism at many points.

For Illich, too, the argument is ultimately theological. "God was the pattern that connected the cosmos" at a time when bare subsistence was accepted as normal and natural, a state we should return to. So long as God ruled the medieval mind, humanity and nature remained in balance. "Man, the agent of disequilibrium," upset the balance after the scientific revolution. Illich regards the concept of an "eco-system which, through multiple feedback mech-anisms, can be regulated scientifically" as a snare and a delusion. Clearly, he implies, a return to a God-centered ascetic world would be preferable.

Theo-ecological rhetoric contains within it more than a hint of the Christian notion of retribution. As the writers Linda Bilmes and Mark Byford have noted, the theological Greens insist "con-sumption is sinful," while environmental blight is seen as "punish-ment for excessive consumerism, lack of spirituality, wastefulness." As in a Sunday sermon, the implication is that we should "repent, and mend our ways." Or, one might add, face fire and brimstone.

This is hardly the place to try to resolve the profound issues raised by the ecology debate—as significant a philosophical debate as that raised by the Enlightenment thinkers at the dawn of the industrial age. What is important, however, is to note the congru-ence between the views of the eco-theologues and the fundamentalist revival, with its deep hostility to secular democracy.

A shared emphasis on absolutes and the belief that sharp restrictions on individual choice may be required (to make people "moral," or to "protect the environment") point ultimately to a common attack on human rights. Indeed, many environmentalists themselves worry openly about the arrival of Green Ayotallahs or "eco-fascists" who impose their particular brand of salvation. Thus, Bahro cautions that "in the deep crises of humanity, charisma always plays a role. The deeper the crisis, the darker the charismatic figure who will emerge. . . . Whether or not we will have a green Adolf depends . . . on how far cultural change advances before the next Chernobyl."

One may admire the integrity and creativity of a thinker like Illich, surely no fascist himself, while recognizing the deeply anti-democratic implications of his search for the absolute, the constant, the static, and the holy. Criticizing the eco-theologues, the French sociologist Alain Touraine warns, "If we reject reason in the name of salvation from ozone depletion, we will court a Green fundamentalism, an eco-theocracy of the Ayatollah Khomeini variety."

If such anxiety sounds too extreme, it may be worth recalling the *Wandervogel* youth movement of the 1920s in Germany, where the Green movement today is most militant. The *Wandervogel* were the hippie-Greens of the Weimar Republic, roaming the countryside with their rucksacks, carrying guitars, wearing flowers, holding Woodstock-like festivals, high on spirituality and preaching a return to nature.

A decade later, Hitler was in control. Hitler also exalted pre-industrial values, picturing the Nazi utopia as one in which "the blacksmith stands again at his anvil, the farmer walks behind his plough." In the words of Professor J. P. Stern of University College, London, Hitler evoked "a pre-industrial rustic idyll." Hitler's ideologists constantly praised the "organic," urged physical fitness, and used biological analogies to justify the vilest race hate. "Hundreds of thousands of youngsters passed through the Youth Movement," writes George L. Mosse in *The Crisis of German Ideology*, "and many of them found it not very difficult to accommodate themselves to the ideological propositions of the Nazis."

Can one really imagine a Neo-Green Party, with armbands, Sam Browne belts, and jackboots, setting out to enforce its own view of nature on the rest of society?

Of course not, under normal conditions. But what if conditions are not "normal"?

Consider the consequences of another Bhopal-like eco-catastrophe set in, say, Seattle, Stuttgart, or Sheffield . . . followed by back-to-back crises elsewhere . . . followed by confusion and monstrous corruption in the disaster relief effort . . . amid fundamentalist cries that the disaster was inflicted by God as punishment for "permissiveness" and immorality. Picture all this occurring in a time of deep economic distress. Imagine an attractive, articulate "Eco-Adolf" who promises not just to solve the immediate crisis but to "purify" the society materially, morally, and politically—if only he is given extraconstitutional powers.

Some of today's eco-theological rhetoric has an absurdist flavor, as did that of the erstwhile Adolf and his ideologists. Nazi propagandists exalted the Middle Ages (especially the time when the Holy Roman Empire dominated Europe) as a period when *Kultur* reached its "highest peak."

Today, a British ecological "fundi," or fundamentalist, writes in a letter to *The Economist* that "the goals of 'fundi' Greens like myself . . . [are to] return to a Europe which existed in the distant past . . . between the fall of Rome and the rise of Charlemagne," in which the basic unit of society "was the rural holding, scarcely larger than a hamlet. . . . The only way for humans to live in harmony with nature is to live at a subsistence level."

What the eco-medievalists normally do not tell us is the political price. They seldom point out that democracy was conspicuously absent from those bucolic villages they hold up for emulation—villages ruled by the cruelest patriarchy, religious mind-control, feudal ignorance, and force. This was the *Kultur* the Nazis glamorized. Not for nothing has the period between the fall of Rome and the rise of Charlemagne become known as the Dark Ages.

By themselves the eco-theologues might be dismissed. They remain a small fringe on the far edge of the environmental movement. But it is a mistake to view them as an isolated or trivial phenomenon. The religious revival and the Green movements alike breed ultras who would be happy to jettison democracy. At their extremes, these two movements may be converging to impose new restrictions on personal and political behavior in the name of both God and Greenness. Together they are pushing for a power shift toward the past.

THE NEW XENOPHOBES

Another characteristic of the Dark Age village was extreme xenophobia—hatred for the foreigner, even for those in the very next village. With the coming of the smokestack era, individual and mass loyalties were gradually transferred from village to nation. But xenophobia, chauvinism, hatred of the outsider, the stranger, the foreigner, continued to be a tool of state power.

Today's shift to a knowledge-based economy requires more cross-national interdependence than the smokestack economy it replaces. Inevitably, this restricts the range of independent action by nations. This, in turn, leads to a xenophobic backlash in everything from commerce to culture.

Today, governments throughout Europe are bracing themselves for an onslaught of imported culture, primarily television and movies, because of the integration of the European market. They are especially jittery about the packaging of news by foreigners.

Le Monde charges that the EC's plan for *Television Without Frontiers* "risks accelerating the implantation of Anglo-Saxon producers and distributors who have taken a decisive lead in the creation of all-European networks."

Europeans are nervous about plans for a Moroccan network to begin satellite broadcasts in Arabic to Europe's 11 million or more mainly Islamic immigrants from North Africa. Concern deepened as Muslin fundamentalists scored voting successes in secular Algeria.

This, however, is only a portent of things to come. Satellite technology and other new media tools are cracking open national cultures. In the opinion of satellite expert Dan Goldin of TRW, the day may well come when home satellite receivers can be sold for a fraction of their already low price, and millions around the world will be able to pick up transmissions from abroad—a Brazilian variety show, a Nigerian newscast, a South Korean drama, a Libyan propaganda program. This cross-communication, however, threatens the "national identity" that governments seek to preserve and propagate for their own self-serving purposes.

When fears of cultural deracination are intensified by large-scale immigration, identity becomes an explosive issue.

The promoters of a European single-market, urging open

borders for capital, culture, and people, seek to displace traditional nationalist sentiments with "supra-nationalism" instead.

But precisely because the new economy is becoming more globally integrated, exporting joblessness, pollution, and culture along with products and services, we see a mounting backlash and the revival of nationalism in the high-tech world.

The Le Penist movement in France, with its viciously anti-Arab propaganda, led by a former legionnaire who terms the Nazi gas chambers "a minor point," appeals to knee-jerk xenophobic emotions. His party holds ten seats in the European Parliament.

The Republikaner Party in West Germany, formed by an ex-Waffen-SS non-com, Franz Schoenhuber, attacks not merely Turkish migrant workers but even ethnic Germans immigrating from Poland and the Soviet Union who are allegedly taking jobs, housing, and pensions away from "real Germans." With links to the Le Penists in France and extremist parties elsewhere in Europe, the Republikaner won eleven seats in the West Berlin legislature in 1989 and six in the European Parliament.

Under banners proclaiming "Germany first," Schoenhuber, like Hitler after the Versailles Treaty, portrayed Germany—now one of the world's richest countries—as a "victim" nation.

Schoenhuber, according to the respected German analyst Josef Joffe, writing in *The Wall Street Journal,* has issued a "call to arms against the rest of the world, which seeks to oppress Germany by shackling it to the past"—meaning that the world won't let Germany forget Hitler's ravages. (Schoenhuber has since quit the party, terming it too extremist.)

Any country continually cudgeled for the sins of a much earlier generation can, of course, expect an eventual backlash, a reassertion of national pride. But pride about what? Instead of urging Germany to become a world leader in developing a more advanced, 21st-century democracy, the neo-nationalists appeal to many of the anti-democratic pathologies of the German past, thus providing neighboring countries good cause for not wanting Germany to forget its crimes.

With the Berlin Wall down and the de facto reunification of Germany well advanced, what happens in Bonn and Berlin (soon, no doubt, to be the country's capital once more) has ramifications throughout Europe, and many all over the continent are watching the Republikaners carefully.

But similar nationalist movements are found all over Western

Europe, from Belgium to Italy and Spain, wherever free-flowing culture and communication and border-crossing migrants threaten the old national self-conceptions.

The resurgence of flag-waving xenophobia, however, is not limited to Europe. In the United States, too, there is a growing nationalist backlash. Fed by a fear that America is in economic and military decline, weary of being told they are too imperialist, materialist, violent, uncultured, etc., etc., even normally apolitical Americans are responding to nationalist demagogy.

Anti-immigration sentiment runs hot, encouraged by eco-extremists who claim the influx of Mexican immigration is damaging to the U.S. environment. This born-again nativism, however, is only one manifestation of a new flag-waving nationalism.

The 1990 ruling of the Supreme Court that burning a flag is a form of free political expression, protected by the U.S. Bill of Rights, led to an outpouring of high-octane emotion. Radio call-in shows were besieged by outraged callers. The White House instantly proposed changing the Constitution to ban the practice.

Another indication of the new mood is Japan-bashing, a popular sport these days among protectionists and ordinary Americans worried about the trade imbalance and the Japanese buy-up of U.S. companies and real estate.

In Japan, meanwhile, a parallel ultra-nationalism is spreading. Resurgent nationalists call for changes in the constitution to permit a more aggressive military buildup. Japan, they say, did "nothing to be ashamed of" during World War II—a view that upsets China and other nearby countries invaded by the Japanese. For suggesting that Emperor Hirohito may have shared responsibility for World War II, the mayor of Nagasaki, Hitoshi Motoshima, became the victim of an attempted assassination. A leading daily, *Asahi Shimbun*, one of whose reporters had previously been murdered, presumably by nationalists, warns that such violence "will lead to fascism."

The ultras claim, moreover, that Japan has a national "soul" and language different from and superior to that of any other nation. The cult of "Yamatoism," which promotes this concept of unique superiority, is called upon to offset a loss of national identity resulting from postwar Westernization.

Having been treated patronizingly by the United States ever since the war, and sick of being criticized by others for economic policies that have brought it tremendous success, some Japanese are willing to listen to the nationalist pitch. This patriotic hubris comes hand in hand with extraordinary financial clout on the world scene and a fast-growing military capability, and is associated with the most anti-democratic forces in Japanese society.

Finally, what makes the widespread resurgence of nationalism truly extraordinary is its reemergence as a powerful political force in the Soviet Union and the Eastern European countries. In fact, rather than democratic uprisings, the upheavals in Eastern Europe could equally well be described as nationalist uprisings among nations bent for nearly half a century to Soviet will.

Reframing the concept of "nation" is one of the most emotional and important tasks to face the world in the decisive decades before us, and maintaining national control over certain functions, rather than allowing them to be either localized or globalized, is essential. But blind tribalism and nationalism are both dangerous and regressive. And when linked to the notion of racial or God-conferred superiority, they give birth to violence or repression.

Significantly, in the U.S.S.R., where ethnic passions rocked the state itself, they are often linked to both environmentalism and religious fundamentalism. Ecological themes are exploited to arouse ethnic sentiment against Moscow. In Tashkent a movement called Birlik, which started up to block the building of an electronics plant, has taken on an Islamic fundamentalist coloration.

Even more significant than the mounting demands of ethnic minorities in the Baltic regions, Armenia, Azerbaijan, Georgia, and other parts of the U.S.S.R. for autonomy or independence is the upsurge of ethnicism in the dominant Great Russian population. Writing about Tolstoi, the historian Paul Johnson described Russian nationalism in words that could apply today. It was, Johnson says, a "chauvinist spirit, the conviction that the Russians were a special race, with unique moral qualities (personified in the peasant) and a God-ordained role to perform in the world."

This attitude is expressed in extreme form in today's anti-Semitic, anti-foreigner Pamyat organization, which claims thirty branches around the Soviet Union, 20,000 members in Moscow alone, and has strong links to both the military and KGB, as well as support from middle-level officialdom. Several of the U.S.S.R.'s best-selling authors and cultural figures are members. Pamyat, now facing criminal prosecution for spreading hate, resembles the Black Hundreds movement, which organized pogroms under the Tsar at the turn of the century.

Pamyat and similar groups portray themselves as merely interested in preserving ancient monuments, or repairing the environment, but have as their goal the re-creation of the same village-based
society that the Green fundamentalists exalt. Some call for a resto-
ration of the Tsarist monarchy, linked to religious orthodoxy.

Like Schoenhuber in Germany, who disclaims anti-Semitism
but mouths Hitler-era lies about Jews, Pamyat claims innocence
but issues virulent diatribes against "International Zionism and
Freemasonry," and its members threaten pogroms.

A Pamyat manifesto lashes out at all who have "reduced our
churches, temples, monasteries, and graves of national heroes of
our Motherland" and who have "reduced the ecology of the country to a catastrophic state." It urges a massive return to the land—
"Down with the giant cities!"—and a revival of the "centuries-old
institution of the ploughman."

Here, then, we find xenophobic ethnicism explicitly linked to
religious fundamentalism and eco-medievalism—all three in a single Dark Age package.

It is a combustible convergence of forces that could blow up in
the face of democracies wherever they now exist. In its worst case,
it conjures up the image of a racist or tribal, eco-fascist, theological
state—a maximal recipe for the suppression of human rights,
freedom of religion, and private property as well.

Such a state seems hard to imagine—except, perhaps, as a
result of some immense crisis and tragedy, an eco-spasm combining ecological upheaval with vast economic crises, terror, or war.

But one need not imagine the worst-case scenario to feel a
chill in the bones. It isn't necessary for such movements, or a
convergence of them, to seize control of a state in order for them
to savagely restrict or destroy a form of democracy that, even in
the high-tech nations, is already fragile because it is increasingly
out of sync with the emerging economy and society.

Governments controlled or heavily influenced by extremists
who put their particular brand of religion, ecology, or nationalism
ahead of democratic values do not stay democratic long.

The system of advanced wealth creation now spreading around
the earth opens expanded opportunities for democracy. For the
first time, as we saw, it makes freedom of expression not just a
political good but an economic necessity. But as the old industrial
society enters its terminal tailspin, counterforces are created that
could destroy both democracy and the option of economic advance.

To save both development and democracy, political systems need to leap to a new stage, as the economy itself is doing. Whether that enormous challenge can be met will decide whether the ultimate powershift that approaches will protect or enslave the individual.

In the Powershift Era ahead, the primary ideological struggle will no longer be between capitalist democracy and communist totalitarianism, but between 21st-century democracy and 11th-century darkness.

PART SIX

PLANETARY POWERSHIFT

29

THE GLOBAL "K-FACTOR"

Few peacetime power shifts have been as dramatic as those following the swift disintegration of the once-monolithic Soviet bloc. Suddenly, immense power, centralized in Moscow for nearly half a century, shifted back to Warsaw, Prague, Budapest, Bucharest, and Berlin. In a few brief spectacular months the "East" splintered.

A second shift has accompanied the breakup of the so-called South. The LDCs, or "less developed countries",* have never been able to form a truly united front vis-à-vis the industrialized world, despite efforts beginning as long ago as the Bandung conference in Indonesia in 1955. In the 1970s the United Nations rang with rhetoric about the common needs of "the South." Programs of "South-South" technological exchange and other forms of cooperation were launched. Campaigns were begun to shift the terms of trade between the North and the South. Power did shift. But not in the way the spokesmen for a united South had hoped.

What happened instead has been the division of the LDCs into distinct groupings with very different needs. One consists of desperately poor countries still mostly dependent on First Wave peasant labor. Another group includes countries—like Brazil, India, and China—that are actually important Second Wave or industrial powers, but saddled with vast populations still scrabbling for subsistence from preindustrial agriculture. Lastly, there are nations like Singapore, Taiwan, and South Korea, which have virtually completed industrialization and are moving swiftly into Third Wave

---

*The term *less developed* is an arrogant misnomer, since many LDCs are highly developed culturally and in other ways. A more appropriate term would be "less economically developed," which is the sense in which it will be used here.

high technology. If power in the East Bloc has splintered, so, too, has power in the so-called South.

The third immense shift of power has been the emergence of Japan and Europe into rivals of the United States, leading to hyper-competition as each fights to dominate the 21st century. The so-called West, too, is now splitting apart.

While politicians, diplomats, and the press still treat these power shifts as distinctly separate phenomena, there is a deep connection among all three. The global structure that reflected the dominance of the Second Wave industrial powers has been shattered like a crystal sphere under the blow of a sledgehammer.

Naturally, such vast historical developments spring from many roots, and no single explanation can completely account for them. To reduce history to any single force or factor is to ignore complexity, chance, the role of individuals, and many other variables. But by the same token, to regard history as a succession of patternless or unrelated accidents is equally reductionist.

The future patterns of global power can only be glimpsed if, instead of looking at each major shift of power as an isolated event, we identify the common forces running through them. And, in fact, we find that all three of these epochal power shifts are closely linked to the decline of industrialism and the rise of the new knowledge-driven economy.

PYRAMIDS AND MOONSHOTS

Advances in science and technology have been so extraordinary since World War II they hardly need elaboration. If nothing had occurred but the invention of the computer and the discovery of DNA, the postwar period might still go down as the most revolutionary in scientific history. But in fact, much more has happened.

We have not only improved our technologies, we have begun to operate at deeper and deeper levels of nature, so that instead of dealing with gross chunks of matter, we can now create a layer of material so incredibly thin that, in the words of *Science*, "the electrons in it are effectively moving in only two dimensions." We can etch lines that are only 20 billionths of a meter wide. We will soon be able to assemble things one atom at a time. This is not "progress," but upheaval.

The U.S. National Academy of Engineering in 1989 listed what it considered the ten most important engineering achievements of the previous twenty-five years. It began the list with the Apollo moon landing, which it ranked in history with the building of the Egyptian pyramids. Next came the development of satellites, micro-processors, lasers, the jumbo jet, genetically engineered products, and other breakthroughs. Since the beginning of the 1950s, when the new wealth-creation system began sprouting in the United States, humans, for the first time in history, opened the pathway to the stars, identified the biological program of life, and invented intellectual tools as important as writing. This is an astonishing set of achievements in what amounts to a single generation.

Nor is it only scientific or technological knowledge that has made, or is about to make, remarkable strides. In everything from organization theory to music, from the study of ecosystems to our understanding of the brain, in linguistics and learning theory, in studies of nonequilibrium, chaos, and dissipative structures, the knowledge base is being revolutionized. And even as this occurs, competing researchers in fields like neural networks and artificial intelligence are providing new knowledge about knowledge itself.

These transformative advances, seemingly remote from the worlds of diplomacy and politics, are in fact inescapably linked to today's geopolitical eruptions. Knowledge is the "K-Factor" in global power struggles.

HAND-ME-DOWN ECONOMICS

Consider, for example, the implications of the knowledge factor for Soviet power.

Today's historic powershift, as we've seen, has made two of the most basic sources of power—violence and wealth—increasingly dependent on the third source: knowledge. Because of the spread of knowledge-based technology and the relatively free circulation of ideas, the United States, Europe, and Japan have been able to leave the socialist nations in the dust economically. But the same technology made possible a vast leap in military power as well.

A fighter airplane today is the equivalent of a computer with wings. Its effectiveness depends almost entirely on the knowledge packed into its avionics and weaponry—and into its pilot's brain. In 1982, Soviet military planners suffered a collective case of ulcers when eighty Soviet-built MiG fighters, flown by the Syrians, were destroyed by Israeli pilots, who lost not a single plane. Soviet-built tanks also did badly against Israeli armor.

Even though the U.S.S.R. had brilliant military scientists, and nukes enough to incinerate the world, it could not keep pace in the race toward super-high-technology conventional weapons or in the dash for strategic defense systems. The growing sophistication of information-based conventional weapons (which, in fact, are not conventional at all) threatened Soviet superiority on the ground in Eastern Europe.

Meanwhile, the extremely knowledge-intensive Strategic Defense Initiative (SDI) threatened to negate the value of Soviet long-range missiles. Critics of SDI complained that it would never work. But the very possibility alarmed Moscow. If SDI could, in fact, block all Soviet nuclear missiles before they hit the United States, they were useless. That would also mean that the United States could launch a first-strike nuclear attack without fear of retaliation. If, on the other hand, as is more reasonable, SDI was only fractionally effective, blocking some but not all warheads, it would leave Soviet war planners wondering which fraction of U.S. missiles would survive. In either case, SDI raised the ante, and made theoretical Soviet use of nuclear weapons, never very likely, even riskier for Moscow.

On the ground and in space, then, the Soviets confronted a double threat.

Faced with these sobering realities, plus its own economic decline, Moscow rationally concluded that it could no longer protect its Eastern European perimeter militarily, except at an unacceptable and skyrocketing cost. For both economic and military reasons, therefore, a reduction of its imperial commitments became necessary.

In the end, what did in the Soviets was not arms or economics, but the K-factor—the new knowledge on which both military strength and economic power are now increasingly dependent.

The same K-factor helps explain the fragmentation of the "developing countries" and the rise of three distinct groupings among them. For example, once the most advanced economies began to shift to computers and information-based technologies, yielding higher value-added products, they transferred many of the old muscle-based, less information-intensive operations to countries like South Korea, Taiwan, Singapore, and now to Thailand and other places. In other words, as Europe, Japan, and the United States moved to Third Wave forms of wealth-making, they passed off the old Second Wave tasks to another tier of nations. This speeded their industrialization and they left the other LDCs behind.

(Many of these "newly industrialized economies," or NIEs, in turn, are now racing to pawn off Second Wave processes on still poorer, more economically backward countries—along with the accompanying pollution and other disadvantages—while they, in turn, try to make the transition to more knowledge-intensive production.) The different speeds of economic development have separated the LDCs from one another.

And as for the inter-capitalist rivalry among Europe, Japan, and the United States, the fabulous success of U.S. postwar policy, which promoted the rebuilding of both the European and Japanese economies, helped both of them restore their shattered industrial structures. This meant the chance for a fresh start and the opportunity to replace old prewar machines with the shiniest new technology, while the United States, whose plants had not been bombed into rubble, still needed to amortize its existing industrial base.

For a variety of reasons, including a future-oriented culture and the regional economic stimulation resulting from the Vietnam War, and, of course, because of the tremendous hard work and creativity of its postwar generation, Japan leaped ahead. Its eyes always focused on the 21st century, its culture always emphasizing the importance of education, business intelligence, and knowledge in general, Japan seized on the computer and all its derivatives in electronics and information technology with an almost erotic passion.

The economic results as Japan transited from the old to the new system of wealth creation were stunning—but they threw Japan into inevitable competition with the United States. In turn, a terrified Europe launched its drive for economic and political integration, after years of dawdling.

We will return to these developments later on, but for here it is only essential to recognize that, at every step, the new knowledge-based system of wealth creation has been either a major contributor to, or a primary cause of, the great historical shift of power now reshaping our world. The global implications of this fact, as we shall see next, are startling.

30

THE FAST AND THE SLOW

One of the greatest power imbalances on earth today divides the rich countries from the poor. That unequal distribution of power, which affects the lives of billions of us, will soon be transformed as the new system of wealth creation spreads.

Since the end of World War II the world has been split between capitalist and communist, North and South. Today, as these old divisions fade in significance, a new one arises.

For from now on the world will be split between the fast and the slow.

To be fast or slow is not simply a matter of metaphor. Whole economies are either fast or slow. Primitive organisms have slow neural systems. The more evolved human nervous system processes signals faster. The same is true of primitive and advanced economies. Historically, power has shifted from the slow to the fast—whether we speak of species *or* nations.

In fast economies, advanced technology speeds production. But this is the least of it. Their pace is determined by the speed of transactions, the time needed to take decisions (especially about investment), the speed with which new ideas are created in laboratories, the rate at which they are brought to market, the velocity of capital flows, and above all the speed with which data, information, and knowledge pulse through the economic system. Fast economies generate wealth—and power—faster than slow ones.

By contrast, in peasant societies economic processes move at a glacial pace. Tradition, ritual, and ignorance limit socially acceptable choices. Communications are primitive; transport, restricted. Before the market system arose as an instrument for making investment choices, tradition governed technological decisions. Tradition, in turn, relied on "rules or taboos to preserve productive techniques that were proven workable over the slow course of biological and cultural evolution," according to economist Don Lavoie.

With most people living at the bare edge of subsistence, experiment was dangerous, innovators were suppressed, and advances in the methods of wealth creation came so slowly they were barely perceptible from lifetime to lifetime. Moments of innovation were followed by what seemed like centuries of stagnation.

The historical explosion we now call the industrial revolution stepped up the economic metabolism. Roads and communications improved. Profit-motivated entrepreneurs actively searched for innovations. Brute force technologies were introduced. Society had a larger surplus to fall back on, reducing the social risks of experimentation. "With technological experimentation now so much less costly," Lavoie points out, "productive methods [could] change much more rapidly."

All this, however, merely set the stage for today's super-fast symbolic economy.

The bar code on the pack of Marlboros, the computer in the Federal Express truck, the scanner at the Safeway checkout counter, the bank's automatic teller, the spread of extra-intelligent data networks across the planet, remotely operated robots, the informationalization of capital, all are preliminary steps in the formation of a 21st-century economy that will operate at nearly real-time speeds.

In due course, the entire wealth-creation cycle will be monitored *as it happens*.

Continual feedback will stream in from sensors built into intelligent technology, from optical scanners in stores, and from transmitters in trucks, planes, and ships that send signals to satellites so managers can track the changing location of every vehicle at every moment. This information will be combined with the results of continuous polling of people and information from a thousand other sources.

The acceleration effect, by making each unit of saved time *more* valuable than the last unit, thus creates a positive feedback loop that accelerates the acceleration.

The consequences of this, in turn, will be not merely evolutionary but revolutionary, because real-time work, management, and finance will be radically different from even today's most advanced methods. Even now, however, well before real-time operations are achieved, time itself has become an increasingly critical factor of production. As a result, knowledge is used to shrink time intervals.

This quickening of economic neural responses in the high-technology nations holds still-unnoticed consequences for low-technology or no-technology economies.

For the more valuable time becomes, the less valuable the traditional factors of production, like raw materials and labor. And that, for the most part, is what these countries sell.

As we shall see in a minute, the acceleration effect will transform all present strategies for economic development.

COMING HOME

The new system for making wealth consists of an expanding global network of markets, banks, production centers, and laboratories in instant communication with one another, constantly exchanging huge—and ever-increasing—flows of data, information, and knowledge.

This is the "fast" economy of tomorrow. It is this accelerative, dynamic new wealth-machine that is the source of economic advance. As such, it is the source of great power as well. To be de-coupled from it is to be excluded from the future.

Yet that is the fate facing many of today's "LDCs," or "less developed countries."

As the world's main system for producing wealth revs up, countries that wish to sell will have to operate at the pace of those in a position to buy. This means that slow economies will have to speed up their neural responses, lose contracts and investments, or drop out of the race entirely.

The earliest signs of this are already detectable.

The United States in the 1980s spent $125 billion a year on clothing. Half of that came from cheap-labor factories dotted around the world from Haiti to Hong Kong. Tomorrow much of this work will return to the United States. The reason is speed.

Of course, shifting taxes, tariffs, currency ratios, and other factors still influence businesses when overseas investment or purchasing decisions are made. But far more fundamental in the long run are changes in the structure of cost. These changes, part of the transition to the new wealth-creation system, are already sending runaway factories and contracts home again to the United States, Japan, and Europe.

The Tandy Corporation, a major manufacturer and retailer of electronic products, not long ago brought its Tandy Color Computer production back from South Korea to Texas. While the Asian plant was automated, the Texas plant operated on an "absolutely continuous" flow basis and had more sophisticated test equipment. In Virginia, Tandy set up a no-human-hands automated plant to turn out five thousand speaker enclosures a day. These supply Japanese manufacturers, who previously had them made with low-cost labor in the Caribbean.

The computer industry is, of course, extremely fast-paced. But even in a slower industry, the Arrow Company, one of the biggest U.S. shirtmakers, recently transferred 20 percent of its dress-shirt production back to the United States after fifteen years of off-shore sourcing. Frederick Atkins Inc., a buyer for U.S. department stores, has increased domestic purchases from 5 percent to 40 percent in three years.

These shifts can be traced, at least in part, to the rising importance of time in economics.

"The new technology," reports *Forbes* magazine, "is giving domestic apparel makers an important advantage over their Asian competitors. Because of fickle fashion trends and the practice of changing styles as often as six times a year, retailers want to be able to keep inventories low. This calls for quick response from apparel makers that can offer fast turnaround on smaller lots in all styles, sizes and colors. Asian suppliers, half a world away, typically require orders three months or more in advance."

By contrast, Italy's Benetton Group delivers midseason reorders within two to three weeks. Because of its electronic network, Haggar Apparel in Dallas is now able to restock its 2,500 customers with slacks every three days, instead of the seven weeks it once needed.

Compare this with the situation facing manufacturers in China who happen to need steel.

In 1988, China suffered the worst steel shortages in memory. Yet with fabricators crying out for supplies, 40 percent of the country's total annual output remained padlocked in the warehouses of the Storage and Transportation General Corporation (STGC). Why? Because this enterprise—incredible as it may seem to the citizens of fast economies—makes deliveries only twice a year.

The fact that steel prices were skyrocketing, that the shortages were creating a black market, that fraud was widespread, and that companies needing the steel faced crisis meant nothing to the managers of STGC. The organization was simply not geared to making more frequent deliveries. While this is no doubt an extreme example, it is not isolated. A "great wall" separates the fast from the slow, and that wall is rising higher with each passing day.

It is this cultural and technological great wall that explains, in part, the high rate of failures in joint projects between fast and slow countries.

Many deals collapse when a slow-country supplier fails to meet promised deadlines. The different pace of economic life in the two worlds make for cross-cultural static. Officials in the slow country typically do not appreciate how important time is to the partner from the fast country—or why it matters so much. Demands for speed seem unreasonable, arrogant. Yet for the fast-country partner, nothing is more important. Delivery delayed is almost as bad as delivery denied.

The increasing cost of unreliability, of endless negotiation, of inadequate tracking and monitoring, and of late responses to demands for up-to-instant information further diminish the competitive edge of low-wage muscle work in the slow economies.

So do expenses arising from delays, lags, irregularities, bureaucratic stalling, and slow decision-making—not to mention the corrupt payments often required to speed things up.

In the advanced economies the speed of decision is becoming a critical consideration. Some executives refer to the inventory of "decisions in process," or "DIP," as an important cost, similar to "work in progress." They are trying to replace sequential decision-making with "parallel processing," which breaks with bureaucracy. They speak of "speed to market," "quick response," "fast cycle time," and "time-based competition."

The increased precision of timing required by systems like "just-in-time delivery" mean that the seller must meet far more rigid and restrictive schedule requirements than before, so that it is easier than ever to slip up.

In turn, as buyers demand more frequent and timely deliveries from overseas, the slow-country suppliers are compelled to maintain larger inventories or buffer stocks at their own expense—with the risk that the stored parts will rapidly become obsolete or unsalable.

The new economic imperative is clear: Overseas suppliers from developing countries will either advance their own technologies to meet the world speed standards, or they will be brutally cut off from their markets—casualties of the acceleration effect.

STRATEGIC REAL ESTATE

The likelihood that many of the world's poorest countries will be isolated from the dynamic global economy and left to stagnate is enhanced by three other powerful factors that stem, directly or indirectly, from the arrival of a new system of wealth creation on the earth.

One way to think about the economic power or powerlessness of the LDCs is to ask what they have to sell to the rest of the world. We can begin with a scarce resource that only a few countries at any given moment can offer the rest of the world: strategic location.

Economists don't normally consider militarily strategic real estate a salable resource, but for many LDCs that is precisely what it has been.

Countries seeking military and political power are frequently prepared to pay for it. Like Cuba, many LDCs now have sold, leased, or lent their location or facilities to the Soviet Union, the United States, or others for military, political, and intelligence purposes. For Cuba, giving the Soviets a foothold ninety miles off the U.S. coast, and heightened political influence throughout Central America, has brought in a $5 billion annual subsidy from Moscow.

For almost half a century the Cold War has meant that even the poorest country (assuming it was strategically located) had something to sell to the highest bidder. Some, like Egypt, managed to sell their favors first to one superpower, then to the other.

But while the relaxation of U.S.-Soviet tensions may be good news for the world, it is decidedly bad news for places like the Philippines, Vietnam, Cuba, and Nicaragua under the Sandinistas, each of which has successfully peddled access to its strategic geography. From now on it is unlikely that the two biggest customers for strategic location will be bidding against each other, as they once did.

Moreover, as logistic capabilities rise, as aircraft and missile range increases, as submarines proliferate, and as military airlift operations quicken, the need for overseas bases, repair facilities, and prepositioned supplies declines.

LDCs must, therefore, anticipate the end of the seller's market for such strategic locations. Unless replaced by other forms of international support, this will choke off billions of dollars of "foreign aid" and "military assistance" funds that have until now flowed into certain LDCs.

The U.S.-Soviet thaw, as we'll see, is a Soviet response to the new system of wealth creation in the high-tech nations. The collapse of the market for strategic location is an indirect consequence.

Even if the great powers of the future (whoever they may be) do continue to locate bases, set up satellite listening posts, or build airfields and submarine facilities on foreign soil, the "leases" will be for shorter times. Today's accelerating changes make all alliances more tenuous and temporary, discouraging the great powers from making long-term investments in fixed locations.

Wars, threats, insurrections will arise at unexpected places. Thus, the military of the great powers will increasingly stress mobile, rapid-deployment forces, the projection of naval power and space operations rather than fixed installations. All this will further drive down the bargaining power of countries with locations to let or lease.

Finally, the rise of Japanese military power in the Pacific may well lead the Philippines and other Southeast Asian countries to *welcome* U.S. or other forces as a counterbalance to a perceived Japanese threat. Carried far enough, this implies even a willingness to *pay* for protection, instead of charging for it.

New outbreaks of regional war or internal violence on many continents will keep the arms business booming. But whatever happens, it will be harder to extract benefits from the United States and the Soviets. This will upset the delicate power balance among LDCs—as between India and Pakistan, for instance—and will trigger potentially violent power shifts *within* the LDCs as well, especially among the elites closely (and sometimes corruptly) linked to aid programs, military procurement, and intelligence operations.

In short, the heyday of the Cold War is over. Far more complex power shifts lie ahead. And the market for strategic locations in the LDCs will never be the same.

BEYOND RAW MATERIALS

A second blow awaits countries that base their development plans on the export of bulk raw materials such as copper or bauxite.

Here, too, power-shifting changes are just around the corner.

Mass production required vast amounts of a small number of resources. By contrast, as de-massified manufacturing methods spread, they will need many more different resources—in much smaller quantities.

Furthermore, the faster metabolism of the new global production system also means that resources regarded as crucial today may be worthless tomorrow—along with all the extractive industries, railroad sidings, mines, harbor facilities, and other installations built to move them. Conversely, today's useless junk could suddenly acquire great value.

Oil itself was regarded as useless until new technologies, and especially the internal combustion engine, made it vital. Titanium was a largely useless white powder until it became valuable in aircraft and submarine production. But the rate at which new technologies arrived was slow. That, of course, is no longer true.

Superconductivity, to choose a single example, will eventually reduce the need for energy by cutting transmission losses and, at the same time, will require new raw materials for its use. New antipollution devices for automobiles may no longer depend on platinum. New pharmaceuticals may call for organic substances that today are either unknown or unvalued. In turn, this could change poverty-stricken countries into important suppliers—while undercutting today's big bulk exporters.

What's more, in the words of Umberto Colombo, Chairman of the EC's Committee on Science and Technology, "In today's advanced and affluent societies, each successive increment in per capita income is linked to an ever-smaller rise in quantities of raw materials and energy used." Colombo cites figures from the International Monetary Fund showing that "Japan . . . in 1984 consumed only 60 percent of the raw materials required for the same volume of industrial output in 1973." Advancing knowledge permits us to do more with less. As it does so, it shifts power away from the bulk producers.

Beyond this, fast-expanding scientific knowledge increases the ability to create substitutes for imported resources. Indeed, the advanced economies may soon be able to create whole arrays of new customized materials such as "nanocomposites" virtually from scratch. The smarter the high-tech nations become about micro-manipulating matter, the less dependent they become on imports of bulk raw materials from abroad.

The new wealth system is too protean, too fast-moving to be shackled to a few "vital" materials. Power will therefore flow from bulk raw material producers to those who control "eyedropper" quantities of temporarily crucial substances, and from them to those who control the knowledge necessary to create new resources *de novo*.

EXPENSIVE CHEAP LABOR

All this would be bad enough. But a third jolting blow is likely to hit the LDCs even harder and change power relations among and within them.

Ever since the smoky dawn of the industrial era, capitalist manufacturers have pursued the golden grail of cheap labor. After World War II the hunt for foreign sources of cheap labor became a stampede. Many developing countries bet their entire economic future on the theory that selling labor cheap would lead to modernization.

Some, like the "four tigers" of East Asia—South Korea, Tai-wan, Hong Kong, and Singapore—even won their bet. They were helped along by a strong work ethic, cultural and other unique factors, including the fact that two bitter wars, the Korean conflict in the 1950s and Vietnam in the 1960s and early '70s, pumped billions of dollars into their region. Some Japanese referred to this dollar influx as the "divine wind."

Because of their success, it is now almost universally believed that shifting from the export of agricultural products or raw mate-rials to the export of goods manufactured by cheap labor is the path to development. Yet nothing could be further from the long-range truth.

There is no doubt that the cheap-labor game is still being

played all over the world. Even now Japan is transferring plants and contracts from Taiwan and Hong Kong, where wages have risen, to Thailand, Malaysia, and China, where wages are still one-tenth those in Japan. No doubt many opportunities still exist for rich countries to locate pools of cheap labor in the LDCs.

But, like leasing military bases or shipping ore, the sale of cheap labor is also reaching its outer limits.

The reason for this is simple: Under the newly emerging system of wealth creation, cheap labor is increasingly expensive.

As the new system spreads, labor costs themselves become a smaller fraction of total costs of production. In some industries today, labor costs represent only 10 percent of the total cost of production. A 1 percent saving of a 10 percent cost factor is only one tenth of a percent.

By contrast, better technology, faster and better information flows, decreased inventory, or streamlined organization can yield savings far beyond any that can be squeezed out of hourly workers.

This is why it may be more profitable to run an advanced facility in Japan or the United States, with a handful of highly educated, highly paid employees, than a backward factory in China or Brazil that depends on masses of badly educated low-wage workers.

Cheap labor, in the words of Umberto Colombo, "is no longer enough to ensure market advantage to developing countries."

HYPER-SPEEDS

Looming on the horizon, therefore, is a dangerous de-coupling of the fast economies from the slow, an event that would spark enormous power shifts throughout the so-called South—with big impacts on the planet as a whole.

The new wealth-creation system holds the possibility of a far better future for vast populations who are now among the planet's poor. Unless the leaders of the LDCs anticipate these changes, however, they will condemn their people to perpetuated misery—and themselves to impotence.

For even as Chinese manufacturers wait for their steel, and traditional economies around the world crawl slowly through their paces, the United States, Japan, Europe, and in this case the Soviets, too, are pressing forward with plans to build hypersonic jets capable of moving 250 tons of people and cargo at Mach 5, meaning that cities like New York, Sydney, London, and Los Angeles will be two and a half hours from Tokyo.

Jiro Tokuyama, former head of the prestigious Nomura Research Institute, and now a senior adviser to the Mitsui Research Institute, heads a fifteen-nation study of what are called the "three T's": telecommunications, transportation, and tourism. Sponsored by the Pacific Economic Cooperation Conference, the study focuses on three key factors likely to accelerate the pace of economic processes in the region still further.

According to Tokuyama, Pacific air-passenger traffic is likely to reach 134 million . . . at the turn of the century. The Society of Japanese Aerospace Companies, Tokuyama adds, estimates that five hundred to one thousand hypersonic jets must be built. Many of these will ply Pacific routes, speeding further the economic development of the region, and promoting faster telecommunications as well. In a paper prepared for the Three T's study, Tokuyama spells out the commercial, social, and political implications of this development.

He also describes a proposal by Taisei, the Japanese construction firm, to build an artificial island five kilometers in length to serve as a "VAA," or "value added airport," capable of handling hypersonics and providing an international conference center, shops, and other facilities to be linked by high-speed linear trains to a densely populated area.

In Texas, meanwhile, billionaire H. Ross Perot is building an airport to be surrounded by advanced manufacturing facilities. As conceived by him, planes could roar in day and night bearing components for overnight processing or assembly in facilities at the airport. The next morning the jets would carry them to all parts of the world.

Simultaneously, on the telecommunications front, the advanced economies are investing billions in the electronic infrastructure essential to operations in the super-fast economy.

The spread of extra-intelligent nets is moving swiftly, and there are now proposals afoot to create special higher-speed fiber optic networks linking supercomputers all across the United States with thousands of laboratories and research groups. (Existing networks, which move 1.5 million bits of information a second, are regarded as too slow. The proposed new nets would send 3 billion bits per second streaming across the country—i.e., three "gigabits.")

The new network is needed, say its advocates, because the existing slower nets are already choked and overloaded. They argue that the project merits government backing because it would help the United States keep ahead of Europe and Japan in a field it now leads.

This, however, is only a special case of a more general clamor. In the words of Mitch Kapor, a founder of Lotus Development Corporation, the software giant, "We need to build a national infrastructure that will be the information equivalent of the national highway-building of the '50s and '60s." An even more appropriate analogy would compare today's computerized telecom infrastructures with the rail and road networks needed at the beginning of the industrial revolution.

What is happening, therefore, is the emergence of an electronic neural system for the economy—without which any nation, no matter how many smokestacks it has, will be doomed to backwardness.

ELECTRONIC GAPS AND DYNAMIC MINORITIES

For the LDCs, as for the rest of the world, power stems from the holster, the wallet, and the book—or, nowadays, the computer. Unless we want an anarchic world, with billions of poverty-stricken people, unstable governments led by unstable leaders, each with a finger on the missile launcher or chemical or bacteriological trigger, we need global strategies for preventing the de-coupling that looms before us.

A study of *Intelligence Requirements for the 1990s,* made by U.S. academic experts, warns that in the years immediately ahead the LDCs will acquire sophisticated new arms—enormous firepower will be added to their already formidable arsenals. Why?

As LDC economic power diminishes, their rulers face political opposition and instability. Under the circumstances, they are likely to do what rulers have done since the origins of the state: They reach for the most primitive form of power—military force.

But the most acute shortage facing LDCs is that of economically relevant knowledge. The 21st-century path to economic development and power is no longer through the exploitation of raw materials and human muscle but, as we've seen, through application of the human mind.

Development strategies make no sense, therefore, unless they take full account of the new role of knowledge in wealth creation, and of the accelerative imperative that goes hand in hand with it.

With knowledge (which in our definition includes such things as imagination, values, images, and motivation, along with formal technical skills) increasingly central to the economy, the Brazils and Nigerias, the Bangladeshes and Haitis must consider how they might best acquire or generate this resource.

It is clear that every wretched child in Northeast Brazil or anywhere else in the world who remains ignorant or intellectually underdeveloped because of malnutrition represents a permanent drain on the future. Revolutionary new forms of education will be needed that are not based on the old factory model.

Acquiring knowledge from elsewhere will also be necessary. This may take unconventional—and sometimes even illicit—forms. Stealing technological secrets is already a booming business around the world. We must expect shrewd LDCs to join the hunt.

Another way of obtaining wealth-making know-how is to organize a brain drain. This can be done on a small scale by bribing or attracting teams of researchers. But some clever countries will figure out that, around the world, there are certain dynamic minorities—often persecuted groups—that can energize a host economy if given the chance. The overseas Chinese in Southeast Asia, Indians in East Africa, Syrians in West Africa, Palestinians in parts of the Mideast, Jews in America, and Japanese in Brazil have all played this role at one time or another.

Transplanted into a different culture, each has brought not merely energy, drive, and commercial or technical acumen, but a pro-knowledge attitude—a ravenous hunger for the latest information, new ideas, skills. These groups have provided a kind of hybrid economic vigor. They work hard, they innovate, they educate their children, and even if they get rich in the process, they stimulate and accelerate the reflexes of the host economy. We will no doubt see various LDCs searching out such groups and inviting them to settle within their borders, in the hopes of injecting a needed adrenaline into the economy.*

Smart governments will also encourage the spread of nongovernmental associations and organizations, since such groups accelerate the spread of economically useful information through newsletters, meetings, conferences, and foreign travel. Associations of merchants, plastics engineers, employers, programmers, trade unions, bankers, journalists, etc., serve as channels for rapid exchange of information about what does and does not work in their respective fields. They are an important, often neglected communications medium.

Governments serious about economic development will also have to recognize the new economic significance of free expression. Failure to permit the circulation of new ideas—including economic and political ideas, even if unflattering to the state—is almost always prima facie proof that the state is weak at its core, and that those in power regard staying there as more important than economic improvement in the lives of their people. Governments committed to becoming part of the new world will systematically open the valves of public discussion.

Other governments will join "knowledge consortia"—partnerships with other countries or with global companies—to explore the far reaches of technology and science and, especially, the possibility of creating new materials.

Instead of pandering to obsolete nationalist notions, they will pursue the national interest passionately—but intelligently. Rather than refusing to pay royalties to foreign pharmaceutical companies on the lofty ground that health is above such grubby concerns, as Brazil has done, they will gladly pay the royalties—provided these funds stay inside the country for a fixed number of years, and are used to finance research projects carried out jointly with a local pharmaceutical firm's own experts. Profits from products that originate in this joint research can then be divided between the host country and the multinational. In this way the royalties pay for technology transfer—and for themselves. Effective nationalism thus replaces obsolete, self-destructive nationalism.

*During World War II the Japanese military actually drafted a plan to bring large numbers of persecuted European Jews to Manchuria, then called Manchukuo, for this purpose. However, the "Fugu Plan," as it was known, was never implemented.

Similarly, intelligent governments will welcome the latest computers, regardless of who built them, rather than trying to build a local computer industry behind tariff walls that keep out not merely products but advanced knowledge.

The computer industry is changing so fast on a world scale that no nation, not even the United States or Japan, can keep up without help from the rest of the world.

By barring certain outside computers and software, Brazil managed to build its own computer industry—but its products are backward compared with those available outside. This means that Brazilian banks, manufacturers, and other businesses have had to use technology that is inefficient compared with that of their foreign competitors. They compete with one hand tied behind them. Rather than gaining, the country loses.

Brazil violated the first rule of the new system of wealth creation. Do what you will with the slowly changing industries, but get out of the way of a fast-advancing industry. Especially one that processes the most important resource of all—knowledge.

Other LDCs will avoid these errors. Some, we may speculate, will actually invest modestly in existing venture capital funds in the United States, Europe, and Japan—on condition that their own technicians, scientists, and students accompany the capital and share in the know-how developed by the resulting start-up firms. In this way, Brazilians or Indonesians or Nigerians or Egyptians might find themselves at the front edge of tomorrow's industries. Astutely managed, the program could well pay for itself—or even make a profit.

Above all, the LDCs will take a completely fresh look at the role of agriculture, regarding it not necessarily as a "backward" sector but as a sector that potentially, with the help of computers, genetics, satellites, and other new technologies, could someday be more advanced, more progressive than all the smokestacks, steel mills, and mines in the world. Knowledge-based agriculture may be the cutting edge of economic advance tomorrow.

Moreover, agriculture will not limit itself to growing food, but will increasingly grow energy crops and feedstocks for new materials. These are but a few of the ideas likely to be tested in the years to come.

But none of these efforts will bear fruit if the country is cut off from participation in the fast-moving global economy and the telecommunications and computer networks that support it.

The maldistribution of telecommunications in today's world is even more dramatic than the maldistribution of food. There are 600 million telephones in the world—with 450 million of them in only nine countries. The lopsided distribution of computers, data bases, technical publications, research expenditures, tells us more about the future potential of nations than all the gross-national-product figures ground out by economists.

To plug into the new world economy, countries like China, Brazil, Mexico, Indonesia, India, as well as the Soviet Union and the East European nations, must find the resources needed to install their own electronic infrastructures. These must go far beyond mere telephone services to include up-to-date, high-speed data systems capable of linking into the latest global networks.

The good news is that today's slow countries may be able to skip over an entire stage of infrastructure development, leap-frogging from First to Third Wave communications without investing the vast sums needed to build Second Wave networks and systems.

The Iridium system, for example, announced by Motorola, Inc., will place 77 tiny satellites into low orbit, making it possible for millions in remote or sparsely populated regions like the Soviet Arctic, the Chinese desert, or the interior of Africa, to send and receive voice, data and digitized images through handheld telephones.

It is not necessary to lay copper or even fiber optic cable across thousands of miles of jungle, ice or sand. The portable phones will communicate directly with the nearest overhead satellite, which will pass the message along. Other advances will similarly slash the huge costs of telecommunications, bringing them within reach of today's impoverished countries. Large scale production and hyper-competition among American, European and Japanese suppliers will also drive costs down.

The new key to economic development is clear.

The "gap" that must be closed is informational and electronic. It is a gap not between the North and the South, but between the slow and the fast.

31

SOCIALISM'S COLLISION WITH THE FUTURE

The dramatic death of state socialism in Eastern Europe and its bloody anguish from Bucharest to Baku to Beijing did not happen by accident.

Socialism collided with the future.

Socialist regimes did not collapse because of CIA plots, capitalist encirclement, or economic strangulation from outside. Eastern European communist governments toppled domino-fashion as soon as Moscow sent the message that it would no longer use troops to protect them from their own people. But the crisis of socialism, as a system, in the Soviet Union, China, and elsewhere was far more deeply based.

Just as Gutenberg's invention of movable type in the mid-15th century led to the diffusion of knowledge and loosened the Catholic Church's grip on knowledge and communication in Western Europe—ultimately igniting the Protestant Reformation—so the appearance of the computer and new communications media in the mid-20th century smashed Moscow's control of the mind in the countries it ruled or held captive.

THE BREAKING POINT

As recently as 1956, Soviet leader Nikita Khrushchev could dream of "burying the West." Ironically, this was the very year when blue-collar workers in the United States were first outnumbered by knowledge and service workers—a shift that signaled the coming decline of the smokestack and the rise of the super-symbolic economy.

Equally ironic is the fact that mind-workers were typically dismissed as "nonproductive" by Marxist economists (and many classical economists as well). Yet it is these supposedly nonproductive workers who, more perhaps than any other, have given Western economies a tremendous shot of adrenaline since the mid-fifties.

Today, even with all their supposed "contradictions" unresolved, the high-tech capitalist nations have swept so far ahead of the rest of the world in economic terms as to render Khrushchev's boast merely pathetic. It was computer-based capitalism, not smokestack socialism, that made what Marxists call a "qualitative leap" forward. With the real revolution spreading in the high-tech nations, the socialist nations had become, in effect, a deeply reactionary bloc led by elderly men imbued with a 19th-century theology. Mikhail Gorbachev was the first Soviet leader to recognize this historic fact.

In a 1989 speech, some thirty years after the new system of wealth creation began to appear in the United States, Gorbachev declared, "We were nearly one of the last to realize that in the age of information science the most expensive asset is knowledge."

He rose to power not just as a remarkable individual, but as representative of a new class of better educated, largely white-collar Soviet citizens—precisely the group despised by earlier leaders. And precisely the group most closely connected with symbolic processing and production.

Marx himself had given the classic definition of a revolutionary moment. It came, he said, when the "social relations of production" (meaning the nature of ownership and control) prevent further development of the "means of production" (roughly speaking, the technology).

That formula perfectly described the socialist world crisis. Just as feudal "social relations" once hindered industrial development, now socialist "social relations" made it all but impossible for socialist countries to take advantage of the new wealth-creation system based on computers, communication, and above all, on open information. In fact, the central failure of the great state socialist experiment of the 20th century lay in its obsolete ideas about knowledge.

THE PRE-CYBERNETIC MACHINE

With minor exceptions, state socialism had led not to affluence, equality, and freedom, but to a one-party political system . . .
a massive bureaucracy . . . heavy-handed secret police . . . government control of the media . . . secrecy . . . and the repression of
intellectual and artistic freedom.

Setting aside the oceans of spurting blood needed to prop it
up, a close look at this system reveals that every one of these
elements is not just a way of organizing people, but also—and
more profoundly—a particular way of organizing, channeling, and
controlling knowledge.

A one-party political system is designed to control political
communication. Since no other party exists, it restricts the diversity
of political information flowing through the society, blocking feedback, and thus blinding those in power to the full complexity of
their problems. With very narrowly defined information flowing
upward through the approved channel, and commands flowing
downward, it becomes very difficult for the system to detect errors
and correct them.

In fact, top-down control in the socialist countries was based
increasingly on lies and misinformation, since reporting bad news
up the line was often risky. The decision to run a one-party system
is a decision, above all, about knowledge.

The overpowering bureaucracy that socialism created in every
sphere of life was also, as we saw in Chapter 15, a knowledge-
restricting device, forcing knowledge into pre-defined compartments or cubbyholes and restricting communication to "official
channels," while de-legitimating informal communication and
organization.

The secret police apparatus, state control of the media, the
intimidation of intellectuals, and the repression of artistic freedom
all represent further attempts to limit and control information
flows.

In fact, behind each of these elements we find a single obsolete assumption about knowledge: the arrogant belief that those in
command—whether of the party or of the state—know what others
should know.

These features of all the state socialist nations guaranteed
economic stupidity and derived from the concept of the pre-

cybernetic machine as applied to society and life itself. Second Wave machines—the kind that surrounded Marx in the 19th century—for the most part operated without any feedback. Plug in the power, start the motor, and it runs irrespective of what is happening in the outside environment.

Third Wave machines, by contrast, are intelligent. They have sensors that suck in information from the environment, detect changes, and adapt the operation of the machine accordingly. They are self-regulating. The technological difference is revolutionary.

While Marx, Engels, and Lenin all bitterly assailed the philosophy of "mechanical materialism," their own thinking, reflecting their era, remained steeped in certain analogies and assumptions based on pre-intelligent machinery.

Thus for Marxian socialists the class struggle was the "locomotive of history." A key task was to capture the "state machine." And society itself, being machine-like, could be pre-set to deliver abundance and freedom. Lenin, on capturing control of Russia in 1917, became the supreme mechanic.

A brilliant intellectual, Lenin understood the importance of ideas. But, for him, symbolic production, too—the mind itself—could be programmed. Marx wrote of freedom, but Lenin, on taking power, undertook to engineer knowledge. Thus he insisted that all art, culture, science, journalism, and symbolic activity in general be placed at the service of a master plan for society. In time the various branches of learning would be neatly organized into an "academy" with fixed bureaucratic departments and ranks, all subject to party and state control. "Cultural workers" would be employed by institutions controlled by a Ministry of Culture. Publishing and broadcasting would be monopolies of the state. Knowledge, in effect, would be made part of the state machine.

This constipated approach to knowledge blocked economic development even in low-level smokestack economies; it is diametrically opposed to the principles needed for economic advance in the age of the computer.

THE PROPERTY PARADOX

The Third Wave wealth-creation system now spreading also challenges three pillars of the socialist faith.

Take the question of property.

From the beginning, socialists traced poverty, depressions, unemployment, and the other evils of industrialism to private ownership of the means of production. The way to solve these ills was for the workers to own the factories—through the state or through collectives.

Once this was accomplished, things would be different. No more competitive waste. Completely rational planning. Production for use rather than profit. Intelligent investment to drive the economy forward. The dream of abundance for all would be realized for the first time in history.

In the 19th century, when these ideas were formulated, they seemed to reflect the most advanced scientific knowledge of the time. Marxists, in fact, claimed to have gone beyond fuzzy-headed utopianism and arrived at truly "scientific socialism." Utopians might dream of self-governing communal villages. Scientific socialists knew that in a developing smokestack society such notions were impractical. Utopians like Charles Fourier looked toward the agrarian past. Scientific socialists looked toward what was then the industrial future.

Thus, later on, while socialist regimes experimented with cooperatives, worker-management, communes, and other schemes, state socialism—state ownership of everything from banks to breweries, rolling mills to restaurants—became the dominant form of property throughout the socialist world. (So complete was this obsession with state ownership that Nicaragua, an imitative latecomer to the socialist world, even created "Lobo Jack," a state-owned disco.) Everywhere, the state, not the workers, thus became the chief beneficiary of socialist revolution.

Socialism failed to meet its promise to improve radically the material conditions of life. When living standards fell in the Soviet Union after the revolution, the decline was blamed, with some justification, on the effects of World War I and counterrevolution. Later the shortfalls were blamed on capitalist encirclement. Still later, on World War II. Yet thirty years after the war, staples like coffee and oranges were still in short supply in Moscow. In the period preceding Gorbachev's perestroika, the diet of a middle-class researcher at a state institute in Moscow was heavily based on cabbage and potatoes. In 1989, four years after the start of Gorbachev's attempt at reforms, the U.S.S.R. had to import 600 million razor blades and 40 million tubes of shaving cream from abroad.

Remarkably, though their number is declining, one still hears orthodox socialists around the world calling for the nationalization of industry and finance. From Brazil and Peru to South Africa and even in the industrialized nations of the West there remain true believers who, despite all historical evidence to the contrary, still regard "public ownership" as "progressive" and resist every effort to de-nationalize or privatize the economy.

It is true that today's increasingly liberalized global economy, uncritically hailed by the great multinational corporations, is itself unstable and could suffer a massive coronary. The distended debt balloon on which it rests could be punctured. Wars, sudden interruptions of energy or resources, and any number of other calamities could cause its collapse in the decades ahead. Under catastrophic conditions, one might well imagine the need for temporary emergency nationalizations.

Nevertheless, incontrovertible evidence proves that state-owned enterprises mistreat their employees, pollute the air, and abuse the public at least as efficiently as private enterprises. Many have become sink-holes of inefficiency, corruption, and greed. Their failures frequently encourage a vast, seething black market that undermines the very legitimacy of the state.

But worst and most ironic of all, instead of taking the lead in technological advance as promised, nationalized enterprises, as a rule, are almost uniformly reactionary—the most bureaucratic, the slowest to reorganize, the least willing to adapt to changing consumer needs, the most afraid to provide information to the citizen, the last to adopt advanced technology.

For more than a century, socialists and defenders of capitalism waged bitter war over public versus private property. Large numbers of men and women literally laid down their lives over this issue. What neither side imagined was a new wealth-creation system that would make virtually all their arguments obsolete.

Yet this is exactly what happened. For the most important form of property is now intangible. It is super-symbolic. It is knowledge. The same knowledge can be used by many people simultaneously to create wealth and to produce still more knowledge. And unlike factories and fields, knowledge is, for all intents, inexhaustible. Neither socialist regimes nor socialists in general have yet come to terms with this truly revolutionary fact.

HOW MANY "LEFT-HANDED" SCREWS?

A second pillar in the cathedral of socialist theory was central planning. Instead of allowing the "chaos" of the marketplace to determine the economy, intelligent top-down planning would be able to concentrate resources on key sectors, and accelerate technological development.

But central planning depended on knowledge, and as early as the 1920s the Austrian economist Ludwig von Mises identified its lack of knowledge or, as he termed it, its "calculation problem," as the Achilles heel of socialism.

How many shoes and what sizes should a factory in Irkutsk make? How many left-handed screws or grades of paper? What price-relationships should be set between carburetors and cucumbers? How many rubles, zlotys, or yuan should be invested in each of tens of thousands of different lines and levels of production?

To answer such questions, even in the simplest smokestack economy, requires more knowledge than central planners can collect or analyze, especially when managers, afraid of trouble, routinely lie to them about actual production. Thus, warehouses filled up with unwanted shoes. Shortages and a vast, shadowy black market became chronic features of most socialist economies.

Generations of earnest socialist planners wrestled desperately with this knowledge problem. They demanded ever more data and got ever more lies. They beefed up the bureaucracy. Lacking the supply-and-demand signals generated by a competitive market, they tried measuring the economy in terms of labor hours, or counting things in terms of kind, rather than money. Later they tried econometric modeling and input-output analysis.

Nothing worked. The more information they had, the more complex and disorganized the economy grew. Fully three quarters of a century after the Russian Revolution the real symbol of the U.S.S.R. was not the hammer and sickle, but the consumer queue.

Today, all across the socialist and ex-socialist spectrum there is a race to introduce market economics, either wholly, as in Poland, or timidly within a planned regimen, as in the Soviet Union. It is now almost universally recognized by socialist reformers that allowing supply and demand to determine prices (at least within certain ranges) provides what the central plan could not—price signals indicating what is or is not needed and wanted in the economy.

However, overlooked in the discussion among economists over the need for these signals is the fundamental change in communication pathways they imply, and the tremendous power shifts that changes in communication systems bring. The most important difference between centrally planned economies and market-driven economies is that, in the first, information flows vertically, whereas in the market, much more information flows horizontally and diagonally in the system, with buyers and sellers exchanging information at every level.

This change does not merely threaten top bureaucrats in the planning ministries and in management, but millions upon millions of mini-bureaucrats whose sole source of power depends on their control of information fed up the reporting channel.

The incapacity of the central planning system to cope with high levels of information thus set limits on the economic complexity necessary for growth.

The new wealth-creation methods require so much knowledge, so much information and communication, that they are totally out of reach of centrally planned economies. The rise of the super-symbolic economy thus collides with a second foundation of socialist orthodoxy.

THE DUSTBIN OF HISTORY

The third crashing pillar of socialism was its overweening emphasis on hardware—its total concentration on smokestack industry and its derogation of both agriculture and mind-work.

In the years after the 1917 revolution, the Soviets lacked capital to build all the steel mills, dams, and auto plants they needed. Soviet leaders seized on the theory of "socialist primitive accumulation" formulated by the economist E. A. Preobrazhensky. This theory held that the necessary capital could be squeezed out of the peasants by forcing their standard of living down to an emaciating minimum and skimming off their surpluses. These would then be used to capitalize heavy industry and subsidize the workers.

Nikolai Bukharin, a Bolshevik leader who paid for his prescience with his life, correctly predicted that this strategy would merely guarantee agricultural collapse. Worse yet, this policy led to the murderous oppression of the peasantry by Stalin, since it was only by means of extreme force that such a program could be imposed. Millions died of starvation or persecution.

As a result of this "industry bias," as the Chinese call it today, agriculture has been a disaster area for virtually all socialist economies and still is. Put differently, the socialist countries pursued a Second Wave strategy at the expense of their First Wave people.

But socialists also frequently denigrated the services and white-collar work. It was not pure coincidence that when the Soviets demanded "socialist realism" in the arts, the walls were soon covered with murals of beefy workers straining muscles in steel mills and factories. Because the goal of socialism everywhere was to industrialize as rapidly as possible, it was muscle-labor that was glorified. Mind-work was for nonproductive wimps.

This widespread attitude went hand in hand with the tremendous concentration on production rather than consumption, on capital goods rather than consumer goods.

While some Marxists, notably Antonio Gramsci, challenged this view, and Mao Tse-tung at times insisted that ideological purity could overcome material handicaps, the fundamental thrust of Marxist regimes was to overrate material production and undervalue products of the mind.

Mainline Marxists typically held the materialist view that ideas, information, art, culture, law, theories, and the other intangible products of the mind were merely part of a "superstructure" which hovered, as it were, over the economic "base" of society. While there was, admittedly, a certain feedback between the two, it was the base that determined the superstructure, rather than the reverse. Those who argued otherwise were condemned as "idealists"—at times a decidedly dangerous label to wear.

Marx, in arguing the primacy of the material base, stood Hegel on his head. The great irony of history today is that the new system of wealth creation, in turn, is standing Marx on his. Or more accurately, laying Marx and Hegel both on their sides.

For Marxists, hardware was always more important than software; the computer revolution now teaches us that the opposite is true. If anything, it is knowledge that drives the economy, not the economy that drives knowledge.

Societies, however, are not machines and they are not computers. They cannot be reduced so simply into hardware and software, base and superstructure. A more apt model would picture them as consisting of many more elements all connected in immensely complex and continually changing feedback loops. As their complexity rises, knowledge becomes more central to both their economic and ecological survival.

In brief, the rise of a new economy whose primary raw material is, in fact, soft and intangible found world socialism totally unprepared. Socialism's collision with the future was fatal.

If orthodox socialism is ready for what Lenin called the "dustbin of history," however, this does not mean that the magnificent dreams that bred it are also dead. The desire to create a world in which affluence, peace, and social justice prevail is at least as noble and widely shared as ever. Such a world cannot rise, however, on old foundations.

The most important revolution on the planet today is the rise of a new Third Wave civilization with its radical new system of wealth creation. Any movement that has not yet grasped this fact is condemned to relive its failures. Any state that makes knowledge a captive freezes its citizens in a nightmare past.

32

THE POWER OF BALANCE

The Powershift Era has only begun and already, it would appear, the future is up for grabs. With the "East" in upheaval, the "South" increasingly divided, and the leading powers of the "West"—Europe, Japan, and America—on a collision course, we face a frantic, endless round of summits, conferences, treaties, and missions as diplomats meet to construct a new global order.

No matter how much hammering, sawing, and wordsmithing they do, however, the new architecture of world power will depend less on their words than on the quantity and quality of power each brings to the table.

Are the United States and the Soviet Union both now global has-beens? If so, how many new "superpowers" will arise to take their place?

Some speak of a world organized around Europe, Japan, and the United States. Others see the world broken into six or eight regional blocs. Still others believe the bipolar world is turning into a five-sided star, with China at one of the points, India at another. Will the new Europe stretch from the Atlantic to the Soviet border—or beyond? No one can solve these puzzles with certainty. But the powershift principle can help.

It reminds us that while many other factors—from political stability to population growth—all count, violence, wealth, and knowledge are the three main rivers from which most other power resources flow, and each is now in the process of being revolutionized.

Take violence.

THE DEMOCRATIZATION OF DEATH

So much has been written about "peace breaking out" that world attention has drifted away from the menacing fact that as the two former superpowers scale down their arms, other nations are racing to fill the gap.

India, for example, despite its image as a backward, peace-loving land, has been the world's biggest arms buyer since 1986, purchasing in 1987 more weapons than warring Iran and Iraq combined. This policy has drawn fire from the Japanese and a sharp riposte from New Delhi. India already possesses nuclear weapons and is hoping to build missiles able to deliver them to a distance of 1,500 miles. Pakistan, which is also nearing nuclear capability, has a short-range missile built with Chinese help.

According to CIA Director William Webster, fully fifteen countries will be manufacturing ballistic missiles within a decade. Many are in the tense Middle East. Egypt, Iraq, and Argentina are partners in a missile-making project.

Beyond this lie a number of terrifying scenarios. Soviet nukes are located in Azerbaijan and other Muslim republics where ethnic fighting has broken out, leading some experts to speculate on the nightmarish possibility that a breakaway republic might seize some of these weapons. Asks one alarmed U.S. official: "Will the fourth-biggest nuclear power be Kazakhstan?"

So serious are the risks that Moscow has reportedly begun withdrawing nuclear arms from the tense Baltic region, and a top Soviet official, speaking privately to the author, has said: "I used to be against SDI [Washington's Strategic Defense Initiative whose goal is to intercept and destroy incoming nuclear missiles]. But now I'm *for* SDI. If the U.S.S.R. splits apart, the world could suddenly find itself confronted with ten more nuclear-armed countries."

In fact, a civil war in the Soviet Union—or any other nuclear power—raises the possibility that rebel forces might seize the weapons, or that rebel and loyalist forces might each seize part of the nuclear arsenal.

Even more ominously, some "developing countries"—Iraq and Libya are not alone—are designing plants to manufacture chemical and bacteriological weapons as well. In short, the present distribution of weapons in the world, and especially nuclear weapons, is neither fixed nor stable.

A key source of state power, therefore, the capacity for hyper-violence that was once concentrated in a few nations, is now becoming democratically but dangerously dispersed.

At the very same time, the nature of violence itself is undergoing profound change, becoming increasingly dependent on such knowledge-intensive technologies as microelectronics, advanced materials, optics, artificial intelligence, satellites, telecommunications, and advanced simulation and software. Thus, whereas the first F-16 fighters needed 135,000 lines of computer programming, the Advanced Tactical Fighter now on the drawing boards will require 1,000,000 lines. These changes in world military systems do more than merely shift power from here to there; they revolutionize the nature of the global game.

Shintaro Ishihara, a former Cabinet member in Japan, blew up a storm in Washington recently with a brief book called *The Japan That Can Say No,* which consisted of speeches he and Akio Morita, co-founder of Sony, had made on various occasions. In it Ishihara pointed out that to radically improve the accuracy of their nuclear weapons the United States and the U.S.S.R. alike would need extremely advanced Japanese-made semiconductor technology.

Referring to the United States, he said, "It has come to the point that no matter how much they continue military expansion, if Japan stopped selling them the chips, there would be nothing more they could do. If, for example, Japan sold chips to the Soviet Union and stopped selling them to the U.S., this would upset the entire military balance. Some Americans say that if Japan were thinking of doing that, it would be occupied. Certainly, this is an age where things could come to that."

Ishihara's remarks underscored the growing dependence of violence on knowledge, a reflection of today's historic powershift.

THE OCEAN OF CAPITAL

The second leg of the power triad—wealth—as previous chapters have documented, is also experiencing deep transformation as the new system for wealth creation spreads across the planet.

As corporations integrate their production and distribution across national boundaries, acquire foreign firms, and draw on brainpower from around the entire world, they inevitably need fresh sources of capital in many countries. They also need it fast. Thus we see a race to "liberalize" capital markets so that investments can flow more or less freely across national frontiers.

As noted earlier, the result is a surging ocean of capital free of restraining walls. This, however, shifts power away from central banks and individual nations, undermining sovereignty and introducing new dangers of financial fibrillation on a worldwide scale.

As we wrote in *The New York Times* shortly after the October 1987 Wall Street crash: "Building a single completely open financial system, subject to minimal regulation, is like building a supertanker without airtight compartments. With adequate dividers or safety cells, a big system can survive the breakdown of certain parts. Without them, a single hole in the hull can sink the tanker."

Since then, Alan Greenspan, chairman of the U.S. Federal Reserve Board, also has warned that the creation of multinational securities firms that buy, sell, underwrite, and invest in many nations increases the risk of large-scale breakdown. "A loss by one or more of these firms," Greenspan declared, could result in "transmitting a disturbance" from one country to another.

As finance is globalized, nations risk losing control over one of the keys to their power. The proposed all-European currency, for example, would reduce the flexibility of individual nations to cope with their own unique economic problems. Another proposal would arm the EC commissioners with far greater control over the budgets of Europe's supposedly sovereign nations than the federal government of the United States exerts over its fifty states—a centralizing power shift of massive proportions.

While this power redistribution is going on, the entire wealth system becomes, as we've seen, super-symbolic. Like violence, wealth, too, is shifting and being transformed at the same time.

THE NEW ARCHITECTURE OF KNOWLEDGE

This takes us to the third leg of the power triad: knowledge.

The wildfire spread of the computer in recent decades has been called the single most important change in the knowledge system since the invention of movable type in the 15th century or even the invention of writing. Paralleling this extraordinary change has come the equally astonishing spread of new networks and media for moving knowledge and its precursors, data and information.

Had nothing else changed, these twin developments alone would warrant the term *knowledge revolution*. But as we know, other, related changes are transforming the entire knowledge system or "info-sphere" in the high-tech world.

The hyper-speed of change today means that given "facts" become obsolete faster—knowledge built on them becomes less durable. To overcome this "transience factor," new technological and organizational tools are currently being designed to accelerate scientific research and development. Others are intended to speed up the learning process. The metabolism of knowledge is moving faster.

Equally important, the high-tech societies are beginning to reorganize their knowledge. As we've seen, the everyday know-how needed in business and politics is growing more abstract every day. Conventional disciplines are breaking down. With the help of the computer, the same data or information can now easily be clustered or "cut" in quite different ways, helping the user to view the same problem from quite different angles, and to synthesize meta-knowledge.

Meanwhile, advances in artificial intelligence and expert systems provide new ways to concentrate expertise. Because of all these changes, we see rising interest in cognitive theory, learning theory, "fuzzy logic," neurobiology, and other intellectual developments that bear on the architecture of knowledge itself.

In short, knowledge is being restructured at least as profoundly as violence and wealth, meaning that all the elements of the power triad are in simultaneous revolution. And each day the other two sources of power themselves become more knowledge-dependent.

This, then, is the turbulent background against which the rise and fall of civilizations and of individual nations needs to be seen, and it explains why most current power assessments will prove misleading.

THE ONE-LEGGED SOVIET

Diplomats like to talk about the balance of power. The powershift principle helps us gauge not only the balance of power but the "power of balance."

Nations (or alliances) can be divided into three types: those whose power is based predominantly on a single leg of the violence-wealth-knowledge stool, those whose power rests on two legs, and those whose global clout is balanced on all three of the main sources of power.

To judge how well the United States, Japan, or Europe will fare in the global power struggles to come, we need to look at all three of these sources of power, focusing special attention on the third: the knowledge base, since this will increasingly determine the value of the other two.

This knowledge base includes far more than conventional items like science and technology or education. It encompasses a nation's strategic conceptions, its foreign intelligence capabilities, its language, its general knowledge of other cultures, its cultural and ideological impact on the world, the diversity of its communication systems and the range of new ideas, information, and imagery flowing through them. All these feed or drain a nation's power and determine what quality of power it can deploy in any given conflict or crisis.

Going beyond the triad, the powershift principle introduces a further useful insight by asking about the *relationship* of violence to wealth to knowledge in any given period.

If we look at the power of balance, as distinct from the balance of power, we discover that throughout the Cold War, the power of the United States has been extremely broadly based. America not only had massive military might but supreme economic clout, and the world's best supply of power-knowledge, ranging from the finest science and technology to a popular culture much of the world wished to emulate.

By contrast, Soviet power was, and remains, totally unbalanced. Its claim to superpower status derived exclusively from its military. Its economy, a shambling wreck at home, counted for little in the world system. While its R&D was excellent in a few defense-related sectors, its general technological know-how was backward, cramped by paranoid secrecy. Its telecommunications were abominable. Its education system was mediocre, its centrally controlled media, tightly censored and backward.

Over the long run of the Cold War, it was the power-balanced United States, rather than the one-legged Soviet Union, that won the endurance race.

This insight, only half-understood by the main global players, helps explain much of what Europe, the United States, and Japan are doing as they race toward their coming collision.

33

TRIADS: TOKYO—BERLIN— WASHINGTON

Until recently Japan was a one-legged nation.

If a nation's global influence springs mainly from military potential, wealth, and knowledge, Japan's, until very recently, rested on one leg of the power triad, much like that of the Soviet Union. Instead of nuclear weapons and the equivalent of the Red Army, Japan had cash. And more cash.

But one-legged stools are notoriously unstable. And even wealth has its limitations. For this reason, Japan today is pursuing the power of balance.

THE JAPANESE GUN

At first bullied into military spending by Washington, Japan has recently needed little prodding to expand its armed forces. What has been unthinkable since Hiroshima—the notion of a nuclear-armed Japan—is no longer regarded as entirely out of the question. It has become, instead, a noticeable gleam in the eye of some Japanese hawks.

Japan's military budget is now the third-largest in the world, after that of the United States and the Soviet Union. Its hawks, according to their critics, now want to expand the military's role beyond Japan's immediate territorial waters; to write a mutual security pact with a neighboring country, giving Japan a definite role as regional policeman; and to equip the navy with an aircraft carrier so Japanese power can be projected over a much wider radius.

Japan's budding military-industrial complex is champing at the bit to build its own fighter aircraft, missiles, and other advanced weaponry. Companies like Fuji Heavy Industries, Kawasaki Heavy Industries, Nissan, Mitsubishi, and Komatso all produce military goods under U.S. license. After acrimonious negotiations with the United States, a joint project is under way to build the FSX advanced fighter plane using active phased array radar, sophisticated composite materials, and other advanced technologies. Japan is also engaged in research on missile defense.

Japan is neither aggressive nor irresponsible. Its military, since World War II, has been firmly under civilian control, and every survey shows the Japanese public to be far more peace-loving than Americans. Nevertheless, it is hard to say how long that sentiment will last as frictions rise between Washington and Tokyo. It is by no means clear what role the Japanese military might play in Southeast Asia if (1) U.S. forces were further weakened or withdrawn; and (2) war or revolution threatened Japan's huge investments in the region.

With political unrest flaring from Beijing and Hong Kong to Manila, Japan's neighbors in the region have one worried eye cocked on Japan's rearmament and the other on America's post-Vietnam retrenchment, its troop withdrawals from South Korea, and its defense cutbacks in general.

Japan is now driving toward military self-sufficiency, preliminary to suggesting, in the most courteous way, that U.S. forces are no longer needed in Japan—or in the region.

In 1988 former Prime Minister Noboru Takeshita put Japan's military buildup in sharp perspective. Japan, he told the Japanese Defense Academy, needed military power to match its enormous new economic clout. Japan is racing to balance its triad.

THE ECONOMIC GODZILLA

The second leg of Japanese power—its wealth—is already so well documented it needs little elaboration here. In 1986, Japan became the world's biggest creditor nation. In 1987 the combined value of all stocks on the Tokyo Stock Exchange shot past that of all New York Stock Exchange stocks. The world's largest banks and securities firms are now Japanese. Japanese buy-ups of prime American real estate, including landmarks like Radio City Music Hall and companies like Columbia Pictures, have ignited anti-Japanese passions in the United States. The same thing is happening in Europe and Australia. Meanwhile, the U.S. government has become dependent on Japanese investors for nearly a third of the funds needed to finance its deficit, raising fears that a sudden pullout of this support could destroy the U.S. economy.

The accumulation of such facts has given rise to predictions that Japan will become an economic Godzilla and dominate the earth for the next fifty years.

Yet Japan's economic rocket cannot orbit forever. The drive to export goods, and especially capital, will run into progressively stiffer resistance and worsened terms for trade and investment. In turn, friction will rise in the richer nations, driving more Japanese investment into the less economically developed countries, where both risks and rewards are potentially higher.

If large numbers of U.S. troops are brought home from Europe, as appears likely, the U.S. budget deficit could decline, further strengthening the dollar and lowering the yen, which in turn would slow overseas expansion. This would, among other things, drive up Japan's costs for oil, which is traded in dollars.

Japan's savings rate, already dropping, will decline further as consumers seek more amenity and leisure, and as the fast-growing older population eats into savings put aside during its working years. In turn, both these developments point toward higher interest rates and slower growth over the long term.

Worse yet, as every Japanese knows, the Japanese economy is perched atop an immense real estate bubble, waiting to explode at the slightest pinprick. When it does, the impact will send shock waves through the already unstable Tokyo Stock Exchange and radiate instantly to Wall Street, Zurich, and London.

Japan, moreover, has a long-neglected backlog of social and political problems. Its discredited political system, corrupt and cumbersome, finds both major parties out of sync with the new realities. (The Liberal Democratic Party depends too heavily on rural voters and needs a stronger urban base. The Socialists are urban, but unable to shake off their obsolete economic and political dogmas.)

The decades ahead will find a Japan far less stable than at present, for the era of linear growth is ending.

THE *JUKU* RACE

More important than either arms or wealth is the knowledge on which both are increasingly dependent. Japanese pupils often go to a *juku,* or cram school, after school hours to improve their grades. Japan, as a nation, has been enrolled in one big *juku* for decades, working overtime to expand the country's ultimate power source—its knowledge base.

Ever since 1970, Japan has thrown itself consciously and enthusiastically into the race to create an information-based economy. It started building its technological R&D capacity even earlier. In 1965 the number of scientists and engineers per 10,000 members of the work force was roughly a third that in the United States. By 1986 the ratio had surpassed that in America. The "knowledge-density" of its work force has been skyrocketing.

Japan is pushing ahead in every advanced field from biotechnology to space. It has ample capital for R&D, and for investments in high-tech start-up firms anywhere in the world. It is advancing frontiers in superconductivity, materials, and robotics. In 1990 it became the third nation, after the United States and the U.S.S.R., to send an unmanned spacecraft to the moon. Its successes in semiconductor chip manufacture have been astonishing.

But the world's scientific-technological marathon is only starting, and Japan's general technological base still lags. Japan even now spends 3.3 times more money for royalties, patents, and licenses for foreign technology than it takes in from the sale of its own. Sixty percent of that is paid to the United States. Japanese weakness is evident in fields like parallel computing architectures, computational fluid dynamics, phased array, and other advanced radar-related technologies.

Moreover, Japan, which is so advanced in the manufacture of computer chips and hardware, continues to be weak in the increasingly crucial field of software. Its much ballyhooed attempt at a great leap forward—the "fifth generation project"—has so far proved disappointing.

Financed by MITI, the Ministry of International Trade and Industry, the project was described as Japan's equivalent of sputnik, the Soviets' first space probe. Such was the advance enthusiasm that, in 1986, Dr. Akira Ishikawa of Aoyama Gakuin University in Tokyo said the Japanese saw the fifth generation project as "nothing short of a mandate for their survival, a means of . . . self-sufficiency." By 1988 it was already apparent that the project was in deep trouble, plagued by vague planning, technical problems, and a failure to produce significant commercial spinoff products. By 1989 it was reporting modest results. Even more significant, perhaps, Japan is behind in the development of "meta"-software, used for producing software itself.

In a recent survey, 98 percent of Japanese CEOs conceded U.S. supremacy in software; 92 percent agreed that the United States was still in the lead in artificial intelligence and in supercomputers; 76 percent felt the same way about computer-aided design and engineering.

In the early laps of the R&D race, therefore, the United States is slipping. Japan is gaining fast, but there are still many laps to go.

Knowledge-power, however, is not just a matter of science and technology. This is something Japan understands much better than the United States. As in chess and war, so in commercial or scientific rivalry: "Know your adversary" is still a vital rule. And here Japan is light-years ahead.

Japan knows infinitely more about the United States than the United States knows about Japan. Because Japan was militarily and politically dependent on the United States for decades, American decisions had an enormous impact on Japan. Japan *needed* to know America inside out.

For decades, therefore, Japanese have been journeying all over the United States, from Silicon Valley to Washington and Wall Street, from Harvard and MIT to Stanford, visiting thousands of businesses, government offices, laboratories, schools, and homes, consciously learning as much as possible about what makes America tick—not just commercially or politically, but culturally, psychologically, socially. This was not so much an exercise in business espionage (although some clearly took place) as an expression of Japan's deeply ingrained curiosity about the outside world and its search for a role model.

Following three hundred years of isolation from the rest of the planet, Japan, after the Meiji revolution, rushed to make up for its enforced ignorance and has become the most avid newspaper-reading nation in the world, the most inquisitive about foreign attitudes, the most eager to travel.

This intense curiosity has contrasted sharply with American provincialism. With the arrogance of the world's dominant power, with a domestic market so large it could afford to treat exports as peripheral, with the condescension of a conqueror and the unconscious racism of its primarily white skin, the United States bothered to learn little about Japan beyond some exotica in which geishas and mixed public bathing figured large. Sushi came later.

While 24,000 Japanese students hastened to study in the United States, fewer than 1,000 Americans bothered to make the reverse trip.

Japan, in fact, works harder than any other nation at expanding its general knowledge, and this helps explain why it has been so good at marketing its wares in the United States, and why U.S. firms would have double difficulty penetrating the Japanese market even if all trade barriers vanished overnight.

Yet Japan's overall knowledge base is still deficient in several dimensions. Reflecting its own racist values, it is naïve about ethnicity and fails to understand its significance in a global economy.

Japan's much-vaunted education system, which many U.S. educators and business leaders naïvely hold up as a model, is itself savagely criticized at home for its overregimentation and creativity-crushing methods. At the lower levels, teachers' unions and the educational bureaucracy snuff out any proposed innovation. Its higher education lacks the renowned quality of its manufactured goods. Japan makes better Acuras than university graduates.

Japan leads the world in spreading extra-intelligent electronic networks, and in developing high-definition television, but it lags behind both the United States and Europe in deregulating the media and allowing the full development of cable television and direct broadcast satellite, which would diversify the imagery and ideas so necessary in spurring innovation in a culture.

Where Japan is weakest of all, however, is in cultural exports. Japan today has great writers, artists, architects, choreographers, and film makers. But few are known outside Japan, and even they exercise little influence.

In pursuit of balanced power, Japan has launched a major cultural offensive—beginning in fields directly linked to the economy, like fashion and industrial design. It is now moving on to the popular arts as well, including television, movies, music, and dance, and to literature and the fine arts. The recent creation of the Praemium Imperiale awards, intended to be the Japanese equivalent of the Nobel Prize and sponsored by the Japan Art Association, indicates Japan's determination to play a significant role in world cultural affairs.

Japan faces a tremendous obstacle, however, in spreading its ideas and culture abroad. This is its language. Some nationalist Japanese scholars insist there is something mystical and untranslatable about Japanese, that it has a unique "soul." In truth, as poets and translators know, all languages are incompletely translatable, since the very categorization schemes and analogies embedded in them differ. But the fact that only 125 million people on the face of the earth speak Japanese is a significant drawback for Japan's pursuit of balanced world power. This is why Japan, more perseveringly than any other nation, presses on with research into computerized translation.

Another, even greater, challenge facing Japan is how to cope with the coming de-massification of a society that has been propagandized into believing that homogeneity is always a virtue. More than a decade ago anthropologist Kazuko Tsurumi of Sophia University pointed out that there is more diversity in Japan than its leaders acknowledge. But this was diversity within the framework of a homogenizing Second Wave society. As Japan enters the Third Wave era it will face potentially explosive heterogenizing pressures.

Its antagonism to social, economic, and cultural diversity is directly related to its greatest long-term weakness of all.

Today's Japanese are no longer the "economic animals" they were once accused of being, and their national power no longer rests on a single leg of the power triad. But in the most important power competition—the generation and diffusion of ideas, information, imagery, and knowledge—they still lag behind the United States.

With these various power resources to deploy, Japan's business and political leaders lack a clear international strategy. A consensus exists at the top about certain key domestic goals. These include expansion of the domestic economy and reduction of the need to export, improvement of the quality of life through increased leisure, and reclamation of the heavily fouled environment.

But Japan's elites are deeply split over foreign economic policy, uncertain about what, if any, world role Japan should play in the future. One strategy presupposes that the world will break into regions and that Japan's role should be to dominate the East Asian/Pacific Region. This means concentrating investment and foreign aid there. It means quietly preparing for the role of regional police power. Such a policy reduces Japan's vulnerability to American and European protectionism.

A second approach suggests that Japan concentrate instead on the developing economies, wherever they may be. A variation of this approach proposes that Japan focus on creating the electronic infrastructures needed by these countries if they are to plug into the world economy. (Such a strategy fills a critical need for the "slow" countries of the world, draws on Japanese technological strengths, and helps lock these economies electronically into Japan's.)

A third strategy, perhaps the most widely held at present, sees Japan's mission as global, unconfined to any particular region. Its backers push for a "global mission," not because of some messianic vision of world domination but because they believe the Japanese economy is too big, too varied, too fast-growing to be contained within a single region or country group.

It is this "globalist" faction that urged the dispatch of navy ships to help the United States and its allies protect the Persian Gulf during the Iran-Iraq war. It is this group that favors making loans to Eastern Europe, playing a larger and larger diplomatic role on the world stage, assuming dominant positions in the International Monetary Fund, the World Bank, and other global institutions.

When Japan makes its decision among these three strategies, it will not be clear-cut. The Japanese way is frequently to split differences. Yet astute observers will be able to judge which way the bamboo stick falls. At that point, the world will first begin to feel the real impact of Japan's thrust toward tomorrow.

THE NEW *OST-STRATEGIE*

The conflict within the capitalist world will intensify as Japan's ambitions collide with those of the other main players, the United States and Europe, calling to mind these lines written on August 23, 1915:

"A United States of Europe is possible . . . but to what end? Only for the purpose of suppressing socialism in Europe, of jointly protecting . . . booty against Japan and America."

Their author was an obscure revolutionary named Vladimir Ilich Lenin, not yet the master of the Soviet Union. What would he make of today's events?

Like the crack-up of communism, the rush to European integration was triggered by the arrival of the Third Wave, with its new system of wealth creation. Says Gianni de Michelis, chairman of the EC's Council of Foreign Ministers: "Integration was the political response to the necessity of moving from an industrial to a post-industrial society." De Michelis forecasts an enormous economic boom as the market economy is extended to Eastern Europe. But the picture is not quite so rosy.

The collapse of Marxist-Leninist governments in Eastern Europe has given their people a taste of freedom and a whiff of hope. But it also changes the terms of the three-way struggle between Europe, the United States, and Japan, creates a power vacuum, and launches Western Europe on a new, unexpected strategy.

Let us assume the region stays peaceful, despite boiling ethnic hatreds in Yugoslavia, Bulgaria and Romania, and elsewhere. Assume that demagogues do not ignite border disputes among Germans, Poles, Hungarians, or Romanians, and that there will be no military repressions, civil wars, or other upheavals. Assume further that the Soviet Union does not fly into furious fragments. (A Soviet newspaper speculates that the very "concept" of a Union of Soviet Socialist Republics could "disappear from the political map of the world.")

If, against the odds, relative stability prevails, the most likely prospect for Eastern Europe is that as the Soviets withdraw, the Western Europeans will move in. And that, for all practical purposes, will mean the Germans.

Life for the East Europeans under West European tutelage could hardly be as bad as that which they suffered under the Soviets and under Hitler before them. The new velvet colonialism could even bring them much higher living standards. What it will not do, for a very long time at least, is allow Eastern Europe to move beyond the smokestack phase.

The Eastern Europeans will cherish their hard-won independence, and by uniting in some form of federation they might enhance their bargaining power vis-à-vis the West. U.S. Secretary of State James Baker proposed a Polish-Hungarian-Czech association. But not even a revived Austro-Hungarian empire and a reborn Emperor Franz Josef (some young Czechs want Vaclav Havel, the playwright-president of the new Czechoslovakia, to be named "king") or, for that matter, a "United States of Eastern Europe" can prevent this new form of satellitization from taking place.

The reason becomes obvious the moment we compare Central Europe's power triad—its military, economic, and knowledge resources—with those available to its Western neighbors.

The European Community, even without the incorporation of additional states, brings overwhelming triadic power to the Continental table.

To glimpse its enormous military potential, ignore NATO and the Warsaw Pact, and imagine the withdrawal of all but a few U.S. and Soviet troops from Europe. West Europeans are still left in command of immense military muscle.

As early as October 1988, West German Chancellor Helmut Kohl proposed the creation of an all-European army. Though he sang of partnership with the United States, the strains of "Yankee Go Home" could clearly be heard. With the Soviet threat presumably diminished, the Germans no longer think American protection necessary. It is true that a complete pullout by the Americans would double the costs of the West European military establishment. But that cost could be trimmed, spread over more countries, and made quite tolerable. The result would be a heavily muscled and armored New Europe.

If there were any doubt as to who will command tomorrow's Euro-Army, a few numbers should dispel it. Until now the French and the West Germans were almost evenly matched in conventional forces. The French military numbered 466,000; the West German Bundeswehr, 494,000. The French had twenty-one submarines; the West Germans, twenty-four. The French had nine squadrons of Mirage and Jaguar ground attack fighters; the West Germans had twenty-one squadrons of Tornados, F4-Fs, and Alphas.

However, German reunification totally skews the picture. With East and West German forces merged, Germany's military expenditures would be 40 percent greater, her army nearly 50 percent larger, and her ground attack fighter capability nearly three times greater than that of France. Reunification puts paid to the French policy voiced by former President Giscard d'Estaing, who said,

"French forces should be an equivalent of size to the other forces on our continent, that is, the German army."

Of course, France has nuclear arms—its famed *force de frappe*, and England, too, has an independent nuclear capability. But it is reasonably certain that Germany could acquire a nuclear capability overnight should it choose to—a fact fully understood by France, England, and the rest of the world.

Even more destabilizing to any intra-European military balance is the fact that, just before they were required by treaty to destroy them, the Soviets secretly transferred twenty-four SS-23 medium-range missiles to East Germany. With complete reunification, these presumably become the property of the merged German military, the last thing the Soviets had in mind.

While all the talk among European politicians is of unity, sweetness and light, therefore, generals on all sides are carefully weighing these numbers. Fighting capabilities cannot be inferred from bean-counting, and no one seriously believes in a replay of 1870, 1914, or 1939. But even this crude comparison makes it plain that, except perhaps under the direst emergency—one calling it the nuclear card into play—it is Germany that will, so to speak, call the shots in any Euro-military.

Today's Germans are not Nazi-fodder. They are steeped in affluent, middle-class democratic values, and they are anything but militaristic. Nevertheless, should Western forces ever be called upon to put down unrest in Eastern Europe, the ultimate decision will be made in Berlin, not Paris or Brussels.

For all Washington's constant carping about European reluctance to "share the burden" of defense, the New Europe is now a major military power all by itself.

EUROPE'S MORNING AFTER

Tomorrow's Euro-army will sit on a gigantic economic base, the second leg of the power triad. Gross figures for the EC, even without adding to its twelve members, are huge. With a population of 320 million it boasts a gross national product almost equal to that of the United States, and one and a half times that of Japan.

In aggregate, the EC nations account for 20 percent of world trade, more than either the United States or Japan.

As with military matters, Europe's key financial decisions will once more be made in Berlin, in the German finance ministry and the Deutschebank, a dominance reflecting economic realities. The combined German economy of $1.4 trillion is one and a half times that of the next-biggest European country, France.

Resigned to these power imbalances but fearful of them, West Europeans, led by France, urge a stronger, tighter EC federation on the assumption that it will limit Germany's freedom of action. But the stronger and more centralized the EC itself becomes as it acquires a common currency and central bank and takes on the role of environmental policeman, the stronger, not weaker, the influence of a combined Germany over the whole European apparatus.

The emergence of this Germano-centric system is, however, only part of an unfolding *Ost-Strategie* of breathtaking scope.

For the emerging economic strategy being developed by governments and corporations in the EC is to take advantage of cheap labor in Czechoslovakia, Hungary, Poland, and other East European countries and use it for low value-added mass production. The goods produced are not primarily for the East Europeans, but are intended for export to Western Europe.

In a nutshell, smokestacks in the East, computers and consumer goods in the West—with a unified Germany acting now not merely as the core of the Western community, but as manager for this entire continental system.

Execution of this broad economic strategy, which shifts hegemonic power over Eastern Europe from the Soviets to the West Europeans and Germans, will occupy the decades immediately ahead, and will be fraught with upsets and difficulties.

This fast-crystallizing *Ost-Strategie* presupposes that the Soviet Union will remain preoccupied with its own internal affairs, and that it will have to turn its military attentions to the Muslim regions on its South and to China and the Pacific, rather than toward Europe. Or that economic deals can be made with the U.S.S.R. that will soften its resistance to the Germanization of the East. This will depend on internal politics within the Soviet Union, as well as on unpredictable events in China and Asia generally.

The *Ost-Strategie* also presupposes that the EC itself can deliver on its glowing promises for Western Europe—a 4.5 to 7 percent growth rate, and 2 million to 5 million new jobs in the twelve member nations. More efficient production. Enhanced competitivity of world trade. Higher profits.

Yet EC planning is still heavily premised on obsolete notions about economies of scale, which apply far more readily to smokestack manufacture than to advanced economies organized around information and service activities.

Moreover, while the new system for wealth creation thrives on (and generates) heterogeneity, emphasizing customization and localization of production, segmentation of markets and de-massification of finance, the EC steamroller, despite rhetoric to the contrary, is intended to flatten out differences.

The Eastern end of the strategy faces major problems as well. To begin with, it takes for granted political stability in the quasi-colonies. Yet the rush toward mass democracy, with parliaments and multiple parties, does not guarantee sausages or ham on the table.

If desperate economic conditions do not significantly improve quickly, the infatuation with parliaments, parties, and voting could degenerate into chaos, charges of corruption, extraparliamentary terrorism, and a return to the kind of fascist or military regimes common in the region before World War II—perhaps with the support of foreign investors for whom stability and order is a paramount requirement.

After the initial euphoria about capital from the West, Eastern Europeans, on the morning after, will increasingly resent their new-style colonial status. Resentment will boil over into resistance. Economic scarcity will be blamed on foreign investors, "imperialists," and local scapegoats. Initial emergency loans will be followed by further emergency loans to keep the economies afloat. Down the line will come demands for loan-repayment moratoria and cancellations.

Even if none of this comes to pass, the root assumption of the *Ost-Strategie*, the importance of cheap labor, needs to be severely questioned. Cheap labor, as we've seen, is now increasingly expensive. With labor costs declining as a component of total cost, the savings will be minimal except in the most backward industries.

Similarly, as we've seen, slow economies cannot plug into fast economies easily. In Poland, until recently, it could take a month to six weeks merely to transfer funds from one bank to another. The entire Eastern metabolism is slower than that required by the

West, and its electronic infrastructure is virtually nonexistent. All this will make the *Ost-Strategie* more costly than it would appear.

Finally, if a significant amount of smokestack work *is* actually transferred to the East, West European governments can expect increased pressure from their own blue-collar trade unions, increased demands for social benefits and protectionism at home.

In Germany, in particular, this implies growing support for the political opposition. Like the neo-Nazi right, Social Democrats will sound nationalist themes in attacking the transfer of jobs to "non-Germans" who work for less than union wages. Greens, meanwhile, will oppose the transfer of pollution to a region that is already one of the most polluted on earth.

Should a Social Democratic Green coalition actually govern Germany, and thus heavily influence the rest of Europe, it would point to a slowdown in technological development on the Continent, since the Social Democrats fear its impact on employment, and the Greens are larded with Luddites and technophobes.

A European Bank for Reconstruction and Development has been created with funds supplied by many Western nations and Japan. Under the innovative leadership of Jacques Attali, the EBRD could lay down key beachheads for technological and economic advance in Eastern Europe. But it won't be easy.

Commercial and political ardor for the *Ost-Strategie* will therefore cool in the coming decade as Europe's deep problems begin to emerge. Europe has enormous wealth, but—so far—a questionable strategy for how to use it.

FROM LEFTISM TO SEMIOLOGY

Even more than in the United States and Japan, the future of European power will depend on its "third leg"—its knowledge base.

Measured by the number of Nobel Prizes and distinguished research laboratories and institutes, Western Europe has little to worry about. It has strength in nuclear energy, aerospace, and robotics, and has stuck a hesitant toe into superconductor research. The EC, which long treated science and technology as a poor relative, has stepped up its funding, especially of cross-border research projects. Science and technology are "in."

Here again, Germany leads. West German scientists enjoy the largest R&D budgets in Europe, and hold 2.5 times as many U.S. patents as either the British or the French. Since 1984, West Germans have been on the Nobel Prize science list every year, for things like the scanning-tunneling microscope or the quantum Hall effect.

Yet Europe, including Germany, trails both Japan and America in the crucial fields of computers and information technology, notably chip manufacture and supercomputers. The recent failure of Nixdorf—once West Germany's hottest computer firm—and its absorption by Siemens, along with the difficulties faced by Norsk Data in Norway and Philips in Holland, underscore Europe's embarrassing weakness in these fields.

In the related field of telecommunications, progress is suffocated by the stubborn refusal of various national PTTs—the post office and telecom ministries—to give up their monopoly control.

Meanwhile, bad as American schools are, Europe, too, has severe educational problems. Its school systems are overcentralized, formalistic, and rigid. And while Europe's cultural exports are greater and more prestigious than those of Japan, Europe lags far behind the United States as an originator of emulated life styles, art, and popular culture. One may, of course, argue that Europe's culture is aesthetically or morally superior to that of the United States, depending upon the criteria applied. But in terms of national power in today's fast-changing, video-drenched world, it is U.S. culture and popular culture that still make the running.

Ideologically and intellectually, Western Europe's prime postwar exports have been a quasi-Marxist leftism and, for a time, existentialism, followed by structuralism and, more recently, semiology. These are now waning in the world intellectual market.

In their place, however, Europe is now taking a strong lead in promoting a new political product. Europe's main ideological export in the years immediately ahead will be a green version of social democracy. This is extremely important and could find immensely receptive markets in the United States, Japan, Eastern Europe, and the Soviet Union, if it is not distorted and dominated by the ecological lunatic fringe.

Finally, whereas Japan is steeped in future-consciousness, and America focuses on the "now," Europe is still heavily past-oriented. A standing joke claims it requires five Britons to replace a burnt-out light bulb—one to screw it in, the other four to say how much better the old one was.

For all these reasons, Western Europe is unlikely to be a truly balanced Great Power until it devotes as much drive to developing its knowledge base as it does to reconfiguring its military and integrating its economy.

Europe has a grand, overarching strategy that aims at shifting regional and world power. This strategy—reborn, rather than freshly invented—is to control what the geopoliticians of the past called the planet's "heartland."

THE WOUNDED GIANT

This takes us to that wounded giant, the United States.

Of course, for the United States even more than for its global competitors, the military leg of the triad is crucial. The armed forces of Europe and Japan are both still primarily regional forces, with limited capacity for operations far from home. By contrast, those of the United States and the Soviet Union, despite cutbacks, both have global outreach.

With the U.S.S.R. troubled internally, however, and its Red Army needed to deal with threatened secessions, ethnic troubles, and potentially unstable borders from Iran all the way to China, the U.S. military has the most resources available for projecting power at a distance (for example, fourteen aircraft carriers with their assorted support ships, compared with four carriers for the Soviets, six for the Europeans). It is precisely the capacity for global projection that differentiates the American forces from all others.

America's tremendous armed might, firmly under civilian guidance and supported by able, educated officers, is, however, shackled to an obsolete strategic view of the world, still overfocused on the Soviet threat to Western Europe. The result is profound confusion about vital national interests and priorities—a form, as it were, of brain failure at the top.

Because of this, congressional pressures for cuts in defense spending, driven by local politics and largely haphazard, are unrelated to any coherent worldview.

The collapse of America's grand strategy also means that

much of its defense expenditure goes toward building the wrong weapons systems and putting them in the wrong places at the wrong time—a waste that dwarfs defense-contractor overruns or the proverbial "$700 gold-plated hammers." It also means that, apart from small ventures like the overthrow of Manuel Noriega in Panama, the United States is reacting to the great world events of our time rather than initiating them, as it once did.

The withdrawal of nearly all U.S. forces from Europe is likely. Less discussed is a possible redeployment toward the Pacific in the light of changed strategic conditions—the great uncertainties in China, the rearmament of Japan, the civil war in the Philippines, and the continued Soviet interest in the region. This shift from Europe toward a "Pacific strategy" would favor the navy and air force as against the army, whose primary focus has been Western Europe. Many of Japan's nervous neighbors would privately welcome such a redeployment.

The United States cannot police the entire tumultuous and highly dangerous world, either on its own behalf or anyone else's, but its unique capability suggests that it may, in alliance with other nations or international organizations, squelch regional conflicts that threaten world peace. In the dangerous decades ahead, many other nations may want just such a firefighter on duty.

THE DECLINING TWINS

The formulation of a new military strategy will also shape that other leg of the power triad, America's economy. Skinning the U.S. military down from a Second Wave force based on mass to a Third Wave force based on mobility, speed, and reach, the military equivalent of miniaturization, could pump new energy into the U.S. economy.

Ad hoc defense cuts, made under pork-barrel pressures from Congress, could destroy key research and development projects and slow down technological advance in the American economy, which has, until now, benefited from Pentagon contracts.

But the same troop withdrawal that could double Europe's military costs could, by the same token, help reduce the U.S. budget deficit, meaning less reliance on Japanese finance. It would create at least temporary unemployment. But it would also tend to lower interest rates and increase investment.

There is no guarantee that freed-up federal funds would necessarily be channeled to overdue social renovation, but some at least would find their way into education, day care, job training, and other uses that, intelligently planned, could help spark next-generation economic gains.

Much tooth-gnashing and wailing has taken place over America's relative economic decline—actually a measure of the success of its post–World War II strategy for putting Japan and Europe back on their feet. The fact is that, despite misconceptions, the United States still represents about the same share of Gross World Production that it did fifteen years ago.

(The big decline in this indicator came just after the war, when the destroyed European and Japanese economies came back on stream. Since the mid-1970s, the United States has roughly held its own.)

But manufacturing is no longer the most important gauge of an economy's importance. In the services and information sectors, which represent the leading edge of the super-symbolic economy, the United States outpoints not only Europe but Japan. As a result, unemployment in the United States has proved a less persistent problem than in Europe.

The trade imbalance, too, which for a time caused near panic in Washington, needs to be reconsidered in the light of the new economy. First, the widespread impression that U.S. exports have fallen is incorrect. During the 1980s, American exports to the world actually rose 61 percent. The problem was that imports rose one and a half times faster. Exports to Japan alone jumped 114 percent, but imports soared over 200 percent. That disparity is now narrowing. But far more important, an economy shifting toward domestic services may be quite healthy, even though many of its new products are not exportable—medical care, for example, or education.

More serious than America's much-lamented "twin deficits," both likely to decline, are the institutional obsolescence and social instability eroding American society and threatening to tear families, communities, and ethnic groups apart, and the spread of drugs in a society whose members are alienated from the state and from one another.

THE WOODY ALLEN IMPACT

Far more vital for U.S. power over the long run than its mass manufacturing base is its knowledge system or info-sphere.

A look at this third leg of the power triad contradicts those who would hastily write off the immense residual power of the United States. Overfocusing on arms and money, they ignore or underestimate the role of knowledge in national power.

Thus, the first enormous advantage that the United States holds at present is simply language. English is the whole world's language in international science, commerce, aviation, and scores of other fields. Until computer translation makes languages transparent to one another, the fact that hundreds of millions of human beings can understand at least some English gives American ideas, styles, inventions, and products a powerful thrust in the world.

Another strength is America's still-strong scientific and technological base. A great deal has been written about the declining percentage of patents being won by Americans, and other signs of scientific and technical infirmity.

After World War II the United States for all practical purposes was the *only* major industrial state able to engage in scientific or technical research on a large scale. Under the circumstances, it is hardly reasonable to expect the United States to continue to hold the same percentage of patents it did in the past.

The United States has lost its virtual monopoly. But its scientific and technical base still towers over that of its rivals. According to the National Science Foundation, U.S. private and public R&D spending runs about $120 billion a year, which is more than the budgets of Japan, Germany, France, and the United Kingdom combined. It is roughly three times that of Japan.

U.S. corporate R&D alone is slightly under $70 billion, much of the rest coming from the Pentagon, a great deal of whose research, despite arguments to the contrary, feeds into the civilian economy. (According to Samuel Fuller, chief of research at Digital Equipment, many product lines, from personal computers to workstations, sprang from basic science funded by the Defense Advanced Research Projects Agency.)

The United States still fields twice as many active research scientists and engineers as Japan, although the Japanese total is skyrocketing and Japanese nonacademic researchers tend to be younger.

The sheer size of America's effort does not guarantee quality. Moreover, with defense cuts likely and American corporations shifting resources from basic to more product-oriented research, the directions of change are not favorable. Still, though clearly challenged, the U.S. lead in high technology, and especially information technology, is still significant.

Japanese progress in computers and memory chips has been phenomenal, and three of its firms—Fujitsu, NEC, and Hitachi—have made dazzling progress. Today, Fujitsu nips at the heels of Digital Equipment, the world's second-largest computer manufacturer, and NEC and Hitachi are not far behind. The Japanese control 50 percent of the market for computer components and an amazing 85 percent of the market for memory chips.

When it comes to computers, as such, however, U.S. manufacturers dominated 69 percent of the world market, the other 31 percent being divided almost evenly by European and Japanese firms. The United States supplies fully 62 percent of all the world's PCs.

Among the world's top twenty computer firms in 1988, ten were American, six European, and only four Japanese. IBM alone was more than twice the combined size of Japan's Big Three together. Digital Equipment was almost as large as Europe's Big Three. In the increasingly important field of computer services, as distinct from machines, nine of the world's top ten firms are American, one European, and not a single one Japanese. (The Japanese share of the service market, only 10.6 percent in 1988, is actually projected to shrink as that of the United States grows.)

Similarly, it is true that Japan's progress in supercomputers has been remarkable, while U.S. supercomputer makers are in trouble. But once again the Japanese lead in hardware; the Americans, in systems and applications software. The race is not over.

In memory chip manufacture, Japanese mass production has decimated its American competition. But IBM was the first to announce a 16-million-bit chip, four times larger than the most advanced chips, and well ahead of the Japanese competition. Moreover, the direction of change is not so much toward mass production as toward chip customization and specialization, where design skills and sophisticated software count for more—precisely the fields of Japanese weakness. As for software itself—a $50 billion business now growing exponentially—the United States has a grip on 70 percent of the world market.

We cannot expand here on other fields, like superconductivity, telecommunications, materials, and biotechnology, but it is far too early to judge outcomes in the world's science and technology race.

Moreover, as time goes on the most important thing about a country's scientific and technological base may not be what information is in it at any given moment, but the speed with which it is continually renewed and the richness of communication carrying specialized know-how to those who need it and acquiring knowledge swiftly from all over the world. It is not the stocks but the flows that will matter.

An acknowledged disaster area for America is its factory-style school system, devastated by drugs, violence, and alienation. Unfortunately, schools are in trouble outside the United States as well, especially in the inner cities. Does one find truly good inner-city schools anywhere? Brixton? Bijlmermeer? Berlin? The education crisis is not an American monopoly.

What gives American schools an edge, despite everything, is that they are less centralized than those in Europe and Japan, and not subject to the dictates of a national ministry of education. This makes them, at least potentially, more open to experiment and innovation.

Unfortunately, the knee-jerk response of the American business and scientific communities is to call for more math and science, more lock-step learning, more Ph.D.'s. Misinformed about actual educational conditions in Japan, most would be amazed to learn that Japan's leap to the high-tech frontier, from 1975 to 1988, took place with only a small increase in the number of engineering and science Ph.D.'s.

Offsetting America's educational wasteland, however, is a key source of America's global power—its unquantified but enormous cultural impact on the planet. This is not a matter of quality—which can, of course, be passionately debated. It is simply fact that culture in one form or another flows outward from the United States. Thus, more American books are translated abroad than foreign books are translated by American publishers. From one point of view this is unfortunate, since it deprives Americans of valuable ideas and insights. But it reflects America's enormous surplus in cultural trade.

For good or ill, vast multitudes around the planet hunger to adopt Western, but also specifically American, life styles, attitudes, fashions, ideas, and innovations. It has been suggested that the global appeal of American popular culture derives from its multi-ethnic origins—fed by the Jewishness of Woody Allen, the Blackness of Bill Cosby, the Italianness of characters like Colombo or film directors like Martin Scorsese, the Japaneseness of "Pat" Morita in *The Karate Kid*, the Cubanness of Desi Arnaz, and the WASPness of Clint Eastwood.

The surging influence of these images, along with the rich flow of science and technology rather than just economic or military power, is what makes the United States so threatening to the hard-liners who control China today or to the Ayatollahs who run Iran. American movies and television programs, not Japanese or Soviet or European, are the most watched around the world. The other major powers are simply not in the running.

Broadly speaking, the United States continues to be a rich source of innovations in science, technology, art, business, imagery, and knowledge in its broadest sense. This advantage may dwindle in the decades ahead, but other nations or regions will find it harder to overtake this American cultural lead than to build a new weapon system or to integrate their economies.

A review of the power triad, therefore, suggests that while the United States has severe problems, it is by no means a paper tiger. In the approaching decades it will be internally racked by social, racial, and sexual protests as the pace of power-shifting accelerates at home and abroad. But America's internal troubles will not, in all likelihood, compare with the upheavals that are to be expected in Europe, the least stable of the three great contenders for world power. Nor will Japan escape political and social turmoil as the world around it is shaken to the core.

Such quick-stroke assessments are admittedly impressionistic, and all of them are legitimately arguable, point by point. But taken together they suggest that the United States holds the most balanced power of any of the three great capitalist centers in the world, and that it still holds the lead in precisely that element of the power triad that is becoming most important—knowledge.

A CHOICE OF PARTNERS

Not only are most forecasts about global power based on overly simple assumptions, they misdefine power. The influential theory of Paul Kennedy, author of *The Rise and Fall of the Great Powers*, for example, which popularized the idea of American decline, essentially measures national power in terms of wealth and military capability alone. Kennedy alludes to, but undervalues, the impact of ideology, religion, and culture, all of which are becoming more important than ever. He vastly underestimates the role of knowledge—which, in fact, has now become the dominant source of both economic wealth and military strength. This is the central powershift of our time.

Moreover, power, as we've seen, is not just a matter of how much but of how good—quality of power may be as important as its quantity, and a nation's power must be related to its own goals, not merely to the power of other nations. What might be adequate for one purpose, reflecting one set of values, might be inadequate for another.

Unlike Europe, whose focus is regional, and Japan, which is hesitating between a regional and a global role, the United States is committed to a global role. Having led a global coalition for the past half-century, America can hardly imagine narrowing its ambitions to a single region. But more than psychology is involved. The U.S. economy is linked into so many parts of the world, and now depends upon so vast a variety of relationships, that to be cut off from access to any significant part of the world economy would be devastating. No American political leader can allow that to happen.

The same may turn out to be true for Japan—and perhaps for Europe as well. Thus, any serious threats of protectionism—in response, say, to an economic crisis—would totally destabilize relations among the three great capitalist centers. What's more, three is an unstable number. Parties of three frequently split into a two and a one.

Of course, many other nations and regions are already fighting for a place in the 21st-century power system. Strange new alliances and strategies will appear. Countries long relegated to the back pages of history will suddenly loom into our consciousness. But even now, European leaders are approaching Washington with what amounts to plans for a new alliance, no longer aimed at Moscow.

Some proposals are limited to specific fields, like high-definition television, or to technology generally. But broader terms are clearly in mind. The German daily the *Stuttgarter Zeitung* voices the common belief that "closer ties between Europeans and Americans can only be of mutual benefit ... in coordinating policy ... toward their joint competitor Japan."

But what if American long-range strategists were blind and permitted history to swing in the opposite direction—toward a tacit alliance (and economic division of the globe) between Japan and a Germanicized Europe? Japanese companies like JVC are already rushing to relocate their European headquarters in Berlin. Mitsubishi has already forged links with Messerschmitt.

The United States, even if integrated into an all–North American common market, could not for long survive this global squeeze play, the result of which might be nothing less catastrophic than World War III.

A reinvigorated U.S.-Japanese alliance, however, could produce a sharply different outcome.

U.S.-Japanese relations have never been worse since World War II. Indeed, the gap between the United States and Japan can only widen so far before dangerous sparks arc across it. Irresponsible jingos in both Tokyo and Washington, playing for easy votes and money, are deliberately stoking dangerous emotions.

If Shintaro Ishihara, a former Cabinet member, can speculate about a future in which the United States reoccupies Japan to prevent the sale of advanced chips to the Soviet, he is, by implication, speculating about outright war, voicing an incredible thought not far from consciousness in both countries. He and his American counterparts who picture Japanese and American missiles pointed at each other should remember that he who rides the tiger cannot get off.

In a world of sudden turnabouts and surprises, no fantasy can be ruled out. But the remotest risk of such confrontation should send horrors down the spine even of those who are equally weary of American superpowerdom and Japanese competition. Such a struggle could plunge the entire earth into a nightmare from which it might not recover for centuries.

The growing hostility between these two Pacific powers could only be heightened if Europe turned protectionist, forcing them into even fiercer competition in the rest of the world. Which is why the idea of a "Fortress Europe" closed to outside competition is the equivalent of a death threat to world peace.

In this highly volatile situation, America can play the coquette, allowing itself to be used as a "card" to be played by Europe or Japan in their global competition. It can play the role of mediator. Or it can forge an alliance to dominate the early decades of the 21st century. But with whom?

It is precisely here that the "power triad" analysis proves most revealing. For if we once more look at violence, wealth, and knowledge, we can glimpse the power consequences of any given lineup.

It tells us, for example, that a de facto U.S.-European alliance would weld together great military power (the old NATO, plus). It would bring together huge markets and great wealth (much of it, however, based on rust-belt manufacture and assumptions). It would merge America's science and technology with Europe's and it would assemble vast cultural power. Long cultural and ethnic ties would make this convergence natural.

Such an alliance, aimed at Japan, would call up memories of the 1930s, further accelerate Japanese rearmament, install hawks in power, and drive Japan deeper toward the developing countries as less favorable markets for its goods and capital. Militarily it could lead to a Soviet-Japanese deal and even toward some new form of Chinese adventure. For Japan to be frozen out of Europe or even, if it is imaginable, the United States, would be yet another equivalent of setting off a global time bomb.

By contrast, cold calculation also shows that a de facto alliance between the United States and Japan, despite their current tensions, would produce quite different consequences for the planet. This turnabout should not be discounted in a world in which public opinion can shift overnight and in which the United States finds itself defending Mikhail Gorbachev.

Strange as it sounds, an American-Japanese alliance to balance the power on the European "heartland" would bring together what are currently the world's first- and third-biggest military budgets; its two largest economies; and its two fastest-growing scientific and technical bases. Such a combination could form a strategic duopoly or condominium encompassing within it the fastest-growing economies in the world—those of the Pacific region, the "heart-sea" counterpart of the "heart-land."

There is, moreover, one last awesome factor differentiating the two alliances, between which the United States may find itself torn. This difference is so little discussed in Washington, Tokyo, or the European capitals that strategists in the richest and most powerful nations tend to forget it. Yet over the long run it holds potentially enormous significance in the great game of nations.

Any Euro-American alliance without Japan is basically a mono-racial, all-white power coalition in a world in which the white race is a dwindling minority. By contrast, a United States–Japan alliance, for all the racism in both those nations, is an interracial power coalition. That difference cannot but register on the rest of the planet's populations.

History does not run along railroad tracks to a pre-set future. In the Powershift Era, a period of revolutionary upheaval on the planet, many other permutations of power are possible. Europe is already worrying about the Muslim pressure on its southern flank. China could erupt in civil war. Any number of other wild-card scenarios can be imagined. Surely the rest of the world will not sit idly by as Europe, Japan, and the United States divide up the spoils. Yet strategists in Washington, Tokyo, Brussels, and Berlin may soon have to choose sides in the great triadic competition for world power.

The decision that Washington makes (consciously or by default) will shape the future of the entire rest of the planet, from China and the U.S.S.R. to the Middle East, Africa, and Latin America.

What, then, should we conclude about this inter-capitalist struggle for world power? Which of the three great contenders will triumph in history's next great powershift?

The answer, as we'll see next, is that we are asking the wrong question.

34

THE GLOBAL GLADIATORS

Asking which nations will dominate the 21st century is an exciting game. But it is, in fact, the wrong question to ask—or at least the wrong form in which to ask it—because it overlooks what could turn out to be the biggest change in global affairs since the rise of the nation-state: the coming of the Global Gladiators.

A new group of power-seekers are leaping onto the world stage and seizing sizable chunks of the clout once controlled by nations alone. Some are good; some, decidedly evil.

THE RESURRECTION OF RELIGION

When a blood-besotted Ayatollah Khomeini called for a martyr to murder Salman Rushdie, whose novel *The Satanic Verses* Khomeini denounced as blasphemous, he sent a historic message to all the world's governments. That message was instantly communicated via satellite, television, and print. The message, however, was totally misunderstood.

One may argue that Rushdie's book was in bad taste, that it deliberately offended many Muslims, that it derided an entire religion, that it violated the Koran. Indeed, Khomeini said these things. But that was not his real message.

Khomeini was telling the world that the nation-state is no longer the only, or even the most important, actor on the world stage.

Superficially, Khomeini seemed to be saying that Iran, itself a sovereign state, had the "right" to dictate what the citizens of other equally sovereign nations could or could not read. In claiming this right, and threatening to enforce it with terrorism, Khomeini suddenly catapulted censorship from a matter of domestic concern to the level of a global issue.

In a world that is witnessing the globalization of the economy and the globalization of the media, Khomeini was demanding the globalization of mind-control.

Other religions, in past eras, have asserted a similar right, and burned heretics at the stake. But in threatening cross-border assassination, Khomeini was doing more than attacking Salman Rushdie —a British citizen. He was challenging the most fundamental right of any nation-state, the right to protect its citizens at home.

What Khomeini was really telling us was that "sovereign" states are not sovereign at all, but subject to a higher Shiite sovereignty, which he alone would define—that a religion or church had rights that supersede those of mere nation-states.

He was, in fact, challenging the entire structure of "modern" international law and custom, which until then had been based on the assumption that nations are the basic units, the key players on the global stage. This assumption pictured a planet neatly divided into states, each with its flag and army, its clearly mapped territory, a seat in the U.N., and certain reasonably defined legal rights.

It is no accident that, to much of the world, Khomeini seemed a cruel throwback to the preindustrial era. He was. His assertion of the rights of religion over nation-states paralleled the doctrine medieval Popes expressed during centuries of bloody church-state conflict.

The reason this is important is that we may well be circling back to the kind of world system that existed before industrialism, before political power was packaged into clearly defined national entities.

That pre-smokestack world was a hodgepodge of city-states, pirate-held ports, feudal princedoms, religious movements, and other entities, all scrambling for power and asserting rights that we, today, assume belong only to governments. What we might now call nations were few and far between. It was a heterogeneous system.

By contrast, the nation-state system that evolved during the smokestack centuries was far more standardized and uniform.

We are now moving back to a more heterogeneous global

system again—only in a fast-changing world of high technology, instantaneous communication, nuclear missiles, and chemical warfare. This is an immense leap that carries us forward and backward at the same time, and propels religion once more to the center of the global stage. And not just Islamic extremism.

A totally different case in point is the growing global power of the Catholic Church. Papal diplomacy has figured recently in major political changes from the Philippines to Panama. In Poland, where the church won admiration for its courageous opposition to the communist regime, it has emerged as a dominant force behind the first noncommunist government. Vatican diplomats claim that the recent changes all across Eastern Europe were, in large measure, triggered by Pope John Paul II.

The Pope is no fanatic and has reached out to other religions. He has spoken out against interethnic violence. Yet echoes of a long-distant pre-secular past are heard in his call for a "Christian Europe" and his repeated criticisms of Western European democracies.

The Pope's policies call to mind a long-forgotten document that was circulated in European capitals in 1918 urging the creation of a Catholic superstate made up of Bavaria, Hungary, Austria, Croatia, Bohemia, Slovakia, and Poland. The Pope's proposed Christian (though presumably not exclusively Catholic) Europe today embraces all of Europe, from the Atlantic to the Urals, with a population of nearly 700 million people.

Such religious stirrings are part of the gathering attack on the secular assumptions that underpinned democracy in the industrial era and kept a healthy distance between church and state. (If Europe is Christian, as distinct from secular, where do nonbelievers fit in, or Hindus or Jews, or the 11 million Muslim immigrants encouraged to come to Europe to serve as cheap labor in the recent past? (Some Muslim fundamentalists actually dream of Islamicizing Europe. Says the director of the Institute of Islamic Culture in Paris: "In a few years Paris will be the capital of Islam, just as Baghdad and Cairo were in other eras.")

The emerging global power game in the decades ahead cannot be understood without taking into account the rising power of Islam, Catholicism, and other religions—or of global conflicts and holy wars among them.

THE EMPIRE OF COCAINE

Religions are not the only forces rising up to challenge the power of nation-states as such. In his massive examination of the global narcotics business, James Mills writes: ". . . the Underground Empire today has more power, wealth, and status than many nations. It flies no flag on the terrace of the United Nations, but it has larger armies, more capable intelligence agencies, more influential diplomatic services than many countries do."

The ability of a drug cartel to corrupt, terrorize, and paralyze the Colombian government for years, having first shifted its balance of trade, suggests what other outlaw groups, not necessarily narcotics traffickers, may also be able to do before long.

A measure of the cartel's menace was the enormous security provided U.S. President Bush and the leaders of Peru, Bolivia, and Colombia when they met at the so-called "drug summit" in Cartagena. The Colombians supplied a squadron of fighter-bombers, a fleet of navy ships, frogmen, antiterrorist SWAT teams, and thousands of soldiers. All this force was ranged not against a hostile nation, but against a network of families.

Governments find it increasingly difficult to deal with these new actors on the world stage. Governments are too bureaucratic. Their response times are too slow. They are linked into so many foreign relationships that require consultation and agreement with allies, and must cater to so many domestic political interest groups, that it takes them too long to react to initiatives by drug lords or religious fanatics and terrorists.

By contrast, many of the Global Gladiators, guerrillas and drug cartels in particular, are non- or even pre-bureaucratic. A single charismatic leader calls the shots quickly, and with chilling—or killing—effect. In other cases, it is unclear who the leaders really are. Governments stagger away confused from conflicts with them. With whom can one make a deal? If a deal is possible, how is one to know if the people making it can actually deliver? Can they really return hostages, stem the flow of drugs, prevent bomb attacks on embassies, or cut down on piracy?

The few international laws that have reduced global anarchy in the past are totally inadequate to deal with the new global realities.

In a world of satellites, lasers, computers, briefcase weapons, precision targeting, and a choice of viruses with which to attack people or computers, nations as we now know them may well find themselves up against potent adversaries, some no more than a millionth their size.

THE DISPERSED "OPPRESSOR"

Just as nations are proving inept in coping with terrorists or religious frenzy, they are also finding it harder to regulate global corporations capable of transferring operations, funds, pollution, and people across borders.

The liberalization of finance has encouraged the growth of some six hundred mega-firms, which used to be called "multinationals" and which now account for about one fifth of value added in agriculture and industrial production in the world. The term *multinational*, however, is obsolete. Mega-firms are essentially non-national.

Until the recent past, globe-girdling corporations have typically "belonged" to one nation or another even if they operated all over the world. IBM was an unquestionably American firm. Under the new system for creating wealth, with companies from several countries linked into global "alliances" and "constellations," it is harder to determine corporate nationality. IBM-Japan is, in many ways, a Japanese firm. Ford owns 25 percent of Mazda. Honda builds cars in the United States and ships them to Japan. General Motors is the largest stockholder in Isuzu. Writes management consultant Kenichi Ohmae: "It is difficult to designate the nationality of . . . global corporations. They fly the flag of their customers, not their country."

What is the "nationality" of Visa International? Its headquarters may be in the United States, but it is owned by 21,000 financial institutions in 187 countries and territories. Its governing board and regional boards are set up to prevent any one nation from having 51 percent of the votes.

With cross-national takeovers, mergers, and acquisitions on the rise, ownership of a firm could, in principle, switch from one country to another overnight. Corporations are thus becoming more truly nonnational or transnational, drawing their capital and management elites from many different nations, creating jobs and distributing their streams of profit to stockholders in many countries.

Changes like these will force us to rethink such emotionally charged concepts as economic nationalism, neocolonialism, and imperialism. For example, it is an article of faith among Latin Americans that Yankee imperialists siphon "superprofits" from their countries. But if tomorrow "superprofits" from a Mexican operation were to go to investors dispersed throughout Japan, Western Europe, and, say, Brazil (or even someday China), who exactly is the neocolonialist?

What if a transnational is nominally based in Macao or, for that matter, Curaçao, and its stock is owned by 100,000 continually changing shareholders from a dozen countries, trading in half a dozen different stock exchanges from Bombay and Sydney to Paris and Hong Kong? What if even the institutional investors are themselves transnational? What if the managers come from all over the world? What country, then, is the "imperialist oppressor"?

As they lose their strictly national identities, the entire relationship between global firms and national governments is transformed. In the past, "home" governments of such companies championed their interests in the world economy, exerted diplomatic pressure on their behalf, and often provided either the threat (or the reality) of military action to protect their investments and people when necessary.

In the early 1970s, at the behest of ITT and other American corporations, the CIA actively worked to destabilize the Allende government in Chile. Future governments may be far less ready to respond to cries for help from firms that are no longer national or multinational but truly transnational.

If so, what happens when terrorists, guerrillas, or a hostile nation threaten the people and facilities of one of the great transnationals? To whom does it turn for help? Does it meekly walk away from its investments?

THE CORPORATE CONDOTTIERI

Military might is the one thing nation-states have had that other contenders for power typically lacked. But if state or inter-governmental forces cannot impose order, the day may dawn when perfectly ordinary transnational corporations decide it is necessary to put their own brigades into the field.

Fantastic as this may sound, it is not without historical prece-dent. Sir Francis Drake waged war not merely on Spanish ships laden with silver, but on towns all along the Pacific coast of South America, Central America, and Mexico. He was financed by pri-vate investors.

Is it entirely fanciful to imagine 21st-century corporate ver-sions of the Italian condottieri?

In *The Apocalypse Brigade* the novelist Alfred Coppel has pic-tured precisely this situation—one in which a mega-oil company organizes its own army to protect oil fields from an anticipated terrorist strike. The company acts on its own because it cannot get its home government to protect its interests.

Extreme as this fictional scenario may seem, there is a certain logic to it. The inability of states to stop terrorism, despite all the armies at their command, has already forced some major corpora-tions to take matters into their own hands, hiring trained drivers, armed bodyguards, high-tech security specialists, and the like. And when Iran took some of his employees hostage, billionaire Ross Perot hired ex–Green Berets to penetrate Iran and rescue them. From here it is only a short step to mercenary troops.

THE U.N.-PLUS

Clearly we are heading for chaos if new international laws aren't written and new agencies created to enforce them—or if key Global Gladiators, like the transnational corporations, religions, and similar forces, are denied representation in them.

Proposals are coming hot and fast for all sorts of new global institutions to deal with ecology, arms control, monetary matters, tourism, telecommunications, as well as regional economic concerns. But who should control these agencies? Nation-states alone?

The less responsive to their needs governments and inter-government organizations become, the more likely it is that transnational firms will end-run governments and demand direct participation in global institutions.

It is not too hard to imagine a Global Council of Global Corporations arising to speak for these new-style firms and to provide a collective counterbalance to nation-state power. Alternatively, major corporations may demand representation in their own names, as part of a new class of membership within organizations like the United Nations, the World Bank, or GATT.

Given the growing diversity and power of Global Gladiators, the United Nations, which until now has been little more than a trade association of nation-states, may eventually be compelled to provide representation for nonstates, too (beyond the token consultative role now granted to certain nongovernmental groups, or NGOs).

Instead of one-nation–one-vote, it may well have to create additional categories of voting membership for transnational companies, religions, and other entities, which would vastly broaden its base of support in the world. On the other hand, if the nation-states who own and operate the U.N. refuse to widen representation, counterorganizations may arise as global corporations multiply and gather strength.

But whether or not such speculations prove correct in the future, the new Global Gladiators—corporate, criminal, religious, and other—already share increasing *de facto* power with nation-states.

NEW-STYLE GLOBAL ORGANIZATIONS

The question of whether some non-national "gladiators" ought to be represented in world bodies is closely related to the design of new organizations on the world scene. A key question facing the architects of the new global order is whether power should flow vertically or horizontally.

A clear example of vertical organization is the European Community, which seeks to build, in effect, a supra-government that would, according to its critics, reduce the present countries of Europe to the status of provinces rather than sovereign nations—by imposing supra-national controls over currency, central banking, educational standards, environment, agriculture, and even national budgets.

This traditional vertical model seeks to solve problems by adding another echelon to the power hierarchy. It is "high-rise" institutional architecture.

The alternative model, congruent with the emerging forms of organization in the business world and the advanced economies, flattens the hierarchy rather than extending it upward. It will be based on networks of alliances, consortia, specialized regulatory agencies, to accomplish ends too large for any single state. In this system there is no higher level of top-down control, and specialized agencies are not grouped hierarchically under a nonspecialized central body. It is the equivalent of "low-rise" architecture. It parallels the flex-firm.

Around the world today, the EC is being closely watched and, very often, taken as the only model for regional organization. Thus, the proposal to clone the EC is loudly heard, from the Maghreb and the Middle East to the Caribbean and the Pacific. A more revolutionary approach would be to lace existing organizations in each of these regions together, without imposing a new layer of control. The same might be done between nations.

Japan and the United States, for example, are so closely intertwined economically, politically, and militarily, that decisions in one have immediate high-impact consequences in the other. Under these circumstances, the day may arrive when Japan will demand actual voting seats inside the Congress of the United States. In return, the United States would no doubt demand equivalent representation in the Japanese Diet. In this way would be born the first of many potential "cross-national" parliaments or legislatures.

Democracy presupposes that those affected by a decision have a right to participate in making the decision. If this is so, then many nations should, in fact, have seats in the U.S. Congress, whose decisions have greater impact on their lives than the decisions of their own politicians.

As the world goes global, and the new system for wealth creation spreads, demands for cross-national political participation—and even cross-national voting—will bubble up from the vast populations who now feel themselves excluded from the decisions that shape their lives.

But whatever form the global organizations of tomorrow assume, they will have to pay more attention, both positive and negative, to the Global Gladiators.

To what extent should groups like religions and global corporations, as well as transnational trade unions, political parties, environmental movements, human rights organizations, and other such entities from the civil society be represented in the institutions now being planned for the world of tomorrow?

How can one keep a crucial separation between church and state at the global level to avoid the fearsome bloodshed and oppression that has so often resulted from their fusion? How might terrorists or criminals, warlords and narco-killers be quarantined? What legitimate global voice might be given to national minorities oppressed at home? What missile defense or chemical-warfare defense measures should be regional or global, rather than left to purely national responsibility?

No one can afford to be dogmatic in answering these dangerous questions of the not-so-far-off future. The questions themselves sound strange, no doubt, in a world that still conceives of itself as organized around nation-states. But at the dawn of the smokestack era, nothing sounded stranger, more radical, more dangerous than the ideas of French, English, and American revolutionaries who thought that people and parliaments should control kings, rather than the reverse, and that lack of representation was cause for rebellion.

In many countries, such ideas may provoke passionate objection on patriotic grounds. The proto-fascist French writer Charles Maurras in the 19th century expressed the traditional view that "of all human liberties, the most precious is the independence of one's country." But absolute sovereignty and independence have always been mythical.

Only countries willing to opt out of the new system of wealth creation forever can avoid plugging into the new global economy. Those who do connect with the world will necessarily be drawn into an interdependent global system populated not by nations alone, but by newly powerful Global Gladiators as well.

We are witnessing a significant shift of power from individual or groups of nation-states to the Global Gladiators. This amounts to nothing less than the next global revolution in political forms.

The shift toward hetrogeneity in the emerging world system will sharply intensify if giant nations splinter, as now seems eminently possible. The Soviet Union is fast-fracturing, with Gorbachev desperate to hold the parts together in a much-loosened framework. But some pieces will almost surely flake off and assume strange new forms in the decades to come. Whether part of the Post-Soviet Union or not, some regions will inevitably be drawn into the economic vortex of a German-dominated Europe; others into the nascent Japanese sphere of influence in Asia.

The backward republics, still dependent on agriculture and raw material extraction, may huddle together in a loosened federation. But rational economic considerations could easily be swept aside by a tidal wave of religious and ethnic strife, so that the Ukraine, the Russian republic, and Byelorussia merge into a giant mass based on Slav culture and a revivified Orthodox church. Islam could glue some of the Central Asian republics together.

China, too, could split up, with its most industrially developed regions in the South and East severing their ties with the great peasant-based China, and forming new kinds of entities with Hong Kong, Taiwan, Singapore, and perhaps a reunified Korea. The result might be a giant new Confucian Economic Community, countering the rise of Japan, while further strengthening the significance of religion as a factor in the world system.

To assume that such changes will happen without civil war and other conflicts, or that they can be contained within the obsolete frame of a nation-based world order, is both shortsighted and unimaginative. The sole certainty is that tommorrow will surprise us all.

What is brilliantly clear, then, is that as the new system of wealth creation moves across the planet it upsets all our ideas about economic development in the so-called South, explodes socialism in the "East," throws allies into killer competition, and calls into being a new, dramatically different global order—diverse and risk-filled, at once hopeful and terrifying.

New knowledge has overturned the world we knew and shaken the pillars of power that held it in place. Surveying the wreckage, ready once more to create a new civilization, we stand, all together now, at Ground Zero.

CODA:

FREEDOM, ORDER, AND CHANCE

This book has told the story of one of the most important revolutions in the history of power—a change that is now reshaping our planet. Over the past generation millions of words have been devoted to upheavals in technology, society, ecology, and culture. But relatively few have attempted to analyze the transformation in the nature of power itself—which drives many of these other changes.

We have seen how, at every level of life, from business to government and global affairs, power is shifting.

Power is among the most basic of social phenomena, and it is linked to the very nature of the universe.

For three hundred years Western science pictured the world as a giant clock or machine, in which knowable causes produced predictable effects. It is a determinist, totally ordered universe, which, once set in motion, pre-programs all subsequent actions.

If this were an accurate description of the real world, we would all be powerless. For if the initial conditions of any process determine its outcome, human intervention cannot alter it. A machine-like universe set in motion by a Prime Mover, divine or otherwise, would be one in which no one has power over anything or anyone. Only, at best, an illusion of power.

Power, in short, depends on cracks in the causal chain, events that are not all pre-programmed. Put differently, it depends on the existence of chance in the universe and in human behavior.

Yet power cannot operate in an entirely accidental universe either. If events and behavior were really random, we would be equally helpless to impose our will. Without some routine, regularity, and predictability, life would force upon us an endless series of random choices, each with random consequences, and thus make us powerless prisoners of fortune.

Power thus implies a world that combines both chance and necessity, chaos and order.

But power is also linked to the biology of the individual and the role of government or, more generally, the state.

This is so because all of us share an irrepressible, biologically rooted craving for a modicum of order in our daily lives, along with a hunger for novelty. It is the need for order that provides the main justification for the very existence of government.

At least since Rousseau's *Social Contract* and the end of the divine right of kings, the state has been seen as party to a contract with the people—a contract to guarantee or supply the necessary order in society. Without the state's soldiers, police, and the apparatus of control, we are told, gangs or brigands would take over all our streets. Extortion, rape, robbery, and murder would rip away the last shreds of the "thin veneer of civilization."

The claim is hard to deny. Indeed, the evidence is overwhelming that in the absence of what we have earlier described as vertical power—order imposed from above—life quickly becomes a horror. Ask the residents of once-beautiful Beirut what it means to live in a place where no government has sufficient power to govern.

But if the first function of the state is to ensure order, how much is enough? And does this change as societies adopt different systems of wealth creation?

When a state imposes iron control over everyday life, silences even the mildest criticism, drives its citizens into their homes in fear, censors the news, closes the theaters, revokes passports, knocks on the door at 4:00 A.M. and drags parents from their screaming children—who is served? The citizen in need of a modicum of order—or the state itself, protecting itself from outrage?

When does order provide necessary stability for the economy— and when does it strangle needed development?

There are, in short, to analogize from Marx, two kinds of order. One might be called "socially necessary order." The other is "surplus order."

Surplus order is that excess order imposed not for the benefit of the society, but exclusively for the benefit of those who control the state. Surplus order is the antithesis of beneficial or socially necessary order. The regime that imposes surplus order on its suffering citizens deprives itself of the Rousseauian justification for existence.

States that impose surplus order lose what Confucians called the "Mandate of Heaven." Today they also lose their moral legitimacy in an interdependent world. In the new system now emerging, they invite not only the attention of global opinion but the sanctions of morally legitimate states.

The widespread opprobrium directed at the Chinese hardliners after the Beijing massacre in 1989—a wave of criticism joined in by the United States, the European Community, Japan, and most other nations of the world—was timid. Each country coolly pondered its economic interests in China before announcing a position. The U.S. President almost immediately dispatched a secret mission to smooth over ruffled relations between the two governments.

Nevertheless, despite all the opportunism and *realpolitik,* the entire world, in effect, voted on the moral legitimacy of the hardliners' regime. The world said, loud enough for Beijing to hear, that it considered the regime's murderous behavior an overreaction and an attempt to impose surplus order.

Beijing angrily replied that the rest of the world had no right to intervene in its internal affairs and that the morality of the critics could also be questioned. But the fact that so many countries were compelled to speak out—even if diffidently, and even if their private policies contradicted their public expressions—suggests that global opinion is growing more articulate, and less tolerant of surplus order.

If so, there is a hidden reason.

The revolutionary new element—a change brought about by the novel system of wealth creation—is a change in the level of socially necessary order. For the new fact is that, as nations make the transition toward the advanced, super-symbolic economy, they need more horizontal self-regulation and less top-down control. Put more simply, totalitarian control chokes economic advance.

Student pilots often fly with white knuckles tightly gripping the controls. Their instructors tell them to loosen up. Overcontrol is just as dangerous as undercontrol. Today, as the crises in the Soviet Union and other countries demonstrate, the state that attempts to overcontrol its people and economy ultimately destroys the very order it seeks. The state with the lightest touch may accomplish the most, and enhance its own power in the process.

This may—just may—be bad news for totalitarians. But enough ominous signs darken the horizon to dispel facile optimism.

Those who have read this far know that this book offers no utopian promises. The use of violence as a source of power will not soon disappear. Students and protesters will still be shot in plazas around the world. Armies will still rumble across borders. Governments will still apply force when they imagine it serves their purposes. The state will never give up the gun.

Similarly, the control of immense wealth, whether by private individuals or public officials, will continue to confer enormous power on them. Wealth will continue to be an awesome tool of power.

Nevertheless, despite exceptions and unevenness, contradictions and confusions, we are witnessing one of the most important changes in the history of power.

For it is now indisputable that knowledge, the source of the highest-quality power of all, is gaining importance with every fleeting nanosecond.

The most important powershift of all, therefore, is not from one person, party, institution, or nation to another. It is the hidden shift in the relationships between violence, wealth, and knowledge as societies speed toward their collision with tomorrow.

This is the dangerous, exhilarating secret of the Powershift Era.

ASSUMPTIONS
BIBLIOGRAPHY
NOTES
ACKNOWLEDGMENTS

ASSUMPTIONS

Because the subject is so fraught with both personal and political controversy, any book on power should be expected to lay out its main assumptions and, preferably, to make plain the underlying model of power on which it is based. No such statement can ever be complete, since it is impossible to define—or even to recognize—all one's assumptions. Nevertheless, even a partially successful effort can be useful to both writer and reader.

Here, then, are some of the assumptions from which *Powershift* springs.

1. Power is inherent in all social systems and in all human relationships. It is not a thing but an aspect of any and all relationships among people. Hence it is inescapable and neutral, intrinsically neither good nor bad.

2. The "power system" includes everyone—no one is free of it. But one person's power loss is not always another's gain.

3. The power system in any society is subdivided into smaller and smaller power subsystems nested within one another. Feedback links these subsystems to one another, and to the larger systems of which they are part. Individuals are embedded in many different, though related, power subsystems.

4. The same person may be power-rich at home and power-poor at work, and so forth.

5. Because human relationships are constantly changing, power relationships are also in constant process.

6. Because people have needs and desires, those who can fulfill them hold potential power. Social power is exercised by supplying or withholding the desired or needed items and experiences.

7. Because needs and desires are highly varied, the ways of meeting or denying them are also extemely varied. There are, therefore, many different "tools" or "levers" of power. Among them, however, violence, wealth, and knowledge are primary. Most other power resources derive from these.

8. Violence, which is chiefly used to punish, is the least versatile source of power. Wealth, which can be used both to reward and punish, and which can be converted into many other resources, is a far more flexible tool of power. Knowledge, however, is the most versatile and basic, since it can help one avert challenges that might require the use of violence or wealth, and can often be used to persuade others to perform in desired ways out of perceived self-interest. Knowledge yields the highest-quality power.

9. The relationships of classes, races, genders, professions, nations, and other social groupings are incessantly altered by shifts in population, ecology, technology, culture, and other factors. These changes lead to conflict and translate into redistributions of power resources.

10. Conflict is an inescapable social fact.

11. Power struggles are not necessarily bad.

12. Fluctuations caused by simultaneous shifts of power in different subsystems may converge to produce radical shifts of power at the level of the larger system of which they are a part. This principle operates at all levels. Intra-psychic conflict within an individual can tear a whole family apart; power conflict among departments can tear a company apart; power struggles among regions can tear a nation apart.

13. At any given moment some of the many power subsystems that comprise the larger system are in relative equilibrium while others are in a far-from-equilibrial condition. Equilibrium is not necessarily a virtue.

14. When power systems are far-from-equilibrial, sudden, seemingly bizarre shifts may occur. This is because when a system or subsystem is highly unstable, nonlinear effects multiply. Big power inputs may yield small results. Small events can trigger the downfall of a regime. A slice of burnt toast can lead to a divorce.

15. Chance matters. The more unstable the system, the more chance matters.

16. Equality of power is an improbable condition. Even if it is achieved, chance will immediately produce new inequalities. So will attempts to rectify old inequalities.

17. Inequalities at one level can be balanced out at another level. For this reason, it is possible for a power balance to exist between two or more entities, even when inequalities exist among their various subsystems.

18. It is virtually impossible for all social systems and subsystems to be simultaneously in perfect balance and for power to be shared equally among all groups. Radical action may be needed to overthrow an oppressive regime, but some degree of inequality is a function of change itself.

19. Perfect equality implies changelessness, and is not only impossible but undesirable. In a world in which millions starve, the idea of stopping change is not only futile but immoral.
    The existence of some degree of inequality is not, therefore, inherently immoral; what *is* immoral is a system that freezes the maldistribution of those resources that give power. It is doubly immoral when that maldistribution is based on race, gender, or other inborn traits.

20. Knowledge is even more maldistributed than arms and wealth. Hence a redistribution of knowledge (and especially knowledge about knowledge) is even more important than, and can lead to, a redistribution of the other main power resources.

21. Overconcentration of power resources is dangerous. (Examples: Stalin, Hitler, and so on. Other examples are too numerous to itemize.)

22. Underconcentration of power resources is equally dangerous. The absence of strong government in Lebanon has turned that poor nation into a synonym for anarchic violence. Scores of groups vie for power without reference to any agreed conception of law or justice or any enforceable constitutional or other restrictions.

23. If both overconcentration and underconcentration of power result in social horror, how much concentrated power is too much? Is there a moral basis for judging?

The moral basis for judging whether power is over- or under-concentrated is directly related to the difference between "socially necessary order" and "surplus order."

24. Power granted to a regime should be just sufficient to provide a degree of safety from real (not imagined) external threat, plus a modicum of internal order and civility. This degree of order is socially necessary, and hence morally justifiable.
Order imposed over and above that needed for the civil society to function, order imposed merely to perpetuate a regime, is immoral.

25. There is a moral basis for opposing or even overthrowing the state that imposes "surplus order."

BIBLIOGRAPHY

The following books have been consulted during the writing of *Powershift*. They are grouped by subject for convenience, although many deal with more than a single topic.

THE PHILOSOPHY OF POWER

[1] Aron, Raymond. *Main Currents in Sociological Thought,* Vol. II. (New York: Basic Books, 1967.)

[2] ———. *Politics and History.* (New Brunswick, N.J.: Transaction Books, 1984.)

[3] Bentham, Jeremy, and John Stuart Mill. *The Utilitarians.* (New York: Anchor Books, 1973.)

[4] Berger, Peter L., and Richard John Neuhaus. *To Empower People.* (Washington, D.C.: The American Enterprise Institute for Public Policy Research, n.d.)

[5] Bodenheimer, Edgar. *Power, Law and Society.* (New York: Crane, Russak, n.d.)

[6] Bogart, Ernest L., and Donald L. Kemmerer. *Economic History of the American People.* (New York: Longmans, Green, 1946.)

[7] Bottomore, T. B. *Elites and Society.* (New York: Basic Books, 1964.)

[8] Burnham, James. *The Machiavellians.* (New York: John Day, 1943.)

[9] Calvert, Peter. *Politics, Power and Revolution.* (Brighton, Sussex: Wheatsheaf Books, 1983.)

[10] Canetti, Elias. *Crowds and Power.* (New York: Seabury Press, 1978.)

[11] Crozier, Brian. *A Theory of Conflict.* (London: Hamish Hamilton, 1974.)

[12] Duyvendak, J. J., ed. *The Book of Lord Shang.* (London: Arthur Probsthain, 1963.)

477

[13] Field, G. Lowell, and John Higley. *Elitism*. (London: Routledge & Kegan Paul, 1980.)

[14] First, Ruth. *Power in Africa*. (New York: Pantheon Books, 1970.)

[15] Galbraith, John Kenneth. *The Anatomy of Power*. (Boston: Houghton Mifflin, 1983.)

[16] Hutschnecker, A. *The Drive for Power*. (New York: M. Evans, 1974.)

[17] Janeway, Elizabeth. *Man's World, Woman's Place*. (New York: Delta Books, 1972.)

[18] ———. *Powers of the Weak*. (New York: Alfred A. Knopf, 1980.)

[19] Jouvenel, Bertrand de. *On Power*. (Boston: Beacon Press, 1969.)

[20] Keohane, Robert O., and Joseph S. Nye. *Power and Interdependence*. (Boston: Little, Brown, 1977.)

[21] Kontos, Alkis, ed. *Domination*. (Toronto: University of Toronto Press, 1975.)

[22] Kropotkin, Peter. *Kropotkin's Revolutionary Writings*. (New York: Vanguard Press, 1927.)

[23] Machiavelli, Niccolò. *The Prince*. (New York: Pocket Books, 1963.)

[24] May, Rollo. *Power and Innocence*. (New York: Delta Books, 1972.)

[25] Milgram, Stanley. *Obedience to Authority*. (New York: Harper Colophon, 1974.)

[26] Mills, C. Wright. *The Power Elite*. (New York: Oxford University Press, 1956.)

[27] More, Sir Thomas. *Utopia*. (New York: Washington Square Press, 1965.)

[28] Mudjanto, G. *The Concept of Power in Javanese Culture*. (Jakarta: Gadjah Mada University Press, 1986.)

[29] Nagel, Jack H. *The Descriptive Analysis of Power*. (New Haven: Yale University Press, 1975.)

[30] Nietzsche, Friedrich. *The Will to Power*. (New York: Vintage Books, 1968.)

[31] Osgood, Robert E., and Robert W. Tucker. *Force, Order, and Justice*. (Baltimore and London: The Johns Hopkins Press, 1967.)

[32] Pye, Lucian W., with Mary W. Pye. *Asian Power and Politics*. (Cambridge, Mass.: The Belknap Press, Harvard University Press, 1985.)

[33] Rueschemeyer, Dietrich. *Power and the Division of Labour*. (Cambridge: Polity Press, 1986.)

[34] Russell, Bertrand. *A History of Western Philosophy*. (New York: Simon and Schuster, 1972.)

[35] ———. *Power*. (London: Unwin Paperbacks, 1983.)

[36] Rustow, Alexander. *Freedom and Domination.* (Princeton: Princeton University Press, 1980.)

[37] Siu, R.G.H. *The Craft of Power.* (New York: John Wiley and Sons, 1979.)

[38] Tzu, Sun. *The Art of War.* (Oxford: Oxford University Press, 1963.)

[39] Waal, Frans de. *Chimpanzee Politics.* (New York: Harper & Row, 1982.)

[40] Wing, R. L. *The Tao of Power.* (Garden City, N.Y.: Doubleday, 1986.)

BUREAUCRACY AND SOCIAL ORGANIZATION

[41] Becker, Gary S. *A Treatise on the Family.* (Cambridge, Mass.: Harvard University Press, 1981.)

[42] Chackerian, Richard, and Gilbert Abcarian. *Bureaucratic Power in Society.* (Chicago: Nelson-Hall, 1984.)

[43] Crozier, Michel. *L'entreprise à l'écoute.* (Paris: Interéditions, 1989.)

[44] Dale, Ernest, *The Great Organizers.* (New York: McGraw-Hill, 1960.)

[45] Davis, Stanley M. *Future Perfect.* (Reading, Mass.: Addison-Wesley, 1987.)

[46] Denhart, Robert B. *In the Shadow of Organization.* (Lawrence: The Regents Press of Kansas, 1981.)

[47] Donzelot, Jacques. *The Policing of Families.* (New York: Pantheon, 1979.)

[48] Dror, Yehezkel. *Public Policymaking Reexamined.* (New Brunswick, N.J.: Transaction Books, 1983.)

[49] Galbraith, John Kenneth. *The New Industrial State.* (New York: New American Library, 1985.)

[50] Goldwin, Robert A., ed. *Bureaucrats, Policy Analysis, Statesmen: Who Leads?* (Washington, D.C.: American Enterprise Institute for Public Policy Research, 1980.)

[51] Gross, Ronald, and Paul Osterman, eds. *Individualism.* (New York: Laurel, 1971.)

[52] Heald, Tim. *Networks.* (London: Hodder & Stoughton, Coronet Books, 1983.)

[53] Heilman, Madeline E., and Harvey A. Hornstein. *Managing Human Forces in Organizations.* (Homewood, Ill.: Richard D. Irwin, 1982.)

[54] Hyneman, Charles S. *Bureaucracy in a Democracy.* (New York: Harper and Brothers, 1950.)

[55] Kahn, Robert L., and Elise Boulding, eds. *Power and Conflict in Organizations.* (New York: Basic Books, 1964.)

[56] Kennedy, Marilyn Moats. *Office Politics.* (New York: Warner Books, 1980.)

[57] ———. *Powerbase.* (New York: Macmillan, 1984.)

[58] Knight, Stephen. *The Brotherhood.* (London: Granada Books, 1985.)

[59] Le Play, Frederic. *On Family, Work, and Social Change.* (Chicago: University of Chicago Press, 1982.)

[60] Mant, Alistair. *Leaders We Deserve.* (Oxford: Martin Robertson, 1983.)

[61] Mills, C. Wright. *White Collar.* (New York: Oxford University Press, 1956.)

[62] Mintzberg, Henry. *Power In and Around Organizations.* (Englewood Cliffs, N.J.: Prentice-Hall, 1983.)

[63] Nachmias, David, and David H. Rosenbloom. *Bureaucratic Government USA.* (New York: St. Martin's, 1980.)

[64] Palazzoli, Mara Selvini, et al. *The Hidden Games of Organizations.* (New York: Pantheon Books, 1986.)

[65] Quinney, Richard. *The Social Reality of Crime.* (Boston: Little, Brown, 1970.)

[66] Rosenberg, Hans. *Bureaucracy, Aristocracy and Autocracy.* (Boston: Beacon Press, 1958.)

[67] Toffler, Alvin. *Future Shock.* (New York: Bantam Books, 1971.)

[68] ———. *Previews and Premises.* (New York: Bantam Books, 1983.)

[69] ———. *The Third Wave.* (New York: Bantam Books, 1981.)

[70] Weber, Max. *Economy and Society,* Vols. I and II. (Berkeley: University of California Press, 1978.)

[71] Welch, Mary-Scott. *Networking.* (New York: Warner Books, 1980.)

[72] Yoshino, M. Y., and Thomas B. Lifson. *The Invisible Link.* (Cambridge, Mass.: M.I.T. Press, 1986.)

BUSINESS/ECONOMICS/FINANCE

[73] Adams, Walter, and James W. Brock. *Dangerous Pursuits.* (New York: Pantheon Books, 1989.)

[74] Aguren, Stefan, et al. *Volvo Kalmar Revisited: Ten Years of Experience.* (Stockholm: Efficiency and Participation Development Council, 1984.)

[75] Aliber, Robert Z. *The International Money Game.* (New York: Basic Books, 1973.)

[76] Applebaum, Herbert. *Work in Non-Market and Transitional Societies.* (Albany: State University of New York Press, 1984.)

[77] Attali, Jacques. *Les trois mondes.* (Paris: Fayard, 1981.)

[78] Batra, Raveendra N. *The Downfall of Capitalism and Communism.* (London: Macmillan Press, 1978.)

[79] Baudrillard, Jean. *The Mirror of Production.* (St. Louis: Telos Press, 1975.)

[80] Belshaw, Cyril S. *Traditional Exchange and Modern Markets.* (London: Prentice-Hall, 1965.)

[81] Bhagwati, Jagdish. *Protectionism.* (Cambridge, Mass.: M.I.T. Press, 1988.)

[82] Brenner, Y. S. *Theories of Economic Development and Growth.* (London: George Allen & Unwin, 1966.)

[83] Bruck, Connie. *The Predators' Ball.* (New York: Simon and Schuster, 1988.)

[84] Canfield, Cass. *The Incredible Pierpont Morgan.* (New York: Harper & Row, 1974.)

[85] Casson, Mark. *Alternatives to the Multinational Enterprise.* (London: Macmillan Press, 1979.)

[86] Clough, Shepard B., Thomas Moodie, and Carol Moodie, eds. *Economic History of Europe: Twentieth Century.* (New York: Harper & Row, 1968.)

[87] Cornwell, Rupert. *God's Banker.* (New York: Dodd, Mead, 1983.)

[88] Crowther, Samuel. *America Self-Contained.* (Garden City, N.Y.: Doubleday, Doran, 1933.)

[89] Denman, D. R. *Origins of Ownership.* (London: George Allen & Unwin, 1958.)

[90] Diwan, Romesh, and Mark Lutz, eds. *Essays in Gandhian Economics.* (New Delhi: Gandhi Peace Foundation, 1985.)

[91] Dressler, Fritz R. S., and John W. Seybold. *The Entrepreneurial Age.* (Media, Pa.: Seybold Publications, 1985.)

[92] Ehrlich, Judith Ramsey, and Barry J. Rehfeld. *The New Crowd.* (Boston: Little, Brown, 1989.)

[93] Evans, Thomas G. *The Currency Carousel.* (Princeton, N.J.: Dow Jones Books, 1977.)

[94] Frank, Charles R., Jr. *Production Theory and Indivisible Commodities.* (Princeton: Princeton University Press, 1969.)

[95] Friedman, Alan. *Agnelli.* (New York: New American Library, 1989.)

[96] Galbraith, John Kenneth. *Money: Whence It Came, Where It Went.* (Boston: Houghton Mifflin, 1975.)

[97] Giarini, Orio, ed. *Cycles, Value and Employment.* (Oxford: Pergamon Press, 1984.)

[98] ———. *The Emerging Service Economy.* (Oxford: Pergamon Press, 1987.)

[99] ———, and Jean Remy Roulet, eds. *L'Europe face à la nouvelle économie de service.* (Paris: Presses Universitaires de France, 1988.)

[100] Giarini, Orio, and Walter R. Stahel. *The Limits to Certainty: Facing Risks in the New Service Economy.* (Geneva: The Risk Institute Project, n.d.)

[101] Gibb, George Sweet, and Evelyn H. Knowlton. *The Resurgent Years: 1911–1927.* (New York: Harper and Brothers, 1956.)

[102] Gregerman, Ira B. *Knowledge Worker Productivity.* (New York: A.M.A. Management Briefing, 1981.)

[103] Gurwin, Larry. *The Calvi Affair.* (London: Pan Books, 1983.)

[104] Gwynne, S. C. *Selling Money.* (New York: Weidenfeld and Nicolson, 1986.)

[105] Herman, Edward S. *Corporate Control, Corporate Power.* (New York: Cambridge University Press, 1981.)

[106] Jackson, Stanley. *J. P. Morgan.* (New York: Stein and Day, 1983.)

[107] Jones, J. P. *The Money Story.* (New York: Drake Publishers, 1973.)

[108] Josephson, Matthew. *The Robber Barons.* (New York: Harcourt, Brace & World, 1962.)

[109] Kahn, Joel S., and J. R. Llobera. *The Anthropology of Pre-Capitalist Societies.* (London: Macmillan Press, 1981.)

[110] Kamioka, Kazuyoshi. *Japanese Business Pioneers.* (Singapore: Times Books International, 1986.)

[111] Kanter, Rosabeth Moss. *Men and Women of the Corporation.* (New York: Basic Books, 1977.)

[112] Keen, Peter G. W. *Competing in Time.* (Cambridge, Mass.: Ballinger, 1986.)

[113] Kenwood, A. G., and A. L. Lougheed. *The Growth of the International Economy 1820–1960.* (London: George Allen & Unwin, 1973.)

[114] Keynes, John Maynard. *The General Theory of Employment, Interest, and Money.* (New York: Harbinger Books, 1964.)

[115] Kindleberger, Charles P. *Manias, Panics, and Crashes.* (New York: Basic Books, 1978.)

[116] Knowles, L.C.A. *The Industrial and Commercial Revolutions in Great Britain During the Nineteenth Century.* (New York: E. P. Dutton, 1922.)

[117] Kornai, Janos. *Anti-Equilibrium*. (Amsterdam: North-Holland Publishing, 1971.)

[118] Kotz, David M. *Bank Control of Large Corporations in the United States*. (Berkeley: University of California Press, 1978.)

[119] Lamarter, Richard Thomas de. *Big Blue*. (New York: Dodd, Mead, 1986.)

[120] Lavoie, Don. *National Economic Planning: What Is Left?* (Cambridge, Mass.: Ballinger, 1985.)

[121] LeClair, Edward E., Jr., and Harold K. Schneider. *Economic Anthropology*. (New York: Holt, Rinehart and Winston, 1968.)

[122] Lens, Sidney. *The Labor Wars*. (Garden City, N.Y.: Doubleday, 1973.)

[123] Levin, Doron P. *Irreconcilable Differences*. (Boston: Little, Brown, 1989.)

[124] Levinson, Harry, and Stuart Rosenthal. *CEO*. (New York: Basic Books, 1984.)

[125] Loebl, Eugen. *Humanomics*. (New York: Random House, 1976.)

[126] Maccoby, Michael. *Why Work*. (New York: Simon and Schuster, 1988.)

[127] Madrick, Jeff. *Taking America*. (New York: Bantam Books, 1987.)

[128] Mattelart, Armand. *Multinational Corporations and the Control of Culture*. (Atlantic Highlands, N.J.: Humanities Press, 1982.)

[129] Mayer, Martin. *The Bankers*. (New York: Weybright and Talley, 1974.)

[130] McCartney, Laton. *Friends in High Places: The Bechtel Story*. (New York: Simon and Schuster, 1988.)

[131] McQuaid, Kim. *Big Business and Presidential Power*. (New York: William Morrow, 1982.)

[132] Meyers, Gerald C., and John Holusha. *When It Hits the Fan*. (London: Unwin Hyman, 1986.)

[133] Mises, Ludwig von. *Human Action*. (New Haven: Yale University Press, 1959.)

[134] Mohn, Reinhard. *Success Through Partnership*. (New York: Doubleday, 1986.)

[135] Monden, Yasuhiro, et al. *Innovations in Management*. (Atlanta: Industrial Engineering and Management Press, 1985.)

[136] Moskowitz, Milton. *The Global Marketplace*. (New York: Macmillan, 1988.)

[137] Mueller, Robert K. *Corporate Networking*. (New York: Free Press, 1986.)

[138] Naniwada, Haruo. *The Crisis*. (Tokyo: The Political Economic Club, 1974.)

[139] Naylor, R. T. *Hot Money*. (New York: Simon and Schuster, 1987.)

[140] Noonan, John T., Jr. *Bribes*. (New York: Macmillan, 1984.)

[141] Nussbaum, Arthur. *A History of the Dollar*. (New York: Columbia University Press, 1957.)

[142] O'Driscoll, Gerald P., Jr., and Mario J. Rizzo. *The Economics of Time and Ignorance*. (Oxford: Basil Blackwell, 1985.)

[143] O'Toole, Patricia. *Corporate Messiah*. (New York: William Morrow, 1984.)

[144] Peacock, William P. *Corporate Combat*. (New York: Facts on File, 1984.)

[145] Polanyi, Karl. *The Great Transformation*. (Boston: Beacon Press, 1957.)

[146] Pye, Michael. *Moguls*. (New York: Holt, Rinehart and Winston, 1980.)

[147] Raymond, H. Alan. *Management in the Third Wave*. (Glenview, Ill.: Scott, Foresman, 1986.)

[148] Robertson, James. *Power, Money and Sex*. (London: Marion Boyars, 1976.)

[149] ———. *Profit or People?* (London: Calder & Boyars, 1974.)

[150] Ropke, Wilhelm. *Economics of the Free Society*. (Chicago: Henry Regnery, 1963.)

[151] Saeed, Syed Mumtaz. *The Managerial Challenge in the Third World*. (Karachi: Academy of Ideas, 1984.)

[152] Sampson, Anthony. *The Money Lenders*. (New York: Viking Press, 1981.)

[153] Schumpeter, Joseph A. *Ten Great Economists*. (New York: Oxford University Press, 1965.)

[154] Sculley, John, with John A. Byrne. *Odyssey: Pepsi to Apple*. (New York: Harper & Row, 1987.)

[155] Singer, Benjamin D. *Advertising and Society*. (Don Mills, Ontario: Addison-Wesley, 1986.)

[156] Smith, Adam. *The Wealth of Nations*. (New York: Modern Library, 1937.)

[157] Sobel, Robert. *IBM, Colossus in Transition*. (New York: Bantam Books, 1981.)

[158] ———. *The Money Manias*. (New York: Weybright and Talley, 1973.)

[159] Soule, George. *Ideas of the Great Economists*. (New York: Mentor Books, 1955.)

[160] Staaf, Robert, and Francis Tannian. *Externalities*. (New York: Dunellen, n.d.)

[161] Stadnichenko, A. *Monetary Crisis of Capitalism*. (Moscow: Progress Publishers, 1975.)

[162] Stevens, Mark. *The Accounting Wars*. (New York: Macmillan, 1985.)

[163] Stewart, Alex. *Automating Distribution: Revolution in Distribution, Retailing and Financial Services*, Japan Focus. (London: Baring Securities, 1987.)

[164] Toffler, Alvin. *The Adaptive Corporation*. (New York: Bantam Books, 1985.)

[165] Tosches, Nick. *Power on Earth*. (New York: Arbor House, 1986.)

[166] Toyoda, Eiji. *Toyota: Fifty Years in Motion*. (Tokyo: Kodansha, 1987.)

[167] Woo, Henry K. H. *The Unseen Dimensions of Wealth*. (Fremont, Cal.: Victoria Press, 1984.)

[168] Zaleznik, Abraham, and Manfred F. R. Kets de Vries. *Power and the Corporate Mind*. (Boston: Houghton Mifflin, 1975.)

[169] Zuboff, Shoshana. *In the Age of the Smart Machine—The Future of Work and Power*. (New York: Basic Books, 1988.)

MEDIA

[170] Bailey, George. *Armageddon in Prime Time*. (New York: Avon Books, 1984.)

[171] Barnouw, Erik. *Mass Communication*. (New York: Rinehart, 1956.)

[172] Biryukov, N. S. *Television in the West and Its Doctrines*. (Moscow: Progress Publishers, 1981.)

[173] Enzensberger, Hans Magnus. *The Consciousness Industry*. (New York: Seabury Press, 1974.)

[174] Freches, José. *La guerre des images*. (Paris: Éditions Denoel, 1986.)

[175] Gourevitch, Jean-Paul. *La politique et ses images*. (Paris: Edilig, 1986.)

[176] Grachev, Andrei, and N. Yermoshkin. *A New Information Order or Psychological Warfare?* (Moscow: Progress Publishers, 1984.)

[177] Orwell, George. *1984*. (New York: New American Library, 1961.)

[178] Ranney, Austin. *Channels of Power*. (New York: Basic Books, 1983.)

[179] Stephens, Mitchell. *A History of the News*. (New York: Viking Press, 1988.)

[180]   Whittemore, Hank. *CNN: The Inside Story.* (Boston: Little, Brown, 1990.)

POLITICS, GOVERNMENT, AND THE STATE

[181]   Allison, Graham T. *Essence of Decision.* (Boston: Little, Brown, 1971.)
[182]   Bennett, James T., and Thomas J. DiLorenzo. *Underground Government.* (Washington, D.C.: Cato Institute, 1983.)
[183]   Bergman, Edward F. *Modern Political Geography.* (Dubuque, Ind.: William C. Brown, 1975.)
[184]   Boaz, David, ed. *Left, Right, and Babyboom.* (Washington, D.C.: Cato Institute, 1986.)
[185]   Bruce-Briggs, B., ed. *The New Class?* (New York: McGraw-Hill, 1979.)
[186]   Cao-Garcia, Ramon J. *Explorations Toward an Economic Theory of Political Systems.* (New York: University Press of America, 1983.)
[187]   Capra, Fritjof, and Charlene Sprentnak. *Green Politics.* (New York: E. P. Dutton, 1984.)
[188]   Carter, April. *Authority and Democracy.* (London: Routledge & Kegan Paul, 1979.)
[189]   Chesneaux, Jean. *Secret Societies in China.* (Ann Arbor: University of Michigan Press, 1971.)
[190]   Coker, F. W. *Organismic Theories of the State.* (New York: AMS Press, 1967.)
[191]   Commager, Henry Steele, ed. *Documents of American History.* (New York: F. S. Crofts, 1943.)
[192]   Crozier, Michel. *The Trouble With America.* (Berkeley: University of California Press, 1984.)
[193]   Ford, Franklin L. *Political Murder.* (Cambridge, Mass.: Harvard University Press, 1985.)
[194]   Franck, Thomas M., and Edward Weisband, eds. *Secrecy and Foreign Policy.* (New York: Oxford University Press, 1974.)
[195]   Gingrich, Newt. *Window of Opportunity.* (New York: Tor Books, 1984.)
[196]   Greenberger, Martin, Matthew A. Crenson, and Brian L. Crissey. *Models in the Policy Process.* (New York: Russell Sage Foundation, 1976.)
[197]   Greenstein, Fred I., ed. *Leadership in the Modern Presidency.* (Cambridge, Mass.: Harvard University Press, 1988.)

[198] Henderson, Nicholas. *The Private Office.* (London: Weidenfeld and Nicolson, 1984.)

[199] Hess, Stephen. *The Government/Press Connection.* (Washington, D.C.: The Brookings Institution, 1984.)

[200] Johnson, Chalmers. *Revolutionary Change.* (Boston: Little, Brown, 1966.)

[201] Kernell, Samuel, and Samuel L. Popkin. *Chief of Staff.* (Los Angeles: University of California Press, 1986.)

[202] King, Anthony, ed. *The New American Political System.* (Washington, D.C.: American Enterprise Institute for Public Policy Research, 1979.)

[203] King, Dennis. *Lyndon LaRouche and the New American Fascism.* (New York: Doubleday, 1989.)

[204] Krader, Lawrence. *Formation of the State.* (Englewood Cliffs, N.J.: Prentice-Hall, 1968.)

[205] Kyemba, Henry. *State of Blood.* (London: Corgi Books, 1977.)

[206] Laski, Harold J. *The American Democracy.* (New York: Viking Press, 1948.)

[207] ———. *Authority in the Modern State.* (Hamden, Conn.: Archon Books, 1968.)

[208] Lebedoff, David. *The New Elite.* (New York: Franklin Watts, 1981.)

[209] Lindblom, Charles E. *Politics and Markets.* (New York: Basic Books, 1977.)

[210] Mafud, Julio. *Sociologia del peronismo.* (Buenos Aires: Editorial Americalee, 1972.)

[211] Matthews, Christopher. *Hardball.* (New York: Summit Books, 1988.)

[212] Morgan, Robin. *The Anatomy of Freedom.* (Garden City, N.Y.: Doubleday, Anchor Press, 1984.)

[213] Navarro, Peter. *The Policy Game.* (New York: John Wiley and Sons, 1984.)

[214] Nelson, Joan M. *Access to Power.* (Princeton: Princeton University Press, 1979.)

[215] Neustadt, Richard E. *Presidential Power.* (New York: John Wiley and Sons, 1960.)

[216] Oppenheimer, Franz. *The State.* (New York: Free Life Editions, 1914.)

[217] Perlmutter, Amos. *Modern Authoritarianism.* (New Haven: Yale University Press, 1981.)

[218] Perry, Roland. *Hidden Power.* (New York: Beaufort Books, 1984.)

[219] Ponting, Clive. *The Right to Know.* (London: Sphere Books, 1985.)

[220] Reed, Steven R. *Japanese Prefectures and Policymaking.* (Pittsburgh: University of Pittsburgh Press, 1986.)

[221] Regan, Donald T. *For the Record.* (San Diego: Harcourt Brace Jovanovich, 1988.)

[222] Reszler, André. *Mythes politiques modernes.* (Paris: Presses Universitaires de France, 1981.)

[223] Rubin, Barry. *Secrets of State.* (New York: Oxford University Press, 1985.)

[224] Sagan, Eli. *At the Dawn of Tyranny.* (New York: Random House, 1985.)

[225] Savas, E. S. *Privatizing the Public Sector.* (Chatham, N.J.: Chatham House, 1982.)

[226] Spencer, Herbert. *The Man vs. the State* (London: Watts, 1940.)

[227] Stockman, David A. *The Triumph of Politics.* (New York: Harper & Row, 1986.)

[228] Straussman, Jeffrey D. *The Limits of Technocratic Politics.* (New Brunswick, N.J.: Transaction Books, 1978.)

[229] Tower, John, et al. *The Tower Commission Report: President's Special Review Board.* (New York: Times Books, 1987.)

[230] Wolferen, Karl van. *The Enigma of Japanese Power.* (New York: Alfred A. Knopf, 1989.)

[231] Woronoff, Jon. *Politics the Japanese Way.* (Tokyo: Lotus Press, 1986.)

RELIGION

[232] Appel, Willa. *Cults in America.* (New York: Holt, Rinehart and Winston, 1983.)

[233] Bakunin, Michael. *God and the State.* (New York: Dover Publications, 1970.)

[234] Barthel, Manfred. *The Jesuits.* (New York: William Morrow, 1984.)

[235] Breton, Thierry. *Vatican III.* (Paris: Robert Laffont, 1985.)

[236] Chai, Ch'u, and Winberg Chai. *Confucianism.* (New York: Barron's Educational Series, 1973.)

[237] Gardner, Martin. *The New Age: Notes of a Fringe Watcher.* (New York: Prometheus Books, 1988.)

[238] Hoffer, Eric. *The True Believer.* (New York: Harper & Row, 1966.)

[239] Holtom, D. C. *The National Faith of Japan.* (London: Kegan Paul, Trench, Trubner, 1938.)

[240] Illich, Ivan. *Celebration of Awareness.* (New York: Doubleday, 1970.)

[241] Levi, Peter. *The Frontiers of Paradise.* (New York: Weidenfeld & Nicolson, 1987.)

[242] Lo Bello, Nino. *The Vatican Papers.* (London: New English Library, 1982.)

[243] Martin, Malachi. *The Jesuits.* (New York: Linden Press, 1987.)

[244] Mortimer, Edward. *Faith and Power.* (New York: Vintage Books, 1982.)

[245] Murakami, Shigeyoshi. *Japanese Religion in the Modern Century.* (Tokyo: University of Tokyo Press, 1983.)

[246] Murphy, Thomas Patrick, ed. *The Holy War.* (Columbus: Ohio State University Press, 1976.)

[247] Pipes, Daniel. *In the Path of God.* (New York: Basic Books, 1983.)

[248] Rodinson, Maxime. *Islam and Capitalism.* (New York: Pantheon Books, 1973.)

[249] Sardar, Ziauddin. *Islamic Futures.* (London: Mansell Publishing, 1985.)

[250] Schultz, Ted, ed. *The Fringes of Reason.* (New York: Harmony Books, 1989.)

[251] Swidler, Leonard, ed. *Religious Liberty and Human Rights in Nations and in Religions.* (Philadelphia: Ecumenical Press, 1986.)

[252] Thomas, Gordon, and Max Morgan-Witts. *Pontiff.* (New York: Doubleday, 1983.)

[253] Tsurumi, Kazuko. *Aspects of Endogenous Development in Modern Japan,* Part II, *Religious Beliefs: State Shintoism vs. Folk Belief.* (Tokyo: Sophia University, 1979.)

[254] Wright, Robin. *Sacred Rage.* (New York: Linden Press, 1985.)

[255] Yallop, David A. *In God's Name.* (New York: Bantam Books, 1984.)

MILITARY

[256] Aron, Raymond. *On War.* (New York: W. W. Norton, 1968.)

[257] Baynes, J.C.M. *The Soldier in Modern Society.* (London: Eyre Methuen, 1972.)

[258] Best, Geoffrey. *War and Society in Revolutionary Europe, 1770–1870.* (Bungay, U.K.: Fontana Paperbacks, 1982.)

[259] Blight, James G., and David A. Welch. *On the Brink.* (New York: Hill and Wang, 1989.)

[260] Creveld, Martin Van. *Command in War.* (Cambridge, Mass.: Harvard University Press, 1985.)

[261] Cross, James Eliot. *Conflict in the Shadows.* (Garden City, N.Y.: Doubleday, 1963.)

[262] De Gaulle, Charles. *The Edge of the Sword.* Translated by George Hopkins. (Westport, Conn.: Greenwood Press, 1975.)

[263] Dixon, Norman. *On the Psychology of Military Incompetence.* (London: Futura Publications, 1976.)

[264] Fletcher, Raymond. *£60 a Second on Defence.* (London: Macgibbon & Kee, 1963.)

[265] Ford, Daniel. *The Button.* (New York: Simon and Schuster, 1985.)

[266] Gabriel, Richard A. *Military Incompetence.* (New York: Hill and Wang, 1985.)

[267] Geraghty, Tony. *Inside the S.A.S.* (New York: Ballantine Books, 1980.)

[268] Kaplan, Fred. *The Wizards of Armageddon.* (New York: Simon and Schuster, 1983.)

[269] Levy, Jack S. *War in the Modern Great Power System 1495–1975.* (Louisville: University of Kentucky Press, 1983.)

[270] Hart, Liddell *Europe in Arms.* (London: Faber and Faber, 1957.)

[271] Mackenzie, W.J.M. *Power, Violence, Decision.* (Middlesex: Penguin Books, 1975.)

[272] Millis, Walter. *The Martial Spirit.* (Cambridge, Mass.: Literary Guild of America, 1931.)

[273] Morison, Samuel Eliot. *American Contributions to the Strategy of World War II.* (London: Oxford University Press, 1958.)

[274] Moro, Comodoro R. Ruben. *Historica del conflicto del Atlantico sur.* (Buenos Aires: Escuela Superior de Guerra Aerea, 1985.)

[275] Organski, A.F.K., and Jacek Kugler. *The War Ledger.* (Chicago: University of Chicago Press, 1980.)

[276] Pfannes, Charles E., and Victor A. Salamona. *The Great Commanders of World War II,* Vol. III, *The Americans.* (Don Mills, Ontario: General Paperbacks, 1981.)

[277] Portela, Adolfo, et al. *Malvinas su advertencia termonuclear.* (Buenos Aires: A-Z Editora, 1985.)

[278] Price, Alfred. *Air Battle Central Europe.* (New York: The Free Press, 1987.)

[279] Rivers, Gayle. *The Specialist.* (New York: Stein and Day, 1985.)

[280] Sadler, A. L., trans., *The Code of the Samurai*. (Rutland, Vt., and Tokyo: Charles E. Tuttle, 1988.)

[281] Sharp, Gene. *The Politics of Nonviolent Action*. (Boston: Porter Sargent, 1973.)

[282] Starr, Chester G. *The Influence of Sea Power on Ancient History*. (New York: Oxford University Press, 1989.)

[283] *Defense of Japan*. White Paper from the Defense Agency, Japan, translated into English by the *Japan Times*. (Tokyo: Japan Times, 1988.)

[284] *Discriminate Deterrence*. (Washington, D.C.: The Commission On Integrated Long-Term Strategy, 1988.)

[285] *The Military Balance, 1989–1990*. (London: International Institute for Strategic Studies, 1989.)

[286] *A Quest for Excellence*, Final Report to the President. (Washington, D.C.: The President's Blue Ribbon Commission on Defense Management, 1986.)

[287] *Strategic Survey, 1988–1989*. (London: International Institute for Strategic Studies, 1989.)

GLOBAL RELATIONSHIPS

[288] Adams, James. *The Financing of Terror*. (London: New English Library, 1986.)

[289] Amin, Samir. *Accumulation on a World Scale*. (New York: Monthly Review Press, 1974.)

[290] Bibo, Istvan. *The Paralysis of International Institutions and the Remedies*. (New York: John Wiley and Sons, 1976.)

[291] Blazy, Jean-Claude. *Le petit livre rouge du nationalisme*. (Paris: Nouvelles Éditions Debresse, n.d.)

[292] Booth, Ken. *Strategy and Ethnocentrism*. (London: Croom Helm, 1979.)

[293] Brown, Lester R., et al. *State of the World, 1990*. (New York: W. W. Norton, 1990.)

[294] Burnham, James. *The War We Are In*. (New Rochelle, N.Y.: Arlington House, 1967.)

[295] Burstein, Daniel. *Yen!* (New York: Simon and Schuster, 1988.)

[296] Buruma, Ian. *God's Dust*. (New York: Farrar Straus & Giroux, 1989.)

[297] Chafetz, Ze'ev. *Members of the Tribe*. (New York: Bantam Books, 1988.)

[298]   Close, Upton. *Behind the Face of Japan.* (New York: D. Appleton-Century, 1934.)

[299]   Colby, Charles C., ed. *Geographic Aspects of International Relations.* (Port Washington, N.Y.: Kennikat Press, 1970.)

[300]   Crenshaw, Martha, ed. *Terrorism, Legitimacy, and Power.* (Middletown, Conn.: Wesleyan University Press, 1983.)

[301]   Davidson, William H. *The Amazing Race.* (New York: John Wiley and Sons, 1984.)

[302]   Dorpalen, Andreas. *The World of General Haushofer.* (Port Washington, N.Y.: Kennikat Press, 1942.)

[303]   Elon, Amos. *The Israelis—Founders and Sons.* (New York: Holt, Rinehart and Winston, 1971.)

[304]   Emmott, Bill. *The Sun Also Sets.* (New York: Times Books, 1989.)

[305]   Gilpin, Robert. *U.S. Power and the Multinational Corporation.* (New York: Basic Books, 1975.)

[306]   ———. *War and Change in World Politics.* (Cambridge: Cambridge University Press, 1981.)

[307]   Glenn, Edmund S., and Christine Glenn. *Man and Mankind.* (Norwood, N.J.: Ablex Publishing, 1981.)

[308]   Hall, Edward T., and Mildred Reed Hall. *Hidden Differences.* (New York: Anchor Press, 1987.)

[309]   Harris, Marvin. *Culture, People, Nature,* 2d ed. (New York: Harper & Row, 1975.)

[310]   Hofheinz, Roy, Jr., and Kent E. Calder. *The Eastasia Edge.* (New York: Basic Books, 1982.)

[311]   Hoyt, Edwin P. *Japan's War.* (New York: McGraw-Hill, 1986.)

[312]   Huppes, Tjerk. *The Western Edge.* (Dordrecht, the Netherlands: Kluwer Academic Publishers, 1987.)

[313]   Kaplan, David E., and Alec Dubro. *Yakuza.* (Menlo Park, Cal.: Addison-Wesley, 1986.)

[314]   Margiotta, Franklin D., and Ralph Sanders, eds. *Technology, Strategy, and National Security.* (Washington, D.C.: National Defense University Press, 1985.)

[315]   Mende, Tibor. *From Aid to Re-colonization.* (New York: New York University Press, 1981.)

[316]   Miller, Abraham H. *Terrorism and Hostage Negotiations.* (Boulder, Col.: Westview Press, 1980.)

[317]   Miller, Roy Andrew. *Japan's Modern Myth.* (New York: Weatherhill, 1982.)

[318]   Morita, Akio, and Shintaro Ishihara. *The Japan That Can Say "No."* (Washington, D.C.: English translation and edition attributed to the Pentagon, 1989.)

[319] Morita, Akio, Edwin M. Reingold, and Mitsuko Shimomura. *Made in Japan.* (New York: E. P. Dutton, 1986.)

[320] Nakdimon, Shlomo. *First Strike.* (New York: Summit Books, 1987.)

[321] Nixon, Richard. *No More Vietnams.* (New York: Arbor House, 1985.)

[322] Ohmae, Kenichi. *Beyond National Borders.* (Homewood, Ill.: Dow Jones–Irwin, 1987.)

[323] ———. *Triad Power.* (New York: Free Press, 1985.)

[324] Palmer, John. *Europe Without America?* (Oxford: Oxford University Press, 1987.)

[325] Park, Jae Kyu, and Jusuf Wanandi, eds. *Korea and Indonesia in the Year 2000.* (Seoul: Kyungnam University Press, 1985.)

[326] Pepper, David, and Alan Jenkins, eds. *The Geography of Peace and War.* (New York: Basil and Blackwell, 1985.)

[327] Priestland, Gerald. *The Future of Violence.* (London: Hamish Hamilton, 1974.)

[328] Pujol-Davila, José. *Sistema y poder geopolítico.* (Buenos Aires: Ediciones Corregidor, 1985.)

[329] Rangel, Carlos. *The Latin Americans: Their Love-Hate Relationship with the United States.* (New York: Harcourt Brace Jovanovich, 1979.)

[330] ———. *Third World Ideology and Western Reality.* (New Brunswick, N.J.: Transaction Books, 1986.)

[331] Rosecrance, Richard. *The Rise of the Trading State.* (New York: Basic Books, 1986.)

[332] Said, Abdul A., and Luiz R. Simmons, eds. *The New Sovereigns.* (Englewood Cliffs, N.J.: Prentice-Hall, 1975.)

[333] Sampson, Geoffrey. *An End to Allegiance.* (London: Temple Smith, 1984.)

[334] Soto, Hernando de. *The Other Path.* (New York: Harper & Row, 1989.)

[335] Sterling, Claire. *The Terror Network.* (New York: Berkley Books, 1981.)

[336] Strausz-Hupe, Robert. *Geopolitics.* (New York: G. P. Putnam's Sons, 1942.)

[337] Suter, Keith. *Reshaping the Global Agenda.* (Sydney: U.N. Association of Australia, 1986.)

[338] Talbott, Strobe. *Deadly Gambits.* (New York: Alfred A. Knopf, 1984.)

[339] Tsurumi, Shunsuke. *A Cultural History of Postwar Japan.* (London: KPI, 1987.)

[340] Walter, Ingo. *Secret Money.* (London: George Allen & Unwin, 1985.)

[341] Wanandi, Jusuf. *Security Dimensions of the Asia-Pacific Region in the 80's.* (Jakarta: Centre for Strategic and International Studies, 1979.)

[342] Wiarda, Howard J. *Ethnocentrism in Foreign Policy.* (Washington, D.C.: American Enterprise Institute for Public Policy Research, 1985.)

[343] Wyden, Peter. *Wall.* (New York: Simon and Schuster, 1989.)

[344] Young, George K. *Finance and World Power.* (London: Thomas Nelson, 1968.)

SOCIALISM AND MARXISM

[345] Aganbegyan, Abel, ed. *Perestroika 1989.* (New York: Charles Scribner's Sons, 1988.)

[346] Althusser, Louis, and Etienne Balibar. *Reading Capital.* (New York: Pantheon Books, 1970.)

[347] Amalrik, Andrei. *Will the Soviet Union Survive Until 1984?* (New York: Perennial Library, 1970.)

[348] Baldwin, Roger N., ed. *Kropotkin's Revolutionary Pamphlets: A Collection of Writings by Peter Kropotkin.* (New York: Dover Publications, 1970.)

[349] Brzezinski, Zbigniew. *The Grand Failure: The Birth and Death of Communism in the 20th Century.* (New York: Charles Scribner's Sons, 1989.)

[350] ———, and Samuel P. Huntington. *Political Power: USA/USSR.* (New York: Viking Press, 1963.)

[351] Cohen, Stephen F. *Bukharin and the Bolshevik Revolution.* (New York: Alfred A. Knopf, 1973.)

[352] ———, and Katrina Vanden Heuvel. *Voices of Glasnost.* (New York: W. W. Norton, 1989.)

[353] Daniels, Robert V. *Russia: The Roots of Confrontation.* (Cambridge, Mass.: Harvard University Press, 1985.)

[354] De Brunhoff, Suzanne. *Marx on Money.* (New York: Urizen Books, 1976.)

[355] d'Encausse, Helene Carrere. *Confiscated Power.* (New York: Harper & Row, 1982.)

[356] Fine, Ben, and Laurence Harris. *Rereading Capital.* (London: Macmillan Press, 1979.)

[357] Fletcher, Raymond. *Stalinism.* (Heanor, U.K.: Byron House Publications, n.d.)

[358] Frankel, Boris. *Beyond the State? Dominant Theories and Socialist Strategies.* (London: Macmillan Press, 1983.)

[359] Friedgut, Theodore H. *Political Participation in the USSR.* (Princeton: Princeton University Press, 1979.)

[360] Frolov, I. *Global Problems and the Future of Mankind.* (Moscow: Progress Publishers, 1982.)

[361] Gorbachev, Mikhail. *Selected Speeches and Articles.* (Moscow: Progress Publishers, 1987.)

[362] Grachev, Andrei. *In the Grip of Terror.* (Moscow: Progress Publishers, 1982.)

[363] Hamrin, Carol Lee. *China and the Challenge of the Future.* (San Francisco: Westview Press, 1990.)

[364] James, Donald. *The Fall of the Russian Empire.* (New York: Signet Books, 1982.)

[365] Kraus, Richard Curt. *Class Conflict in Chinese Socialism.* (New York: Columbia University Press, 1981.)

[366] Lichtheim, George. *The Origins of Socialism.* (New York: Frederick A. Praeger, 1969.)

[367] Loebl, Eugen. *Stalinism in Prague.* (New York: Grove Press, 1969.)

[368] Marx, Karl. *Capital,* Vol. I. (New York: International Publishers, 1939.)

[369] ———, F. Engels, and V. Lenin. *On Historical Materialism, A Collection.* (Moscow: Progress Publishers, 1972.)

[370] McMurtry, John. *The Structure of Marx's World-View.* (Princeton: Princeton University Press, 1978.)

[371] Muqiao, Xue. *China's Socialist Economy.* (Beijing: Foreign Languages Press, 1981.)

[372] Pan, Lynn. *The New Chinese Revolution.* (Chicago: Contemporary Books, 1988.)

[373] Possony, Stefan T., ed. *The Lenin Reader.* (Chicago: Henry Regnery, 1966.)

[374] Poster, Mark. *Foucault, Marxism and History.* (Oxford: Polity Press, 1984.)

[375] Rigby, T. H., Archie Brown, and Peter Reddaway, eds. *Authority, Power and Policy in the USSR.* (London: Macmillan Press, 1980.)

[376] Sassoon, Anne Showstack. *Approaches to Gramsci.* (London: Writers and Readers Publishing Cooperative Society, 1982.)

[377] Sherman, Howard. *Radical Political Economy.* (New York: Basic Books, 1972.)

[378] Sik, Ota. *The Communist Power System.* (New York: Praeger Publishers, 1981.)

[379] Starr, John Bryan. *Continuing the Revolution: The Political Thought of Mao.* (Princeton: Princeton University Press, 1979.)
[380] Wilson, Dick. *The Sun at Noon.* (London: Hamish Hamilton, 1986.)
[381] Zamoshkin, Yu. A. *Problems of Power and Management Under the Scientific Technological Revolution.* (Moscow: Soviet Sociological Association, 1974.)

FASCISM

[382] Beradt, Charlotte. *The Third Reich of Dreams.* (Wellingborough, U.K.: Aquarian Press, 1985.)
[383] Friedlander, Saul. *Reflections on Nazism.* (New York: Avon Books, 1984.)
[384] Glaser, Hermann. *The Cultural Roots of National Socialism.* (Austin: University of Texas Press, 1978.)
[385] Gregor, A. James. *The Fascist Persuasion in Radical Politics.* (Princeton: Princeton University Press, 1974.)
[386] ———. *The Ideology of Fascism.* (New York: The Free Press, 1969.)
[387] Hitler, Adolf. *Mein Kampf.* (Boston: Houghton Mifflin, 1971.)
[388] Laqueur, Walter. *Fascism: A Reader's Guide.* (Berkeley: University of California Press, 1976.)
[389] Lewin, Ronald. *Hitler's Mistakes.* (New York: William Morrow, 1984.)
[390] Mosse, George L. *The Crisis of German Ideology.* (London: Weidenfeld and Nicolson, 1964.)
[391] Reveille, Thomas. *The Spoil of Europe.* (New York: W. W. Norton, 1941.)

INTELLIGENCE AND ESPIONAGE

[392] Aburish, Said K. *Pay-Off: Wheeling and Dealing in the Arab World.* (London: Andre Deutsch, 1986.)
[393] Andrew, Christopher. *Secret Service.* (London: Heinemann, 1985.)
[394] ———, and David Dilks, eds. *The Missing Dimension.* (Chicago: University of Illinois Press, 1984.)
[395] Ball, Desmond. *Pine Gap.* (Sydney: Allen & Unwin, 1988.)
[396] ———, J. O. Langtry, and J. D. Stevenson. *Defend the North.* (Sydney: George Allen and Unwin, 1985.)

[397] Brown, Anthony Cave. *Bodyguard of Lies.* (New York: Bantam Books, 1976.)

[398] ———. *"C".* (New York: Macmillan, 1987.)

[399] Burrows, William E. *Deep Black.* (New York: Random House, 1986.)

[400] Caroz, Yaacov. *The Arab Secret Services.* (London: Corgi Books, 1978.)

[401] Costello, John. *Mask of Treachery.* (New York: William Morrow, 1988.)

[402] Coxsedge, Joan, Ken Coldicutt, and Gerry Harant. *Rooted in Secrecy.* (Capp, Australia: Balwyn North, 1982.)

[403] Deacon, Richard. *"C": A Biography of Sir Maurice Oldfield.* (London: McDonald, 1985.)

[404] ———. *A History of the Russian Secret Service.* (London: Frederick Muller, 1972.)

[405] Donner, Frank J. *The Age of Surveillance.* (New York: Alfred A. Knopf, 1980.)

[406] Felix, Christopher. *A Short Course in the Secret War.* (New York: Dell Publishing, 1988.)

[407] Garwood, Darrell. *Undercover: Thirty-five Years of CIA Deception.* (New York: Grove Press, 1985.)

[408] Godson, Roy. *Intelligence Requirements for the 1980's.* (Lexington, Mass.: Lexington Books, 1986.)

[409] Halamka, John D. *Espionage in the Silicon Valley.* (Berkeley, Cal.: Sybex, 1984.)

[410] Henderson, Bernard R. *Pollard: The Spy's Story.* (New York: Alpha Books, 1988.)

[411] Knightley, Phillip. *The Second Oldest Profession.* (New York: W. W. Norton, 1986.)

[412] Laqueur, Walter. *A World of Secrets.* (New York: Basic Books, 1985.)

[413] Levchenko, Stanislav. *On the Wrong Side.* (Washington, D.C.: Pergamon-Brassey's, 1988.)

[414] Levite, Ariel. *Intelligence and Strategic Surprises.* (New York: Columbia University Press, 1987.)

[415] Marenches, Count de, and Christine Ockrent. *The Evil Empire.* (London: Sidgwick and Jackson, 1986.)

[416] Pacepa, Ion. *Red Horizons.* (London: Hodder and Stoughton, Coronet Books, 1989.)

[417] Perrault, Gilles. *The Red Orchestra.* (New York: Pocket Books, 1969.)

[418] Phillips, David Atlee. *Careers in Secret Operations.* (Bethesda, Md.: Stone Trail Press, 1984.)

[419] Pincher, Chapman. *Too Secret Too Long.* (New York: St. Martin's Press, 1984.)

[420] Plate, Thomas, and Andrea Darvi. *Secret Police.* (London: Robert Hale, 1981.)

[421] Prouty, Fletcher L. *The Secret Team.* (Englewood Cliffs, N.J.: Prentice-Hall, 1973.)

[422] Richelson, Jeffrey. *American Espionage and the Soviet Target.* (New York: Quill, 1987.)

[423] ———. *Foreign Intelligence Organizations.* (Cambridge, Mass.: Ballinger, 1988.)

[424] ———. *The U.S. Intelligence Community.* (Cambridge, Mass.: Ballinger, 1985.)

[425] Rositzke, Harry. *The KGB.* (New York: Doubleday, 1981.)

[426] Seth, Ronald. *Secret Servants.* (New York: Farrar, Straus and Cudahy, 1957.)

[427] Shevchenko, Arkady N. *Breaking with Moscow.* (New York: Alfred A. Knopf, 1985.)

[428] Shultz, Richard H., and Roy Godson. *Dezinformatsia.* (New York: Berkley Books, 1986.)

[429] Suvorov, Viktor. *Inside Soviet Military Intelligence.* (New York: Berkley Books, 1984.)

[430] ———. *Inside the Aquarium: The Making of a Top Spy.* (New York: Berkley Books, 1987.)

[431] Toohey, Brian, and William Pinwill. *Oyster.* (Port Melbourne, Australia: William Heinemann, 1989.)

[432] Turner, Stansfield. *Secrecy and Democracy.* (Boston: Houghton Mifflin, 1985.)

[433] West, Nigel. *The Circus.* (New York: Stein and Day, 1983.)

[434] ———. *Games of Intelligence.* (London: Weidenfeld and Nicolson, 1989.)

[435] Woodward, Bob. *Veil.* (New York: Simon and Schuster, 1987.)

[436] Wright, Peter, and Paul Greengrass. *Spycatcher.* (New York: Viking Press, 1987.)

KNOWLEDGE AND SOCIETY

[437] Afanasyev, V. *Social Information and the Regulation of Social Development.* (Moscow: Progress Publishers, 1978.)

[438] Alisjahbana, S. Takdir. *Values As Integrating Forces in Personality, Society and Culture.* (Kuala Lumpur: University of Malaya Press, 1966.)

[439] Attali, Jacques. *Noise*. (Minneapolis: University of Minnesota Press, 1985.)

[440] Bacon, Francis. *A Selection of His Works*. (Indianapolis: Bobbs-Merrill Educational Publishing, 1965.)

[441] Bok, Sissela. *Secrets*. (New York: Vintage Books, 1984.)

[442] Cherry, Kittredge. *Womansword*. (Tokyo: Kodansha International, 1989.)

[443] Cirlot, J. E. *A Dictionary of Symbols*. (New York: Philosophical Library, 1962.)

[444] Coser, Lewis A. *Men of Ideas*. (New York: Free Press, 1970.)

[445] Curtis, James E., and John W. Petras, eds. *The Sociology of Knowledge*. (New York: Praeger, 1970.)

[446] De Huszar, George B., ed. *The Intellectuals*. (Glencoe, Ill.: Free Press of Glencoe, 1960.)

[447] Doi, Takeo. *The Anatomy of Dependence*. (Tokyo: Kodansha International, 1985.)

[448] Duke, Benjamin. *The Japanese School*. (New York: Praeger, 1986.)

[449] Ekman, Paul. *Telling Lies*. (New York: W. W. Norton, 1985.)

[450] Everhart, Robert B., ed. *The Public School Monopoly*. (Cambridge, Mass.: Ballinger, 1982.)

[451] Feigenbaum, Edward, Pamela McCorduck, and H. Penny Nii. *The Rise of the Expert Company*. (New York: Times Books, 1988.)

[452] Foster, Hal. *Postmodern Culture*. (London: Pluto Press, 1985.)

[453] Foucault, Michel. *Power, Truth, Strategy*. (Sydney: Feral Publications, 1979.)

[454] Gardner, Howard. *The Mind's New Science*. (New York: Basic Books, 1985.)

[455] Gouldner, Alvin W. *The Future of Intellectuals and the Rise of the New Class*. (New York: Continuum Books, 1979.)

[456] Habermas, Jurgen. *Knowledge and Human Interests*. (Boston: Beacon Press, 1968.)

[457] Hansen, Robert H. *The Why, What and How of Decision Support*. (New York: AMA Management Briefing, 1984.)

[458] Hoffman, Lily M. *The Politics of Knowledge*. (Albany: State University of New York Press, 1989.)

[459] Keren, Michael. *Ben Gurion and the Intellectuals*. (Dekalb, Ill.: Northern Illinois University Press, 1983.)

[460] Kindaichi, Haruhiko. *The Japanese Language*. (Rutland, Vt.: Charles E. Tuttle, 1978.)

[461] Konrad, George. *Antipolitics*. (New York: Harcourt Brace Jovanovich, 1984.)

[462]   Konrad, George, and Ivan Szelenyi. *The Intellectuals on the Road to Class Power.* (New York: Harcourt, Brace Jovanovich, 1976.)

[463]   Kraemer, Kenneth L., et al. *Datawars.* (New York: Columbia University Press, 1987.)

[464]   Lakatos, Imre, and Alan Musgrave, eds. *Criticism and the Growth of Knowledge.* (London: Cambridge University Press, 1979.)

[465]   Lamberton, D. M., ed. *Economics of Information and Knowledge.* (Middlesex, U.K.: Penguin Books, 1971.)

[466]   Lyotard, Jean-François. *The Post-Modern Condition.* (Minneapolis: University of Minnesota Press, 1984.)

[467]   Machlup, Fritz. *Knowledge: Its Creation, Distribution, and Economic Significance,* Vol. I. (Princeton: Princeton University Press, 1980.)

[468]   ———. *The Production and Distribution of Knowledge in the United States.* (Princeton: Princeton University Press, 1962.)

[469]   Noer, Deliar. *Culture, Philosophy and the Future.* (Jakarta: P. T. Dian Rakyat, 1988.)

[470]   Ohmae, Kenichi. *The Mind of the Strategist.* (New York: Penguin, 1983.)

[471]   Ong, Walter J. *Orality and Literacy.* (London: Methuen, 1982.)

[472]   ———, ed. *Knowledge and the Future of Man.* (New York: Clarion Books, 1968.)

[473]   Paulos, John Allen. *Innumeracy.* (New York: Hill and Wang, 1988.)

[474]   Popper, K. R. *The Open Society and Its Enemies,* Vol. I. (London: Routledge and Kegan Paul, 1962.)

[475]   Powers, Richard Gid. *Secrecy and Power: The Life of J. Edgar Hoover.* (New York: Free Press, 1987.)

[476]   Scott, D. R. *The Cultural Significance of Accounting.* (Columbia, Mo.: Lucas Brothers, n.d.)

[477]   Singer, Kurt. *Mirror, Sword and Jewel.* (Tokyo: Kodansha International, 1973.)

[478]   Sowell, Thomas. *Knowledge and Decisions.* (New York: Basic Books, 1980.)

[479]   Strehlow, T.G.H. *Songs of Central Australia.* (Sydney: Angus and Robertson, 1971.)

[480]   Swetz, Frank J. *Capitalism and Arithmetic.* (La Salle, Ill.: Open Court, 1987.)

[481]   Taylor, Stanley. *Conceptions of Institutions and the Theory of Knowledge.* (New Brunswick, N.J.: Transaction, 1989.)

[482]   Tefft, Stanton K. *Secrecy: A Cross-Cultural Perspective.* (New York: Human Sciences Press, 1980.)

[483]   Van den Berg, Jan Hendrik. *Medical Power and Medical Ethics.* (New York: W. W. Norton, 1978.)

[484]   Whitehead, Alfred North. *The Function of Reason.* (Boston: Beacon Press, 1958.)

COMPUTERS AND COMMUNICATIONS

[485]   Acco, Alain, and Edmond Zuchelli. *La peste informatique.* (Paris: Éditions Plume, 1989.)

[486]   Arnold, Erik, and Ken Guy. *Parallel Convergence: National Strategies in Information Technology.* (London: Frances Pinter, 1986.)

[487]   Ashby, W. Ross. *Design for a Brain.* (London: Chapman and Hall, 1978.)

[488]   Berlin, Isaiah. *Against the Current.* (New York: Viking Press, 1955.)

[489]   Berlo, David K. *The Process of Communication.* (New York: Holt, Rinehart and Winston, 1960.)

[490]   Cherry, Colin. *World Communication: Threat or Promise?* (London: Wiley-Interscience, 1971.)

[491]   Civikly, Jean M. *Messages.* (New York: Random House, 1974.)

[492]   Duncan, Hugh Dalziel. *Communication and Social Order.* (London: Oxford University Press, 1962.)

[493]   Goodman, Danny. *The Complete HyperCard Handbook.* (New York: Bantam Books, 1987.)

[494]   Goulden, Joseph C. *Monopoly.* (New York: Pocket Books, 1970.)

[495]   Hemphill, Charles F., Jr., and Robert D. Hemphill. *Security Safeguards for the Computer.* (New York: AMA Management Briefing, 1979.)

[496]   Johnson, Douglas W. *Computer Ethics.* (Elgin, Ill.: Brethren Press, 1984.)

[497]   Kaligo, Al, Lou Baumbach, and Joe Garzinsky. *Telecommunications Management: A Practical Approach.* (New York: AMA Management Briefing, 1984.)

[498]   Kitahara, Yasusada. *Information Network System.* (London: Heinemann Educational Books, 1983.)

[499]   Landau, Robert M. *Information Resources Management.* (New York: AMA Management Briefing, 1980.)

[500]   Levy, Steven. *Hackers.* (New York: Dell, 1984.)

[501]   Marchand, Marie. *The Minitel Saga.* (Paris: Larousse, 1988.)

[502] McLuhan, Marshall, and Bruce R. Powers. *The Global Village.* (New York: Oxford University Press, 1989.)

[503] Mortensen, C. David. *Communication.* (New York: McGraw-Hill, 1972.)

[504] Pool, Ithiel de Sola. *Technologies of Freedom.* (Cambridge, Mass.: Belknap Press of Harvard University Press, 1983.)

[505] Poppel, Harvey L., and Bernard Goldstein. *Information Technology.* (New York: McGraw-Hill, 1987.)

[506] Shannon, Claude, and Warren Weaver. *The Mathematical Theory of Communication.* (Urbana: University of Illinois Press, 1949.)

[507] Smith, Alfred G., ed. *Communication and Culture.* (New York: Holt, Rinehart and Winston, 1966.)

[508] Spacks, Patricia Meyer. *Gossip.* (Chicago: University of Chicago Press, 1985.)

[509] Strassman, Paul A. *Information Payoff.* (New York: Free Press, 1985.)

[510] Tarde, Gabriel. *On Communication and Social Influence.* (Chicago: University of Chicago Press, 1969.)

[511] Wilcox, A. M., M. G. Slade, and P. A. Ramsdale. *Command Control and Communications.* (New York: Brassey's Defense Publishers, 1983.)

[512] Wilmot, William W., and John R. Wenburg. *Communicational Involvement: Personal Perspectives.* (New York: John Wiley and Sons, 1974.)

[513] Winograd, Terry, and Fernando Flores. *Understanding Computers and Cognition.* (Reading, Mass.: Addison-Wesley, 1986.)

SCIENCE AND TECHNOLOGY

[514] Colombo, Umberto, et al. *Science and Technology Towards the XXI Century and Their Impact Upon Society.* (Milan: The Pirelli Group, n.d.)

[515] Drexler, K. Eric. *Engines of Creation.* (New York: Anchor Press, 1986.)

[516] Dryakhlov, Nikolai. *The Scientific and Technological Revolution: Its Rss. Design for a Brain.* (London: Chapman and Hall, 1978.)

[517] Illich, Ivan. *Tools for Conviviality.* (New York: Harper & Row, 1973.)

[518] Langone, John. *Superconductivity: The New Alchemy*. (Chicago: Contemporary Books, 1989.)

[519] Melvern, Linda, David Hebditch, and Nick Anning. *Techno-Bandits*. (Boston: Houghton Mifflin, 1984.)

[520] Mendelssohn, Kurt. *The Secret of Western Domination*. (New York: Praeger, 1976.)

[521] Muroyama, Janet H., and H. Guyford Stever, eds. *Globalization of Technology*. (Washington, D.C.: National Academy Press, 1988.)

[522] Nicolis, G., and I. Prigogine. *Self-Organization in Nonequilibrium Systems*. (New York: John Wiley and Sons, 1977.)

[523] Prigogine, Ilya. *From Being to Becoming*. (San Francisco: W. H. Freeman, 1980.)

[524] ———, and Isabelle Stengers. *La nouvelle alliance*. (Paris: Éditions Gallimard, 1979.)

[525] ———. *Order Out of Chaos*. (New York: Bantam Books, 1984.)

[526] Tuck, Jay. *High-Tech Espionage*. (London: Sidgwick and Jackson, 1986.)

[527] *The Scientific-Technological Revolution and the Contradictions of Capitalism*. International Theoretical Conference, Moscow, May 21–23, 1979. (Moscow: Progress Publishers, 1982.)

HISTORY AND BIOGRAPHY

[528] Allen, Frederick Lewis. *The Lords of Creation*. (New York: Harper & Brothers, 1935.)

[529] Attali, Jacques. *A Man of Influence*. (Bethesda, Md.: Adler & Adler, 1987.)

[530] Ayling, S. E. *Portraits of Power*. (New York: Barnes and Noble, 1963.)

[531] Braudel, Fernand. *Afterthoughts on Material Civilization and Capitalism*. (Baltimore: Johns Hopkins University Press, 1977.)

[532] ———. *Capitalism and Material Life 1400–1800*. (New York: Harper Colophon Books, 1973.)

[533] ———. *The Mediterranean*, Vol. I. (New York: Harper & Row, 1972.)

[534] ———. *The Mediterranean*, Vol. II. (New York: Harper & Row, 1972.)

[535] ———. *On History*. (London: Weidenfeld and Nicolson, 1980.)

[536] ———. *The Structures of Everyday Life*, Vol. I. (New York: Harper & Row, 1981.)

[537] Burke, John. *Duet in Diamonds.* (New York: G. P. Putnam's Sons, 1972.)

[538] Bury, J.P.T., ed. *The New Cambridge Modern History.* (Cambridge: Cambridge University Press, 1971.)

[539] Cashman, Sean Dennis. *America in the Gilded Age.* (New York: New York University Press, 1984.)

[540] Center for Medieval and Renaissance Studies, UCLA. *The Dawn of Modern Banking.* (New Haven: Yale University Press, 1979.)

[541] Chernow, Ron. *The House of Morgan.* (New York: Atlantic Monthly Press, 1990.)

[542] Cook, Don. *Charles De Gaulle.* (New York: G. P. Putnam's Sons, 1983.)

[543] Cooper, A. Duff. *Talleyrand.* (London: Cassell, 1987.)

[544] Corey, Lewis. *The House of Morgan.* (New York: G. Howard Watt, 1930.)

[545] Crankshaw, Edward. *The Fall of the House of Habsburg.* (New York: Penguin Books, 1983.)

[546] Crozier, Brian. *The Masters of Power.* (Boston: Little, Brown, 1969.)

[547] Curtin, Philip D. *Cross-Cultural Trade in World History.* (Cambridge: Cambridge University Press, 1984.)

[548] Custine, Marquis de. *Journey for Our Time: The Journals of the Marquis de Custine.* (London: George Prior, 1980.)

[549] Dodd, Alfred. *Francis Bacon's Personal Life-Story,* Vol. I. (London: Rider, 1949.)

[550] ———. *Francis Bacon's Personal Life Story,* Vol. II. (London: Rider, 1986.)

[551] Elias, Norbert. *Power and Civility.* (New York: Pantheon Books, 1982.)

[552] Eyck, Erich. *Bismarck and the German Empire.* (New York and London: W. W. Norton, 1950.)

[553] Febvre, Lucien, and Henri-Jean Martin. *The Coming of the Book.* (London: New Left Books, 1984.)

[554] Green, A. Wigfall. *Sir Francis Bacon.* (Denver: Alan Swallow, 1952.)

[555] Hammer, Armand, with Neil Lyndon. *Hammer.* (New York: G. P. Putnam's Sons, 1987.)

[556] Hook, Sidney. *Out of Step.* (New York: Carroll & Graf, 1987.)

[557] Isaacson, Walter, and Evan Thomas. *The Wise Men.* (New York: Simon and Schuster, 1986.)

[558] Johnson, Paul. *Intellectuals.* (New York: Harper & Row, 1988.)

[559]   Kapuscinski, Ryszard. *The Emperor*. (New York: Harcourt Brace Jovanovich, 1983.)

[560]   ———. *Shah of Shahs*. (New York: Harcourt Brace Jovanovich, 1985.)

[561]   Kennedy, Paul. *The Rise and Fall of the Great Powers*. (New York: Random House, 1987.)

[562]   Kerr, Clark, et al. *Industrialism and Industrial Man*. (Harmondsworth, U.K.: Penguin Books, 1973.)

[563]   Kula, Witold. *An Economic Theory of the Feudal System*. (London: NLB, 1976.)

[564]   Lacouture, Jean. *The Demigods*. (New York: Alfred A. Knopf, 1970.)

[565]   Markham, Felix. *Napoleon*. (New York: Mentor Books, 1963.)

[566]   Mazlish, Bruce. *James and John Stuart Mill*. (New York: Basic Books, 1975.)

[567]   McNeill, William H. *The Pursuit of Power*. (Chicago: University of Chicago Press, 1982.)

[568]   Mee, Charles L., Jr. *The End of Order*. (New York: E. P. Dutton, 1980.)

[569]   Metcalfe, Philip. *1933*. (Sag Harbor, N.Y.: Permanent Press, 1988.)

[570]   Millar, Fergus. *The Emperor in the Roman World*. (Ithaca, N.Y.: Cornell University Press, 1977.)

[571]   Myers, Gustavus. *History of the Great American Fortunes*. (New York: Modern Library, 1937.)

[572]   Nicholls, A. J. *Weimar and the Rise of Hitler*. (London: Macmillan, 1979.)

[573]   Nixon, Richard. *Leaders*. (New York: Warner Books, 1982.)

[574]   ———. *The Memoirs of Richard Nixon*. (New York: Grosset and Dunlap, 1978.)

[575]   Norwich, John Julius. *Venice: The Rise to Empire*. (London: Allen Lane, 1977.)

[576]   Nystrom, Anton. *Before, During, and After 1914*. (London: William Heinemann, 1915.)

[577]   Schevill, Ferdinand. *A History of Europe*. (New York: Harcourt Brace, 1938.)

[578]   Schlereth, Thomas J. *The Cosmopolitan Ideal in the Enlightenment Thought*. (Notre Dame, Ind.: University of Notre Dame Press, 1977.)

[579]   Schmidt-Hauer, Christian. *Gorbachev*. (Topsfield, Mass.: Salem House, 1986.)

[580]   Seward, Desmond. *Napoleon and Hitler*. (New York: Viking Press, 1988.)

[581]   Stephenson, Carl. *Mediaeval Feudalism.* (Ithaca: Cornell University Press, 1967.)

[582]   Stern, J. P. *Hitler.* (London: Fontana/Collins, 1975.)

[583]   Tapsell, R. F. *Monarchs, Rulers, Dynasties and Kingdoms of the World.* (London: Thames and Hudson, 1983.)

[584]   Thompson, E. P. *The Making of the English Working Class.* (New York: Vintage Books, 1963.)

[585]   Walker, James Blaine. *The Epic of American Industry.* (New York: Harper & Brothers, 1949.)

[586]   Ward, J. T. *The Factory System,* Vol. I. (Newton Abbot, U.K.: David and Charles, 1970.)

[587]   Weatherford, Jack. *Indian Givers.* (New York: Crown Books, 1988.)

[588]   Wendt, Lloyd, and Herman Kogan. *Bet A Million!.* (Indianapolis: Bobbs-Merrill, 1948.)

[589]   Wheeler, George. *Pierpont Morgan and Friends.* (Englewood Cliffs, N.J.: Prentice-Hall, 1973.)

[590]   Wilson, Derek. *Rothschild: The Wealth and Power of a Dynasty.* (New York: Charles Scribner's Sons, 1988.)

[591]   Wilson, George M. *Radical Nationalist on Japan: Kita Ikki 1883–1937.* (Cambridge, Mass.: Harvard University Press, 1969.)

[592]   Wittfogel, Karl A. *Oriental Despotism.* (New Haven: Yale University Press, 1964.)

NOTES

Bracketed [ ] numbers indicate items listed in the accompanying Bibliography. Thus, in the Notes, [1] will stand for the first item in the Bibliography: Aron, Raymond. *Main Currents in Sociological Thought.*

A PERSONAL PREFACE

PAGE

xix   Institute for Scientific Information, correspondence with author, January 5, 1978.

xx   Re *The Third Wave* in China, see [363]. Also "Alvin Toffler in China: Deng's Big Bang," by Andrew Mendelsohn, *New Republic,* April 4, 1988.

CHAPTER 1   THE POWERSHIFT ERA

5   "GM Is Tougher Than You Think," by Anne B. Fisher, *Fortune,* November 10, 1986.

5   Re fading U.S. computer dominance, *Datamation,* June 15, 1988.

6   "Gephardt Plans to Call for Japan-Style Trade Agency," *Los Angeles Times,* October 4, 1989.

6   For MITI, see following from *Japan Economic Journal:* "MITI Fights to Hold Influence as Japanese Firms Go Global," April 1, 1989; "Icy Welcome for MITI's Retail Law Change," October 21, 1989; "Japan Carmakers Eye Growth Despite MITI Warning," October 21, 1989; "Trade Policy Flip-Flop Puts MITI on Defensive," January 20, 1990.

7–8   Medical material based in part on interviews with staff of
        The Wilkerson Group, medical management consulting
        organization, New York; also Wendy Borow, Director of
        American Medical Association Division of Television, Ra-
        dio and Film; and Barry Cohn, television news producer,
        AMA, Chicago.

9   Poster quote from [374] p. 53.

CHAPTER 2   MUSCLE, MONEY, AND MIND

On definitions: There are as many definitions of power as there are cherry blossoms in Japan, and all are fraught with difficulty. One of the most famous is Bertrand Russell's statement that "Power may be defined as the production of intended effects." Perfectly sensible, clear, and precise.

Unfortunately, even this simple sentence is spiked with hidden booby traps.

First, we need to know what is "intended" (not so easy to specify, even for the person whose intentions they are). Next, we need to understand the "effects" so we can compare these with the intentions. Yet every act itself has many second, third, and "nth" order consequences, some intended, others not. What counts as an "effect" and what doesn't?

Then, too, we need to know whether what happens was actually "produced" by the actions taken. This implies a knowledge of causality that is frequently beyond our grasp.

Finally, a rich irony pops its beady eyes out of a hole in the ground:

The more numerous and varied the intentions, the greater the odds that only a fraction of them will be realized and the more difficult it becomes to determine what actually "produced" them all. In this sense, according to Russell's perfectly plausible-sounding definition, the more limited one's intentions, the greater the range of control one may exercise.

If producing a desired effect, with minimum (identifiable) side effects, is a definition of power, then the person whose goals are most narrowly defined and whose awareness of side effects is most rudimentary will be defined as most powerful.

Despite such a cautionary example (and the knowledge that our own definition is not without conceptual difficulties) we need at least a loose working definition sufficient for our purposes. In these pages the term *power* will mean the ability to mobilize and use violence, wealth, and/or knowledge, or their many derivatives, to motivate others in ways we think will gratify our needs and desires.

13 The three legendary symbols of power still play a part in Japanese ritual. When Emporor Hirohito died in 1989, the imperial sword, jewel, and mirror, passed down from emperor to emperor, were transferred to his son, Emperor Akihito ("What Sort of Peace in Heisei?" *Economist*, January 14, 1989). For background on *san shu no jingi*, see *Encyclopedia of Japan* (Tokyo: Kodansha Publishing House) listing for "Imperial Regalia." See also [239] pp. 124–131.

13 For symbolic meanings of *mirror*, [443] p. 201.

Power is embedded not only in Japanese legend but in the language itself. Japanese, like many other languages, contains honorifics that require one to identify her or his position in the pecking order every time the lips move. It is almost impossible to speak without addressing one's words up to a superior or down to an inferior. The language thus assumes the existence of a power hierarchy. While the ideogram for a male symbolizes a rice field and strong legs, that for a woman is a submissive, kneeling figure. Such symbols reflect and perpetuate patriarchal power. *Womansword* [442], subtitled *What Japanese Words Say About Women,* is a rich source of examples. But Japanese is not the only language laden with implicit power meanings. Javanese, for example, has two "levels": *ngoko,* which is spoken to inferiors, and *krama,* to superiors. Each in turn has subtle levels within levels (*cf.* [28]).

13 Re Boesky: "Suddenly the Fish Gets Bigger," *Business Week,* March 2, 1989.
13 Re Klaus Fuchs: [411] pp. 263–264.
15–16 *Cuba* (United Artists, 1979.)
17 Military dependence on computers: "Real Time Creates 'Smart' Flight Simulators," by Richard E. Morley and Todd Leadbeater, *Defense Science,* November 1988.

CHAPTER 3 BEYOND THE AGE OF GLITZ

25 The syndicated "Doonesbury" cartoon strip by Garry Trudeau has savagely satirized real estate tycoon Donald Trump,

whose best-selling *The Art of the Deal* was produced with writer Tony Schwartz. Chrysler chairman Lee Iacocca's best-seller was written for him by William Novak. For presidential rumors, see "Iacocca for President?" *Washington Post,* December 13, 1987, and "Starwatch" (column by Jeannie Williams), *USA Today,* October 26, 1989.

26   Re the "takeover frenzy" of the 1980s, now in temporary remission, see "The World Catches Takeover Fever," *New York Times,* May 21, 1989, and "Attack on Corporate Europe," *The Times* (London), October 1, 1989. See also [73] and [127].

27   Smokestack moguls: "America's Sixty Families," *New Republic,* November 17, 1937. Contrast them with "The Forbes Four Hundred," by Harold Seneker, et al., *Forbes,* October 23, 1989.

27   Labor unions and business takeovers: "Move Over Boone, Carl, and IRV—Here Comes Labor," *Business Week,* December 14, 1987.

28–29   Re Gilded Age: [539] pp. 34–37, 50–51; also [537] pp. 70–71, 164–167, 170–171; [588] pp. 10–11; and [206] p. 64.

29   Weingarten quote: interview with author.

29   For Iacocca's feud see his mega-best-seller published by Bantam in 1984.

29   Ross Perot and GM: [123] pp. 280–289.

30   On the Italian battle between old and new money power, and the role of Carlo de Benedetti, Gianni Agnelli, and Enrico Cuccia: "The Last Emperor," *Euromoney,* October 1988. Also [95] throughout.

30   For French and German cross-border acquisitions, see "Europe's Buyout Bulge," *New York Times,* November 6, 1989. Also interview with Philippe Adhemar, Financial Minister, the French Embassy, Washington, D.C.

30   The Spanish melo-farce is reported in "A Success Story Turns Sour," *Financial Times,* February 25/26, 1989.

33   The consultant's tale is from [64] pp. 3–7.

CHAPTER 4   FORCE: THE YAKUZA COMPONENT

37   Selyunin is quoted in "Lenin Faulted on State Terror, and a Soviet Taboo Is Broken," *New York Times,* June 8, 1988.

37–38   Some accounts of labor violence in the United States will be found in [108] pp. 212–213; [122] pp. 7 and 55–63.

38   "Violence at Motorola in Korea," *Financial Times,* December 31, 1988.

38   "Firms Gang Up to Quiet Stockholder Meeting Louts," *Japan Economic Journal,* July 2, 1988; also, "Japan's Sokaiya Fail to Trap Juiciest Prey," *Financial Times,* June 27, 1989.

38–39   "Japanese Fund Manager Found Buried in Concrete," *Financial Times,* October 19, 1988.

39   Re strongarm tactics in Japanese real estate: "Shadow Syndicate," by Kai Herrman, *20/20* (London), February 1990; and "No Vacancy: Soaring Land Prices in Japan Slam Door on Housing Market," *Wall Street Journal,* October 13, 1987.

39   U.S. lawyer with baseball bat: "Nippon Steal," by Eamonn Fingleton, *Euromoney,* October 1988.

39   "Snakes Alive in Korean Cinemas," *Financial Times,* October 5, 1989.

39   Re loan sharks: [313] pp. 167–168.

39   "Silkwood: The Story Behind the Story," *New Statesman,* May 4, 1984.

41   De Gaulle is quoted in [546] p. 31.

41   Japan's Recruit scandal summarized: "Takeshita Hears the Thud of the Axes," *Economist,* February 18, 1989, and "Will the Recruit Scandal Just Go Away?" *Business Week,* June 12, 1989.

41–42   German scandal: "A Deadly Game of Dirty Tricks," *Newsweek,* October 26, 1987. Also, "A Pair of Bad Smells," *Economist,* October 17, 1987.

42   For pachinko politics: "A Pinball Bribery Scandal Rocks 2 Japanese Political Parties," *New York Times,* October 13, 1989; "Pinball Scandal Threatens Political Upsets in Japan," *Financial Times,* October 12, 1989.

CHAPTER 5 WEALTH: MORGAN, MILKEN . . . AND AFTER

45–46   For Morgan, see [544] pp. 12, 49, 176–177, 191, 213–214, 236–240, 255–258, 354, 396, 403. Also, [106] pp. 13, 82, 98–99, 114, 125–127, 173, 312, front matter and Postscript; and [84] p. 99; also [541].

46–47   For Milken, Connie Bruck's *The Predator's Ball* [83] is a scathing portrait of Milken and the high-yield or junk bond business he created, but by no means adequate analytically. The simplest and most balanced short explanation of the Milken junk bond phenomenon is "Bearing Down on Milken," by David Frum, *National Review*, March 19, 1990; other important sources include "How Mike Milken Made a Billion Dollars and Changed the Face of American Capitalism," by Edward Jay Epstein, *Manhattan, inc.*, September 1987. See also [92] pp. 14–17, 232–233, 236–238; "A Chat With Michael Milken," by Allan Sloan, *Forbes*, July 13, 1987; "Milken's Salary Is One for Record Books," *Wall Street Journal/Europe*, April 3, 1989; "Lynch Law," by Andrew Marton, *Regardie's*, March 1990; and "Caught Up in a Morality Tale," by Richard Starr, *Insight*, March 5, 1990.

47   Early history of Drexel: [589] pp. 124–125.

48   Milken's involvement with trade unions: "Move Over Boone, Carl, and IRV—Here Comes Labor," *Business Week*, December 14, 1987; also "The Mercenary Messiah Strikes Again," by Mark Feinberg, *In These Times*, June 7–20, 1989.

49   U.S. shift to service-information economy: "A New Revolution in the U.S. 'Class Structure' and Labor Force," *Fortune*, April 1958.

49–50   Structural impact of Milken: "How Milken Machine Financed Companies, Takeover Raids," *Los Angeles Times*, March 30, 1989; also "High-Stakes Drama at Revlon," *New York Times*, November 11, 1985; "A Chat with Michael Milken," by Allan Sloan, *Forbes*, July 13, 1987; and "'Junk Bond' Genius Inspires Loyalty From Some, Hostility From Others," *Los Angeles Times*, March 30, 1989.

51   Milken's indictment: "'Junk Bond' King Milken Indicted for Stock Fraud," *Los Angeles Times*, March 30, 1989; also "Predator's Fall," *Time*, February 26, 1990, on the collapse of Drexel; "Lynch Law," by Andrew Marton, *Regardie's*, March 1990.

51–52   Re battle to restrict or relax credit, see "Junk Bonds—A Positive Force in the Market," *New York Times*, November 23, 1987.

52   On Milken's democratizing capital: [83] p. 350.

52   Re breaking up rather than agglomerating: author interview with Milken; also with Dean Kehler, Managing Director,

Investment and Banking, of now-defunct Drexel Burnham Lambert. See also "The New Buy-Out Binge," *Newsweek*, August 24, 1987.

53   For remark about "information age," see "A Chat With Michael Milken," by Allan Sloan, *Forbes*, July 13, 1987. Also Milken and Kehler interviews with author.

55   Salomon's agonies: [92] pp. 351 and 356–359.

55–56   The savings and loan mess: "Can the Thrifts be Salvaged?" *Newsweek*, August 21, 1989; "Up to $100 Billion Extra Sought for S&L Rescues," *Los Angeles Times*, November 1, 1989.

56   Re foreign exchange trading: "What Moves Exchange Rates," a brilliant analysis by Kenichi Ohmae in *Japan Times*, July 29, 1987.

57   The power of central banks: "Concept of a Central Bank Gains Support in Europe," *New York Times*, June 13, 1989.

CHAPTER 6 KNOWLEDGE: A WEALTH OF SYMBOLS

63   Re early money: [536] pp. 442–443; also [141] p. 3.

On money and desire: Money is ordinarily seen as a way to fulfill need or desire. But money has also been the great liberator of desire.

In pre-money cultures the person with a chicken to spare, and a desire for a blanket, first had to find someone who had a blanket and then, among all blanket owners, had to locate the one willing to take a chicken in exchange. Desires had to match.

The invention of money changed all that. Because it is fungible, and can be converted into a virtually unlimited number of satisfactions, money unleashed the acquisitive imagination. Those who had it suddenly developed desires they never knew they had. Previously unimagined and even unimaginable possibilities suddenly loomed before one's eyes. Money fed the imaginative spirit of the human species.

Money also encouraged clever men and women to identify the desires of others, whether coarse or overrefined, and to package for sale the things, services, and experiences that would fulfill them. This made money convertible into a still wider range of desirables and therefore, in turn, made it even more useful than before. (This self-reinforcing process, once unleashed, is like a chain reaction, and explains how money became so important in human social development.)

The original invention of money also greatly increased the efficiency of wealth as a tool of power. It strengthened the hand of the rich by radically simplifying control of behavior. Thus money made it possible to reward (and punish) people without even bothering to inquire into their desires, so that a factory owner didn't need to know if the worker desired a blanket, a chicken, or a Cadillac. It didn't matter; sufficient money could buy all or any of them.

In agrarian civilizations, apart from the wealthy—whose desires ran the range from exquisitely aesthetic to perversely sensual, from metaphysical to militaristic—the range of collective desires was so small and cramped it could be summed up in two words: bread (or rice) and land.

By contrast, in smokestack societies, once the basic needs of the population were met, collective desires seemed to multiply. Desire exploded out of its ghetto and colonized new regions, as a relentless progression turned the luxuries of one generation into the "necessities" of the next.

This expansion of desire was just as evident in supposedly anti-acquisitive socialist societies as it was in the openly acquisitive capitalist nations. It was, and continues to be, the basis for the mass consumer society. And it explains why, in the industrial world, the paycheck became the most basic tool of social control.

Today, the structure of desire is in upheaval. As we move beyond smokestack culture we see not the limitation of desire, but its further extension into new, more rarefied, increasingly nonmaterial regions, along with its growing individualization.

63	For William Potter: [6] p. 154
63	On paper money: [96] p. 51.
64	Visa data from company.
64	"Smart Cards: Pocket Power," *Newsweek*, July 31, 1989; also *Economist*, April 30, 1988.
64	French work on smart cards: "A New Technology Emerges on the World Stage," *French Advances in Science and Technology* (newsletter), Summer 1986; also "Bull's Smart Cards Come Up Trumps," *Financial Times*, September 30, 1987.
64	61 million: "Smart Cards: Pocket Power," *Newsweek*, July 31, 1989.
65	NTT cards: "Putting Smart Money On Smart Cards," *Economist*, August 27, 1988.
65	U.S. Department of Agriculture project: "Smart Cards: Pocket Power," *Newsweek*, July 31, 1989.

65–66   Schools: "Debit Cards for Pupils to Use in Cafeterias," by Susan Dillingham, *Insight,* August 21, 1989.

66   Joseph Wright quote: "U.S. Plans Wide Use of Credit Cards," *New York Times,* March 1, 1989.

67   Hock quote: from interview with author.

67   Loss of central bank control: "Designer Currency Dangers," by David Kilburn, *Business Tokyo,* May 1988.

67   Plastic money in South Korea: "A State of Siege for Corporate Korea," by Michael Berger, *Billion Magazine* (Hong Kong), September 1989.

CHAPTER 7   MATERIAL-ISMO!

70   U.S. agricultural work force: *Statistical Abstract of the United States 1989* (U.S. Department of Commerce), p. 376.

70   U.S. manufacturing work force: "Flat Manufacturing Employment for 1990's," by Michael K. Evans and R. D. Norton, *Industry Week,* October 2, 1989; also "The Myth of U.S. Manufacturing," *Los Angeles Times,* October 22, 1989.

70   On xenophobic economics: "America's Destiny Is in Danger," by June-Collier Mason, *Industry Week,* June 6, 1988.

71   U.S. service work force: "End Sought to Barriers to Trade in Services," *New York Times,* October 25, 1989.

71   "Exports of Services Increase to $560 bn," *Financial Times,* September 15, 1989.

75   Expert systems and CD-ROM: "HP and Ford Motors," by John Markoff, *Windows,* vol. 1, no. 1, Fall 1987.

76   CSX: interview with Alex Mandl, Chairman, Sea-Land Service, Inc.

77   Intelligence level in different corporations: personal communication from Dr. Donald F. Klein.

78   GenCorp data: "The (New) Flat Earth Society Gathers in Shelbyville," by Brian S. Moskal, *Industry Week,* October 2, 1989.

80   Re Soviet planner mentality in West: "Is There a British Miracle?" *Financial Times,* June 16, 1988.

80   For Giarini, see [100] throughout; for Loebl, [125]; for Woo, [167]. Weisskopf's views are in Walter A. Weisskopf, "Reflections on Uncertainty in Economics," *The Geneva Papers,* vol. 9, no. 33, October 1984.

81   On Prométhée: "From Trade to Global Wealth Creation," Thinknet Commission special issue, *Project Prométhée Perspectives,* No. 4, Paris, December 1987.

CHAPTER 8   THE ULTIMATE SUBSTITUTE

84   Literacy and numeracy: [480] pp. 282–283, and 338; also "Capitalism Plus Math: It All Adds Up," *Los Angeles Times,* May 13, 1989.

86   On short-run production: "Manufacturing: The New Case for Vertical Integration," by Ted Kumpe and Piet T. Bolwijn, *Harvard Business Review,* March-April 1988. Also, "Kicking Down the Debt," *Time,* November 7, 1988, and "Customized Goods Aim at Mass Market," *Japan Economic Journal,* October 1, 1988.

87   Re new materials: "Materials Battle Heats Up," by Thomas M. Rohan, *Industry Week,* October 2, 1989; "Plastics and Ceramics Replace Steel as the Sinews of War," *New York Times,* July 18, 1989; and "Project Forecast II" in *Assault Systems,* vol 1, no. 1.

87   Superconductivity: [518] pp. 166–173.

88   Re GE: "Electronic Data Exchange: A Leap of Faith," by Neal E. Boudette, *Industry Week,* August 7, 1989.

88   1.3 trillion documents: "Throwing Away the Paper-Based System," *Financial Times,* April 26, 1989.

89   Merloni material: interview with author.

89–90   Textile and apparel industries: "EDI, Barcoding Seen the Way to Save Millions," *Daily News Record,* March 11, 1987.

90   NHK Spring Company: "Just in Time Computers," by Peter Fuchs, et al., *Business Tokyo,* May 1988.

90   Merloni on funds transfer and telecommunications: interview with author.

90   Author interview with Michael Milken.

CHAPTER 9   THE CHECKOUT BATTLE

96   For Bic-Gillette rivalry: author interviews with Tom Johnson, Director of Research, Nolan Norton & Co., consultants; Gillette Company Annual Report 1988; and [136] pp. 69–73.

96–97   On Gillette marketing: Johnson interviews; and "Marketing's New Look," *Business Week,* January 26, 1987.

98   Introduction of retail bar coding: author interview with Harold Juckett, Executive Director, Uniform Code Council, Inc. Also "UPC History," document supplied by Uniform Code Council.

98–99   International data on bar coding: mainly drawn from International Article Numbering Association.

99   Battle for retail shelf space: "Supermarkets Demand Food Firms' Payments Just to Get on the Shelf," *Wall Street Journal*, November 1, 1988; "Want Shelf Space at the Supermarket? Ante Up," *Business Week*, August 7, 1989; and "Stores Often Paid to Stock New Items," *USA Today*, August 26, 1987.

99   Gillette: Kavin W. Moody, Corporate Director, Management Information Systems, Gillette Company, interview.

99–100   Retail computer models: interviews with Tom Johnson, Director of Research, Nolan Norton & Co.; also "At Today's Supermarket, the Computer Is Doing It All," *Business Week*, August 11, 1986.

100   Plan-a-Grams: "At Today's Supermarket, the Computer Is Doing It All," *Business Week*, August 11, 1986.

100   Re Toys "R" Us: "Stores Rush to Automate for the Holidays," *New York Times*, November 28, 1987.

100–01   Wal-Mart policies: Tom Johnson interviews; also "Make That Sale, Mr. Sam," *Time*, May 18, 1987.

102   Interview with Max Hopper, Senior Vice-President, American Airlines; also [112] pp. 4–5.

103   Marui reference is drawn from [163]—i.e., "Automating Distribution: Revolution in Distribution, Retailing and Financial Services," the best, most definitive English-language report on Japanese developments in these related fields, prepared by Alex Stewart for Baring Securities Ltd., London, 1987.

104   Electronic shelves: Tom Johnson interviews; also "At Today's Supermarket, the Computer Is Doing It All," *Business Week*, August 11, 1986, and "Electronic Prices," by George Nobbe, *Omni*, November 1987.

104   Smarter shelves: Tom Johnson interviews.

105   Retailers dominant: [163].

105   Retailing as information process: "Small Stores and Those Who Service Them in Times of Structural Change," *Japan Times*, July 13, 1987.

CHAPTER 10 EXTRA-INTELLIGENCE

107   Morse material from [585] pp. 102–103.

108   Re McDonald's ISDN network, see AT&T advertisement, *Datamation*, October 1, 1987. Volvo net described in same issue.

108   Du Pont and Sara Lee: "When Strategy Meets Technology," by Therese R. Welter, *Industry Week*, December 14, 1987.

108   Figures on PCs from International Data Corporation, which defines *personal computer* to include everything that runs MS-DOS, from low-end hobby units to workstations.

109   Western Union's early days: [494]; also [585] p. 108.

109   Western Union versus AT&T: [494] pp. 34–35.

111   U.S. share of telephones: Anthony Rutkowski, Senior Counsel, International Telecommunications Union (Geneva); also "Rewiring the World," *Economist*, October 17, 1987.

111–12   Re telephone company breakup: [164] p. xxii–xxiii.

114   Neural networks: "Government Researchers Work to Nail Down Building Blocks for Neural Networks," *Defense News*, January 11, 1988.

115   Re Minitel: See *Teletel Newsletter* #5 (1989 Facts and Figures), France Telecom (Paris); and *Teletel Newsletter* #2 (International); "France Hooked on Minitel," *Financial Times*, December 13, 1989. Also, interviews with Manuel Barbero, France Telecom International (New York); Olivier Duval, Études Systèmes et Logiciels (Paris); and [501] throughout.

117   Sabre System: interview with Max Hopper, Senior Vice-President, American Airlines.

117   Numbers of Value Added Networks: "Rewiring the World," *Economist*, October 17, 1987; "Competition Endangering Small VAN Operators," *Japan Economic Journal*, April 2, 1988.

CHAPTER 11 NET POWER

119   Nippon Life: "Networking Global Finance," *Business Tokyo*, May 1988; also, "Japanese Networks Expand After Deregulation," by Robert Poe, *Datamation*, November 1, 1987.

119–20   Re Dai Ichi and Meiji Insurance: "Japanese Networks Expand After Deregulation," by Robert Poe, *Datamation*, November 1, 1987.

120   Burlington Industries: [505] p. 49.

121   Auto industry networks: "Electronic Data Interchange: A Leap of Faith," by Neal E. Boudette, *Industry Week*, August 7, 1989; and "Auto ID & EDI: Managing in the 90's," *Industry Week*, August 24, 1989.

121   Shiseido's electronic networks: [163] p. 10.

121–22   Effects on wholesalers: interview with Monroe Greenstein, Bear, Stearns and Co., Inc. (New York), and [163] pp. 10–13.

122   Hospital and drugstore networks: "Origin of the Species," by P. Gralla, *CIO* magazine. January/February 1988; also [112] pp. 46–49.

123   Japanese warehousing: [163] pp. 9, 12, 13, and 23.

124   Petroleum industry network: "MITI to Establish Oil Information Network," *Japan Economic Journal*, December 26, 1987.

124   Wool industry networks: "Woolcom Move in Paperless Trading 'Predatory Pricing' " and "Push for Closer Links," *Financial Review* (Sydney), September 4, 1989.

124–25   U.S. textile and apparel industries: "Spreading the Bar Code Gospel," *Women's Wear Daily*, September 1986; "Auto ID & EDI: Managing in the 90's," *Industry Week*, August 24, 1989; "Apparel Makers Shift Tactics," *New York Times*, September 21, 1987.

125   Battle between AT&T, KDD, and British Telecom: "A Scramble for Global Networks," *Business Week*, March 21, 1988.

125   GE's electronic services: "Messenger of the Gods," by Alyssa A. Lappen, *Forbes*, March 21, 1988. Also, "Fast Forward," by Curtis Bill Pepper, *Business Month*, February 1989.

126   Hairdresser credit card: "NTT Data to Provide Telecom VAN Service," *Japan Economic Journal*, April 1, 1989.

127   Merrill Lynch Cash Management Account: [112] p. 97.

127–28   Seibu cash dispensers: [163] p. 75.

125–28   British Petroleum: [112] p. 92.

CHAPTER 12   THE WIDENING WAR

131   High definition TV: "Consortium Set Up for New TV," *New York Times*, January 26, 1990; "Japan Tunes In While Europe Talks," *Financial Times*, April 21, 1988.

131   Levine quote: "Networks Urge Slow Shift to Sharper TV Picture System," *Los Angeles Times*, June 24, 1988.

132   European views on HDTV: "La guerre des normes," *Le Monde Diplomatique* (Paris), September 1987; and "TV Makers Take on Japanese," *Financial Times*, January 27, 1988. See also "High-Definition War," by John Boyd, *Business Tokyo*, May 1988.

132   A key roundup on the technical aspects of the HDTV contest: "Chasing Japan in the HDTV Race," by Ronald K. Jurgen, *IEEE Spectrum*, October 1989. See also "A Television System for Tomorrow," *French Advances in Technology and Science*, Winter 1987.

132   Europeans court U.S. for alliance against Japanese standards: "Bonn Calls for Joint US-Europe Effort in TV Technology Race," *Financial Times*, May 16, 1989.

132   Re different models around the world: "Firms Are Ready to Meet Any HDTV Format," *Japan Economic Journal*, October 22, 1988; and "Japan Tunes In While Europe Talks," *Financial Times*, April 21, 1988.

133   Markey quote: "Networks Urge Slow Shift to Sharper TV Picture System," *Los Angeles Times*, June 24, 1988.

133   IBM's early ability to impose order on the computer industry: "Living With Computer Anarchy," by Nawa Kotaro, *Japan Echo* (Tokyo), (special issue, 1986.)

134   Re Ada software standards: See issues of *Defense Science*.

134–35   On UNIX battle: "Computer Standards Row May Be Costly for Makers and Users," *Financial Times*, January 23, 1989; "Hopes Rise for World Computer Standard," *Financial Times*, July 12, 1988; "Standards by Fiat," by Esther Dyson, *Forbes*, July 11, 1988; and "Apollo Aims for Eclipse of the Sun," *Financial Times*, July 12, 1988. Also, "OSF à la vitesse Mach," by Patrice Aron and Guy Hervier, *01 Informatique* (Paris), November 24, 1989.

135   Open Software Foundation: "OSF à la vitesse Mach," by Patrice Aron and Guy Hervier, *01 Informatique* (Paris), November 24, 1989; "Computer Gangs Stake out Turf," *New York Times*, December 13, 1988; "Apollo Aims for

Eclipse of the Sun," *Financial Times,* July 12, 1988, and "Standards by Fiat," by Esther Dyson, *Forbes,* July 11, 1988. Also, "The Power and Potential of Computing Standards," *Financial Times,* May 26, 1988.

136   GM's standards battle: "Manufacturing Automation's Problem," by Parker Hodges, *Datamation,* November 15, 1989.

136–37   IBM's standards for computer-to-computer communication: "Japan Shifts on Computer Networks," *New York Times,* October 22, 1988; "IBM Europe Backs a Computer Language Pushed by Its Rivals," *Wall Street Journal,* May 2, 1986.

137   Open System Interconnection fight: "IBM Europe Backs a Computer Language Pushed by Its Rivals," *Wall Street Journal,* May 2, 1986; "Informatique: IBM en échec," *Le Monde Diplomatique* (Paris), September 1987.

137   U.S. protests European standards: interview with Donald S. Abelson, Director, Technical Trade Barriers, Office of the U.S. Trade Representative; also, his remarks on "The U.S. Government's View of Standards Trade Policy" before the General Assembly of the Association Française de Normalisation (AFNOR) (Paris), April 24, 1986.

139   Standards as trade barriers: "West Germany Climbs Down Over Purity of Sausages," *Financial Times,* January 18, 1988; see also Abelson speech cited above.

140   Messine's thoughtful article: "Au coeur des stratégies industrielles," *Le Monde Diplomatique* (Paris), September 1987.

CHAPTER 13   THE EXECUTIVE THOUGHT POLICE

141   Characteristics of corporate "chief information officers" drawn from survey reported in "CIOs in the Spotlight," by Lew McCreary, *CIO,* September 1989.

141   Ryan, Schefer, and Johnson: "Migration Path," by Kathleen Melymuka, *CIO,* September 1989.

142   Sales of information technology: "Charting the Champs," by Parker Hodges; and "At the Top of the IS Peak," *Datamation,* June 15, 1988.

143–45   Merrill conflict: interview with Gerald H. Ely, Vice-President, Merrill Lynch Capital Markets.

145–46   Re Bank of America: "BankAmerica Is Computing More Trouble," *American Banker,* July 16, 1987; "Bank of America's Plans for Computer Don't Add Up," *Los Angeles Times*, February 7, 1988; and "BankAmerica Asks 2 Officials to Quit, Sources Assert," *Wall Street Journal*, October 22, 1987.

148   "Worlds more to lose": Harry B. DeMaio, senior manager, Deloitte & Touche, quoted in "Security, Meet Reality," by Meghan O'Leary, *CIO* magazine, September 1989.

149   Re computer downsizing: Klein quoted from "Honey, I Shrunk the Mainframe!" by Kathleen Melymuka, *CIO* magazine, September 1989.

149   Gassman quoted from "The Politics of Network Management," by Susan Kerr, *Datamation*, September 15, 1988.

CHAPTER 14   TOTAL INFORMATION WAR

153–54 Espionage at Texas Instrument: "The Case of the Terminal Secrets," by Skip Hollandsworth, *D* magazine, November 1986.

154   Hollstein: "Telecommunications Crime," by Nat Weber, *Across the Board*, February 1986.

155   "Designing a chip . . .": [409] p. 50.

155   Xerox: "Corporate Spies Snoop to Conquer," by Brian Dumaine, *Fortune*, November 7, 1988.

155   Service products: "Reverse Engineering a Service Product," by Robert E. Schmidt, Jr., *Planning Review*, September/ October 1987.

156   On full-time sleuths: "George Smiley Joins the Firm," *Newsweek*, May 2, 1988.

156   Society of Competitor Intelligence Professionals: "Intelligence Experts for Corporations," *New York Times*, September 27, 1988.

156   Marriott's spies: "Corporate Spies Snoop to Conquer," by Brian Dumaine, *Fortune*, November 7, 1988.

156   Sheller-Globe case: "Demystifying Competitive Analysis," by Daniel C. Smith and John E. Prescott, *Planning Review*, September/ October 1987.

156–57 Defense contracting scandals: "Pentagon Fraud Inquiry: What Is Known to Date," *New York Times*, July 7, 1988; also, "Pentagon Halts Pay on $1 Billion in Contracts," *Los Angeles Times*, July 2, 1988; and "The Pentagon Up for Sale," *Time*, June 27, 1988.

157   "Anything goes" attitude: "Never Mind MIS; Consider MI5," by L.B.C., *Business Month*, February 1989.

159   GE: "Keeping Tabs on Competitors," *New York Times,* October 28, 1985.

160   On West German computer spies: "Byteman Blows the Whistle on the Sysop Cops," *Los Angeles Times Book Review,* November 19, 1989. Also "The Quest for Intruder-Proof Computer Systems," by Karen Fitzgerald, *IEEE Spectrum,* August 1989.

161   Fake orders into rival firm's computers: "Computer Crime Patterns: The Last 20 Years (1990–2010)," by Joseph F. Coates, *Datamation,* September 15, 1987.

161–62 Counterintelligence technologies: "The Quest for Intruder-Proof Computer Systems," by Karen Fitzgerald, *IEEE Spectrum,* August 1989.

CHAPTER 15   THE CUBBYHOLE CRASH

166   Toshiba's "underground research" and Tandem: "Firms Try to Make Corporate Structure Flexible," *Japan Economic Journal,* February 27, 1988.

167   On Pentagon incomprehensibility: "Entities of Democracy" (excerpts from a speech by Secretary of the Navy John F. Lehman, Jr., to the Sea-Air-Space Exposition banquet in Washington, D.C., April 3, 1985), *New York Times,* April 6, 1985.

168–69 Bhopal disaster: "Bhopal: A Tragedy in Waiting," by Gary Stix, *IEEE Spectrum,* June 1989.

169   Poisoned chocolate: "Candy with a Deadly Taste," by Peter McGill, *MacLean's* (Toronto), October 22, 1984.

169   1989 stock market crash: "The Dow Plunges 190 Points, About 7%, in a Late Selloff; Takeover Stocks Hit Hard," *New York Times,* October 14, 1989.

175   Non-hierarchical data: "Firms Seek to Gain Edge with Swift Grip on Data," by Ivy Schmerken, *Wall Street Computer Review,* July 1987.

175–76 Hyper-media: interview with Bill Atkinson, HyperCard creator. Also "A Conversation with Bill Atkinson" in [493] pp. xxi–xxxii, and pp. 1–14.

CHAPTER 16   THE FLEX-FIRM

180   Italian "miracle": "A Pattern of 'Putting Out,' " *Financial Times,* March 7, 1989, and "In Italy, an Industrial Renaissance Thrives," *Christian Science Monitor,* April 7, 1987.

180–81   New interest in family firms: "Family Business: A Hot Market," by Sharon Nelton, *Nation's Business,* September 1988. For alternative view: "The Decline of the Family Empire," *World Executive Digest* (Hong Kong), July 1987.

181   EC attitude: "Small Is No Longer Beautiful When It's Alone," *Financial Times,* July 4, 1988.

181   Dynamism of small firms: "Is Your Company Too Big?" *Business Week,* March 27, 1989. An example of how new technology helps in "The Fewer Engineers per Project, the Better," *IEEE Spectrum,* by C. Gordon Bell, February 1989.

181   Povejsil quote: "Corporate Strategy for the 1990's," by Walter Kiechel III, *Fortune,* February 29, 1988.

183   The media discover the flexible firm: "A Glimpse of the 'Flex' Future," *Newsweek,* August 1, 1988.

185   Birth and death life-cycles in business: "Changing Corporate Behavior: 1, Diversification," *Japan Economic Journal,* Summer 1988.

187   Hewlett-Packard's Jepson: "At Seatrain, the Buck Stops Here . . . and Here, Too," by William H. Miller, *Industry Week,* March 7, 1988.

189   Saeed's comment on the relationship of business organization to family life is from his thought-provoking book, [151] p. 53.

CHAPTER 17   TRIBAL CHIEFS AND CORPORATE COMMISSARS

191   Census as "pulsator": interview with Maury Cagle, U.S. Bureau of the Census; and "Census Bureau Scrambling to Fill Jobs Here," by Adam Lashinsky, *Crain's Chicago Business,* March 19, 1990.

192–93   SAS example from [279] p. 24.

193   David Stirling on the four-man module: [267] pp. 2–3 and 7–8.

193   Southern California Edison: "Information Systems for Crisis Management," by Thomas J. Housel, Omar A. El Sawy, and Paul F. Donovan, *MIS Quarterly,* vol. 10, no. 4, December 1986.

194   Continental Illinois and A. H. Robins: [132] pp. 22 and 33.

194   Checkerboard organization in Austria: "Austria's Jobs Carve-Up Keeps Bank Post Vacant," *Financial Times,* July 7, 1988.

196–97   Re "skunkworks": "The New Product Development Game," by Hirotaka Takeuchi and Ikujiro Nonaka, *Harvard Business Review,* January/February 1986.

198   Self-start teams: Interview with David Stone, Digital Equipment Corporation (Geneva).

201   Corning, Inc.: "The Age of the Hierarchy Is Over," *New York Times,* September 24, 1989.

201–02   Key thinking on networks: "The Network Alternative," proposal developed by Anthony J. N. Judge of the Union of International Associations (Brussels). Judge's matrix, showing international networks on one axis and global problems on the other, is found in *Yearbook of World Problems and Human Potential,* published by the above organization in 1976.

202   Re NETMAP: "A Business Profile," NETMAP brochure, and "Corporations Reshaped by the Computer," *New York Times,* January 7, 1987; also, remarks of Les Berkes, NETMAP vice-president at Nolan & Norton seminar, November 20, 1987, New York.

CHAPTER 18   THE AUTONOMOUS EMPLOYEE

205   General Electric plant: "Smart Machines, Smart Workers," *New York Times,* October 17, 1988.

205–206   Ford Australia: "Bringing More Brain Power to Bear," *Financial Times,* March 23, 1988.

206   Chrysler-Mitsubishi and Mazda: "How Does Japan Inc. Pick Its American Workers?" *Business Week,* October 3, 1988.

209   Misuse of computers: "Report Says Computers Spy On 7 Million Workers in U.S.," *New York Times,* September 28, 1988.

210   Re separation of thinking and doing: "Japanese Organizational Behavior" by Teruya Nagao, in [135] p. 34.

210–11   Hewitt quote from "Getting Set for Implementation," special CIM report, by Therese R. Welter, *Industry Week,* November 2, 1987.

211   Mohn quote from original English-language ms. of [134]. For European attitudes, see "La redécouverte du 'capital humain,' " *Le Monde* (Paris), October 5, 1988. Attitudes of young workers: "Jeunes: ce qu'ils croient," by Roselyne Bosch, *Le Point* (Paris), June 16, 1987, and "Families More Important," *Business Tokyo,* May 1988.

211–12   GenCorp Automotive: "The (New) Flat Earth Society Gathers in Shelbyville," by Brian Moskal, *Industry Week,* October 2, 1989.

212   Ware quote: from interview with author.

213   Stone quote: from interview with author.

214   Brother Industries: "Creativity in Japan: Some Initial Obser-
         vations," by Dr. Nigel Holden, *Creativity and Innovation,*
         April-June 1986.

215   On shop-floor power flowing downward: "Why Managers
         Resist Machines," *New York Times,* February 7, 1988. See
         also [169] throughout, for fine-grain study of complexities
         introduced by new computerized technology.

215   Human-relations model: "Japanese Organizational Behav-
         ior," by Teruya Nagao, in [135] p. 27.

CHAPTER 19   THE POWER-MOSAIC

218   Takeovers and mergers: [73] pp. 11–15.

222–23   On layoffs: "General Semantics as a Diagnostic Tool in the
         Management of Radical Workforce Reduction," by Harold
         Oaklander, at 50th Anniversary Conference, Institute of
         General Semantics, Yale University, July 28, 1988.

223   IBM PROFS system: IBM Public Relations (Armonk, N.Y.).

224   Vertical integration in oil industry: [101] pp. 3–7.

224   Vertical integration in steel industry: [44] pp. 114–115 and
         126–129.

224   Air freight operations: "Pan American World Airways to
         Contract Out All Belly Freight Space on Transcontinental
         Flights," *Journal of Commerce,* November 1, 1985.

224   Ford and GM outsourcing: "Original Auto Parts Will Grow
         2–3% . . ." *Metalworking News,* August 27, 1987.

224   AMA: "Vertical Integration of Multinationals Becomes Ob-
         solete," *Management Today,* June 1986.

225   IBM's chip manufacture: "How the Computer Companies Lost
         Their Memories," by George Gilder, *Forbes,* June 13, 1988.

225   M.I.T. study: "Electronic Markets and Electronic Hierarchies:
         Effects of Information Technology on Market Structures
         and Corporate Strategies," by Robert I. Benjamin, Thomas
         W. Malone, and Joanne Yates, Sloan School of Manage-
         ment, Massachusetts Institute of Technology, April 1986.

226   Small business in U.S.: "The Inc. 100," *Inc.* magazine, May
         1989.

226   On trilateral consortia: [322] p. 89.

226–27   Lamborghini, from his "Technological Change and Strategic
         Alliances" paper at International Management Institute/

European Foundation for Management Development conference, Brussels, June 4–5, 1987.

227   Atlanta airport data from "Hartsfield Atlanta International Airport Economic Impact Report," 1987, based on data prepared by Deloitte, Haskins & Sells and Martin, Murphy, Harps and Syphoe for City of Atlanta Department of Aviation. Also "Fact Sheet" of Airport Commissioner's Office.

228–29   Sculley quotes from [154] pp. 96–97.

229   Matsushita's relations with suppliers: "Manufacturing Innovations Save 'Shitauke,' " *Japan Economic Journal,* January 16, 1988.

230   Re VAX and Lotus users groups: "The Number of User Groups Is Adding Up," by Judith A. Finn, *Digital Review,* April 18, 1988.

230   IBM users: "Council Unites Top IBM User Groups," by Paul Tate, *Datamation,* September 15, 1987.

CODA   THE NEW SYSTEM FOR WEALTH CREATION

234   Two trillionths of a second: "New Chips Offer the Promise of Much Speedier Computers," *New York Times,* January 4, 1989.

236   On concurrent processing and simultaneous engineering: "Strategic Alliances Make Marketing & Manufacturing an International Game," by George Weimer, et al., *Industry Week,* November 21, 1988 ("Integrated Manufacturing" section).

236   On just-in-time: "Added Value Emanating from Acronyms," *Financial Times,* December 13, 1989.

237   Motorola's Team Bandit: "State-of-the-Art CIM in 18 Months?" by John H. Sheridan, *Industry Week,* December 5, 1988.

237–38   Japanese auto industry advantage: "Time—The Next Source of Competitive Advantage," by George Stalk, Jr., *Harvard Business Review,* July-August 1988.

237–38   Re Toyota and bank speedup: "Fast-Cycle Capability for Competitive Power," by Joseph L. Bower and Thomas M. Hout, *Harvard Business Review,* November-December 1988.

CHAPTER 20   THE DECISIVE DECADES

Governments have always manipulated information and knowledge. They have used many different tactics for inducing or compelling consent. Today, as computers and the media proliferate, the tools of control (and of popular resistance) are multiplying and becoming more subtle. To place this political development in perspective, it helps to look into the history of the state.

While certain tribal groups like the Ifugao of the Philippines, or the Nuer and Kung! Bushmen of Africa may have survived without any semblance of a state, today virtually every human on the planet is a citizen—or more bluntly a subject—of one state or another. And the state is commonly regarded as the most powerful of all social institutions.

Theories of the state abound. Alexander Rustow, the German economist, has maintained that the state arose out of the "higher hunting cultures, with their chieftancy and their strict organization for the chase and war." The historian Karl Wittfogel speculated that the need for large irrigation projects, which in turn required the mobilization and control of large masses of workers, led to the highly organized state. According to Engels's theory, elaborated in Lenin's *State and Revolution,* the state arose when people were first divided into classes. The state was an instrument used by one class to oppress another. For Marxists, therefore, the state is the "executive arm" of a ruling class.

Whatever theory one chooses to believe, it seems reasonable that a key political turning point was reached when tribal or village groups first passed the economic subsistence point. Once a community could produce and store a food surplus, some defense was needed to protect it against outside raiders and from those within the community who might try to grab it for their own use.

The first great powershift in history comes when the community chooses a "protector," usually male, from among its strongest members. It is easy to imagine this "strongman" demanding part of the community surplus in return for his protective services.

The next step in the formation of the state comes when the protector uses part of the wealth he has extracted from the population to "hire" warriors now directly beholden to him, not the community. The protector himself is now protected.

The second great powershift occurs when the task of extracting tribute or taxes is systematized, with "collectors" appointed to gather the wealth. This step, once taken, creates a self-reinforcing feedback and speeds things up, greatly increasing the power of the rulers and their supporters. The more wealth they can extract, the more soldiers they can afford, and the harder they can then squeeze the community for still more wealth.

With this added wealth, of course, the embryonic state moves to a new level. Its ruler now commands two of the three main tools of social control: violence and wealth, rather than just violence alone.

This means those in control no longer need to intimidate and dominate by force exclusively. They can now use part of the "take" extracted from the community to reward faithful followers and build political support. To the low-quality power based on violence, therefore, the ruling individual or clique now adds the far more versatile form of power based on wealth.

The next powershift occurs when clever rulers discover they can enhance their power, and actually reduce the cost of soldiers to protect them, if they can mind-wash their people. By seducing or terrorizing the population into believing an appropriate mythology, religion, or ideology, it becomes possible to persuade one's subjects that the existing power system is not only inevitable and permanent, but morally right and proper, if not actually divine. Used this way, knowledge —in the form of myth, religion, and ideology, truth as well as falsehood—becomes a key political weapon.

One might even argue that this is the moment at which the state is born—that, until this point, there are only embryonic, half-formed anticipations of the state. The state, in short, is not fully a state until it commands all three of the basic tools of social control: knowledge, as well as wealth and the potential for violence.

While this schematic is clearly speculative and grandly oversimplified, it provides a plausible explanation for the origin of the state and integrates it with the new theory of power.

246–47   Crupi quote from "Political Risk Begins at Home," *Across the Board,* January 1986.

247   Queen's worry: "Scottish Nationalism Threatens British Unity," *Los Angeles Times,* December 25, 1988.

247   Hapsburgs in Central Europe: [545] pp. 26, 27, and 422.

249   Tokyo earthquake impact: "The Japanese Earthquake Explained" (first published, September 1923), *Natural History,* April 1980; "When the Big One Hits Tokyo . . ." by Edith Terry, *World Press Review,* December 1989, and "How a Tokyo Earthquake Could Devastate Wall Street," by Michael Lewis, *Manhattan, inc.,* June 1989.

250   On growing interethnic battles in U.S.: "New Interethnic
        Conflict Replaces an L.A. History of Biracial Politics," *Los
        Angeles Times,* January 7, 1990; "Shake-Up at Latino Sta-
        tion Sparks Protest," *Los Angeles Times,* June 6, 1989; "Cu-
        bans, not Haitians, Offered Legal Status: Blacks 'Outraged,' "
        by Kathleen Kelly, *National Catholic Reporter,* February 24,
        1984; "Showdown on Middle Neck Road," by Robert Spero,
        Present Tense, May–June 1989; "Swapping Lessons," *Los
        Angeles Times,* January 11, 1990; "Rapping Solo," *Billboard,*
        January 13, 1990.
252   Hitler's first Nazi meeting: [580] p. 54.
252–53 On pivotal minorities: [103] see throughout, especially Chap-
        ter 12 on P-2 Lodge; also [95] p. 16; [165] pp. 3–4, and
        throughout, under "Gelli"; "The Roots of Kahanism," *Ha'am*
        newspaper, University of California at Los Angeles, January–
        February 1987; "Links of Anti-Semitic Band Provokes
        6-State Parley," *New York Times,* December 27, 1984; "Neo-
        Nazis Dream of Racist Territory," *New York Times,* July 5,
        1986; "The Charmer," *New York* magazine, October 7,
        1985; "Lyndon LaRouche: From Marxist Left to Well-
        Connected Right," by John Mintz, *Washington Post National
        Weekly,* February 25, 1985; "LaRouche Fringe Stirs in Ger-
        many," *New York Times,* June 30, 1986; [203] throughout.
253   On hate group proliferation: "Rioting in the Streets: Déjà
        Vu?" by William L. Tafoya, *C(riminal) J(ustice)—the Americas,*
        December 1989–January 1990.
254–55 Re the proliferation of "holy wars": "High-Intensity Aggres-
        sive Ideologies as an International Threat," by Yehezkel
        Dror, *Jerusalem Journal of International Relations,* vol. 9, no.
        1, 1987.

CHAPTER 21   THE INVISIBLE PARTY

256   Atwater's comment made to author.
256   Tsurumi article: "A Bureaucratic Hold on Japan," *Los Ange-
        les Times,* January 25, 1988.
257–58 Rival ministries in Tokyo: "Turf Battles and Telecom," by
        Kazuhisa Maeno, *Journal of Japanese Trade and Industry,* no.
        5, 1988. On intra-ministerial rivalries, see the unusually
        rich *Conflict in Japan* by Ellis S. Krauss, Thomas P. Rohlen,

and Patricia G. Steinhoff, eds. (Honolulu: University of Hawaii Press, 1984), p. 298.

258   Mexico privatization plans: "First State of the Nation Report," President Carlos Salinas de Gortari (Mexico City), November 1, 1989.

259   Mobil divestitures: "Integrated—and Determined to Stay That Way," by Toni Mack, *Forbes*, December 12, 1988, and "Less Is Less," *Forbes*, April 4, 1988.

259–60 Sabotage in Japan: "Paralysis on the Tracks," *Time*, December 9, 1985.

260   Privatization of NTT: "Hold the Phone," by Richard Phalon, *Forbes*, October 17, 1988; "Japan's Spending Spree," *World Press Review*, January 1990; see also, "Deregulation, Privatization Spur JAL to Diversify Operations," by James Ott and Eiichiro Sekigawa, *Aviation Week and Space Technology*, May 8, 1989.

260   Privatizations in many countries: "Can a Privatized Matra Do Better on Its Own?" by Jennifer L. Schenker, *Electronics*, February 18, 1988; "Why Bonn Just Can't Let Go," *Business Week*, April 4, 1988; "A Choice Menu from Jacques Chirac," by Michael McFadden, *Fortune*, January 5, 1987; "How Many Bureaucrats to Install a Phone?" by Richard C. Morais, *Forbes*, September 19, 1988; "Air Canada Comes of Age," *MacLean's* (Toronto), April 25, 1988.

261   Popkin on fewer hierarchies: [201] pp. 227–228.

263   Kohl ignores Foreign Ministry: "Ostpolitik Pays Belated Dividend for Germany's Elder Statesman," *Financial Times*, December 14, 1989.

CHAPTER 22   INFO-TACTICS

266   Johnson on freedom of information: [194] pp. 3–4.

266   20 million secret documents: "The Future of Intelligence," by Walter Laqueur, *Society*, November–December 1985.

266–67 CIA quote: [194] p. 24.

267   Recruit-Cosmos leaks: "Gentlemanly Press Gets Gloves Dirty," *Insight*, December 4, 1989.

267   Pattie quote from "Tory Thought Curbed by 'Fear of Leaks,'" *Times* (London), October 10, 1986.

267–68 Gergen on White House leaks: "Secrecy Means Big Things Get Little Thought," *Los Angeles Times*, November 27, 1986.

268   Kissinger role in telephone taps: [574] p. 388.

269   Vietnam report: [421] p. 6.

269   Re Zimmerman telegram: [397] p. 18.

270–71 Shultz-Kelly back-channel fight: "Shultz Calls Envoy Home, Saying He Dealt in Secret," *Los Angeles Times*, December 9, 1986; "Shultz Warning Envoys to Stop Bypassing Him," *New York Times*, December 18, 1986.

271   Kissinger-South Korea case is described in Seymour M. Hersh's critical volume *The Price of Power* (New York: Summit Books, 1983), pp. 42–43.

272   Kissinger-Dobrynin back-channel: [427] pp. 153 and 193.

272   Cuban missile back-channel: [407] pp. 146–147.

272–73 The Double-Channel Tactic: [427] p. 205.

275   Re Red Brigade case: [435] p. 129.

275   AIDS: See "Soviets, At Last, Face up to AIDS," *Los Angeles Times*, April 22, 1989; also "The KGB's New Muscle," *U.S. News and World Report*, September 15, 1986.

275   Reversal in Jerusalem: "Peres Office, in Israeli Infighting, Bars Shamir Message to Embassies," *New York Times*, January 15, 1987.

276   Churchill on authentic data: [398] p. 292.

CHAPTER 23   META-TACTICS

278   Sununu as computer-wise governor: "The Granite State of the Art," *Time*, January 27, 1986.

279   Computer-aided software engineering: "From CASE to Software Factories," by Herbert Weber, *Datamation*, April 1, 1989.

280   Profits like sausages and GM: "Cute Tricks on the Bottom Line," by Gary Hector, *Fortune*, April 24, 1989.

282   Mafia amputates finger: [485] p. 74.

282   U.S. Justice Department list of computer crimes: "Electronic Capers," by J. A. Tujo, *Information Executive*, vol. 2, no. 1, 1985.

283   Congressional letters vanish: "Two Cases of Computer Burglary," *New York Times*, March 21, 1986.

284   South Korean elections: "Observers Allege Computer Fraud in S. Korea Poll," *Financial Times*, December 21, 1987.

284–85 Election Watch case: "Electronic Elections Seen as Invitation to Fraud," *Los Angeles Times*, July 4, 1989.

286   Stockman: [227] p. 92.
286–87 Re Census: "Analyzing the Figures That Shape Our Daily Lives," by Richard Lipkin, *Insight,* May 22, 1989; "Political Power and Money at Stake in Census Undercount Fight," *Washington Post,* January 11, 1988; "False Signals on Inflation," *Newsweek,* July 28, 1986; "Measuring Money," by John Roberts, *National Westminster Moneycare* magazine (London), October–November 1986; also, author interview with Jack Keane, Director, U.S. Bureau of the Census, and staff.
289   Rona quote: "Spy Satellites: Entering a New Era," *Science,* March 24, 1989.
290   Inferencing capabilities and expert systems: "Car and Plane Makers Fuel Up with CAD, AI," and "Oil Companies Exploit as Much as Explore IS," both in *Datamation,* November 15, 1989. See also, "New Shells for Old Iron," by John J. Popolizio and William S. Cappelli, *Datamation,* April 15, 1989.
292   How models are used and misused: [463] pp. 9–10 and 31–32.
292   How many in poverty?: "Taking the Measure, or Mismeasure, of It All," *New York Times,* August 28, 1984.
292   Hot deck imputation: "Hide and Seek," *Atlantic,* December 1988.
292   Census lawsuit: "Accord on Census May Bring Change in Minority Data," *New York Times,* July 18, 1989.

CHAPTER 24   A MARKET FOR SPIES

296   Ancient Egyptian spies are cited in [403] p. 111.
296   Baden-Powell's butterflies: [394] pp. 7–8.
296   Captain Giichi Tanaka's tale is in [394] pp. 21–23.
296   Mass spying: [426] p. 83.
297   The use of "Rabcors" is described in [417] p. 6.
297   Richard Sorge's life story is told in [404] pp. 325–343.
298   The coverage provided by remote sensing systems: [399] p. xvi.
298   Listening to limos and Lop Nor: "Exit Smiley, Enter IBM," *The Sunday Times* (London), October 31, 1982.
300   U.S. intelligence "community": [424] and [422] throughout; [434] Chapters 1 and 2. Also, interview with Alfred Kingon, Kingon International, former White House Cabinet Secretary.
300   Re Soviet intelligence: [404] throughout; [434] Chapters 4 and 5; also, though somewhat dated, [425]. And [526] pp. 166–167 focuses on technological espionage.

300–01   French intelligence: [415] throughout; [434] Chapter 7; [423] Chapter 6.

301   German intelligence: "Smiley Without People: A Tale of Intelligence Misjudgments," *Der Tagesspiegel* (Berlin), January 6, 1990; also [434] pp. 3, 113, 127, 130, and 182; [423] pp. 127–147 and 254–257.

301   Japanese intelligence: [423] Chapter 8; see also [426] for history.

301   Trans-Siberian incident: [423] p. 255.

301–02   New Zealand's "ex-communication": "British Ban Kiwis From Intelligence Briefings," *The Sunday Times* (London), May 4, 1986.

302   The Harper espionage story is from [434] p. 165.

302–03   Argentina's dilemma: author's interviews, Buenos Aires.

303   East European collaboration with Moscow after ouster of Communist governments: "It's Still Business as Usual for Spies, Even as the Eastern Bloc Rises Up," *New York Times*, December 31, 1989.

303   U.S. intelligence to South Africa: "U.S. Is Said to Have Given Pretoria Intelligence on Rebel Organization," *New York Times*, July 23, 1986; also "Query on CIA Tie to Mandela Case Deflected," *Los Angeles Times*, June 13, 1990.

303   Australian aid to CIA in Chile: [402] pp. 24–25.

303   French-Portuguese and French-Moroccan collaboration: [415] pp. 79–80, 71–73.

303   Romanian-PLO collaboration: [416] pp. 13, 15–35, and 92–99.

303   Israeli collaboration with U.S.: [424] pp. 205–207.

303   U.S.-Soviet collaboration: "Ex-KGB Aides to Join U.S. Talks on Terrorism," *Los Angeles Times*, September 25, 1989.

304   Effect of intelligence swapping on civil liberties: [411] p. 373.

305   Iraqi warplane story: "The 300-Million-Dollar Disaster" in *The Voice of the Arab World* (London), undated; also [392] throughout.

305–06   NSA and GCHQ "watch lists": "Exit Smiley, Enter IBM," *The Sunday Times* (London), October 31, 1982.

306   Olmer quotes: interview with author.

308–09   Ceausescu's nuclear scam: [416] pp. 292–297.

309   One operation can pay the whole intelligence budget: [415] pp. 41–42.

309   KGB in Tokyo: [413] pp. 103–104.

309   Line X position in KGB Table of Organization: [434] p. 87.

310   On CoCom: "Appeal for CoCom Blacklist to be Overhauled," commentary, *Frankfurter Rundschau*, November 29, 1989 (translated in *The German Tribune*, December 10, 1989); "American Hypocrisy Highlighted in CoCom Rule Implementation," *Japan Economic Journal*, July 2, 1988; "A Challenge for High-Tech Censors," *Financial Times*, October 19, 1988; "U.S. Set to Ease European Defence Technology Curbs," *Financial Times*, January 29, 1988. And [526] p. 15.

311   Eco-war: "Turkey's Stranglehold on the Euphrates Irks Its Neighbours," *Financial Times*, January 3, 1990.

312   Bechtel-CIA relations: [130] p. 117.

312   200 U.S. spies under "business cover": "Business Pose by U.S. Spies Reported," *New York Times*, February 28, 1974.

312–13 Lack of U.S. pressure on citizens to spy: [434] p. 49.

315   Five nations: author interview with Kevin Corbley, Media Coordinator, EOSAT (Earth Observation Satellite Company).

315   Landsat and SPOT satellites: "Space Cameras and Security Risks," by David Dickson, *Science*, January 27, 1989; "Civilians Use Satellite Photos for Spying on Soviet Military," *New York Times*, April 7, 1986. Corbley interview. *Spotlight*, vol. 3, no. 2, June 1989 (SPOT Image Corporation); also SPOT Data Products and Services (catalog); and SPOT Surveillance brochure (which advises potential customers: "Before taking any decision concerning a target located deep inside a zone inaccessible to reconnaissance planes and RPVs [i.e., remotely piloted vehicles]" rely on SPOT images to analyze the target, the "threats" surrounding it, and the route leading to it. SPOT also offers "penetration assistance," pointing out that "passage under radar and missile coverage calls for in-depth study of the penetration route," in the form of SPOT 3-dimensional images.

315–16 The processing and enhancement of remote sensing images for commercial and military purposes is a growing business. See EOSAT "Directory of Landsat-Related Products and Services—United States Edition, 1988," and "Directory of Landsat-Related Products and Services—International Edition, 1989," from EOSAT, Lanham, Maryland.

316   Space Media Network: brochure from Space Media Network. Also, "Photos Prove '57 Nuclear Disaster," *Chicago Tribune*, December 1, 1988; "Satellite Photos Appear to Show Construction of Soviet Space Shuttle Base," *New York Times*, August 25, 1986; and Space Media Network "List of Media Projects."

316   Poor-country satellite and missile development: "Star Wars,"
       by Sterett Pope, *World Press Review,* December 1989.
317   Acceleration effect in intelligence: "E. European Events Out-
       run Intelligence Analysts, Panel Told," *Los Angeles Times,*
       December 13, 1989.
318   Conrad, from his *Under Western Eyes,* 1911.

CHAPTER 25   THE INFO-AGENDA

320   McFarlane in Tehran: "Iran Says McFarlane Came on Se-
       cret Mission to Tehran," *Washington Post Foreign Service,*
       November 11, 1986; "Cloak and Dagger," *Newsweek,* No-
       vember 17, 1986; "Reagan's Backdoor Hostage Deal with
       Iran," *U.S. News & World Report,* November 17, 1986;
       "Cake Delivered to Iranians Was Strictly Kosher," *Los An-
       geles Times,* February 27, 1987.
321   "Federal Information: Who Should Get It, Who Shouldn't?"
       by Diane Sherwood, *The World & I,* January 1990.
322   Layoff numbers: "Heading for an Override?" *Time,* July 18,
       1988.
322   Fairness issue: "Heading for an Override?" *Time,* July 18,
       1988; "Closing Law's Key Provisions," by Martha I. Finney,
       Nation's Business, January 1989; and "72–73 Senate Vote
       Approves Notice of Plant Closings," *New York Times,* July
       7, 1988.
323   Osaka citizens: "Group Seeks Access to City's Information,"
       Japan Times, August 29, 1989.
323–24 Freedom of information legislation: "Role of Access Coordi-
       nators Under Scrutiny," *Transnational Data and Communica-
       tions Report,* March 1989; also, "International FOI Roundup,"
       Transnational Data Report, June 1985. This journal keeps a
       running check on "FOI" developments.
324–25 Congressional inquiry: "Transportation Secretary Assails Pub-
       licizing of Terrorist Warnings," *New York Times,* April 13,
       1989.
325   Northwest case: "Northwest Planned to Disclose Bomb Threat
       at the Gate," *Los Angeles Times,* December 30, 1989; "North-
       west Warns Flight's Ticket Holders of Threat," *New York
       Times,* December 29, 1989.
325   AIDS: "AIDS: Who Should Be Tested?" *Newsweek,* May 11,
       1987; "As AIDS Spooks the Schoolroom—," *U.S. News and*

World Report, September 23, 1985; "Putting AIDS to the Test," *Time,* March 2, 1987; "Mandatory Testing for AIDS?" *Newsweek,* February 16, 1987.

326–27 Does one country have a right to know about another?: "Sweden Protests to Moscow Over Lack of Warning," *Financial Times,* April 30, 1986; "Russians Pressed to Give Full Details of Nuclear Disaster," *The Times* (London), April 29, 1986.

327 Stansfield Turner article: "The U.S. Responded Poorly to Chernobyl," *New York Times,* May 23, 1986.

327 Libya chemical weapons incident: "Libyan Plant Sparks Storm in Bonn," *Washington Post,* January 19, 1989; "West Germany in Libya Probe," *Financial Times,* January 14/15, 1989; "Senator Assails Bonn in Libya Scandal," *Los Angeles Times,* January 29, 1989; "Vigilance, Luck Expose Libya Plant," *Los Angeles Times,* January 22, 1989.

328 Tape pirates: "Thai Copyright War Divides Washington," *Financial Times,* January 27, 1989.

328 Book piracy: "Barbary Book Pirates," by Sterett Pope, *World Press Review,* June 1986; "La book connection," by Rémy Lilliet, *L'Express,* March 29, 1985; also, "Copyright Holders Name 12 Pirate Nations," *Financial Times,* April 25, 1989.

328 *Indiana Jones:* "High-Tech Tactics Slow Film Piracy," *New York Times,* January 29, 1986.

328–29 Taiwan teenagers: "Pulling the Plug on Pirate Videos," *Los Angeles Times,* January 8, 1990.

329 Stealing software: "Psst! hey, mister, want to buy some software cheap?" by Christopher Johnston, *PC Computing,* October 1988; and "Thai Copyright War Divides Washington," *Financial Times,* January 27, 1989.

330 Japanese attitude on intellectual property: "Putting a Price on Intellect," by Yuji Masuda, *Journal of Japanese Trade and Industry,* no. 5, 1988.

330 EC attitude: "Brussels Plan for IPR Control," *Financial Times,* July 4, 1989.

330 Harlan Cleveland quoted from *WFSF Newsletter* (World Future Studies Federation), July 1989.

331 Maldistribution of information quote from [332] p. v.

331 Pharmaceuticals: "Whose Idea Is It Anyway?" *Economist,* November 12, 1988.

CHAPTER 26 THE IMAGE MAKERS

332 Early newspaper history from [171] pp. 5–6, and [179] pp. 203–205.

332–33 On the rise of "public opinion": [538] p. 14.

333–34 CNN impact: "Watching Cable News Network Grow," *New York Times,* December 16, 1987; "Triumphant Ted," by Joshua Hammer, *Playboy,* January 1990; see also CNN documents: "The Growth of a Global Network," "Milestones," "Live Reporting," and [180] throughout.

333–34 Fidel Castro: Turner showed tape privately to author.

336 New TV networks and services in U.S.: "Cable," by Paula Parisi, *Hollywood Reporter,* 1989–1990 TV Preview; also " 'Channel One' Could Whittle Away at Net and Syndie Teen and Coin," by Verne Gay, *Variety,* June 14–20, 1989.

336 Number of channels available: [68] p. 281; and, "Technology Adds Choices and Programming Needs," *New York Times,* July 24, 1989.

337 Direct broadcast satellite: "One Hundred and Eight Channels by 1993? Stay Tuned, America," *International Herald Tribune,* February 22, 1990.

337 Rise of independent stations and syndicates: "The Future of Television," *Newsweek,* October 17, 1988.

337 Iger quote: "Technology Adds Choices and Programming Needs," *New York Times,* July 24, 1989.

337 "Hardly anyone remembers" quote from author interview with Al Burton, Executive Producer, Universal Television, and President, Al Burton Productions.

338 European satellite channels: "Tube Wars," by Fred V. Guterl, *Business Month,* December 1988.

338 BSB and Sky rivalry: "BSB Inks 5-Year Output Deal with Orion; Rumors of Oz' Bond Pulling Out Abound," by Elizabeth Guider, *Variety,* June 14–20, 1989; and "Activate the Death Star," *Economist,* July 8, 1989.

338 French television: "Off-Screen TV: Scandal, Sex, Money," *New York Times,* January 18, 1988; "Boost for Cable TV Industry in France," *Financial Times,* February 9, 1990; "France's New Television Order," by Adam Glenn, *Broadcasting,* August 24, 1987; "Commercial TV, Mon Dieu!" *Time,* March 17, 1986; and "Le Defi Disney," by John Marcom, Jr., *Forbes,* February 20, 1989.

338 German television: "New German TV: Idiot Culture or Breath of Air?" *New York Times,* February 11, 1985; "Tube Wars,"

by Fred V. Guterl, *Business Month,* December 1988.

339   Advertising agency mergers: "WPP, the New Giant of . . .
PR?" *Business Week,* May 29, 1989; "Upbeat View at Saatchi
New York," *New York Times,* June 21, 1989. Things were
looking less "upbeat" by 1990.

339–40   Failure of "global sell" strategy: "Marketers Turn Sour on
Global Sales Pitch Harvard Guru Makes," *Wall Street Journal,*
May 12, 1988; "The Overselling of World Brands," *Finan-
cial Times,* December 21, 1988; and "Why the Single Mar-
ket Is a Misnomer—and the Consequences," *Financial Times,*
December 21, 1988.

341   Sony in Hollywood: "$3 Billion Bid for Columbia by Sony,"
Los Angeles Times, September 26, 1989. This initial report
underestimated the actual price. Two days later, on September 28, 1989, in "Sony Has High Hopes for Columbia Pictures," the *New York Times* estimated the price at $3.4 billion.
"Sony Goes to Hollywood," *The Sunday Times* (London),
October 1, 1989, calculated the deal at "almost $5 billion."

341–42   Murdoch empire: "Four Titans Carve Up European TV," by
William Fisher and Mark Schapiro, *Nation,* January 9/16,
1989; and "Tube Wars," by Fred V. Guterl, *Business Month,*
December 1988.

342   Maxwell profiled: "Larger Than Life," *Time,* November 28,
1988; see also, "Four Titans Carve Up European TV," by
William Fisher and Mark Schapiro, *Nation,* January 9/16,
1989, and "Business Goes Global," *Report on Business
Magazine—The Globe and Mail* (Toronto), February 1989.

343   Mohn and Bertelsmann profiled: "Reinhard Mohn," *Nation,*
June 12, 1989; see also [134] throughout; "Business Goes
Global," *Report on Business Magazine—The Globe and Mail*
(Toronto), February 1989; and "Bertelsmann Philosophy,"
Bertelsmann brochure.

CHAPTER 27   THE SUBVERSIVE MEDIA

347   Mexicans' legal victory: "Mexicans Who Sued Deputies Win $1
Million," *Los Angeles Times,* January 25, 1990; and "Video-
tape Is Centerpiece of 'Victorville 5' Brutality Lawsuit," *Los
Angeles Times,* January 9, 1990.

347–48   Czech rebels' videos: "The Czechoslovak Pen Defies the Party
Sword," *Financial Times,* November 28, 1989.

348   Political use of television and videocassettes: excellent roundup in "TV, VCRs Fan Fire of Revolution," *Los Angeles Times*, January 18, 1990.

348   Ceausescu once invited the author to "spend my vacation with me and we can watch *Kojak* together." The surprise invitation came after a long meeting between the Romanian President and the Tofflers, attended by Harry Barnes, then U.S. Ambassador to Bucharest. The year was 1976. The end of the Ceausescu story is told in "How the Ceausescus Fell: Harnessing Popular Rage," *New York Times*, January 7, 1990.

349   The role of TV in the Philippines: "Playing to the TV Cameras," *U.S. News and World Report*, March 10, 1986.

349–50   Romanian revolution: "How the Ceausescus Fell: Harnessing Popular Rage," *New York Times*, January 7, 1990; "Romanian Revolt, Live and Uncensored," *New York Times*, December 28, 1989; also, "Message of the Media," *Financial Times*, December 30, 1989.

353   Dresden out of reach of West German TV: "The Long Journey out of the Valley of the Ignorant," *Stuttgarter Zeitung*, December 19, 1989.

353   Role of Voice of America: Testimony of Richard Carlson, Director VOA, before subcommittee of House Foreign Affairs Committee, U.S. Congress, June 15, 1989; also, "Old Men Riding a Tiger and Feeling Paranoid," *Los Angeles Times*, January 8, 1990.

355   Christianity in South Korea: "Chun's $21 Million Apology," *Newsweek*, December 5, 1988; also, "Papal Nod to a Christian Boom," *Time*, May 14, 1984.

355   Khomeini's use of tape recordings: "The Ayatollah's Hit Parade," *Time*, February 12, 1979.

356   Politics of wall posters: "Peking's Posters Point Finger of Protest to the Party," *Financial Times*, June 17, 1988.

356   Summary accounts of Chinese student uprising: See [363] pp. 219–220; "State of Siege," *Time*, May 29, 1989; and, for a socialist perspective, "China's Long Winter," by Anita Chan, *Monthly Review*, January 1990. Also, "Watching China Change," by Mark Hopkins, *Columbia Journalism Review*, September/October 1989.

357–58   The new role of "meta-news" is seen in media coverage of media coverage—knowledge about knowledge again. See "The Revolution Will Not Be Televised," *Los Angeles Times*,

May 22, 1989; "China Allows Foreign Broadcasters to Re-sume News Transmission," *New York Times,* May 24, 1989; "China Lets World Hear but Not See," *New York Times,* May 21, 1989.

357–58   Political use of new media: ". . . As Chinese in U.S. Pierce a News Blockade," *New York Times,* May 24, 1989; also, "TV, VCRs Fan Fire of Revolution," *Los Angeles Times,* January 18, 1990; "Phones, Faxes: Students in U.S. Keep Lines of Communication Open," *Los Angeles Times,* June 6, 1989.

358   First "citizen jamming" efforts: "Chinese Students in U.S. Seeking to Foil 'Tip' Lines," *Los Angeles Times,* June 11, 1989.

CHAPTER 28   THE "SCREENIE" GENERATION

360–61   Slave golfer: author interviews with Gordon Stulberg, Chair-man, and Bernard Luskin, President, American Interac-tive Media Corporation; also company documents.

361   Network games: "Computer Company Plans to Bring TV Viewers Into the Action," *Los Angeles Herald Examiner,* Feb-ruary 11, 1988.

361   Gilder: "Forget HDTV, It's Already Outmoded," *New York Times,* May 28, 1989; and "IBM-TV?" by George Gilder, *Forbes,* February 20, 1989.

363–64   Faxes and billions of pages: U.S. Congressman Edward J. Markey in "Ban Fax Attacks; They Are Costly," *USA Today,* May 31, 1989.

366   AT&T breakdown: "President Reagan Declares Martin Lu-ther King, Jr., Day," *Jet,* January 23, 1989; AT&T Pin-points Source of Service Disruption," *New York Times,* January 17, 1990; and "AT&T Fiasco: Tense Fight With Haywire Technology," *Los Angeles Times,* January 19, 1990.

367–68   Moritz on "screenies": Letter to author from Jeffrey M. Moritz, President, National College Television.

CODA: YEARNINGS FOR A NEW DARK AGE

373   The God-Is-Dead controversy: "Toward a Hidden God," *Time,* April 8, 1966.

375   Azerbaijan links to Muslim fundamentalism: Accounts of the 1989 uprising in Azerbaijan and the massacre of Ar-

menians in Baku differ widely as to the role of the Communist Party local leadership, Moscow's delay in using troops to restore order, and the character of the Azeri movement. "Baku: Before and After," by Igor Beliaev, *Literaturnaya Gazeta International*—"The Literary Gazette" (Moscow), March 1990; "Iran Warns Against 'Harsh' Soviet Moves in Azerbaijan," *Los Angeles Times*, January 18, 1990; "Fundamentalism Blamed for Uzbeck Rioting," *Financial Times*, June 14, 1989; "Soviets Are At Loss About Ethnic Unrest," *Wall Street Journal*, July 21, 1989; and, "Teheran Is Said to Back 'Islamic Seal' but Not Separatism in Azerbaijan," *New York Times*, January 21, 1990.

375 Fundamentalists in Israel: See "Israel's Cultural War," *The Christian Century*, July 16–23, 1986. For relationships to early German romanticism, see [303] pp. 60–63.

377 Splits in the Green Party and in Green ideology: "Greens Trade Insults at Birthday Party," *Handelsblatt* (Dusseldorf), January 15, 1990, reports on declining status of German Greens as major parties adopt some of their policies. Ideological-philosophical divide in world ecology movement is best delineated in the Spring 1989 *New Perspectives Quarterly (NPQ)*, which brings together many of the leading thinkers of the ecology movement and frames the key philosophical issues. Edited by Nathan Gardels, *NPQ* is consistently among America's most challenging periodicals.

378 Bahro is from "Theology Not Ecology"; and Sachs, from "A Critique of Ecology"; both in *NPQ*, Spring 1989.

379 Illich is from "The Shadow Our Future Throws," *NPQ*, Spring 1989; [517] pp. 101–102; and [240] p. 181.

379 Bilmes and Byford are quoted from "Armageddon and the Greens," *Financial Times*, December 30–31, 1989.

380 Bahro on a "green Adolf": See "Theology Not Ecology," *NPQ*, Spring 1989.

380 Touraine's counter to ecological anti-reason: "Neo-Modern Ecology," *NPQ*, Spring 1989.

380 On German romanticism and back-to-naturism: "The Dangers of Counter-Culture," by John de Graff, *Undercurrents 21*, April/May 1977; see also [582] pp. 50–55; [384] especially Chapter 11; also [390] p. 188.

381 Nazi exaltation of the Middle Ages: [391] p. 50, and adjoining map.

381 "Green Tribe" (letter from Ron James), *Economist*, July 29, 1989.

382   Worry over Anglo-Saxon TV: "Vers un marche mondial de l'information télévisée," by Yves Eudes, *Le Monde Diplomatique* (Paris), June 1988; "Hollywood Predominance Reflects Sad State of European Industry," *Süddeutsche Zeitung* (Munich), January 6, 1990.

382   Plummeting price of satellite dishes: interview with Dan Goldin, satellite expert, TRW, Inc.

383   Le Pen on Nazis and death camps: "French Rightist Belittles Gas Chambers," *New York Times*, September 16, 1987; see also "Le Front National et le drapeau nazi dans le champ belge à Rotterdam," *Le Soir* (Brussels), November 30/December 1, 1985; and, "Europeans Showed Dissatisfaction With Ruling Parties," *Los Angeles Times*, June 24, 1989.

383   Germany's Republikaners: "Europe's Grand Parties in a Tightening Vise," *Wall Street Journal*, June 26, 1989; "Extreme Rightists Win Frankfurt Council Seats," *Los Angeles Times*, March 13, 1989; "Germany's Republikaners Start a Rumble on the Far Right," *Wall Street Journal*, July 24, 1989; and "Is Extremist or Opportunist Behind Bonn Rightist's Tempered Slogans?" *New York Times*, June 27, 1989; also "Millstone Instead of Milestone for Republicans," *Süddeutsche Zeitung* (Munich), January 15, 1990; "Former Nazi Quits as W. German Party Leader, Blaming Extremists," *Los Angeles Times*, May 26, 1990.

384   Eco-vandals and anti-immigrationists: "Saboteurs for a Better Environment," *New York Times*, July 9, 1989; see also, debate in pages of *Earth First!* (Canton, N.Y.), a publication of eco-extremists.

384–85   Japanese nationalist sentiment: "A New Japanese Nationalism," by Ian Buruma, *New York Times Magazine*, April 12, 1987; "Mayor Who Faulted Hirohito Is Shot," *New York Times*, January 19, 1990; "Attack on Nagasaki Mayor Stirs Fears of Speaking Out," *New York Times*, January 21, 1990; "Rightist Held in Shooting of Blunt Nagasaki Mayor," *Los Angeles Times*, January 19, 1990; "Japanese See a Threat to Democracy in Shooting of Nagasaki Mayor," *Los Angeles Times*, January 20, 1990.

384   "Yamato-ism" and supposed uniqueness of Japanese language: "The 'Japan as Number One' Syndrome," by Kunihiro Masao, *Japan Echo* (Tokyo), volume XI, no. 3, 1984; "A New Japanese Nationalism," by Ian Buruma, *New York Times Magazine*, April 12, 1987. See also [460] for

leading expression of Japanese linguistic uniqueness, a concept with important political and nationalist resonance, and [317], especially Chapters 7 and 12, for a refutation.

385–86   Great Russian chauvinism: [558] p. 110. See also the prescient [347] pp. 38–39 on messianic component of Slavophile nationalism and its origins, and [548] throughout.

385–86   Pamyat's green camouflage and anti-Semitism: "The Secret of Pamyat's Success," *Wall Street Journal,* April 3, 1989; "Ideological Terror" (letter), *Present Tense,* November/ December 1989; the January 18, 1990, break-in, during which thugs broke into a meeting of the Moscow Central Writers Club and shouted threatening anti-Semitic slogans, was even condemned by the Soviet Public Anti-Zionist Committee, whose "outrage" is voiced in "Statement," *Literaturnaya Gazeta International*—"The Literary Gazette" (Moscow), March 1990. More general comments and reports in "Right-Wing Russians," *Christian Science Monitor,* June 18, 1987; "Anxiety Over Anti-Semitism Spurs Soviet Warning on Hate," *New York Times,* February 2, 1990; "Yearning for an Iron Hand," *New York Times Magazine,* January 28, 1990; "Anti-Semitic Rallies Prompt Protest," *Washington Post,* August 14, 1988; and "Don't Underestimate Anti-Semitic Soviet Fringe" (letter), *New York Times,* April 3, 1989. See also [352] pp. 66 and 86.

The split between secular reformers in the Soviet Union and the messianic Russian Christian nationalists is reflected by the difference between two great and courageous dissident figures—on the one hand, the late Nobel Prize winner and human-rights campaigner, Andrei Sakharov, who was a Western-oriented small "d" democrat, and on the other, Aleksandr Solzhenitsyn, who combines Great Russian nationalism with religious mysticism and a distinct hostility to democracy.

386   Schoenhuber: "Is Extremist or Opportunist Behind Bonn Rightist's Tempered Slogans?" *New York Times,* June 27, 1989.

CHAPTER 29   THE GLOBAL "K-FACTOR"

392   Intervening at deeper levels of nature: "A Small Revolution Gets Under Way," by Robert Pool, *Science,* January 5, 1990.

393   Most important breakthroughs: "Academy Chooses 10 Top Feats," *The Institute* (Institute of Electrical and Electronics Engineers), February 1990.

394   Comment on Soviet techno-military defeat: "Dithering in Moscow," *New York Times*, December 14, 1989.

CHAPTER 30   THE FAST AND THE SLOW

397–98 On tradition as an instrument for selecting technology: [120] p. 30.

398   On reduced risk in innovation: [120] p. 35.

399–400 Fading U.S. reliance on foreign cheap labor in apparel industry: "Made in the U.S.A.," by Ralph King, Jr., *Forbes*, May 16, 1988.

400   Tandy case: author interview with John Roach, Chairman, Tandy Corporation.

400   Arrow, Atkins, and *Forbes* quote are from "Made in the U.S.A.," by Ralph King, Jr., *Forbes*, May 16, 1988.

400   Benetton turnaround time: "Fast Forward," by Curtis Bill Pepper, *Business Month*, February 1989.

400–01 Chinese steel response-time: "Bureaucracy Blights China's Steel Industry," *Financial Times*, December 16, 1988.

404   On declining energy required for each unit of output: "The Technology Revolution and the Restructuring of the Global Economy," by Umberto Colombo, in "Proceedings of the Sixth Convocation of the Council of Academies of Engineering and Technological Sciences," in [521] pp. 23–31.

405   On new composites: "A Small Revolution Gets Under Way," by Robert Pool, *Science*, January 5, 1990.

406   Japan shifting investment away from Taiwan, Hong Kong: "Political Reforms Pave Way," *Japan Economic Journal*, October 1, 1988.

406   Umberto Colombo: from [521] p. 25.

407   On faster jets and the "three T's" project: "Moving Toward a Supersonic Age," by Jiro Tokuyama, Center for Pacific Business Studies, Mitsui Research Institute (Tokyo), 1988.

407   Perot's airport: "Can Ross Perot Save America?" by Peter Elkind, *Texas Monthly*, December 1988.

408–09 On poor-country arms race: "Becoming Smarter on Intelligence," by Henrik Bering-Jebsen, *Insight*, December 26, 1988–January 2, 1989.

409–10 Re dynamic minorities: "Foreigners in Britain, New Blood," *Economist,* December 24, 1988.

410–11 Brazil on pharmaceutical royalties: "Brazil: A Practical Guide to Intellectual Property Protection," *Business America,* January 18, 1988; and "Whose Idea Is It Anyway?" *Economist,* November 12, 1988.

412 World distribution of telephones: data from Anthony Rutkowski, Senior Counsel, International Telecommunications Union (Geneva).

CHAPTER 31 SOCIALISM'S COLLISION WITH THE FUTURE

413 For Gutenberg's impact, see "A Red Square Reformation," by Robert Conot, *Los Angeles Times,* March 11, 1990.

413 Khrushchev's famous taunt to the West was made to a group of Western diplomats and reported in "We Will Bury You," *Time,* November 26, 1956.

413–14 The 1956 turning point of the U.S. economy, from its Second Wave manufacturing base toward its present Third Wave service-information base, was spotted in "A New Social Revolution," *Fortune,* April 1958, which reported 1956 figures on the work force. Figures were based on a study by Murray Wernick, an economist at the U.S. Federal Reserve Board.

414 Gorbachev on "the age of information science": from remarks by Gorbachev before the Soviet Central Committee on February 5, 1990, provided by Tass English Language service. For rise of white-collar class in U.S.S.R. see "Gorbachev Politics," by Jerry F. Hough, *Foreign Affairs,* Winter 1989–90; also, "Médias sovietiques: censure glasnost," *Le Point,* March 12, 1990.

414 On current crisis of communism as reflection of Marx's concept of the "relations of production" obstructing the "means of production": Author argued this in 1983 in [68] p. 78; also in "Future Shock in Moscow," *New Perspectives Quarterly,* Winter 1987; in "A Conversation with Mikhail Gorbachev" (series) by Heidi and Alvin Toffler, *Christian Science Monitor,* January 5, 6, 7, 1987; and, following a meeting with then-Communist Party chief Zhao Ziyang in Beijing, in "Socialism in Crisis," *World Monitor,* January 1989. The same thesis is taken up by Yegor Ligachev, a

Soviet Politburo member and rival of Gorbachev, in *World Marxist Review* (Prague), July 1987, and by Valentin Fyodorov, Vice-Rector, Moscow Institute of Economics, in "Ignorance Is Bliss," *Literaturnaya Gazeta International*—"The Literary Gazette" (Moscow), March 1990.

416   Lenin's assumptions about the role of knowledge and culture are summed up in his 1905 statement that "Literary activity must become part of the overall proletarian cause, a 'cog and screw' in the united and great social-democratic mechanism."

417   For 19th-century utopians and socialists: see [366].

418   Razor blades in U.S.S.R.: "El fracaso del marxismo-leninismo," *El Heraldo* (Mexico City), December 3, 1989.

419   Socialism's "calculation problem": see [133] Chapter 26, entitled "The Impossibility of Economic Calculation Under Socialism," especially pp. 698–699; also [120] pp. 52–65 and 241.

420   Poland's "cold turkey" shift to market economics: "East Europe Joins the Market and Gets a Preview of the Pain," *New York Times,* January 7, 1990.

420–21 Squeezing agriculture: [377] pp. 212–229; also, more detailed reconstruction of debates about Preobrazhensky's socialist primitive accumulation (sometimes translated as "primitive socialist accumulation") in [351] pp. 163–180.

422   Is the dream dead? Belatedly awakening to the rise of a new, Third Wave system of wealth creation and its social correlatives, some Western socialists and communists are trying to regroup around new themes. See: "It's the End of the Road for Communism," extract from the speech of Martin Jacques, editor of *Marxism Today,* reported in *The Sunday Times* (London), November 26, 1989. Jacques stresses ecology, gender equality, an end to central planning, the support of the "civil society." Opposing individualism, however, he sums up with: "Socialism is about interdependence, about solidarity, about equality" and a "rebirth of collectivism."

CHAPTER 32   THE POWER OF BALANCE

424   India's military muscle: "India Rejects Japanese Criticism," and "Last Indian Contingent Leaves Maldives," both in *Jane's Defence Weekly,* November 18, 1989; also, "The Awak-

ening of an Asian Power," *Time*, April 3, 1989; and, "India Is Reportedly Ready to Test Missile With Range of 1,500 Miles," *New York Times*, April 3, 1989.

424 Spread of missiles: "Third World Missile-Making Prompts Campaign by C.I.A.," *New York Times*, March 31, 1989.

424 Capture of nukes by Islamic extremists or military rebels: "U.S. Worried by Nuclear Security in Unstable Soviet Empire," *Los Angeles Times*, December 15, 1989.

425 Ishihara's famous quote about Japan's potential for tilting the world power balance by selling advanced chips to the U.S.S.R: [318] pp. 3–5. Also, "Seeing a Dependent and Declining U.S., More Japanese Adopt a Nationalistic Spirit," *New York Times*, September 1, 1989.

426 Dangers of a financial collapse: "A Post-Panic System," by Alvin Toffler, *New York Times*, October 25, 1987; Greenspan's qualms are reported in "Market Globalization Risky, Greenspan Says," *Los Angeles Times*, June 15, 1989.

426 Central controls over national budgets and fiscal policies were proposed in the Delors Report, which was approved unanimously by a committee of EC central bankers and experts in April 1989. See: "Sovereignty and Fiscal Policy," *Financial Times*, July 18, 1989.

CHAPTER 33 TRIADS: TOKYO—BERLIN—WASHINGTON

430 Japanese military spending: Pressed by Washington to "share the burden" of defense, Japan's military budget has climbed steadily, bypassing that of France and West Germany, and standing either above or just below that of the U.K., depending on currency conversions and other factors. Only the U.S. and the U.S.S.R. clearly outrank Japan—but, to put matters in perspective, they do so massively. For more detail, see [285]. Also: "The State of Japan's Military Art," by Katherine T. Chen, *IEEE Spectrum*, September 1989; "Guess Who's Carrying a Bigger Stick?" by Peter Hartcher, *World Press Review*, July 1988; and [283].

431 On rise of a new military-industrial complex in Japan: "The State of Japan's Military Art," by Katherine T. Chen, *IEEE Spectrum*, September 1989; "The Sun Also Rises Over Japan's Technology," *Economist*, April 1, 1989. Also, take

account of discussions on joint venturing in defense field between Mitsubishi and Germany's Daimler-Benz (which owns Messerschmitt and Deutsche Aerospace). These have caused misgivings among many Europeans, as in "Colossal mariage," *Le Point* (Paris), March 12, 1990.

431   Takeshita on need to balance economic power with military clout: "Japan: A Superpower Minus Military Power," *Los Angeles Times*, September 11, 1988.

432   Comparative savings rates: "Japanese Thrift? The Stereotype Suffers a Setback," *Business Week*, August 14, 1989; and "U.S. Is Getting What It Asked for in Japan," *Los Angeles Times*, February 7, 1990.

433   Rising percentage of scientists and engineers in work force: "R&D in Japan vs. the United States," *IEEE Spectrum*, February 1989.

434   Fifth generation disappointment: "What Happened to the Wonder Child?" by Stuart Dambrot, *Business Tokyo*, February 1989; and " 'Fifth Generation Computer' Makes U.S. Debut," *Los Angeles Times*, October 12, 1989.

434   Survey of Japanese CEOs: "Technology Leadership: The Votes Are In," *Information Industry Insights* (Booz-Allen Hamilton), issue 18, 1988.

435   Newspaper readership: "Millions a Day," by Annamaria Waldmueller, *World Press Review*, April 1988.

435   Numbers of foreign students: "U.S. Failing to Close Its Education Gap With Japan," *Los Angeles Times*, January 7, 1990.

437–38   Lenin on united Europe: from *Sotzial-Demokrat*, no. 44, August 23, 1915. See his collected works.

439   All-Europe army: "Kohl Praises Prospect of European Army," *Financial Times*, December 14, 1988.

439   Possible costs to Europe of a U.S. military pull-out: [287] p. 37.

439–40   French and German military figures are from [286] pp. 47–48 and 59–64; for discussion of possible budget cuts, "Changing Attitudes in a Changing Europe Leave the Bundeswehr at the Crossroads," *Die Zeit* (Hamburg), December 22, 1989.

439–40   French policy of balancing West German arms: "Return of 'The German Menace,' " by Wolfgang J. Koschnick, *Worldview*, January/February 1977.

441–42   For EC's "glowing promises," see "Social Dimension of the Internal Market," a report of the Commission of the European Communities (Brussels), September 14, 1988, especially p. 4.

443 R&D increases: "Brussels Proposes Big Rise in High-Tech Research," *Financial Times,* July 26, 1989.

444 German patents and prizes: "Ein Wissenschaftswunder?" *Economist,* November 11, 1989.

444 Nixdorf's demise and Norsk's troubles: "Siemens Takeover of Nixdorf Creates a Giant," *Die Welt* (Bonn), January 13, 1990; and "Norsk Data Suffers Further Losses," *Financial Times,* February 7, 1990.

445 For heartland theory, see [336] and [302].

445 On carriers and their battle groups, see [286].

447 U.S. imports and exports: from "U.S. Foreign Trade Highlights, 1988," U.S. Department of Commerce; also, press release of U.S. Bureau of the Census, February 16, 1990, entitled "U.S. Merchandise Trade: December, 1989." See also: "New ITA Report Shows Major Improvement in U.S. Trade Performance in 1988," in *Business America,* November 6, 1989, pp. 6 and 12.

448 Patents: U.S. patents issued to residents of foreign countries have increased steadily since 1965, when only 23 percent went to non-U.S. residents. This percentage had doubled by 1989.

448 Relative numbers of engineers and scientists: "R&D in Japan vs. the United States," *IEEE Spectrum,* February 1989.

449 Computer industry comparisons: "Chiffres clés de l'informatique mondiale," by Michel Solis and Benedicte Haquin, *01 Informatique* (Paris), November 24, 1989; and "Staying American," *Economist,* August 19, 1989.

449 IBM's 16 million-bit chip: "IBM Announces Memory Chip Breakthrough," *Los Angeles Times,* February 11, 1990.

449 Growth of software market: "Competitive Software Industry Suits Up for Global Hardball," by Jeff Shear, *Insight,* July 10, 1989.

450 Ph.D.'s: Japan found it needed to increase its number of master's degree holders instead. The figures, 1975–1988: B.A.'s up 17 percent; Ph.D.'s, up 26 percent; but M.A.'s, up fully 84 percent.

453 Re Europe/U.S. vs. Japan: "The Changing Nature of the Relationship with America," in *Stuttgarter Zeitung,* January 19, 1990, expresses a widespread European view.

CHAPTER 34   THE GLOBAL GLADIATORS

456   Rushdie case: "Unrighteous Indignation," by Christian C. Muck, *Christianity Today,* April 7, 1989; "Hunted by an Angry Faith," *Time,* February 27, 1989; "Freedom-to-Write Bulletin," March 1989 (PEN American Center); and "PEN Defends Rushdie," Spring 1989 (International PEN USA Center West).

458   Catholic diplomacy: "Inextricably Involved," *America,* May 23, 1987; "No Place to Run," *Time,* January 8, 1990; "Pope Warns Against Divisions in the East," *New York Times,* January 14, 1990; "Pope Urges United Christian Europe," *International Herald Tribune,* August 22, 1989.

458   1918 document: [234] p. 256; "Pope, Visiting France, Calls for a United Europe," *New York Times,* October 9, 1988.

460   600 multinationals: "Come Back Multinationals," *Economist,* November 26, 1988.

460   Re non-nationality of global corporations: "Borderless Economy Calls for New Politics," by Kenichi Ohmae, *Los Angeles Times,* March 26, 1990; also, "Who Is Us?" by Robert Reich, *Harvard Business Review,* January–February 1990.

462   Sir Francis Drake: [587] pp. 28–29.

462   Perot's hostage rescue: "Ross Perot to the Rescue," by Ron Rosenbaum, *Esquire,* December 1980; also, "Perot's Mission Impossible," *Newsweek,* March 5, 1979.

465   Maurras quote, from [291] p. 6.

ACKNOWLEDGMENTS

No work of this scope can be written without the support of many people—friends, sources, and numerous outside experts who patiently offered insight and clarification. Our first thanks must go to Alberto Vitale, the former chairman, and Linda Grey, president and publisher, of Bantam Books for their endless, good-humored patience and enthusiasm for the project. During all the years of preparation Alberto and Linda steadfastly refused to hurry us, insisting instead that we take all the time necessary to do the best book possible.

That patience is appreciated and, we hope, will now be rewarded. Special credit must go, too, to Bantam executive editor Toni Burbank, whose deep understanding of this book and detailed editorial suggestions have made *Powershift* more integrated and readable than it might otherwise have been.

Strong support has come, too, for more than a decade, from Perry Knowlton of Curtis Brown, Ltd., our literary agency. From the start we have always been able to count on Perry for gentle, helpful advice about the business of publishing.

A similar vote of thanks must go to one of our oldest and most erudite friends, Dr. Donald F. Klein, director of research, New York State Psychiatric Institute, for his similarly detailed—but far more tart and challenging—criticisms all along the way.

Robert I. Weingarten and Pam Weingarten helped us understand certain financial headlines as they unfolded during the writing, while Al and Sally Burton helped keep us in touch with changes in television and the media. No better guides exist.

Sociologist Benjamin D. Singer of the University of Western Ontario plied us with journal articles, suggestions and enthusiasm throughout.

Tom Johnson of Nolan, Norton, Inc., and James P. Ware of the Index Group, both outstanding business consultants, contributed insights into some of the organizational changes and "info-wars" now changing the way business works.

From start to finish, Juan Gomez has been a more-than-model aide, maintaining our extensive research collection (amazingly able to put his finger on the most obscure journal article or clipping in our files), courteously fending off intrusions during the writing, arranging our complex travel schedule, and helping us with great intelligence, responsibility, and good cheer at every step. *Para* Juan, *muchas gracias.*

Words cannot express our feelings for our daughter, Karen, who worked under high pressure during the final weeks of manuscript preparation, double-checking and updating data in several key chapters, helping to prepare the notes and bibliography, and overseeing the index—in our case a more than mechanical matter, since its categories are designed for conceptual compatibility with the indices in *Future Shock, The Third Wave,* and our other works as well.

Finally, no such list can be complete without special thanks to Deborah E. Brown, who came aboard in the final months to perform a fine-grained, final fact-check on the manuscript, assuring that it is as up-to-date and correct as possible.

In a work of such broad scope, some errors and misinterpretations are inevitable. In addition, the continually accelerating pace of change means that many details risk obsolescence in the interval between the time they are written and the time they are read. It goes without need for elaboration that ultimate responsibility for any error remains with the authors, and not with the many people who have gone out of their way to assist them.

INDEX

A. H. Robins Company, 194
ABC (American Broadcasting Companies), 5, 336–37
Abcarian, Gilbert, 479
Abelson, Donald S., 137, 521
Abstraction, 279, 289, 293
Abu Dhabi, 56
Aburish, Said K., 305, 496
Acceleration, xviii, xix, xxi, 11, 32, 54–56, 110, 117, 123, 168, 178, 195, 214, 218, 222–23, 235–36, 237–38, 262, 263, 317, 350, 397–402, 409, 419, 427; in media, 350
Acceleration effect, 238, 398–99; in economy, 234
Access Tactic, 273. *See also* Info-tactics
Acco, Alain, 501
Accounting, 32, 62, 157–58, 171–72, 195, 203, 226, 231, 280–81; knowledge assets, 159, 231
Activism, electronic, 364–66
Acura (automobile), 435
Ada (software), 134
Adams, James, 491
Adams, Walter, 480
Adams, William, 349
Addison's disease, 8
Adhemar, Philippe, 510
Ad-hocracy, 191, 239, 264
Advanced Tactical Fighter (aircraft), 425
Advertising, 25, 48, 50, 81, 97, 258, 260, 280, 333–34, 338–39, 340, 343, 359, 363, 365
AEG (company), 308
Aerospace industry, 17, 115, 215, 218, 260, 305, 306, 393–94, 403–4, 407, 433, 443
Afanasyev, V., 498
Afghanistan, 219
Africa, 56, 303, 306, 310, 412, 455
African National Congress, 303
African-Americans, 52, 249, 250, 253, 451. *See also* Ethnicity; Minorities; Race and racism
Aganbegyan, Abel, 494
Aging, 10, 231, 432
Agnelli, Gianni, 30, 510
Agrarian society (First Wave), xx, 10, 28, 36, 63, 206–7, 244–45, 391, 405, 417, 421, 466
Agriculture, 46, 52, 70, 74, 266, 307, 420, 460, 466; as advanced industry (Third Wave), 411. *See also* Agrarian society (First Wave); Farmers

Aguren, Stefan, 480
AIDS, 275, 325–26
Aiken, South Carolina, 322
Air Canada, 260
Air Line Pilots Association, 227
Aircraft industry. *See* Aerospace industry
Airlines, 48, 65, 117, 227, 260, 324–25, 407. *See also names of individual carriers*
Airports, 227, 260, 407
Akihito, Emperor, 509
Akzo (company), 218
Alaska, 248, 377
Albania, 247, 249
Alcocer, Alberto, 30
Alcohol and alcoholism, 103, 196, 262, 340
Alfonsin, Raul, 302
Algeria, 382
Aliber, Robert Z., 481
Alienation, 61, 450
Alisjahbana, S. Takdir, 498
Allen, Frederick Lewis, 503
Allen, Woody, 451
Allende, Salvador, 303, 461
Alliances, 452–53, 464
Allied-Signal, Inc., 87
Allison, Graham T., 486
Alpha (aircraft), 439
Alphabet, 85
Alsace-Lorraine, 247
Althusser, Louis, 494
Amalrik, Andrei, 494
Amaterasu-omi-kami, 13, 34
Amazon, 311
Ambrose, Saint, 84–85
American Airlines, 117
American Express Company, 64, 67
American Hospital Supply, 122
American Interactive Media, 360–61
American Management Association, 224
American Public Power Association, 87
American Revolution, 370
American Society for Industrial Security, 154
American Telephone & Telegraph Company (AT&T), 28, 45, 110–12, 125, 131, 134–35, 145, 235, 364, 366; divestiture, 111–12
Amin, Samir, 491
AMR Corp., 117
Amstrad (company), 342
Analogy, 85, 370, 436
Anderson, Howard M., 238

555

ABOUT THE AUTHOR

One of the world's best-known social thinkers, Alvin Toffler is the author of *Future Shock, The Third Wave, Previews and Premises, The Adaptive Corporation,* and other works that are read in more than fifty countries. His ideas have drawn comment from world leaders from Richard Nixon to Mikhail Gorbachev, and have significantly influenced contemporary thought.

At various times a Visiting Professor at Cornell University, a Washington correspondent, and a Visiting Scholar at the Russell Sage Foundation, Toffler earlier spent five years as a factory worker in an auto plant, a steel foundry, and other shops in heavy industry.

His books have won the McKinsey Foundation Book Award for their distinguished contribution to management literature in the United States; the Golden Key Award in China; and the prestigious Prix du Meilleur Livre Étranger in France.

Toffler works in close intellectual partnership with his spouse, Heidi Toffler, who holds an honorary doctorate in law and has been awarded the Medal of the President of the Italian Republic for her own contributions to social thought. He has been named a Fellow of the American Association for the Advancement of Science and an Officier de l'Ordre des Arts et Lettres in France.